Routledge Handbook of International Law and the Humanities

This Handbook brings together 40 of the world's leading scholars and rising stars who study international law from disciplines in the humanities – from history to literature, philosophy to the visual arts – to showcase the distinctive contributions that this field has made to the study of international law over the past two decades.

Including authors from Australia, Canada, Europe, India, South Africa, the UK and the USA, all the contributors engage the question of what is distinctive, and critical, about the work that has been done and that continues to be done in the field of 'international law and the humanities'. For many of these authors, answering this question involves reflecting on the work they themselves have been contributing to this path-breaking field since its inception at the end of the twentieth century. For others, it involves offering models of the new work they are carrying out, or reflecting on the future directions of a field that has now taken its place as one of the most important sites for the study of international legal practice and theory. Each of the book's six parts foregrounds a different element, or cluster of elements, of international law and the humanities, from an attention to the office, conduct and training of the jurist and jurisprudent (Part 1); to scholarly craft and technique (Part 2); to questions of authority and responsibility (Part 3); history and historiography (Part 4); plurality and community (Part 5); as well as the challenge of thinking, and rethinking, international legal concepts for our times (Part 6).

Outlining new ways of imagining, and doing, international law at a moment in time when original, critical thought and practice is more necessary than ever, this Handbook will be essential for scholars, students and practitioners in international law, international relations, as well as in law and the humanities more generally.

Shane Chalmers is a University of Melbourne McKenzie research fellow and Program Director in Law and Art at the Institute for International Law and the Humanities (IILAH), Melbourne Law School. He is the author of *Liberia and the Dialectic of Law: Critical Theory, Pluralism, and the Rule of Law* (Routledge, 2018) and a forthcoming critical literary-legal history of the colonisation of Australia.

Sundhya Pahuja is a professor and the Director of Melbourne Law School's Institute for International Law and the Humanities (IILAH), the University of Melbourne. Sundhya has written widely on the history, theory and practice of international law in both its political and economic dimensions.

Routledge Handbook of International Law and the Humanities

Edited by Shane Chalmers and Sundhya Pahuja

Routledge
Taylor & Francis Group
LONDON AND NEW YORK

First published 2021
by Routledge
2 Park Square, Milton Park, Abingdon, Oxon OX14 4RN

and by Routledge
605 Third Avenue, New York, NY 10158

Routledge is an imprint of the Taylor & Francis Group, an informa business

British Library Cataloguing-in-Publication Data
A catalogue record for this book is available from the British Library

Library of Congress Cataloging-in-Publication Data
A catalog record for this book has been requested

ISBN: 978-0-367-42074-1 (hbk)
ISBN: 978-0-367-77345-8 (pbk)
ISBN: 978-1-003-17091-4 (ebk)

Typeset in Bembo
by Apex CoVantage, LLC

In memory of Peter Fitzpatrick

Contents

Figures

Contributors

Tom Andrews is a lecturer at the La Trobe Law School, Australia. His recently submitted doctorate describes the transformation of criminal procedure jurisprudence in the context of the British Empire. He also writes on the politics of contemporary cities. Tom lives, researches and teaches critical criminology on the un-ceded lands of the Wurundjeri People.

Matilda Arvidsson is an associate professor in international law and a researcher in international law, legal theory and history at the Department of Law, University of Gothenburg. Her research concerns human-other intersections and the embodiment of law in its various forms.

Olivia Barr is a senior lecturer at the Melbourne Law School. She writes in jurisprudence, and her cross-disciplinary work engages with geography, anthropology, philosophy, architecture and contemporary public art practices. Olivia's research focuses on questions of inheritance, especially ongoing relations between Anglo-Australian common law and Aboriginal law in Australia. Olivia recently published *A Jurisprudence of Movement: Common Law, Walking, Unsettling Place* (Routledge, 2016).

Kathleen Birrell is a McKenzie postdoctoral fellow at Melbourne Law School. She is the author of *Indigeneity: Before and Beyond the Law* (Routledge, 2016). Her research adopts critical legal methodologies to consider relationships between law and materiality, and rights, obligations and jurisprudential encounters in the Anthropocene. She completed a PhD (Law) at Birkbeck, University of London.

Ruth Buchanan is a professor at Osgoode Hall Law School, at York University in Toronto, Canada and a senior fallow at Melbourne Law School. Her current research projects include a co-edited *Handbook on International Law and Development* (with Pahuja and Eslava); an investigation into the uses of visual media in both the practice and the pedagogy of international law and development; and a collaborative project on Indigenous cinema, time and ideas of apocalypse.

Hilary Charlesworth is a Melbourne laureate professor at the Melbourne Law School. She is also a distinguished professor at the Australian National University. In 2019, she delivered the general course of The Hague Academy of International Law on 'The Art of International Law'.

Matthew Craven is a professor of international law at SOAS, the University of London, senior fellow at Melbourne Law School and a member of the Advisory Council of the Institute for Global Law and Policy at Harvard University. His books include the prize winning *The*

Decolonisation of International Law (Oxford University Press, 2007), *Time, History and International Law* (Martinus Nijhoff, 2007), and *International Law and the Cold War* (Cambridge University Press, 2019).

Julia Dehm is a senior lecturer at the La Trobe Law School, Australia. She was previously a postdoctoral fellow at the Rapoport Center for Human Rights and Justice at the University of Texas in Austin and a resident fellow at the Harvard Law School's Institute for Global Law and Policy. Julia is the Co-Editor in Chief of the *Journal of Human Rights and the Environment* and an associate member of the Institute for International Law and the Humanities (IILAH). Her monograph, *Reconsidering REDD+: Authority, Power and Law in the Green Economy*, is forthcoming with Cambridge University Press.

Sara Dehm is a lecturer at the Faculty of Law, University of Technology Sydney. She researches and writes on the history and theory of international law's regulation of human mobility and the subjects of migration, with a focus on questions of international administration, knowledge production and changing regimes of border controls.

Debolina Dutta teaches at the Jindal Global Law School and works in the areas of feminist jurisprudence, law and humanities, sexuality and postcolonial theory. She has previously worked as a human rights educator and a sexual rights activist. She is currently finishing a book titled *Rule of Laughter*, which looks at feminist humour in sex workers' activism.

Maria Elander is a senior lecturer at La Trobe Law School. Her research in international criminal justice engages with theories in cultural and feminist legal studies. She is particularly interested in questions of representation and its limits relating to victimhood, gender and the visual.

Peter Fitzpatrick's scholarship and teaching has transformed the study of law in the fields of legal philosophy and law and social theory. His book, *The Mythology of Modern Law* (Routledge, 1992), opened a new field of study for understanding the relation between law and myth and influenced a generation of scholars concerned with the relation between law, race and empire, while his more recent work on Michel Foucault has opened a new way of understanding law in the work of Foucault. Peter passed away as this book was going to print; it is in his memory that the volume is dedicated.

Sunil Gangopadhyay†, born in 1934 in Faridpur (now in Bangladesh), is one of the doyens of modernist Bangla literature. He moved to Calcutta (now Kolkata) at the age of 2 or 3 before the Partition of India. He studied science at the University of Calcutta and was later invited to attend the Iowa Writers' Workshop. He lived and worked in Calcutta until his death in 2012, by which time he amassed great popularity.

Ann Genovese is an associate professor at Melbourne Law School. As an Australian historian, jurisprudent and jurisographer, she researches the relationship between law and history as disciplines and practices; the nature of legal archives and the responsibilities of custodians and writers towards them; and the sources, forms and techniques necessary to show how Australian people have lived with their law.

Christopher Gevers teaches international law and legal theory in the School of Law, University of KwaZulu-Natal, and is a PhD candidate at Melbourne Law School. His current research focusses on Third World Approaches to International Law, critical race theory, and law and literature. Since 2015 he has been a faculty member of the Institute for Global Law & Policy at Harvard Law School. His most recent publications appear in Craven, Pahuja & Simpson (eds) *International Law and the Cold War* (2019), Heller et al (eds) *Oxford Handbook of International Criminal Law* (2019) and the *London Review of International Law*.

Lee Godden is a professor at Melbourne Law School and long-term member of the Institute for International Law and the Humanities (IILAH). Her research interests include environmental law and heritage, the intersections of settler law and the law of Aboriginal peoples and Torres Strait Islanders, and comparative research on native title and land rights in former British colonial countries. As a lawyer and geographer, she has a fascination with how space is materialised in law and the implications that that confluence holds for conceptions of the body. From 2013–2015, she was an Australian Law Reform Commissioner leading a review of the Native Title Act 1993 (Cth).

Ben Golder teaches law and social theory, public law, and the politics of human rights, at the Faculty of Law at the University of New South Wales. He researches and writes in the field of critical legal theory and contemporary political theory and sits on the editorial boards of *Law & Critique*, *Contemporary Political Theory* and the *Australian Journal of Human Rights*. His last book was *Foucault and the Politics of Rights* (Stanford, 2015) and recent published work has examined the function of metaphor in the field of human rights and the stakes of legal performativity.

Kate Grady is a senior lecturer in law at SOAS University of London, where she researches international law and critical legal theories.

Judith Grbich is a visitor to the Institute for International Law and the Humanities (IILAH) at Melbourne Law School, an adjunct associate professor at Griffith Law School, Griffith University, and past Editor in Chief of the *Australian Feminist Law Journal: A Critical Legal Journal*. She has practised law, and taught taxation law and legal theory to both law and humanities students in Australia. She has been President of the Law and Literature Association of Australia, and a council member of Institute for Postcolonial Studies. Her current project within international taxation law involves a retrieval of medieval and early modern dramatic contestations of monetary knowledges, and has a focus on the historiography of monetary things.

Adil Hasan Khan is a McKenzie fellow at the Melbourne Law School, where he is undertaking a research project on the intersections between international law and disasters, with a focus on South Asia, as well as a jurisprudential history of nineteenth- and twentieth-century South Asian traditions of international law. His research straddles the fields of jurisprudence, international legal histories of the South, ethics, and international law and development. He completed his PhD at the Graduate Institute of International and Development Studies (IHEID) in Geneva.

Jeffery G Hewitt is an assistant professor at Osgoode Hall Law School, York University and is mixed-descent Cree. His research is mainly community-based, and his areas of interests include Indigenous legal orders, constitutional law, international law, human rights, art and law. He has delivered numerous guest lectures to a variety of audiences.

Henry Jones is an associate professor at Durham University School of Law. His research focuses on the history and spatiality of international law. Specifically, he has written about the historical creation and governance of maritime space, the creation of territory through property in English colonialism, and the co-constitutive relationship between law and space at an international scale. He is currently writing a book about international law and geography.

Richard Joyce is a senior lecturer in the Faculty of Law at Monash University, Australia. His main research interests are in the history and theory of international law, with a particular focus on sovereignty, violence and responsibility. He is the author of *Competing Sovereignties* (Routledge, 2013).

Anne-Charlotte Martineau is a tenured researcher (French National Center for Scientific Research) and works at the École Normale Supérieure in Paris. She has held positions at the Max Planck Institute in Luxembourg and Law Faculty of the University of Leiden, and completed her PhD at the University of Helsinki and Sorbonne University, with a thesis on the debate on the fragmentation of international law. Her current research revisits the role of international law and lawyers in the establishment, justification and maintenance of slavery.

Mark McMillan is a Wiradjuri man, Indigenous jurisprudent and legal scholar. His current research focuses on Indigenous nation building and Indigenous international law.

Shaun McVeigh is a professor of law at Melbourne Law School and Kent Law School. As a jurisprudent and jurisographer, he currently researches the conduct of the office of jurisprudent and the quality of lawful relations within the common law tradition.

Stewart Motha is professor of law at Birkbeck School of Law, University of London, United Kingdom. He is a former Managing Editor of *Law & Critique*, and published *Archiving Sovereignty: Law, History, Violence* (University of Michigan Press, 2018). For his podcast, visit countersignisapodcast.com.

Vasuki Nesiah is professor of practice at NYU. She writes on the history and politics of human rights, humanitarianism, international criminal law, global feminisms and decolonisation. Her current project, *Reading the Ruins: Slavery, Colonialism and International Law*, focuses on international legal history, including reparations claims. She is a founding member of Third World Approaches to International Law (TWAIL).

Gregor Noll is a professor of international law at the Department of Law, School of Business, Economics and Law, Gothenburg University. His research covers migration law, the law of armed conflict, the impact of artificial intelligence on law and the theory of international law. Noll held the Pufendorf Chair at Lund University from 2012–2016. Together with an interdisciplinary team of colleagues, he edited and published *War and Algorithm* (Rowman and Littlefield, 2019) analysing emergent forms of warfare from the perspective of critical theory, philosophy, legal studies and visual studies.

Dianne Otto is a professorial fellow at Melbourne Law School. She held the Francine V McNiff Chair in Human Rights Law 2013–2016 and was the Director of the Institute for International Law and the Humanities (IILAH) 2012–2015. Her research, in the field of public international law and human rights law, covers a broad field including addressing gender, sexuality and race inequalities in the context of international human rights law; the UN Security Council's peacekeeping work; the technologies of global 'crisis governance'; threats to economic, social and cultural rights; and the transformative potential of people's tribunals and other NGO initiatives. Her recent publications include *Queering International Law: Possibilities, Alliances, Complicities, Risks* (editor, Routledge 2018).

Alice Palmer is a senior fellow teaching at the Melbourne Law School and a member of the Institute for International Law and the Humanities (IILAH). Her chapter in this volume draws on her PhD research at the University of Melbourne on images of aesthetic value in international environmental law, for which she received an Australian Government Research Training Program Scholarship. Alice was previously the Director of the Foundation for International Environmental Law and Development (FIELD), a not-for-profit organisation in the UK that assisted developing country governments and advocacy organisations in their use of international law to protect the environment.

James E K Parker has been a member of Melbourne Law School's Institute for International Law and the Humanities (IILAH) since 2009, first as a doctoral student and now as an associate professor. His book *Acoustic Jurisprudence: Listening to the Trial of Simon Bikindi* (OUP, 2015) was awarded the Penny Pether Prize (ECR) for scholarship in law, literature and the humanities in 2017. James is also co-curator of *Eavesdropping* (2018, 2019) and an associate curator at Liquid Architecture, an Australian organisation for artists working with sound. His current project is on the laws and politics of machine listening.

Connal Parsley is a senior lecturer in Law at Kent Law School. He is Co-director of the AHRC-funded Law and the Human Network, and the Kent Summer School in Critical Theory, and a deputy director of the Centre for Critical Thought. Connal's interdisciplinary research in critical legal, political and visual cultural theory addresses human life, legal personhood, and authority in a technological world. He is the translator of several works by contemporary Italian thinkers Roberto Esposito, Giorgio Agamben and Emanuele Coccia. Connal is currently completing a project on the utility of Giorgio Agamben's thought in reshaping legal thinking for the coming technological age.

Laura Petersen is a PhD candidate at the Institute for International Law and the Humanities at Melbourne Law School, University of Melbourne. Her research is cross-disciplinary, combining approaches to jurisprudence with literature and visual and public art. Laura's PhD thesis examines practices of *Wiedergutmachung* ('making good again') in Germany after the NS Regime and the Holocaust.

Sara Ramshaw is an associate professor at the University of Victoria Faculty of Law, Canada. Her research explores arts-based approaches to law and legal pedagogy, and she is particularly interested in the relationship between improvised artistic practices and justice.

Sophie Rigney is a senior research associate at the Indigenous Law Centre, University of New South Wales, researching constitutional reform and the *Uluru Statement from the Heart*. She is also an adjunct lecturer in law at the University of Tasmania. She is from settler and migrant heritage and lives on Muwinina land (Hobart, Australia).

Isobel Roele teaches law at Queen Mary University of London, where she is Co-director of the Centre for Law and Society in a Global Context. Isobel writes about international organisation and modernism, and is especially interested in the artwork and management structures of the United Nations.

Gerry Simpson is a professor of international law at the LSE. He is currently writing *Lawful Interregnum*, a book on the Cold War (with Sundhya Pahuja and Matthew Craven). His latest book, *The Sentimental Life of International Law*, will be published in 2021. His chapter in this book, 'the atomics', is drawn from a longer meditation on nuclearism, also titled *the atomics*.

Oishik Sircar teaches at the Jindal Global Law School and works in the areas of critical jurisprudence, queer theory, and law and aesthetics. He is the author of *Violent Modernities: Cultural Lives of Law in the New India* (OUP, 2021).

Cait Storr is Chancellor's Postdoctoral Research Fellow at the University of Technology Sydney, Australia. She researches the relationship between property and territory in the history of imperialism and international law, with a focus on resource extraction in international domains. She has held positions as Early Career Academic Fellow at Melbourne Law School, and lecturer at the University of Glasgow. Her doctoral thesis was awarded the University of Melbourne Chancellor's Prize, and published as *International Status in the Shadow of Empire: Nauru and the Histories of International Law* (Cambridge University Press, 2020).

Valeria Vázquez Guevara is a PhD candidate at Melbourne Law School and a member of the Institute for International Law and the Humanities (IILAH). Valeria's research is concerned with how international law 'works' after violent conflict, and what sort of post-conflict society it shapes, especially in the Global South.

Introduction

Practice, Craft and ethos: inheriting a tradition

Shane Chalmers and Sundhya Pahuja[1]

> I also wrote a book "On Faith, Hope, and Love" since the one to whom it was written had asked me for a little treatise of mine that he might always have it "at hand" – the kind of book the Greeks call an *enchiridion*. . . . This book begins: "I cannot tell you, my dearest son Laurence."
>
> Augustine's Testimony Concerning the *Enchiridion*[2]

In one sense this Handbook comes late to a 500-year-old conversation.[3] This is a conversation about the humanistic study of law. Each of the authors in this book is concerned to join that conversation, and to take up an inheritance of the traditions of thought in which law is part of humanistic study. Those traditions are varied,[4] and the authors each contribute to the conversation and take up their inheritance in different ways. But within those traditions, questions of training and transmission have always been central,[5] and so it seems fitting for the community

1 The authors would like to acknowledge the advice of Shaun McVeigh in shaping this chapter, as well as the input from Adil Hasan Khan and Sara Ramshaw.

2 Albert Cook Outler, ed., *Augustine: Confessions and Enchiridion* (Louisville, Kentucky: Westminster John Knox Press, 2006), 26.

3 Although we can assure our publishers that it is all new.

4 See, e.g., Shaun McVeigh, "Critical Approaches to Jurisdiction and International Law," in *The Oxford Handbook of Jurisdiction in International Law*, eds. Stephen Allen, et al. (Oxford: Oxford University Press, 2019); Peter Goodrich, *The Laws of Love: A Brief Historical and Practical Manual* (New York: Palgrave Macmillan, 2007); James Turner, *Philology: The Forgotten Origins of the Modern Humanities* (Princeton: Princeton University Press, 2014); Philip Selznick, *A Humanist Science: Values and Ideals in Social Inquiry* (Stanford, CA: Stanford University Press, 2008); Donald R. Kelley, *The Human Measure: Social Thought in the Western Legal Tradition* (Cambridge: Harvard University Press, 1990).

5 This is a theme frequently taken up in the work of Shaun McVeigh. See, e.g., Shaun McVeigh, "Reciprocal Relations: Formations of the Office of Legal Scholar," *Jindal Global Law Review* 9, no. 2 (2018); Shaun McVeigh, "Office and Persona of the Critical Jurist: Peripheral Legal Thought (Australia)," in *Searching for Contemporary Legal Thought*, eds. Justin Desautels-Stein and Christopher Tomlins (Cambridge: Cambridge University Press, 2017); Ann Genovese, Shaun McVeigh and Peter D. Rush, "Lives Lived with Law: An Introduction," *Law Text Culture* 20 (2016).

of scholars who contribute to this book to find ourselves joined together, and to our readers, in the genre of instruction.

The Handbook

The Handbook is part of a wider genre of instructional writing. Sharing an etymology with manuals (at least in the European context), both are works designed to be 'on hand' for review, instruction, help or reference.[6] There are many traditions of handbook writing, from the texts of late antiquity in Europe known as *enchiridia*,[7] and *vademecum*,[8] to related books from imperial China,[9] and the decidedly hard-to-carry scientific handbooks of the nineteenth century.[10] Across the variation we can detect two broad ambitions which seem to emerge, and by the nineteenth century become somewhat distinct traditions.[11] For heuristic purposes, we could say that one tradition aspires to present in the Handbook an encyclopaedic knowledge about a scientific field; while the second tradition aims to gather and curate the experiential knowledge generated through practice, to serve as a basis for training.[12]

In the encyclopaedic tradition, the Handbook's purpose is to present an authoritative account of the field that strives to be comprehensive and coherent. The result is designed to reassure; with this book to hand, one might navigate the field. In this, the aesthetic form of the work, and the form of authority to which it lays claim, go hand in hand.[13] Its formal elements signal order, mastery and completeness. These elements include front matter attesting to the professional standing of its editors and authors, and the aesthetic arrangement of the work. The Handbook's title offers a neat encapsulation of the field. Its table of contents registers and communicates its parameters, its categories and its idioms. The promise is both that there is a field that can be surveyed and mapped, and that *this* book has covered the terrain, explored its features, encountered its natives. And now, under the sign of the field's proper name, it offers up a reliable guide.[14] The authority to which such handbooks appeal is closely related to the kind of authority that grounds occidental modern law.[15] Like the encyclopaedic handbook, modern law is supposed to be autonomous, its authority transcending its makers rather than being dependent upon them. Similarly, modern law is said to be coherent, characterised by unity rather than

6 Angela Creager, Mathias Grote and Elaine Leong, eds., *Learning by the Book: Manuals and Handbooks in the History of Science* (forthcoming).

7 A Latin rendition of the Greek word *enkheiridion*, literally 'in the hand', popular as a Stoic literary genre and perhaps best known through the work of Augustine (thanks to Adil Hasan Khan for this point).

8 A book designed to 'go with me' (literally, '*vade mecum*').

9 See Martha Hanson's contribution to Creager, Grote and Leong, *Learning by the Book*.

10 See Creager, Grote and Leong, *Learning by the Book*.

11 See James A. Secord, "Science, Technology and Mathematics," in *The Cambridge History of the Book in Britain Volume 6: 1830–1914*, ed. David McKitterick (Cambridge: Cambridge University Press, 2009), 443–74.

12 See generally, Creager, Grote and Leong, *Learning by the Book*. See for example (with respect to medical handbooks), Axel C. Hüntelmann, "Medical Knowledge and the Manual Production of Casebook-Based Handbooks," *Learning by the Book Blog Series*, accessed June 1, 2018, https://historyofknowledge.net/2018/06/01/manual-production-of-casebook-based-handbooks/.

13 Pardon the pun.

14 See also Alrun Schmidtke, "The Handbook as Genre: Conflicting Concepts in 1950's Physics Publishing," *Learning by the Book Blog Series*, accessed May 31, 2018, https://historyofknowledge.net/2018/05/31/the-handbook-as-genre/; Lorraine Daston and Peter Galison, *Objectivity* (New York: Zone Books, 2007).

15 See Peter Fitzpatrick, *The Mythology of Modern Law* (Abingdon: Routledge, 1992).

plurality. Modern law, like the encyclopaedic handbook, seeks exteriority, promising to guide us from some standpoint external to both its makers and the (social) field.[16]

The second tradition of handbooks is the technical manual. These are often the artists', physicians' and craftspersons' manuals, which take up their etymological inheritance in the hand which makes and shapes. In this tradition, practical knowledge forms the basis of the text, and authority finds its feet in the shared practices of a community.[17] The purpose of the Handbook in this tradition is to provide technical instruction, or to describe how to do something, often in the context of an apprenticeship or in the company of a teacher. As in the encyclopaedic tradition, the aesthetic form of the work and the asserted form of authority are closely connected. Such works are often arranged in a contingent and provisional way. One famous example, the seventeenth-century *Pictoria, Sculptoria et quae Subalternarum Artium*, 'edited' by Theodore de Mayerne, was made up of 170 loose leaves of paper of various sizes, written in large part by 'miscellaneous hands' and gathered together over 25 years by de Mayerne, and bound as a single volume only after his death.[18] In it, paint recipes are annotated, crossed out and rewritten; diagrams are offered; experiments are reported; letters from artists are inserted; conversations are recorded. And all of this in six different languages. And yet, while the manuscript was far from being a unified and coherent artists' rule book, it was a preeminent authority on the craft of painting in its day and remained so for decades. The force of its authority derived not from a claim to having mastered its object through transcending it, but from its experiential nature, and its source within a particular community of practitioners.[19] This type of authority resonates with a rather different jurisprudential tradition, one in which law is understood to be 'discursive, performed, assumed, located, relational, and material'.[20] In Margaret Davies' account, in this broad tradition the authority of law is understood to be 'intrinsically plural – differentiated by different knowledges, subjectivities, locations, performances'.[21]

The changing styles and traditions of handbooks can be observed historically to reflect changing scholarly relationships to textuality.[22] In the early modern period, in both Christianity

16 See also Margaret Davies, *Law Unlimited: Materialism, Pluralism, and Legal Theory* (Abingdon: Routledge, 2017).

17 For an interesting reflection on why the distinction we are drawing should not be understood as a distinction between practice and theory, see Richard Parry, "*Episteme* and *Techne*," in *Stanford Encyclopedia of Philosophy (Summer 2020 Edition)*, ed. Edward N. Zalta, https://plato.stanford.edu/archives/sum2020/entries/episteme-techne/.

18 As a matter of content, the de Mayerne manuscript provides a guide to artistic techniques, including recipes for making 'pigments, oils and varnishes', as well as standards and procedures for 'the priming and preparation of surfaces for painting' and 'the repair and conservation of paintings': see the British Library catalogue entry, "Sir Theodore de Mayerne, Pictoria, sculptoria et quae subalternarum artium," Sloane MS 2052, www.bl.uk/manuscripts/FullDisplay.aspx?ref=Sloane_MS_2052.

19 The pages emanated from some of the most reputable workshops in Europe. The hands may have been miscellaneous, but they were the hands of artists and craftspeople with years of training and practice. Some were of 'major' renown, others were almost unknown. See Jenny Boulboullé, "The Manual as Artifact: On Artists' Manuals and Craftsmen's Handbooks," *Learning by the Book Blog Series*, accessed June 4, 2018, https://historyofknowledge.net/2018/06/04/manual-as-artifact/; Jo Kirby, "The Painter's Trade in the Seventeenth Century: Theory and Practice," *National Gallery Technical Bulletin* 20 (1999): 11–12. For an English translation, see Donald C. Fels, Jr, ed., *Lost Secrets of Flemish Painting: Including the First Complete English Translation of the de Mayerne Manuscript, BM Sloane 2052* (Floyd, VA: Alchemist Inc, 2004).

20 Davies, *Law Unlimited*, 89.

21 Ibid. See also Margaret Davies, "The Ethos of Pluralism," *Sydney Law Review* 27 (2005); Roderick A. Macdonald, "Custom Made – for a Non-Chirographic Critical Legal Pluralism," *Canadian Journal of Law and Society* 26, no. 2 (2011).

22 Matthew Melvin-Koushki, "*How to Rule the World*: Occult-Scientific Manuals of the Early Modern Persian Cosmopolis," *Journal of Persianate Studies* 11, no. 2 (2019).

and Islam for instance, there were transformations in the production and reception of manuals of instruction. Authors began to write books as standalone sources of knowledge, and readers began to read them as such.[23] This included texts written for royal readers across the Islamo-Christian world, which encouraged a quest to control the world scientifically and imperially.[24] In the nineteenth century, European imperial expansion coincided with decreasing publishing costs and increasing literacy rates. Instructional literature was central to the civilising project,[25] and the encyclopaedic style of handbooks flourished during this period.[26] Imperial power in Europe was co-produced with imperial knowledge, and the rise of this style of handbook was historically implicated in the rearrangement of knowledge. Certain forms of knowledge were made more widely available to increasingly literate publics in Europe and its imperial centres alongside the dissemination of printed works to the colonies, while other forms of knowledge were displaced through mass education in both metropole and colony.[27]

These displacements of knowledge were also displacements of laws.[28] And the two horizons of ambition and their divergence in the nineteenth century can be felt in the instructional literature about law and jurisprudence too. In the English context, Sugarman argues that the invention in the nineteenth century of the 'textbook tradition' was key not only to the reshaping of juristic concerns amongst lawyers, but to the constitution of a new social consciousness about state, society and politics.[29] These new instructional works were part of a 'revolution' in legal education during which time the new academic lawyers 'fundamentally reconceptualized the form and content of English law'.[30] This new tradition took legal education and academic writing away from the practices of lawyers and the palimpsestual form of the Common Law, toward a codification of the law which sought clarity, precision and the separation of legal 'science' from other disciplines. In colonial contexts, too, this new tradition has been felt, from across Africa to the settler-colonies of Australia and Canada, through a legal education that has sought to transmit not only the codified rules of the Common Law, but its 'spirit', as a 'cultural heritage' freighted with British values.[31]

23 Ibid.

24 Ibid.

25 See, e.g., Thomas Babington Macaulay, "Minute by the Hon'ble T B Macaulay, dated the 2nd February 1835," known as the 'Macaulay minute on education in India'. See also Gauri Viswanathan, *Masks of Conquest: Literary Study and British Rule in India* (Oxford: Oxford University Press, 1998).

26 For example, one of the most important English-language contributions, *Chambers's Encyclopaedia: A Dictionary of Universal Knowledge for the People*, appeared mid-century, in 1859.

27 Consider the example of language; see Ngũgĩ wa Thiong'o, *Decolonising the Mind: The Politics of Language in African Literature* (Nairobi: East African Educational Publishers, 1981); Chinweizu, Onwuchekwa Jemie and Ihechukwu Madubuike, *Toward the Decolonization of African Literature, Volume 1: African Fiction and Poetry and Their Critics* (Washington, DC: Howard University Press, 1987).

28 See Ibid. See also the children's film, *The Secret of Roan Inish* (1994), for a moving depiction of the mutual displacement of both Gaelic language and Brehon Law through practices of education, and disciplining children out of speaking their mother tongue – 'the night of the sword and the bullet was followed by the morning of the chalk and the blackboard' (wa Thiong'o, *Decolonising the Mind*, 9).

29 David Sugarman, "Legal Theory, the Common Law Mind and the Making of the Textbook Tradition," in *Legal Theory and Common Law*, ed. William Twining (New York: Blackwell, 1986): 26–62.

30 Ibid., 54.

31 See W. Wesley Pue, "Educating the Total Jurist?" *Legal Ethics* 8, no. 2 (2005): 213–14, discussing Lord Denning, "Legal Education in Africa: Sharing Our Heritage," *Law Society Gazette* 58 (1961). See also John A Harrington and Ambreena Manji, "'Mind with Mind and Spirit with Spirit': Lord Denning and African Legal Education," *Journal of Law and Society* 30 (2003); W. Wesley Pue, "Planting British Legal Culture in Colonial Soil: Legal Professionalism in the Lands of the Beaver and Kangaroo," in *Shaping Nations: Constitutionalism and Society in Australia and Canada*, eds. Linda Cardinal and David Headon (Ottawa: University of Ottawa Press, 2002): 91–116.

All of this is to draw attention to the relationship between styles of handbooks, traditions of transmission and instruction, and accounts of authority, knowledge and law. Our account is too clean to be true of course, but it is meant to be heuristic rather than historical. The point is not to construct a schematisation that sets the styles of a humanistic study of law against a corresponding handbook style. Instead, we seek to locate this particular Handbook within these overlapping genres of instructional writing, and to gesture to the entangled traditions of thought that they carry.

The field

Perhaps the most visible point at which the forms of knowledge, authority, laws and handbooks come together is in the 'field' in which they promise to guide the reader. Far from simply registering an existing field, handbooks actively participate in their creation. This is true of both traditions of handbooks, though they participate in field-making in different ways. In the encyclopaedic tradition, the gesture is toward 'mapping' the field by identifying its definitive markers (today publishers often ask the editors of a proposed handbook to demonstrate that it will be 'field defining'). The resulting representation seems to present an observable connection to an existing body of knowledge. But the relation between handbook and object is less one of connection than co-production,[32] and by linking description, instruction and authorisation (both scientific and juridical), handbooks shape not only how the world is known but also how it is actualised.[33] An analogy can be drawn here with maps, and many examples could be cited, of maps which clearly reveal the link between description and authorisation.[34] Just one handbook which exemplifies this work, of description or authoring, and authorisation, is the *Manuale Legum sive Hexabiblos* (Manual of Laws in Six Books), also known as the *Procheiron Nomon* (Handbook of the Laws), compiled by the Byzantine jurist Constantine Harmenopoulos, in 1345.[35] This Handbook was a survey of a number of the most important existing law books of the period, organised into a mapping and projection of Byzantine law, which had great influence on imperial and state legal systems for over five centuries, right into the nineteenth century.[36]

32 Sheila Jasanoff, "The Idiom of Co-production," in *States of Knowledge: The Co-Production of Science and the Social Order*, ed. Sheila Jasanoff (Abingdon: Routledge, 2004), 1–12. Co-production refers to the way that the normative and descriptive are co-produced.

33 Think of the 1494 map based on the Treaty of Tordesillas, which divided the world into two spheres of authority, one Spanish, one Portuguese, or the 1884–1885 Berlin West Africa Conference maps, which shaped Africa through its division into spheres of European authority. See Antony Anghie, *Imperialism, Sovereignty and the Making of International Law* (Cambridge: Cambridge University Press, 2004), 91; Matthew Craven, "Between Law and History: The Berlin Conference of 1884–1885 and the Logic of Free Trade," *London Review of International Law* 3, no. 1 (2015): 31–59.

34 See Shaunnagh Dorsett, "Mapping Territories," in *Jurisprudence of Jurisdiction*, ed. Shaun McVeigh (Abingdon: Routledge, 2006); Boaventura de Sousa Santos, "Law: A Map of Misreading. Toward a Postmodern Conception of Law," *Journal of Law and Society* 14, no. 3 (1987): 279–302.

35 Marie Theres Fögen, "Harmenopoulos, Constantine," in *The Oxford Dictionary of Byzantium*, ed. Alexander P. Kazhdan (Oxford: Oxford University Press, 1991). The German translation, first published in 1564, is the *Handbuch und auszug Kayserlicher und Bürgerlicher Rechten* ('Handbook of Imperial and Civil Laws').

36 Of course this facility of maps to describe and re-describe 'reality', and their power to reconstitute it in ways that subvert the given or 'natural' state of things, can be a critical resource as much as an imperial one, as Boaventura de Sousa Santos has shown in "Law: A Map of Misreading." Historically, projects of resistance also took up this mode, engaging dialectically with the colonisation of knowledge by taking up the aesthetic forms of a particular style of knowledge claim in order to contest the claim to authority. The same is true of the encyclopaedic

Handbooks in the technical tradition also participate in creating a field. But perhaps rather than mapping the field from an objective or external standpoint, they could be read as stitching together an image of the field from inside a community of practice. The analogy here might be quilting.[37] Quilting is a craft that requires the sensibilities and techniques of a craftsperson. It is a patchwork craft, which emphasises the fragment as both singularly important and integral to the whole. Quilting also tends to be a communal, inter-subjective project, involving many hands holding many threads. In contrast to the act of mapping an object, the act of quilting embodies a practice of collective story telling that produces, records and transmits a patchwork of community knowledge.[38] It is this communal production that gives the quilt its authority, as a cultural medium for representing and creating social knowledge.

When it comes to handbooks of law and jurisprudence, the field-making work of each tradition also has a 'juris-dictional' effect, insofar as it speaks the law.[39] This can be true for handbooks in both traditions. The extent to which that juris-diction, or enunciation of law, joins in displacing other laws outside a particular tradition will vary from hand to hand and book to book,[40] and may not correspond neatly with the two traditions of handbooks. When the handbook of a legal field claims to be authoritative, coherent or comprehensive, it is participating in authoring and authorising both the legal 'field' and the law on which it is based. In other words, not only what the law is, but what law 'itself' is. So, for example, a handbook of the history of international law with an encyclopaedic aim has the effect not only of circumscribing a scholarly field in a particular way,[41] but participates in speaking the law 'itself' by its implication that what it is describing should properly be considered international law.[42] The lower horizon of ambition reflected in the Handbook as manual could allow the possibility of reporting from 'within' a field of shared legal practice without a necessary claim to the universality of that account of the field, but its effects on the displacement of rival laws would depend too on the accounts of law carried with them, and types of claim being made for those accounts.[43]

Over the past decade, an increasing number of volumes has begun to offer accounts of the field of 'law and the humanities' or its subfields.[44] At the same time, there has been a push

handbooks, which can be taken up in ways that subvert their claim to authority. Examples include the forthcoming *Handbook of Third World Approaches to International Law*, which uses the form of the encyclopaedic handbook to help create a field of resistance, or the forthcoming *Oxford Handbook on International Law and Development*, which works to redescribe and thereby subvert an existing field.

37 There are many varied traditions of quilting, but they share some important characteristics, from the centuries-old tradition of Ralli quilting in South Asia to the decades-old tradition of colonial quilting in the United States.

38 See, e.g., Linda Chalmers, "Ikat Sequences and Social-Cultural Patterns: The Impact of Industrialization on the Lives of Iban Artisans in Sarawak" (PhD Thesis, James Cook University, North Queensland, 1993) on how the ikat textile work of Iban women in Sarawak reproduces systems of social knowledge.

39 Peter Rush, "An Altered Jurisdiction: Corporeal Traces of Law," *Griffith Law Review* 6 (1997); Shaunnagh Dorsett and Shaun McVeigh, *Jurisdiction* (Abingdon: Routledge, 2012).

40 An effect that Robert Cover has called 'jurispathic'; see Robert Cover, "The Supreme Court, 1982 Term – Foreword: *Nomos* and Narrative," *Harvard Law Review* 97 (1983).

41 Rose Parfitt, "The Spectre of Sources," *European Journal of International Law* 25, no. 1 (2014).

42 Sundhya Pahuja, "Letters from Bandung," in *Bandung, Global History, and International Law: Critical Pasts and Pending Futures*, eds. Luis Eslava, Michael Fakhri and Vasuki Nesiah (Cambridge: Cambridge University Press, 2017), 552–73.

43 For an example of this approach, see Ann Genovese and Shaun McVeigh, "Nineteen Eighty Three: A Jurisographic Report on *Commonwealth v Tasmania*," *Griffith Law Review* 24 (2015).

44 See, e.g., Simon Stern, Maksymilian Del Mar and Bernadette Meyler, *The Oxford Handbook of Law and Humanities* (Oxford: Oxford University Press, 2020); the six volume survey produced by Gary Watt, ed., *A Cultural History of Law* (London: Bloomsbury, 2019); Austin Sarat, Matthew Anderson and Cathrine O. Frank, eds.,

to expand the imagined parameters of the field beyond an Anglo-centric focus, by pluralising the positions of its practitioners as well as its geographical and jurisdictional focus.[45] This efflorescence has been accompanied by discussions about the canonisation of the field, as well as the importance of resisting canonisation given the traditions of thought being taken up.[46] In general, these volumes seek to avoid the horizon of ambition associated with the encyclopaedic tradition. The editors of *The Oxford Handbook of Law and Humanities*, for example, express this through the form of the invitation they describe as having been extended to proposed contributors, which requested that they 'bring their own subjectivity to bear' rather than attempt to produce objectively-distanced 'reviews' of 'the literature'.[47]

Across these volumes, different inflections are given to what the idea of the 'field' of law and the humanities might be. Alongside the relatively widely shared intellectual concern to avoid the reification of particular forms of legal knowledge, we can sense the political, institutional and social imperatives at play in the need to have, and be able to name, a field at all, rather than simply to conduct research within broader fields of law, legal theory, legal studies or jurisprudence. Some of these material imperatives are connected to the way a felt desire for scholarly community adapts to changing research interests. Others are patterned by the changing nature of the university and the increasing need for scholars to be able to explain and justify their work, describe their networks and name their tribes to people outside their scholarly community.

In all of this, one frequently observed inflection given to the field is a focus on disciplinarity 'itself', and the need to articulate the joining of law to humanistic disciplines in substantive, methodological or formal ways. For those who focus on disciplinarity, one story would trace the 'origins' of the field to the United States, where the historical disaggregation of traditions of thought into 'disciplines', and the subsequent rise of law and economics in US legal academia, created for many scholars an ethical and political imperative for a different, and differently oriented kind of inter-disciplinarity.[48] This formation is reflected in the names of early journals

Law and the Humanities: An Introduction (Cambridge: Cambridge University Press, 2010); and the special issue of *International Journal of Law in Context* 5, no. 3 (2009) on 'socio-legal studies and the humanities'. For an indication of recent work in the sub-fields of law and literature and law and the visual, see Elizabeth S. Anker and Bernadette Meyler, eds., *New Directions in Law and Literature* (Oxford: Oxford University Press, 2017); Lorna Hutson, ed., *The Oxford Handbook of English Law and Literature, 1500–1700* (Oxford: Oxford University Press, 2017); Jani McCutcheon and Fiona McGaughey, eds., *Research Handbook on Art and Law* (Cheltenham: Edward Elgar, 2020); Desmond Manderson, ed., *Law and the Visual: Representations, Technologies, Critique* (Toronto: University of Toronto Press, 2018).

45 See the special issue of *Law & Literature* 31, no. 2 (2019) on 'law and the humanities in China' edited by Marco Wan. See also Greta Olson, "De-Americanizing Law and Literature Narratives: Opening Up the Story," *Law & Literature* 22, no. 2 (2010).

46 See Sara Ramshaw, "Law and Humanities: A Field without a Canon," *Law, Culture and the Humanities* (2019), https://doi.org/10.1177/1743872119886235; Hyo Yoon Kang, "Is There (Should There Be) a Law and Humanities Canon?" *Law, Culture and the Humanities* (2019), https://doi.org/10.1177/1743872119857063; Cathrine O. Frank, "Literacies for a New Canon," *Law, Culture and the Humanities* (2019), https://doi.org/10.1177/1743872119893320. See also Costas Douzinas, "A Humanities of Resistance: Fragments for a Legal History of Humanity," in *Law and the Humanities: An Introduction*, eds. Austin Sarat, Matthew Anderson and Cathrine O. Frank (Cambridge: Cambridge University Press, 2010).

47 Simon Stern, Maksymilian Del Mar and Bernadette Meyler, "Introduction," in *The Oxford Handbook of Law and Humanities*, eds. Simon Stern, Maksymilian Del Mar and Bernadette Meyler (Oxford: Oxford University Press, 2020), xxi.

48 See Jack M. Balkin and Sanford Levinson, "Law and the Humanities: An Uneasy Relationship," *Yale Journal of Law & the Humanities* 18, no. 2 (2006): 166–72; Christopher Tomlins, "Framing the Field of Law's Interdisciplinary Encounters: A Historical Narrative," *Law and Society Review* 34, no. 4 (2000); Julie Stone Peters, "Law, Literature, and the Vanishing Real: On the Future of an Interdisciplinary Illusion," *PMLA* 120, no. 2 (2005).

identifying with this field in the US, such as *Cardozo Studies in Law and Literature* (now *Law & Literature*), and indeed by the name of the nascent field itself, 'law and the humanities'. Others embrace an explicitly 'transdisciplinary' approach.[49] For these scholars, their work is not the product of an encounter between disciplines, but an 'engagement with' the objects, sites and traditions more habitually claimed by one or other humanistic disciplines.[50]

But from the beginning,[51] scholars seeking institutional shelter under the umbrella of 'law and the humanities' did not understand themselves only through a lens of disciplinary encounter. The Australian journal, *Law Text Culture*, for example, focused from the outset on what might be called the whereabouts of law – its objects and sites – rather than on the disciplinary identities of those who study law. The possibilities offered by this inflection can be seen in the first volume, and indeed the first article of the first volume, which took 'Aboriginal traditional and customary law' as the centre point of its intervention in the field. Others still have pointed to method, rather than discipline or object, as a way of understanding what unites scholars in the field. For Desmond Manderson, for example, whether one's object of study is an artwork or a roadway, what matters is not the object's type (i.e., whether it is properly 'humanistic' material), but how one approaches it. This approach could be described as a 'method', an orienting sensibility[52] or an attitude.[53] For Manderson, the approach implies an attention to the singularities, representational qualities and constitutive power of the object of study,[54] but it might also imply an attention to discontinuities, a sensitivity to the marginal and a reflexivity.[55]

For scholars in this volume, drawn together in the field of international law and the humanities, we could perhaps best describe what we have in common as an ethos. In this, we share with many an emphasis on practice, but join questions of method explicitly to the formation of a particular community. Etymologically, ethos implies a link between one's own character and the habits and customs of the group.[56] An ethos is cultivated through the transmission of tradition through a training in conduct.[57] In an institutional sense, this happens each day at the Institute for International Law and the Humanities in Melbourne, from where both editors write. And it is not a coincidence that an emplaced community is at the core of a handbook such as this one. But IILAH, as it is known, is also a focal point and node in a more virtual community, in which

49 On the shift from an interdisciplinary to a transdisciplinary identity, and in a way anticipating it, see the conclusion to Peters, "Law, Literature, and the Vanishing Real," 450–51; Dermot Feenan, "Foreword: Socio-Legal Studies and the Humanities," *International Journal of Law in Context* 5, no. 3 (2009): 235–42.

50 See the Call for Papers, *Routledge Handbook of Cultural Legal Studies* (2020).

51 As early as the 1990s.

52 See, e.g., Desmond Manderson, "Bodies in the Water: On Reading Images More Sensibly," *Law & Literature* 27, no. 2 (2015): 279–93.

53 See Panu Minkkinen, "Critical Legal Method as 'Attitude'," in *Research Methods in Law, 2E*, eds. Dawn Watkins and Mandy Burton (Routledge, 2017), 146–69; Balkin and Levinson, "Law and the Humanities," 161–63.

54 Desmond Manderson, "Ad 2014: A Review Essay of Eve Darian-Smith, *Laws and Societies in Global Contexts – Contemporary Approaches*," *Law and Humanities* 8, no. 1 (2014).

55 Thus, the editors of *The Oxford Handbook of Law and Humanities* connect the field to a sensitivity to 'the irregular and the unpatterened', which they also call 'an attitude of respect for, or a responsiveness to, the anomaly, to particularity, to idiosyncrasy' (which corresponds with Manderson's point about being attentive to singularities). Other examples that they give are reflexivity, or a sensitivity to 'our blind spots'; and, in a Benjaminian vein, a sensitivity to life's refuse ('the humanities look, with delicacy and care, through the garbage bins of history'). Stern, Del Mar and Meyler, *Oxford Handbook*, xxiii.

56 Coming from the Greek for character, custom or habit.

57 See McVeigh, "Formations of the Office of Legal Scholar"; McVeigh, "Office and Persona of the Critical Jurist"; McVeigh, "Critical Approaches." See also Davies, "The Ethos of Pluralism."

the members are joined together by a particular ethos. In this context, ethos denotes shared ways of doing things, such that both these practices, and the manner in which the practices are shared, become aspects of how we take up an inheritance of the traditions of the humanistic study of law. A more elegant way of describing all this is to say that the scholars in this book can all be understood in their various ways to be grappling with what Shaun McVeigh calls 'the character and transmission of forms of authority'.[58]

As we shall see, the 'international', and what that implies, inflects that task and shapes the traditions we join in different ways for the different scholars gathered together here. In the context of our strong sense of a shared ethos, and awareness that those we invited were each, in different ways, taking up an inheritance of the humanistic study of law, our invitation to contributors was quite open in terms of form. The result is that, rather than a collection of formally consistent chapters, the Handbook is made up of reflections, illustrations, experiments, exposés, tales, cautions and dialogues, of varying sizes and styles, all of which address the authors' senses of the craft of the jurisprudent of international law and the humanities and how to transmit that sense, as much as the topical knowledge they contribute.

But commissioning the works is only half the task. Editors of a handbook also have a duty to care for the scholarship that has been entrusted to them, and to fulfil the responsibility to organise and present that scholarship. Part of this presentation has been the explanation that you have just read, of why we have sought to situate this Handbook in the technical traditions of the craftsperson or artisan, rather than attempt to produce an authoritative guide to a jurisprudential field. The other part of the presentation is to explain how we have arranged the chapters.

The chapters

We have arranged the chapters into six parts,[59] under the headings Formation, Sense, World-making, History-telling, Community and Concepts for our Time. With each part, we have sought to highlight some of the ways in which the authors have taken up the 'international' as an aspect of their inheritance of the traditions of the humanistic study of law. The parts may be suggestive, too, of wider tendencies in the field. But still, we hope that for the reader each chapter also sits in the Handbook like the sheaves of paper in the de Mayerne manuscript. We have arranged and bound them in this way, but it is provisional, and they could be moved differently in relation to each other to draw out different things.

Formation

The first part begins with a collection of chapters that each take up the 'international' in terms of international law as a disciplinary formation. Each of the authors is concerned with the

58 McVeigh, "Critical Approaches," 183.

59 In curating the chapters, we draw inspiration from the concept of the constellation. For Theodor Adorno, inheriting the concept from his friend and mentor Walter Benjamin, the constellation offered a model for arranging knowledge that could be representational without appealing to a transcendent authority. As a mode of representation, a constellation offers an image of its 'object' – in this case the field of 'international law and the humanities' – by coming at it indirectly, and relationally, from multiple, interconnected points. The effect is to highlight features of the field, while remaining suggestive and open, creating an impression rather than a sense of having grasped the thing in itself. We did contemplate making a quilt, but that seemed harder than arranging stars.

responsibilities that come with practising as a jurist in this discipline, whether through writing, scholarship, advising or advocacy,[60] and with inhabiting the office of the international, or transnational, jurisprudent. These chapters also attend to what we have become accustomed to calling the conduct of diplomatic, or international, relations, but which we might think of as the modes of conduct that the discipline offers for the meeting of laws and societies.

In Chapter 1, Shaun McVeigh draws on a collaboration with Ann Genovese and Mark McMillan, on treaties between Indigenous and non-Indigenous Australians, to address the question of 'the appropriate conduct (*officia*) of public life and office, and the creation of ways of co-existence between peoples and nations'. McVeigh does not advance a singular normative approach in response to this question, but instead offers examples drawn from a rich archive of Indigenous and non-Indigenous traditions. He shows us how these traditions offer 'different sets of duties, and conducts of disciplinary life', which might aid in the negotiation and conduct of relations between peoples and nations. In a different sense, the formation of the discipline is also the focus of Gregor Noll's contribution (Chapter 2). Like McVeigh, Noll examines the European inheritance of the discipline's traditions, not only to understand one possible genealogy – which Noll traces back to monastic orders – but also to retrieve modes of conduct that might guide international jurisprudents in their disciplinary work today. For Noll, a central problem of that inheritance is the discipline's attempt at secularisation within Europe. This 'failed' secularisation both inheres in the discipline, and points to a way of conducting research that is not limited to any particular area of knowledge: it is instead inherently interdisciplinary. This problem, and the productive possibility, of the secularisation of the discipline also animates Adil Hasan Khan's contribution (Chapter 3). Like Noll's account, Hasan Khan's chapter is framed by debates over the intersection between theology, politics and law in the formation of the discipline. Like McVeigh (and drawing on his thought), Hasan Khan is concerned with receiving the traditions of the conduct of public office, and in particular traditions of 'civility', which might guide the jurisprudent in cultivating conditions of cohabitation. Here Hasan Khan is animated by a concern with the lawful coexistence of peoples in South Asia, and the ways in which South Asian traditions may offer a different international legal disciplinary force and formation that rivals the projects of colonial modernity.

The next two chapters turn from what we might think of as the formation of a discipline, to the ways in which (international) law relates to the formation of subjects. Gerry Simpson's account of growing up during the Cold War under the threat of nuclear annihilation (Chapter 4) is an intimate, personal reflection on how international legal nuclearism shaped him as an international lawyer, not only as someone who has taken up the discipline of international law as a profession, but as someone who has already been disciplined by its nuclear imperatives since childhood. In the same register – of being born into a legal world – Judith Grbich's study of the 'characters of private international law' (Chapter 5) offers an account of how Europeans came to learn 'to inhabit a world of financial things'. As Grbich shows through her genealogy of money in Europe, understanding globalised financial practices today requires understanding how we are interpellated by images, in this case, images of exchange, which in Grbich's account can be illustrated by sixteenth-century Tudor systems of governance.

The final chapter in this part crosses both of these registers – of the formation of the discipline, and of the discipline's generative force. The chapter is a collaboration between the late Peter Fitzpatrick and four of his former doctoral students, who are now themselves teachers

60 See Andrew Fitzmaurice, "Context in the History of International Law," *Journal of the History of International Law / Revue d'histoire du droit international* 20, no. 1 (2018).

(Chapter 6). The chapter takes the form of an unfinished fragment by Fitzpatrick, a meditation on the discipline of international law, received as a parting gift, followed by responses from his former students, Sundhya Pahuja, Richard Joyce, Kathleen Birrell and Ben Golder. The result is a reminder that scholarship, like law, is only ever 'finished', or fulfilled, in community. But more than that, the chapter exemplifies the ways in which scholarly training in the humanistic study of law draws the attention of the novice to the intellectual formations of the discipline, as well as to the responsibilities and modes of conduct that come with inhabiting the office of the jurisprudent.

Sense

The chapters that we have grouped together in the second part of the Handbook offer six reflections on what we may know or feel the 'international' to be. While all of the chapters in this Handbook are oriented toward practice, the chapters in this part are explicitly reflexive. Like the paint recipes in the de Mayerne manuscript, these chapters report on three experiments with how we might sense, and know, the international (by Palmer, Parker and Andrews) and three demonstrations of how the international may be as much a sensibility as something sensed (Barr, Petersen and Golder).

Alice Palmer (Chapter 7) begins by addressing the persistent trope that there is no law in international law. In response to this trope, Palmer wonders whether an interdisciplinary encounter between international law and the humanities might help us to see this absent law. As she puts it: '[m]ight the humanities – and more specifically visual art – be used in the service of international law, to generate an image of international law where there is some law to be seen and, even better, applied to some purpose?' The answer she offers emerges through her analysis of a performance artwork and its relation to international environmental law – an answer that offers a way of seeing, and knowing, international law as law. In the chapter by James Parker that follows (Chapter 8), we are similarly invited to sense international law in a way that we might not have before, in this case through its sounds and silences. By putting two sonic artworks in conversation with each other (John Cage's *4'33"* and Lawrence Abu Hamdan's *Saydnaya (the missing 19dB)*), as well as with jurisprudential thought, Parker offers an account of the relationship between sound and silence, listening, and international law that foregrounds 'the complex ways in which sound and silence are connected to techniques of domination, power and resistance'. Alongside Palmer's experiment in seeing international law, and Parker's practicum in listening to law, we have placed Tom Andrews' chapter, which invites us to 'think with procedure' (Chapter 9). In this chapter, Andrews argues that a turn to the humanities enables us to apprehend the 'forms, modes, methods and structures of the conduct of juridical processes'. Grounded in a study of Jeremy Bentham's own attempts to constrain and order the conduct of juridical office, Andrew's chapter opens up the possibility of a jurisprudence of procedure that is attentive to 'the arrangement of the responsibilities and activities of law in terms of the quality of how the patterning, intensity, provenance, and choice of conduct might be proscribed, resisted, nominated, de-essentialised or chosen'. Taken together, these three chapters can be read as a series of cross-disciplinary encounters that offer ways to heighten our sense of the features of the 'international', to denaturalise, rearrange and potentially reimagine them.

The next three chapters turn from sense to sensibility. The first of these, by Olivia Barr (Chapter 10), takes the form of a reflection on how she has approached her research into the ongoing colonisation of Australia. By taking us along with her on her research journey over the past decade, Barr's chapter becomes both guide and companion to 'creative method-making'. The term that unites her scholarly practices is 'wayfaring', an approach that embraces getting lost as much as discovering one's way, that is sometimes meandering, sometimes path-breaking and always sensitive to how one walks with law. In a similar way, Laura Petersen (Chapter 11) offers a reflection on research method, as well as communication, through an account of 'foot notes' that explores the opportunities and challenges of connecting 'form and content' in scholarship. For Petersen, the footnote is more than a simple referencing technique. As a form of legal writing, the footnote itself does legal work through the representation of authority. But more than that, footnoting is a sensibility. For Petersen, footnoting is 'a grounded method for undertaking legal research outside of texts – literally as "foot notes"', a claim that she grounds in her own research practice of producing a walking video for her doctoral project. In the final chapter of this part, Ben Golder (Chapter 12) addresses the question of how we might understand the relationship between human rights and the humanities. Golder's answer is less concerned with uncovering the proper relationship as it is with showing us the operation, and importance, of two particular modes of critique: genealogy and performativity. By staging an encounter between human rights law and the humanities in disciplinary terms, Golder offers us an experiment in what we might think of as performative genealogy, made possible by returning the study of law to a less habitual humanistic tradition.

World-making

In the third part of the Handbook we have gathered together chapters that take up the 'international' as a mode of world-making. The first, by Cree scholar Jeffery G Hewitt (Chapter 13), focuses on how the authority of Anglo-European international law is generated and sustained through visual and textual media, while Indigenous international law is, in the Anglo-European imaginary, cast as a cultural artefact. Through a reading of two artefacts – a painting in the British Museum by Gerard ter Borch, representing an origin story of European international law, and the exhibition of North American wampum in museums – Hewitt shows how the former, European artwork, is granted legal force while the latter, Indigenous legal object, is stripped of its legality through its museological framing. The result is both argument and illustration of the ways in which different kinds of international laws are differentially authorised and de-authorised through the treatment of material culture. The chapter highlights too the Global North's ongoing legal illiteracy when it comes to Indigenous laws, national and international. The chapter that follows, by Hilary Charlesworth (Chapter 14), is also concerned with how the authority of international law, and its mythology, is generated and sustained by images. In this case, Charlesworth's focus is on international human rights law following the creation of the Universal Declaration of Human Rights (UDHR), and specifically, a UNESCO-curated travelling exhibition in 1950, which illustrated the UDHR and introduced it to the world. On one level, the exhibition worked to 'shore up the claims that the rights in the UDHR had a universal origin'. But as Charlesworth's reading shows, the images also exceeded their intended meaning and revealed something more about 'the specificity of the human at the centre of international human rights law'. It is a reminder of how the authority of international law might rely on visual images, but the same images can work to subvert that authority.

Like the chapters by Hewitt and Charlesworth, the next two chapters are concerned with the racist construction of the modern international legal order, and its decolonisation. However, for both Christopher Gevers, writing from South Africa, and Debolina Dutta and Oishik Sircar, writing from India, the question is how the literary practices of authors in the Global South can work to unmake the colonial world and its international law. Central to Gevers' concerns (Chapter 15) is the way in which the disciplines of international law and literature are co-implicated in the construction of the 'modern' international legal order, and how African writers have worked to contest this construction and to make different legal worlds through their literary practices. To show this, Gevers offers an historical-contextualist reading of two novels, by John Buchan, and W. E. B. Du Bois, which track, in Gevers' words, 'the worldmaking, and *unmaking*, practices' of international law in the early twentieth century. For Gevers, the practices of both disciplines – international law and literature – are more than just 'entangled', historically and theoretically: they are inseparable. One must consider the source, and force, of literature in order to more fully understand the work of international law in the world. In a similar way, law and literature are inseparable for Dutta and Sircar (Chapter 16), just as they are inseparable in the short story by Bengali writer, Sunil Gangopadhyay, which forms the core of their chapter. Gangopadhyay's story, which appears here for the first time in English translation, unfolds in a fictional nineteenth-century British-India. At its centre is the head of a lawyer, Benimadhab Laskar, which, as Dutta and Sircar elaborate in their Afterword, becomes an 'artefact for juridical and medical enquiry'. For Dutta and Sircar, the importance of this 'law story' is its ability to 'unlimit' a legal world in which 'sole interpretative authority' is granted to the coloniser. By unlimiting this legal world, Gangopadhyay's story works to decolonise both law and literature.

In the final chapter of this part, Isobel Roele (Chapter 17) keeps in focus the question of authoring and authorising a world, while honing in more specifically on the question of responsibility. 'We are all engaged in world-making: the choice we have is about whether our world-making is reflective and collaborative, or not'. Roele draws this conclusion from her encounter with another work of art, Paul Nash's *We Are Making a New World* (1918). Standing before this painting at Tate Britain, Roele finds herself implicated not only in the European world-making projects of the twentieth century, but in the one that is unfolding around her: Brexit. For Roele, Nash's painting is a visceral reminder that, while world-making is 'violent, messy, and unlikely to end happily', it is also 'inescapable, something we cannot opt-out of and are bound to do'. What this means for Roele, as it does for each of our contributors in different ways, is that co-creation implies shared responsibility for what is created.

History-telling

In part four we move from 'world-making' to 'history-telling'. Two concerns in particular run through the chapters here. One is how international law is implicated in the construction of History as world narrative, and by extension, how such history-telling has been, and continues to be, contested, especially by jurisprudents in the Global South (Craven, Nesiah, Motha, Martineau). The second concern is with how history-telling can be used as a technique in the analysis of international law, and more specifically, how it can be a mode of witnessing the 'international' (Storr, Jones, Buchanan). Although animated by slightly different concerns, the chapters here share an attention to the particularities of time and place, and of people and authorship, which shape any historical account. And in their own ways, each of the seven chapters is an argument against the kind of history-from-nowhere that tends to animate some traditions of history writing in the discipline of international law, and that continues to authorise the discipline's imperial ambitions and movements.

The first exemplification comes with Matthew Craven's analysis (Chapter 18) of twentieth-century decolonisation. In his argument, decolonisation was not simply a spatial and jurisdictional reconfiguration of the globe involving the overthrow of empire and the birth of new nation-states, but a temporal one. For Craven, temporality was the 'central problematic' of decolonisation. For those who resisted colonisation, it was not only the 'spatial ambit' of empire which had to be addressed, but 'its temporal structure'. As he shows through his reading of several Third World international jurisprudents, the question of what it meant to be 'contemporary' was one of their driving concerns. This resulted from an experience of being made non-contemporaneous with the European and North American world. In a similar way, Vasuki Nesiah (Chapter 19) is concerned with how postcolonial statehood has been constructed under a regime of debt which has shaped postcolonial sovereignty and set the political horizon for 'independent' states. Nesiah explores the case of Haiti, which successfully liberated itself from France only to find that France and her allies would not grant recognition to the newly independent nation-state, unless Haiti compensated France, and French slaveholders, for the loss of their slaves. In Nesiah's argument, the resulting sovereign 'debt' naturalised the violent and coercive nature of that event, patterning it into the background and focusing our attention instead on the 'indebted' sovereign. In this way, the story becomes one about a 'self-inflicted' wound as sovereign act, rather than a coercive ordering of the 'international'. Nesiah thinks with the concept of 'odius debt' and the 2006 film *Bamako* to explore the ways in which resistance to the global regime of Third World debt could be made thinkable through stories which interrupt how the world functions. These are stories which would be carried, performed and actualised through legal doctrines and demands.

In the next chapter, Stewart Motha (Chapter 20) returns to the question of how the history of international law has been narrated. Focusing on the Chagos litigation that has unfolded over the last two decades in UK courts, and in particular the International Court of Justice's *Advisory Opinion on the Chagos Archipelago* (2019), Motha questions how the cases have been interpreted and narrated alternatively in the genres of 'romance' or 'tragedy'. By interrogating the generative power of these narrative forms, while offering a different 'style' for 'narrating the relation between colonial pasts and decolonised futures', Motha reminds us of how 'reading cases to ascertain their literariness and what literature enables in law' is one of 'the major contributions of the humanities to the study of international law'. Like Craven, Nesiah and Motha, the chapter by Anne-Charlotte Martineau (Chapter 21) is concerned with how history is narrated, in this case in support of competing claims and positions on the history of slavery. At its centre is a caution against abolitionist narratives, which focus on the triumph of international law in ending slavery, as a mode that yet again 'privileges a history in which Europe gets to play the hero'. Instead of celebrating the role of international law in ending slavery, Martineau argues, the focus should be on understanding the discipline's role in creating and enabling slavery.

The next three chapters in this part turn from a concern with how international law is implicated in the construction of History, to how history as a technique of knowledge production is used in the construction of international law. In her contribution, Cait Storr (Chapter 22) focuses on the regulation and governance of space resource extraction. Storr shows how this unfolding extra-terrestrial subfield of international law is not a wholly new frontier, but rather a continuation and intensification of terrestrial resource exploitation. For Storr, 'the advent of a commercial space resource industry signals neither an escape from terrestrial jurisdiction nor a failure of international law, but a predictable evolution of its extractivist logic'. In drawing out this continuity, Storr is not only making an argument about the international law of space resource extraction; she is making an argument for historical analysis as a critical tool that can show us the deep historical structures of the international legal order. In a similar way, Henry Jones (Chapter 23) argues that histories of the future, and not just of the past, can offer a way of witnessing present developments in international law. Like Storr, Jones focuses on space resource extraction, but he does so by turning to a work of science fiction to think through a potential future history in which the colonial violence of 'occidental law' is 'repeated on a new set of facts' – the colonisation of Mars. While Jones' law-in-literature analysis offers a way of seeing how international law works to produce 'space', and highlights the problematic relationships between international law and technology, his historiography can also be read as an exercise in imagining the world, and its international laws, differently.

The idea that an encounter with a literary text can be a productive moment for historical international legal analysis also animates Ruth Buchanan's contribution (Chapter 24). In the final chapter in this part, Buchanan returns to the past – her past – to offer a reflection on how film, and more specifically our encounters with it, can offer both a mode of 'critical (counter) history', and an archive of international law. The film that captures Buchanan's imagination – for the reason that it captures an international legal imagination – is *Local Hero*, a film that revolves around a development project in Scotland in the 1980s. On one hand, this film is an archival witness 'of the common sense of its own historical moment'; on the other hand, as Buchanan shows, the affective encounter with this film-as-witness enables the international jurisprudent to 'make sense of a world in which the international ownership and operation of extractive industry has expanded to the point at which its consequences – in terms of environmental destruction, species loss and climate change – have become an existential threat to humanity.'

Community

Informing each of the chapters in this Handbook is an attention to plurality and being-in-common as both empirical 'fact' and normative concern. But whilst these concerns have been largely in the background of the chapters presented so far, they take the foreground in the next six chapters. Here the studies range from a focus on the international regulation of the family and jurisdictional techniques of inclusion/exclusion, to nation-building projects and encounters between different laws and societies.

Dianne Otto (Chapter 25) begins this part with an account of how international human rights law, over the past 25 years, has worked to deny recognition, 'and thus full humanity', to different family formations, including 'Indigenous families, extended families, female-headed families, polygamous families and "queer" families, to name but a few'. The question that drives Otto's study is why it is still 'unthinkable' in international law for communities around the world to form families of their own choosing, despite enormous efforts on the part of activists and jurisprudents to make legal definitions of the family more inclusive. Through a genealogy of international human rights law, Otto shows the politics that underpin its concept of the 'family', and how this concept goes to the very 'survival of the nation-state in an increasingly interdependent world'. But more than that, Otto points to how 'queer kinship relations offer a starting point for reconceiving "families" as a site of freedom and redistributive economics, as well as a place of human belonging and care'. Staying with the problem of international law's role in perpetuating violence against communities who are seen to threaten the nation-state, Sara Dehm (Chapter 26) draws on the work of Achille Mbembe to examine the relationship between international law's concept of the 'state' and people seeking asylum. For Dehm, this relationship, and the violence it perpetuates against refugees, calls for two lines of inquiry. The first requires being attentive to 'international law's entanglement in colonial histories', and in particular, what Mbembe has termed the 'necropolitical' spaces of state border regimes. The second involves 'interrogating international law's categories of political belonging and state responsibility that allow for the differential allocation of rights and status towards refugees in their care'. While Dehm draws on the example of the Australian state's detention of refugees on Manus Island, the next chapter, by Kate Grady (Chapter 27) is concerned with how the ideas and practices of incarceration travel across different legal spaces. Through her analysis of the relationship between international law and these 'carceral spaces', Grady develops what she terms a 'carceral geography', that is, 'a combination of geography, criminology and penology which examines places and practices of incarceration, their distributional geographies and social and spatial relations'. While the starting point of such a geography is the prison as a site of international law, the end is to draw out the ways in which international law connects such sites in the creation of a 'carceral archipelago', under the influence of the logics of colonialism and capitalism – and how international jurisprudents might resist this project.

The next two chapters turn to consider the relationship between nation-building and international law. Of particular interest to Lee Godden (Chapter 28) is how nation-building is mediated by bodily sacrifice, in this instance the extra-territorial sacrifice of soldiers killed in wars fought on foreign soil. The case that Godden focuses on is the Australian government's efforts to take the state's founding myth of national sacrifice in the First World War, which had been grounded in the battles fought and lost in Gallipoli, and re-ground it on the Western Front, in the region around Villers-Bretonneux in France. Central to the government's efforts, Godden shows, is international law; just as bodily sacrifice is seen to mediate the creation of the national origin myth, so too international law is seen to mediate the commemoration of the sacrificed, or what Godden calls the 'archival performance' of nationhood. And yet, as Godden also highlights, such nation-building obscures, and is resisted by, other narratives of national origins, such as the one told through the recognition of 'native title' in the case of *Mabo*. For our next author, Valeria Vázquez Guevara (Chapter 29), a similar dynamic is observed in a very different context: Chile after the 1973–1990 dictatorship. Like Godden, Vázquez Guevara is concerned with how international law is implicated in a nation-building project that renders invisible other accounts of national belonging. In this case, the focus is Chile's 1990 Truth Commission (TC), and how international human rights law informs the TC's work 'in shaping social and institutional relations' after the dictatorship. Through an ethnography of Chile's *Museo de la Memoria y los Derechos Humanos* (Museum of Memory and Human Rights), Vázquez Guevara shows how this cultural institution continues this work in a way that visibly subordinates other 'lawful truths' to a national truth that obtains its authority from international law. If this is an example of laws meeting badly, then the final chapter in this part, by Sophie Rigney (Chapter 30), points to the possibility of a more hopeful encounter. The site of this encounter is children's literature, a site that offers an archive for understanding the discursive construction of law, as well as the ways in which different laws meet, and might meet better. To explore this, Rigney analyses two Australian children's books, *The Complete Adventures of Snugglepot and Cuddlepie* (May Gibbs) and *Welcome to Country: A Traditional Aboriginal Ceremony* (Aunty Joy Murphy), focusing on how each depicts, although in fundamentally different ways, 'law, lawlessness, lawfulness, and the meeting of laws'. Reading these books as international jurisprudents, Rigney argues, not only 'compels us to consider the racist ways in which international law has denied Indigenous laws', but on the hopeful note, how 'we can create meeting places between European/settler colonial and Indigenous international laws'.

Concepts for our times

The final part of the Handbook focuses on the urgent task of thinking, and rethinking, international legal concepts for the challenges of our times. Kathleen Birrell and Julia Dehm (Chapter 31) begin with an account of how scholars in international law and the humanities have begun to rethink key concepts in the field in response to the 'Anthropocene', a concept that itself poses 'critical questions about the futures we wish to collectively build'. While international jurisprudents have been slower to address this task, Birrell and Dehm find a rich body of scholarship in the humanities and social science that can assist to 'unsettle and pluralise' a discipline that holds onto European Enlightenment ideals of mastery and continues to pursue a universalising law. This is necessary, Birrell and Dehm argue, if we are to discover 'new collective possibilities and encounters within and between communities as well as scholarly disciplines', and achieve 'a more responsive, radical and open international law'. The next two chapters remain with the 'Anthropocene', but focus on how it unsettles one concept in particular – that of the 'human'. For Matilda Arvidsson (Chapter 32), the question of 'who, or what, is the human of international humanitarian law' might have long haunted the discipline, but with the accelerating use of 'intelligent technologies' in warfare, the notion of human agency, and the conceptual separation of the 'human' from its 'others' (whether animal or technological), can no longer be backgrounded. By taking targeting in intelligent warfare as her example, and drawing on posthumanist feminist analysis, Arvidsson issues a call 'for an ethical and normative order worthy of our time'. This would be an 'international posthumanitarian legal ordering able to recognise subjectivity and accountability of "non-human" entities in warfare alongside and in conjunction with "human" and "more-than-human" entities, not as separate and superior/subordinate, but as relationally responsible posthuman becomings'. Like Arvidsson, the next chapter, by Connal Parsley (Chapter 33), seeks to unsettle, or 'unlimit', the concept of the human in the field of international humanitarian law. Parsley's starting point is Gregor Noll's observation that 'legal paradigms of normativity' are 'fundamentally incompatible' with emergent machine learning technologies being used and developed for Lethal Autonomous Weapons Systems. With this in mind, Parsley examines how the concept of Meaningful Human Control (which is supposed to regulate the Lethal Autonomous Weapons Systems) assumes, on one side, a non-automated 'human', and on the other side, an automated 'machine', resulting in an understanding of authority and responsibility that rests with the 'human' over the 'machine'. But what happens, Parsley asks, if the conceptual divide between human/machine is no longer tenable? Indeed the problem, as Parsley shows, is that the notion of 'Meaningful Human Control' reproduces an historical concept of the human (as non-automated) at a time when it is least tenable. By registering this problem, the chapter reminds us that the Western imagination, and its discipline of international law, remains limited by 'an instituted image of regulatory and decision-making authority that is deeply premised on the separation of the human from the technological', and that 'it falls to a "new (law and) humanities" – in which law, science and the human are indistinguishable – to discover a new criterion of value and evaluation that does not insist on anthropogenically separating human life from technology'.

The next chapter, by Sara Ramshaw (Chapter 34), takes us deeper into the question of the humanity of machines, to ask whether, or to what extent, machine listening can increase Access to Justice in the international subfield of family law. As she writes: can machines 'ever listen deeply and attentively to the singularity of a family law case such that they are able to offer the creative and bespoke solutions that Family Justice demands?' To answer that question, Ramsaw draws on her work in improvisation studies, 'attentive listening' and creative approaches to Family Justice. The result is both an overview of some of the key issues at stake in thinking through the humanity of machines, and a reason for thinking that '(machine) listening as improvisation might offer some hope for the future of international Family Justice'. Staying with the conceptual construction of humanity, but changing fields from international Family Justice to international criminal justice, Maria Elander (Chapter 35) focuses our attention on the ways in which international criminal courts and tribunals are implicated in the constitution of the 'victim'. In particular, she questions 'how practices of international criminal justice represent victims of atrocity – if and when representation is understood as a practice of subject formation', and how this contributes to 'our understanding of the constitution of victim, for and in international criminal justice'. To answer these questions, Elander examines two cases, one from the International Military Tribunal in Nuremberg, the second, the Eichmann trial in Jerusalem. While the first case highlights the ways in which a victim's identity changes over time, the second shows how 'subject formation is not simply a power imposed on a person', but is 'negotiated and can be resisted'.

From the concept of humanity, we turn in the final chapter of the Handbook to a concept that has remained at the centre of 'modern' international law since the creation of its origin myths in the Peace of Westphalia: sovereignty. In this chapter, Richard Joyce (Chapter 36) responds to the resurgence of fascism and extreme right-wing populism around the world by asking whether the concept of sovereignty might be rethought in a way that renders it 'useless for the purposes of fascism' and 'useful for the formulation of revolutionary demands in law'. While acknowledging the concept's imperialist, and indeed fascist, history, Joyce refuses to simply give it up, recognising that the concept is still used by Indigenous peoples and independence movements around the world. Instead, Joyce re-reads, with the help of Walter Benjamin, the Western and anti-colonial canon on 'sovereignty', in order to theorise the concept in a way that can resist colonial, imperial, fascist configurations of law and community, and work for an international law, and a humanity, that is responsive to the challenges of justice of our times.

Conclusion

Rather than facilitating instruction toward mastery by representing the field as a totality, we hope that this Handbook of international law and the humanities serves as a basis for training and inspiration, by drawing together 36 works of scholarship that exemplify the practice, craft and ethos of this field. The result is an invitation to readers to reflect on the experiments of others, and to perhaps try out something similar. Although we are inspired by the de Mayerne manuscript, we cannot mimic its loose-leaf form in the printed version of this Handbook (although, ironically, the electronic format that most people will encounter may in fact allow the kind of creative rearrangement of chapters that the loose leaves of the seventeenth century permitted). But like the recipes in that manuscript, the chapters in this Handbook seek to provide guidance based on experimentation, about the many ways in which we can take up an inheritance of the humanistic study of law without foreclosing either its means or ends.

Formation

1

Modus Vivendi

Office of transnational jurisprudent

Shaun McVeigh with Ann Genovese and Mark McMillan[1]

Introduction

The concerns of this chapter take up two long-standing topics in the disciplines of law and of the humanities: the appropriate conduct *(officia)* of public life and office, and the creation of ways of co-existence between peoples and nations. We have taken up this topic as part of a response to the formulation of lawful (as opposed to lawless) relations expressed in the transnational, pan-Aboriginal, *Uluru Statement from the Heart.*[2] This statement was delivered in 2017 by Aboriginal Constitutional Convention to the Australian people, and by extension to the Commonwealth of Australia.[3] Here we consider the quality of relations of law that might be sustained within the office, or role, of the transnational jurisprudent and diplomat of the common law tradition.[4]

The *Uluru Statement from the Heart* presents a significant affirmation of the spiritual and material understanding of Aboriginal sovereign existence and continuing obligations to country.

1 This chapter is co-authored. It is written, for the most part, from the standpoint of Shaun McVeigh as a jurisprudent of the common law tradition of Australia and of England and Wales. It forms part of an Australian Research Council funded project titled 'Indigenous Leaders: From Encounter to Treaty' IN182100065. In a different idiom and with a different address, the investigation of this chapter draws material from advice on the public law obligations of the state of Victoria given to the Department of Premier and Cabinet by Mark McMillan with David Frost, Ann Genovese, Shaun McVeigh and Maureen Tehan in June 2018. The jurisographical concerns of this chapter have been developed further in a collaborative research project with Ann Genovese and Peter Rush titled 'Lives Lived with Law'. Thanks also to Olivia Barr and Adil Hasan Khan respectively for their conversation on walking and movement and eloquence and civility.

2 *Uluru Statement from the Heart*, accessed May 20, 2020, https://ulurustatement.org.

3 In this chapter there is no formal terminology of the designation 'Aboriginal', 'Indigenous', 'First Nations' and 'Peoples of Australia' beyond affiliation by people, place and language. We have followed usage in public documents where one designation is used. All carry histories of colonial encounter.

4 While clear enough for many purposes, the terminology of the diplomat belongs to the nineteenth century and the formalisation of state-centred diplomacy. Here it must do the work of cognates ambassador, emissary and so on. The term jurisprudent is not a regularly used figure in contemporary common law discourse. We use the figure and term 'jurisprudent' to emphasise the care for the conduct of lawful relations and to maintain a link with jurisprudence as a genre of prudential writing that links practical wisdom and judgment.

It also makes important political assertions for the importance of both a representative political voice for Aboriginal people and a truthful account of law and the relationship between Indigenous and non-Indigenous peoples of Australia. To date (2020), the Commonwealth of Australia has rejected this invitation. However, the Australian State of Victoria has chosen to accept, and respond to the invitation. What we wish to emphasise is the character of the invitation to enter into treaty relations, since it is an invitation to join an already existing transnational network of agreements amongst Aboriginal peoples and nations. The *Uluru Statement* invites people of the common law tradition to join these relations.

The first response of Victoria to the *Uluru Statement* has been presented in the Advancing the Treaty Process Act 2018 (Vic).[5] It invites the Aboriginal people of Victoria (rather than First Nations) to enter into a treaty process within the sphere of the law of the State of Victoria. The disjuncture of laws and fora is familiar to common law colonial relations and transnational agreements. We are interested in how this positioning of authority is addressed within a common law conduct of office.[6] To do so we concentrate on the forms of practice, and inherited protocols of acknowledgment and meeting, that reside within that tradition. We also reflect on the ways in which such forms and comportments might transmit the aspiration of conducting (transnational) lawful relations amongst peoples of law, within 'Australia', or at least Victoria.

In order to set our account of the office of jurisprudent in motion, we follow three conceits that shadow the common law as a tradition. We would summarise these as 'understand your obligations', 'know your tradition' and 'act appropriately'. The first conceit we relate to relations of transnational and international law. While this is not usually the case, we treat engagements between Indigenous peoples and 'settler colonial states' in two ways. One is as an aspect of international and transnational law. The other is as an existing law of nations between Indigenous peoples (or, more polemically, an Indigenous international or transnational law).[7] The second conceit is that the writings of jurisprudence provide a training in the conduct of the office jurisprudent. This training, we argue, still finds meaningful expression within the idioms of university humanities and international law scholarship. For us, it is the rhetorical tradition, and the resources and the valency of the cultivation of eloquence that is the centre of this tradition. Like the term civility, eloquence is often understood only in negative terms (genteel comportment and fine words and nothing more). We investigate some of the more positive inflections of eloquence within humanist traditions of rhetorical education. These formulations associate eloquence with the consideration of the form, style and genre of comportment and communication. Eloquence, understood in this way, matters because the broad tradition of rhetorical education has been central to the training in appropriate conduct for public life. It remains important too within the contemporary conduct of law and diplomacy. The third conceit we follow in this essay is that there are public obligations to be performed by a transnational jurisprudent of the common law tradition in Australia – and that these need deliberate attention.

The approach we take here to the cultivation of the persona, or public character, of the jurisprudent and their conduct of office is broadly jurisographical.[8] Rather than presenting a

5 *Advancing the Treaty Process with Aboriginal Victorians Act 2018* (Vic).

6 Shaunnagh Dorsett and Shaun McVeigh, *Jurisdiction* (London: Routledge, 2012), 98–99.

7 Mark McMillan and Sophie Rigney, "The Place of the First Peoples in the International Sphere: A Logical Starting Point for the Demand for Justice by Indigenous Peoples," *Melbourne University Law Review* 39, no. 3 (2016): 981–83; Ravi de Costa, *A Higher Authority: Indigenous Transnationalism and Australia* (Sydney: University of New South Wales Press, 2006).

8 Ann Genovese, Shaun McVeigh and Peter Rush, "Lives Lived with Law: An Introduction," *Law Text Culture* 20 (2016): 1–6.

normative or critical-historical account of the conduct of lawful relations as might a legal critic, historian or theorist, as jurisographers we focus on how jurisprudents have addressed what it means to inherit, and write with, different sets of duties, and conducts of disciplinary life.[9] In doing so we attend to some of the forms of the writing of jurisprudence (not only from jurists, judges and legal scholars) as resources for addressing how jurisprudents are trained into relations of law. Treated together in this way, jurisprudential writings offer and operate as a handbook (cautionary and otherwise) that addresses the training in conduct for those holding offices that emanate from the arrival of the common law tradition in Australia.

As jurisographers and legal scholars, we also write our own accounts of jurisprudence, including what is offered here, with a certain openness about our own sources and collaborations.[10] To make clear the thread of our concern with the quality of lawful relations in this chapter, we have deployed the figure of the jurisprudent and diplomat, or, more expressly, jurisprudent *as* diplomat, as an exemplar of relations that are, as yet, more imagined than realised. In this respect, we are also taking up the invitation of the editors of this collection in a literal way and present this chapter as an aid to meeting well enough, rather than as a normative idealisation of treaty relationships. Accordingly, we proceed through histories, glosses and examples of conduct to address the challenge that treaty presents in our own time and place, as a formation of relations between Indigenous and non-Indigenous nations and peoples.

As noted by June Oscar, a Bunuba Woman, Elder, ambassador and Australian social justice commissioner, when a 'treaty' is understood that way, it must begin from an understanding that the institutions of government and justice of Australia remain a part of 'the web of Imperial power'.[11] The work of the office of the transnational jurisprudent of Australia, as elsewhere, is drawn through this web; as is the consideration of conduct of office and training in eloquence and civility that might suggest ways to meet that are adequate to the task.

The three sections of this chapter add commentary to known aspects of the public office of the jurisprudent in terms of the assumption of obligation, repertoires of conduct and performance of relationship. We have divided up some familiar topics in order to give texture to the formulation of the obligations of the office of the transnational jurisprudent of the common law tradition.

Office, treaty and the creation of forms of public obligation

Our first note addresses the ways in which transnational relations of law might give shape to the office of transnational jurisprudent. It focusses on the obligations of meeting, as does the whole chapter. Our example follows the different ways the understanding of treaty relations is presented in the *Uluru Statement from the Heart* and the Advancing the Treaty Process Act. We do so to consider the ways their proposed relationship can be understood as presenting horizons of, and for, the conduct of an office. For the jurisprudent of the common law tradition decisions have to be made about how to engage with different sources of authority and to live with different kinds of commitments of lawful conduct in relation to place and each other.

9 Ann Genovese, "Inheriting and Inhabiting the Pleasures and Duties of Our Own Existence: The Second Sex and Feminist Jurisprudence," *Australian Feminist Law Journal* 38, no. 1 (2013): 41–45.

10 Ann Genovese and Shaun McVeigh, "Nineteen Eighty Three: A Jurisographic Report on Commonwealth v Tasmania," *Griffith Law Review* 24, no. 1 (2015): 68–72.

11 June Oscar, "Encountering Truth: The Real Life Stories of Objects from Empire's Frontier and Beyond," in *Encounters: Revealing Stories of Aboriginal and Torres Strait Islander Objects from the British Museum*, ed. Australian National Museum (Canberra: Australian National Museum Press, 2015), 23.

For moderns living with the (colonial-settled) common law of Australia, political and legal relations are shaped around a civil authority and forms of government that are generally understood in terms of the maintenance of civil peace, the scope of public administration and, in a diffuse way, juridical and equitable ordering of life lived in public. Since the 1990s, accounts of the conduct of lawful relations have also acknowledged transnational responsibilities established by agreement-making and treaties between non-Aboriginal and Aboriginal peoples.[12]

Within the university, the concern with how such responsibility can be acknowledged is usually considered in terms of authority and its sources, scope and transmission, and meaning. Here, we address instead a limited and quite worldly concern with the horizons of responsibility that might be established through the active practice of entering into treaty relations between the First Nations of Australia and the Commonwealth and states of Australia. Accordingly, we follow a limited range of obligations associated with meeting-well. There are many other forms of lawful relation that can be addressed, even when such relations are limited to those that can be addressed historically (and jurisprudentially) within a common law tradition.

Over the last 40 years, the site for the conduct of lawful relations between Indigenous and non-Indigenous peoples in Australia has increasingly been shaped by Western international law and, most notably, the United Nations Declaration on the Rights of Indigenous Peoples (UNDRIP), the Permanent Forum of Indigenous Issues and the political and diplomatic engagements of Indigenous land rights movements.[13] This horizon, however, is not clearly organised around the acknowledgment of an Indigenous international law or an understanding of Indigenous jurisdictions within international law. For the most part, UNDRIP is directed towards existing states and acknowledged as customary international law.[14] In doing so it leaves open the instantiation of lawful relations to the signatories of the treaty.

The *Uluru Statement from the Heart* also draws on the language of human rights, as well as that of transitional justice. However, it draws both of these into established genres of agreement-making and into the engagement of substantive recognition of lawful relations. It does so by holding a proposed, or reformed, relation to a commitment to formal association (political voice through constitutional amendment), truthfulness (through truth and reconciliation commissions) and ceremony (as the continuing obligation of (treaty) relationship). While the *Uluru*

12 Marcia Langton and Lisa Palmer, "Treaties, Agreement Making and the Recognition of Indigenous Customary Polities," in *Honour Among Nations? Treaties and Agreements with Indigenous People*, eds. Marica Langton, et al. (Melbourne: Melbourne University Press, 2004), 3435.

13 For a participant history of the political engagements in the Indigenous international domain see: James (Sa'Ke'j) Youngblood Henderson, *Indigenous Diplomacy and the Rights of Peoples: Achieving UN Recognition* (Vancouver: Purich Publishers, 2008). Jens Dahl and Shiri Pasternak note how little international and transnational Indigenous struggle and representation passes through the United Nations. They also note the complexity of relations between Indigenous and non-Indigenous engagement in plural sites of engagement, see Jens Dahl, *The Indigenous Space and Marginalized Peoples in the United Nations* (Basingstoke: Palgrave-Macmillan, 2012); Shiri Pasternak, *Grounded Authority: The Algonquins of Barriere Lake Against the State* (Minneapolis: University of Minnesota Press, 2017). Tom Mayor notes the transnational character of the continent of Australia and draws the language of law from there, see Tom Mayor, *Finding the Heart of the Nation: The Journey of the Uluru Statement Towards Voice, Treaty and Truth* (Melbourne: Hardy Grant Publishing, 2019). Aileen Moreton-Robinson provides a direct critique of the international horizon of the United Nations and their international law as an aspect of 'white sovereignty'; see Aileen Moreton-Robinson, "Virtuous Racial States: The Possessive Logic of Patriarchal White Sovereignty and the United Nations Declaration of the Rights of Indigenous Peoples," *Griffith Law Review* 20, no. 3 (2011): 641–58.

14 Sylvanus, Barnabas, "The Legal Status of the United Nations Declaration on the Rights of Indigenous Peoples (2007) in Contemporary International Human Rights Law," *International Human Rights Law Review* 6, no. 2 (2017): 242–61.

Statement has mostly been received in Australia as a constitutional document, it is better understood as providing an Indigenous transnational horizon through which the obligations of the engagement of lawful relations are made visible. The proposed relation is encapsulated in a language that resonates with old understandings of law and the common law: first that sovereignty is understood through a spiritual connection to the land, and, second, that 'this ancient sovereignty can shine through as a fuller expression of Australia's nationhood'.[15] One invitation then, addressed to the people of Australia, is the acknowledgement of the presence of an ancient sovereignty and law. Another invitation is issued to transform the common law of Australia and to realise a fuller relationship of law for all Australians. This transformation is one of laws – both transnationally and nationally.

In the Treaty Process Act, the State of Victoria committed itself to entering into treaty relations with the Indigenous people of Victoria. We treat this as a matter of authority and conduct as well as one of protocol and comportment. The Act accepted the challenge of finding an appropriate 'meeting place of law' with Aboriginal Victorians – and of establishing public offices and office-holders capable of so doing. This established the State of Victoria's own horizon of obligations concerning its conduct towards and relationship with Aboriginal Victorians. It draws on the language of UNDRIP to describe the relationship in terms of 'self-determination' and 'empowerment'. In the preambular commitments to the Act, the State declared its own comportment as 'walk[ing] alongside', 'work[ing] in partnership', 'tak[ing] each step forward on the pathway to treaty together'; relationally, as 'work[ing] collaboratively' with Aboriginal people; and, dispositionally, as always in 'good faith'. The language of 'walking alongside' invokes a language of Christian fellowship, as does 'good faith'. This comportment might give a different inflection to the tone of an earlier, longstanding, understanding of relationship in terms of conquest and settlement.

What has proven hard to recognise, we argue, is that the political ordering of the State of Victoria, and its government, is also and already obligated through laws of Aboriginal peoples and nations. In one respect the Treaty Process Act continues the old tradition of the common law by not directly acknowledging Aboriginal sovereignty or laws. This repeats the general situation established by those who live with the common law tradition of Australia and its international law.[16] Nevertheless, it is possible to articulate a sense of the public obligation that binds the institutions of the university and the State within a network of responsibilities of relationship. Analogously, the *Uluru Statement* and the political and institutional arrangements that led to its creation, recast the obligations of an Indigenous law of nations, in order to create an Indigenous public law amenable to engagement with the public and administrative law of Australia (or at least the State of Victoria).

We close this section by pluralising some of the horizons of agreement-making. While the *Uluru Statement* draws on a variety of ways of understanding dispute and agreement-making, it is certainly not the only form of relationship through which Aboriginal and non-Aboriginal jurisprudence and diplomacy have been engaged.[17] The establishment of diplomatic relations

15 Megan Davis, "The Long Road to Uluru: Walking Together: Truth Before Justice," *Griffith Review* 60 (2018): 43–45.

16 Irene Watson, *Aboriginal Peoples, Colonialism and International Law: Raw Law* (London: Routledge, 2016). See also Shaunnagh Dorsett and Shaun McVeigh, "Just So: 'The Law which Governs Australia Is Australian Law'," *Law and Critique* 13 (2002): 289–309.

17 The *Uluru Statement* joins a tradition of petitions and declarations; see Karen O'Brien, *Petitioning for Land: The Petitions of First Peoples of Modern British Colonies* (London: Bloomsbury, 2019), 151–61. For an account of contemporary petitioning and how it joins a tradition of law see Yunupingu Gallarrwuy, *Tradition, Truth and*

can also be understood as an aspect of Indigenous agreement-making. As Kombumerri, Wakka Wakka political philosopher Mary Graham notes, the development of treaty processes for Traditional Owners and Aboriginal peoples starts from within Aboriginal knowledge and governance systems.[18] These relations are further shaped by the acknowledgement of an Indigenous transnational law between Indigenous nations independently of the Commonwealth of Australia and its understanding of law.[19]

We have set some horizons of the meeting or engagement of transnational laws. They can be considered in both institutional and ideational terms. Within Western idioms they articulate forms of authority and jurisdiction through which lawful relations can be negotiated and conducted.[20] The Treaty Process Act invites consideration of the mode and way the State (of Victoria) might respond. There is no sense here that these horizons and associated obligations can be arranged without remainder or conflict.

Conducts of office and life

Our second gloss steps back from the meeting of laws and focuses on the cultivation of the persona and training in conduct of meeting well. We do so by attending to what Ann Genovese has called a 'conduct of life' tradition.[21] As a matter of conduct, a training within the common law tradition must be sufficient to act with plural authorities and contested transnational horizons and be capable of forming and maintaining relations of law. There is no shortage of criticism of the resources of the common law tradition. Humanist training is most often cultivated in opposition to rival forms of training. The cultivation of the arts of relationship has barely begun to be directed to the responsibilities in articulating relations of non-Indigenous and Indigenous jurisprudences and law. If the Treaty Process Act does invite a new relationship of law then, we argue, one source of training emerges in the rhetorical emphasis given to the importance of eloquence.

One articulation of how a jurisprudent might respond is expressed in the Act's 'guiding principles for the treaty process'. This frames the conduct of the treaty process in general terms of administrative process and ethical precepts of public service: 'fairness', 'equality', 'transparency', 'honesty' and 'integrity' – all of which play on the promise of transformation and accountability (responsibility).[22] One version of transformation is that such commitments are the expression of a jurisprudence of public administration. They are held in place by legislation and monitored

Tomorrow (Melbourne: Black Inc, 2008). A different practice of anti-colonial diplomacy was practiced through the Aboriginal Tent embassy starting in 1972; see Gary Foley, Andrew Schaap and Edwina Howell, *The Aboriginal Tent Embassy: Sovereignty, Black Power, Land Rights and the State* (London: Routledge, 2013). For an account that addresses contemporary treaty practice in Aotearoa/New Zealand, see Carwyn Jones, *New Treaty, New Tradition: Reconciling New Zealand and Maori Law* (Vancouver: University of British Columbia Press, 2016).

18 Mary Graham, Morgan Brigg and Polly Walker, "Conflict Murri Way: Managing Through Place and Relatedness," in *Mediating Across Difference: Oceanic and Asian Approaches to Conflict Resolution*, eds. Morgan Brigg and Roland Bleiker (Honolulu: University of Hawai'i Press, 2011), 75–99.

19 Shino Konishi, "First Nations Scholars, Settler Colonial Studies and Indigenous History," *Australian Historical Studies* 50, no. 3 (July 2019): 285–304.

20 See Nicole Roughan, *Authorities: Conflicts, Cooperation, and Transnational Legal Theory* (Oxford: Oxford University Press, 2013), 163–71.

21 Ann Genovese, "On Australian Feminist Tradition: Three Notes on Conduct, Inheritance and the Relations of Historiography and Jurisprudence," *Journal of Australian Studies* 38, no. 4 (October 2014): 430–44; Wilhelm Hennis, *Max Weber's Central Question* (Newbury: Threshold Press, 2000), 30–33.

22 *Advancing the Treaty Process with Aboriginal Victorians Act 2018* (Vic), ss 22–26.

for their reasonableness by public judicial oversight. This might be thought of as a promise to change through continuing a potentially effective practice of government. However, these commitments also draw on a terminology that shapes a legal conscience recently re-inherited from Christian thought.[23] Here the transformation turns on the quality of 'good faith' or intention in the process. Our response is to treat the concern with conscience as a substantive concern within the art of meeting well-enough. Process is treated as a protocol for those who are meeting. Taking a cue from the early modern humanist Italian rhetorician, jurisprudent and university scholar, Giambattista Vico (1688–1744), we understand one of the obligations of the jurisprudent as attending to an art of office capable of realising a common relation of law and life. Our choice of Vico as interlocuter sharpens both the account of eloquence and institutions and allows some thematic links to be developed in shaping the conduct of office around eloquence and civility.

As a professor of rhetoric, Vico bound life to law by paying attention to the traditions that hold the living in place through the institutions of the dead, the living and the yet to be born.[24] For Vico eloquence was the proper communication and realisation of practical wisdom and a training for young noblemen in conduct for public life.[25] While the language of rhetoric, eloquence and civility is not at the forefront of contemporary political and legal education, the relationship between eloquence and what is honourable and useful, and what is civil and what is barbarous, still shadows the office of contemporary jurisprudents and ambassadors of the common law tradition. In many circumstances, even invoking tradition or civility in such terms, especially a common law civility, would be to invite rebuke.[26] Our response here does not seek to reduce this complicity with civilising projects and effects. Rather, we aim to present a reminder of the multivalent (and ambivalent) traditions of office and conduct through which jurisprudents have been inducted into public life. (One aspect of complicity directs attention to the accomplishment of alliances made in the complication or folding in of relations.)[27]

For early moderns and moderns (post-seventeenth century), the conduct of public life and the conduct of lawful relations through office have most typically been understood in terms of the institutions of public life – church, state and, perhaps, the United Nations. The offices of the church exemplified by the priest and prophet and ordered around liturgy and the ceremonial realisation of the life of Christ and those of the state are formed by the governor, judge, legislator, administrator and soldier, and ordered around civil peace, good government and public administration. The institutional life of the United Nations is shaped around an international

23 Peter Goodrich, *Languages of Law* (London: Weidenfeld and Nicolson, 1991); Talal Asad, *Secular Translations* (New York: Columbia University Press, 2018), 13–18, 113–15; Ian Hunter, "English Blasphemy," *Humanity* 4, no. 3 (2014): 403–7.

24 In *Jurisprudence as Movement: Common Law, Walking, Unsettling Place* (London: Routledge, 2017), Olivia Barr traces a similar relation between the common law, movement and the relation to the dead. See also Robert Harrison, *The Dominion of the Dead* (Chicago: University of Chicago, 2003), 84–86.

25 Giambattista Vico, "On the Study Methods of our Time," in *On the Study Methods of Our Time*, trans. and ed. Elio Gianturco (Ithaca: Cornell University Press, 1990), 77–79. Such a training must enable (the young) to make well-judged distinctions between ferocity (violence), avarice and courage (ambition), wealth and wisdom, see *Giambattista Vico, The New Science of Giambattista Vico,* trans. Thomas Goddard Bergin and Max Harold Fisch (Ithaca: Cornell University Press, 1976), 62. See also Franics Mootz, "Vico and Imagination: An Ingenious Approach to Educating Lawyers with Semiotic Sensibility," *International Journal for the Semiotics of Law* 22, no. 1 (2009): 11–22.

26 Ian Duncanson, *Historiography, Empire and the Rule of Law* (London: Routledge, 2012), 164–96.

27 John Docker, *The Origins of Violence: Religion History and Genocide* (London: Pluto Press, 2008), 161–74.

civil administration and public service.[28] It is relatively recent that a significant turn has been made away from institutions. The office of the jurisprudent has been developed within all three institutions across long periods of time. Our test here is that their institutional and disciplinary inheritance can still be illuminated through reference to Renaissance and early modern training in eloquence and civility.[29]

This brief diversion into the training in the conduct of lawful relations and diplomacy presumes great generality ('there is a tradition that is capable of inheritance') and specificity (there are forms of 'spiritual exercise' and 'training in conduct' that are adequate to the task at hand). Eloquence, as a general term, can be drawn upon in the cultivation of the persona of the speaker, as well as in the formal fashioning of the style of argument and the quality of communication and listening in the conduct of civic life.[30] The Renaissance elevation of eloquence and persuasion in the *studia humanitatis*, for example, provided a model of the scholar-jurisprudent's engagement with forms of office and public life by linking decorum and eloquence with honour, honesty and morality (*honestas*).[31] Whereas dignity (and later decorum) were related to the conduct of office, eloquence in its various forms directed attention to the cultivation of the persona of the scholar.[32] Humanist eloquence, and its rhetorically inflected ethics, also sustained

28 Anne Orford, *International Authority and the Responsibility to Protect* (Cambridge: Cambridge University Press, 2011).

29 David Saunders, *Anti-Lawyers: Religion and the Critics of the Law and State* (London: Routledge, 1997), 121–40; Keith Thomas, *In Pursuit of Civility* (New Haven: Yale University Press, 2018), 32–49.

30 Charles Guérin, "Philosophical Decorum and the Literarization of Rhetoric in Cicero's Orator," in *Literary and Philosophical Rhetoric in the Greek, Roman, Syriac and Arabic Worlds*, ed. Frédérique Woerther (Hildesheim: Georg Olms Verlag, 2009), 119–39. Although not central to the contemporary canon of Anglophone international law, there is broad tradition of Renaissance jurisprudence that still resonates with the rhetorical ethics established in the training jurisprudents (with or without acknowledgement of inheritance). One formulation, exemplified by the Italian poet Torquarto Tasso (1544–1595), would make the role of the ambassador one of mediation in the name of the honourable or the good, and an expression of the humanist or Christian values of the peacemaker and the law of nations. Another formulation, found in the work of the Italian jurist Alberico Gentili (1552–1608), would make the ambassador the useful agent of the prince subject to the laws between nations (states). A third formulation from the work of Michel de Montaigne (1533–1592) turned attention away from the authority of the prince and of law and instead focused the honour of the ambassador on the person. Montaigne moves furthest from a shared formulation of a *ius gentium* and closest to the maintenance of the complicity of relations of amity and civility necessary to engage lawful relations. We have drawn on Montaigne's studied indifference to the larger claims made on office and his sense of improvisation in responding to the conduct of public life, see Garrett Mattingly, *Renaissance Diplomacy* (London: Jonathan Cape, 1955), 201–29; Timothy Hampton, *Fictions of Embassy Literature and Diplomacy in Early Modern Europe* (Ithaca: Cornell University Press, 2009), 67–70; Hugo Freidrich, *Montaigne* (Berkeley: University of California Press, 1991), 208–9, 313–16.

31 Paul Kristeller, *Renaissance Thought and Its Sources* (New York: Columbia University Press, 1979), 241–42; John Baker, "The Third University 1450–1550: Law School or Finishing School?" In *The Intellectual and Cultural World of the Early Modern Inns of Court*, eds. Jayne Archer, Elizabeth Goldring and Sarah Knight (Manchester: Manchester University Press), 8–41.

32 Piyel Haldar, "The Tongue and The Eye: Eloquence and The Language of Office in Some Renaissance Emblems," in *Genealogies of Legal Vision*, eds. Peter Goodrich and Valerie Hayaert (New York: Routledge, 2015), 152–78. More generally, Peter Goodrich has argued that the training methods of Renaissance humanist jurists have continued to provide a contemporary, though rarely acknowledged, training in the conscience and comportment of the jurisprudent and diplomat. A humanist legal education follows a training in eloquence and public memory (rhetoric), the elaboration of the visual ordering of law (emblematics and chorography), the practice of shared understanding and commentary (hermeneutics and exegesis), the responsibility for the sources and meaning of words (philology) and casuistry (as judgment on particular actions in the world), see Peter Goodrich, *Legal Emblems and the Art of Law: Obiter Depicta as the Vision of Governance* (Cambridge: Cambridge University Press, 2014); Anthony Carty and Jing Tan, "Confucianism and Western International Law in 1900: Li Hongzhang and Sir Ernest Satow Compared: A Case Study of the Crisis of Russia in Manchuria (1900–01),"

the forms of comportment, ritual and ceremony that carried the conduct of office.[33] Eloquence, for some, also became the means by which the philosophical understanding of the good life was instituted and transmitted.[34] In this way it joined a spiritual to a temporal engagement of the world.

The training in eloquence and civility, whether for university, court or embassy, has not been passed on uncontested. What are the 'proper' kinds of eloquence, and the character of the 'eloquent' courtier, have been highly contested.[35] One important contest over eloquence as the vehicle of *honestum* was the emergence of forms of civil jurisprudence in the seventeenth century. In part as a consequence of sectarian religious wars that devastated Christian Europe, the training of jurists and diplomats became engaged in the cultivation of a persona capable of subordinating themselves to, and organising their conduct around, forms of de-sacralised civil authority of sovereign princes.[36] The civil settlement of England and Wales, for example, was organised around a confessional (Anglican) civil authority. In this settlement, aspects of equity and religious law were folded into the common law.

In this way the common law gained a jurisdiction and a jurisprudence in some matters of conscience (relating especially to children and marriage). However, in common law jurisprudence, *honestum* became associated with religion and religious morality, and separated from *decorum* now associated with manners, and *justum* associated with state law.[37] In such accounts eloquence became a matter of useful persuasion rather than an art of public life.

For Ian Hunter, the training in conduct of modern officials can still be understood both in terms of rival formations of authority and conduct.[38] The de-sacralised training of state and civil service was based on an array of techniques to live within the constraints of a conduct of life defined by institutional office. Such a civil persona is shaped around the tasks of occupying several different offices, often with conflicting obligations.[39] The office of common law jurist is one such civil office – albeit one with a specialist legal conscience. The task of these jurists is to govern and resolve disputes without resort to religious principles. Their service is shaped through the requirements of the civil bureau, formal rationality and procedures, and the

---

in *Morality and Responsibility of Rulers European and Chinese Origins of a Rule of Law as Justice for World Order*, eds. Anthony Carty and Janne Nijman (Oxford: Oxford University Press, 2018), 435–53.

33 We would treat the distinction between eloquence as false speech (of courtiers) and plain communication polemical.

34 Piyel Haldar, "Equity as a Question of Decorum and Manners: Conscience as Vision," *Pólemos* 10, no. 2 (2016): 311–13.

35 Whilst the theme of the hypocrisy of courtiers and ambassadors is common, it is worth remembering that hypocrisy is not always considered a vice. The link between virtues, civility and eloquence becomes a theme in the literatures of the eighteenth-century 'Republic of Letters', and it can still be felt in the teaching of humanities. See Annette Baier, *Death and Character: Further Reflections on Hume* (Cambridge, MA: Harvard University Press, 2008): 35–57; Marc Fumaroli, *The Republic of Letters*, trans. Lara Vergnaud (New Haven: Yale University Press, 2018), 212–17; Mattingly, *Renaissance Diplomacy*, 222–29. For a modern iteration, see Costas Constantinou, "Between Statecraft and Humanism: Diplomacy and Its Forms of Knowledge," *International Studies Review* 15 (2013): 141–62.

36 Ian Hunter, "The Figure of Man and the Territorialisation of Justice in 'Enlightenment' Natural Law: Pufendorf and Vattel," *Intellectual History Review* 23, no. 3 (2013): 289–92.

37 Saunders, *Anti-Lawyers*, 85.

38 Hunter, "Figure of Man," 293. Hunter considers the training of the public official in the practice of empirical historiography rather than eloquence to be central to this task, Ian Hunter, "The Mythos, Ethos, and Pathos of the Humanities," *History of European Ideas* 40, no. 1 (2014): 31–34.

39 Jeffrey Minson, *Questions of Conduct: Sexual Harassment, Citizenship, Government* (Basingstoke: Palgrave Macmillan, 1993), 26–29.

concerns of government and commerce. In a formulation made visible by Max Weber, the training of the civil worker and, differently, the university jurist is shaped in two ways. First by limiting the relation between knowledge and politics (legal science cannot provide authority for political action) and second by working within a milieu with 'no ultimate ends or value' (the jurist is to address the due process of justice not justice itself).[40] While the legal conscience of the civil jurisprudent of the common law tradition may not be so austere, it still directs attention, and life, to the limited horizon of public administration.

The rival account of the jurist as keeper of the conscience of humanity, also cultivated through forms of training, is more closely aligned with the spiritual exercises of classical philosophy and Christian theology and metaphysics than with the historical and administrative training of civil authority.[41] The cultivation of the persona of the cosmopolitan found, for example, in the work of Immanuel Kant, continues this tradition.[42] The ambition of such jurists was, and is, to train themselves and others to transform the material world or restore a moral world.

Our brief return to Renaissance rhetoric and jurisprudence is, in part, a reminder of the resources of a tradition. It is easy to underestimate the institutional work that has contributed to the fashioning of civil and religious personae within the common law tradition. It is also a reminder that it is easy to over-estimate the sense in which the personae cultivated within a tradition are appropriate to present realities. As Hunter has argued, the traditions and idioms within which jurisprudence is written, including our own, are still intimately concerned with the contests of religion and civil peace.[43] These traditions, however, have not necessarily made colonialism (or its inheritance) a central concern of their own forms of government or self-government.[44] It is not necessarily the case that training in moral conscience will make available forms of engagement that are adequate to the task of responding fully to the *Uluru Statement from the Heart.*

This section opened with a comment on the work of Giambattista Vico's quest to link law and life through institutions (*res*) – places, styles of action, and laws of association and gathering in birth, marriage and death.[45] For Vico, the task of the disciplines of philology and jurisprudence was to find the basic words that would make this possible.[46] In an 'age of man' as equals, it was eloquence that maintained such a relation. The challenge of the *Uluru Statement*, for the transnational jurisprudent of the common law, is not simply to recognise that there are other peoples and laws in what is now 'Australia'. It is also, we argue, to respond from within a tradition to the understanding that another law and spiritual relation to land 'shines through' the existing state law of Australia.

40 Max Weber, "Science as Vocation," in *Max Weber: The Vocation Lectures,* eds. David Owen and Tracy B. Strong (Indianapolis: Hackett Publishing Company, 2004), 28–30.

41 A theme elaborated in Samuel Moyn, *Christian Human Rights* (Philadelphia: Penn Press, 2015).

42 Martti Koskenniemi, "A History of International Law Histories," in *The Oxford Handbook of the History of International Law,* eds. Bardo Fassbender and Anne Peters (Oxford: Oxford University Press, 2012), 943–45. It is also the implicit theme of Martti Koskenniemi, *The Gentle Civilizer of Nations: The Rise and Fall of International Law 1870–1960* (Cambridge: Cambridge University Press, 2001).

43 Ian Hunter, *Rival Enlightenments* (Cambridge: Cambridge University Press, 2001), Ch 1.

44 Shaunnagh Dorsett, *Juridical Encounters Māori and the Colonial Courts 1840–1852* (Auckland: University of Auckland Press, 2017), 271–80; Peter Rush, "Deathbound Doctrine: Scenes of Murder and Its Inheritance," *Studies in Law, Politics, and Society* 16 (1997): 96–99.

45 Harrison, *Dominion of the Dead,* 81; Jeffrey Barnouw, "The Critique of Classical Republicanism and the Understanding of Modern forms of Polity in Vico's *New Science,*" *Clio* 9, no. 3 (1980): 402–4.

46 Vico, *New Science,* §238–41; Harrison, *Dominion of the Dead,* 79–81.

Training in conduct

The third gloss of this chapter addresses the contemporary cultivation of appropriate conduct for the transnational jurisprudent in realising lawful relations. As elsewhere, our examples of meetings hold to the passage of relations rather than an essence. Our attention is directed to the cultivation of *modus vivendi* and the prudence of meeting rather than to the ethical form of reconciliation and critical reflection.[47]

To begin, we draw attention to the political training carried by the *Uluru Statement* itself. Megan Davis has addressed questions of conduct in terms of leadership and the intellectual resources and political courage necessary to maintain relations.[48] Tom Mayor, a Torres Strait Islander born on Larrikea Country, and also a delegate to the Convention has written about the training involved in listening through discussion during his experience of travelling with the *Uluru Statement* around the country.[49] Both Davis and Mayor frame their conduct in terms of the political virtues of courage and experience, and comradeship and struggle. A non-Indigenous political leader, we argue, might be expected to be no less engaged in addressing their own law.

Indigenous and non-Indigenous historians have charted, and participated in, many of the forms of transnational agreement-making in Australia. A training in lawful relations has been addressed narratively through the conducts of life, examined historiographically ('How have people of law conducted themselves in the past?'), and also questioned critically, where the conducts of office are viewed through the obligations and comportments of the Indigenous and non-Indigenous historians who write about relations of law in the present ('How have historians participated in and witnessed agreement making?').[50]

Within Indigenous diplomatic jurisprudences, there have been a number of responses to forms of non-Indigenous and Indigenous agreement-making. Kombumerri, Munaljahlai jurisprudent Christine Black considers the whole domain of human rights and responsibilities to be a matter of diplomacy in the sense that the rights and responsibilities of humans are constantly met in consideration of relationship.[51] She also emphasises the ways that the obligations of Indigenous jurisprudence are set within a cosmology of relationships rather than solely within a pragmatics of negotiation. In this respect the understanding of rights and responsibilities is bound into that of the protocols of the conduct of relations between, say, the living, the dead and the yet to be born; or, the land and those who move within it. In her consideration of the diplomacy and jurisprudence of Senior Law Man Bill Neidjie, Black, relates that all questions of relationships are shaped around the need to keep the law (*Djang*), the energy (*phūsis* and *energeia*) that animates existence in relationship.[52] Diplomacy and jurisprudence give shape to

47 Michel de Montaigne, *The Essays of Michel de Montaigne*, trans. and ed. Michael Screech (Harmondsworth: Penguin, 1987), 907–8.

48 Megan Davis, "Listening but Not Hearing: When Process Trumps Substance," *Griffith Review* 51 (2016): 84–87.

49 Mayor, *Finding the Heart of the Nation*, 1–4, and with Jill Gallagher, 143–51. For a political (and critical) account of non-Indigenous transnational law see Muthucumaraswamy Sornarajah, "On Fighting for Global Justice: The Role of a Third World International Lawyer," *Third World Quarterly* 37, no. 11 (2016): 1972–89.

50 Ann Curthoys, Ann Genovese and Alexander Reilly, *Rights and Redemption: History, Law and Indigenous People* (Sydney: University of New South Wales Press, 2008), 219–25. See more generally, Konisho, "First Nations Scholars."

51 Christine Black, *The Land Is the Source of the Law* (London: Routledge, 2011), 11–21.

52 Ibid., 33–40. The designation 'Senior Law Man' is given by Black to show status and office (as one might a High Court Judge), see Ibid., 186. Bill Neidjie's reflection on law (*Djang*) is found in Bill Neidjie, *Story About Feeling* (Broome: Magabala Books, 1989).

this balancing through the creation and maintenance of dyadic, witnessed relationships. In this account the offices and immediate horizons of conduct, including those expressed through the common law tradition, are patterned back into a concern with maintaining the law not with the accommodation of state interests in a *modus vivendi*.

Another response to the horizons of Indigenous and non-Indigenous transnational engagements, presented in the register of diplomacy and jurisprudence, is to repose a concern with the conduct of lawful relations through an Indigenous law of public offices. Here the acknowledgement of the obligations of the law of more than one nation is posed from within a public office. As Wiradjuri jurisprudent Mark McMillan has noted, if the public offices of the states and Commonwealth of Australia are to be understood as obligated to more than one law, then the modes of authorisation of tradition through scholarship, advice and judgment are also presented according to more than one form of authority.[53] This situation is also true of the university and the office of scholar. In this context, McMillan has argued for the naming of an office of Indigenous jurisprudent within the university and government as well as being an aspect of an Aboriginal public law and life. For McMillan, it is an office he occupies both as a Wiradjuri jurisprudent with plural sources of authority and obligations of collaboration and witness as well as common law jurisprudent.[54] The training for each law is different; one is directed to the obligations of country and the other towards the forms of Western national and international laws.

For many non-Indigenous legal scholars, the challenge is how to acknowledge the forms of relation, exchange and obligation within a common law tradition that canvasses a relatively small range of concerns when compared to the obligations that might be met through an Indigenous jurisprudence. Two examples of patterning of relationship between peoples and laws are given here. The first renovates aspects of Renaissance models of appropriate conduct and the second returns to the institutional understanding of office.

Returning to Vico as a source for enlivening forms of public life, the 'public worker' British-Australian scholar and designer Paul Carter directs attention to an *eros* of lawfulness which requires a training in the realisation of protocols of just passage, and the cultivation of an art of arrangement of meetings.[55] The education of Carter's transnational public worker, including the jurisprudent and diplomat, is existential.[56] As an art of association and its narration, Carter's sense of jurisprudence and diplomacy can also be considered in terms of an eloquence that seeks relations and equivalences (the public worker is a dramaturg).[57] For example, in reporting on a public design project on Arrente land and in the city of Alice Springs, Northern Territory, Australia, Carter starts from the observation that in many modern accounts of treaty, reconciliation, community and transnational life are shaped by strongly held accounts of present or future unity. In an important formulation, Emile Durkheim presented such unity in terms of *religio* as an

53 Mark McMillan, "Koowarta and the Rival Indigenous International: Our Place as Indigenous Peoples in the International," *Griffith Law* Review 23, no. 1 (2014): 110–12.

54 Ibid., 122.

55 *Eros* is often associated in Greek mythology with primordial forms of desire and existence that bring life out of chaos (Hesiod, *Theogany*). Later forms humanise desire but eros still carries with the impulse to create. This is the sense of *eros* that Plato, in *The Symposium*, suggests is needed in order to undertake a training in philosophy, see Pierre Hadot, *Philosophy as a Way of Life* (Oxford: Blackwell Press, 1995), 55. The understanding of service for the public worker differs according to religious and civil ordering.

56 Paul Carter, *Decolonising Governance: Archipelagic Thinking* (London: Routledge, 2019), 59; Margaret Kemarre Turner, *Iwenhe Tyetrrtye: What It Means to Be an Aboriginal Person* (Alice Springs: IAD Press, 2010), 18–19.

57 Paul Carter, *Places Made After Their Stories: Design and the Art of Choreotopography* (Crawley: University of Western Australia Press, 2015), 55–58.

ecstatic religious and social binding. While there are philosophical and theological sources for such kinds of argument, Carter also notes the ways that Durkheim drew on Arrernte knowledge as evidence. As a critic he notes both the inaccuracy of Durkheim's understanding of Arrernte knowledge and the way in which it passes over the 'difficult' histories of colonial, transnational and contemporary meetings.[58]

In presenting his own understanding of the obligations of meeting in Alice Springs, Carter also turns to Arrernte knowledge to think again about what those who live with the common law of Australia bring to a meeting (or treaty) place. Drawing on Akarre elder Margaret Kamarre Turner's characterisation of *utyerre, as* 'a big twirl of string that holds us there with our families', Carter reflects on the ways in which a meeting place might open a storied network of meeting and dispersal.[59] Translating the dramaturgy of meeting into an idiom of humanistic education, Carter shapes eloquence, as did Vico, as ontological and poetic (where the ability to hold or find a proper place is understood in terms of movement (*energeia*) rather than possession); phenomenological and rhetorical (where the narrative of physical and symbolic modes of existence of, for example, trees, are held in relation); as choreographical in the cultivation of the practices of meeting; and as diplomatic (in maintaining forms of co-existence through many different forms of distance).[60] Such comportments and abilities might also require dispositions of observance, restraint and care – as well as an ability to judge how to live with distinctions of complicity and appropriation.

Where Turner has written of *utyerre* as a vein or root that holds and moves homelands and kin, and trees and plants, Carter holds his meeting place to surfaces.[61] However, this is not the surface of the geometric forms of a master plan. It is an involuted surface of innumerable islands (archipelagos of land and sea) patterned regionally and transnationally into relations of exchange.[62] Carter's account draws attention to the importance of creating relations. His work as a writer and designer is set against the rationalism and violence of the state. In this respect his work can be read as a quest for a romantic escape from civil order. It does not seek reconciliation but a *modus vivendi* established through (non-state) islands of relationships. However, it can also be read less romantically as a training in how to meet, second time round, with a sense of the place of lawful relations.

Most of the interlocutors in this section find the authority of law apart from the civil authority of the state: Black patterns law back into the cosmos (*phūsis*) and arranges her own meetings on country; McMillan follows the patterns of two laws and trains jurisprudents in both forms of responsibility; Carter imagines his law sustained through exchange (custom) and the material bond of language (ceremony and place). At the end of the second section of this chapter, we noted the way the civil jurisprudence traditions described the ways training in conduct was shaped by the ways in which office was subordinated to forms of civil authority (jurisdiction) and the empirically described limits of institutional life.[63] Within such idioms close attention is paid to the invocation of a moral or living law that draws on Christianised forms of conduct.

58 Paul Carter, *Meeting Place: The Human Encounter and the Challenge of Coexistence* (Minneapolis: Minnesota University Press, 2013), 113–15.

59 Turner, *Iwenhe Tyetrrtye*, 154; Carter, *Places Made After Their Stories,* 108–9; Kirsten Anker, "Law As . . . Forest: Eco-logic, Stories and Spirits in Indigenous Jurisprudence," *Law Text Culture* 21 (2017): 191–213.

60 Carter, *Meeting Place*, 108–9.

61 Turner, *Iwenhe Tyetrrtye*, 15–17; Carter, *Decolonising Governance*, 42.

62 Carter, *Decolonising Governance*, 40.

63 Hunter, "The Mythos," 11–15.

Such contemporary forms of address, Hunter has argued, invite irresolvable spiritual conflict.[64] The same can be said of a training in conduct that orientates thought and action to the romanticism of a reconciled polity arranged around an identity or isomorphy of laws.[65] We have also noted how such formulations have rendered questions of transnational relations of law collateral and insubstantial. The last part of the section returns to some of those concerns to consider the comportment of officials who remain within their civil offices.

Writing within an idiom of civic humanism, Jeffrey Minson has argued that while offices subject to civil authority are generally viewed as 'disenchanted' and subject only to instruction, this need not be the case for all offices.[66] For Minson, it is through the pluralisation of offices that it is possible to maintain a sense of the variety of obligations assumed in time and place.[67] The Renaissance concern with 'humanism' and philanthropy (love of man), for example, can be understood as an aspect of the 'office of humanity' rather than as a general attribute of dignity or equality.[68] For Minson, it directs attention to the appropriate conduct of the humanist scholar in relation to the education of the student.[69] Other offices have different forms of training and expectations of appropriate conduct. Offices too can be occupied in different ways, and with different obligations, by Indigenous and non-Indigenous jurisprudents (and by men and women).[70]

Conclusion

There is no doubt that the accounts of training and conduct offered in this chapter represent rival accounts to the conducts of office set within different traditions and located within common law thought. We have sought, however, to draw out some of the different commitments to rhetorical education and the training of eloquence. The engagement by Megan Davies and the officials who drafted the Treaty Process Act is significantly, and necessarily, different to the understanding of meeting place presented by Carter. What is less visible, perhaps, is that the *Uluru Statement* imagines that the people who live within the common law tradition have, or should have, the ability to understand the ways in which an Indigenous jurisprudence might 'shine through' an Australian law and nation. The focus in this chapter has been on the ways in which a rhetorical tradition of eloquence maintains repertoires of lawful relations. It also offers cautions about how to take responsibility for the comportments of the offices of jurisprudent and diplomat. As the jurist-diplomats of the sixteenth and seventeenth centuries were aware, the obligations of office were, and are, considerable.

We close with a note on examples. This chapter has proceeded jurisographically through the use of examples. It has not offered a dialectical critique of current understandings and configurations of international or transnational legal thought. It has assumed that a failure to

64 Ibid., 22–24.

65 Weber, "Science as Vocation," 29–30.

66 Jeffrey Minson, "How to Speak Well of the State: A Rhetoric of Civil Prudence," *UC Irvine Law Review* 4 (2014): 437–44.

67 Minson, *Questions of Conduct*, 28.

68 Jeffrey Minson, "S. Toussaint, Humanismes Antihumanismes, Paris: Les Belles Lettres, 2009," *Cromohs* 14 (2009): 2.

69 Ibid., 12–13.

70 Genovese, "Inheriting and Inhabiting," 55–57. See also John Borrows, "Heroes, Tricksters, Monsters and Caretakers: Indigenous Law and Legal Education," *McGill Law Journal* 61, no. 4 (June 2016): 795–846.

attend to non-Indigenous and Indigenous relations in Australia and elsewhere will present an inadequate account of the conduct of lawful relations within a common law tradition. While we have opinions on the quality of rival accounts of conduct, we have been concerned here with the ways in which eloquence, as speech and comportment, can carry meaning as part of a training in conduct. Our own examples were chosen to make visible what is brought into lawful relationship.

2

Life in the ruins

International law as doctrine and discipline

Gregor Noll

In this contribution I examine how the monastic order as a historical predecessor has shaped the discipline of international law and discuss the problems relating to the discipline's attempts at secularisation.

1.

Some years ago I conducted empirical research on the principle of proportionality in international humanitarian law (IHL). Put simply, the principle entails that civilian casualties in an attack shall be proportionate to the military advantage achieved. I interviewed persons working with IHL in academia, militaries and the International Committee of the Red Cross and studied IHL treaty law, cases and doctrine. Doctrinal literature made a big issue of proportionality. To my surprise, though, it simply did not answer the question of *how* proportionality should be assessed. Amongst my sources, there was overwhelming consensus that such assessments must nonetheless be carried out, even though one and the same scenario might engender widely varying results even amongst IHL lawyers within the same military organisation.

Agnosticism on what procedure is demanded by the law is paired with forceful expressions of allegiance to the principle of proportionality, which one prominent IHL lawyer described as 'fundamental'. Where legal doctrine falls silent, it appears that legal discipline continues to operate, and, indeed, operates in a more proper sense of the word. Doctrine and discipline reflect two rather different understandings of learning. We do not know what the law demands of us: this seems to escalate the importance that we practice it. On a day-to-day basis, this practice is carried out in the spatial and social seclusion of a military organisation, where legal advisers assist 'responsible military commanders' to assess proportionality. In this particular context, there is a confluence of the order of the military as well as the order of the law in the term 'discipline'.

Does this not remind us of something? I come to think of a monastic order, whose members live and practise in spatial and social seclusion. Looking back at the origins of the monastic order, in the classical antiquity, it seems obvious that monastic discipline is the central normative factor in the lives of the monks and nuns. The monastic discipline comprises spiritual rules on daily conduct, often mirroring the life of the founder of the order or laid down by the founder himself. Discipline enables a small group to gather around questions to which explicit religious rules have no answer. Where doctrine operates at a universal level, discipline is always particular. While doctrine purports to be substantive, discipline necessarily verges on the procedural. While doctrine deals with that which has been revealed in the law already, discipline prepares for revelation to come.

2.

You will recognise the pattern I just described from similar constellations in areas other than IHL. Let me account for another example. In the field of asylum, judges, decision-makers and counsel told me that credibility assessments are decisive for an important part of the caseload. This is so because there is usually little or no other evidence apart from the testimony of the asylum seeker. Hence, credibility becomes a central issue, without norms of international law, doctrine or case law detailing how credibility is to be assessed. As with a proportionality assessment in the military context, it is no exaggeration that a credibility assessment may form a matter of life and death. Credibility assessments are carried out in the spatial and social seclusion of authorities, courts, or within the UNHCR, governed by discipline rather than by doctrine.[1] The way credibility is assessed seems to be deeply engrained in these organisations, which brings critics to use phrases like 'the culture of disbelief'.[2] There are a number of empirical studies showing how specific courts or authorities clam up and form epistemic communities. The court or local authority creates its own practice which can depart quite significantly from other units within the same court system or authority.[3] This is not anarchy in the making, but the result of an order of strong discipline and weak doctrine.

This type of phenomenon is open to the critique of undermining legal certainty. The criticism implies that legal certainty is created by central actors successfully streamlining norm implementation. The doctrinal legal tradition is an antidote: from the hive of case law and practice, tenets and general principles are identified which counteract the particularity of discipline and unify the law. The uniting power of doctrine lives off the pluralism of discipline. Doctrine is closely related to a central power, while discipline thrives in closed spaces shared with brothers and sisters.

Again, it is helpful to think of Christian monastic life which has been in institutional competition with the medieval Catholic Church as well as with early modern state power. We are soon struck by how different the monastery and the Church are in their normative construction. The monasteries of classical antiquity institutionalised a significant degree of obliviousness to the outside world, all while Christianity was becoming the officially recognised religion in the Roman Empire and the Church allied itself with the imperial central power. These monasteries spread to the deserts of the Middle East, while the Church was centralising a considerable amount of power in Rome and Constantinople. The normative heritage of early monasteries can be traced back to *The Sayings of the Desert Fathers and Mothers. Abbas* (fathers) and *ammas*

1 Olga Jubany, "Constructing Truths in a Culture of Disbelief. Understanding Asylum Screening from Within," *International Sociology* 26, no. 1 (January 2011): 74.

2 Ibid.

3 One significant large-scale study of US practice has the topical name 'Refugee Roulette' and draws the conclusion that the assigning of decision-maker is the most outcome-determining moment in the asylum procedure: Jaya Ramji-Nogales, Andrew Schoenholtz and Philip Schrag, "Refugee Roulette: Disparities in Asylum Adjudication," *Stanford Law Review* 60, no. 1 (November 2007): 295. The principle of proportionality in IHL is more difficult to examine due to confidentiality of military organisations. However, I think that the outcome variations of proportionality assessments are not necessarily smaller than those of asylum claim decisions.

(mothers) give concrete examples from life in Christ's footsteps. These texts revolve around persons more than norms: the collections of sayings were organised alphabetically after the person who in them appeared to be the teacher.[4] Here we have reached the core of the term discipline, consisting of being a disciple. And being a disciple releases centrifugal forces.

The contrast to *Codex iuris canonici*, the normative heritage of the Catholic Church, could hardly be more distinct. Its historical source is Gratian's *Concordantia discondantium canonum* from the mid-twelfth century, whose title can be translated freely to 'the work which gives accordance to rules that don't accord' – the core of the doctrinal mission. Gratian's person exemplifies how doctrine emerges where religious power becomes secular. He was a jurist who distinguished himself as a teacher at the University of Bologna, where he contributed to the establishment of canon law as its own legal discipline. Bologna was at the time considered to be the leading centre of learning in medieval Europe.[5] Lifeworks and aphorisms from monastery founders are collected in the sayings characterising the collection of norms as, above all, diverse. By contrast, the works of Gratian are driven by the aspiration to unify the law. We now witness the emergence of two types of ideal teachers. On the one hand we have the disciplinary teacher embodied first by the Desert Fathers and Mothers and later by monastery founders such as Benedict of Nursia, Francis of Assisi and Dominic of Osma. In their works the norm is concretised to the degree that norm and life amalgamate.[6] On the other hand we have the doctrinal teacher whose agenda is to abstract norm from life to express it in purer form. In both cases it is about making a divergence disappear. The strategy of doctrine is abstraction; the strategy of discipline is concretion.[7]

3.

Peter Goodrich, professor of jurisprudence at Cardozo Law School, has added to the discussion on scholarly discipline and jurisdiction in an article published in 2010.[8] After exemplifying how legal power needs to convince us of its historical ascendancy to cast itself as legitimate, Goodrich says this:

> [T]he support of power by chronicles and histories, by the simple assertion of age, does display a limit of law, a joining of legality with the humanist discipline par excellence at precisely that moment when law is least independent and so most vulnerable in the sense of depending upon another jurisdiction. The identity of law, its authenticity, is here expressly a matter of historical method, of narrative recollection.[9]

4 Samuel Rubenson and Riksbankens Jubileumsfond, *Det tidiga klosterväsendet och den antika bildningen: Slutrapport från ett forskningsprogram* (Stockholm: Makadam Förlag, 2016), 19.

5 Ulrich Nonn, *Mönche, Schreiber und Gelehrte. Bildung und Wissenschaft im Mittelalter* (Darmstadt: Wissenschaftliche Buchgesellschaft, 2012), 102.

6 Agamben has pointed out that the four fathers describe their own rules as *vita vel regula*, that is the life or the rule. There is no difference between rule and life, life and rule. '[B]oth *rule* and *life*', Agamben writes, 'lose their familiar meaning in order to point in the direction of a third thing': Giorgio Agamben, *The Highest Poverty: Monastic Rules and Form-of-Life* (Stanford, CA: Stanford University Press, 2013), xii.

7 'Etymologically, discipline, as pertaining to the disciple or scholar, is antithetical to doctrine, the property of the doctor or teacher; hence, in the history of the words, doctrine is more concerned with abstract theory, and discipline with practice or exercise': Oxford English Dictionary, 'discipline, n'.

8 Peter Goodrich, "Disciplines and Jurisdictions: An Historical Note," *English Language Notes* 48, no. 2 (Fall/Winter 2010): 153.

9 Ibid., 156.

We recognise this sideways shift from the difficult questions of law such as proportionality and credibility assessments. The core capability of doctrine to transform an array of single norms into a coherent system is only of limited resource; at best, it tends to account for a plurality of possible solutions. A dogmatic lawyer can then turn to an auxiliary form of scholarship – outside of the law – to produce an authoritative result which legal scholarship cannot produce in itself. Replacing credibility assessments with estimates of probability is an example of this. Formalising proportionality assessments through mathematic formulas is another. This turn to auxiliary scholarship is precisely what Goodrich describes as rule rather than exception. At a closer glance legal scholarship seems to turn into a science of history. What Goodrich calls 'historical method' becomes leading and not just auxiliary when determining the law.

Let us consider an analogous situation. In IHL, proportionality assessments settle whether the taking of life by those in power is just or unjust. The vagueness and open-endedness of the law leaves this question to be settled by military commanders instead of international lawmakers. A military commander bases her decision to a large extent on earlier practice, passed down by superiors, or by the silent imitation of the actions of superiors.[10] We witness how discipline, an imitation of superiors, emerges as a normative principle. Discipline becomes a normativity bound by persons rather than by an abstract language.

To justify military conduct as lawful, earlier cases must be remembered, organised and accounted for in more explicit terms. And with that, the transition is made from the exclusive jurisdiction of the law to the broader jurisdiction of scholarship. Scholarship provides for 'historical method' and 'narrative recollection' to uphold law's authority. Armed forces usually organise a branch that deals with the scholarship of war, with a varying degree of autonomy. International legal scholarship plays a significant role in that scholarship of war.[11]

However, when it comes to hard cases, international legal scholarship is incapable of providing clear-cut answers through its abstraction techniques. One of the most widely spread English-language textbooks on the laws of war is Yoram Dinstein's *The Conduct of Hostilities under the International Law of Armed Conflict*, published in multiple editions. Dinstein explains the content of the proportionality principle through a long casuistry of contemporary warfare situations.[12] In Goodrich's words, here is 'a joining of legality with the humanist discipline', namely contemporary history, 'at the moment when law is least independent'.[13] And the snake's head – the concrete question of legality of a certain military attack – meets its tail in the form of a presentist enumeration of earlier military practice. A closer analysis of his list of cases reveals them to be disparate and inconclusive. Even though the doctrinal legal scholar assumed the role of the chronicler, the substantive void of doctrine persists. The shift from warfare to a science of war, and from legal scholarship to contemporary history, lead us into a circle of self-referentiality.

10 Documents laying down 'military doctrine' usually merge established earlier practice with policy-driven guidelines. The parallel to legal doctrine is readily apparent.

11 In Sweden this task is conducted by the Swedish Defence University which was earlier a part of the national armed forces but is now a state-run university since 2008. The Royal Swedish Academy of War Sciences, under the protection of His Majesty the King, is not bound to the state. The charter of the Academy states that its aim is to 'further sciences of importance to the defence of the motherland' [author's translation]. Both the Swedish Defence University and the Royal Swedish Academy of War Sciences work to a great extent with questions of international law.

12 Yoram Dinstein, *The Conduct of Hostilities Under the Law of International Armed Conflict*, 2nd ed. (Cambridge: Cambridge University Press, 2010), 128–38.

13 Goodrich, "Disciplines and Jurisdictions: An Historical Note," 156.

Now we are in the domains of discipline, where great teachers are followed and their teachings are conformed to. The military decision-maker, using Dinstein's textbook on international law, is assured of two things: the principle of proportionality entails a substantial difference between the just and the unjust, and the decision to take a life on the basis of the principle of proportionality is a legal exercise of power. In the worst-case scenario, this does not mean anything else than that the reader's power to take a life in war is authorised by following in the footsteps of Dinstein. The failure of doctrinal authority is compensated by increasing disciplinary authority, resting on an apodictic base.

4.

Is legal scholarship not about a certain *method*, to be taught and adhered to, which guarantees scholarly legitimacy and disciplinary identity? In Goodrich's account, the framing of 'chronicles and histories' becomes the full stop where legal scholarship turns into historiography. To be sure, we are provided with rules on the sources of law and on interpretation. But difficult cases such as proportionality and credibility assessments are not determined in the sphere of these rules but are subject to the ability of the decision-maker to make a convincing argument based on the intention of involved parties, on custom or on reasonableness. Generally, an advanced ability to use historical material is needed when arguing with parties' intent, custom or reasonableness. It seems that legal method must go beyond itself when the chips are down.

Thus, the tension between doctrine and discipline manifests itself in methodological questions as well. Method entails the application of abstract rules. To apply a method might mean to follow in the footsteps of the teacher. Finding our own path is yet another, instantaneous way to practise a method.[14] In the second and third meanings we are faithful to the metaphorical meaning of the Greek *metodos*, meaning 'way'. What determines whether the legal scholar follows or leads? The answer is charisma, the teleological meaning being divine alms, or, in Max Weber's secular remake, the ability to attract admiration and followers. Both forms give charisma a transcendental base. Followers can follow either a person or, equally, a question evading its answer.

Here, we might consider the importance of scholarship's demand for originality. When research is evaluated, it is discussed to what extent a researcher's contribution possesses a degree of originality. Originality is thought to reflect the personal creativity of the researcher, her ability to find new methods, perspectives or explanations. There is an alternative interpretation. The demand is for the researcher's ability to let the origin – Latin's *origo* – emerge. In that respect originality is related to charisma: they both display a strong connection to the transcendental.[15]

5.

My examples seem to suggest that there are unaccounted remnants of spirituality at work in the discipline of IHL lawyers and refugee lawyers. Why remnants of spirituality? We are living in secular times, and so is the discipline of international law. Etymologically, *saeculum* means 'span

14 See, for example, Chapter 10 in this volume by Olivia Barr, "Wayfaring Methods."

15 Is a secular form of originality possible? 'Only a thought that does not conceal its own unsaid – but constantly takes up and elaborates it – may eventually lay claim to originality': Giorgio Agamben, *The Signature of All Things: On Method* (New York: Zone Books, 2009), 8.

of time' and secular also means 'not belonging to a religious order'. So it is the same thing to say that international law is a temporal order and that it is a secular order.

Monastic orders were, and continue to be, temporal orders seeking to reflect a transcendental order. In that attempt, the monastic movement inserted itself into a vertical structure going all the way up from the Church to the Creator. The Creator formed a metaphysical point towards which the temporal orders of monks and nuns were organised. Divine will, the doctrines of the Church and the discipline of the order formed a universe.[16] Metaphorically speaking, our universities live on in the ruins of this universe.

6.

Academia and the academic functions of monasteries have complemented each other over time. The Academy of Athens, founded by Plato and originally located in a place called Hekademia, was closed by Emperor Justinian I in 529. In the same year, Benedict of Nursia founded a monastery in Montecassino, which is generally regarded as heralding the monastic movement in Christianity at large (which was by the way, the same monastery in which Wittgenstein was interned as a prisoner of war in 1918). Reformation ended a period of extraordinary growth of monastic orders, which were fulfilling academic functions. Schools and institutions for higher education were established, and the monasteries held libraries and kept chronicles. After reformation, these functions were performed within an increasingly secular academia located at universities, and we see the discipline of law, including public international law, emerging in a trajectory leading up to today and beyond. So it seems that we have just about bracketed a period in which academic disciplines were under the custodianship of Christianity. That is not saying that the transcendental structure it once consolidated can be placed in brackets.

7.

If we seek contemporary expressions of the inability of doctrine to keep us aligned with a central reference point, the discourse on fragmentation is one obvious example. During the Noughties international lawyers began worrying about the increasing complexity in the international legal framework and started discussing the fragmentation of international law into a number of self-contained regimes. These regimes seemed to optimise their own systemic goals. International economic law optimises economic growth, international human rights law optimises human dignity, and international environmental law optimises sustainable development. Naturally, these goals can be subsumed under an assumed systemic goal of international law (the preservation of an international order of peace and security would be one possible candidate; there are others), but apparently the international lawyers of the Noughties did not feel that this subsumption would suffice to dampen the anxiety caused by the loss of disciplinary identity. Notably, sub-systemic goals such as economic growth, human dignity and sustainable development have managed to establish themselves as fairly plausible transcendental positions. International law as a cohesive discipline does not have a more convincing story on transcendence with which to supplant these sub-systemic goals. My point is not that international law should be kept together, nor that it should fragment into various smaller disciplines. The point is

16 The monasteries could present themselves as resting upon divine authority, which enabled (and enables) a non-hierarchical laterality as opposed to subordination under Church authority.

that disciplinary practice always releases centrifugal forces, and that it is hard to stop disciplinary entrepreneurs from founding new monasteries. This is, of course, supported by the lack of a common transcendental reference point.

8.

In another paragraph of his article Goodrich writes:

> The state cannot be censor of itself, as the unfortunate history of international law generally indicates. It needs an alien will within.[17]

. . . and so does the individual monk, to censor himself, so does the individual nun, to censor herself. The monastic discipline provides the basis for this censorship as 'an alien will within'. What is alien is its relation to the divine, and it wills a life at the threshold of the temporal.

What are the chronicles, what is revealed in the chronicles and histories? A Christian metaphysics would answer that creation is the gradual revelation of the divine in the world. A secular metaphysics short-circuits at this point, and falls into self-referentiality: what is revealed is no longer divine creation, but the will of the secular sovereign in the world. A radically secular chronicler of international law cannot be the 'alien will within', censoring the state. Why? Because there is, strictly speaking, nothing to reveal, nothing to justify against an alien standard. All that remains is, using Goodrich's terms, an 'acclamatory and choral relation of legal academics to State and law'.[18] Without the divine providing normative guidelines for censure, a radically secularised doctrine is sent in sideways movements finally turning into circular movements. Discipline will take on an apodictic function: through a socially complex role-play the predecessors of discipline will identify a certain historical occurrence as just or unjust. Such a predecessor, enjoying enough actual authority, will be elevated to a source of law in all but her name. Of a law to come, that is. The temporal-normative movement within is analogous to hermits' and monastery saints' aspiration to live in the Kingdom of God. Also present here is the threat of self-referentiality. The sacred person knows what is sacred since he or she practices it. The divine as the fully alien is its counterweight.

Consequently, discipline opens up for two kinds of self-referentiality, one immanent and one transcendental. The monastic discipline combined temporal and divine and broke the circle of self-referentiality. Since the divine is categorically different from the temporal, a combination of the two cannot refer to the same unit, to the same 'self'. The secularised academy is deprived of this possibility.

9.

Yet, we cannot expect that the structures inherited from monastic life will be irrelevant for us, that we are unperturbed by our life in the ruins. Though the vertical relationship to the Creator is abolished due to secularisation, the routines of the old days will remain, if only to provide a stabilising function. We will retain parts of our Christian *habitus*, and repress the factual lack of its metaphysical foundation into the subconscious.

17 Goodrich, "Disciplines and Jurisdictions: An Historical Note," 159.
18 Ibid.

It works like this: first, we think the sovereign as a worldly power, which would therewith be fully existing in time. Yet, over and above that, we also take a mental detour up to the position of the divine, find it empty and ricochet back to the sovereign from there. But we do not tell anybody, least of all ourselves, that we do this. By this detour through the transcendental, we carry on its dust to the sovereign who now possesses structural attributes previously reserved for its Creator. A veritable taboo has been established. All possibilities for 'critique', that is the ability to make judgments of worldly powers' conduct, are therewith gone. What is more, the divine revelation earlier sought in history has now made a covert move into the history produced by that sovereign. With our sources of law, canons of interpretation and norms of collision, we legal scholars now work to reveal in time once again what already has been revealed in time by the sovereign. This is how formalism became so important, since it takes place where the transcendental manifested itself in the world.

Accordingly, there is an increased risk of secular international legal scholars vacating their position as chronicling censors to a chronicling chorus. But this is not what we experience in our academic workplace, is it? The term 'critical thinking' is written into a growing number of syllabi, strategic plans and vision documents at my university. Surely, it cannot be right that we have vacated the position of censure?

Let us look at another word proliferating in academia. It is the term 'interdisciplinarity'. When meaning can no longer be derived from the vertical relationship to the divine, we seek it, first, in the discipline itself. Due to the self-referentiality of an intra-disciplinary practice of revelation, we find ourselves limited and frustrated in this exercise. So we start to project on other disciplines the possession of the truth that we are unable to reveal within our discipline. Yet, the other disciplines play the same game of projection. Leaving the self-referentiality of law, we find the self-referentiality of history, anthropology, political sciences, etc.

As no truth is to be found in the other disciplines either, we will be inclined to seek it between the disciplines or beyond them – hence our great hopes for interdisciplinarity, cross-disciplinarity and transdisciplinarity.[19] As long as the metaphysical reasons for our lateral move towards interdisciplinarity are not realised, interdisciplinarity and its siblings will remain unable to provide us with a vantage point for critical thinking. The acclamatory chorus will simply be enlarged with new members from other disciplines, enabling ever louder incantations.

So, what should we be looking for? The type of research which emphasises the process of secularisation in its own practice, empirical as well as theoretical. It will not be able to limit itself to one area of knowledge but will be an interdisciplinary practice which simultaneously examines its disciplinary pre-conditions as well as the research matter.

10.

Towards the end of his text, Goodrich nevertheless admonishes legal scholars to 'offer censure'.[20] But how is censure possible? Perhaps only through the alienation from ourselves as disciplinary practitioners. The transcendental relationship we once had to God then transforms into a relationship with the alienness of how my own cognitive possibilities and limitations have been shaped by history and become a part of my body.

19 'All interdisciplinarity, one might argue, is disciplinary symptom: somatization, in the disciplinary body, of some invisible pain': Julie Stone Peters, "Law, Literature, and the Vanishing Real: On the Future of an Interdisciplinary Illusion," *PMLA* 120, no. 2 (2005): 448.

20 Goodrich, "Disciplines and Jurisdictions: An Historical Note," 159.

Let me revert to the question of proportionality in IHL, which engenders such intense disciplinary activity within militaries. The lexical root of 'proportionality' is the Latin noun *proportio*, which, in turn, is a translation of the Greek noun *analogia* (ἀναλογία). To deal with something *ana logos* means to deal with it according to a due *logos*. The Greek *ana* literally means 'up to', implying a vertical relationship. The ἀ in ἀναλογία (*analogia*) indicates the 'first', the *entem*, the pure essence, while the ν (n) indicates that the two entities ontologically share a common origin.

Traditionally, lawyers use the terms 'analogy' when reasoning on relevant commonalities of two cases, while they use 'proportionality' when reasoning on the relative weight of conflicting principles. Both proportionality and analogy rest on the possibility to represent the whole through its parts. While the *alpha* of *analogia* was made to refer to God in the Christian tradition, there was, and is, a tradition of Christian thought that emphasised the ultimate unknowability of God. My awareness of the transcendental possibilities of use and misuse of proportionality assessments is a small step towards alienating myself as a legal scholar.

'What is needed', Goodrich writes, 'is not just expertise in law . . . but also a sense of the purpose and conscience that history and practice have given these norms by virtue of what has been done with them and to *whom*'.[21] So what is this conscience, this knowing-together of something that is radically different, in the discipline of international law? Knowledge of transcendental misuse alone is not enough to grasp the phenomenon of proportionality and credibility. The question of what the legal norms have done and 'to whom' is the empirical mission to live the discipline as much in the self as in the world.

21 Ibid. (emphasis added).

3

Receiving traditions of civility, remaking conditions of cohabitation

A genealogy of politics, law and piety in South Asia

Adil Hasan Khan[1]

Introduction

From December 2019 to March 2020, India witnessed widespread protests against the passage of the Citizenship Amendment Act (CAA) and the associated proposal to create a National Register of Citizens (NRC), on the grounds that these laws and policies fundamentally endangered the conditions supporting civic cohabitation.[2] These measures of the right-wing Hindu regime have been widely perceived to be part of a larger project to eventually exclude various others, especially Muslims and Dalits, from the citizenry.

These vibrant protests (only cut short by the COVID-19 enforced national lockdown) were accompanied by various protest slogans, poetry and chants, memorably including public recitals of the Preamble of the Constitution of India.[3] Some of these protest practices ended up raising

1 I want to acknowledge the generous comments and guidance provided by Upendra Baxi, Rustom Bharucha, Rajshree Chandra, Julia Dehm, Debolina Dutta, Ratna Kapur, Shaun McVeigh, Usha Natarajan, Moin Ahmad Nizami, Sundhya Pahuja, Shalini Randeria, Rahul Rao, Jeff Redding, Silvia Suteu and Ntina Tzouvala. I also want to thank the editors of this edited volume for their inordinate support and unflagging patience throughout the process of writing of this chapter. Finally, I want to acknowledge that an earlier version of this chapter has been published as an online reflection by the *Third World Approaches to International Law Review* (TWAILR), and to thank the editors of the *Review* for their insightful comments and helpful feedback on that version.

2 See Rohit De and Surabhi Ranganathan, "We Are Witnessing the Rediscovery of India's Republic," *The New York Times*, December 27, 2019, www.nytimes.com/2019/12/27/opinion/india-constitution-protests.html.

3 Many of these peaceful protestors, especially the young Muslim students amongst them, have since faced a veritable witch hunt at the hands of the National Capital Region's (Delhi's) police services. Several protest organisers, including a heavily pregnant graduate student, have been jailed during the pandemic lockdown. The main charges against these student activists are that they conspired to 'incite' the violent pogrom that was unleashed in late February, primarily by right-wing Hindu mobs against the Muslim residents of North-Eastern Delhi, in the wake

hackles in certain quarters, for being seditious, anti-national, anti-Hindu, 'extremist' (Islamist extremism) and religious (anti-secular). In a thought-provoking piece, Rahul Rao has suggested that the debate over the use of 'religious' chants in these political protests – such as '*Allahu akbar*' ('God is great') or '*La ilaha illallah*' ('There is no God but Allah') – have 'exposed a fault line' amongst proponents of secularism.[4] Following an analysis of some of the public debate that the chants elicited, Rao critiques the narrow concept of secularism that struggles with any expressions of piety in the public sphere. Rao also contrasts this with practices of secularism on display in these very protests that do not 'merely tolerate religious difference but exists precisely to enable the practice of piety by those who wish to practice it'. Cross-religious solidarities ('fraternity'), Rao suggests, have the potential to contest ongoing right-wing projects of dismantling cohabitation.

In this chapter I take Rao's instructive line of inquiry further by showing how the principle of secularism that Rao critiques forms a part of a larger project of modernity. I argue that in order to formulate an alternative project of enabling cohabitation, we must not only re-appraise our concept of the secular, but also simultaneously re-conceive the associated concepts of politics, law and religion, and how they all relate to one another. This constellation of concepts forms inter-linked parts of the transformational project of modernity.[5]

One pivot around which this re-configuration of religion and politics operates in modernity's project has been articulated by modern secularists, who, in the modern national state, sought to privatise religion by confining it to autonomous forms of *belief* protected within the domain of the private sphere. Relatedly, in the *colonial* public sphere, modern secularists sought to construct religion as a marker of essentialised group identity on the basis of which civic and limited political rights could be claimed.[6] The other pivot gets articulated by modern anti-secularists, who have sought to extend a politicised religion's autonomous obligations into the public sphere.

Pertinently, when it comes to the practice of the Hindu right in postcolonial India, we are confronted with how these two modern modes of re-configuring politics and religion get potently combined so as to facilitate the determination of the national public sphere by one set of religious norms, while simultaneously policing the appearance of any practices of other religious communities.[7] In fact, as Ratna Kapur shows, this paradoxical combination is achieved by construing secularism itself as representing a public norm uniquely supplied by a homogenised (and monotheistic) version of Hinduism and its laudatory commitment to religious tolerance, while complementarily arguing for this doctrine to be interpreted as requiring

---

of these anti-CAA/NRC protests. See Hanan Zaffar and Majid Alam, "Despite a Lockdown, India Is Cracking Down on Student Activists Who Were a Part of Anti-CAA Protests," *Vice*, April 22, 2020, www.vice.com/en_in/article/epgyx7/india-cracks-down-on-anti-caa-students-despite-lockdown.

4 Rahul Rao, "Test of Faith: The Anti-CAA Protests Shake the Bounds of old Indian Secular Morality," *The Caravan*, January 30, 2020, https://caravanmagazine.in/politics/caa-protests-shake-old-bounds-indian-secular-morality.

5 See Talal Asad, *Formations of the Secular: Christianity, Islam, Modernity* (Stanford, CA: Stanford University Press, 2003).

6 See Saba Mahmood, *Religious Difference in a Secular Age: A Minority Report* (Princeton: Princeton University Press, 2016).

7 Saba Mahmood, in her work on postcolonial Egypt, has shown how this combination is certainly not unique to right-wing Hindu majoritarian in India. See Saba Mahmood, "Religious and Civil Inequality," in *Religious Difference in a Secular Age: A Minority Report*, ed. Saba Mahmood (Princeton: Princeton University Press, 2016), 149–80.

the strict maintenance of formal equality in order to prevent any recognition of group rights or protection for the public expression of religious practices of other religious communities.[8] As she observes:

> The result is that the project of secularism becomes a project about assimilating religious minorities rather than about the protection of the rights of religious minorities.[9]

For international legal scholars, the argument put forward here might initially (and erroneously) resonate with recent critical treatments of the relationship between politics, international law and religion. In these writings, the mainstream liberal narrative of a secular international law as the *other* of ('irrational') religion – one that enables the rational management and/or overcoming of religious practices and religious identity within the public sphere – is contested.[10] What then follows is an anti-secularism that instead attempts to reveal how international law is essentially made up of 'secularised theological concepts',[11] a critique that ends up universalising and anachronistically essentialising a particular conception of international law and religion.[12] By collapsing international law and religion into one another and suggesting a certain inescapable (and ahistorical) rigidity to this formation, these critical scholars end up positing a dialectical account of politics. For them, there is a (juridical) politics that is determined by this oppressively theological (read: Catholic) international law, and a counter-politics that is antinomian, messianic and driven by the singular demands of an interior conscience that founds justice (read: Protestant).[13] This critical formulation leaves no room for a rival configuration of the relationship between politics, international law and religion, whereby there might be a politics that is neither fully determined by religion and international law (utopia), nor entirely bereft of an ethic (apology).[14] In other words, it remains blinded to *another* international law that might assist in the cultivation of conditions of cohabitation.

8 See Ratna Kapur, "A Leap of Faith: The Construction of Hindu Majoritarianism Through Secular Law," *The South Atlantic Quarterly* 113, no. 1 (2014): 109. See also Brenda Cossman and Ratna Kapur, "Secularism's Last Sigh? The Hindu Right, the Courts, and India's Struggle for Democracy," *Harvard Journal of International Law* 38, no. 1 (1997): 113–70.

9 Ratna Kapur, "The 'Ayodhya' Case: Hindu Majoritarianism and the Right to Religious Liberty," *Maryland Journal of International Law* 29 (2014): 305–65, 317.

10 See David Kennedy, "Losing Faith in the Secular: Law, Religion, and the Culture of International Governance," in *Religion and International Law*, eds. Mark W. Janis and Carolyn Evans (The Hague: Martinus Nijhoff Publishers, 1999), 309–20; Reut Yael Paz, "Religion, Secularism, and International Law," in *The Oxford Handbook of The Theory of International Law*, eds. Anne Orford and Florian Hoffman (Oxford: Oxford University Press, 2016), 923–38; Martti Koskenniemi, "International Law and Religion: No Stable Ground," in *International Law and Religion: Contemporary and Historical Perspectives*, eds. Martti Koskenniemi, et al. (Cambridge: Cambridge University Press, 2017), 3–21.

11 Carl Schmitt, *Political Theology: Four Chapters on the Concept of Theology*, trans. George Schwab (Cambridge: The MIT Press, 1985), 36.

12 This critical scholarship is distinct from a more (celebratory) revivalist set of anti-secular interventions that have sought to embrace the unique 'Christian heritage' of international law. However, the obvious overlap lies in their shared positing of the existence of solely *one* international law (and not a plurality of rival traditions). See Raphael Domingo and John Witte Jr. eds., *Christianity and Global Law* (Abingdon: Routledge, 2020).

13 See Duncan Kennedy, "A Semiotics of Critique," *Cardozo Law Review* 22, no. 4 (2001): 1147–89.

14 For an articulation of such a rival configuration in legal scholarship see Jeffrey Minson, "How to Speak Well of the State: A Rhetoric of Civil Prudence," *UC Irvine Law Review* 4, no. 1 (2014): 437–70; Ann Genovese, Shaun McVeigh and Peter D. Rush, "Lives Lived with Law," *Law Text Culture* 20, no. 1 (2016): 1–13.

To search for alternatives, we must undertake an exercise in genealogy that unpacks the colonial histories of projects of modernity in India, over the course of the late nineteenth and early twentieth centuries. It is these histories, and their absent-mindedly naturalised legacies in contemporary times, that we must reckon with to illuminate alternative practices of living and struggling together.

These alternative traditions are those of civility. Civility here refers to those historically conjoined arts of training selves and others – such as rhetoric, ritual and jurisprudence – that seek to cultivate cohabitation.[15] With the emergence of the project of modernity, the twinned domains of these arts – the *psychi* and the *polis* – have been differentiated, with one considered to be the proper concern of the disciplines of moral philosophy and aesthetics (wherein politics is a 'passionate' contest of moral obligations), and the other, of the social sciences (wherein politics is a 'rational' calculus of interests).[16] I briefly describe certain traditions of civility practiced in early modern Mughal *Hindustan* in the penultimate section, before concluding this chapter.

Iqbal and his worlds

A key event in the unleashing of the project of colonial modernity in South Asia lay in the catastrophic aftermath of the failed revolt of 1857 against the colonial regime. This aftermath brought about the formal extinguishment of the Mughal *Hindustan* as well as intense colonial violence, especially against Muslim inhabitants of the capital city Dilli, whom the colonial regime identified as the group most responsible for an uprising conceived as having been the outcome of 'religious grievances'.[17] While this was accompanied by renewed claims by colonial authorities that their successes stemmed from the superiority of their civilisation, as Karuna Mantena has shown, it also marked 'a definitive turning point in the transformation of British imperial ideology'.[18] A prior imperial policy assumed the eventual disappearance of the 'backward' and 'corrupt' traditions of the colonised in the face of a beneficial English civilisation. This was displaced with a rival imperial policy that advocated studying and managing the purportedly 'recalcitrant belief and customs', including by way of the technique of 'non-interference' and indirect rule, which relied on creating 'native religious authorities' over the newly constructed realm of the 'personal'. This response set the terms for the British Raj's colonial governance projects, as well as the 'native' and nationalist participation in it, taking the form of a 'politics of interest'.[19] For politics in this mode, 'religious identity' became the primary basis for both the claiming and distribution of state violence, state protection, resources, employment, education and, over the course of time, limited representation in government.

15 For an account of the *humanities* as forming a part of the traditions of civility, see Jeffrey Minson, "In the Office of Humanity," *Cyber Review of Modern Historiography* 14 (2009): 1–19.

16 See Michel Foucault, *The Hermeneutics of the Subject: Lectures of the College De France 1981–1982* (New York: Picador, 2005). Here it is also instructive to keep in mind how colonial modernity's institution of a separation between law and ethics forms a part of this broader separation. See Talal Asad, "Thinking About Law, Morality, and Religion in the Story of Egyptian Modernization," *Journal of the Interdisciplinary Study of Monotheistic Religion* 1 (2005): 13–24.

17 Thomas R. Metcalf, *Aftermath of Revolt: India 1857–1970* (Princeton: Princeton University Press, 1964), 46–91. On the use of the term '*Hindustan*' (and not 'India'), see Manan Ahmed Asif, *The Loss of Hindustan: The Invention of India* (Cambridge, MA: Harvard University Press, 2020).

18 Karuna Mantena, *Alibis of Empire: Henry Maine and the Ends of Liberal Imperialism* (Princeton: Princeton University Press, 2010), 1.

19 Markus Daechsel, *The Politics of Self-Expression: The Urdu Middle-Class Milieu in Mid-Twentieth Century India and Pakistan* (Abingdon: Routledge, 2006), 19–35.

In the wake of this crisis, many members of an emergent Muslim middle-class intelligentsia felt a need to respond to a purported 'civilisational decline' *vis-à-vis* the colonising West through a re-working of their inherited Mughal Indo-Persian traditions. Investment in what got termed as 'religious revivalism' was evidenced in what were otherwise seemingly rival heirs to the Mughal traditions: the modernising liberal educational reformist Aligarh Movement and the 'traditional revivalist' Deoband school.[20] Both Aligarh and Deoband, by effecting a division of labour, began construing religious education as being specialised and distinctive from training for so-called 'worldly affairs' (*dunya*), thus revealing how this religious revivalism operated within the terms set by the colonial 'politics of interests'.[21] The college at Aligarh took up the task of providing 'modern western education' to elite Muslims to take up 'secular' roles in the service of the colonial state and to participate in the colonial public sphere (for which they were in competition with members of other religious communities). The seminary at Deoband took up the task of training specialised religious scholars, teachers and jurists who did not seek any association with the colonial public sphere, and instead made the personal sphere the proper domain for the application of this specialised religious knowledge.[22] However, by the early twentieth century, there also emerged an anti-colonial anti-secular politics responding to this problematic of civilisational decline. This included theologians associated with Deoband committing to anti-colonial political solidarity with other Indian religious communities.[23]

With the famous poet and London-trained barrister Muhmmad Iqbal, and his influential re-conceptualisation of religion and its expansive role in politics, we have a rival anti-colonial anti-secular politics being articulated. This significantly comes across in his 1930 Madras Lectures (later published as *Reconstruction of Religious Thought in Islam*),[24] and his famous Presidential Address at the All India Muslim League Annual Conference in the same year.[25] One is immediately struck by affinities between Iqbal's Islam as religion, and Reformation Protestantism, a parallel that Iqbal himself draws. Similarities include conceiving religion in terms of self-expression of an authentic interior self of the believer and its personal responsibility to a transcendental God, one that did not require any intercession by way of ritual, mystical guides or institutions. For Iqbal, the extant Sufi orders, and their mediative rituals, acted much as the monastic orders and the Catholic Church had done to provoke the ire of Protestant reformers, on account of

20 See Brannon D. Ingram, "Crises of the Public in Muslim India: Critiquing 'Custom' at Aligarh and Deoband," *South Asia: Journal of South Asian Studies* 38, no. 3 (2015): 403–18.

21 See Brannon D. Ingram, "'Modern' Madrasa: Deoband and Colonial Secularity," *Historical Social Research* 44, no. 3 (2019): 206–29; Margrit Pernau, *Ashraf into Middle Classes: Muslims in Nineteenth-Century Delhi* (Oxford: Oxford University Press, 2013), 269–95. Jamal Malik, "Sufi Amnesia in Sayyid Ahmad Khan's *Tahdib al-Akhlaq*" in *Sufism East and West: Mystical Islam and Cross-Cultural Exchange in the Muslim World*, eds. Jamal Malik and Saeed Zarrabi-Zadeh (Leiden, Boston: Brill, 2019): 76–103.

22 This co-constitutive separation between secular and religious education gets illuminatingly contrasted when we examine the more contiguous character of both the curriculum and the possible offices of employment available to graduates even in the pre-revolt Dilli College, originally a Madrasa founded under Mughal patronage in the late seventeenth century, which had since been re-formed by the British East India Company (from 1828 to 1857). See Margrit Pernau, "Maulawi Muhammad Zaka Ullah: Reflections of a Muslim Moralist on the Compatibility of Islam, Hinduism and Christianity," in *Idées religieuses, engagement et projets de société en Asie du Sud moderne et contemporaine*, ed. Catherine Clémentin-Ojha (Paris: Centre d'Etudes de l'Inde et de l'Asie du Sud, 2011): 31–47.

23 See Maulana Hussain Ahmad Madani, *Composite Nationalism and Islam* (Delhi: Manohar, 2005). See also Barbara D. Metcalf, *Hussain Ahmad Madani: The Jihad for Islam and India's Freedom* (Oxford: Oneworld, 2009).

24 Muhammad Iqbal, *Reconstruction of Religious Thought in Islam* (New Delhi: New Taj Office, 1980).

25 Muhammad Iqbal, "Presidential Address. Allahabad Session. December 1930," reproduced in *The All India Muslim League and Allama Iqbal's Allahabad Address, 1930*, ed. Nadeem Shafiq Malik (Lahore: Iqbal Academy Pakistan, 2013), 272.

their alleged enchanted (i.e., 'superstitious') admixture of other worldliness with life in this world. Religion, as he conceived it, was a distinct transcendental system to be kept pure of any immanent mediations, but as these universal truths ('spirit') it also provided the grounds for *inspiring* an individual's conduct in *all* spheres of life.[26]

Thus, for Iqbal, religious piety takes the form of 'an Islamic version of the Protestant ethic',[27] which ultimately emphasises the immense personal responsibility of every individual to act as this transcendental God's representative (*Khalifa*) in a disenchanted world.[28] Through their masterful actions these divine representatives must create an Islamic polity that would successfully protect their religion in this world, while expressing unshakable *faith* in their own *personal* salvation in the next. Assumed by this injunction is a reorganisation of the relationship between religion and civilisation that renders them to be coeval, with civilisation (*Tahzib*) construed as the enduring worldly achievements of immanent actions (though requiring defending). Religious civilisation (e.g., Islamic civilisation) is conceived as an actualisation of this divine man's inherent powers to act, create and self-express, which becomes the defining quality and achievement of an exclusive community (*Umma*) within an assumed world order. For Iqbal, this 'politics of self-expression'[29] promised to overcome the perceived 'civilizational decline' *vis-à-vis* the colonial Christian West, provided the 'original spirit' of Islam could be revived (here civilisational 'originality' was strongly analogised with personal 'interiority' and 'authenticity').

Azad's legacy

With the jurist and theologian Abul Kalam Azad we find one of the most influential displays of the aforementioned (and Deoband-associated) anti-colonial anti-secular politics which fundamentally contested this configuration of religious groups as essentially isolated and self-contained actors (both by Iqbal, as well as those practising the 'politics of interest'). Here was an anti-secular politics wherein religious obligations are taken to primarily demand *fraternity* with other religious groups, with the *telos* of politics being sociability. Notably, Azad displayed a more optimistic spirit that, rather than anxiously obsessing on decline, evinced confidence in sociable creativity forming a major part of the Indian Muslim's civilisational inheritance. These points prominently come across in his Address at The Bengal Provincial Khilafat Conference in 1920 (titled *Khilafat aur Jaziratul-Arab*) and his acclaimed Urdu translation and commentary on sections of the Quran, *Tarjuman ul-Quran* (1930–32).[30]

This variant of politics came to the fore with the launching of the All India Khilafat and Non-Cooperation Movement in 1919–1920, with Azad as one of its chief ideologues. This inaugural mass movement of anti-colonial Indian nationalism espoused a pan-Islamic anti-imperial solidarity and grounded the Khilafat movement on the preservation of an explicitly religious symbol – the

26 See Iqbal Sevea Singh, *The Political Philosophy of Muhammad Iqbal: Islam and Nationalism in South Asia* (Cambridge: Cambridge University Press, 2012).

27 C. M. Naim, "Prize Winning *Adab*: A Study of Five Urdu Books Written in Response to the Allahabad Government Gazette Notification," in *Moral Conduct and Authority: The Place of Adab in South Asian Islam,* ed. Barbara D. Metcalf (Berkeley: University of California Press, 1984), 314.

28 Francis Robinson, "Other-Worldly and This-Worldly Islam and the Islamic Revival. A Memorial Lecture for Wilfred Cantwell Smith," *Journal of the Royal Asiatic Society* 3, no. 14 (2004): 53–54.

29 Daechsel, *The Politics of Self-Expression.*

30 Maulana Abul-Kalam Azad, *Khilafat and Jaziratul-Arab: The Address of Maulana Abul-Kalam Azad Delivered at The Bengal Provincial Khilafat Conference, February 28, 1920,* trans. Mirza Abdul Qadir (Bombay: Central Khilafat Committee of India, 1920); Mawlana Abul Kalam Azad, *The Tarjuman al-Quran: Volume One. Surat-Ul-Fatiha,* trans. Syed Abdul Latif, 3rd ed. (Hyderabad: Dr. Syed Abdul Latif's Trust for Quranic & Other Cultural Studies, 1981).

office of the Ottoman Sultan as the *Amin al-Muminin* (Commander of the Faithful) and the custodian of the sacred places of Islam, that is to say the *Khalifat* as an institution. This institution was perceived to be particularly threatened after the First World War on account of the moves by the British and allied powers to dismember the Ottoman Empire. However, Azad's articulation of pan-Islamism was expressly linked with an anti-colonial national solidarity between Hindus and Muslims in India, and Azad's speeches and writings had as their focus the creation of this plural national community. Meeting, living and struggling together with other religious communities was expressly grounded by Azad in Quranic injunctions and narrated Prophetic *exemplum* ('*Hadith*'). He argued that Indian Muslims were bound by religious law to non-cooperation with the British, and to cooperation with their Hindu allies – a community he deemed analogous to the '*umma wahida*' that Muslims, under Prophet Muhammad, had formed with allied Jewish tribes in Medina by entering into a Covenant ('*ahad nama*'), known as the 'Constitution of Medina' (he further developed upon these ideas in the aftermath of the *Khilafat* movement in the *Tarjuman*).[31]

Minority futures

The subsequent demise of the *Khilafat* movement (with the abolition of the Caliphate by the Turkish Republic in 1924) did not end mass political mobilisation efforts by anti-colonial nationalist elites.[32] When coupled with further colonial reforms in terms of allowing for greater participatory representation in provincial governments for these nationalist parties, the overwhelming role of numerical strength in determining the outcomes of a colonial 'politics of interest' became ever more acute.[33] For Muslims, such a politics naturally raised the problem associated with their status as a minority and the disadvantage this created in terms of engaging in formal representative rule.[34] Iqbal and Azad again provided rival responses to it.

Iqbal's solution, through his 'politics of self-expression', ultimately expressed a lack of faith in any possible future in which inter-community cohabitation did not descend into majoritarianism. As a minority, very much divided across different possible fault-lines (e.g., caste, class, language and religious practices), the only way out of this conundrum was to achieve overarching pan-Islamic unity by way of successful vertical and horizontal mobilisation. This is a mode of politics that seeks to achieve such mass mobilising unity around this abstracting category of a supra-national religious identity, through an exhortation of the passions which appeal to the personal responsibility of each individual to the cause of their isolated *Umma*.[35] However, in order to achieve this, religion was sought to be stripped of all lived histories that illuminate distinctions, variations and cross-pollinations, and forcefully melded into a homogenous and dis-embedded abstract national community, denying history and the claims of sociability.[36]

31 On the exemplarity of this treaty for other Muslim religious scholars also advocating such a co-habitational nationalism see Barbara D. Metcalf, "Maulana Husain Ahmad Madani and the Jami'at 'Ulama-i-Hind': Against Pakistan, Against the Muslim League," in *Muslims Against the Muslim League*, eds. Ali Usman Qasmi and Megan Eaton Robb (Cambridge: Cambridge University Press, 2018), 44.

32 See Gail Minault, *The Khilafat Movement: Religious Symbolism and Political Mobilization in India* (New York: Columbia University Press, 1982).

33 See Faisal Devji, *Muslim Zion: Pakistan as a Political Idea* (Cambridge: Harvard University Press, 2013), 49–88.

34 For the role of (a particular) international law in the making of this problematique see Mohammad Shahabuddin, "Minorities and the Making of Postcolonial States in International Law," *Third World Approaches to International Law Review, Reflections* 18 (2020).

35 See Julia Stephens, "The Politics of Muslim Rage: Secular Law and Religious Sentiment in Late Colonial India," *History Workshop Journal Issue* 77 (2013): 45–64.

36 See Devji, *Muslim Zion*, 89–122.

With Azad, both the minority problem, and its solution, were not formulated in such abstractive terms. He expressed an optimism in certain minority rights being duly protected in any future postcolonial state – suggesting a limited harking back to a 'politics of interests'. However, this optimism in the possibilities of cross-denominational solidarity ultimately drew succour from the lived histories of cohabitation in India. In his effort to learn, rather than abstract from, these lived histories, Azad revealed that his politics was not entirely confined to the terms set in place by the project of modernity. It is to some of these other histories of traditions of cohabitation from Mughal *Hindustan* to which I now briefly turn.

Receiving Mughal civility

Prominent amongst the arts associated with traditions of civility in the Mughal *Hindustan* were that of *Siyasi Akhlaq* (arts of political governance)[37] and *Sufi Adab* (arts of religious piety).[38]

Siyasi Akhlaq aimed to achieve a virtuous disposition for *both* the political governors and, relatedly, the polity. One was not achievable without the other, and both demanded a cultivation of states of moderation of extremes, and a balancing of competing desires, chiefly associated with discerning the norms of justice (*'adl'*).[39] Most significant here is the virtue of temperance or self-limitation (with non-observance of limits considered be an attribute of the vice of tyranny). The primary manifestation of this virtue was to limit the chauvinistic glorification of one's religion, including through its compulsory propagation by the ruler, as this would imperil the balance and harmony required for the peaceful cohabitation of plural denominations (*sulh-i kull*),[40] all of whom were assumed to subscribe to ultimately irreconcilable faiths. Such temperance is evocatively captured by the following didactic couplets penned by Nur al-Din Qazi al-Khaqani in his important early seventeenth-century contribution to *Akhlaq* literature, the *Akhlaq-i Jahangiri*:

> *Know that it is Justice, not Infidelity or Faith*
> *that ensures the safety of the country;*
> *for the world is better served by justice without Faith*
> *than by the tyranny of a Faithful king.*[41]

Unlike the self-control associated with tolerance, secularism's *ur*-principle for reckoning with religious difference, the virtue of self-limitation sought by *Siyasi Akhlaq*, requires a more positive limit on the self.[42] Temperance extended further to relativising the politico-ethical norms

37 See Muzaffar Alam, *The Languages of Political Islam: India 1200–1800* (New Delhi: Permanent Black, 2004); Mehrzad Boroujerdi, ed., *Mirror for the Muslim Prince: Islam and the Theory of Statecraft* (Syracuse: Syracuse University Press, 2013); Rajeev Kinra, *Writing Self, Writing Empire: Chandra Bhan Brahman and the Cultural World of the Indo-Persian State Secretary* (Oakland: University of California Press, 2015).

38 See Barbara D. Metcalf, ed., *Moral Conduct and Authority: The Place of Adab in South Asian Islam* (Berkeley: University of California Press, 1984).

39 See Margrit Pernau, "The Virtuous Individual and Social Reform: Debates Among North Indian Urdu Speakers," in *Civilizing Emotions: Concepts in Nineteenth-Century Asia and Europe*, eds. Margrit Pernau, et al. (Oxford: Oxford University Press, 2015), 170–71.

40 See Rajeev Kinra, "Handling Diversity with Absolute Civility: The Global Historical Legacy of Mughal Sulh-I Kull," *The Medieval History Journal* 16, no. 2 (2013): 251–95.

41 Translation from Persian reproduced from Alam, *The Languages of Political Islam*, 73.

42 For precedents within the Indic tradition see Rajeev Bhargava, "Beyond Toleration: Civility and Principled Coexistence in Asokan Edicts," in *Boundaries of Toleration*, eds. Charles Taylor and Alfred Stepan (New York: Columbia University Press, 2014), 173–202.

drawn from any single exemplary tradition (for example, Quranic verses or the Islamic Prophetic exemplary conduct), by instead eclectically drawing upon a plurality of exemplary precedents, including the Indo-Persian traditions of kings, and the Greek and Indo-Persian wisdom literature.[43]

If self-limitation was the *telos* of the *Siyasi Akhlaq* arts, then porosity and syncretism were key features of the *Sufi Adab*. Thus, *Sufi Adab* practices of rituals, spiritual exercises and everyday courtesies frequently drew upon other Indic religious practices and idioms of piety, to achieve mystical illumination and cultivate spiritual selves – and thus be considered truly *civilised*. This openness of *Sufi* practices of piety was itself enabled by the *Sufi* theological doctrine of *Wahdat ul-Wujud* ('Unity of Being'), which emphasised the immanent presence of the divine in all existence, and thus accommodated different interpretations of non-dualism underlying several Indic traditions of piety.[44] Additionally, this piety of self-transformation was not one of ascetic renunciation, but put emphasis on virtuous everyday worldly conduct with co-habiting others as being essential to achieving spiritual character.[45] Contrary to Iqbal's negative characterisation of this form of piety, this is not an *other worldly* ethic but a different way of being *in this world* with others. Instead of ethical practices of isolated divine representatives struggling to secure worldly success in order to *protect* their religion and to promote its glory (with faith in their personal salvation in the next world), *Sufi Adab* entails worldly training undertaken by relational beings aimed at achieving union with the divine, both in this world, and in the next.

It is my argument that both *Siyasi Akhlaq* and *Sufi Adab*, often complementarily, trained selves and others in the conduct and care for 'lawful relations'[46] and were thus vital 'forms of jurisprudence' associated with the traditions of civility.

Conclusion

Politics, law and religion are historical concepts – formed, modified and related by diverse practices of reception and transmission – and not some universal timeless categories.[47] However, in historicising politics, law and religion, and their relationship, the aim of this genealogy has not been to neatly periodise these concepts and practices into before and after early modern, colonial modern and postcolonial eras. Such an exercise would commit the error of treating colonial modernity as a *period*, instead of being a *project* aimed at creating a particular form of life.

Instead, our ongoing efforts to create traditions of civility today should be mindful of this re-descriptive history. This historical illumination may allow us to be more receptive to alternative conceptions of meeting and struggling together with others which belong to the rival project of

43 See Muzaffar Alam, "*Shari'a* and Governance in the Indo-Islamic Context," in *Beyond Turk and Hindu: Rethinking Religious Identities in Islamicate South Asia*, eds. David Gilmartin and Bruce B. Lawrence (Gainesville: The University Press of Florida, 2000), 216–45; Said Amir Arjomand, "Perso-Islamicate Political Ethic in Relation to the Sources of Islamic Law," in *Mirror for the Muslim Prince: Islam and the Theory of Statecraft*, ed. Mehrzad Boroujerdi (Syracuse: Syracuse University Press, 2013), 82–106.

44 See Moin Ahmad Nizami, *Reform and Renewal in South-Asian Islam: The Chishti-Sabris in 18th and 19th Century North India* (Cambridge: Cambridge University Press, 2011), 1–4.

45 Ira M. Lapidus, "Knowledge, Virtue, and Action: The Classical Muslim Conception of *Adab* and the Nature of Religious Fulfillment in Islam," in *Moral Conduct and Authority: The Place of Adab in South Asian Islam*, ed. Barbara D. Metcalf (Berkeley: University of California Press, 1984), 60–61.

46 Genovese, McVeigh and Rush, "Lives Lived with Law," 2.

47 The inspiration for this methodological orientation remains Michel Foucault. See Foucault, *The Hermeneutics of the Subject*; Michel Foucault, *The Use of Pleasure: Volume 2 of The History of Sexuality*, trans. Robert Hurley (New York: Vintage Books, 1990).

civility. Traditions of civility, such as *Akhlaq* and *Adab*, while non-hegemonic in an age divided between the 'complicity of the contraries'[48] that is secularism and anti-secularism, continue to be practised by, and associated with, other forms of life. They require cultivation, and learning, by more of us today, so as to enable the necessary conditions for cohabitation.

For international legal scholars, this is a call to trouble the assumption that the *other* of a colonial international law can only be conceived in messianic and antinomian terms. We need to consider what international laws of civility are, and what modes of international cohabitation they enable.[49]

48 Frédéric Gros, "Course Context," in *The Hermeneutics of the Subject: Lectures of the College De France 1981–1982*, ed. Michel Foucault (New York: Picador, 2005), 524.

49 For an exemplary instance of such an exercise see Sundhya Pahuja, "Letters from Bandung," in *Bandung, Global History, and International Law: Critical Pasts and Pending Futures*, eds. Luis Eslava, Michael Fakhri and Vasuki Nesiah (Cambridge: Cambridge University Press, 2017), 552–73.

4
the atomics

Gerry Simpson

The Cold War was a nuclear war. And I grew up in the midst of this nuclear war. The fallout was everywhere. Nuclearism infected our fantasies, our houses, our birthday parties.[1] But, for me, this was not simply a temporal coincidence. I spent the third night (and most subsequent nights until I left home at 17) of my life in an 'atomic house'. My atomic house was a greyish-white, pebbledash, Scottish council house affair meshed with a half-hearted gesture in the direction of post-war architectural modernity. It was on a street called Howburn Road, just round the corner from John F. Kennedy Drive, and it was surrounded by hundreds of other identikit, classless, atomic houses. It took me a while to appreciate that houses could be built, or look, any other way. For most of my toddlerhood, houses *were* atomic houses. This was Levittown on the Pentland Firth: a made-up place where, at night, dreams of escape (to London, to America, to *Inverness*) vied for sub-conscious attention with nuclear nightmares.[2] Everyone I knew grew up in an atomic house, and it didn't take me long to learn that the people who lived in them were called – by the locals – 'atomics'.

I was an atomic, living in an atomic house in the middle of an atomic war.[3]

In one recurring dream (I used to have it every Christmas Eve, as I dozed waiting for my sisters – older and less interested in Santa Claus – to awaken), I would look up at the sky and see large Soviet planes circling above my garden at 34,000 feet. The fact that these planes were called 'bears' and carried in their undercarriages the means to vaporise the Highlands of Scotland hardly helped. The dream was a repeated circling. These bears circled my dreams.

1 For a feverish account: Martin Amis, *Einstein's Monsters* (London: Johnathan Cape, 1987).

2 Levittowns were Cold War housing projects facilitated by the US 1948 Housing Bill and celebrated as instant communities for the lower middle classes (men returning from the war) or derided as bland and soulless new suburbs (the *ur-text* is Richard Yates, *Revolutionary Road* (Boston: Little, Brown & Company, 1961)). For a more nuanced picture, see Mike Davis, *City of Quartz* (London: Verso, 1990).

3 For an American experience: Kristen Iverson, *Full Body Burden: Growing Up in the Nuclear Shadow of Rocky Flats* (London: Harvill Secker, 2012).

Occasionally, like a projection of my subconscious, actual Soviet bombers would appear in the actual sky and be chased away by American Phantom jets in little pretend dogfights. Down below, I would enact this balletic aerial combat with Second World War Airfix kit. Alongside nuclear extinction, everyone was obsessed with WWII. All the talk at Miller Academy Primary School was of Hurricanes, Spitfires, Messchershmits and Nazis. It was a way of distracting us from the horrors of nuclear war, from what Lynn Emanuel has called the 'suave, brilliant wattage of the bomb'.[4]

Like most children, I was worried about dying.

As a teenager, I used to devour books with titles like *The Third World War*. In the more geopolitically alert of these novels, this conflict invariably broke out in and over Yugoslavia. Tito's wooing of the West and fear of the Soviets – and then the reverse – provoked a stand-off and then a war and then a world war.[5] It was all plausible, seamless and scary. Reading these thrillers precipitated a period when I was obsessed with the mechanics of nuclear war. What would be the last thing I would see? There were lots of people to ask. The father of one of my friends – a scientist with interests in nuclear annihilation – told me at a 13th birthday party that I would see a tiny object, like a bottle top, in the sky spinning towards me and then, a microsecond later, I would be obliterated. I didn't sleep for weeks, maybe months. Walking to school, I would scan the sky for small spinning objects. I lived in a state of nuclear terror. In J.O. Morgan's book-length poem, 'Assurances', about the activities of Airborne Nuclear Command during the Cold War, nuclear-armed Vulcan bombers circle Soviet targets. Morgan, too, has a sense of what these missiles will resemble as they descend to Earth like

> thirty black specks all converging little
> clusters moving over the map of the land
> each one extinguished with a small white flash.[6]

Yuri Andropov, who was to become the General Secretary of the Communist Party and leader of the Soviet Union, once described the American policy elite as 'atomaniacs'. There were quite a few atomaniacs around my hometown. Indeed, in some respects, we were all atomaniacs, or nuclear conscripts. There was a comedy show at the time called 'Not the Nine O' Clock News' which featured a sketch in which schoolchildren living near a nuclear power station go to school with a warm radioactive glow around their little bodies (this was a play on a breakfast cereal commercial that was shown at the time). We were those children and because it was cold, and because it was dark when we went to school and dark when we left school, the glow seemed like it might be a good thing. When I went to university, I adopted a series of Leftish poses on virtually every question: trade unions, anti-Thatcherism, the Sandinistas, the inadvisability of privatisation and the awfulness of Tories. Some of these hardened into political commitments. But, around my Left friends, I had a problem. They were not keen on

4 Lynn Emanuel, "The Planet Krypton" from her collection, *The Dig* (Urbana: University of Illinois Press, 1992).

5 For example John Hackett, *The Third World War: August 1985* (New York: Macmillan, 1978); John Hackett, *The Third World War: The Untold Story* (New York: Macmillan, 1982); Kenneth Macksey, *First Clash: Combat Close-Up in World War Three* (Berkley: Berkley Publishing Group, 1988) (note: first published in 1985 by Arms & Armour Press in London; all other novels cited are the original editions).

6 J. O. Morgan, *Assurances* (London: Johnathan Cape, 2018), 29.

nuclear energy, or the nuclear industry. Like them, I was totally against nuclear war and, like the World Court in The Hague ten years later, I thought it a bad idea in almost every respect.[7] But nuclear energy was different. It was the passage to free and clean electric power. At high school I remember learning a lot about the Aberfan Disaster when, in 1966, 116 Welsh schoolchildren were suffocated under a collapsing heap of coal dust that had been carelessly stacked just next to their classrooms. They were just like us and they were victims of a dirty, expensive, dying and dangerous industry that was about to be declared obsolete. That was the past; we were the future. I just didn't yet know how long the future would be. I knew nothing at all about isotopic waste or trillion-year half-lives.

But I had another compelling reason to be in favour of nuclear energy. Every weekday morning at around 7.00 am, I would hear a car come to a halt outside our house. Three men would be waiting in the car in the dark, smoking cigarettes. Then my father would emerge from the house and after a muffled flurry of greetings and laughter, he would climb into the car and speed away. It wasn't hard to imagine him being detained by the KGB or leaving on a Carre-esque mission behind enemy lines. In his ordinary handsomeness, he looked like a character from *Tinker-Tailor-Soldier-Spy*: someone wrestling with his conscience before betraying his best friend.

In fact, he *was* fighting the Cold War. Every day. He worked in a nuclear power station called Dounreay situated, not accidentally, on the furthermost reaches of the already obscure Scottish North Coast.

My mother used to say that she had no idea what he did because he never talked about it. My experience was a bit different. For one thing, he took me to Dounreay and had me stand on top of the reactor while explaining what would happen if it exploded (Scotland would be over, and it was strongly implied that I would be too). Later we were obliged to handle – using enormous mechanical arms behind thick lead screens – what he claimed were pieces of plutonium (but I must be misremembering that). He told me that one tiny piece of plutonium, if touched by every person in Caithness, would kill them all. I can safely say I have never touched a piece of plutonium since, not even at a party. Mostly, though, he spoke about the promise of nuclear energy. The idea, as far as I could figure out, was to fast breed nuclear energy through a fusion process that would – and this was the masterstroke – consume its own waste. There would be so much clean energy that a lot of it would have to be sold to the French, or the Russians. Meanwhile, the National Grid would be powered, not by some child-endangering and dirty coal station, but by Dounreay and its technologically advanced white heat. Lights could be left on all day, cars would become electrically powered and dirt cheap to run, and I might acquire an electric blanket. And there would be no more Aberfans.[8]

Dounreay had its own disasters, of course. As it turned out. There is a beach in nearby Reay, a village surprisingly untransformed by the close presence of a nuclear power station. The beach abutted a golf course, also called Reay. I remember the course well. It was

7 'In view of the unique characteristics of nuclear weapons, to which the Court has referred above, the use of such weapons in fact seems scarcely reconcilable with respect for such requirements. Nevertheless, the Court considers that it does not have sufficient elements to enable it to conclude with certainty that the use of nuclear weapons would necessarily be at variance with the principles and rules of law applicable in international armed conflict in any circumstance', International Court of Justice, *Legality of the Threat or Use of Nuclear Weapons,* Advisory Opinion, July 8, 1996, ICJ Reports 1996, para 95.

8 There is, inevitably, a literature, see especially, Louise Walsh's novel, *Black River: A Novel on the Aberfan Disaster 1966* (Llanrwst: Gwasg Carreg Gwalch, 2016).

the scene of one of my greatest triumphs when I won the Thurso Gala Cup there after a distinctly flukey 18 holes of golf. The Gala Cup was named after the local Thurso Gala, a mid-summer event for which the whole town was in sun-soaked attendance. There was something vaguely Americanised about Thurso, and the Gala felt like one of those New Jersey State Fairs that Bruce Springsteen wrote about (Springsteen was hugely popular in Thurso, I think, for that reason. We could readily imagine racing in the streets in our Cortinas and Escorts, or, in my case, a rather fancy and feminine, gold and crimson Raleigh bicycle). The climax of the Gala was the crowning of the Gala queen and her two princesses (there was no Gala king). My sister was the most beautiful Gala princess Thurso had ever seen. I can still remember how she looked in her pink, high-necked midi dress sporting a distinctly *avant la lettre* pixie haircut. She was miserably lovely, or loveably miserable. I was so proud of her, but I couldn't work out why she was so unhappy to have been chosen as a princess. I think I imagined that she was disappointed not to be queen. But that, for her, would have been even worse.

The beach next to the golf course was one of those wild, unkempt Northern beaches. Not quite pretty and not the sort of beach where swimming was exactly encouraged. It is called Sandside and it has been closed for 20 years. According to reports, 285 traces of *plutonium* have been found, since 1985, in or under the sand. But that wasn't the only accident to afflict Dounreay. Long after I had left Scotland, I watched an episode of the BBC investigative documentary series, *Panorama*, about an explosion at Dounreay. A 30-ton plug had been blown 25 feet into the air in an accident (my Dad confirmed this story later to me). There was contemporaneous footage of a man in a JCB Digger filling the hole with mud and large stones.

Of course, the atomics all attended an atomic high school. There were three primary schools: Pennyland Primary School (exclusively for atomic children), Mount Pleasant (for the unpleasant local toughs) and Miller Academy (a mixture of toughs and atomics). It was somehow appropriate that I attended the mixed school. There had been a mix-up at my birth, after all. My mother was convinced that she had gone home with the wrong baby. In the cot next to mine was John Budge, already preparing to become the most feared boy at school and the leader of an outfit called the 'bare belly gang'. Whenever I was naughty, she would tell me that I was really John Budge. I was only partly radioactive, mildly tough. In any case, as I was subsequently informed, my mother and father had had a nuclear accident, a fusion, maybe a fission. Whatever it was, I was the result: an unexpected third child to go with my two elder sisters.

I was born nuclear in 1963 just a few months after the October Crisis when the world had nearly come to an end. I can remember where I was when John Kennedy nearly killed me (I'm paraphrasing Christopher Hitchins here): I was in the second trimester of my mother's pregnancy.

I had no idea that JFK and Castro were conspiring to kill me. Even later, I wasn't entirely sure who was trying to blow my brains out. I had some vague ideas about who the enemy was, largely gleaned from the *Sunday Express*. Later, my ideas became more advanced. While my friends were playing Cowboys and Indians, I was playing 'UN Forces under US Command and Control' v 'North Koreans with Chinese Support'. I didn't stop to wonder how this arrangement worked. The UN and the US seemed pretty much the same to me at that age – a vaguely pro-Western thing to be supported in the struggle against the Soviets. There was a lengthy battle one frigid afternoon in the North of Scotland. The UN Forces were pinned back but the North Koreans lost a lot of men in the ensuing wave of attacks (53,000). My thinking continued to develop. In one of my early years at high school, our teacher, Miss Mackenzie, asked us to prepare a talk to give to the class on our return from the Easter vacation. I spent hours researching my topic: 'The Korean War and its Aftermath'. The speech was far too long and was a casualty of its own casualty figures. No one wanted to hear how many New Zealanders had been wounded at Pusan.

The numbers were meaningless. But then they were pretty meaningless in Henry Kissinger's and Robert McNamara's hands too. One familiar approach to speaking about nuclear war was through rationality (or maybe we should describe it as ultra-rationality or, even, irrationality).[9] Anyone who has studied nuclear deterrence will know that, after a while, these ways of thinking and speaking begin to coincide. The central paradox in a system of thought and signs riven with paradoxes is that when it comes to nuclear war, the more rational the tone, the more irrational the substance. Henry Kissinger's memo to Richard Nixon, for example, sent around the time of the SALT talks, lists the number of expected dead after a nuclear exchange in a cold, affectless, tone that strives for technocratic neutrality but topples into numerical insanity.[10] A million dead is a statistic, one dead is a tragedy, 100 million dead begins to look like a very black comedy.[11] The numbers don't add up (or, perhaps that is the problem: they do). At one point, Kissinger compares the percentage of Soviet citizens (41%) who would die 'promptly' (as if turning up to parent-teacher interviews) in the absence of an ABM agreement to those who would die (39%) if there had been/was (the tenses are hard to figure out here, perhaps nuclear war has no tense) an agreement.[12] At one point there is a footnote (footnote 3) that states: 'The calculations were done using a method which does not take into account fatalities above 142 million.' Pity the person who is the 142 millionth and one to die. Not even a statistic, far less a tragedy. Meanwhile, Cold War doyen, Casper Weinberger, assured readers of the *New York Times* that the United States had no intention of fighting to win a nuclear war but that 'our policy requires that, if necessary, we prevail in denying victory to the Soviets'.[13] Such circumlocutions (often combined with euphemism (yield, population centres) and infantilism ('Little Boy', 'Big Boy')) are the very stuff of nuclear strategy, and enough has been written about them elsewhere.[14] They have been parodied in film (*Dr Strangelove*), in literature (*Gravity's Rainbow*) and in song (Tom Lehrer, Randy Newman).[15]

Nuclear talk was dominated for a long time by hawks and abolitionists. Or hawks who became abolitionists. After all, nuclear war has a habit of making apostates out of its cheerleaders. In the end, everyone is an abolitionist. Paul Nitze, that most predatory of hawks, ended his

9 There are some born-again evangelical groups who revel in the prospect of nuclear war as a kind of prelude to the Second Coming and who seem to be getting closer and closer to the centre of power in the United States.

10 Even the word 'exchange' has a strange ring to it here, suggesting that the two superpowers had merely entered into some sort of agreement to swap nuclear weapons by exploding an equivalent number over each other's territory. SALT refers to the then ongoing Strategic Arms Limitation Treaty talks.

11 Top Secret Letter from Henry Kissinger to Richard Nixon, May 23, 1969, in *National Security Archive George Washington University*, accessed March 18, 2020, http://nsarchive.gwu.edu/NSAEBB/NSAEBB60/abm01.pdf.

12 I write this as Donald Trump announces that the United States will withdraw from the *Intermediate Range Nuclear Forces Agreement*, United States of America and the Union of Soviet Socialist Republics, signed December 8, 1987, 1657 UNTS 2. See Julian Borger and Martin Pengelly, "Trump Says U.S. Will Withdraw from Nuclear Arms Treaty with Russia," *The Guardian*, October 21, 2018, www.theguardian.com/world/2018/oct/20/trump-us-nuclear-arms-treaty-russia.

13 Caspar W. Weinberger and Theodore H. Draper, "On Nuclear War: An Exchange with the Secretary of Defence," *The New York Review of Books*, August 18, 1983, www.nybooks.com/articles/1983/08/18/on-nuclear-war-an-exchange-with-the-secretary-of-d/.

14 See Amis, *Einstein's Monsters*.

15 For example Thomas Pynchon, *Gravity's Rainbow* (New York: Viking Press, 1973).

writing life with an op-ed in the *Washington Post* calling for the removal of nuclear weapons.[16] The Four Horsemen of the Anti-Apocalypse (Sam Nunn, Henry Kissinger, George Schulz and William Perry) famously called for general disarmament in two letters to the *Wall Street Journal* in January 2007 and 2008.[17] Robert MacNamara, meanwhile, made a late-career swerve in the direction of peace and anti-nuclearism.[18] In this, he resembled President Reagan who went to Reykjavik apparently convinced that nuclear weapons could be banned and un-loved.[19]

This man, McNamara, had nearly ended my life, before I even had a life (though about a decade ago and just a few months before he died, he bought me lunch in Vienna; all is forgiven).

In late 2018, I was living on my own in an apartment in the East Village. On the 1st of December, I went for a swim at a local club then came home to my apartment and thought: 'why don't I do what everyone does when they are at home alone? I'll watch an old film on YouTube.' It wouldn't be quite true to say I had *never* done this. My daughter, Hannah, and I had got through about 20 minutes of an eight-hour documentary called *The Battle of Chile* once. But that was it. Because I was researching atomic annihilation, I happened upon an old made-for-TV film called *The Day After*. Thinking it might be rubbishy in an interesting anthropological way I settled down with a cup of coffee and some toast slathered in *Sarabeth Red Berry Jam* and began watching it. It was immediately far better than I had anticipated. Almost everything from the Reagan era feels very dated now (even Keith Richards was wearing horrible white slacks in those days) but this wasn't. It begins with some vague, off-screen mutterings about tensions in East Germany and then three military types get into a helicopter and begin travelling across the plains of Kansas. They fly low over ordinary life: people going about their business feeding cattle, riding horses, driving cars, in their houses making love. This 5-minute segment is followed by the more conventional architecture of the horror film: we are introduced to people who will die (I'm sorry about that and should have issued a spoiler alert; in fact maybe the world should now come with a spoiler alert. 'Everyone will die, in the end.' Of course, everyone does die in the end, but the planet usually carries on in a way I find comforting when I think about mortality). People like Jason Robards and someone from *Starsky and Hutch*. These people are getting laid, going to college, planning babies, giving birth and quarrelling. The whole scene is permeated by a mid-to-late century American decency. A father discovers his daughter has been out having sex with her boyfriend. And *he* apologises to *her*. It's that kind of film.

Later there is a very nasty ratcheting up of tension in the geopolitical world. Reports filter through in an aesthetically pleasing, indirect way. Sage commentators are heard speaking about Berlin and about NATO's outmatched ground forces (most of this turned out to be poppycock). Then a boy looks up at the sky (at 45.53), sees the planes circling overhead. Then it ends.

This was my Cold War childhood. There was a nuclear submarine base close by where sailors were taught how to end planetary life (I didn't know then that the number of submarines used by each side was governed by the Strategic Arms Limitation Treaty (SALT I) signed in 1972

16 Paul Nitze, "A Threat Mostly to Ourselves," *The New York Times*, October 28, 1999, www.nytimes.com/1999/10/28/opinion/a-threat-mostly-to-ourselves.html.

17 George P. Shultz, William J. Perry, Henry A. Kissinger and Sam Nunn, "A World Free of Nuclear Weapons," *The Wall Street Journal*, January 4, 2007, www.wsj.com/articles/SB116787515251566636; George P. Shultz, William J. Perry, Henry A. Kissinger and Sam Nunn, "Toward a Nuclear-Free World," *The Wall Street Journal*, January 15, 2008, www.wsj.com/articles/SB120036422673589947.

18 Errol Morris, *The Fog of War: Documentary* (New York: Sony Pictures Classics, 2003).

19 The phrase is from Schultz: 'I have never learned to love the bomb,' quoted in Sverre Lodgaard, *Nuclear Disarmament and Non-Proliferation: Towards a Nuclear-Weapon-Free World?* (Abington: Routledge, 2010), 197.

between the United States and the USSR in Article 3 of the Interim Agreement). There were NATO early warning radar stations at West Murkle (opened in 1963, the year of my birth) and at Forss (governed by the NATO Agreements)[20] as well as a large American model village for the use of US Navymen.

But in the various conversations around town and with my father, an acronym kept appearing: 'IAEA'. I would repeat it as if I knew what it meant. The IAEA was on its way to inspect, an IAEA official had been spotted in the local pub.

This, it turned out, was the International Atomic Energy Authority (an international organisation tasked with regulating the use and movement of nuclear fuels).[21] This is how I grew up then: an atomic in an atomic house in an atomic war governed by atomic law; the child of a thoroughly legalised, cold, nuclear war.

20 See J. B. Gunn, "The History and Legacy of the United States Naval and Communication Station in Thurso, Scotland," in *Defence Sites II: Heritage and Future*, eds. C. A. Brebbia and C. Clark (Ashurst: WIT Press, 2014).

21 Lawrence Scheinman, *The International Atomic Energy Agency and World Nuclear Order* (Abingdon: Routledge, 2015).

5

Tender images

Characters of private international law in the humanities

Judith Grbich

How images are imbricated in the work of law has been one question of recent scholarship in the visual arts. The legal scholar Goodrich has written of the *mos britannicus* and linked technologies of print to the work of early modern lawyers of the common law and their maxim *pro lectione picture est*, 'the picture takes the place of knowing how to read, and an accompanying norm that gave the image – the painting – priority over its material support, the page and the ink.'[1] In Goodrich's scholarship the early modern English lawyers practiced a *mos Britannicus* – the habit of an English common law – within a broader theological and juridical tradition, and within also a broader technological and aesthetic tradition. Manderson has posed time, art and law as partners in an interdisciplinary dance, a *danse macabre*, in which we are before the image, as in Kafka's story 'Before the Law'. He argues that 'law . . . is a form that structures time – and vice versa – and we experience both "before the image".'[2] Manderson, art historian and *jurisprude extraordinaire*, has focused on how 'death makes law matter', and takes the *danse macabre* genre of art and allegory from medieval Europe to interrogate some early modern and contemporary legal practices of death, jurisprudence, colonialism and judgment. In these and many other recent works on aesthetics and law, art and objects, jurisprudential boundaries of public and private – of public things and private things – have been profoundly shaken as the disciplines of the humanities are brought back to law. Persons and properties are being re-arranged,[3] and old notions of property as based on land or territory being abandoned, as images in the work of law are found to predate the Renaissance and the early moderns' return to the classical age. It is not so much a 'new materialism', nor an 'old materialism', but an even older materialism, one which has remained lingering in images.

1 Peter Goodrich, "Faces and Frames of Government," in *Law and the Visual: Representations, Technologies, and Critique*, ed. Desmond Manderson (Toronto: University of Toronto Press, 2018), 51–74, 55.

2 Desmond Manderson, *Danse Macabre: Temporalities of law in the Visual Arts* (Cambridge: Cambridge University Press, 2019), 2.

3 Jennifer Beard and Sundhya Pahuja, "Before the Beginning: A Disclosure of Law's Foundation," *Australian Feminist Law Journal* 19 (2003): 1–10; Jennifer Beard, *The Political Economy of Desire: International Law, Development and the Nation State* (Oxford: Routledge, 2007); Sundhya Pahuja, *Decolonising International Law: Development, Economic Growth and the Politics of Uncertainty* (Cambridge: Cambridge University Press, 2011); Yoriko Otomo, *Unconditional Life: The Postwar International Law Settlement* (Oxford: Oxford University Press, 2016).

The literary theorist and art historian W. J. T. Mitchell has argued that the very notions of art objects and non-art objects is a division 'forged in the colonial encounter'.[4] He has claimed that 'both art and objecthood are imperial (an imperious) categories, and that aesthetics as a quasi science or artistic judgment is a separation of the redeemed from the damned, the purified from the corrupt and the degraded object'. While he does go on to argue that the age of imperialism is over, and that 'the age of disembodied, immaterial virtuality and cyberspace is upon us', he also suggests that we are therefore 'compelled to think about material objects'. But this seems a far too brief sketch of the history of any aesthetic judgment imbricated in the thingness of objects, and for this purpose I want to look at an early modern practice of imperialism, an imperialism of Elizabeth I of England, over Ireland. Ireland had in effect been colonised by the English and Scots for some 50 years by 1601.

Turning to the humanities in private international law and to questions of aesthetics and iconographic regimes raises different questions about things, movement and ownership than one would pursue in the textbooks of international law. One can link the classic textbooks of private international law to the empire-building of European nations, and understand the textbook writers as creating foundations for moving financial things around the globe. We take for granted the role of the textbook writers in the facilitation of dispute-settling rules for the European trading nations, and can understand the dissemination of written rules as one of the twentieth-century practices of maintaining colonial and postcolonial empires. Earlier forms of the compendiums on ensuring the security of things travelling between nations, from the early nineteenth century, had focused on the laws of ownership being in conflict, with Savigny,[5] Story[6] and Reddie[7] devising textbooks for instruction on the laws themselves. The later nineteenth century works of Westlake,[8] Lorimer[9] or Foote[10] laid out the possibilities of movable things having been separated from their owners, who would be looking to embassies, navies and treasuries for passage home. But the aesthetics or images of movement at each stage of this textbook tradition can tell a different story. My focus in this chapter is not on movement, but instead upon financial things.

Perhaps the monetary characters of international law textbooks never moved at all, and questions of their *domicile*[11] were simply an alibi for further Crown and corporate plunder through currency manipulations? Maybe twenty-first century off-shore financial practices involve *archipelago* tactics[12] little changed from the Tudor aggression over its Atlantic *archipelago* of Ireland,[13] that is,

4 W. J. T. Mitchell, "Empire and Objecthood," in *What do Pictures Want? The Lives and Loves of Images*, ed. W. J. T. Mitchell (Chicago: University of Chicago Press, 2005), 145–68, 147.

5 Friedrich Karl Von Savigny, *A Treatise on the Conflicts of Laws, and the Limits of Their Operation in Respect of Place and Time*, trans. William Guthrie (London: Stevens and Sons, 1869).

6 Joseph Storey, *Commentaries on the Conflicts of Laws, Foreign and Domestic in Regard to Contracts, Rights and Remedies*, 2nd ed. (London: Maxwell, 1841).

7 James Reddie, *Inquiries in International Law Public and Private*, 2nd ed. (London: Blackwell, 1851).

8 John Westlake, A *Treatise on Private International Law with Principal Reference to Its Practice in England*, 4th ed. (London: Sweet and Maxwell, 1905).

9 James Lorimer, *The Institutes of the Law of Nations: A Treatise of the Jural Relations of Separate Political Communities* (London: Blackwood and Sons, 1883).

10 John Alderson Foote, *Foreign and Domestic. A Concise Treatise on Private International Jurisprudence* (London: Sweet and Haynes, 1878).

11 A. V. Dicey, *The Law of Domicile as a Branch of the Law of England* (London: Stevens and Sons, 1879).

12 Vanessa Ogle, "Archipelago Capitalism: Tax Havens, Offshore Money, and the State, 1950s – 1970s," *American Historical Review* 122, no. 5 (December 2017): 1431–58.

13 Brendan Bradshaw and John Morrill, eds., *The British Problem, c.1534–1707: State Formation in the Atlantic Archipelago* (London: MacMillan Press, 1996).

as the imaginal[14] regimes of cultural lives in the Home Counties of England, or in more modern times, the Hamptons of New York? Recent international law scholarship has introduced a focus on law's objects, in projects designed to discover the background stories of how the 'things' of law seemed to have a life of their own. 'Things in themselves' have had a long genealogy in continental philosophy, and more broadly in contemporary cultural studies,[15] each attempting to mine the historical practices of writing, rhetoric and genre to flesh out different ways of being human in the twenty-first century. My focus upon the characters of private international law brings together these projects, with a study of the background story to that 'thing' of English law known as 'money' or 'currency' – a story about money's ontological and historiographical heritage in the theological, juridical and cultural practices of sixteenth-century Tudor governance of resources. Tudor money was not only a chattel but also part of other imaginal practices of a juridical theology which relied upon images of exchange for the transformation of moralities, substances and souls into something different. I argue that Tudor and subsequent Stuart governance used a form or figure of exchange which retained its usefulness in the succeeding centuries – an image or picture memorialising the scriptural accounts of Magdalene's entreaty to God – an image of Mary Magdalene entreating the crucified Christ to appear before her. My study is also taking up the challenge of recent international law scholarship to think of the history of international law differently.[16] Rather than finding anything of a monetary kind my chapter engages with images of exchange, images in which the reader learns how to inhabit a world of financial things, a world in which financial practices are made to change within the human structures of imaginal beings. But then the reader really already knows how to inhabit this world; my chapter is a reminder. It is apologetically a Western and a Judeo-Christian story about English juridical politics, but it could be inhabited differently where it has been imagined differently. And it clearly can be imagined differently elsewhere.[17] We do not all live in the Home Counties or Hamptons of the imagination.

My chapter proceeds by retrieving certain early seventeenth-century English dramatic representations about the authority and meaning of Tudor and Stuart practices of debasement of coinage, and its effects upon commercial and accounting practices. Just as words, images and metallic substances vie for significance and authority in the cultural imagination of the people of the Tudor 'british' archipelago, so in Shakespearean dramatisation of monetary characters and their narratives, metaphor and image pose a commoner's questions to his Sovereign about Royal finance, and trade, and religion. Shakespearean plotting of his character's capacities for procreation and generation, I argue, pose for his audience questions of the morality of debased coinage, while the narratives of substitution and the 'proper lover' reference contemporary religious conflicts around iconoclasm and forbidden images of the Beloved. My chapter then leaves this issue of the proper 'dealing' between a believer and one's God, to proceed to a discussion of Richard Hooker's attempt to settle religious discontent in Elizabethan England with his many-volumed 1591 *Of Laws of Ecclesiastical Polity*, and concludes with an analysis of the 1611 frontispiece image to the *Laws* in which Mary Magdalene is depicted holding her Bible on high and receiving within the Light of God. While my chapter does present the bare bones of scriptural

14 Chiara Bottici, *Imaginal Politics: Images Beyond Imagination and the Imaginary* (New York: Columbia University Press, 2014).

15 Arjun Appadurai, "Introduction: Commodities and the Politics of Value," in *The Social Life of Things: Commodities in Cultural Perspective*, ed. Arjun Appadurai (Cambridge: Cambridge University Press, 1986), 3–63.

16 Jean d'Aspremont, "Critical Histories of International Law and the Repression of Disciplinary Imagination," *London Review of International Law* 7, no. 1 (2019): 89–115.

17 Irene Watson, "The Power of Muldarbi and the Road to Its Demise," *Australian Feminist Law Journal* 11 (1998): 28; Irene Watson, *Aboriginal Peoples, Colonialism and International Law: Raw Law* (London: Routledge, 2015).

records of Christian belief, it is not about English theology of the sixteenth century, nor even about Christian belief, but about how Hooker's ontotheological framing of Western metaphysics, and his presentation of Elizabethan governance as including the Christian Trinity – the pattern of the Father, the Son, and the Spirit or Holy Ghost – remains within twenty-first century framing of the actions of financial characters. In addition, Hooker's patterning of the religious rites of the 'Last Supper' or Eucharist – his arrangement of the paradox of the form of the exchange and the sign of the substance – also remains as an incarnational hermeneutics of English jurisprudence and Western financial accounting, always entrapping the viewer within various images of the Word.[18]

A more traditional approach to this study of law's things and their phenomenal 'movements' might begin with the work of the United Nations Commission on International Trade Law and their work on Secured Transactions, or the UNIDROIT Convention on Substantive Rules for Intermediated Securities, or even the current UK Law Commission's reference into Intermediated Securities. I could look at the work of the international advisory agency, the Financial Stability Board, and its development of global regulatory standards for digital currencies. Each has in common a problem of the 'thingness' of a security, or the interposition of a new owner into a payment system where the 'thing' in question is being held by another. Electronic payment systems and cryptocurrencies have challenged governmental regulators' abilities to conceptualise and manage the commercial dealings of both corporations and national entities. The 'crypto' or secret and hiddenness of currencies seems to have taken over global financial technologies as the players of a new worlding find a tightening of the possibilities for contravening national taxation collections for corporate entities. Crypto-assets now have a market of their own. In countries where cryptocurrencies are banned, a new technology of 'stablecoin' such as Tether can be bought with cash, and facilitate entry into the crypto exchange market.[19] Facebook's digital currency project is fashioning a *Libra*, in an attempt to create a privately owned global payments system.

In bringing questions of iconography and aesthetics to these practices of global monetary technologies, the aim is to work with some images of the hiddenness of aspects of traditional monetary systems, to interrogate secrets which seem always to have been in plain view. A cultural literacy in iconography raises different questions about the history of international law, and the history of international law as a practice of imperialism. The 'movement' of securities in global economies and fiscal practices – including tax avoidance practices – can be understood as 'imaginal' in the sense of 'that which is made of images'.[20] Global financialisation seems to take international law further into the realm of private dealing, at the same time removing governance by humans and by democratic institutions.

Of coins, numbers, emblems and procreation

The English imperialism of Elizabeth I took a modern form in her 1601 Proclamation of 24 May whereby a debased form of currency minted in the London Tower should be the lawful and current money of the kingdom of Ireland. The rebellion in Tyrone led by Hugh O'Neill was to be put down by removing his ability to buy weapons, by removing Irish coin with a good silver content attractive to foreign suppliers and replacing coinage in Ireland with the debased coinage

18 The Holy Bible, John, 1.1: 'In the beginning was the Word, and the Word was with God, and the Word was God.'

19 Olga Kharif, "The Cryptocurrency That Out-Trades Bitcoin," *The Age*, October 4, 2010.

20 Chiara Bottici, "Imagination, Imaginary, Imaginal: Towards a new Social Ontology?" *Social Epistemology* 33, no. 5 (2019): 433–41, 436.

minted in London. The added advantage was Elizabeth's collection of the old good silver coinage, and her ability to pay her troops in Ireland with the new 'mixed' or debased currency.[21]

While this was a successful monetary policy for Elizabeth I a certain merchant, one Brett of Drogheda, had reason to complain when the London merchant Gilbert refused to accept the agreed payment of 100 pounds sterling in fulfilment of the contract conditions for the supply of goods to Brett. The agreement was made in April 1601 before the Proclamation, and Brett tendered his payment of 100 pounds sterling at the correct time in the new mixed money, but after the introduction of this debased Irish currency. The Privy Council judgment in *Brett v. Gilbert*[22] remains good law for the rule that legal tender requires the use of 'the authority of the prince, the stamp and the value'. Gilbert had to accept the Irish mixed money as they were the 'current and lawful money of England' and had been proclaimed as Elizabethan coin and stamped with the identifier of the Crown – 'the usual stamp of the arms of the crown, and the inscription of her royal stile'. The value of the silver and bronze coin was held to be that stamped and signified by the image of the Crown and proclaimed as such under the Royal Prerogative. Legally the weight and purity of the named coin was that settled in the proclamation.

The Elizabethan Irish coinage of 1558, the Billon Groat, had a crowned and mantled bust of the Queen on the obverse, and circled with the Latin words, 'Elizabeth by the Grace of God Queen of England, France and Ireland'. On the reverse was stamped a crowned harp with crowned initials each side, E and R, encircled by the Latin words, 'I have made God my helper'. The debased coinage of 1601 included those 'tokens' named as shillings, sixpences, threepences, pennies and halfpennies. The obverse on the penny was Elizabeth's coat of arms with the initials E and R each side. On the reverse was the crowned harp, sitting between two parts of the date, 16 and 01. The Latin words remained the same as the earlier issue. Regardless of the quantity of silver which the Crown might decide to make up the coinage – or absence of silver in the case of the copper penny – Royal Proclamation and stamp or impression were held sufficient for a legitimate currency, in other words, monetary nominalism continued to rule the day, as it had for several centuries. English monarchs had made Irish coinage it seems at least since King Edward VI. What was new was debasement by the Crown as a practice of imperialism had arrived with a Privy Council judgment as to its legality.

We are left with this particular fusion of art and law, and its confusions. Is the image of the 'Crown' – the bust of the Queen, or her coat of arms – on the face of the coin sufficient to signify its value? Does the word or letters E R signify the value? In this heady mix, words, sovereign visages and other emblemata vie for significance, in addition to the legally excluded quantity and weight of silver or other alloy. What was settled by the Privy Council clearly did not satisfy either the merchants of London or the playwrights of the period for whom these same money questions created endless comedies. Many of the jokes used the conventions of book keeping and the new arithmetic of Arabic numerals, where the arrangement of the columns of double entry accounting produced amazement at the profits seemingly 'unearned' and the generative capacity of the figure of zero, the Arabic number of 'nought'. The use of zero in settling accounts was likened to the forbidden pleasure of using a character of prostitution. Zero could be used to give pleasures unimaginable, she could make some-thing out of no-thing, and

21 Hans Scott Pawlisch, *Sir John Davies and the Conquest of Ireland: A Study in Legal Imperialism* (New York: Cambridge University Press, 1985), Ch 8, 'The Case of Mixed Money', 142–57.

22 *Gilbert v Brett* (1605) Davis 18; an English translation appears at (1605) 2 *Howells State Trials* 114–30, and Sir John Davies, *A Report of cases and matters in law, resolved and adjudged in the King's Courts in Ireland.* Collected and digested by Sir John Davies, translated into English, Dublin (1762) *Eighteenth Century Collections Online*, Gale, CW1244 38949, 48–77.

it didn't seem proper. Shakespeare's *Much ado about Nothing*, had a lot to say about the morals of the 'nothing' which men used to make much of themselves.

With the accession of James I on the death of Elizabeth in 1603 a new coin for England was issued by the King, the Angel, and Shakespeare amongst other playwrights, makes merry with his characters of Angelo and Lucio in his 1604 play *Measure for Measure*.[23] Angelo and Lucio enact several financial and sexed plots with the joking words 'desire', 'bottom', 'satisfaction', 'touching' and 'point'. The Angel coin had an image of Archangel Saint Michael on one side, slaying a dragon, and on the other an image of an English galley ship in full sail, the ship bearing the King's arms, and the legend 'by thy cross save us, Christ Redeemer'. Much of the play's comedy is focused around the performance of things of measure, and how they are visually arranged in practices of commercial accounting books, to make things even more confusing, or hilarious, for the Jacobean audience. The play instructs James I on some difficult questions about royal finances, practices of revenue farming, coinage losses, the merits of trading with foreigners, the morality of taking security in commercial dealings and the public's anxieties about the likely effect of James's religious commitments on the enforcement of anti-usury laws. The humanities had come to the Exchequer whether James liked it or not.

In Act 1, Scene 2, there is a dialogue between Lucio (*lucre*?) as a character of finance and two gentleman, in which ethical questions are raised by the practices of commercial accounting, as if these practices were the journal of a seafaring captain, a journal recording the practices of entering the transactions already made in another book – the memorial or chronicle of each venture's business transactions. Is it stealing to have raised more money than one began with? The accounting imagery of seafaring crosses over into ones of sickness and disease, as the doing of commercial profits becomes likened to the 'doing' of a woman, a woman who is not your wife. As the gentlemen question just how much their actions are morally tainted, or not, through the metaphors of disease and purchase, by 'three thousand dolours a year', or a 'French crown', Mistress Overdone from the bawdy house announces the performance of another 'making' with an even higher measure. Claudio has been sent to prison for an offence 'worth five thousand of you all', for getting his bride-to-be Julietta, with child. Punning upon 'made', as in making an excess, Claudio's Julietta is 'a woman with maid by him'.[24] Procreation, generation and the character of the proper lover were the comedic tropes of playwrights and poets, as well as the moral questions which constituted the 'new science'[25] of the Exchequer and the Church.

Shakespeare and other playwrights of early seventeenth-century England mixed the figuration of words, numbers and images in the same way the Privy Council had read the legitimacy of the debased coinage for plundering Ireland, and the same way in which the Tudor and Stuart religious settlement had pictured the authority of the state – in a theological imagery open to cultural change. The impressions of sovereigns or saints on coinage, these images of holy persons, were as much part of a legal practice of governance as they were spiritual or ecclesiastical. James I's Angel coin was current money, and yet still part of the older practice of distribution to the unfortunates suffering from scrofula (the king's evil). It was to be hung around their necks in the ceremony of the royal touch, and, being 'touched' by the King, they would be cured. But new forms of governance were being made, new kinds of royal patronage were being made into things which could be traded, and new kinds of payments became monetary, provided

23 William Shakespeare, "Measure for Measure," in *William Shakespeare: Complete Works*, eds. Jonathan Bate and Eric Rasmussen (Basingstoke: MacMillan, 2007), 155–214.

24 Ibid. Act 1, Scene 2, line 67, 163.

25 Michel de Certeau, *The Mystic Fable, Volume One, The Sixteenth and Seventeenth Centuries*, trans. Michael B. Smith (Chicago and London: University of Chicago Press, 1992), 79–112.

they fulfilled the legal requirements of proclamation and impression, regardless of the absence of precious metal of any kind. In a short space of time monied things passed from copper and silver, to paper, and eventually would arrive in the digital age as propertied objects capable of human possession, as if plucked out of thin air. But this quick summary of the aesthetic regimes of Tudor England requires a longer dialogue with some images of a certain cultural 'dealing' between the believer and one's God – we might call them the practices of tendering, or the use of images of tender, the 'tender images'.

Re-arranging the bodies in Tudor England

Richard Hooker's *Of Laws of Ecclesiastical Polity*[26] was written in the late 1580s, and published in 1591 in England. Hooker was a humanist scholar and Anglican clergyman writing in the hope of settling civil discontent in Elizabethan England, where nonconforming Puritans were challenging the authority of the Crown. Asking questions about art or aesthetics at the time of Elizabeth is to enter the politics of the European Renaissance at a single point. Then, as now, the Western imaginary of the Judeo-Christian princes was populated by images of virgin births, angelic messengers, Godly fathers, a messianic Son and numerous communities of faith who shared a theological belief in a heavenly origin and a heavenly return. They differed about who would return to Heaven, whether this was a return willed or 'predestined' by God, and whether God had left any space for human free will in the process of the return to Heaven. Could a human being decide to be good and to do good works and influence his chances of returning to Heaven? Or were the redeemed and the non-redeemed already decided by God, so that mankind's efforts could be commendable but ultimately make no difference? Could the clergy assist in some way to obtain forgiveness for your sins, and were you nevertheless destined to remain in the sinful state into which you were born, as set out in the Bible as the problem of 'original' sin following the expulsion from the Garden of Eden? They all agreed on a heavenly origin of the human being. These theological characters of the Judeo-Christian heritage were depicted in artworks; adorned church and monastery walls; and were carved, engraved and printed in the new media of the early moderns.

My purpose in visiting Hooker is to set out one story of an imperial and international sovereignty, which conveniently comes with a pictorial representation – an engraved frontispiece – and is a good enough account of a twenty-first-century imperial or international sovereignty. Hooker's 1591 political theology of the British polity not only remains a good account of the present constitutional arrangement of the United Kingdom as an international player, albeit an ideological one,[27] but also contains within it the structural matters of private international law, those characters of private law who appear to move around the globe as our financial actors, having their home and measures in national exchequers and their lives in global markets. We have been given a picturing of these patterns – in the form of the frontispiece of the *Laws* since the 1611 edition. I would mention that it isn't really surprising that Hooker's 1591 settlement of the 'laws' of the 'ecclesiastical polity' of Britain remains current, as he has largely argued from the legal requirements of political authority set out in the Tudor legislation begun as the 1559 *Act of Uniformity*, legislation whose authority remains largely intact. But the pictures have changed. And so I propose to read the jurisprudence through and with the changes in pictures.

26 Richard Hooker, *Of the Lawes of Ecclesiastical Polity, The Folger Library Edition of the Works of Richard Hooker, Books I to IV*, ed. Georges Edelen (Cambridge: Harvard University Press, 1977) ('FLE').

27 Robert Eccleshall, "Richard Hooker and the Peculiarities of the English: The Reception of the *Ecclesiastical Polity* in the Seventeenth and Eighteenth Centuries," *History of Political Thought* 11, no. 1 (1981): 63–117.

The British Archbishop of Canterbury, Dr Rowan Williams, on delivering a lecture in 2005 at The Temple Church, London, 'The Richard Hooker Lecture', remarked that:

> Hooker's treatise is thus a good deal more than a museum piece. It poses some very central questions about the nature and purpose of law, questions which bear on many current questions about how to manage a multi-cultural and multi-religious state without adopting an oppressive insistence upon public secularity.[28]

Dr Williams had been invited to give the lecture at the Temple Church, associated with the London Inns of Court, and the same church at which Hooker had delivered a series of lectures in the 1580s. As Williams remarked:

> Hooker spent some formative – if appallingly difficult – years in the atmosphere of the Inns of Court. It would be nice to think that his valuation of certain habits of thought and relationship was nurtured here – his concern for responsible interpretation, his concern for the possibilities of (in every sense,) civil speech.[29]

But first, what are the laws of 'ecclesiastical polity' according to Hooker? Hooker gives us a deeply humanist account of the authority of the Elizabethan establishment. At its simplest level he sketches the early modern learning from the Greek and Roman classics, and their reception in third- and fourth-century Christian philosophies, and later ninth-century polishing touches. From Aristotle's *Categories*[30] on the division of things and their names, he moves to Plato's classifications in the *Timaeus*[31] of the things of God brought into being by the movement of God from nothing or chaos into the universe. Just as the classical scholars moved from a study of the names of things as a practice of logic, towards a theological belief in the many things of God as a divinely created ontology, so Hooker followed the neoplatonic synthesis which was developing in the fourth-century works of St Augustine, such as the *City of God*[32] and *On Christian Teaching*.[33] Augustine had argued that use of the correct methods of interpretation in scripture could assist the person 'blown away from their homeland by the adverse winds of their own perverted characters' and, to learn of the truth of God's creation was a process, 'a trek, or a voyage to our homeland, though progress towards the One who is ever present is not made through space, but through integrity of purpose and character'.[34] As Augustine, and others, moved the study of human understanding from practices of language and logic, to disciplines of ontology and theology, the methods of dialectic and syllogism became understood as not simply practices of reason, but also methods of finding the realities of being.

Hooker's scholarship within sixteenth-century English humanism was a skilful synthesis of Thomas Aquinas and Augustine, Ciceronian rhetoric and laws, the recently re- discovered work

28 Dr Rowan Williams, Archbishop of Canterbury, *The Richard Hooker Lecture – Richard Hooker (c1554–1600): The Laws of Ecclesiastical Polity Revisited*, October 26, 2005, http://aoc2013.brix.fatbeehive.com/articles.php/2107/the-richard-hooker-lecture-richard-hooker-c1554-1600-the-laws-of-ecclesiastical-polity-revisited.

29 Ibid.

30 Aristotle, "The Categories," in *The Basic Works of Aristotle*, ed. Richard McKeon (New York: Random House, 1941), 3–37.

31 Plato, "Timaeus," in *The Dialogues of Plato*, vol. 2, trans. B. Jowett (New York: Random House, 1937), 3–68.

32 John O'Meara, ed., *Saint Augustine, City of God*, trans. Henry Bettenson (London: Penguin, 1972).

33 Saint Augustine, *On Christian Teaching*, trans. R. P. H. Green (Oxford: Oxford University Press, 1997).

34 Ibid., 13.

of the 'Egyptian' Mercury Trismegistus, and the neoplatonic Italian renaissance works of Marcello Ficino. It is not my intention to provide an outline of Hooker's eight volumes of the *Laws*, but instead to argue that it is possible to find in these volumes an ontology of human being, arranged as a progression from the fallen and sensual matter of the human to the Godly and eternal essence of the Divine; or to put this another way, a progression from the Being of God, from Oneness or Unity, to all those essences of Life found in the creatures of the Garden – angels, to the creatures outside of the Garden, the fallen ones of mankind. My chapter is not about Hooker's sixteenth-century theology, but about the ontotheological framing of Western metaphysics, about the re-arranging of the '*corpus mysticum*' or mystical body of the Western Church in early modern Europe,[35] and its effects upon notions of the juridical which remain embedded in Western cultural practices of global finance. My point is that the framing of 'money' and law within an onto-theology of technicism did not disappear with any seventeenth-century Cartesian or Hobbesian theorisation of the human in a secular state, it just remains out of sight, out of thought, but able to be discerned in the progress of the imaginal, the image, and the transitional things of cultural works. And perhaps it isn't even a technicism, more an ethno-poetics, if one hasn't moved to any post-Cartesian settlement of embodiment as separate from the mind. In Hooker's onto-theology for Elizabethan imperialism, imagination is embodied, never separate, always imaginal, the things of God retain their Unity with the Being of God, we fallen creatures await the outcome of Judgment Day and the return of our souls to 'home'. 'Home' is the Being of God. The human being is suspended in time, between 'paradise lost' and 'paradise gained', but the soul returns home only for some, those 'predestined' to return. The Protestant Reformation turned on these questions of whether reading scripture without priestly assistance was sufficient to enhance ones return, or whether a priestly hierarchy was also necessary for the forgiveness of one's sins. Hooker's *Laws* was written to remove the conflict within Tudor England on the legal settlement of these questions, as he explained in his lengthy Preface.

Hooker's *Laws* describes a hierarchy of creatures, or things made by God, which nevertheless are both not God and with God. Each creature has a divinity which may return to God, as the soul in the case of humans. The purpose of God's making of these things is to enjoy his handiwork, and to ensure their return home to Heaven – a return assisted by God's own pattern for life as set out in the biblical works of scripture, and the conditional act of Judgment Day. Medieval and early modern theology dwelt upon the contradictions of how man could be redeemed, that is, return to God as a saved soul on Judgment Day, and whether the works of man, his will to do good, could influence the pre-ordained pattern for each life. Hooker's work set out a settlement of this issue of 'predestination' as one settled by God before Creation, not influenced by man, work, priests or penance, but conditional only upon faith in Christ as redeemer, and God's knowledge at Creation, his foresight of which fallen creatures would remain fallen: 'we are . . . justified by faith without works, by grace without merit.' Hooker aimed to settle a major controversy of Protestant theology – predestination,[36] and reconcile the various competing communities of faith. Theologies of all churches were to be reconciled, in Hooker's works, by his positioning of ecclesiastical laws of all churches as eternal laws which could change over time and in different communities. Present differences of church practices, ritual, liturgy and governance were in this work, things 'mutable' to God. But they were not 'mutable' to the Elizabeth establishment, and hence his structuring of the different kinds of laws

35 de Certeau, *The Mystic Fable,* 79–112.

36 Richard Hooker, "*The Dublin Fragments,* Notes Toward a Fragment on Predestination, Grace and Free Will, the Sacraments, and Predestination," in *The Folger Library Edition of The Works of Richard Hooker*, vol. IV, ed. John E. Booty (Cambridge: Harvard University Press, 1982), 101–67.

which had the authority of God, but were nevertheless changeable. The words 'church' and 'commonwealth' applied to different dominions and different jurisdictions, but 'with us' English, said Hooker, they are the 'one and self same multitude . . . that no person appertaining to the one can be denied to be also of the other'.[37]

Hooker sets out a hierarchy of laws, the neoplatonic synthesis, with eternal law of God as that changeless action of God existing in his creation of the world and the creatures. Eternal law includes the internal operations of God – the work of the pattern of three in the Trinity, that is, the Father and his generation of the Son, and the procession of the Spirit. Eternal law also includes the divine law as revealed in scripture, and natural law as found in natural things. Viewed externally by human creatures it appears to us that God has created the world through intellect, as the classical fathers had confirmed. He had provided a pattern for human governance in the scriptural stories of Moses, and given to fallen creatures the laws of reason, positive laws of peoples, laws of civil and ecclesiastical governance, and the international law of nations. This hierarchical classification of laws and things is a synthesis of Cicero's *Republic*, his *Laws*, Old Testament narratives of early Judaic kingship, all held together within a phenomenal whole by Hooker's patterning of the performance of the Christian rite or sacrament of the 'Last Supper', and the scriptural rendering of the meaning of Christ as the 'Word'. In what we might understand now as a phenomenal practice of political belief, the believer joins an invisible community of the Church by the performance of the sacrament of remembrance, that is, the 'Last Supper' or Eucharist, and experiences the transference of the soul towards God, as one reads of belief in 'Christ as the Word' being redemptive.[38] This is a settlement of a centuries old theological re-arrangement of the placing of the sacramental body of Christ, in relation to the body of the Church and to the historical body of Jesus, and has been theorised recently by the French Jesuit philosopher De Certeau as a 'new science' of the secret, a visible instituting of some institution as the home of the 'mystical'.[39] In Hooker's structuring of Elizabethan politics and theologies it is as if God has proclaimed and impressed his pattern of Christ upon each human soul, and it remains for the fallen human being to read the scriptural 'Book of Life' wherein 'the law of God is proposed unto men as a glasse wherin to behold the staines and spottes of their sinfull soules. By it they are to judge themselves.'[40]

As Shakespeare's *Measure for Measure* makes plain, one is using a shared pattern or social imagination, with which to look at oneself, as outlined in the biblical book of *Matthew*, Chapter 7, 'with what measure ye mete, it shall be measured to you again'. Measuring one's sins within the glasse of divine law is a spiritual judgment, but it is also political – poverty as sin remains as neoliberal darlings of twenty-first-century political imaginaries, used to lash some into submission. Incarnational hermeneutics remain alive and well as the imaginal processes by which the human being inhabits a world of financial things and spiritual things, that is, the politics of global economies and international laws.

The 'tender images' of Marianna and Magdalene

The detailed frontispiece to Hooker's *Laws* re-publication of 1611 was engraved by William Hole, and commissioned by William Stansby, who combined the five volumes of the *Laws* into one book for the first time (see Figure 5.1). The frontispiece was repeated in 11 subsequent editions through to 1723, and again in *Volume III* of the 1981 *Folger Library Edition of the Works of Richard Hooker.*

37 Hooker, *Laws*, Book 8, Ch 1.2, FLE Vol. III, 319.
38 Ibid. Book 5, part 55.7 FLE II, 231.
39 de Certeau, *The Mystic Fable,* 85–90.
40 Hooker, *Laws*, Book 8, Ch 6.9, FLE III, 397.

Figure 5.1 Engraved title page of Hooker's *Of the Laws of Ecclesiastical Polity*, 1662 edition (reduced). The title page first appeared in William Stansby's edition of the Lawes, Books I-V, and the Sermons and Tractates in 1611; it was engraved by William Hole.[41]

41 Richard Hooker, *Of the Laws of Ecclesiastical Polity, the Folger Library Edition of the Works of Richard Hooker, Books VI to VIII*, vol. III (Cambridge: The Belknap Press of Harvard University Press, 1981), frontispiece.

The frontispiece gives an emblematic picturing of the eternal law governing all, as outlined in the Hooker text. The eternal law of God is shining down upon three figures: King James as the spiritual father of positive laws, upon St Stephen's Chapel at the Palace of Westminster – the chapel which served as the chamber of the House of Commons from 1547 to 1834, and upon Mary Magdalene. Below these figures are the emblems of Hope, Charitie, and Justice, suggesting that the missing emblem of Faith is bestowed upon Mary Magdalene in the top left corner.[42]

Centuries of Magdalene narratives and artworks had depicted Mary Magdalene as the woman of tears, from the biblical story of Christ's crucifixion and resurrection. She is grief stricken and reaches out to touch her loved one, her Beloved – the risen Christ, who has been crucified and laid within a sepulchre, and now appears before her. In the biblical account she is instructed by Christ 'Touch me not,' *noli me tangere*.[43] Renaissance artworks of the 'Magdalene Penitent' had proliferated for some two centuries before this frontispiece;[44] the puzzle is to read why it seemed appropriate as a figure in Jacobean and Protestant governance. The earlier 'Magdalene art' portrays her kneeling in grief and the figure of Christ risen, or simply her gazing upon the risen Christ. As Protestantism gains ground in Europe sometimes she is a solitary figure in artworks, sometimes with the skull as a *memento mori* – the cultural message of 'remember you will die', and a whip or scourge to flay the sinner in oneself. In Hooker's *Laws* frontispiece she is receiving the light of God into a book held high, in addition to the skull and the whip, and she is fully clothed. As the Magdalene art genre moves towards the nineteenth century she is likely to be less clothed, a figure of desire, but often still reading her book.

Hole's 1611 engraving of the Magdalene receiving the light of God into her book would have been an easy image for Elizabethan and Jacobean believers to understand. Shakespeare's staging of the morality of monarchical projects and commercial practices in his *Measure for Measure* used the character of Marianna, an abandoned woman in his story, in a comedic substitution of one lover for another in Angelo's bed. He was playing with a centuries old Magdalene tradition of devotional texts in which Mary's tears are patterned as monetary things,[45] and had juxtaposed the pattern of the devotional texts against the pattern of an Elizabethan coinage or payments order. The Magdalene tears genre flourished in Elizabethan England as Roman Catholic priests were forbidden to celebrate Mass, and such celebrations became capital offences from the 1570s. Just as the Logos theology of Christ as the Word was understood as a form of salvation, and reading the pattern of Christ in the Bible could save the soul, so the Mary's tears genre posed her tears as able to 'buy' the presence of Christ, her Beloved. Mary and her tears became an image of an exchange, whereby the human 'things' of God – human beings – became incorporated into a scriptural economy. Jacobean audiences would understand that her tears of faith were the means of ensuring the return of her soul to Heaven. While the devotional literature had a deeply religious meaning, it also co-opted commercial meanings and practices in ways which entangled human incorporation within the invisible body of the Church, with incorporation of the human being within the visible and invisible bodies of the financial world.

42 Debora Kuller Shuger, *The Renaissance Bible: Scholarship, Sacrifice, and Subjectivity* (Berkeley: University California Press, 1998), 258.

43 *Holy Bible*, John, Ch 20:17; 'Jesus saith unto her, Touch me not: for I am not yet ascended to my Father: but go to my brethren, and say unto them, I ascend unto my Father, and your Father; and to my God, and your God.'

44 Giotto's fresco *Noli me tangere* of 1304 at the Scrovegna Chapel, Padua, Italy; Fra Angelico's *Noli me tangere* of 1438 at Sant Marco, Florence, Italy; Antonio Allegri da Correggio's *Noli me Tangere* of 1525 at Correggio, Reggio Emilia, Italy.

45 Robert Southwell, "Mary Magdalenes Funeral Tears," in *The Works of Southwell*, ed. W. Jos Walter (London: Keating and Co, 1822), 11–84.

The Elizabethan payments Order for coinage was like the spiritual patterning of Christ as God's payment Order. In Christian theologies God exchanged his Son for the sins of fallen believers; this exchange carried the biblical promise of eternal life for the believer. Mary Magdalene as Faith is an image of that exchange. Hooker's readers would easily understand the Magdalene image as the imaginal making of the life of each human being, albeit an everlasting life after one's temporal life.

As payments systems changed, from coin to paper, images of Magadalene and her book retained their social imaginality, their ability to incorporate the human imagination within the social imaginary, and to make things differently. Images of Magdalene and Marianna continued to be made and changed throughout the following centuries; new stories of exchange and substitution gave her new characters of her desire. We have learnt to stand before these 'tender images' and ponder their current lives in the imagined economies of financial globalisation, the off-shore tax havens and the apparent fading of state sovereignty. Might not further scholarship on the *mos Magdalena* and the *mos Britannicus* – the habits of Magdalene juridical imaginaries – provide resources for new strategies against the precarity of human friends of these characters of private international law and their off-shore homelands of the mind.

6
A training in conduct

Peter Fitzpatrick with Sundhya Pahuja, Richard Joyce, Kathleen Birrell and Ben Golder

Editors' preface

We end this part with a chapter that embodies each of the qualities of 'international law and the humanities', from encounter to plurality to responsibility. But above all, this chapter models the quality of scholarly training that is at the regenerative heart of this field. As the contributors to this chapter show, such a training is about more than intellectual development: it is about how to conduct oneself as a scholar of law, with a sense of care for the law, which is also to say, for others. Such a training is about respect, and love, as much as protocol and doctrine; a responsiveness to the ever-changing faces of the law, as much as a determined attention to the histories, traditions, canons and practices without which there would be nothing new. It is about the teacher as master, as much as teachers as students.

Like the law, this chapter began with one intention, before taking on new meaning. The intention was for Peter Fitzpatrick to contribute a sole-authored chapter reflecting his learning in, and contributions to, the field of international law. Since that commission, Peter was diagnosed with cancer, and on the eve of submitting the manuscript, he left us. In the spirit of generosity that suffused his life, Peter offered the fragment that he had already written. Like law, like life, this fragment is 'unfinished', a beginning without end; and like law, like life, it is a work that can only ever be fulfilled in community. To this 'end' we invited four of Peter's students, who are now each themselves teachers, to respond to Peter's fragment. The result, we believe, is a window into the training in conduct that continues to be one of Peter's greatest gifts to us all.

Ultimate legality: (de)constructing international law

Peter Fitzpatrick

The Bell within the steeple wild
The flying tidings told –
How much can come
And much can go,
And yet abide the World!

Emily Dickinson[1]

1 Emily Dickinson, "There Came a Wind like a Bugle," in *The Poems of Emily Dickinson*, ed. R. W. Franklin (Cambridge, MA: The Belknap Press of Harvard University Press, 1999), 591.

An impossible introduction

The focal obsession of this chapter will be with Derrida's deconstruction, his most prominent contribution to, and encapsulation of, poststructural philosophy. This may not at first seem a promising prospect since Derrida finds deconstruction itself to be impossible. Nonetheless, and this will be the guiding conundrum, 'deconstruction is possible as an experience of the impossible'; it presents 'an impossible possibility'.[2]

So, along with Derrida, '[l]et us begin by the impossible'.[3] And let us compound the impossible by looking briefly for now at some of the oft-noted improbabilities of international law. A leading contender is summarised by Bauman: '[i]n a world fully and exhaustively divided into national domains, there was no space left for internationalism.'[4] That is hardly conducive to an international law which, drawing on a standard text, 'is primarily a system regulating the rights and duties of states inter se'.[5] Yet, as that same standard text would add, international law extends 'beyond' this 'traditional definition of international law' to include a more expansive diffusion of 'certain rules of law relating to individuals and non-state entities so far as the rights or duties of such individuals and non-state entities are the concern of the international community'.[6] All of which could provoke reluctant agreement with the ancestor figures of (English) legal positivism for whom international law, not having any overarching and cohering authority, had at best an attenuated existence.[7] Their successor-in-title, Hart, would allow international law to be only a matter of particular laws, lacking as it does any 'system'.[8] An abundance of impossibilities remains, but that sketch should for now serve to evoke the aptness of deconstruction in making the impossibilities possible, something the chapter considers next.

International law and deconstruction do share many sins. Like international law, deconstruction does not accommodate any predominant authority that would endow it with an enduring and invariant coherence, with any persistent positivity. For deconstruction, any entity is integrally and illimitably tied to alterity – to what it can ever and otherwise become. Yet, and contrary to the common equation of deconstruction and postmodernism, deconstruction does not leave the identity in a state of diffuse indeterminacy. Deconstruction is also construction. It determinately makes and remakes the entity in and as a connective persistence. The relational range of possible connection is infinite. The more an entity endures as the apparent same, the more thoroughly adaptive the responsive connection has to be. Lampedusa positions the point neatly in his novel *The Leopard* where the Prince decrees from his Sicilian fastness that, even after the *Risorgimento*, the 'resurgence' accompanying Italian unification, everything will have to stay the same; to which his nephew Tancredi responds: 'If we want things to stay as they are, things will have to change.'[9]

That rebuttal of positivist relegation may itself be intrinsically challenged by asking just what coherence is endowed by deconstruction with its related but seemingly contrary dimensions of infinite responsiveness and resolved determinacy. And those dimensions are, for Derrida,

2 Jacques Derrida, "Force of Law: The 'Mystical Foundation of Authority'," in *Acts of Religion*, ed. Gill Anidjar and trans. Mary Quaintance (New York: Routledge, 2012), 243, 264.

3 Jacques Derrida, *Given Time, 1. Counterfeit Money*, trans. Peggy Camuf (Chicago: The University of Chicago Press, 1992), 6.

4 Zygmunt Bauman, *Modernity and the Holocaust* (Cambridge: Polity Press, 1989), 53.

5 I. A. Shearer, *Starke's International Law*, 11th ed. (London: Butterworths, 1994), 4.

6 Ibid., 3.

7 Thomas Hobbes, *Leviathan* (Chicago: Encyclopedia Britannica, 1952), Chapter 30; John Austin, *The Province of Jurisprudence Determined: Lectures in Jurisprudence*, vol. 1, 2nd ed. (London: John Murray, 1861), 177.

8 H. L. A. Hart, *The Concept of Law*, 1st ed. (Oxford: Oxford University Press, 1961), 231.

9 Giuseppe Di Lampedusa, *The Leopard*, trans. Archibald Colquhoun (London: Vintage Books, 2010), 19.

contrary, seeing as he did the relation between them as aporetic.[10] Yet for deconstruction the relation has to be combinative and generative. Derrida would transcend such an impossibility with what may seem like another by attributing to that relation something of a spiritual 'force' even as it is supposedly secular.[11] The term Derrida most frequently employs for this force is 'messianic', the adjectival being stressed so as to set the 'messianic' apart from some ultimately resolving 'messianism'; that is from an ultimately resolving eschatology, divine or otherwise.[12] Rather, what 'messianic' imports is a 'structure of experience', not a set structure but, with the adjectival fused into the now 'messianicity', an impelling 'universal structure', an opening of 'experience', and opening to the future, always 'to come', an opening to 'the other'.[13]

That would still make it difficult to know how messianicity could be perceptively grasped, or known, or brought to bear. And for present purposes, it would remain difficult to know how something as distinct as law could in this setting be cognisable and operatively amenable. The answer that will be offered to both concerns will be community, along with community and law as mutually integral, with international law being most aptly so. This will involve some extension into poststructural philosophy and some posthumous persuasion of Derrida to shelve his objection to the term 'community'.

What comes next is a more extensive depiction of international law which then meshes with an accommodating deconstruction and, finally, the two are jointly embedded in community. International law thence emerges, contrary to positivist prescription, as a paradigm of law.

The mysteries of international law

The distinctions between history and myth can be elusive, but with the following two 'histories' of international law myth becomes conspicuously triumphant. The most commonly invoked historiographic attribution is, as Pahuja has it, the 'myth of origin' extracted from the Peace of Westphalia.[14] This was a series of treaties agreed to by a collection of European nations in 1648 ending a prolonged war of religion – a compact term for a series of wars. Borrowing Lesaffer's summary: 'historians and international lawyers alike have for a long time been quite unanimous in calling the Peace Treaties of Westphalia of 1648 the very birth certificate of the modern European state system and the modern law of nations.'[15] For Koskenniemi that birth equates to 'the founding myth of the system', the society of these nations, of these independent states, 'would now arise from itself and not from any religious, moral or political notions of the good external to it'.[16]

10 Derrida, "Force of Law," 244, 251–58.

11 'Force' here is borrowed from Derrida, "Force of Law."

12 Jacques Derrida, *Specters of Marx: The State of the Debt, the Work of Mourning, and The New International*, trans. Peggy Kamuf (New York: Routledge, 1994), 59, 167–68.

13 Ibid., 168; Jacques Derrida, "The Villanova Roundtable: *A Conversation with Jacques Derrida*," in *Deconstruction in a Nutshell: A Conversation with Jacques Derrida*, ed. John D. Caputo (New York: Fordham University Press, 1997), 22; John D. Caputo, "The Messianic: Waiting for the Future," in *Deconstruction in a Nutshell: A Conversation with Jacques Derrida*, ed. John D. Caputo (New York: Fordham University Press, 1997), 162.

14 Sundhya Pahuja, *Decolonising International Law: Development, Economic Growth and the Politics of Universality* (Cambridge: Cambridge University Press, 2011), 132.

15 Randall Lesaffer, "Peace Treaties from Lodi to Westphalia," in *Peace Treaties and International Law in European History: From the Late Middle Ages to World War One,* ed. Randall Lesaffer (Cambridge: Cambridge University Press, 2004), 9.

16 Martti Koskenniemi, "What Is International Law For?" In *International Law*, ed. Malcolm D. Evans, 5th ed. (Cambridge: Cambridge University Press, 2018), 29.

This 'history' spectacularly conforms to Foucault's depiction of how modernist history takes on 'a suprahistorical perspective: a history whose function is to compose the finally reduced diversity of time into a totality fully closed upon itself'.[17] The enduring ancestral text that fits this scenario for international law is provided by Vattel in the mid-eighteenth century when he elevates an 'unlimited and unconditional power' of the sovereign state territorially assured, so that none of the member states of the international 'yield . . . rights to the general body', each sovereign state being 'independent of all the others'.[18] Entities having such power, and as Nancy would affirm, would be unable to relate in terms of any commonality, of any community, and could only subsist as a deific 'communion' – a communion of deific substitutes.[19] A down-to-earth secular existence would thence be denied international law: 'in a world fully and exhaustively divided into national domains, there was no space left for internationalism.'[20] So Nietzsche, along with many after him, sees the death of God as enabling state to become a 'new idol' able to act like 'the ordaining finger of God'.[21] And aptly Pahuja would add: 'the dimensions of international law after god's death remain what we might call "theological".'[22] That could be seen as enabling international law's unbound universality and even its transcendence.[23]

And that could be seen as endowing the 'national spirit' of international law were it not for the imperative secularity supposedly intrinsic to it.[24] The constitutive strategy avoiding this conundrum and enabling an occidental modernity (and a strategy which will be returned to at times in the rest of the paper) could be called a negative universal reference. A universalised comprehensive identity it achieved, not by the 'positive' ascription of qualities, but by an incorporated rejection of their invented contrary, a scenario of significance in and for international law.[25] For example, and for Walker, the 'founding mythology' of Westphalia marked 'a moment at which another world was ordained in opposition to' the modern: 'a world, in part, deemed bereft of civilization and thus legitimately subject to colonial exploitation'.[26] Staying with Vattel as an exemplar, there is a 'national society' grounded in a primitive state of nature which did not count in terms of sovereignty because it lacked a secure hold on demarcated, agricultural territory, and that inadequacy made it lawful to colonise and take possession of the land.[27]

The negative reference is also impelled beyond exclusion. Whilst an appropriated universal excludes utterly, still the universal has to be all-inclusive. Accounts of international law equating it with the civilised, or with its 'civilising mission', provide an indicative instance of both exclusion and inclusion. With the marker of civilisation, there is historically both an overlap between

17 Michel Foucault, "Nietzsche, Genealogy, History," in *Language, Counter-Memory, Practice*, trans. Donald F. Bouchard and Simon Sherry, ed. Donald F. Bouchard (Ithaca: Cornell University Press, 1977), 152.

18 Emer de Vattel, *The Law of Nations or the Principles of Natural Law Applied to the Conduct of the Affairs of Nations and Sovereigns*, vol. 3, trans. C. G. Fenwick (Washington: Carnegie Institute, 1916), 9.

19 Jean-Luc Nancy, *The Inoperative Community*, trans. Peter Connor and Lisa Garbus (Minneapolis: University of Minnesota Press, 1991), 15.

20 Bauman, *Modernity and the Holocaust*, 53.

21 Friedrich Nietzsche, *Thus Spoke Zarathustra*, trans. Adrian Del Caro (Cambridge: Cambridge University Press, 2006), 34–35 (First Part "On the New Idol").

22 Pahuja, *Decolonising International Law*, 132.

23 Ibid., 254–60, *et passim*.

24 For the term see Martti Koskenniemi, *The Gentle Civilizer of Nations: The Rise and Fall of International Law 1870–1960* (Cambridge: Cambridge University Press, 2002), 13, 14.

25 Ruth Buchanan and Sundhya Pahuja, "Law, Nation, and (Imagined) International Communities," *Law Text Culture* 8 (2004): 137–66.

26 R. B. J. Walker, *After the Globe, Before the World* (London: Routledge, 2010), 131, 132.

27 Vattel, *The Law of Nations*, 9. A more extensive account can be found in Peter Fitzpatrick, *Modernism and the Grounds of Law* (Cambridge: Cambridge University Press, 2001), 157–58.

and a shift from civilisation as denoting absolute difference and civilisation as the standard of a condition to be achieved by the excluded through 'improvement' or, later, 'development', and constantly in the discourse of international law, by way of 'progress'.[28] Such progress with its impelling inclusion also extended to the repositories of the universal whose modernist transformation was set radically against its inadequate mediaeval predecessor. Yet the supposed transformation was a distorted negation of the mediaeval and its relation to the modern more a matter of continuity than ruptural difference.[29]

Vattel's formulaic elevation of the origin of international law was both belated and, in effect, derivative. The earlier and once subdued contribution of Francisco de Vitoria has been undergoing an apt revival.[30] The impelling setting is summarily provided by Anghie: 'European international law could not have become universally applicable if not for colonialism. Colonialism justified itself as a civilizing mission.'[31] This generative colonialism emerged out of the Hispanic colonisation of the Americas in the sixteenth century along with its expanding into a singular constitution of the world embedded in and by Europe, thence elevating 'the New World, America, the land of freedom, i.e. land free for appropriation by Europeans'.[32] It was Vitoria who, appropriately enough, derived this end from the *jus gentium* of Roman law:

> Vitoria argued that the *jus gentium* of the Roman texts, in which it meant the law shared by all peoples, should be understood also as *jus inter gentes*, that is, a set of rules governing the relations between one people and another.[33]

The prescription has persisted, but this origin also was infused with a negative universal reference. The *jus inter gentes* would include 'the American Indians' but also and utterly exclude them if they did not comply with the conditions of their colonisation – exclude them to the point of justifying their elimination.[34]

Law, like love

Sundhya Pahuja

In *Modus Vivendi*, their chapter for this volume, McVeigh, Genovese and McMillan ask how a transnational jurisprudent of the common law tradition might conduct themselves well.

28 Thomas Skouteris, *The Notion of Progress in International Law Discourse* (The Hague: T. M. C. Asser Press, 2009).

29 Richard Joyce, "Westphalia: Event, Memory, Myth," in *Events: The Force of International Law*, eds. Fleur Johns, Richard Joyce and Sundhya Pahuja (Abingdon: Routledge, 2011). And recent historical engagements with such 'periodization' and the quality of the mediaeval have shown it to be more politically and legally refined and effective. A survey of such engagements can be found in Peter Fitzpatrick, "Being Originary: Periodization and the Force of Feminine Law," *The Australian Feminist Law Journal* 38, no. 1 (June 2013): 25–35.

30 Kojo Koram, "The Vitorian Recovery and the (Re)turn Towards a Sacrificial International Law," *London Review of International Law* 6, no. 3 (November 2018): 443–70.

31 Antony Anghie, "Law, Concepts of the International," in *Encyclopedia of Western Colonialism Since 1450*, ed. Thomas Benjamin (Detroit: Macmillan Reference USA, 2007), 727.

32 Carl Schmitt, *The Nomos of the Earth in the International Law of the Jus Publicum Europaeum*, trans. G. L. Ulmen (New York: Telos Press, 2003), 97.

33 Peter Stein, *Roman Law in European History* (Cambridge: Cambridge University Press, 1999), 94–95.

34 Francisco de Vitoria, "On the American Indians (*De Indis*)," in *Francisco de Vitoria: Political Writings*, eds. Anthony Pagden and Jeremy Lawrance, trans. Jeremy Lawrance (Cambridge: Cambridge University Press, 1991), 231, 282–83, 285–86, 291–92.

Although he might be surprised to hear himself described as a 'transnational jurisprudent', Peter Fitzpatrick is a model for such conduct. His exemplarity does not reside primarily in a list of qualities (though one could compile an embarrassingly long list with ease). Instead, it can be found in the way Peter thinks and writes law from within a humanist tradition, 'caring for the conduct of law',[35] whilst responding to the obligations created by the imperial history and foundations of modern law.

This is thinking and writing grounded in responsibility. Peter is fond of recalling the 'archaic' spelling, 'responsability', because it reminds us that responsibility is, above all, responsive. For him, law, like love,[36] 'responds' to the world, in both its fixity and change. And so too should the jurisprudent. Fitzpatrick's 'responsability', emplaced, yet expansive, oriented toward justice, yet attentive to empire, both cleaves to the best, and acknowledges the 'worst'. Three books written by Peter make this clearer than I could.[37] Each of them appears regularly in my own reading, teaching and writing. Together the books tell a story of the colonial and postcolonial journey of modern law, its violent institution and stabilisation in the colony, its mythic dimensions and foundation-less grounds. Throughout this trajectory, we find the other, abject, yet resistant,[38] 'constituted' by modern law, but always in excess, endlessly cast out, but critical to the self-grounding of modern law's authority.[39]

But those who people the Occident's 'other' are, in Peter's hands, never mere objects of scholarship, but among those to whom the 'responsability' is owed. And so, although his engagement with modern law is always critical, this is no scorched-earth jurisprudence in which no green shoots of law may be found. Not for Fitzpatrick a critical dialectic and its transcendence, nor a displacement from bad 'law' to a good 'political'. Instead he always reminds us that 'Law is We':[40] just as there can be no law without community, there can be no community without law. The task of the occidentally trained jurisprudent is to find, and take up, what is good and what is just in occidental law.

But this fragment – like the body of work for which it yearns – whispers with each breath, that 'justice is impossible'. The 'community' which joins us can also mark a limit, a line of decision, about who is inside and who may be kept out, who must be sacrificed. This community-as-colony can 'justify elimination'. Peter's early work drew out this genocidal tendency of modern law precisely in the context of the colony and settler-colony, but also in the nation-state in general. The historical and the theoretical are deftly interwoven in that work to reveal both the technologies of occidental imperial domination, and the jurisprudential practices which authorise and sustain them.

Peter often jokes that he 'knows nothing' about international law. And yet in retrospect, it seems that it was always only a matter of time before international law came to know him.

35 Shaun McVeigh, "Critical Approaches to Jurisdiction and International Law," in *The Oxford Handbook of Jurisdiction in International Law*, eds. Stephen Allen, et al. (Oxford: Oxford University Press, 2019).

36 See W. H. Auden, "Law Like Love," in *Poetry of the Law: From Chaucer to the Present*, eds. David Kader and Michael Standford (Iowa City: University of Iowa Press, 2010), 108–9. See also, Peter Fitzpatrick, "Law Like Poetry – Burnt Norton," *Liverpool Law Review: A Journal of Contemporary Legal and Social Policy* 23, no. 3 (2001): 285–88.

37 The three books are P. Fitzpatrick, *Law and the State in Papua New Guinea* (London: Academic Press, 1980); P. Fitzpatrick, *The Mythology of Law* (London: Routledge, 1992); P. Fitzpatrick, *Modernism and the Grounds of Law* (Cambridge: Cambridge University Press, 2001).

38 Peter Fitzpatrick, *Law as Resistance: Modernism, Imperialism, Legalism* (Burlington: Ashgate, 2008).

39 Peter Fitzpatrick and Patricia Tuitt, eds., *Critical Beings: Law, Nation and the Global Subject* (Burlington: Ashgate, 2003).

40 Auden, "Law Like Love," 109.

The door may at first have been opened by sovereignty, a term central to Peter's work, and as I read him, treated as both technology and concept. In earlier works, sovereignty was positioned as the pivot between history and theory. Later, he showed it to be the pivot between nation and inter-nation. It was at this point for me that Peter's jurisprudence met international law most explicitly.[41] The theological dimensions of a putatively secular law, the need for a transcendent referent to secure modern (international) law's grounds, the false opposition between universality and particularity, the centrality of race and civilisation to modern law's claims to authority; all were yet to become familiar ideas within the canon of international law.

I think it was roughly at this point in the chronology of his work that I became Peter's PhD student. My training until then had largely been in how to take up the office of cosmopolitan bureaucrat, learning the rituals and rites of those who would save the post-Cold War world with free trade and human rights. I began to gain a sense that there might be different traditions available, and different worlds to be made, during my LLM at UBC under the guidance of Mickelson, Buchanan, Pue, Boyd and Borrows. They were a dream team for a young scholar of international law. But it was Peter who trained me to think of international law as part of a humanist tradition, and Peter who modelled for me most profoundly the jurisprudent schooled in the 'humanities inflected jurisprudence of the common law tradition'.[42] For the international jurist, the responsibilities of office in this tradition must be understood as being owed not only to those within a community, but to those whom the community must encounter, and with whom it must treat. But against my cosmopolitan training until that point, I learnt from Peter that this responsibility is not to save, but to encounter. It is not deific, but mundane. There is no 'view from nowhere'.[43]

For me, one element of Peter's interest in international law lay in the absence of an overarching sovereign. The idea of a law which does not transcend maintains its fascination, even in this fragment. But if inter-national law has no cohering authority, yet we occidentals struggle to find the 'inter', or between. 'Infused with a negative universal reference', the 'between' itself levitates, and threatens to transcend. It seems we have never been modern.[44] And the 'new' international law, like the 'new imperialism',[45] claims to speak on behalf of Humanity.[46] But there is no transcendent humanity, no sacred law upon which we can rely. Despite its claims, Europe has no direct line to the gods, not even the god of progress. This potent fragment distils this lesson.

But still, no earth scorched of law. For although international law may be the child of empire, we may yet encourage its oedipal tendencies.[47] So we were trained by Peter, not to have faith

41 Peter Fitzpatrick, "'Gods Would Be Needed . . .': American Empire and the Rule of (International) Law," *Leiden Journal of International Law* 16, no. 3 (2003): 429–66.

42 McVeigh, "Critical Approaches."

43 Sheila Jasanoff, *Designs on Nature: Science and Democracy in Europe and the United States* (Princeton: Princeton University Press, 2005), 266.

44 Bruno Latour, *We Have Never Been Modern*, trans. Catherine Porter (Cambridge, MA: Harvard University Press, 1993).

45 C. C. Elridge, *Disraeli and the Rise of a New Imperialism* (Cardiff: University of Wales Press, 1996).

46 This is Fitzpatrick paraphrasing Schmitt: 'he who speaks on behalf of humanity, cheats'. Peter Fitzpatrick, "Is Humanity Enough? The Secular Theology of Human Rights," *Law, Social Justice, and Global Development* 1 (2007): 1–14.

47 Peter Fitzpatrick, "Latin Roots: Imperialism and the Making of Modern Law," *CLAVE: A Counter-Disciplinary Journal of Race, Culture and Power* 2 (2006): 1–18. See also Peter Fitzpatrick, "Latin Roots: The Force of International Law as Event," in *Events: The Force of International Law*, eds. Fleur Johns, Richard Joyce and Sundhya Pahuja (Abingdon: Routledge, 2011), 43–54.

in law, but to show fidelity to it;[48] not to solve law's mysteries, but to find in them the 'generative mythos'[49] of law's capacity to be other than what it is. We learnt that our responsibility as jurisprudents must include an attention to history and to the material, and have a sense of place. We must be vigilant against the tendency of law to declare itself just, of justice to declare itself Right, and of community to become colony. Our duty is not to save the Other with (our) law, or (our) knowledge, but to meet lawfully with those who live by other laws.

But lest this sounds rather dry, these abstract lessons were accompanied by more embodied and prosaic practices of training. In the rather liturgical secularity of Peter's supervision, we learnt to read slowly and with care. And after the combative rituals of frank intellectual exchange, ceremonies of conviviality were always held.[50] It is in this combination of the intellectual and the embodied, seriousness and lightness, erudition and humility, that Peter exemplifies the jurisprudent who both cares for the conduct of law, and is infinitely responsive to those in his care.

Ultimate legality, infinite critique

Richard Joyce

> [I]n the silence you don't know, you must go on, I can't go on. I'll go on.
>
> Samuel Beckett, 'The Unnameable'[51]

This chapter is not finished. Questions it raises, and those which will occur to readers (including this one) in the months and years to come, will remain unanswered. Expressions which, with Fitzpatrick's characteristic economy, complexity and range, could have encapsulated its themes will forever remain unformed. The chapter begins with the impossible, introduces mysteries and ends now without a conclusion.

What is it that we inherit, those who receive this unfinished work? For those of us asked to provide comments on it, and who 'cannot not be its heirs',[52] how can we do justice to this fragment? What should we make of it, and with it?

The chapter's 'focal obsession'[53] is one of long standing within Fitzpatrick's work: Derrida's deconstruction. It begins with reference to the English positivists. Hart is named, not for the first time, perhaps because positivism gets half of law's story right, or else because 'a radicalization is always indebted to the very thing it radicalizes'.[54] Here, the reference to Hart is by way of allusion to the positivist tradition of scepticism towards international law as a legal system proper. The destruction, not just deconstruction, of Hartian positivism, is done elsewhere.[55]

48 In practical terms, this training in the profane was always rather liturgical. This was its pleasure. The ritual of the reading group, and ceremony of conciliation afterwards. The journeys to Sturry, and the beauty of the Kentish-Brazilian garden.

49 Peter Fitzpatrick, "Still Not Being Modern: Law and the Insistence of Myth," *Australian Feminist Law Journal* 43, no. 2 (2017): 232.

50 Drinks at the pub, of course.

51 Samuel Beckett, *Molly Malone Dies the Unnameable (3 novels)* (London: John Calder, 1915), 418.

52 Derrida, *Specters of Marx*, 91.

53 See page 76 above.

54 Derrida, *Specters of* Marx, 92.

55 Fitzpatrick, *Modernism and the Grounds of Law*, 97–99; Fitzpatrick, *The Mythology of Modern Law*, Chapter 6.

The chapter then considers the affinities between international law and deconstruction – most pointedly the absence of any 'predominant authority that would endow [either] with an enduring and invariant coherence, any persistent positivity'.[56] These affinities are elaborated in the section enticingly subtitled 'the mysteries of international law'. Among other things, this discussion reflects how Fitzpatrick's pioneering engagement with poststructural theory and law drew him towards international law as a field of inquiry and analysis. Or perhaps it is the effect of his theoretical engagements drawing international law scholars to him.

As Fitzpatrick sets them out, we see how certain crucial elements of international law seem so apt for explanation through the lens of deconstruction – the apparent foundational independence of its constituent actors, the absence of a centralised authority, the importance of myths of origin, the claim to universality, the recourse to theology in spite (or precisely because) of a claimed secularism and the dependence on a negative referent. Deconstruction, we see, offers us a mode of holding the contradictions, paradoxes and conundrums of international law in place, allowing us to see the work they do in constituting what international law *is*, while also pointing towards the impelling force of what it might ever become. This by way of deconstruction's, and international law's, 'related but seemingly contrary dimensions of infinite responsiveness and resolved determinacy'.[57]

But is international law particularly apt for explanation, analysis and action through deconstruction in a way which national law is not? While the chapter contains indications to the contrary, the answer ultimately is no. The central claims about international law being made in this chapter are also made about modern law in general in Fitzpatrick's broader canon, especially (when read together) his major works, *The Mythology of Modern Law* and *Modernism and the Grounds of Law*.[58] The only element which appears especially apposite to international law is the absence of a centralised authority.

Even that element is perhaps less apposite than it seems. It can be rendered also as indicative of an absence of solid grounds, of law made in and by entities forming a community without a pre-existing foundation or pre-determined end, and without an ever-enduring site of authority. These are, for Fitzpatrick, essential characteristics of modern law in general. And so, Fitzpatrick suggests that 'international law . . . emerges, contrary to positivist prescription, as a paradigm of law'.[59] It takes more effort to expose the groundlessness of national law, and to think through its implications, but the quality of groundlessness is common to both systems. So too does national law combine the aporetic, generative relation of responsiveness and determinacy.

The important challenge Fitzpatrick sets before us, which he modestly attributes to deconstruction, but is really the product of his own original development of deconstruction in the context of legal theory, is how the impelling force generated by that relation can be 'perceptively grasped, or known, or brought to bear', and specifically, how 'law' so understood could be 'cognisable and operatively amenable'.[60]

Two related, preliminary modes by which we might approach an answer are offered. One draws on Derrida's own terminology of 'messianic', referring not to a 'resolving eschatology', but, as Derrida puts it, 'a structure of experience' – the experience of an opening to the future, or of the future as openness.[61] The other is by reference to 'community', in which 'community

56 See page 76 above.
57 Ibid.
58 Fitzpatrick, *Modernism and the Grounds of Law*; Fitzpatrick, *The Mythology of Modern Law*.
59 See page 77 above.
60 Ibid.
61 Ibid.

and law [are] mutually integral'.[62] Time did not permit Peter to pursue this challenge any further in this piece. And I cannot say that space alone prevents me from attempting to do so here.[63] We can say, at least, that both are ways of articulating the experience of the infinity of social relations, and necessarily then, of law. With that infinity comes a responsibility to make interventions which put that openness to work – in other words, to put into thought and action that which Peter discovered about law in his scholarly life.

From where would we draw the inspiration and conviction to pursue such interventions, if they are indeed to be based on that which lies, mysterious and, in many ways, unnameable, at the heart of law and of social existence? One Derridean answer might be 'justice'.[64] But another might be responsibility itself.

If responsibility, then, to whom, and before what? The answer to that question would vary for all of Fitzpatrick's readers, and even within each reader it would vary between contexts. For this particular reader, at this particular moment, in this particular place, the responsibility is to Peter himself. It is one of inheritance, and debt. Indeed, there 'is no inheritance without a call to responsibility'.[65] What is it that we, his students, have inherited from Peter? How will we discharge our debts to him?

Certainly we have inherited an ethos of scholarly comportment, of companionship, care and craft. But also a body of work, unfinished, like this chapter. Interrupted too soon, as it would inevitably have been. A body of work so rich, a set of provocations so powerful, that completion is impossible. Peter has set down an inexhaustible challenge: to account for the infinite nature of social life, and law's role in it. What greater gift could a teacher give his students?

I, for one, will never be able to repay my debts to Peter, scholarly and personal. They, too, are infinite. But if there is one thing that Peter has taught us, it is to confront the infinite head on, unflinchingly and together. If, with Valéry and Auden, we might say that a 'poem is never finished; it is only abandoned',[66] then our privileged responsibility is never to abandon Peter's poem. Its rhythms and mysteries are those of life itself.

Law, for the time being

Kathleen Birrell

The epigraph to Peter's fragment, an excerpt from Emily Dickinson's 'There Came a Wind Like a Bugle',[67] lyrically captures an intellectual legacy defined by an attentiveness to the constitutive oscillations of the world. Dickinson affirms the abiding rhythms of life and death through the wild pealing of a steeple bell in the midst of a storm, which tells the tidings of birdsong, a reference to Keats' immortal nightingale and the anguish of the mortal poet.[68] In resonant response, Fitzpatrick insists upon the abiding rhythms of law, constitutively oscillating between determinacy and indeterminacy, universality and particularity, exclusion and inclusion, possibility and

62 Ibid.

63 See Ben Golder's contribution to this chapter below.

64 Derrida, "Force of Law."

65 Derrida, *Specters of Marx*, 91.

66 W. H. Auden, *Collected Poems* (Franklin Center, PA: The Franklin Library, 1978), xxiv.

67 Dickinson, "There Came a Wind Like a Bugle," 591.

68 See more fulsome discussion in Jamie Heit, *Liturgical Liaisons: The Textual Body, Irony, and Betrayal in John Donne and Emily Dickinson* (Cambridge: The Lutterworth Press, 2017), 96.

impossibility. The perpetual comings and goings that 'yet abide the World' are, for Fitzpatrick, expressed in the mutual constitution of law and its others, law and community, and the ultimate plurality of commonality.[69] The enduring preoccupation so deftly encapsulated in this epigraph epitomises the manner in which Peter conducted his life as a scholar, teacher and mentor. His intellectual legacy is marked by a gentle insistence, his pedagogical approach by patient precision, and his scholarly guidance by companionable constancy. In this short response, I will reflect upon this legacy and conduct and their sustained influence on my own intellectual formation.

The law elaborated in Fitzpatrick's vast scholarly contribution is, in his earlier work, a mythology that is nonetheless 'vibrantly operative in modernity'.[70] In later work, he continues this project and is concerned to situate this law as both in and beyond modernity[71] and, further, as comprising mutually suffusing dimensions.[72] A Derridean concern with an iterative law, the text and force of which are constituted by an interminable responsiveness, and the 'impossible' experience of justice in the perpetual movement between the 'calculable and incalculable',[73] provide a critical premise. This law is constituted by the determinate fusion of 'what is determinately here' and a 'responsiveness to what is ever beyond, even if that determination is only and ever "for the time being"'.[74] With reference to Auden, for whom 'poetry makes nothing happen', insofar as 'it brings nothingness into happening', Fitzpatrick cites Blanchot, for whom law is formulated by exteriority.[75] Indeed, reading Derrida and Nancy, he emphasises the determinacy and responsivity of literature, as of law, between which '[a]ffinities loom'.[76] And yet further, drawing upon Nancy, he dwells upon the plurality of singularity[77] and, with reference to law, the constitution of law by its other, '[t]he law of abandonment'.[78] The fragment for this chapter draws upon these generative philosophical engagements, with an insistent focus on the aporetic[79] and 'seemingly contrary'[80] dimensions of law and the revelation of this law and community as 'mutually integral',[81] with international law its most apposite example.

The dimensions of law elaborated in Fitzpatrick's work, alongside the philosophical tradition from which this elaboration draws, have infused and sustained my own work, both in my doctoral research under Peter's exemplary supervision and in my current projects. My doctorate and monograph explored the animation of indigeneities within textual imaginaries, juridical and literary, through an examination of Indigenous subjectivities and laws before and beyond a

69 Peter Fitzpatrick, "Ultimate Plurality: International Law and the Possibility of Resistance," *Inter Gentes* 1, no. 1 (2016): 16.

70 Fitzpatrick, *The Mythology of Modern Law*, ix.

71 Fitzpatrick, *Modernism and the Grounds of Law*.

72 Ibid., 102.

73 Derrida, "Force of Law," 233. See also Fitzpatrick, *Modernism and the Grounds of Law*.

74 Peter Fitzpatrick, "Bare Sovereignty: *Homo Sacer* and the Insistence of Law," in *Politics, Metaphysics and Death: Essays on Giorgio Agamben's Homo Sacer*, ed. Andrew Norris (Durham, NC: Duke University Press, 2005) 53; see also 62. See also Fitzpatrick, *Modernism and the Grounds of Law*, 44–45; Peter Fitzpatrick, "Reading Slowly: The Law of Literature and the Literature of Law," in *Reading Modern Law: Critical Methodologies and Sovereign Formations,* eds. Ruth Buchanan, Stewart Motha and Sundhya Pahuja (London: Routledge, 2012), 206.

75 Fitzpatrick, "Reading Slowly," 195, 204.

76 Ibid., 199. See also Maurice Blanchot, *The Madness of the Day*, trans. Lydia David (Barrytown: Station Hill Press, 1981), 16; Maurice Blanchot, "Literature and the Right to Death," in *The Station Hill Blanchot Reader: Fiction and Literary Essays*, ed. George Quasha (Barrytown: Station Hill Press, 1999), 365–66.

77 Jean-Luc Nancy, *Being Singular Plural* (Stanford, CA: Stanford University Press, 2000).

78 Jean-Luc Nancy, *The Birth to Presence*, trans. Brian Holmes (Stanford, CA: Stanford University Press, 1993), 44.

79 Derrida, "Force of Law," 244, 251–58.

80 [cross-reference to Peter Fitzpatrick's section in this chapter].

81 Ibid.

non-Indigenous (common law) juridical tradition and as evoked in Indigenous literary jurisprudences. My current research builds upon and extends this work, now contextualised by the existential crisis of climatic catastrophe. Its focal concern is encounters between juridical, political and cultural narratives, and ensuing constructions of right and obligation. Where Fitzpatrick's scholarship elaborates an operative duality of the law in which I am trained, this premise allows me to imagine an ethics of encounter between laws, as between subjectivities both human and more-than-human, which require a responsivity to authority, legitimacy and transformation from a variety of sources. The modes of conduct adequate to ethical encounters, in order to meet well,[82] might be informed by an attentiveness to our 'being-with', a plurality that inheres in our singularity.[83] Fitzpatrick's reading of law and community, each rendered 'determinately operative' yet also and necessarily 'responsively open to the illimitability of relation',[84] provides a possible philosophical foundation for ethical encounter. Indeed, returning to Derrida, we are called to a radical 'response-ability', an 'active responsibility, which "assigns [us] even in [our] liberty"'.[85] This imperative is illuminated by the Anthropocenic realisation of our 'mineralogical dimension' and of humans as 'geologic subjects',[86] and further amplified by the multispecies entanglements and assemblages revealed by a global pandemic. Its enactment requires the acknowledgment and fulfilment of mutual obligation, which both precedes and exceeds right.

In all, my greatest intellectual debt to Peter is a methodological training deeply informed by his scholarship. The discipline of slow and careful reading reflects his revelation of the duality of modern law, the latter comprehensible as itself 'a device for reading slowly'.[87] Alongside this discipline, his scholarly conduct privileged enduring intellectual companionship and community, and attentive and generous teaching, which affirmed a lived concern with the mutuality of 'being-together'.[88] In closing, I return to Dickinson and the perpetual rhythms of life and death, the comings and goings that 'yet abide the World', within which we are all enmeshed and enriched. It is this rhythm that articulates and animates Fitzpatrick's rendering of law and community, in accordance with which an end is 'terminal', yet 'only and ever "for the time being"'.[89]

Peter as teacher

Ben Golder

'Ultimate Legality: (De)constructing International Law', or, at any rate, the unfinished and suggestive fragment of it that we have here, is resonant with possibility. 'For the avoidance of doubt',

82 Shaunnagh Dorsett and Shaun McVeigh, "Conduct of Laws: Native Title, Responsibility, and Some Limits of Jurisdictional Thinking," *Melbourne University Law Review* 36, no. 2 (2012): 493.

83 Nancy, *Being Singular Plural*. See also Jean-Luc Nancy, "Of Being-in-Common," in *Community at Loose Ends*, eds. Miami Theory Collective (Minneapolis: University of Minnesota Press, 1991), 2, 6.

84 Peter Fitzpatrick, "Myth and the Mystical: Legal Theology in a 'Modern' World" (Keynote Presentation at the Mythology of Modern Law at 25 Years Conference, Melbourne Law School, May 2017).

85 Jacques Derrida, *Limited Inc.* (Evanston: Northwestern University Press, 1988), 130. See also Fitzpatrick, *Modernism and the Grounds of Law*, 76–77. See further Upendra Baxi, "Towards a Climate Justice Theory," *Journal of Human Rights and the Environment* 7, no. 1 (2016): 12; Donna Haraway, *Staying with the Trouble: Making Kin in the Chthulucene* (Durham, NC: Duke University Press, 2016), 2.

86 Kathryn Yusoff, "Geologic Life: Prehistory, Climate, Futures in the Anthropocene," *Environment and Planning D: Society and Space* 31, no. 5 (2013): 779–95.

87 Ruth Buchanan, Stewart Motha and Sundhya Pahuja, "Introduction," in *Reading Modern Law: Critical Methodologies and Sovereign Formations*, eds. Ruth Buchanan, Stewart Motha and Sundhya Pahuja (London: Routledge, 2012), 2.

88 Fitzpatrick, "Myth and the Mystical."

89 Fitzpatrick, "Reading Slowly," 206.

as Peter would sometimes say with tongue firmly planted in cheek, rolling his poststructural eyes at the vain semantic conceits of lawyers, I use 'suggestive' in a positive sense (evocative, referential, generative of ideas) and not the somewhat contrary sense which, as his doctoral student, it took me too long to realise actually meant something more akin to 'not quite there, yet'. ('Intriguing' was a close synonym of 'suggestive' in Peter's coded and avuncular idiom – never for him the brutal judgment of 'half-baked' or 'inchoate'. But Peter was never straightforward when a more sinuous, and interesting, approach lay open.) Here I intend 'suggestive' not in its well-meaning, shock-softening supervisorial sense, instead intimating something wider, something beyond, something altogether more expansive and capacious. Just as a fragment implies a whole, so too does this piece index and refer to an encompassing body of scholarship and teaching whose 'relational range of possible connection is infinite', as the present fragment aptly has it.[90]

Others have reflected and will reflect better than I can on Peter's scholarship and on his intellectual legacy,[91] so I want to focus instead on the possibly less remarked upon qualities of Peter as a teacher. I never saw Peter teach an undergraduate tutorial or a masters seminar. So I do not mean that type of teaching. Rather, I mean 'teaching' in the widest possible sense (as a question of training or conduct as a scholar, as a question of intellectual formation). As his former doctoral student, collaborator, co-author and now friend, I experienced and continue to experience his teaching at close quarters.

What does Peter teach us? What do we learn from him and his writings? The question is a little misconstrued, perhaps. Assuredly, we learn and will *continue* to learn many actual things (Peter's books, especially *Modernism and the Grounds of Law*, demand and repay multiple readings). His legal theoretical insights into modern law's perduring mythological dimensions and its 'seemingly contrary dimensions of infinite responsiveness and resolved determinacy' are, justly, well known.[92] So too his many discussions, developed throughout his work but particularly pertinent to international law, of the 'strategy' of 'negative universal reference' whereby 'an occidental modernity' was enabled to achieve 'a comprehensive identity . . . not by the "positive" ascription of qualities, but by an incorporated rejection of their invented contrary'.[93] And much, much else besides.

But Peter's influence on many of us (students, readers, scholars, friends) is irreducible to substantive theoretical insights about law or even to that infectious, signature mode of expressing them (so luxuriant and idiosyncratic a prose style as almost calculated to subvert the anonymity of academic peer review). Rather, I think Peter teaches us (through patient exemplarity) a particular mode of scholarly engagement defined by an attentively rigorous creativity. Like many a Fitzpatrickianism, this might not immediately seem 'a promising prospect', might be 'improbable,' even.[94] Attentive rigour and creativity are, after all, themselves two quite different modes of scholarly engagement that pull in very different directions. The former orients one reverently, centripetally, to the text and its pathology is like a kind of stale, Casaubonian scholasticism (something Foucault once memorably lampooned as the 'warm freemasonry of useless erudition').[95] The latter orients one breathlessly away from the text and its pathology is like a kind of cavalier insouciance, untrammelled by regard for extant scholarship and the historical record (ahem,

90 See page 76 above.

91 See, for example, Ruth Buchanan, Stewart Motha and Sundhya Pahuja, eds., *Reading Modern Law: Critical Methodologies and Sovereign Formations* (London: Routledge, 2012).

92 See page 76 above. See further Fitzpatrick, *The Mythology of Modern Law*; Fitzpatrick, *Modernism and the Grounds of Law*.

93 See page 78 above. See further Fitzpatrick, '"Gods Would Be Needed'," 429.

94 See page 76 above.

95 Michel Foucault, *"Society Must Be Defended": Lectures at the Collège de France, 1975–1976*, trans. David Macey (Harmondsworth: Penguin, 2004), 5.

Foucault himself, sometimes). Avoiding both pathologies, Peter's work (im)possibly brings deep textual erudition and creative playfulness into relation. Peter's *oeuvre* is steeped in the texts of what we might call the poststructural canon, and this fragment itself is a neat conspectus of these references, with Nietzsche, Foucault, Derrida and Nancy all called in aid, alongside the obligatory poem (here Dickinson, often Auden or Eliot),[96] and the glancing jibe at HLA Hart.[97]

And yet Peter's Derrida, Peter's Nancy, Peter's Foucault, for all that, are distinctive and recognisable creatures. Crucially, Peter's creative rewritings and reworkings are studied and often understated ones, performed and reperformed iteratively across a number of different texts and contexts through the words of his sources. Not so much for Peter the monstrous Deleuzian buggery as the more gentle and dialogic 'posthumous persuasion'[98] of his textual interlocutors.[99] This latter mode of engagement demands a very patient and constant attunement to the canon, to the generous inhabiting of one's scholarly references, but at the same time a countervailing attunement to the world constantly made anew, and the desire (indeed, imperative) to rewrite in light of that.

Peter would always write chidingly on doctoral drafts that the standard exculpatory resort of scholars ('there is not time to develop the point here') would not avail us and would have to go. I seem to remember it was one of the few things he expressly forbade (rather than suggest cryptically that a particular point was 'suggestive' in its current formulation). But I am afraid (sorry, Peter) that time and space have almost run out and I cannot here tease out the ways in which Peter's generative generosity implied and relied upon a community, and the many ways in which he fostered that community in his writing and in his life. So, instead, I will finish with an anecdote. Elisabeth Young-Bruehl tells a story about Hannah Arendt in her biography which captures something of what I have been discussing:

> I had produced a translation of a cryptic saying of Aristotle's. Hannah Arendt checked her copy of a standard Latin translation and compared it to my effort, disapprovingly. She then checked a German translation and became skeptical about the Latin. Finally, she sat back, rendered her verdict on my translation, and made a statement about her thinking style: "Ja, well, my dear, it's not exactly right, but then maybe Aristotle would think it more interesting than wrong."[100]

We are not quite there, yet.

96 See Fitzpatrick, "Law Like Poetry," 285.

97 See Tara Mulqueen, "Naturalising the Myth: Hart, Biopolitics, and the Body Corporate," *Australian Feminist Law Journal* 34, no. 2 (2018): 251 on the more sustained demolition job.

98 See page 77 above.

99 That is, to 'tak[e] an author from behind and giv[e] him [*sic*] a child that would be his [*sic*] own offspring, yet monstrous'. See Gilles Deleuze, "Letter to a Harsh Critic," in *Negotiations: 1972–1990*, trans. Martin Joughin (New York: Columbia University Press, 1997), 6.

100 Elisabeth Young-Bruehl, *Hannah Arendt: For Love of the World*, 2nd ed. (New Haven: Yale University Press, 2004), 1.

Sense

7

Absent images of international law

Alice Palmer

Absent law

For Peter Goodrich, a 'lack' of law in international law leaves international lawyers no choice but 'to turn to other disciplines and discourses'.[1] There is, otherwise, 'nothing to say'.[2] For the lacuna that is international law, Goodrich cites Ed Morgan. 'International law is', Morgan states, 'the law that is used up'.[3] It is perhaps not surprising that when he addressed a theory of 'international law and image' a decade later, Goodrich spoke to 'law and image' as the legitimate precursor to an international unlaw.[4] His disdain for international law had not waned, it would seem, in the intervening years.

The claim that international law is 'no law at all'[5] is commonly endorsed by scholars who are not, it perhaps goes without saying, international lawyers. The charge of law's absence typically focusses on the political nature of international law: it's international relations, no more, no less.[6] In its crudest form, the argument points out that there is no central command and no jail for states.[7] This is a long-time debate that has been readily settled by an expansive understanding of 'law' that befits the horizontal authority of inter-state cooperation.[8]

1 Peter Goodrich, "On the Relational Aesthetics of International Law: Philosophy of International Law, Anthony Carty," (Review Article) *Journal of the History of International Law* 10, no. 2 (2008): 321, 323.
2 Ibid.
3 Ed Morgan, *The Aesthetics of International Law* (Toronto: University of Toronto Press, 2007), 15.
4 Peter Goodrich, "The International Signs Law," in *The Oxford Handbook of the Theory of International Law*, eds. Anne Orford, Florian Hoffmann and Martin Clark (Oxford: Oxford University Press, 2016), 365.
5 Goodrich, "Relational Aesthetics," 323.
6 For example Nikolas Rajkovic, "Interdisciplinarity," in *Concepts for International Law: Contributions to Disciplinary Thought*, eds. Jean d'Aspremont and Sahib Singh (Northampton: Edward Elgar Publishing, 2019), 490; Jan Klabbers, "The Bridge Crack'd: A Critical Look at Interdisciplinary Relations," *International Relations* 23 (2009): 119.
7 Cf Anthony D'Amato, "Is International Law Really 'Law'?" *Northwestern University Law Review* 79 (1984): 1293.
8 Martii Koskenniemi, "Law, Teleology and International Relations: An Essay in Counterdisciplinarity," *International Relations* 26 (2012): 3; Harold Hongju Koh, "Why Do Nations Obey International Law?," (Review Article) *The Yale Law Journal* 106, no. 8 (1997): 2599.

Figure 7.1 'South China Sea Arbitration, Photograph from Jurisdictional Hearing – July 2015 – Hearing in Session'. Source: Permanent Court of Arbitration, 'Arbitration between the Republic of the Philippines and the People's Republic of China' (Press Release, 13 July 2015).

But as time wears on, and the cracks in international law are tested by a climate stressed planet, it seems fair to ask just how much law there is in all this. Russia and China thumb their noses at the Permanent Court of Arbitration in matters concerning the United Nations Convention on the Law of the Sea.[9] Places are set at the respondent's table for the guests that will never arrive (see Figure 7.1). The United States casts aside the Paris Agreement on climate change – an instrument lacking in law if there ever was one.[10] Japan rejects first the International Court of Justice,[11] and then international 'law' itself, as it withdraws from the International Convention on the Regulation of Whaling,[12] and sets off to hunt whales unwittingly entering

9 Opened for signature December 10, 1982, 1833 *UNTS* 397 (entered into force November 16, 1994); Arctic Sunrise Arbitration (*Netherlands v Russia*) PCA Case No 2014–02 (PCA 2015); South China Sea Arbitration (*Philippines v China*) PCA Case No 2013–19 (PCA 2016).

10 Emily Holden, "Trump Begins Year-Long Process to Formally Exit Paris Climate Agreement," *The Guardian*, November 5, 2019, www.theguardian.com/us-news/2019/nov/04/donald-trump-climate-crisis-exit-paris-agreement; note also Jacob Werksman, "A Moment in the Sun: Does the Paris Agreement on Climate Change Mark an Evolution or an Extinction of International Environmental Law?" In *Conversation with Alice Palmer, IILAH Seminar* (Melbourne: Melbourne Law School, October 23, 2017).

11 *Japan's Declaration Recognizing as Compulsory the Jurisdiction of the International Court of Justice Under Article 36, paragraph 2, of the Statute of the Court 15 October 1946* (October 6, 2015).

12 *International Convention on the Regulation of Whaling*, opened for signature December 2, 1946, 161 UNTS 72 (entered into force November 10, 1948), *Japan – Note Verbale* (December 26, 2018).

its territorial waters. International law was quite literally erased, leaving blank the space it had once marked on the Japanese whaling vessel.[13]

Meanwhile, fires burn, forests are felled, coal is sold and rivers run dry as the international law that protects biodiversity is found, yet again, to have done no such thing at all.[14] The only good news story of recent times is the expanded scope of international laws on trade in hazardous waste to cover certain plastics – only agreed, like so many international environmental laws, when the problem littered the front stoop of rich states.[15]

Indeed, international environmental law is possibly the branch of international law that can most concentrate the minds of those sceptical about the presence of 'law' in international law. For if international law *writ large* challenges the expectations of some jurisprudents, then international environmental law is an example *in extremis*. This is a field where not only does something called 'soft' law abound but it is fostered and hailed as international law gone well.[16] This is a fragment of international law – admittedly one of many – where the causes of the problems at the heart of international agreement continue unabated while the band plays on.

My point for the purposes of the present volume is this: if international law – at least in the guise of international environmental law – is 'no law at all', then what might a scholarly engagement with the humanities do for that law? If indeed there is no law, then to speak of 'international law and the humanities' as an inter-disciplinary field of study is a misnomer. There is nothing *inter* about it. By this reckoning, scholars writing on aesthetic jurisprudence should perhaps describe their field of inquiry, quite simply, as 'the humanities'.[17] Not in recognition that law is born of a humanist tradition,[18] just acknowledging that on the topic of 'international law', there is 'nothing to say'.[19] Or might the humanities – and more specifically visual art – be used in the service of international law, to generate an image of international law where there is some law to be seen and, even better, applied to some purpose? If the absence of law denies international law an image, can visual art provide it – and to what end?

Absent art

I was thinking on this when I stood in the Friedenssaal of the Münster Rathaus as a visitor to Alexandra Pirici's *Leaking Territories* (2017) (Figure 7.2). Plain clothes performers moved about the space, sometimes apart, sometimes united as their individual figures made together one

13 Jake Sturmer and Yumi Asada, "Japan Scrubs 'Research' from Its Whaling Ship as It Returns to Commercial Hunting," *ABC News*, July 2, 2019, www.abc.net.au/news/2019-07-02/japan-resumes-commercial-whaling-after-30-year-hiatus/11266966.

14 See Secretariat of the Convention on Biological Diversity, *Global Biodiversity Outlook 4: A Mid-Term Assessment of Progress Towards the Implementation of the Strategic Plan for Biodiversity 2011–2020* (2014); Intergovernmental Science-Policy Platform on Biodiversity and Ecosystem Services (IPBES), *Global Assessment Report on Biodiversity and Ecosystem Services*, May 2019.

15 Conference of the Parties to the *Convention on the Control of Transboundary Movements of Hazardous Wastes and Their Disposal*, Decision BC-14/12, "Amendments to Annexes II, VIII and IX to the Basel Convention" (May 2019).

16 Sumudu Atapattu, "International Environmental Law and Soft Law: A New Direction or a Contradiction?," In *Non-State Actors, Soft Law and Protective Regimes: From the Margins*, ed. Cecilia Bailliet (Cambridge: Cambridge University Press, 2012), 200.

17 Costas Douzinas, "A Short History of the British Critical Legal Conference or, the Responsibility of the Critic," *Law and Critique* 25, no. 2 (2014): 187; Andrea Bianchi, "Law and Literature," in *International Law Theories* (Oxford: Oxford University Press, 2016), 287.

18 See J. E. G. de Montmorency, "Law & the Humanities: A Lecture," delivered at University College, Gower Street, November 24, 1922 (Oxford: Oxford University Press, 1923).

19 Goodrich, "Relational Aesthetics," 323.

Figure 7.2 Alexandra Pirici, *Leaking Territories*, Friedenssaal in Historischen Rathaus Münster, Prinzipalmarkt 10, Skulptur-Projekte 2017. Photo Credit: LWL-Museum für Kunst und Kultur, Münster/Skulptur Projekte Archiv/Henning Rogge.

body. They would pause, strike a pose, then morph to another tableau, taking turns in a soliloquy. 'Here we are . . .', a performer would commence, before describing the 'here' in terms of a there, or a then, or a that, rendering us – the six performers and the 30 or so visitors – relative to the near and far of the past, present and future. The Arab Spring. The refugee crisis. Tiananmen Square. The invention of the atomic bomb. The small pox vaccine. Wars. A ghetto. A changing climate. A climate changed.

But the 'here' was the ancient Friedenssaal or 'Peace Hall', a timber-lined room studded with portraits of the envoys who negotiated the recognition of sovereign states in a treaty that would bring peace to Westphalia.[20] An instrument often cited as the first act of modern international law.[21] And the 'here' was also me, an international lawyer, of sorts, participating in a work of art. Contested 'art' at that: possibly 'performance' art, as part of a 'sculpture' festival. The work was literally figurative but pointedly conceptual. Through performers and visitors, the concepts were embodied yet the artist herself was physically absent. I was at a loss to know myself. Which is, of course, exactly what a great artwork will do.

20 France-Holy Roman Empire, *Treaty of Münster*, October 24, 1648, 1 CTS 271.

21 Stephen Neff, *Justice Among Nations* (Harvard: Harvard University Press, 2014), 139–40.

It seemed particularly interesting that the Münster Sculpture Project, a decennial festival of site-specific sculpture commissioned from international artists and hosted by a university town in Germany, had extended the brief to performance. Transience, and the absence of static media typically associated with sculpture, made *Leaking Territories* a particular outlier in the genre. It was not a first for the Münster Sculpture Project, where organic, dynamic, ephemeral and intangible manifestations of sculpture have been welcomed to the fold.[22] Performance can, however, be seen by some in aesthetic philosophy as a stretch too far for sculpture, if not for visual art itself. In old guard thinking, performance is theatre, but if it is visual art, it does not have the markings of sculpture made from inanimate media manipulated by the artist and positioned on a pedestal for posterity.[23] Pirici, in her practice and her talk on her practice, lays to rest any such arcane parameters for art, where 'performance' is even a misnomer.[24]

Absent theory

The marginalisation of performance art in the thinking on the arts nevertheless echoes the marginalisation of international law in the thinking on law that I described at the outset. Performance art, like international law, does not tick the boxes created for the principal discipline by the conventional academy. Yet a distancing of art from performance art, as antiquated as that might be, might also have some corollary in the vexed relations between international environmental law and critical legal theory.

Scholarship in international environmental law has a fondness for thinking that does positivism proud. Not everyone, of course. Karin Mickelson has, for example, persistently examined the workings of international environmental law through critical theory.[25] It is, however, not common for scholars to theorise international environmental law from a critical vantage. As Andreas Kotsakis observes, environmental law, including its international incarnations, is twice blighted when 'legal scholarship's fear of [critical] theory becomes intertwined with ecology's suspicion against theorising in the face of environmental catastrophe'.[26] The wariness probably goes both ways though. Perhaps because international environmental law is so dedicated in its instrumental mission, and because the dogmatic intricacies of the field created in that mission are not readily mastered by the generalist scholar, critical theorists of grand scheme international law tend to give international environmental law a wide berth.[27]

22 For example Suzan Phiipsz, *The Lost Reflection* (sound installation, Münster Sculpture Project, 2007); Rosemarie Trockel, *Less Savage Than Others* (tree installation, Münster Sculpture Project, 2006–2007).

23 Robert Hopkins, "Sculpture," in *The Oxford Handbook of Aesthetics*, ed. Jerrold Levinson (Oxford: Oxford University Press, 2003), 572; see also Tanya Augsburg, "Interdisciplinary Arts," in *The Oxford Handbook of Interdisciplinarity*, ed. Robert Frodeman (Oxford: Oxford University Press, 2017), 131.

24 Alexandra Pirici, "Are You Alive or Not? Looking at ART through the lens of THEATRE" (Lecture at Conference-Festival, Theatre De Brakke Grond, Curated by Claire Bishop, March 22, 2015); see also Bree Richards, "Double Take: The Choreographic (Re)turn in Contemporary Art," *Art Monthly Australia* 271 (July 2014): 14.

25 Karin Mickelson, "South, North, International Environmental Law, and International Environmental Lawyers," *Yearbook of International Environmental Law* 11, no. 1 (2000): 52. See also Usha Natarajan and Kishan Khoday, "Locating Nature: Making and Unmaking International Law," *Leiden Journal of International Law* 27 (2014): 573.

26 Andreas Kotsakis, "On the Relation Between Scholarship and Action in Environmental Law: Method, Theory, Change," in *Research Methods in Environmental Law: A Handbook*, eds. Andreas Philippopoulos-Mihalopoulos and Victoria Brooks (Northampton: Edward Elgar Publishing, 2017), 338, 340.

27 Cf Stephen Humphreys and Yoriko Otomo, "Theorizing International Environmental Law," in *The Oxford Handbook of the Theory of International Law*, eds. Anne Orford, Florian Hoffmann and Martin Clark (Oxford: Oxford University Press, 2016), 797.

Figure 7.3 Alexandra Pirici, *Leaking Territories*, Friedenssaal in Historischen Rathaus Münster, Prinzipalmarkt 10, Skulptur-Projekte 2017. Photo Credit: LWL-Museum für Kunst und Kultur, Münster/Skulptur Projekte Archiv/Henning Rogge.

There are calls for more critical legal scholarship for the environment, notably with respect to environmental law.[28] But the same need for critical incursions is apparent in respect of international environmental law.[29] The failure of that law to address the problems that threaten the very existence of states, let alone the habitats that bridge their borders, demands the kind of reorientation that critical theory can foster.[30]

It was visual jurisprudence, or 'imaginal law',[31] that I had in mind as a theory for international environmental law while I observed *Leaking Territories* (Figure 7.3). The idea of 'image' for law takes many forms in the legal literature. Desmond Manderson, for example, conceives

28 Andreas Philippopoulos-Mihalopoulos, "Critical Legal Thinking in Environmental Law," in *Law and Ecology: New Environmental Foundations*, ed. Andreas Philippopoulos-Mihalopoulos (New York: Routledge, 2011), 18.

29 Tim Stephens, "What is the Point of International Environmental Law Scholarship in the Anthropocene?," In *Perspectives on Environmental Law Scholarship: Essays on Purpose, Shape and Direction*, ed. Ole W. Pedersen (Cambridge: Cambridge University Press, 2018), 121.

30 Cait Storr, "Islands and the South: Framing the Relationship Between International Law and Environmental Crisis," (Review Article) *European Journal of International Law* 27, no. 2 (2016): 519.

31 Desmond Manderson, "Introduction: Imaginal Law," in *Law and the Visual: Representations, Technologies and Critique*, ed. Desmond Manderson (Toronto: University of Toronto Press, 2018), 3. See also Costas Douzinas and Lynda Nead, eds., *Law and the Image: The Authority of Art and the Aesthetics of Law* (Chicago: University of Chicago Press, 1999); Richard Sherwin, *Visualizing Law in the Age of the Digital Baroque: Arabesques and Entanglements* (London: Routledge, 2011); Peter Goodrich and Valérie Hayaert, eds., *Genealogies of Legal Vision* (London: Routledge, 2015).

of image for law as conceptual and physical.[32] His 'conceptual' images are abstractions. By contrast, Manderson's 'physical' images are material 'artworks, photographs, representations, and the like'.[33] This idea of 'image' extends to visual representations of law, visual technologies in law and aesthetic critiques of law where 'image' includes art images.[34] The image 'of' law, for example, might be a conceptual image that assumes material form in the artworks, photographs and films depicting the law or used in legal process.

Leaking Territories made images of international law and, to my mind, of international environmental law. And the law made images for *Leaking Territories*. The site-specific artwork was burnished by the historic signs of law all about it – obviously, the portraits of treaty negotiators, and the judge's bench too. Later I would see other signs – Moses carved into a wooden window niche and, the likely legal significance of which is supposed but intriguing nonetheless, an embroidered slipper and a severed hand in a vitrine at one end of the hall.[35] But the name of the site – the Peace Hall – was the ultimate pall of international legal meaning. The celebration of reconciled states in that space jarred with the mentions of international and civil conflict in the performance itself. Conflict laying waste, and born from the wasting, of environments.[36]

The artwork facilitated a movement in time and space, between events and things. In the process, it generated both conceptual and physical images that made an image in my mind. These images were, in many ways, uncomfortable and more complex critical representations of international environmental law than those created by international environmental lawyers themselves.

I consider my interrogation of international law through 'image', including images from artworks like *Leaking Territories*, to fall within the realm of a critical theory. But whether my approach, or any one of the many approaches assumed by jurisprudents of imaginal law, is 'critical' is open for debate.[37] The lines between what is, and what isn't, infect visual jurisprudence and 'international law' alike. Even if an approach embraced in the name of imaginal law is not formally grounded in Critical Legal Studies, it can, if done well, work more on the side of critical reflection than offerings of 'a cultural gloss to future corporate lawyers'.[38] In the very least, the task of reading law in images, and seeing images of law, 'interrupts the straightforward story of legal governance and bypasses it in favour of a more uncomfortable one'.[39]

Absent lawyers

A reorientation of law through a critical theory for a higher purpose should appeal to international environmental lawyers. It serves, perversely, the 'heroic vision' of international environmental law

32 Manderson, "Introduction: Imaginal Law," 4, citing Chiara Bottici. See also Desmond Manderson, *Danse Macabre: Temporalities of Law in the Visual Arts* (Cambridge: Cambridge University Press, 2019), 16.

33 Manderson, "Introduction: Imaginal Law," 4.

34 Ibid.; see also Jessica Silbey, "Images in/of Law," *New York Law School Law Review* 57 (2012–2013): 171.

35 The shoe might have belonged to the wife of a diplomat attending the peace negotiations in 1648, and the hand might have been from an alleged victim of murder, tendered in evidence to a seventeenth-century court, see Annette Gresing, "Town Hall of the Peace of Westphalia," *Münster Marketing*, 2017, www.stadt-muenster.de/fileadmin//user_upload/stadt-muenster/80_tourismus/pdf/muenster-historisch_en.pdf.

36 Note United Nations Environment Assembly of the United Nations Environment Programme, Resolution 2/15. *Protection of the Environment in Areas Affected by Armed Conflict* UN Doc UNEP/EA.2/Res.15 August 4, 2016.

37 See for example Peter Goodrich, "Imago Decidendi: On the Common Law of Images," *Art and Law* 1, no. 1 (2017): 1. See further distinction between 'modern' and 'postmodern' jurisprudence in Costas Douzinas, Ronnie Warrington and Shaun McVeigh, *Postmodern Jurisprudence: The Law of the Text in the Texts of the Law* (London: Routledge, 1991).

38 Douzinas, "A Short History," 193.

39 Alison Young, *Judging the Image: Art, Value, Law* (New York: Routledge, 2004), 10.

as a normative project that 'is not only beneficial to the planet and mankind' but to international law itself.[40] It appears that a Messianic complex touches international lawyers in general.[41] But again, international environmental lawyers do it particularly well: we're a voice for the 'more-than-human',[42] 'individuals who are passionately concerned about the state of the global environment'.[43] As Mickelson points out, such evangelism can be problematic, particularly where the 'more-than-human' sidelines the less-than-rich humans.[44] However, the state of crisis that drives that normative project is real, and, as Mickelson has also observed, possibly instrumental to state cooperation on the environment.[45] As champions of the cause, international environmental lawyers are obvious recruits to any theoretical approaches that might help law to mend the broken world.

This turgid image of international environmental law, and the lawyers that work it, contrasts with the image of international law and international lawyers that Goodrich painted back in 2008.[46] It was the unseen international lawyer that had been the target of Goodrich's ire when he wrote on the lack of law in international law. The lack of 'law' was either a product of, or exacerbated by, a lack of international lawyers in the public realm. He berated international lawyers for their absence (along with their law) from spheres of influence. International lawyers should, he said, borrow from the theory of 'relational aesthetics' and socialise international law – so that international law might become something from nothing. Specifically, he called on jurists to use 'judgments' as a 'social interstice', unpacking for the public the ways in which international law facilitates 'democratic ways of being together'.[47]

What to make of the call to demonstrate 'democratic ways of being together' through the judgments of international courts and tribunals? It would, at best, be a hard task. Most decisions would probably be characterised as inherently undemocratic, or as irrelevant to democratic outcomes.[48] When it comes to international environmental law, prospects for using judgments to foster democracy might be better – though they could also be worse. The endorsement of environmental assessments in the *Pulp Mills* case, for example, lends itself to an analysis of popular participation.[49] But how to democratise judgments involving undemocratic states – or for states that don't even show up, or for the states that show up but are ignored?[50]

Gerry Simpson later took Goodrich to task on his image of the absent international lawyer, pointing out that Goodrich's source (Richard Posner's survey of 'public intellectuals') had missed the many international lawyers who do engage in public commentary – including an

40 Mario Prost and Alejandra Torres Camprubí, "Against Fairness? International Environmental Law, Disciplinary Bias, and Pareto Justice," *Leiden Journal of International Law* 25 (2012): 379, 381.

41 See Martii Koskenniemi, "Between Commitment and Cynicism," in *International Law as a Profession*, eds. Jean D'Aspremont, T. Gazzini, A. Nollkaemper and W. Werner (Cambridge: Cambridge University Press, 2017), 38.

42 Sarah Whatmore, "Geographies of/for a More Than Human World: Towards a Relational Ethics," in *Hybrid Geographies: Natures, Cultures, Spaces*, ed. Sarah Whatmore (London: Sage, 2002), 146; Christopher Stone, "Should Trees Have Standing? Towards Legal Rights for Natural Objects," *Southern California Law Review* 45 (1972): 450.

43 Mickelson, "South, North," 80.

44 Ibid.

45 Karin Mickelson, "Between Crisis and Complacency: Seeking Commitment in International Environmental Law," *Netherlands Yearbook of International Law* 44 (2013): 139.

46 Goodrich, "Relational Aesthetics."

47 Ibid., 341.

48 See generally Hilary Charlesworth, "Democracy," in *Concepts for International Law: Contributions to Disciplinary Thought*, eds. Jean d'Aspremont and Sahib Singh (Northampton: Edward Elgar Publishing, 2019), 164.

49 *Pulp Mills on the River Uruguay (Argentina v Uruguay) (Judgment)* [2010] ICJ Rep 14.

50 See Jutta Brunnée, "The United States and International Environmental Law: Living with an Elephant," *European Journal of International Law* 15, no. 4 (2004): 617.

international environmental lawyer.[51] But I think it would be true to say that most international environmental lawyers working in the field are ghost writers. The image of the international environmental lawyer is the object of their ventriloquism – a tree, a river, an island. This might be a problem if it means that their agenda – that barrow that they push, the cause that drives them to do what they do – is promoted with impunity. As advisors, though, they serve the advised, and it is possibly for the states and other participants that make and implement international environmental law on that advice to be held to account in a 'democratic' way of being together that can be found in international law.[52]

That goes to one of the ways in which international environmental law has improved on international law: scholars often point to the extent of non-state participation in the making of international environmental law, and the international environmental laws that facilitate non-state participation in environmental decision-making, as a democratic direction for international law.[53] Yet the sidelining of the state in international environmental law takes us back to the question of just how much 'law' there is in international environmental law if the main agent, the state, and the founding principle, sovereignty, is rendered increasingly irrelevant to its making and implementation. International environmental law's 'improvement' on international law is to undo it.

More than Goodrich's entreaty, it is the rise of the non-state that appears to be bringing international environmental lawyers out on the streets – not only are they visible, but they can be seen doing something not quite like international law. Farhana Yamin, one of the founders of Extinction Rebellion, is also an international environmental lawyer. For a long time, she has advised small island states in climate change negotiations.[54] Over many years, she has made a major investment in the formal institutions of international environmental law. Now she is also gluing herself to the offices of a major oil company and spruiking civil disobedience to spur policy action on climate change.[55]

International law absent states is, I suggest, the new image of international environmental law. It is an image made by or with international environmental lawyers,[56] but well supported by international environmental law itself: the Paris Agreement is in some respects the side event to the many networks of laws, policies and practices of sub-state and non-state actors addressing climate change.[57]

51 Gerry Simpson, "The Sentimental Life of International Law," *London Review of International Law* 2 (2014): 1.

52 See Farhana Yamin, "NGOs and International Environmental Law: A Critical Evaluation of Their Roles and Responsibilities," *Review of European, Comparative and International Environmental Law* 10, no. 2 (2001): 149, 159.

53 For example Kal Raustiala, "The Participatory Revolution in International Environmental Law," *Harvard Environmental Law Review* 21 (1997): 537; cf Daniel Bodansky, "The Legitimacy of International Governance: A Coming Challenge for International Environmental Law?" *The American Journal of International Law* 93, no. 3 (1999): 596, 619; see also Kishan Khoday and Usha Natarajan, "Fairness and International Environmental Law from Below: Social Movements and Legal Transformation in India," *Leiden Journal of International Law* 25, no. 2 (2012): 415.

54 See for example Keith Perry, "Lawyers Help Island Nations Keep Afloat," *The Guardian*, December 13, 2000, www.theguardian.com/uk/2000/dec/13/christmasappeal2000.keithperry.

55 BBC, *BBC News Night*, April 29, 2019, www.youtube.com/watch?v=xNg7SdRmhtI.

56 Andrew Anthony, "Farhana Yamin: 'It Took 20 Minutes to Unglue Me from Shell's Office. It Was a Bit Painful'," *The Guardian*, May 19, 2019, www.theguardian.com/environment/2019/may/19/farhana-yamin-extinction-rebellion-unglue-shell.

57 See for example Edith Brown Weiss, "Rule of Law for Nature in a Kaleidoscopic World," in *Rule of Law for Nature: New Dimensions and Ideas in Environmental Law*, ed. Christina Voigt (Cambridge: Cambridge University Press, 2013), 27; Khoday and Natarajan, "Fairness"; Jutta Brunnée, "International Environmental Law and Community Interests: Procedural Aspects," in *Community Obligations Across International Law*, eds. Eval Benvenisti and Georg Nolte (Oxford: Oxford University Press, 2018).

Absent artists

The concept of 'relational aesthetics' promoted by Goodrich for law is difficult to distil when it is removed from the context of the art practices that prompted the curatorial moniker.[58] In any event, art theory and practice has moved on to other ways of democratising aesthetics.[59] *Leaking Territories* was a form of social art practice – at least to the extent that it integrated the viewing public (Figure 7.4). We followed the performers around the space, we moved, or didn't (there is one in every crowd), when they walked or rolled towards us. At the end, they invited us to speak. I felt very unsure of what I was in that project. Alison Young described her participation in Spencer Tunick's *nudeadrift* as 'not a critical writing about art; instead, this is art as the writing of bodies, of my body'.[60] Lying naked on a rock in a public place surrounded by naked strangers while Tunick took photographs, Young was made very aware of the different acts of writing, making and being art.[61]

I've thought a lot about what Young felt, and I thought about it again when I participated in *Leaking Territories*. In my writing and teaching on international law, I discuss visual art and I also use the ways – I dare say methods – of understanding images that are taught in aesthetic philosophy.[62] But I am very conscious, in my engagement with the arts, that my 'expertise' is in law – international law – international environmental law. I do not view art as whimsy, an irreverent folly, or light relief from the constraints of international law. Art is serious and, as an international lawyer, I do not presume to know all there is to know of it. I rely on art experts. I think that when lawyers, including international lawyers, write about law and art, their understanding of law is informed by aesthetics but it remains a writing on law. Just as I would not view an artist's intervention on international law – *Leaking Territories*, say – a study in international law, I would not call my writing on international law and art a study in aesthetics.

This thinking about law and aesthetics might be problematic for my contributions to legal theory. I come dangerously close to wedding myself to the disciplinary boundaries that are collapsed by critical approaches.[63] I do not subscribe, though, to hard interfaces between disciplines. International law is undoubtedly a pluri-disciplinary construct of societies, cultures, economics and power that leak into one another. But to write of those constructs, through a lens of the arts, is not to assume the mantle of another discipline. It is to look through it. So it is for me true, then, that it is not inter-disciplinary research that I do when I do law and humanities. Not because there is no international law to speak of, as Goodrich might have it, but because there is so very much to say about international law. What I write is not necessarily what international lawyers would call international law. They might not see image as international law

58 Nicolas Bourriaud, *Relational Aesthetics*, trans. Simon Pleasance, Fronza Woods with the participation of Mathieu Copeland (France: Les presses du réel, 2002).

59 See Claire Bishop, "Antagonism and Relational Aesthetics," *October* 110 (Fall 2004): 51; Catherine de Zegher and Gerald McMaster, eds., *All Our Relations: 18th Biennale of Sydney* (Sydney: Biennale of Sydney, 2012); note also Mattin with Dania Burger, Dafni Krazoudi, Danai Liodaki, Smaragda Nitsopoulou, Ioannis Sarris and Eleni Zervou, *Social Dissonance* (Kassel: Durational Concert, Documenta Kassel, 2017).

60 Alison Young, *Judging the Image: Art, Value, Law* (New York: Routledge, 2005), 3.

61 Ibid., 1.

62 For example Alice Palmer, "Image and Art in the *Whaling in the Antarctic* Case," in *Research Handbook on Art and Law*, eds. Jani McCutcheon and Fiona McGaughey (Northampton: Edward Elgar, 2020), 408; Alice Palmer, "Legal Dimensions to Valuing Aesthetics in World Heritage Decisions," *Social & Legal Studies* 26, no. 5 (2017): 581.

63 Rajkovic, "Interdisciplinarity."

Figure 7.4 Alexandra Pirici, *Leaking Territories*, Friedenssaal in Historischen Rathaus Münster, Prinzipalmarkt 10, Skulptur-Projekte 2017. Photo Credit: LWL-Museum für Kunst und Kultur, Münster/Skulptur Projekte Archiv/Henning Rogge.

and, if they do, they might not see aesthetic theory as relevant to their understanding of those images in international law.

Whereas I say they are, and it is.

Absent image

Towards the end of *Leaking Territories*, the performers lined up in the centre of the hall. They were, they proclaimed, an 'algorithm', inviting the visitors to enter a term in a search field. They stood inert, with middle-distance stares, a figurative search engine. After a long and, for me, uncomfortable silence, I felt compelled to volunteer one. 'Abstraction', I said, with well-meaning pretention. The performers all turned, walked towards me, and looked me over, before offering improvised meanings for 'abstraction' tailored, they said, to my profile. They talked aesthetic theory like a Wikipedia page well might – what is, what is not, an abstract work of art. One 'pulled up' perfume – 'Abstraction' he said, with an advertiser's tone, 'a new brand of fragrance'. More off-script meanings and associations followed before the performers descended into cyber babble and left the room.

The performers' visual profiling of me had been a bit off. Their impromptu riff on 'abstraction' was impressive, it should be said. But no performer mentioned the abstraction I had in mind at the time: international environmental law. If I am an image of an international environmental

Figure 7.5 **'Stumps on the Valley Caused by Deforestation and Slash and Burn Type of Agriculture of Madagascar'. Photo Credit: Dudarev Mikhail/Shutterstock.com.**

lawyer, I wasn't seen as such, so no connection between my discipline and abstraction need be made. Yet every part of international environmental law is an abstraction. Crucially, it is the abstraction of its subject – the environment – that may well be its undoing.[64] The abstracted environment in international law is invariably one that is gone (Figure 7.5). Colours bleached, species extinct, riverbeds dry, land cleared. A plaque dedicated to the lost Okjökull glacier in Iceland marks absence as the point where 'we know what is happening and know what needs to be done'.[65] International law's agents warn that we risk living in an 'empty world'.[66] So again, it is an image of nothing that we are faced with when we think about international environmental law.

There was comfort for me though, in *Leaking Territories*. For as bleak as many of its images of 'law', the 'international' and the 'environment' were, I felt the art gave me something to work with. As Manderson observed: 'Images are representations that, at the same time that they are

64 Cf Andreas Philippopoulos-Mihalopoulos, *Absent Environments: Theorising Environmental Law and the City* (Abingdon: Routledge-Cavendish, 2007). See also Emily Brady, "The Ugly Truth: Negative Aesthetics and Environment," *Philosophy and Environment: Royal Institute of Philosophy Supplements* 69 (2012): 83.

65 Katrin Jakobsdottir, Prime Minister of Iceland, "Climate Change Is Melting Glaciers Worldwide. Only We Can Stop It," *The New York Times*, August 17, 2019, www.nytimes.com/2019/08/17/opinion/iceland-glacier-climate-change.html.

66 Patrick Greenfield, "Humans Risk Living in an Empty World, Warns UN Biodiversity Chief," *The Guardian*, January 20, 2020, www.theguardian.com/environment/2020/jan/20/humans-risk-living-in-an-empty-world-warns-un-biodiversity-chief-aoe.

unquestionably reminders of an absence – both the absence of the representing subject and of the represented object – are also unmistakeably present to viewers.'[67] *Leaking Territories* made an image of nothing something that I could feel, embody and imagine. I was left thinking that if I go to art, as opposed to legal judgments, to understand international law, I might well see things as they should be rather than how they are.

67 Manderson, *Danse Macabre*, 17.

8

Listening about law in the sonic arts

John Cage's *4'33"* and Lawrence Abu Hamdan's *Saydnaya (the missing 19dB)*

James E K Parker

Introduction

This chapter puts two artworks into conversation, with each other and with jurisprudence. The first is John Cage's *4'33"* (1952): the notorious 'silent piece', comprising – in the standard account – 4 minutes 33 seconds of nothing, Cage's most famous work, and one of the most important compositions of the twentieth century. An enormous amount has been written on it, and its influence, both in music and elsewhere, can hardly be overstated. Cage would have approved. When an interviewer once asked him if *4'33"* was in danger of being taken too seriously, he replied that he didn't think it could.[1] The history of Western music can be divided into the periods BC and AC, Yoko Ono remarked on the centenary of the composer's birth: before Cage and after.[2] Nowhere does the shadow of *4'33"* loom larger than in 'sound art', a growing field of art practice where the piece has become a ubiquitous, even – in an act of 'fabulous retroactivity'[3] – a founding reference.[4] Alan Licht calls Cage sound art's 'godfather'. 'Often when I've given a lecture,' he writes, 'I'll ask the audience to name a sound artist, and they usually say "John Cage", if they say anything at all.'[5] In this way of thinking, the 'event' of Cage in music was also sound art's birth. For anyone concerned about this degree of influence, however, the composer's name is tantalisingly suggestive. The sculptor Walter de Maria built a series of literal cages out of wood and steel according to the composer's exact body measurements.[6] They

1 William Duckworth, *Talking Music* (New York: Schirmer Books, 1995), 13–15.

2 Yoko Ono (@yokoono), September 5, 2012, https://twitter.com/yokoono/status/243304637669720064.

3 'Fabulous' since Cage always thought of himself as a composer and 'retroactive' since the term 'sound art' first appeared at the end of the 1970s and would not be used with any regularity until the late 1990s. Jacques Derrida, "Declarations of Independence," *New Political Science* 7, no. 1 (1986): 10.

4 Marcel Cobussen, Vincent Meelberg and Barry Truax, eds., *The Routledge Companion to Sounding Art* (New York: Routledge, 2017).

5 Alan Licht, *Sound Art Revisited* (London: Bloomsbury Publishing Inc, 2019), 7.

6 www.moma.org/collection/works/81149. See also Dieter Daniels and Inke Arns, *Sounds Like Silence: John Cage – 4'33" – Silence Today* (Leipzig: Spector, 2012), 24.

are tributes of a sort, a kind of visual analogue to *4'33"*: all structure, full of nothing. But the critique hardly needs spelling out. 'Cage as cage,' Christof Migone writes.[7] One of the things I want to do in this chapter is think through the limits of Cage's influential conceptions of sound and silence as epitomised in *4'33"*. This is worth doing in a book on international law and the humanities because, as Cage himself never tired of pointing out – indeed as *4'33"* set out to prove – there is no such thing as silence. For a famously 'silent' piece, *4'33"* is surprisingly loud. 'There is always something to see, something to hear,' Cage explained. 'Until I die there will be sounds. And they will continue following my death.'[8] The implications of this point are significant well beyond music and the sonic arts, as Cage certainly knew. Law and humanities scholarship is only now beginning to reckon with sound's ubiquity, and so its deep entanglement with legal practice and relations, both international and otherwise.[9] But it is important to be clear about what we mean by sound when we think law and sound together, and we should be wary of Cage's own account in this respect. As we will see, *4'33"* provides an ideal way into law-sound relations precisely because it seems, at first blush and in the stories most commonly told about it, to have so little to do with them. Despite and against Cage's own pronouncements, *4'33"* isn't just 'about' music, sound or silence, but law too.

This is not the first piece to remark on the jurisprudential significance of *4'33"*.[10] But it might be the first to approach Cage via the more critical accounts of his work in art history and practice. This possibility first occurred to me on encountering Lawrence Abu Hamdan's *Saydnaya (the missing 19dB)* (2016) in the context of an exhibition I curated with Joel Stern in 2018.[11] Abu Hamdan is a British-Lebanese artist currently based in Dubai. Not only is he one of the most celebrated 'sound artists' working today, and now a joint winner of the Turner Prize,[12] but also, I think, amongst the most original and important. The fact that virtually all of his work is also to do with law is a key part of the reason why. Unlike Cage, Abu Hamdan's work presents itself as already jurisprudential. It works with, on and against legal techniques and idioms; gathers, presents and interprets evidence; stages virtual trials; and makes explicit doctrinal claims; all with a view to intervening in political struggles in which questions of law are directly implicated. 'Forensic listening', he calls it.[13] Because of its subject matter and methodology, Abu Hamdan's work is always heavy, but *Saydnaya (the missing 19dB)* is crushingly so. It is one of several artworks[14] and a major report to have come out of a collaborative project between

7 Christof Migone, *Sonic Somatic: Performances of the Unsound Body* (Berlin: Errant Bodies Press, 2012), 7 ("Sonic Somatic").

8 John Cage, *Silence: Lectures and Writings* (Middletown: Wesleyan University Press, 2011), 8 ("*Silence*").

9 James E. K. Parker, *Acoustic Jurisprudence: Listening to the Trial of Simon Bikindi*, 1st ed. (Oxford: Oxford University Press, 2015) ("*Acoustic Jurisprudence*"). Recent collections include Danilo Mandic, ed., *HEAR* (forthcoming); James Parker, Sara Ramshaw and Mehera San Roque, *The Acoustics of Justice*, special issue of in *Law, Text, Culture* (2020).

10 James E. K. Parker, "The Soundscape of Justice," *Griffith Law Review* 20, no. 4 (2011): 962; Katherine Biber, "How Silent Is the Right to Silence?" *Cultural Studies Review* 18, no. 3 (2012); Sean Mulcahy, "Silence and Attunement in Legal Performance," *Canadian Journal of Law and Society / Revue Canadienne Droit et Société* 34, no. 2 (2019): 191; Marianne Constable, *Just Silences: The Limits and Possibilities of Modern Law* (New Jersey: Princeton University Press, 2005).

11 http://eavesdropping.exposed/; James Parker and Joel Stern, eds., *Eavesdropping: A Reader* (Wellington: City Gallery Wellington, 2019).

12 www.theguardian.com/artanddesign/2019/dec/03/turner-prize-2019-lawrence-abu-hamdan-helen-cammock-oscar-murillo-and-tai-shani-shared.

13 Lawrence Abu Hamdan, "Aural Contract – Forensic Listening and The Reorganization of The Speaking Subject," *Cesura//Acceso* 1 (2014): 200.

14 For instance, *Earwitness Inventory* (2018); *Walled Unwalled* (2018).

Amnesty International and Forensic Architecture, a research agency based at Goldsmiths, University of London.[15] The work concerns an acoustic investigation into Saydnaya Military Prison, 30 kilometres north of Damascus, Syria, where an estimated 13,000 people have been executed by the Assad regime since 2011. Because Saydnaya is inaccessible to independent monitors, the memories of the few survivors to have been released are the only way to learn of, document and condemn the violations taking place there. And since prisoners at Saydnaya are kept in tiny cells, in near total darkness, and at risk of death if they so much as make a sound, those memories are largely auditory. *Saydnaya (the missing 19dB)* is constructed largely of testimony about detainees' auditory experience and its analysis by the artist. We are very far from Cage here. Indeed, *Saydnaya (the missing 19dB)* can be understood precisely as a critique of the twin conceptions of sound and silence advanced by Cage and taken up by his inheritors, in jurisprudence as much as sound art. Abu Hamdan's concern, like that of the survivors whose testimony we hear, is clearly not for sounds 'themselves'. Instead, the work addresses the complex ways in which sound and silence are connected to techniques of domination, power and resistance, including especially by recourse to international law. This recourse, we will also see, is a risk.

4'33"

The impossible inaudible

There are at least three different scores for *4'33"*, and Cage composed many other 'silent' works. But the canonical version remains David Tudor's reproduction of the lost original manuscript, first performed by Tudor at a piano recital in Maverick Concert Hall, Woodstock, in 1952.[16] A performance comprises three movements totalling the 4 minutes 33 seconds of the piece's title, during which any number of instrumentalists on any instruments 'do not play'. The result is unexpectedly loud. The audience sits listening to itself listen (to the sounds of each other breathing, shuffling, coughing, sighing), to the peculiarities of the performance space (creaking floorboards, chairs and rafters, the hum of lighting or ventilation), along with any other sounds able to infiltrate the sanctity of the concert hall (rainfall on the roof, rumbling planes or machinery, buzzing insects and phones, someone talking in the hallway outside). The background becomes the foreground. Not so much silence as the realisation there is no such thing. 'The opposition between sound and silence is replaced with a gradient.'[17] *4'33"* doesn't just expand the field of music, it abolishes it in favour of spontaneous, ubiquitous sound: 'the impossible inaudible' as Douglas Kahn puts it.[18] 'If you want to know the truth of the matter', Cage once explained, 'the music I prefer, even to my own or anybody else's, is what we are hearing if we are just quiet'.[19] 'One may give up the desire to control sound, clear his mind of music and set about discovering means to let sounds be themselves rather than vehicles for man-made theories or expressions of human sentiments.'[20]

15 Amnesty International, *Human Slaughterhouse: Mass Hangings and Extermination at Saydnaya Prison, Syria* (2017) ("*Human Slaughterhouse*"), www.amnesty.org/en/documents/document/?indexNumber=mde24%2f5415%2f2017&language=en.

16 Daniels and Arns, *Sounds Like Silence*.

17 Douglas Kahn, *Noise, Water, Meat: A History of Sound in the Arts* (Cambridge, MA: MIT Press, 1999), 160 ("*Noise, Water, Meat*").

18 Ibid., 158.

19 Richard Kostelanetz, *Conversing with Cage* (Abingdon: Routledge, 2003), 12.

20 Cage, *Silence*, 10.

'Discovering means to let sounds be themselves.'[21] Brian Kane calls this sort of thing 'onto-aesthetics': art or discourse about art in which what is valued is the work's ability to explore or disclose its own ontology.[22] In this instance, the desire to reveal and revel in sound as it actually is. As Clement Greenberg put it in his famous 1960 essay championing modernist painting, a great influence on Cage,[23] 'what had to be exhibited and made explicit was that which was unique and irreducible not only in art in general but also in each particular art. Each art had to determine, through operations peculiar to itself, the effects peculiar and exclusive to itself'.[24] Thus, for Christoph Cox, *4'33"* is important because it points to and embodies music's necessary sonicity, because it 'explore[s] the *materiality* of sound',[25] and because it exposes and teaches us something about sound's nature as a 'ceaseless and intense flow' of vibrant matter that is 'actualised in, but not exhausted by, speech, music and significant sound of all sorts'.[26] Sound, thus, is an 'anonymous flux' that 'precedes and exceeds individual listeners and, indeed, composers, who Cage came to conceive less as *creators* than as *curators* of this sonic flux'.[27] *4'33"* exemplifies this curatorial relationship, Cox says, insofar as it 'simply provides a spatial frame' in which to allow sounds to be – and be appreciated for being – nothing but themselves.[28]

Sound leads elsewhere

As Kane points out, the 'critical thrust' of onto-aesthetics is to 'remove artworks from their cultural contexts (claims about hermeneutics, interpretation, meaning, intention, reception, and so forth) by suturing them to their ontological conditions'. The trouble is they can't, since 'every time some feature of an artwork is claimed to exemplify this or that ontology [is] a moment where the onto-aesthetician begs the cultural basis of such a claim'.[29] With *4'33"*, what's being begged and elided is all the work required to produce the 'spatial frame' Cox refers to. This act of framing is anything but 'simple'. It demands, at the very least: a composer, a score and so a 'work';[30] perhaps a conductor; a performer or performers along with their instruments; the staging of a performance; across three movements; in a soundproofed concert hall;[31] for money; before an audience (urbane, elite, often white) trained in the arts of concert-going, with all

21 Ibid.

22 Brian Kane, "Sound Studies without Auditory Culture: A Critique of the Ontological Turn," *Sound Studies* 1, no. 1 (2015): 2 ("Sound Studies without Auditory Culture").

23 Robert Rauschenberg's 'white paintings' from 1951 were a major influence on Cage. See Seth Kim-Cohen, *In the Blink of an Ear: Toward a Non-Cochlear Sonic Art* (London: A&C Black, 2009), 161–63 ("*In the Blink of an Ear*").

24 Clement Greenberg, *The Collected Essays and Criticism, Volume 4: Modernism with a Vengeance* (1957–1969), ed. John O'Brian (Chicago: University of Chicago Press, 1993), 86 ("*The Collected Essays and Criticism, Volume 4*").

25 Christoph Cox, "Beyond Representation and Signification: Toward a Sonic Materialism," in Margaret Schedel and Andrew V. Uroskie, eds., *Journal of Visual Culture* 10, no. 2 (2011): 145 ("Beyond Representation and Signification").

26 Christoph Cox, "Sound Art and the Sonic Unconscious," *Organised Sound* 14, no. 1 (2009): 19, 22.

27 Cox, "Beyond Representation and Signification," 155.

28 Ibid., 159.

29 Kane, "Sound Studies without Auditory Culture", 159.

30 Jacques Derrida, "Before the Law," in *Acts of Literature,* ed. Derek Attridge (Abingdon: Routledge, 1992).

31 Emily Ann Thompson, *The Soundscape of Modernity: Architectural Acoustics and the Culture of Listening in America, 1900–1933* (Cambridge, MA: MIT Press, 2002) ("*The Soundscape of Modernity*").

its norms – both explicit and implicit – of listenership and comportment,[32] and in particular the extremely recent convention of hushed attention; a certain knowledge of the musical tradition(s) into which Cage is intervening; in many cases, direct knowledge of the work itself, along with the powerful mythology surrounding it. All this and more is required to produce and sustain the 'frame' that will make the next few minutes comprehensible as having to do with sound 'itself', separate and alone.

For Brandon Joseph, therefore, *4'33"* is a 'pure technique of power'. Far from pointing us to sound's essence or materiality, it demonstrates the necessary entanglement of sound, music and listening with 'the operation of discipline or control'.[33] For Douglas Kahn, it is both about the impossibility of silence and itself an act of silencing in which Cage doesn't so much disappear as creator and master of his work as magnify his own presence and authority, extended now to include audience members and other institutional actors in addition to those on stage.[34] Just try whispering to your neighbour during a performance of *4'33"*. It's much harder to get away with than at a gig or the opera. What is at stake here is the distribution and quality of what Brandon LaBelle terms 'sonic agency'.[35] Moreover, once the door has been opened to what Seth Kim-Cohen, riffing on Marcel Duchamp, calls the 'non-cochlear dimensions' of the work, they quickly 'saturate' it.[36] 'The normally supplemental *parerga*', Kim-Cohen writes, borrowing Derrida's term, 'become central to the act of encounter'.[37] 'Contexts impose themselves: past experiences, future expectations, adjacent sounds, other works, institutional settings, curatorial framing. All these influences, and other *parerga* besides, are essential components of our experience of what we call "the work"'.[38] Even if they can't be 'heard'. In order to explore and appreciate these dimensions of the work, Kim-Cohen claims, indeed of any encounter with the sounding world, we must move beyond a concern for sound-in-itself, beyond vibration, beyond even the 'jurisdiction of the ear'[39] towards sound's necessary social-embeddedness; to 'disengage sound thinking . . . from its naturalistic rut'.[40] 'Sound leads elsewhere,' Kahn explains.[41] What he doesn't mention is that this elsewhere includes matters of law and justice. Jurisprudence has much to learn from art theory and history, but they might benefit from a dose of jurisprudence too.[42]

32 Christopher Small, *Musicking: The Meanings of Performing and Listening* (Middletown, CT: Wesleyan University Press, 2011) ("*Musicking*").

33 Branden Wayne Joseph, *Beyond the Dream Syndicate: Tony Conrad and the Arts After Cage (a 'Minor' History)* (New York: Zone Books, 2008), 188.

34 Kahn, *Noise, Water, Meat*, 161.

35 Brandon LaBelle, *Sonic Agency: Sound and Emergent Forms of Resistance* (London: Goldsmiths Press, 2018) ("*Sonic Agency*").

36 Seth Kim-Cohen, "Dams, Weirs, and Damn Weird Ears: Post-Ergonal Sound," in *The Routledge Companion to Sounding Art*, eds. Marcel Cobussen, Vincent Meelberg and Barry Truax (Abingdon: Routledge, 2016), 71, 54 ("Dams, Weirs, and Damn Weird Ears").

37 Jacques Derrida, *The Truth in Painting*, trans. G. Bennington and I. McLeod (Chicago: University of Chicago Press, 1987); Kim-Cohen, "Dams, Weirs, and Damn Weird Ears," 229.

38 Kim-Cohen, "Dams, Weirs, and Damn Weird Ears," 54.

39 Seth Kim-Cohen, *Against Ambience* (London: Bloomsbury Publishing USA, 2013), 73.

40 Michel Chion, *Audio-Vision: Sound on Screen* (New York: Columbia University Press, 1994), 94 ("*Audio-Vision*").

41 Douglas Kahn, "Sound Leads Elsewhere," in *The Routledge Companion to Sounding Art* (Abingdon: Routledge, 2016), 61.

42 Desmond Manderson, *Danse Macabre: Temporalities of Law in the Visual Arts* (Cambridge: Cambridge University Press, 2019) ("*Danse Macabre*").

Listening jurisprudentially

Law is everywhere in *4'33"*, provided you listen out for it. Law is one of the piece's 'other *parerga*', to return to Kim-Cohen's phrase. To begin with, every one of the 'incidental sounds'[43] framed and celebrated by *4'33"* emerges from and into legal worlds, which is another way of saying they're not so incidental. The performance has its conditions of entry, the tickets their contractual terms. Both the composition 'itself' and every version of the score is subject to intellectual property laws, as are any recordings made, official or otherwise, along with the recording formats on which they are made.[44] This matters because these are the parameters according to which the work circulates and its fame and influence accrues. Indeed, they are partly what makes *4'33"* legible *as* a work in the first place, and makes it so fertile when it comes to interrogating the idea of the 'work' itself.[45] Moreover, the concert hall wasn't just built that way. The very features which most affect its acoustic properties – how this performance venue 'sounds': its size and shape, the nature and degree of soundproofing – were all subject to regulations or a sad lack of them.[46] Likewise, the rumbling planes and buzzing phones. Not even the rain on the roof is innocent of law in the age of the Anthropocene, itself partly a function of centuries of legal thought and practice. And as for all the quiet breathing and muffled coughs, if that's all it amounts to, they are the product of a powerful normativity that Brandon Joseph may figure in terms of 'discipline or control' but any good legal pluralist will tell you is also fundamentally a matter of law.[47] We could be even more explicit. Depending, as ever, on the jurisdiction, there are any number of things you could do, say or sing to breach the peace/piece, many of which would get you thrown out or arrested. The fact that you don't is evidence of law's presence as much as its absence. The concert hall is always also a 'lawscape'.[48] Law too is ubiquitous: always speaking, always there in the 'background', all the more potent *because* of its backgrounding, in fact.[49]

Duncan Kennedy once wrote that law school is a training in the reproduction of hierarchy.[50] So is the concert.[51] Or, the concert is also a law school. It too is an institution where relations of authority and faculties of judgment are cultivated and shaped. Contra Cage, one of *4'33"*'s central lessons is this: silence isn't a condition of soundlessness but a powerful institutional effect. This is just as true outside of concert settings as in them. In courtrooms, legislatures and prisons too, silence is the name we give to the attitude of deference, respect or fear reserved for those authorised to govern the soundscape. There is a direct connection between the baton

43 See Cage's thoughts on indeterminacy in general, and for instance at Cage, *Silence*, 260.

44 Jonathan Sterne, *MP3: The Meaning of a Format* (Durham, NC: Duke University Press, 2012) ("*MP3*").

45 Derrida, "Before the Law"; Dennis Kurzon, "Peters Edition v. Batt: The Intertextuality of Silence," *International Journal for the Semiotics of Law – Revue internationale de Sémiotique juridique* 20, no. 4 (2007): 285 ("Peters Edition v. Batt").

46 Thompson, *The Soundscape of Modernity*.

47 Martha-Marie Kleinhans and Roderick A. Macdonald, "What Is a Critical Legal Pluralism?" *Canadian Journal of Law & Society/La Revue Canadienne Droit et Société* 12, no. 2 (1997): 25; Margaret Davies, *Law Unlimited* (New York: Routledge, 2017).

48 Andreas Philippopoulos-Mihalopoulos, *Spatial Justice: Body, Lawscape, Atmosphere* (Abingdon: Routledge, 2014) ("*Spatial Justice*").

49 Illan Wall, "The Ordinary Affects of Law," *Law, Culture and the Humanities* (2019): online, print forthcoming.

50 Duncan Kennedy, *Legal Education as Training for Hierarchy* (London: Pluto Press, 1992).

51 Small, *Musicking*.

and the gavel, as between the conductor, prison guard, legislator and judge.[52] The modes of sanction and enforcement may be different, but the institutional dynamics are largely the same. The concert is just one of many institutions, in fact, that both depend on and entrench an association between silence and civility, noise and disorder, that has a long pedigree in legal and political thought, in the West and elsewhere.[53] *4'33"* sits right on the cusp of these associations. On one level, the work is clearly noisy: dis-ordering. On the piece's first New York City performance in 1954, the publisher Helen Wolff wrote the composer to decry it as 'a schoolboy's prank', advising him not to 'cheapen' his work with a 'trick' intended merely 'to shock and bewilder people'.[54] Cage's response was to insist on the work's value, despite the controversy it was bound to provoke.[55] 'Art, if you want a definition of it, is criminal action,' he wrote years later. 'It conforms to no rules. Not even its own.'[56] But *4'33"* is also a celebration and aestheticisation of noise, a welcoming of noise into the musical fold: not so much a disturbance of the status quo, therefore, as a re-ordering of it. By making noise continuous with silence, it is tamed. Far from undoing the association between silence and civility, *4'33"* doubles down on it.

This association is a major feature of law's sonic imagination and acoustic life;[57] that much is clear. But it also points to the profound 'sonicity' of legal imaginations more generally, which is not quite the same thing. Legal institutions often think *with* sound, even (or especially) when they're not thinking *about* it. For Hillel Schwarz, the history of noise in the West is a history of its becoming a 'root metaphor about our world, our lives, and the meaning of our lives abroad in the world'.[58] We could say the same of silence and its analogues. Consider the United Nations Conference on International Organization, brought to order with three strikes of a gavel on 25 April 1945.[59] Exactly two months later, the Charter of the United Nations was unanimously adopted in an opera house to rapturous applause. Its express purpose and constant refrain is international peace through law. Etymologically, the English 'peace' and the French '*paix*' (French being another working language of the UN) share a common origin in the Latin '*pax/pacem*'. From there, the connotations of silence, order and the end or absence of war arrived together,

52 James E. K. Parker, "The Gavel," in *International Law's Objects*, eds. Jessie Hohmann and Daniel Joyce (Oxford: Oxford University Press, 2018); Carolyn McKay, *The Pixelated Prisoner: Prison Video Links, Court 'Appearance' and the Justice Matrix* (London: Routledge, 2018) ("*The Pixelated Prisoner*").

53 John Picker, "The Soundproof Study," in *The Sound Studies Reader*, ed. Jonathan Sterne (Abingdon: Routledge, 2012); Jacques Attali, *Noise: The Political Economy of Music*, trans. Brian Massumi (Minneapolis: University of Minnesota Press, 1985) (translated from of: *Bruits: Essai sur l'économie politique de la musique* (first published 1977)). For a legal example, see *In Re Dakin* (1887) 13 *Victorian Law Reports* 522 in which Dakin was found in contempt of court for refusing to stop the construction of a notice board in a yard adjoining the Supreme Court of Victoria, which was causing a lot of noise and disturbing proceedings inside.

54 Daniels and Arns, *Sounds Like Silence*, 20.

55 Ibid., 21–22.

56 John Cage, "Diary: Audience 1966," in *A Year from Monday: New Lectures and Writings* (Middletown, CT: Wesleyan University Press, 1967).

57 Jonathan Sterne, *The Sound Studies Reader* (Oxford: Routledge, 2012), 5–7; James E. K. Parker, "Towards an Acoustic Jurisprudence: Law and the Long Range Acoustic Device," *Law, Culture and the Humanities* 14, no. 2 (2018) ("Towards an Acoustic Jurisprudence").

58 Hillel Schwartz, *Making Noise: From Babel to the Big Bang & Beyond* (New York: Zone Books, 2011), 21 ("*Making Noise*").

59 United Nations, "United Nations Conference on International Organization" (1945), https://research.un.org/c.php?g=209174&p=1426445, at 0:57.

complete with legal overtones.[60] Peace wasn't a situation you found yourself in – some state of nature – but precisely a legal achievement: a 'pact'.[61] Hence the Peace of Westphalia, which ended the Thirty Years War: then the loudest war in history. Not only could its field cannons be heard as far as 20 miles away, it also provided the first documented instances of what would later be known as 'shellshock'.[62] The Peace of Westphalia didn't just bring all this to a close. In the common origin myth, it birthed the nation-state and modern system of international law in doing so.[63] The logic cuts both ways. It was Cicero who famously claimed '*silent enim lēgēs inter arma*'. In *Perpetual Peace*, Kant's major work of international law, he translates: 'all laws are silent in the time of war'.[64] For Cicero this was an argument for self-defence. For the US, in the wake of 9/11, a justification for the state of exception.[65] For Kant, as for the UN, along with many of the world's most influential international lawyers, it is an injunction.[66] In this way of thinking, it's not that law *is* always speaking. It *must*. Without law, war. Without war, peace. The silencing of arms depends on the unsilencing of law. Peace too will be an institutional effect.[67]

Sound is never just itself. Neither is law. The positivism and poverty of Cage's own account of *4'33"*, whereby what the work points to and celebrates is a kind of bare sonicity, maps perfectly onto positivist accounts of law. There too legality is imagined as hermetic, nothing but itself, and to be celebrated as such. But law also leads elsewhere, and for very similar reasons. Indeed, this is the premise and wager of all work in law and humanities.[68] For Kim-Cohen, the 'non' in 'non-cochlear' accounts of sound and listening is 'not a negation, not an erasure, not, as Derrida puts it, "absence, negativity, non-Being, lack" . . . [rather] the non-cochlear and the cochlear "pass into one another indefinitely".'[69] The same is true of law. Just as listening must be non-cochlear, jurisprudence must be non-lexical, and an acoustic jurisprudence must be both. To listen to a work like *4'33"* jurisprudentially – as if it opens out to law – is also to think law sonically – as if *4'33"* were already doing jurisprudential work.

Lawrence Abu Hamdan's work is very explicit about this. At least since 2010, his projects have consistently worked with and on a range of testimonial practices, doctrinal categories and forensic methods on which legal institutions often like to claim a monopoly. Indeed, if Cage identified the artist with the criminal – the rule breaker – Abu Hamdan has more in common with the criminal investigator. The crimes in question are typically those of the state.

60 'peace, n.'. OED Online (September 2019), Oxford University Press, accessed October 13, 2019, https://www-oed-com.ezp.lib.unimelb.edu.au/view/Entry/139215?rskey=WAOjpk&result=1.

61 'pact, n'. OED Online (March 2005), Oxford University Press, accessed January 24, 2020, https://www-oed-com.ezp.lib.unimelb.edu.au/view/Entry/135873?rskey=nfo2Q5&result=1#eid.

62 Schwartz, *Making Noise*, 65–66.

63 Sundhya Pahuja, *Decolonising International Law: Development, Economic Growth and the Politics of Universality* (Cambridge: Cambridge University Press, 2011), 111 ("*Decolonising International Law*").

64 Patrick Capps, "The Kantian Project in Modern International Legal Theory," *European Journal of International Law* 12, no. 5 (2001): 1003. NB the German word for peace '*freiden*' [confirm] has the same sonic connotations.

65 Argument of the state in *Hamdi v Rumsfeld* 124 S. Ct. 2633 (2004).

66 See, for instance, Grenville Clark and Louis B. Sohn, *World Peace Through World Law* (Cambridge: Harvard University Press, 1958, 1960, 1966); Hans Kelsen, *Peace Through Law* (Clark, NJ: The Lawbook Exchange Ltd, 2008).

67 Both the International Court of Justice and the Permanent Court of Arbitration, remember, are housed at the Peace Palace in The Hague.

68 This is close to Goodrich's point in Peter Goodrich, "Europe in America: Grammatology, Legal Studies, and the Politics of Transmission," *Columbia Law Review* 101, no. 8 (2001): 2033, 2035.

69 Kim-Cohen, *In the Blink of an Ear*, xxii.

Saydnaya (the missing 19dB)

Violence at the threshold of audibility

You are sitting in a room.[70] Not a concert hall this time, a gallery. The room is dark and empty but for the mixing desk on the floor in front of you and the black speakers mounted beside it. Suddenly, an ear-splitting tone jolts you to attention. One of the faders on the desk moves up, as if by some phantom hand. The artist's voice: 'Boeing 737 aircraft at one nautical mile before landing.' Another tone, not quite so loud, but still uncomfortable, and the fader moves down a notch: '149 glass bottles crash into the back of a garbage disposal truck.' Down again: 'A freight train passes through Utrecht train station.' On and on, quieter and quieter, precisely, methodically: [–] a conversation in a Manchester restaurant; [–] canned music in the lobby of a three-star hotel; [–] frogs croaking throughout the Amazon rainforest in 2010; [–] the few surviving species in 2017; [–] the deathly still of the Chernobyl exclusion zone. Until finally, quietest of all, barely discernible: [–] 'Saydnaya, the Syrian regime prison thirty kilometres north of Damascus' where more than 13,000 people have been executed by representatives of the Syrian state since 2011.[71] 'In Saydnaya, silence is the master,' one survivor explains, their original Arabic still audible beneath the hushed English of the interpreter. 'You can't raise your voice. You can only whisper. And silence is what allows you to hear everything.'

These are the opening minutes of *Saydnaya (the missing 19dB)*, which debuted at the 13th Sharjah Biennial. Already the work is in dialogue with Cage. Here too, the relationship between sound and silence is a gradient. But notice that this gradient is precise and measurable now: scientific; a matter of degrees. It is also overtly political. Each tone indexes an event with a name and a cause or perpetrator, and as the volume diminishes so the violence intensifies until, finally, we arrive at Saydnaya, where the silence is simultaneously a form of domination and of great forensic potential. This dialectic is at the work's heart. As it unfolds, we hear survivor after survivor testify about the ferocious silencing to which they were subjected. This is not the silence of solitary confinement: silence as a function of isolation, as a form of sensory deprivation, or – in an older way of thinking – as a method of 'inspiring' communion with God.[72] At Saydnaya, the silence is collective and brutally enforced. Indeed, it is 'part of the brutality'.[73]

> Once in the cell across from ours the guards heard the voice of a man whispering. We heard them say, "who made the sound? Come forward or I will kill you all." One of the detainees confessed and the guard said, "I'm going to take you to the angel of death." All we could hear were hits landing on his body from a distance without a single cry of pain. The hits were so brutal. Eventually it stopped. We heard him say, "I emptied out a spot for you so you can get more comfortable in there. I took your friend to the angel of death. Whoever wants to join him I'll send you over there too."

70 Alvin Lucier, "I am Sitting in a Room" (1981). See also Joel Stern, "I am Sitting in a Courtroom" (2017), www.youtube.com/watch?v=XoSrykqa4So&list=PLrN3t2eBJmgtAr_owiL5hdhG_fwEncQeb&index=3.

71 Amnesty, *Human Slaughterhouse*, 17.

72 John Frow, "In the Penal Colony," *Australian Humanities Review* 13 (1999), discussing the silent 'Separate Prison' at Port Arthur, in what is now known as Tasmania. The prison was built in 1848–1849, based on principles derived from Jeremy Bentham's famous writings on the panopticon.

73 Lawrence Abu Hamdan, "Saydnaya (the Missing 19db)," in *Eavesdropping: A Reader*, eds. James Parker and Joel Stern (Wellington: City Gallery Wellington, 2019), 49.

Or again:

> You'd be there in total silence for 2 hours and then all of a sudden you hear "vvrrruuu", the shaft opens, and the beatings begin. You hear the beatings, but you don't hear the voices of those being beaten. To scream while you're being beaten is forbidden. In other prisons the guards wouldn't leave the prisoner alone until he screams, but Saydnaya is totally opposite. If you scream the beatings would intensify. So, we could always know if there were new arrivals to the prison if you hear their screams of pain.

Clearly, the beatings are not the only acts of violence here, or even necessarily the 'worst'. The silence remembered by survivors as such a defining feature of their imprisonment is not just 'testimony to the uninhabitable condition of Saydnaya's overcrowded cells', Abu Hamdan claims, but 'a form of torture in and of itself'.

This is an express doctrinal claim now. In context, it is utterly convincing. To begin with, there is something particularly horrific about a form of devoicing so extreme that it denies a person the expression of their own pain. The fact that this silencing also forces detainees to produce the (auditory) conditions of their own and each other's suffering surely involves a certain violence of its own: a terrible complicity. In an essay accompanying the work, Abu Hamdan likens the silence inflicted at Saydnaya to the 'stress positions' used so famously by the US at Guantanamo and other black sites, and the subject of ceaseless lawfare before and since. 'The order of silence restricts prisoners' physical movements and suppresses their respiratory functions', he writes, 'forcing them to remain still, not stretching their muscles for fear of making a sound', since to do so was to risk death. 'When I came out of Saydnaya', one survivor explains, 'I used to speak like someone with a twisted tongue. After whispering so long, my tongue wasn't used to speaking loudly. Speech was very difficult for me.' Even as Saydnaya's deathly silence mutes the body, it intensifies listening. In jurisprudence and the sonic arts, this kind of 'attunement' or 'deep listening' is typically celebrated.[74] At Saydnaya it is part of the horror, an excruciating form of hyper-attention whereby even the quietest sound can be petrifying. Under such conditions, 'detainees develop an acute sensitivity to sound', Abu Hamdan tells us. 'The constant fear of an impending attack makes every footstep sound like a car crash.' Such is the effect of a psychosomatic imprisonment no longer defined by bars and walls but by the institution of silence itself.

Considering how readily this silencing is understood as torture in the gallery, it is worth knowing how controversial it would seem to most international lawyers. There is very little relevant precedent on torture's acoustic dimensions, and the little there is has concerned the deliberate bombardment of detainees with 'loud music' and 'noise'. Though there is authority that such practices may rise to the level of torture, or at least cruel, inhuman or degrading treatment, even here the legality question is complex.[75] And the most recent version of the UN Standard Minimum Rules for the Treatment or Prisoners (the so-called Mandela Rules) contains provisions addressing everything from natural light to food, sanitation, exercise, clothing

74 Pauline Oliveros, *Deep Listening: A Composer's Sound Practice* (New York: IUniverse, 2005) ("*Deep Listening*"); Sara Ramshaw, *Justice as Improvisation : The Law of the Extempore* (New York: Routledge, 2013), 89 ("*Justice as Improvisation*"); Mulcahy, "Silence and Attunement in Legal Performance"; Richard Dawson, *Justice as Attunement: Transforming Constitutions in Law, Literature, Economics and the Rest of Life* (Abingdon: Routledge, 2014).

75 James E. K. Parker, "Sonic Lawfare: On the Jurisprudence of Weaponised Sound," *Sound Studies* 1 (2019) ("Sonic Lawfare").

and bedding, but nothing on acoustic conditions at all.[76] So it matters that *Saydnaya (the missing 19dB)* makes the claim so straightforwardly, without working through the doctrinal niceties. There is a moral clarity to it. In fact, this is how the language of international law is often invoked, especially by NGOs like Amnesty. The allegation of illegality isn't made because the claim already *is* uncontroversial, but in order to make it so: description as prescription. *Saydnaya (the missing 19dB)* deploys the gallery in the service of a normative world to come. Contemporary art as law's avant-garde.

Forensic listening

'Let's all be quiet for a minute. Turn that off.' The room hushes. You shift uncomfortably as your mind turns to the profound difference between the 'silence' you are experiencing, one of several in the work, and the silence being recalled. 'This is how quiet it was in our cell.' Another long pause, as the *parerga* rush in. For the artist and composer George Brecht, a student of Cage's, the key intervention of *4'33"* and other compositions like it was to substitute the virtuoso composer and performer for a 'virtuoso listener'.[77] This is not a bad description of the prisoners at Saydnaya, or indeed of many forced to live through war and conflict.[78] 'My hearing is now a third of what it used to be since I was in Saydnaya,' one survivor tells us. 'I don't rely on it as much now.' For Abu Hamdan, this former acuity is an opportunity. It isn't just a matter of translating survivors' aural memories into oral testimony, as we have seen. *Saydnaya (the missing 19dB)* also makes a bold forensic claim concerning the missing 19dB of the work's title.

'I despise anyone who says that art is about asking questions and not providing answers,' Abu Hamdan explained in a 2018 interview, the year after *Saydnaya (the missing 19dB)* debuted at the 13th Sharjah Biennial. 'You hear that pretty much every day in our profession. Artists who repeat this statement think of this as a radical act. But what if art's radicality is actually about art being an engine for truth production?'[79] Notice that the concern here is not for truth's representation, as in neo-classicism,[80] or its revelation, as in modernist onto-aesthetics, but rather its 'production', which is to say something altogether more contingent and material. In law the word is forensics, though as Eyal Weizman points out, it has not always been law's exclusive property. *Forensis*, he writes, 'is Latin for "pertaining to the forum" and is the origin of the term forensics'.

> The Roman forum to which forensics pertained was a multidimensional space of politics, law, and economy, but the word has since undergone a strong linguistic drift: the forum gradually came to refer exclusively to the court of law, and forensics to the use of medicine and science within it. This telescoping of the term meant that a critical dimension of the

76 UN General Assembly Resolution, United Nations Standard Minimum Rules for the Treatment of Prisoners (the Nelson Mandela Rules), A/RES/70/175 (December 17, 2015).

77 Branden W. Joseph, "Chance, Indeterminacy, Multiplicity," in *Experimentations: John Cage in Music, Art, and Architecture* (London: Bloomsbury Academic, 2016), 27, 237.

78 J. Martin Daughtry, *Listening to War: Sound, Music, Trauma, and Survival in Wartime Iraq* (Oxford: Oxford University Press, 2015) ("*Listening to War*").

79 Mohammad Salemy, "Lawrence Abu Hamdan in Conversation," Interview with Lawrence Abu Hamdan, April 6, 2018, https://ocula.com/magazine/conversations/lawrence-abu-hamdan/.

80 Desmond Manderson, "Diachronic Justice," in *Danse Macabre: Temporalities of Law in the Visual Arts*, ed. Desmond Manderson (Cambridge: Cambridge University Press, 2019), 53.

> practice of forensics was lost in the process of its modernization – namely its potential as a political practice.[81]

It is this political potential that Abu Hamdan is interested in unlocking and exploring. 'Forensic listening' is thus both an appropriation and an expansion of the techniques developed, particularly since the 1980s, by scientists with, for and around legal institutions.[82] Abu Hamdan has been very clear, for instance, about the importance of Peter French's work to his thinking. French is a founding member and the current president of the International Association for Forensic Phonetics and Acoustics as well as one of the field's most experienced expert witnesses, having testified in and authored reports for courts all round the world, including at the trial of Slobadan Milošević. Abu Hamdan first interviewed him in 2010 for his radiophonic work *The Freedom of Speech Itself* (2012), and it is French at least as much as any artist or theorist that Abu Hamdan cites as an influence because of his meticulous concern for sonic materials and how they can be made to speak (*prosopopoeia*[83]) of the social worlds from which they emerge.[84] Forensic listening's material orientation is not out of concern for sounds 'themselves', therefore, but rather what Weizman terms the 'politics in matter'.[85]

From the silence, whispers. Then a low tone, which we recall from the work's start. It is clean sounding; clinical; probably a single sine wave, without harmonics. Abu Hamdan explains,

> I asked each of the survivors to listen to the sound of a test tone, and to match the volume of the tone with the level at which they could whisper to one another in their cells. A barely audible tone of whisper was consistent amongst Samad, Samer and Jamal, but Diab's whisper was 19 decibels greater, the equivalent of being four times louder than the rest.

19 decibels, Abu Hamdan continues, 'is the difference between a jack hammer carving up a pavement and a dishwasher rinsing food off a plate'. And Diab's whisper was 19 decibels louder than the rest, he posits, 'because he was released in 2011 when all the inmates of Saydnaya were freed in order to use the prison exclusively for the political protesters that were starting a revolution across the country'. The tone becomes audible again and quickly grows louder: urgent sounding. 'As a response to these protests, a new era of extreme violence and terror took hold at Saydnaya.' The tone cuts out at its peak. 'A mass murder that can be measured in whispers.'

The claim probably wouldn't hold up in court. All the more reason to make it in a gallery. *Saydnaya (the missing 19dB)* doesn't just displace forensic listening; it takes full advantage of the additional latitude granted by art as a jurisdiction. The argument is not, of course, that the level at which prisoners could safely whisper 'actually' fell by 19dB after 2011. The point is simply to 'give scale' to the difference and so make it 'serviceable', and in public.[86] The measure is

81 Eyal Weizman, *Forensis: The Architecture of Public Truth* (Berlin: Sternberg Press, 2014), 9 ("*Forensis*").

82 Abu Hamdan, "Aural Contract – Forensic Listening."

83 Thomas Keenan, "Getting the Dead to Tell Me What Happened: Justice, Prosopopoeia, and Forensic Afterlives," *Kronos* 44, no. 1 (2018): 21; Susan Schuppli, *Material Witness: Media, Forensics, Evidence* (Cambridge: The Massachusetts Institute of Technology Press, 2020).

84 Lawrence Abu Hamdan, *Aural Contract: Investigations at the Threshold of Audibility* (London: Goldsmiths, 2017), 38.

85 Eyal Weizman, *Hollow Land: Israel's Architecture of Occupation* (London: Verso Books, 2012), 144–46 ("*Hollow Land*").

86 Lawrence Abu Hamdan, "Saydnaya (the Missing 19db)," in *Eavesdropping: A Reader*, eds. James Parker and Joel Stern (Wellington: City Gallery Wellington, 2019), 53; Sheila Jasanoff, "Serviceable Truths: Science for Action in Law and Policy," *Texas Law Review* 93 (2015): 29.

of a psychoacoustic experience and its commitment to memory under conditions of extreme trauma, not sound levels *per se*. So, it isn't only the methods of forensic listening that Abu Hamdan is appropriating and expanding here, but the decibel itself, which now indexes degrees of sonic agency and perceived risk as opposed or in addition to amplitude. The work succeeds to the extent it can make this way of accounting for the violence at Saydnaya seem probative: not simply 'in the absence of other material evidence',[87] but because it captures something 'truer' than conventional legal fora would likely allow.[88]

Critical counter-listening?

Saydnaya (the missing 19dB) works with and on forensics then, just as it does the law of torture. In doing so, it shows up both the poverty and the luxury of Cagean silence, with its putative separation of sound and the social. Silencing emerges instead as a brutal expression of state authority: the gruesome intensification of a dynamic familiar to the world's courtrooms, concert halls and beyond. In this, the work is extremely potent. Like *4'33"*, *Saydnaya (the missing 19dB)* lingers with you. Like *4'33"*, many will 'hear the world differently' because of it:[89] a world in which sound and silence can be weaponised, and in which law and listening are possible modes of resistance. It's on this latter point that I want to finish, because the appeal to law as an idiom of critique or medium for politics is never without its risks. And international law – the norms and institutions of international human rights law, international criminal law and international humanitarian law in particular, since these are the fields in which state torture and killing most obviously register – provides the never-quite-articulated reserve from which *Saydnaya (the missing 19dB)* draws much of its rhetorical and emotional power. The work doesn't just borrow legal techniques and vocabulary, but also international law's symbolic capital, secular virtue and the promise of a cudgel.[90]

As lawyers, activists and scholars of many different stripes have pointed out, however, international law is part of the problem as much as the solution: not just in relation to Syria, and not just when things 'go wrong'.[91] This is true in all sorts of ways, but we could begin with international law's dubious legitimacy. From Westphalia on, the whole edifice of international law is not only rooted in colonialism and its 'civilising mission' but continues it,[92] often by means of a humanitarianism that is increasingly carceral and bellicose as well as 'excessively universalistic and centralised'.[93] Not just that. This 'muscular humanitarianism'[94] tends to occupy

87 Abu Hamdan, "Saydnaya (the Missing 19db)," 54.

88 Eyal Weizman, "Open Verification – e-Flux Architecture – e-Flux," www.e-flux.com/architecture/becoming-digital/248062/open-verification/.

89 Kahn, *Noise, Water, Meat*, 158.

90 Julie Stone Peters, "Law, Literature, and the Vanishing Real: On the Future of an Interdisciplinary Illusion," *PMLA* 120, no. 2 (2005): 442 ("Law, Literature, and the Vanishing Real").

91 Martti Koskenniemi, *From Apology to Utopia: The Structure of International Legal Argument* (Cambridge: Cambridge University Press, 2006) ("*From Apology to Utopia*").

92 Antony Anghie, *Imperialism, Sovereignty and the Making of International Law* (Cambridge: Cambridge University Press, 2005).

93 Frédéric Mégret, "International Criminal Justice: A Critical Research Agenda," in *Critical Approaches to International Criminal Law: An Introduction*, ed. Christine Schwöbel (Abingdon: Routledge, 2014), 17, 30 ("International Criminal Justice").

94 Anne Orford, "Muscular Humanitarianism: Reading the Narratives of the New Interventionism," *European Journal of International Law* 10, no. 4 (1999): 679 ("Muscular Humanitarianism").

'the imaginative space of emancipation' and 'crowd out other ways of understanding harm and recompense'.[95] It can mire political challenges in opaque – indeed fundamentally indeterminate – doctrine, procedure and endless lawfare, funnelling precious resources to lawyers, bureaucrats and other professionals in the Global North all the while.[96] Both international criminal law and international humanitarian law force complex social and historical forces through the myopic lens of criminal accountability and, in doing so, struggle to account both for the structural causes of atrocity and the complicity of the very international community in whose name jurisdiction is asserted.[97] Meanwhile, international human rights law not only 'expresses the ideology, ethics, aesthetic sensibility and political practice of a particular Western Eighteenth-through Twentieth-Century liberalism',[98] but sits all too comfortably with the logics and institutions of contemporary neoliberalism.[99]

The critiques are far too many to repeat, and clearly it is beyond a single artwork to bear them. Nevertheless, to the extent that *Saydnaya (the missing 19dB)* appeals to or draws on the promise of international law, they cannot be ignored. Politics never 'runs clean' of course.[100] Neither does law; nor art. And in other works, Abu Hamdan has turned the methods of forensic listening expressly back on the legal institutions that ordinarily deploy them. For Weizman, law – like forensics – is a *pharmakon*, 'both a cure and a poison', so that the question is not whether to invoke it but how, when and why: a question, in other words, of tactics.[101] There is more to this question than the politics or justice of the cause, which in the case of *Saydnaya (the missing 19dB)* are hard to dispute. A robust 'counter-forensics' would also find ways not to reinforce or celebrate international law, and especially its more insidious dimensions, in the process.[102] The challenge for anyone attempting to critically appropriate law's methods, as Ben Golder argues, is to 'pervert and "performatively undermine"' them in the very process of their employment.[103] 'To employ law as a tactic', he writes, drawing on Foucault,

> is to approach it not as a substantive ideal or a normative system binding on all, but rather as an assemblage of power-knowledge available for appropriation by various social actors that can be, and is, put to varying uses. An instrumental deployment of law (or any other assemblage) is a kind of insubordinate, disobedient, and potentially subversive deployment that plays the game in a way that does not respect the stated purpose of the game and hence troubles and possibly undermines it.[104]

We have already seen how *Saydnaya (the missing 19dB)* works with doctrine and evidence in ways that are both novel and persuasive. The fact that these might struggle to hold up in court is not a failing but a critique: of the paucity of law's sonic imagination, on the one hand, and the

95 David Kennedy, "The International Human Rights Movement: Part of the Problem?" *Harvard Human Rights Journal* 15 (2002): 101, 108 ("The International Human Rights Movement").
96 David Kennedy, *Of War and Law* (Princeton, NJ: Princeton University Press, 2009).
97 Mégret, "International Criminal Justice."
98 Kennedy, "The International Human Rights Movement," 114.
99 Jessica Whyte, "Human Rights and the Collateral Damage of Neoliberalism," *Theory & Event* 20, no. 1 (2017).
100 Gayatri Chakravorty Spivak, *A Critique of Postcolonial Reason* (Cambridge, MA: Harvard University Press, 1999).
101 Eyal Weizman, *Forensic Architecture: Violence at the Threshold of Detectability* (Cambridge, MA: The MIT Press, 2017), 71 ("*Forensic Architecture*").
102 Thomas Keenan, "Counter-Forensics and Photography," *Grey Room* 55 (2014): 58.
103 Ben Golder, *Foucault and the Politics of Rights* (Stanford, CA: Stanford University Press, 2015), 21.
104 Ibid., 117.

limits of ordinary legal processes, on the other. There is something gently subversive too about the failure to address the question of redress or sanctions, with which international law and its critics are almost constitutively obsessed, and which an NGO like Amnesty would never go without mentioning.[105] The risk, of course, is that the work contributes to the desire for further 'humanitarian intervention' in Syria. But there is also something refreshing in the suggestion that a certain justice may be had in the investigative process itself: in this practice of listening-in to Saydnaya, despite and against the efforts of the Syrian state. The justice, perhaps, of a verdict without a sentence.

In the end, it is not Abu Hamdan who delivers it. The final minutes of the work are given over to survivors, who present the results of their own acoustic investigations, developed far away from the methods and institutions of law. Now, finally, the inversion of juridical procedure is unmistakable. Forensic listening appears, in the final analysis, as a technique of resistance available to the least empowered, precisely as a function of their disempowerment in fact, and independent of law's recognition or authorisation. 'Silence is what allows you to hear everything', one man explains again.

> What we figured out from the sounds were that every ten to fifteen days the guards would take a selection of prisoners out of each cell of the prison. We would hear them open the doors of each of the cells to take them out and gather them all and put them in the first two cells of our ring. We would hear the guards saying "lie on top of one another." Once we counted that they had crammed 300 men into one cell. They gathered them here and they keep them crammed inside until the middle of the night. We'd start to fall asleep, then we'd wake up to the noise of their cell opening and the guards cursing and beating them. At around 5 in the morning they'd collect them, put them in trucks, and we would hear the trucks drive off.

Detainees would count how many trucks came and went during the night. 'Once I remember the truck came 10 times. Each time it would park, they would fill it up with prisoners and then drive off.' Detainees began memorising the names of the prisoners whose names were called by the guards, so that if they ever escaped, they could ask about them.

> We asked about them and none of the men were taken to any civil prisons. We don't know where they went. They have disappeared. We would hear the trucks drive off and it would be silent for 15 minutes and then we would hear the truck return empty. . . . So, the sound of these trucks leaving and the fifteen minutes of silence until we heard them coming back empty, this was the sounds of executions.

105 See the "Conclusions and Recommendations" section of Amnesty, *Human Slaughterhouse*.

9

Criminal procedure and the humanities

Questions of method and orientation

Tom Andrews

Introduction

In 1803, Jeremy Bentham had a bad year. After having toiled for some 16 years on the planning, politics and philosophy of rationalising the punishment of imprisonment, his dream of realising the construction and governorship of his panopticon faltered in the very swamp that was set aside for its construction. Bentham was devastated. He interpreted the negotiations as malevolent and conspiratorial,[1] and proclaimed that the cost of the negotiations was that the Treasury and Home Office 'have murdered my best days'.[2] As any observer of institutional life can no doubt glean from their own experiences, problems have a habit of generating rules to prevent their recurrence (here I think of every sign pasted to the walls or appliances of a faculty kitchen). Bentham's attempt at reorganising the procedure of the common law was his respite, his catharsis, to the panopticon project's failure. Given the panopticon's place in criminology and jurisprudence as a model of the regularisation of discipline, this warrants further consideration.

The invention of the panopticon is usually attributed to the wrong Bentham. It was not Jeremy but his brother, the naval engineer Samuel, who came up with both the model and purpose of the inspection house that would capture Jeremy's imagination for the following decade and a half of his working life. Samuel Bentham trained as an engineer and a shipwright, who having failed to obtain employment in England, entered the service of the Russian Prince Grigory Aleksandrovich Potemkin in 1784 after spending a period of time touring the naval and shipbuilding facilities of Europe, venturing as far as Siberia.[3] Specifically, his role was first

1 Bentham Project, Box 120, ff 466–68.

2 Bentham Project, Box 120, ff 466. Quoted in Janet Sempel, *Bentham's Prison: A Study of the Panopticon Penitentiary* (Oxford: Clarendon Press, 1993).

3 Indeed, this proved of some relief to Bentham's father, who was comforted by the knowledge that he had signed a ten-year contract of employment for the running of Potemkin's industries. See Letter 565, from Jeremy Bentham (co-signed with Samuel, although the letter is authored from Jeremy's perspective) to his father Jeramiah explaining the relief that Samuel had found a way of getting money (March 17–28, 1786) in Ian R. Christie, ed., *The Correspondence of Jeremy Bentham: Volume 3 January 1781 to October 1788* (London: Athlone Press, 1971), 460–63.

'to establish a shipyard for the construction of river transports',[4] and to facilitate domestic industry by both 'training men as sailors and shipwrights, and building ships for the Russian navy'.[5] However, he also worked widely and examples of his duties included taking part in a war against Turkey; improving breweries; and assisting Prince Potemkin in the construction and command of a worm-shaped vessel for Catherine the Great's tour of the southern part of her empire.[6] Indeed, so-called Potemkin Villages were thought to be housed and erected daily from this ship of Samuel Bentham's design and piloting.

So what inspired the building of the panoptic inspection house? The inspiration came from the problem of building English ships abroad due to lumber shortages on the British Isles. The Benthams came to understand these problems of construction in a twofold fashion. First, while '[a]t no time . . . did the [Russian] peasants offer Bentham any particular problems of discipline',[7] there was a lack of skilled craftsmen amongst the serfs on Potemkin's estate.[8] Second, to facilitate their training, Samuel had been importing craftspeople from England, who proved 'increasingly difficult to control'.[9] Samuel's solution to the problem of these skilled yet ill-disciplined craftsmen was a circular inspection house occupied by a supervisor.[10] Jeremy, who was at the time working with Samuel in Russia, attending to some of his accounts and administrative responsibilities, was quick to detect the value and generalisability of the invention.

It is worth noting that in a letter to his father, brimming with enthusiasm following his brother's discovery, Jeremy Bentham highlighted that the idea for the inspection house was first considered capable of additional implementation by the *magistracy*.[11] It was Jeremy who realised the potential of the architectural device of asymmetrical and centralised supervision, and argued with enthusiasm for its broader applicability because he recognised its capacity to both generalise and standardise behaviour in an institutional context.[12] Additionally, these early writings also suggest that Bentham sensed from the outset that there was a jurisprudential dimension to this invention; after all, he sought for his father to mention the device to magistrates, on the basis that it could assist in their substantive business or perhaps administration. After contract

4 Ian R. Christie, *The Benthams in Russia 1780–1791* (Oxford: Berg Publishers, 1993), 131.

5 Philip Steadman, "Samuel Bentham's Panopticon," *Journal of Bentham Studies* 14 (2012): 1–30.

6 The implications of the work for the political philosophy of the panopticon project are explored in Simon Werrett's two publications on Samuel Bentham's work and the political philosophy of the Russian Empire: Simon Werrett, "Potemkin and the Panopticon: Samuel Bentham and the Architecture of Absolutism in Eighteenth Century Russia," *Journal of Bentham Studies* 2 (1999): 1–25; Simon Werrett, "The Panopticon in the Garden: Samuel Bentham's Inspection House and Noble Theatricality in Eighteenth-Century Russia," *Ab Imperio* 3 (2008): 47–70.

7 Werrett, "Potemkin and the Panopticon," 6.

8 It perhaps is obvious that ship construction was produced by craftsmen, organised through trades and their respective guilds, prior to Fordist innovations in production; the large warships in contemporary services therefore required considerable skill in manufacturing in addition to the architectural knowledge to design vessels that could sustain the imperial ambitions of Catherine the Great. The solutions worked up to the combined problems of workshop and dock design (architecture), and the need for skilled labour (and mechanical means of simplifying construction methods) were to provide Bentham with the key means for advancement in his naval career.

9 Werrett, "Potemkin and the Panopticon," 6.

10 Interestingly, the problem seems to inhere in the way labour was administered in England – not so much from the perspective of those doing the work, but instead from the entrenched interests of those tasked with the responsibilities and assumption of supervisory roles. Entrenched, pre-bureaucratic forms of management by commissions with distinct but intersecting jurisdictions were the problem that Bentham confronted during his later employment by the Royal Navy.

11 See Jeremy Bentham, "Letter to Jeremiah Bentham (582) (December 18–29, 1786)," in *The Correspondence of Jeremy Bentham: Volume 3 January 1781 to October 1788*, eds. Ian R. Christie (London: Athlone Press, 1971): 509–12.

12 Werrett, "Potemkin and the Panopticon."

negotiations ended, the impulse was strikingly similar: to write a treatise on how to generalise a response that sees the political means of decision-making subject to the abstract ends of utilitarianism. The *Principles of Judicial Procedure* was this answer.[13]

Bentham's insight was that neither the utility of a guiding principle nor the precision of the legislature's language was sufficient to guarantee the translation of a desired action into consequence. And Bentham's solution was to divorce the writing and setting of procedure from the institutional setting of its administration, to assiduously minimise delay, and to formulate a way to subordinate the law of actions and the attendant adjudicative processes to the objective of veridiction and the utility of substantive actions.

The aim of procedure, in other words, was to provide the mechanism for advancing the legislative's calculated expression of a maximised desire.[14] The question of how to make institutions yield to reform is a question as alive today as it was during the nineteenth century. However, in contrast to the focus on the place of suspension and emergency, here Bentham's focus was on the constraint and ordering of the conduct of juridical office. His procedure code, like so much of his writing, languished half-finished for decades only to provide one source of inspiration amongst many to legislative reformers working to legislate British India as well as those jurists mulling over domestic reform in the generations that followed.[15] The published text is, perhaps unsurprisingly, rendered, as a consequence of following his own style guide, a broadly soporific one, punctuated occasionally with moments of corpuscular disappointment, hurt and anger, dulled but not erased, by the intervening years.

1.

The basic question of procedure is itself already and always double, posed in the second order: as the conduct of conduct. How *can* one proceed? How *should* one proceed? Simply, *how* to proceed? A straightforward enough series of questions. An alertness to procedure is to interrogate elements of the practical or the prudential. Procedure discourse is often marked by its technical quality, one that can too readily disavow its theoretical or situated terrain by means of an invocation of the world of action or the 'at hand' acceptability of existing forms of activity. Once considered and proscribed, procedure isn't merely a supplement: it enables as well as constrains, it guides as it circumscribes. Of course, the movements of a procedure already carry within them multiplicities: questions of economy, modulating approaches to certainty, relations between and beyond institutions, and capacities for rhetoric. As such, thinking with the ethics of procedure necessitates thinking about how one might dwell in a procedural space: how one might evoke and invoke not only the premises of that movement, bound iteratively to space and time, ground and life, and to the specificity of questions of the good that arise within its ambit, voiced in its argot.[16] After all, can any response be other than mediated? Thinking with procedure provides a way of following the arrangement of the responsibilities and activities of law in terms of the quality of how the patterning, intensity, provenance and choice of conduct might be proscribed, resisted, nominated, de-essentialised or chosen. To this end, a jurisprudence of procedure, attentive to the humanities, should follow and critique its emergences, interventions,

13 Jeremy Bentham, "Principles of Judicial Procedure," in *The Works of Jeremy Bentham*, eds. John Bowring (Edinburg: William Tait, 1843).

14 Here, it is worth thinking about Jacques-Alain Miller and Richard Miller, "Jeremy Bentham's Panoptic Device," *October* 41 (Summer 1987): 3–29.

15 See Eric Stokes, *The English Utilitarians and India* (Oxford: Clarendon Press, 1959).

16 See Max Weber's 1919 essay, "Politics as a Vocation."

structurings, modes of filiation and attachments to the broad field of the government of human relations to self as well as the government of others in which it operates. And yet, even as procedure arrives, it hovers: arrested in its own temporal and jurisdictional hesitancy: a reflexivity disguised and perhaps ill-digested, and a moment of reflection as well as interpellation into a tradition, a template, of action and one of thought, in place and time, of limit and potential. As a question of law, it is a question of conduct that resonates in the jurisdictional depths of the *how*. To ask such a question is to already have one's conduct subject to a law and simultaneously to recognise that the iteration of conduct is already and always caught in the dynamics of the pattern, template or promise as well as (of necessity) its opposite or its failure; haunted from the start by the tremulous or tremoring memory of failure.[17] To start an inquiry with *how* is to begin to address the problematic of procedure.

To reiterate this argument in slightly more concrete terms: a jurisprudential study of procedure can be made to move away from technical dimensions and towards the humanities if one turns one's attention to the conduct of conduct. Such a jurisprudence seeks to describe the description of a mode of action resolutely and resonantly before the law. Consequently, the study of procedure in a tradition attuned to questions of the humanities will ask questions of a broader ambit of the forms, modes, methods and structures of the conduct of juridical processes. There are two initial comments to make here: first, procedure is not the process. Procedure describes *how* a process is to proceed. The question of how invites re-description and with it, critique. A number of preliminary lines of thought emerge: how can the relationship between means and ends be brought into focus? What might be said about the quality of activity proposed? What might be said of the qualities of those made responsible for that activity? Indeed, how is responsibility parsed and allocated? How is responsibility rendered responsible at all? How does a particular patterning of legal conduct express or represent what that law is? What questions of ethical disposition or decisional authority are further enlivened by asking how? Second, procedure jurisprudence can usefully voice a critique in the interstice opened by second order thinking.[18] Already such questions open up others beyond the domain of the blackletter and the technical: they speak to the techniques of the technical as well as the grammatology of the blackletter.[19] This approach involves following in precise terms the way that the practical, active or prudential are held to a relationship with a law.[20]

Second, the concerns of procedure can be held apart from those that follow evidence law or trial processes. While procedure interfaces with questions of epistemology and philosophy, its analysis can also be productively carried out in an idiom of authority, jurisdiction or technique. When put in this way, procedure scholarship offers a study in the techniques that both enable and constrain the expression of authority in a specifically lawful style. An advantage of holding on to questions of technique in the context of thinking with lawful authority is that it necessitates an understanding of the practical dimension of jurisprudence. In this regard, one's line of questioning can also be turned to think about the stakes and formations of activity that take place when conduct is arranged in a standardised manner. The history of criminal procedure from

17 Jacques Derrida, "Force De Loi: Le Fondement Mystique De L'Autorite/Force of Law: The Mystical Foundation of Authority'," *Cardozo Law Review* 11, no. 5–6 (July–August 1990).

18 On this score, see Niklas Luhmann, *Law as a Social System* (Oxford: Oxford University Press, 2004).

19 Peter Goodrich, *Languages of Law: From Logics of Memory to Nomadic Masks* (London: Weidenfeld, 1990); Jacques Derrida, *Of Grammatology* (Baltimore and London: Johns Hopkins University Press, 1976).

20 In this regard, Sheila Jasanoff's approach to science and technology studies is similar: what is the problem and how does the problem come to be regarded as problematic: Sheila Jasanoff, "The Idiom of Co-Production," in *States of Knowledge: The Co-Production of Science and Social Order*, ed. Sheila Jasanoff (Hoboken: Taylor and Francis, 2004).

the eighteenth century has been double. On the one hand, there is a gradual tendency toward standardised forms that nevertheless still rely on an older language of procedure, for example, the categorisation of offences and the availability of writs are references to the specific letter-writing practices of the courts of common law.[21] On the other hand, contemporary procedure also has a legislative history: one that starts with Bentham but continues apace throughout the British Empire.[22] Procedure addresses the past as offering a template for the furrows of future action.

2.

There is a tendency to parse procedure as a fixed aspect of either legal expression or the practice of a given jurisdiction. As one way of approaching the task or problem of governing one's self or others, the concept of procedure should be interrogated as the outcome of located, partial and political contests to standardise the conduct of a particular type of government.[23] As a concept, we can look to the emergence of procedure through Michel Foucault's method for reading 'the complex interconnection with a multiplicity of historical processes'.[24] While my understanding of procedure has a clear debt to Michel Foucault, aspects of work on this project have been informed by three broad concerns with the legacy of Foucault's work for common law scholars of criminal law. His concern with procedure started from at least the early 1970s,[25] and included a study of a series of transformations in the rationality, manner and art of government, into what he calls the 'ring of truth . . . [that] alethurgic circle that turns around' power and operationalises it.[26] Foucault's research programme recognises a bifurcation of questions of the juridical into what he calls 'jurisdiction' and 'veridiction'. In this, for Foucault, the study of the history of truth becomes the dominant theme, as opposed to the history of conduct. Less satisfyingly, Foucault's work (at least as it is translated into English) assumes that the category of knowledge and conduct called 'procedure' has an epistemological and deontological consistency. In other words, the question of procedure as a particular style of conduct or technique of jurisdiction, needs to be historicised with the same degree of subtlety and attention as the concept of veridiction.[27] A cursory glance at a history of, for example, the changing methods of the trial, the composition of the jury (particularly apropos of witnesses) or the relationship between the writing technologies of indictment, suggests that this is a poor assumption to hold.

21 Cornelia Vismann, *Files: Law and Media Technology* (Stanford, CA: Stanford University Press, 2008).

22 On civil procedure, see Shaunnagh Dorsett, "The First Procedural Code in the British Empire: New Zealand 1856," *New Zealand Universities Law Review* 27, no. 3 (2017).

23 Such an investigation should also consider the standardisation of standards: how isomorphic arrangements of predictable behaviour become invested with jurisprudential or political virtue.

24 Michel Foucault, "Questions of Method," in *Power: Essential Works of Foucault 1954–1984* (New York: Penguin, 2000), 223–38, 225.

25 Michel Foucault, "Truth and Juridical Forms," in *Power: Essential Works of Foucault 1954–1984* (New York: Penguin, 2000), 1–89.

26 Michel Foucault, *On the Government of the Living: Lectures at the Collège de France, 1979–1980* (Hampshire: Palgrave MacMillan, 2014).

27 Consider for example how these tensions are made present in a discussion on methodology conducted in 1978. He describes his project as 'eventalizing singular regimes of practices, so as to make them graspable as different regimes of "jurisdiction" and "veridiction": that to put it in exceedingly barbarous terms is what I would like to do. . . . I would like, in short, to resituate the production of true and false at the heart of historical analysis and political critique' (230). The study of events is one of 'effecting a sort of multiplication or pluralization of causes . . . according to the multiple processes that constitute it' (227).

Finally, Foucault's answers to his questions are located in his own cultural milieu and his own series of interests and concerns. A difference in approach to materials, authors, time-frames and localities comes from writing from the colonial antipodes about the common law. Although this fact apparently did not come to the attention of Foucault, it seems important that the first English-language philosophy of legal procedure was written by Jeremy Bentham.[28] This provides some further evidence that Bentham's contributions to the intellectual organisation, effective deployment as well as clarification of the jurisprudential principles of authority that underpin contemporary procedure should be read as part of a general project directed toward the government of conduct.

3.

How, then, do ideas in the domain of procedure move? A preliminary answer might simply be 'by ship'. This isn't a vexatious response, even though it might appear that way at the outset. But, why should shipping be a less appropriate media technology for facilitating changes in the conduct of lawful relations than the surveillant potentialities of contemporary networked computers or the humble rolling suitcase? After all, a recurrent theme in the early history of procedure jurisprudence is the myriad ways that shipping – as a material practice as much as a mechanism of punishment – intersects with the transformation of criminal procedure. Shipping emerges as both the background of key moments, often and unexpectedly, providing space or a haven for writing.[29] Alternatively as a problem: most literally in the form of a job, in the context of stevedores and the capital momentarily embodied in the form of either the vessels themselves or in the imperial commodities that their hulls sling from the plantations in the West Indies. After all, shipping and its world of logistical entailments all point to an increase in complexity through the advent and iteration of increasingly technical know-how in the domain of not only naval architecture and manufacturing, but also the cartographic, navigational and meteorological sciences, which are themselves applied onboard to govern complexity. From the mid-eighteenth century in the UK, shipping sustains an astonishing problem of things, persons and populations. Consider the logistical problem of victuals at a time when 'the navy's shipboard population in time of war – more than 40,000 men – was greater than that of any British city except for London'.[30] Administrative expertise was purposive knowledge, and its accretion took place over time through the interplay of techniques and solutions that accompanied the form of seafaring empire that Britain was. If procedure is a practical activity, then a burgeoning and unwieldy empire provided the fissile material through which to workshop administrative techniques. These can be understood through the various sites of struggle: both Ireland (in terms of providing Sir Robert Peel with a place to experiment with the organisation of paramilitary police forces before their formal institution in London and export abroad) and India (consider the legislative and codifying hubris that followed the assumption of direct rule following the

28 See Gerald J. Postema, "The Principle of Utility and the Law of Procedure: Bentham's Theory of Adjudication," *Georgia Law Review* 11 (1977): 1392–412.

29 Perhaps equally frequent is the recurrent theme of personal trauma and criminal procedure jurisprudence. This isn't surprising on the face of it, but the particular style of trauma – understood as something which unmakes or re-makes the subject – and the turn toward a writing of either jurisprudence, procedure or both, occurs with a pronounced frequency as providing biographical and authorial context to a number of important texts in the archive looked at here.

30 John Brewer, *The Sinews of Power: War, Money, and the English State, 1688–1783* (London: Unwin Hyman, 1989), 36. He points out a page later: 'their seaborne station made them far more difficult to feed' (37).

first war of independence). Additionally, it is possible to sequence changes under the standard-bearing proper nouns of famous criminal jurists who worked on the imperial project and innovated in the space of jurisprudence and procedure reform: Thomas Macaulay, James Fitzjames Stephen, Henry Sumner Maine and, of course, Jeremy Bentham.

4.

Amongst Jeremy Bentham's preparatory notes for the first English language text concerned entirely with the jurisprudence of legal procedure is a short jot of a note, itself in a table of miscellany, concerning his understanding of the relationship between law and the poetic. Bentham writes:

> No two things can be more hostile to each other than the genius of Poetry and that of law. If a . . . write thing is good in poetry it is bad for law: if a thing is good law, it is bad and you write poetry. The one addresses itself to the imagination, and aims at the properties of wit. [Locke] The other to the reasoning judgement faculty and aims at the properties of to give master of judgement. The aim of the one is to darrk & confound: that of the other is to clear up enlighten and distinguish.[31]

It is fitting that Bentham, as an early exponent of a positivist jurisprudence, had to tarry in the thicket of language in drafting his book on procedure. Few authors, after all, need to make an unironic entry in a ledger reminding themselves, 'No *sesquidpedalia verba* [foot and a half long words], like those extirpated breeded out by Linnaeus'.[32] Perhaps such a scant note-to-self is best dismissed as marginalia, as an aide memoire or as a restatement of some stricture that sits adjacent to the project and text itself. Bentham's note-to-self raises a number of questions of procedure when read in a jurisprudential register: what is the relationship between language and concept when occupying the office of legislator? How exactly do 'notes-to-self' function as a technique of self-government and the government of one's outward responsibilities? How does the conceptual apparatus borrowed from Linneas' biology impose its own order on the organisation of law? In what idiom must a jurist write? How fluid is the genre of legislation? And what are the responsibilities of jurists and legislatures to their readers, both lawyerly and not? After all, Bentham is writing at a time when these questions were still open. As an open antagonist of the common law, its lawyers and judges, one of Bentham's techniques was to engage in flights of fancy and simply ignore and replace the authority of the common law according to his imagination: this is an imagination that ranges from the incisive, deductive and empirical critique and onwards to the baroque.[33]

So far this chapter has argued for a closer engagement with understanding the suite of solutions that criminal procedure has come to offer problems within the broad authority of government by forms of law. It is of course ironic that one of the rote gestures that seems to inaugurate any contribution to the surprisingly slender volume of academic jurisprudence addressed to the theme, problematic and theory of procedure, is to call attention to the lack of sustained scholarly procedural jurisprudence. And while this might, with some important exceptions, formally be the case, this brush-clearing gesture also betrays something of an impoverished sense of how

31 UCL Bentham Project JB/027/140/002. All notation and spellings as per the original.

32 Ibid.

33 See the conclusion later in this chapter for a discussion of one of Bentham's more fantastical schemes.

questions of procedure might be parsed, represented and expressed. While the aim of this chapter is to introduce an example of thinking through criminal procedure in terms of its potential for greater consideration and excavation within the plural traditions, methods and approaches huddled together as the humanities, it is important to acknowledge some of the important work that has been done in this field.

Procedure scholarship is often concerned with supreme court jurisprudence and readings of the criminal law (substantive, evidential and procedural). Often, and particularly in the American context, procedure is considered through the analysis of the translation of principles of constitutional law and its interpretation. To this end, I want to focus on a number of contributions to thinking about procedure that offer some important remedies for styles of thought that might be lost when scholarship is too closely focused on a consideration of technique, case law and procedure doctrine (in terms of the criminal law's substantive, evidential and procedural rules). This is important due to the empirical fact that most criminal cases are not heard in the higher courts of a given jurisdiction, and that it is the rules of procedure which ensure that this is the case. The effect for a body of jurisprudence is that the rules of criminal procedure shape the archive of judgments available to study, and with this gesture, directs attention toward the jurisprudence of those higher courts. Writing momentarily in a more institutionally liberal idiom, this relegates large swatches of the day-to-day operation of state power to either jurisprudential invisibility or inferiority; and in either case this raises a number of questions about the textuality of authority and the authority of legal texts, both as genres of writing as well as writing media and archive, while foregrounding a critique of the rule of law in this same rubric.

Early and now widely cited exemplars of this scholarship that squarely address these questions posed of (and for) criminal procedure include Patricia Carlen's work on the dramaturgical and material functionality of the magistrates' court.[34] This was followed a few years later by Doreen McBarnet's excellent book, *Conviction*,[35] which addressed the way specifically legal procedural rules contributed to and ultimately provided structure for what she called an 'ideology of triviality'.[36] McBarnet argued that this ideology has produced a situation where the overwhelming majority of cases are viewed as legally unimportant, undignified in terms of their process, and treated as evidentially simple. Her argument describes criminal procedure as a dynamic, a mechanism or feedback loop, for attaching the practices of the magistrates' court to the world of law with consequences for how authority is both legally structured and culturally understood. It is the structure of procedural rules that mandates that the bulk of criminal law work, in its institutional reliance on the amateur dispensation of justice (recall that in the UK magistrates are still largely unpaid and require no formal qualifications in law), at once confirms its status as unimportant, and yet simultaneously relies on the authority generated by an image of dignity, carefulness, professionalism and resources of the law that is inculcated in the superior courts.

A rich volume of important scholarship has developed to address the legal history of procedure, particular institutions, and the relationship between procedure and civil society.[37] Norma Landau's study of justices of the peace remains an exemplary work of scholarship focused on

34 Patricia Carlen, *Magistrates' Justice* (London: Martin Robertson, 1976).

35 Doreen McBarnet, *Conviction: The Law, the State and the Construction of Justice* (London: MacMillan, 1981).

36 Ibid. Chapter 4.

37 Examples include Lindsay Farmer, *Making the Modern Criminal Law: Criminalization and Civil Order* (Oxford: Oxford University Press, 2016); Norma Landau, *The Justice of the Peace, 1679–1760* (Berkeley: University of California Press, 1984); Peter King, *Crime, Justice and Discretion in England 1740–1820* (Oxford: Oxford University Press, 2000); John Langbein, *The Origins of the Adversary Criminal Trial* (Oxford: Oxford University Press,

a single institutional form and its mode of conduct.[38] Bruce P Smith has been writing on the relationship between criminal procedure and transformations in the broader economy of the nineteenth century in a way that warrants attention: namely, the use of possession offences to reverse the onus of proof in a changing society.[39] Edward Mussawir's scholarship on the jurisprudence of procedure represents a careful guide for the humanities in thinking with the genres and styles of procedure in ways that remain the work of a jurisprudent who seeks to understand the historical, political, technical and libidinal dimensions of law.[40]

A number of scholars have also attempted to categorise criminal procedure in terms of its various genres. Important work that attempts to think procedure on its own terms includes the broad and deep scholarship of Mirjam Damaška, most famously embodied in his article 'Structures of Authority and Comparative Criminal Procedure',[41] which has developed an influential heuristic for understanding procedure as predicated on the political and social compacts for the acceptability and organisation of public authority rather than trial methods. Robert Cover and Owen Fiss began the task of rethinking procedure scholarship as part of their teaching obligations,[42] and a short book of excerpts, now out of print, was produced as part of this project. The lines of engagement suggested in their introduction to this book remain important: how to interrogate the value of procedure and the values of procedures, the open question of fairness in liberal thought, and the relationship between procedure and justice.

Conclusion

In the closing substantive chapter of her book on the panopticon, Janet Semple muses on the style of utopianism 'J.B.'[43] aspired to. It is at the end of this chapter that we might be better positioned to review and reflect on the place that criminal procedure occupies in the world. Her account draws attention to the parapraxis, or Freudian slips found in marginalia, literally, pencilled in the margins of the boxes of panopticon papers in the Bentham archive at UCL.[44] Her narration of the archival material reads:[45]

> The panopticon was to be the centre of new trading and exploration ventures. Ships would be sent across the oceans of the world to West America, "Cook's shores", and California to collect specimens of plants and seeds, especially valuably hardy timber trees, the raw

2003); Drew Gray, *Crime, Prosecution and Social Relations: The Summary Courts of the City of London in the Late Eighteenth Century* (Basingstoke: Palgrave Macmillan, 2009).

38 Landau, *The Justice of the Peace, 1679–1760.*

39 Bruce Smith, "The Presumption of Guilty and the English Law of Theft, 1750–1850," *Law and History Review* 23 (2005): 133–99.

40 Edward Mussawir, "Justice 'from Room to Room': Toward a Concept of Procedural Space in Kafka's the Trial and the Fictional Work of Western Jurisprudence," in *Spaces of Justice: Peripheries, Passages, Appropriations*, eds. Chris Butler and Edward Mussawir (London: Routledge, 2017), 37–55; Edward Mussawir, "Jurisdiction of Control: Judgment and Procedural Forms in *Thomas v Mowbray*," *Griffith Law Review* 19, no. 2 (2010): 307–29.

41 Mirjam Damaška, "Structures of Authority and Comparative Criminal Procedure," *Yale Law Journal* 84 (1975): 480–544. Note that this is really more attuned to the question of procedure than Herbert Parker's earlier attempt which sought to describe broader orientations of the project of criminal law: Herbert L. Packer, "Two Models of the Criminal Process," *University of Pennsylvania Law Review* 113, no. 1 (November 1964): 1–68.

42 Robert M. Cover and Owen M. Fiss, *The Structure of Procedure* (New York: Foundation Press, 1992).

43 See Janet Semple, *Bentham's Prison: A Study of the Panopticon Penitentiary* (Oxford: Clarendon Press, 1993), 286.

44 Ibid.

45 UCL Bentham 107 / ff 71, 72, 74.

> materials for the woodworking machinery of the panopticon. These new specimens would be propagated in the panopticon nurseries; and the voyages could be made profitable by the sale of these plants and proceeds from the publication of illustrated accounts of the expeditions.[46]

This returns us to Bentham's fragment cited earlier, a caution against the pleasurable oneiric folly of the poetic for the pursuit of enlightenment taxonomy. Behind the order of law lies imagination, the properties of wit and also, the gurgling of the unconscious. Semple's narration of this material is in the service of describing Bentham's adolescent fantasies of the swashbuckling botanist. A more careful reading of these materials might draw attention to the capillary action that these remarks reveal to be operating in both Bentham's panoptic schema and jurisprudential thought. The obvious remark is that the panopticon is envisaged as the centre of an imperialism of Bentham's own founding. This is an imperialism founded on extraction from the antipodes, and predicated on existing shipping technologies, which would be improved by extracting new species of timber, milling and crafting wood in the workshops of his prison. Botany sits closer to Bentham's thought than is widely appreciated.

I have deliberately avoided the technocratic dimensions of procedure to hold attention to its manners of movement, its sense of purpose as well as the quality of deportment that accompanies such voyages in space and time. The example provided by Bentham, and the texts that surround the voicing of procedure in the English language and its traditions of political thought, give us an opportunity to pause and reflect on the historiography of conduct, the politics of the concept of utility and the ambivalent directions of the desire that attends to it.

However, in spite of a short but ever widening literature, my contention for the purposes of this *Handbook* is to point out the existence of a longer, stranger and less well-examined history of juristic attention to questions of procedure and to how one's relationship to law might be conducted. This is a literature concerned with conduct and government, and officeholding as one way of holding on to questions about the other of authority and the manners and methods for conducting public life. In broad terms, its concern is with the repertoire of techniques that have accreted through institutional or official practice, that give shape to appropriate methods for the government of selves and others.

Procedure emerged as one possible solution to a particular arrangement of problems, but one that can and should be read as the prudential or pragmatic dimensions of a jurisprudence that was thoroughly situated in its imperial and governmental contexts.[47] Authority to order and the order of authority are jurisdictional devices.[48] Procedure is one second order technique in this repertoire. Procedure provides a diagram of the ordered world that lawyers imagine. It describes the furrows and orthodoxies of lawful conduct and the institutions that support it. It offers sublime but temporary, inadequate and fallible symbolic order to manage the exigencies of a changing, violent and unpredictable world composed of matter both lawful and not. For these reasons, as a technology of hope as well as an overlaid violence, as a means of projection or hedging of a common future, scholars of jurisprudence and law would do well to curiously and attentively spend time unfurling the question, *how?*

46 See Semple, *Bentham's Prison*, 286.

47 See Nasser Hussain, *The Jurisprudence of Emergency: Colonialism and the Rule of Law* (Ann Arbour: The University of Michigan Press, 2003).

48 Shaunnagh Dorsett and Shaun McVeigh, *Jurisdiction* (Hoboken: Taylor and Francis, 2012), Chapter 4.

10
Wayfaring

Olivia Barr

Always the heartbeat below existence in Australia is the unresolved legal scar of British colonisation. The brutal violence Aboriginal and Torres Strait Islander peoples did – and continue to – experience as a result of the British Empire and its contemporary manifestations is hard to ignore. The legal mechanisms that authorised such violent colonial activities, including those that led to the creation of Australia, continue to be present in our current legal structures. In other words, the colonial project is ongoing. My research tries to understand the present nature of this ongoing project, and how it shapes so much of contemporary life in Australia. To do this, my research looks into the past to understand the role of law in creating and maintaining this inheritance in the present, and also looks to the future to creatively find ways to move forward.

This chapter is a reflection on my approach to this research. In particular it is a reflection on how I found my way into law and humanities research, and the extraordinary gift it offered to creatively explore different research methods. As evidenced in this book, law and humanities is a broad church of scholarship that involves contemplating law from diverse perspectives within the humanities. While often under-appreciated, it is important to recognise that law and humanities scholarship inflects not only the content of legal research, but also its methods. In other words, it not only impacts what we research, but how we go about that research. It is therefore helpful to identify the paths and ways we travel as we seek answers to our research questions, and to notice how these paths often involve navigating unforeseen risks and verdant possibilities.

My aim in this chapter is to outline a guide for what I call 'wayfaring methods', and in doing so, to celebrate the opportunities for creative method-making made possible by law and humanities scholars, and their scholarship. The chapter evolves over five parts. The first part begins with an experience of becoming lost with law after finding doctrine insufficient. The next three parts involve a search, a guide and then a discovery, that there are many different ways of working with law. The final part concludes with some advice on making your own way in legal research with wayfaring methods, and how to navigate the risks while relishing the benefits.

Wayless

There was a moment when I lost my way, and looking back I realise it started with a feeling. Ever since I can remember, I have had a slow-burning feeling of both utter belonging in certain

Australian landscapes, while also being simultaneously ill at ease. For me, the landscape I am most at home in is a mix of pindan earth, dried out dune bushes, grey-green peppermint trees, eye-burning white sand, metallic blue oceans and endless skies. This is a landscape common to the southwest coast of Australia, and like an old pair of favourite winter uggboots, it is a landscape I feel I can always sink into. But even when I do sink into these landscapes of my childhood, and allow myself to feel peacefully at home, there is a discomfort that niggles at the edge of my awareness. This mixture of love and uncertainty of belonging is not a unique feeling. Many non-Indigenous people in Australia are unsure how to relate to the place they call home, despite often deep levels of love and attachment.

Throughout the landscape and contemporary populace there is a quiet uncertainty about what it means to live as a non-Indigenous person on Indigenous land stolen by British forefathers, Land that remains, to this day, unceded sovereign Aboriginal territories. This is a deep-rooted problem, and its associated feelings of dislocated uncertainty manifest in myriad ways. I can feel it, for example, in the undertones of contemporary Australian politics, in the quick anger of politicians, and the topics left unsaid. I can feel it in the difficult and slow-grappling conversations about national identity, from the *Uluru Statement from the Heart* and its call for a Voice,[1] thwarted republicanism, treaty-talk, and increasing calls and steadfast resistance to change the date of Australia Day.[2] Most viscerally, I can feel it in the throat-clearing hesitations of those unsure how to acknowledge Country in a brief but significant ceremony used to open many public events. Whatever the moment, and wherever the experience, once felt, this is a feeling that is hard to shake.

Even with this feeling, though, I am not wayless: I know who I am. Kaya noonakoort. Ngany wadjela yorga who grew up on Whadjuk Noongar Boodja.[3] In other words, I am a whitefella living on Aboriginal Country. Having grown up on Whadjuk Noongar Country, and having had the joy of spending large amounts of time on Yamatji, Gunaikurnai, Gadigal and Darkinjung Country, I now live on Wurundjeri Country but my heart remains in Noongar Country.[4] In other words, who I am is intrinsically linked to where I am, and where I have been. Yet I still feel the feeling. Questions of belonging for non-Indigenous people living on unceded sovereign Aboriginal Country cannot and should never be paralleled to challenges facing Aboriginal peoples in Australia. Yet there is a common inheritance of colonialism that is deeply problematic. This inheritance is problematic not only as a matter of history, but also as a matter of politics, culture and law.

1 The *Uluru Statement from the Heart* is a constitutional document in the form of an artwork telling two Tjukurpa ('Dreaming') stories of the Aṉangu people, the traditional owners of Uluru. The artwork can be viewed here: ANTaR, "Uluru Statement from the Heart," accessed October 31, 2019, https://antar.org.au/stories/uluru-statement-heart. The text included at the centre of the artwork can be more easily read here, accessed October 31, 2019, https://ulurustatement.org/.

2 For a snapshot, see Amnesty International, "Change the Date," accessed October 31, 2019, www.amnesty.org.au/change-the-date/. For a longer analysis, see Stan Grant, *Australia Day* (Sydney: HarperCollins, 2019).

3 This is the language of Whadjuk Noongar Boodja, which translates: 'Hi everyone, I am a non-Indigenous woman who grew up on Whadjuk Noongar Country.' I was born at the start of Bunuru (the hottest part of the year), near the banks of the Derbal Yerrigan (Swan River), and spent most of my childhood in the wardan (ocean, sea). See Rose Whitehurst, ed., *Noongar Dictionary: Noongar to English and English to Noongar*, 2nd ed. (East Perth: Noongar Language and Education Centre, 1997).

4 This is best illustrated by the following map that aims to represent all Indigenous nations. See Australian Institute of Aboriginal and Torres Strait Islander Studies, "AIATSIS map of Indigenous Australia," interactive map, accessed October 30, 2019, https://aiatsis.gov.au/explore/articles/aiatsis-map-indigenous-australia.

It was because of feeling this problem, and a suspicion that Australian law might have something to do with it (whether creating the problem, fixing it or some combination I was unsure), that I found my way to law school at the University of Western Australia hoping to find a small measure of justice. My hope was, and still is, that there might be a way to articulate this problem, and the associated feelings, in order to explain what it is, and to find a way forward: not just for me, but for all of us. However, after a long exploration of both international and Australian law as a student, solicitor, and in law reform both domestically and internationally, I found myself a little disappointed.

As a lawyer trained and practiced in Australian law, I found trying to articulate this deeply problematic issue within a legal idiom difficult. In both international and domestic legal arenas, I was confronted with issues of jurisdictional uncertainty and doctrinal incomprehension. Take, for example, legal questions of the ongoing presence and practice of Aboriginal sovereignty. These questions have been consistently held to be non-justiciable in the High Court of Australia, which effectively closes off all domestic legal avenues for recourse.[5] Yet simultaneously Aboriginal nations, like the Noongar Nation on whose Country I grew up on, do not have standing in international courts, which generally allow standing for states not individuals, because they are not recognised as sovereign states by other UN-sitting sovereign states. Why? Because domestic Australian courts have previously determined the issue of Aboriginal sovereignty is non-justiciable, which effectively closes off all international legal avenues too. A classic catch-22.

Doctrinally, that is, using law's own methods of engaging with the rules of legal doctrine, I found that the legal doors were closed on this problem whichever way I turned. I was increasingly frustrated with inadequate legal answers and relentless obfuscation. After a fairly exhaustive search through study and legal practice, I concluded doctrine was ill-equipped to adequately address the problem I was seeking to understand. Having determined doctrine was insufficient, I found myself as a practising lawyer lacking direction or purpose, with no obvious legal roads or doctrinal paths to follow. Within both domestic and international law, I was drifting without a way forward. I was wayless. After toying with the idea of abandoning law to join the circus, I chose to persist with this deeply problematic issue. The remainder of the chapter is a reflection on how I found my way back into law by utilising the insights and support of law and humanities scholarship, even though that involved walking a mildly unusual path.

Wayfaring

Having lost my way with law, and the resources it could offer doctrinally, I went searching for other ways. I think of this as 'wayfaring'. A wayfarer is a 'traveller by road, esp. one who goes on foot'.[6] For researchers in any discipline, there is a figurative sense in which a person may act as a wayfarer, travelling the paths unseen through new scholarship. There is also a material sense of wayfaring in research, even if footprints mostly involve stepping on and off aeroplanes to visit a conference, archive or field site. Holding onto physical and metaphorical wayfaring, in this part of the chapter I recount my early exploration of different legal research methods.

5 *Coe v Commonwealth* (1979) 24 ALR 118; *Wacando v Commonwealth* (1981) 148 CLR 1; *Mabo v Queensland (No. 2)* (1992) 175 CLR 1; *Coe v Commonwealth* (1993) 118 ALR 193; *Walker v New South Wales* (1994) 182 CLR 45.

6 "wayfarer, n.," *OED Online*, Oxford University Press, accessed October 30, 2019, https://www-oed-com.ezp.lib.unimelb.edu.au/view/Entry/226486?redirectedFrom=wayfarer.

While this is a personal narrative, I am confident it is a fairly common experience when entering legal research. My aim in sharing this story is to lay the foundations for appreciating the enormous possibilities provided by taking a creative or wayfaring approach to method-making in legal scholarship.

When I first embarked on in-depth research in law through a masters by research at the University of British Columbia in Vancouver, Canada, some of the oddest moments of learning occurred when I found myself amid conversations about method, or the more serious and intimidating term 'methodology'. As a lawyer, I had no idea what anyone meant. My guiding thought was: 'surely, we just do law, don't we?' Until that moment, I had never thought about what, as lawyers, we actually do. When I did stop and think, all I could come up with was the practice of sifting through rules in cases and legislation to make arguments and provide advice. I was stubbornly unable to comprehend how what I did as a lawyer by providing legal advice related to what was referred to as 'research method' or 'methodology'. I was even more confused by the quiet suggestion that there was a choice of method. I found myself asking: 'could there really be more than one way of doing law?'

I vividly recall sitting in the weekly research classes taught by Joel Bakan. Each week we delved into an overview of a different legal research method and read an applied example. I discovered in the first class that what I had been doing as a lawyer was called 'doctrinal research' because it was about manipulating rules and doctrines, and I learnt that there were a dozen more weeks of class and hence a dozen more methods to learn. Quickly fascinated, each week I would approach the readings with avid enthusiasm and a dash of sceptical curiosity. Each week I asked myself: 'is this my method?' Though tempted at times, the answer was inevitably 'no'. By the end of the year, during which I had largely researched and written my 40,000-word thesis, I was puzzled to realise that despite a wide-ranging exploration from eco-feminism to empirical methods to law reform, apart from a few near-misses, I still hadn't found my method. No one week had provided the answer. This left the rather unsettling question: 'what I am doing then?' Followed quickly by: 'if I do not have a method, then is my research . . . wrong?'

These are no small worries, and common to many entering legal research. I distinctly remember sitting down with one of my supervisors, Professor Michael Jackson, towards the end of the academic year. We pulled two metal school chairs into the sunshine on the grassy verge at the back of the old UBC law school and sat looking out across the water, past the bald-headed eagles' nests, towards the tips of the local mountains. An extraordinarily beautiful spot. I told him about my hunt for a method and that after a year of enthusiastic searching I had come up short and failed to find an answer. I told him I now had serious doubts about the thesis I had mostly written because I was unsure how to describe my method, and worried this lack of label meant what I did was incorrect, improper or unauthorised. He listened calmly, as is his way, and then told me he had never really understood method either, and that his solution was to just write what he needed to write and not worry about a label. But, if I felt I needed a label, a helpful one to use is the ubiquitous 'mixed method'. He offered further advice by saying that if I do struggle to name a method, I needed something else to shore up my work. He asked me if I knew what my research question was – and I said yes – and he said, well, do you know how to answer that question? And I said yes, and he said that as far as he was concerned, that was what mattered most, even if I wasn't able to articulate my method in familiar terms. So I finished my master's thesis by answering the question of whether there was an inherent right of Aboriginal self-government in Australia, and I did this by using a 'mixed method', which was in effect a doctrinal method relentlessly applied to a supposedly non-doctrinal *sui generis* topic, coupled with a tentative experiment in law and literature.

The reason I share this unsuccessful exploration of different legal methodologies is not because it is unique, but because I suspect it isn't. What I learnt from 'wayfaring' through different methods was to not be afraid of breaking expected norms, categories or labels of what a legal research method ought to be. This was a lesson reiterated during my PhD at Melbourne Law School, where I first embraced law and humanities scholarship with the guidance and support of the Institute for International Law and the Humanities (IILAH). Importantly, with time and practice, I have also learnt when wayfaring to trust my instinct, and to wield my legal judgment in new ways in order to follow the research question wherever it leads.

Waywiser

In the absence of an established or orthodox category of method, the key to not getting too lost when wayfaring amongst methods is to make sure there is a clear and steady guide. A waywiser is an old expression for a guidepost. Whenever I find myself at a cross-roads in my research, unsure of which way to travel or how best to proceed, my waywiser has been my research question. When it comes to using a research question as a guidepost, it is important to ensure the question is framed cleanly. Research questions may appear simple but are notoriously complex to frame. To this end, it is helpful to differentiate between two types of questions. One type captures the impulse or motivation behind the research. In a sense, this is 'the question behind the question', which is effectively the reason for asking a particular research question in the first place. While important, and relevant to shaping the research question, this is not the waywiser. A second type is a more nuanced question that involves a question of law and drives the details of the research. This is the research question. This is the waywiser. While these two types of question are related, they need to be separated to clearly identify the relevant guidepost.

In my own work, the 'question behind the question' is always: 'How do I, as a lawyer trained in Australian law, live on unceded Aboriginal land, and how might I do this well?' This is the unsolvable riddle that lured me into law school and keeps me here. It is what I am trying to understand. In this respect, it is necessarily centred on my own experience, but also contains something more universal. It can be asked by lawyers and non-lawyers alike when conscious of the present injustice of colonisation in Australia. It can also be asked in other settler colonies or in nation-states struggling with complex legal legacies of colonisation, war or genocide. However asked, this is not a legal question *per se*. Yet inherent in this question is a critique of a colonial legal system directly responsible for unauthorised land theft and genocide. In this respect, my 'question behind the question' forms the basic political impulse and ongoing motivation behind my research projects, which in turn helps frame my more detailed research question. While the precise formulation changes from project to project, once shaped cleanly, it is my research question that acts as the guidepost directing the project. While sometimes the guidepost points towards familiar territory, often I find myself pointed in directions I do not anticipate.

One consequence of knowing my 'question behind the question' has been that the key word in my research question is often 'where'? Such as: 'Where is Australian law?' And 'What laws are here?' Perhaps not surprisingly, such questions are not easily answered by doctrinal methods, which tend to focus on questions like: 'Is there a legal right or remedy?', 'Why is there no legal solution?' or 'How can we reform the law to enable X?' etc. The question, 'Where is law?', if ever asked, is only answered doctrinally by an uninterested shrug of 'everywhere, I guess'. In other words, questions about the location of law are not issues addressed by traditional legal research. But for me, having articulated my 'question behind the question', my legal research question shaped into a series of 'where' questions. This did make for unusual waywisers, granted, but having chosen to follow each waywiser as it asked questions of 'where', I found myself pointed in unexpected directions. The challenge then became one of learning to trust my waywiser to guide me, and to bring me back again, even when it pointed me towards some unfamiliar, even wayward, fields.

Wayward

To be wayward is commonly associated with disobedience and intractability. The Oxford English Dictionary defines wayward as 'disposed to go against the wishes or advice of others or what is proper or reasonable' and 'contrary to what is expected or desired'.[7] It also offers a definition of 'conforming to no fixed rule or principle of conduct; capricious, unaccountable; erratic, unpredictable; uncontrollable'. Maybe it is my temperament, political leanings or just the nature of my 'question behind the question', but norm-breaking has always been quite appealing. Not simply for its own sake, norm-breaking is appealing to me in circumstances where it makes sense to break the mould of current expectations because the current rules no longer make sense. While I haven't intentionally aimed to be wayward in my research methods, reflecting back on my research since completing my masters, including a long association with IILAH, I realise that like many others in law and humanities research, my method has not conformed to standard principles and processes. Adopting new and potentially wayward methods has taken my research outside orthodox legal practice and into some unexpected quarters. While wayfaring into disciplinary territories in the humanities, and in my case also the sciences, certainly involves risks elaborated in the final part of this article, such journeys also offer benefits that arise from addressing a research question in new ways. To manage this intentional waywardness and to avoid getting too lost when following a research question into unexpected fields or disciplines, the trick is to hold onto law in the form of a cleanly framed waywiser.

This is best illustrated by an example. My ongoing interest in questions of where and the topic of the location of law has meant that my waywiser often points me towards other disciplines more attuned to 'where' questions, such as geography, architecture and public art. In different ways, these are site-specific humanities disciplines that use research methods attentive to the specific places they study. Put rather bluntly, geography focuses on geo (the Earth) and in doing so addresses meta-questions of where. Architecture and public art direct attention to locations on a smaller scale. Method, in each discipline, is responsive to location and the specific details of each place. An architect, for example, would not use the same design for a building located on a rocky cliff, flat desert plain or insecure coastal land subject to erosion. Likewise, a public artist utilises the particular dynamics of a location to create a work that place-makes the site anew. By following my waywiser to disciplines more attuned to questions of site-specific locations, I have been able to learn new ways of going about place-based research. Returning to my waywiser after these explorations, I have incorporated some of these non-legal methods into my legal research. In other words, the question of 'where' has changed how I go about my work by influencing my method and guiding me towards an increasingly cross-disciplinary practice.

For instance, in my current project on legal places, I focus on a series of sites around the world from Germany, Iceland, Scotland and Australia to investigate how overlapping laws are inherited in particular locations. My method in this particular project is, no surprise, a 'mixed

7 "wayward, adj. and n.," *OED Online*, Oxford University Press, accessed October 30, 2019, https://www-oed-com.ezp.lib.unimelb.edu.au/view/Entry/226525.

method'. This time, though, it involves a series of site visits (architecture, public art), interviews (social sciences, anthropology), archives (history, photography) and analysis of doctrine (law). By investigating these sites using this 'wayward' method, I have been able to notice what laws are situated where, as well as how different laws at times overlap in one location. This has enabled me to develop a greater conceptual understanding of the more general relationship between law and place, which is an understanding simultaneously attentive to the deadlocking of law to location, and its vibrant temporality.

One site in this project on legal places is a much-loved community mural in Redfern, Sydney, Australia.[8] Over a number of years I spent time with this mural and the people involved in its complex story. To work with this site in a manner sensitive to its unique jouissance, I adopted a site-specific method influenced by architecture and art, and to a lesser extent participant-observation practices of anthropology. This involved repeat visits to catalogue the mural's changing nature over time. During each visit I walked alongside the mural to observe its material context, paused, took photographs, sometimes wrote poetry in response, before reflecting on the experience. As research methods, these are all very odd practices for a lawyer previously puzzled by the suggestion law even had a method, let alone multiple ones. However, as a direct result of using site-specific methods drawn from disciplines taking place-based research seriously, I learnt something new about law. I learnt some of the ways law and location intertwine, how this intertwining is unique to each site and how this manifests kaleidoscopically in complex sites hosting multiple laws. More specifically, I learnt:

> Wherever complex sites like this occur, whether in Redfern or an anonymous street corner, my argument is that fractal patterns of different types of law emerge, criss-crossing the physical landscape, creating a particular type of legal place that I have come to think of as a "kaleidoscopic legal place". . . . By focusing on one site at a time, and privileging materiality, it becomes possible to notice that sometimes, in fact often, different laws simultaneously inhabit the same place. . . . [When] different types of law inhabit physical spaces differently, whether state, federal, local, religious or Aboriginal . . . they exhibit distinct legal modes of physical manifestation. For example, in the case of a mural where multiple laws inhabit the same place, some laws materialise in the bricks, some in the pigment shards of long-faded paint, and some in the haptic hand of restoration artists. . . . A kaleidoscopic understanding of the place of law . . . offers a way of seeing how multiple layers of different types of law – such as local regulations, federal mandates and Aboriginal laws of *Country* for example – relentlessly interact to create, and recreate, unique legal places both above and below ground.[9]

While in some ways the concept of 'kaleidoscopic legal places' draws on the content of cross-disciplinary work in legal geography and a lesser extent legal pluralism, the method in identifying such locations remains refreshingly new. By adopting a way of doing research more common in the humanities than legal scholarship, my research on legal place provides a way to heighten the visibility of what is already there: multiple laws embedded in our material landscape. What is most interesting though is that this site-specific method reveals different types of

8 See Olivia Barr, "Legal Footprints," *Law Text Culture* 17 (2017): 214–51; Olivia Barr, "How to Notice Kaleidoscopic Legal Places: Lessons from a Mural, a Street in Redfern, and Walking the City on Aboriginal Country," *Law, Culture and Humanities* (forthcoming).

9 Barr, "How to Notice Kaleidoscopic Legal Places."

law do not inhabit places in the same manner, nor for the same duration. Noticing the quality of distinct legal places, including kaleidoscopic ones, is my response to my guidepost when it asks, 'where is law?'

By following a waywiser as it guided me towards other disciplines, and adopting what might be viewed in some quarters as 'wayward' methods, the practice of noticing legal differences as they manifest in distinct physical locations has become possible. Across different projects, and as a result of the guidepost changing, the method I use changes in response to each specific question. Looking back, what I have learnt from this experience is that embracing a wayward practice of method-making is a positive opportunity that finds and then opens new doors in legal research.

Waymaker

My aim in this reflective chapter has been to make visible my method. As a lawyer my work is unapologetically legal, and more specifically jurisprudential, even though my research is influenced by a number of other disciplines. While my formal training is in law, anthropology and philosophy, the research questions I often circle lead me to grapple with disciplines I have little to no experience in. For instance, alongside 'where' questions I continue to ask, a growing research interest in law's materiality has acted as a bridge to disciplines in the humanities, including geography and architecture again, as well as directing me towards geology and botany in the hard sciences. Over time, and with the support of IILAH and law and humanities scholars worldwide, I have developed confidence in my ability to contemplate law not just on its own terms, and not just from within law's limited range of methods. Reflecting back on this experience, what I have realised is that this movement towards the humanities (and even the sciences) inflects not only the content of my research, but also – and in many ways more importantly – its methods. As explored in this chapter, law and humanities scholarship provides an opportunity to creatively engage in diverse methods of scholarship that open up legal research questions in unimaginable ways. This truly is a wondrous gift. Yet it is a gift that raises a unique set of challenges, including coming to terms with the nimble dance required of all good cross-disciplinary scholarship, ensuring research remains legal despite this dance, as well as an awareness that method is never apolitical.

Law and humanities research comes with the very real risk of enthusiastically but indelicately treading on someone else's disciplinary turf, especially when it is a discipline lawyers rarely visit. When I find myself in scenarios outside my formal training, a measure of uncertainty arises. Often I hesitate before ultimately trusting my waywiser. Yet the uncertainty remains, and I try to manage this by being respectful of other disciplines through a variety of simple practices. Sometimes this involves finding experts willing to engage as collaborators, educators or simply in conversation. I've audited classes, learnt by co-teaching in disciplines I'm not trained in (e.g., architecture), bugged a friend's 12-year-old just back from geology camp to share their new knowledge, and I will soon put myself on a stone-wall making course to better understand the material and haptic construction of a site in my legal place project. I also, of course, read widely, from discipline-specific literature to introductory textbooks.

When I wayfare into other territory, the important point is that I always remain a lawyer writing jurisprudence. While I may pitch my work as cross-disciplinary occasionally, a law question in my waywiser always guides me, so I'm not debilitatingly worried about treading on disciplinary toes. I have, of course, trodden on toes, because method is political. Some historians have been quite grumpy at me when my research engages with historical moments in an unfamiliar manner. I spent a good few years learning to explain how lawyers and historians might wander in the same historical period, and even use similar archival methods at times, but ask quite different questions of the same material. While this was fruitful at times, at others the attempt to open up cross-disciplinary conversations was unsuccessful. On the other hand, architects, geographers and public artists have mostly been delightfully open, if not mildly amused, at my curiosity towards their discipline, and I'm yet to learn much about geologists or botanists. Whether successful or not, the practice of engaging in cross-disciplinary conversations is a useful learning curve itself.

How, then, to manage the challenges involved in taking up creative approaches to method-making, such as the public projection or internal experience of waywardness? The answer is quite simple: hold onto law. When your waywiser leads you to methods more commonly practiced in disciplines outside of law, utilise these methods respectfully while maintaining a steadfast focus on your disciplinary practice in law. Try not to hold back from the challenge, and instead try to navigate any feelings of uncertainty by ensuring the research question remains wholly within the field of jurisprudence: questioning the practice and conduct of law. Keep in mind that contemporary research authorised by law and humanities scholarship is uniquely capable of pushing boundaries and breaking traditional legal norms while refusing to cede the central point that this *is* legal scholarship, even if it might not be familiar yet.

An openness to method, including cross-disciplinary methods in the humanities and the sciences, can propel legal research into quite wonderful directions. If I hadn't followed my research question into unfamiliar disciplinary waters, I feel confident I wouldn't have learnt what I have about law. Questions of location and materiality have been my bridges to other disciplines, but there are many other topics, questions or curiosities that might also act as bridges to unexpected fields. If the opportunity arises, my advice is simple: be open. Be open not just to new concepts and theories, but also to new methods and disciplines. Genuine scholarship and deep learning follows the research question, even if the turf gets a little scary sometimes.

This is why I conclude with the proposition that law and humanities scholars are waymakers. A waymaker is someone who prepares the road or the way as a forerunner, precursor or a prelude. While it is uncomfortably self-indulgent to think of my work in this way, law and humanities scholars often make new paths in legal research by treading somewhere for the first time. This allows others to follow, and to make their own paths by avoiding unfruitful avenues or continuing further along the same track. In a sense, whether it is through the conceptual knitting of new intellectual strands or the adoption of 'wayfaring methods' as I have suggested here, law and humanities scholarship is best understood as a research practice of collective and collaborative waymaking.

11

Foot notes. Reflections on method and form

Laura Petersen

What is your law question? This is the refrain which accompanied my thesis writing. I heard it in different ways over the years, and I know perhaps these were deliberate mishearings – or ways it may not have been intended to be heard. In the beginning, I heard it as a challenge. My chosen objects came out of literature and art but I was writing a doctorate in a law school. I heard it as a way of saying the law needed its own questions, it couldn't be contained within questions from the humanities. It was as if only the 'law' remained. This seemed somewhat fitting for a thesis which was explicitly thematising remainders, the idea of a fragment, and what is left behind. But I am not sure if that way of hearing it was true. As I grew more fluent in the language and origins of contemporary discussions at Melbourne Law School, I heard it differently: what is your law question? The intonation fell on the 'your' – the personal, the possessive – what does it mean to you, to take on the responsibility for asking and having the authority to ask questions of law, and particularly now, in this time, in this place, as an Australian legal scholar working today. What is your law question? Later I heard it differently again, with the focus on the idea of a 'question': a word with an etymology grounded in legal history as an old form of inquest and interrogation. But it also seemed to hold within it a sense of seeking, an openness, a literal quest linked with an institution – an institutional journey of law. I know that is perhaps just another way to describe doing a PhD in a law school. But all of these meanings and meetings of law holding within them the themes of genre, perspective, and authority have stayed with me.

Law is bound by its form.[1]

Law is an aesthetic enterprise. Before the ethical dreams and political ambitions of law can even be articulated, let alone realized, the aesthetics of law have already shaped the medium within which those projects will have to do their work.[2]

1 Ronald K. L. Collins and David M. Skover, "Paratexts," *Stanford Law Review* 44, no. 3 (February 1992): 509, https://doi.org/10.2307/1228974.

2 Pierre Schlag, "The Aesthetics of American Law," *Harvard Law Review* 115, no. 4 (February 2002): 1049, https://doi.org/10.2307/1342629.

This piece offers some personal reflections on method and the communication of research undertaken in the area of law and humanities. It explores the idea of 'foot notes' in two ways. I pay attention to the form of legal writing to notice how the footnote functions as a representation of authority in legal scholarship. However, I also use the term as a way to think about a grounded method for undertaking legal research outside of texts – literally as 'foot notes'. As part of this, I describe the process of making a short video as part of my PhD project. This was intended as a way of recording – for myself – an experience of walking through a street in Berlin. However, it proved also to be a tool in trying to communicate my work to an audience. In this way, I use the idea of a foot note – in both meanings – to explore the potentials and difficulties of trying to express the connection between form and content in scholarly work.

Part one: in the margins

Form in legal scholarship

The verb 'to craft' is often used as a synonym for the practice of writing. All types of writing are the result of wordsmithing: crafting texts into forms, which themselves carry within them particular textual practices. This first section explores one textual practice used in legal scholarship: the footnote.

Thinking about form is not a new approach – as Adam Gearey begins his book on *Law and Aesthetics*, '[f]orm bestows identity and coherence on the phenomenon of study. The idea of form is the prerequisite to the study of any discipline'.[3] But often the formal, structural dimensions of the text do not receive the attention they deserve. I am interested, in particular, in legal marginalia: in genres of commentary, such as the gloss, but also the textual practices of scholarship, including paratexts, headings and footnotes. What fascinates me is the tension between the vessel for knowledge, the form, as a way of necessarily setting limits and constraints but also having a 'performative' or 'productive' nature.[4] For instance, in his seminal work on genre theory, John Frow draws our attention to that double quality which is provoked when one begins to examine the shape of a work: the shape is something that 'both enables and restricts meaning and is a basic condition for meaning to take place'.[5]

Paying attention to form is not a neutral undertaking. In fact, it is a way to notice what may otherwise be taken for granted. Desmond Manderson, a scholar known for his attempts to explicitly perform and subvert formal constraints, writes:

> Formal design or structure – whether of a poem or a statute – is not just the medium through which ideas are expressed but is itself an aspect of meaning. Form and style are not, then, just the receptacles into which abstract propositions of law are bundled but part of what the law says to us. Indeed, exactly because the form of something is often not on the conscious horizon of its authors, it provides us with a revealing glimpse into that which is accepted uncritically within a legal community.[6]

3 Adam Gearey, *Law and Aesthetics* (Oxford: Hart, 2001), 4.
4 John Frow, *Genre*, 2nd ed. (New York: Routledge, 2015), 10.
5 Ibid.
6 Desmond Manderson, *Songs Without Music: Aesthetic Dimensions of Law and Justice* (Berkeley: University of California Press, 2000), 33.

Paying attention to form is therefore a way to get texts to open up their different layers of meaning and ideological impulses. It follows Douzinas et al.'s approach to critique:

> The critical scholar attends to the marginal, the peripheral or the surface precisely so as to recapture the politics which has escaped the text, or has been hidden beneath its ritual paraphernalia.[7]

The footnote, therefore, is a minor but intriguing part of the 'ritual paraphernalia' of legal scholarship.[8]

The footnote

So if the philology of legal scholarship matters, where do footnotes come from? The historiographer Anthony Grafton tracks the footnote back to the Enlightenment era of the creation of social sciences and the beginnings of a particular methodology of history writing, beginning with Leopold von Ranke in the early 1800s.[9] However, texts that could be defined as legal or jurisprudential in nature have footnotes which appear earlier than this, right from the beginning of printing.[10] The print revolution also meant that the cross-referencing of books could begin with ease.[11] Their placement at the bottom of the page led to a shift in understanding about the purpose of these types of annotations – they were now 'subordinate' to the main text.[12] In any

7 Peter Goodrich, Costas Douzinas and Yifat Hachamovitch, "Introduction. Politics, Ethics and the Legality of the Contingent," in *Politics, Postmodernity and Critical Legal Studies. The Legality of the Contingent*, eds. Costas Douzinas, Peter Goodrich and Yifat Hachamovitch (London: Routledge, 1994), 16.

8 Drawing attention to these forms of marginalia within a legal tradition also fits with other scholarship in different domains. In literary studies, for instance, Tribble argues that '[a]nnotations – glosses in the margins and their eighteenth-century successors, footnotes – are consistently undervalued in studies of the history of authorship and publishing. Yet, if rendered visible, the page has much to tell us.' Evelyn B. Tribble, "Like a Looking-Glass in the Frame': From the Marginal Note to the Footnote," in *The Margins of the Text*, ed. David C. Greetham (Ann Arbor: The University of Michigan Press, 1997), 229.

9 Anthony Grafton, *The Footnote: A Curious History* (Cambridge, MA: Harvard University Press, 1997), 34ff.

10 See, for example, Patrick Parkinson, *Tradition and Change in Australian Law* (North Ryde: Law Book Company, 1994), 34.

11 Elizabeth L. Eisenstein, *The Printing Press as an Agent of Change Vol. 1* (Cambridge: Cambridge University Press, 1979), 135.

12 Lawrence Lipking, "The Marginal Gloss," *Critical Inquiry* 3, no. 4 (July 1, 1977): 609–55, https://doi.org/10.1086/447910. See for example: 'As with all aspects of the annotational phenomenon, these early forms were involved with the economics and technology of printing. It was a printing trend, not an authorial trend, that began in the eighteenth century to move annotational reference from the margins to the bottom of the page.' Thomas McFarland, "Who Was Benjamin Whichcote? Or, The Myth of Annotation," in *Annotation and Its Texts*, ed. Stephen A. Barney (New York: Oxford University Press, 1991), 165. However perhaps the positioning of annotations will change once legal scholarship moves primarily onto the screen. In 2015, the *Harvard Law Review* website was updated with a new design: "Harvard Law Review," Harvard University, accessed November 29, 2019, https://harvardlawreview.org/. Fittingly, given the ancient legal tradition of annotations, the main text of article has been designed to appear in the middle of the screen, just like a folio of a medieval manuscript. The footnotes are signalled with subscript but appear alongside the relevant sentence, in the 'margins' of both sides of the webpage and not at the bottom of the page. See the design approach by the web designers: "No Photos in over 127 Years? No Problem," *Upstatement*, accessed November 29, 2019, https://casestudies.upstatement.com/work/harvard-law-review/. In this way, the internet has enabled legal annotation to go back in time before the printing revolution and return to a medieval visual layout which elevates the annotations back up to the same level as the main text.

case, today's contemporary legal scholarship and judicial opinion writing are characterised by their copious use of footnotes.[13]

Regardless of their positioning on the page, footnotes result in an interruption of the reading experience of a text. As the oft-quoted (and mis-attributed) line by John Barrymore bemoans, 'having to look at a footnote was like having to go down to the front door just as you were making love.'[14] Through the convention of a numbered subscript, the reader's gaze is halted and drawn to a reference containing extra-textual material that is at the same time within the page of the work. This material could be personal to the author – an aside, a digression – but usually the footnote contains evidence (or contra-evidence) for the assertions made in the body of the text. These marks designating and linking to texts published beforehand are embedded within the strata of scholarly work; they conform to the geological 'principle of inclusions', where fragments in a rock are older than the rock itself.[15] Legal scholarship is therefore always textually open, gesturing to extra-textual presences and absences in the margins.[16] Footnotes, however, do not only result in a stratification of texts and a shifting of time as part of the reading experience. They also mark the text as being itself part of a particular context, and holding within it certain professional and institutional inheritances.[17] Footnotes in legal scholarship function to rhetorically and practically demonstrate that the writer belongs to a community of scholars and that their work conforms to an important ethos of attribution. Footnotes are the key textual practice which turns a writer into a scholar and the resulting text into an authoritative scholarly argument; they are necessarily 'bound up, in modern life, with the ideology and the technical practices of a profession'.[18] Footnotes, however marginal, are about representations of authority and institutional power.

Furthermore, it must be remarked that in common law judicial opinions, footnotes are *the* textual practice which gives a court its authority. They are the transmitter and rhetorical signifier of legal precedent – the medium through which a judicial decision represents itself as sound law. As Goodrich et al. remind us:

> The half-said or more properly enigmatic quality of the citation, of the influence, borrowing or reception thus itself becomes a question of ethics and interpretation, a matter of the politics of institutional transmission, a question of justice.[19]

13 The spoof or satirical article about the use of footnotes in law seems to be a common way for legal academics to let off steam. Surveying the situation in American law reviews, Joan Magat notes that '[c]riticism of the footnote is just about as old as the footnote itself'. Joan Ames Magat, "Bottomheavy: Legal Footnotes," *Journal of Legal Education* 60, no. 1 (2010): 69. The obsession with footnotes extends to the German legal system, see: Herbert Grziwotz, "Glosse: Der Fußnotenwahn," *Legal Tribune Online*, February 21, 2011, www.lto.de/recht/feuilleton/f/glosse-der-fussnotenwahn/.

14 On the somewhat ironic problems of verification and misattribution of this quotation to Noel Coward and even Austin himself, see Arthur Austin, "Footnote Skulduggery and Other Bad Habits," *University of Miami Law Review* 44 (1990): 1012, footnote 20.

15 Steven Earle, *Physical Geology* (Victoria: BCcampus, 2015), https://opentextbc.ca/geology/.

16 They can also serve as subtle clues to scholarly allegiances; the omission of authors can be more telling than the inclusion. 'To the inexpert, footnotes look like deep root systems, solid and fixed; to the connoisseur, however, they reveal themselves as anthills, swarming with constructive and combative activity.' Grafton, *The Footnote: A Curious History*, 9.

17 'In documenting the thought and research that underpin the narrative above them, footnotes prove that it is a historically contingent product, dependent on the forms of research, opportunities, and states of particular questions that existed when the historian went to work.' Ibid., 23.

18 Ibid., 5.

19 Peter Goodrich, et al., "Introduction: A Philosophy of Legal Enigmas," in *Derrida and Legal Philosophy*, eds. Peter Goodrich, Florian Hoffman, Michel Rosenfeld and Cornelia Vismann (Basingstoke: Palgrave Macmillan, 2008), 10.

Part two: beyond text

This next section takes a different approach and writing style. Here I am interested in what happens when one attempts to do legal scholarship in a genre which goes beyond the 'page'. How do these same questions of authority and inheritance function in different genres? Or, more precisely, how do I present law and humanities research, which relies on a grounded, affective method, in a scholarly text, *without losing the essence of what I am trying to express*? What happens when I am using a different form of evidence, of footnotes, but just ones that are outside of a page – notes made on foot, notes made while moving, notes of moving?[20]

Schöneberg, Berlin

These questions come out of my research centred on an area of Berlin called the Bavarian Quarter in the suburb of Schöneberg. As part of my PhD on the legal and aesthetic practices of restitution, I became interested in public art monuments and memorials in Berlin. As such, I did field research walking the streets and neighbourhoods of Schöneberg over a series of days. In the resulting chapter in my PhD, I invoke the performative and ritualised nature of walking through these streets as a way to argue that walking could be a way of enacting everyday moments of law and of restitution.

I was interested in two memorials in Schöneberg which I will only describe briefly here. Both are deeply embedded within the streetscape. First, *Places of Remembrance* consists of 80 aluminium signs mounted on the side of lampposts which re-print excerpts from regulations from the Nazi regime.[21] They are mounted in everyday locations. These locations are not necessarily 'historical' but are sites which are relevant for the *present* in a way that is connected with the law remembered on the sign. These sites range from the post office, shops in the shopping strip, apartment buildings in residential streets, as well as in front of institutions such as the courthouse, a church and a school. Present day buildings therefore become overlaid and imbued with spectres of the past, activated by a walker passing by. I follow the way that walking and moving in the streets of Schöneberg becomes a spatial and temporal 'contact point' for restitutive legal stories after the Nazi period: constructing sites which encourage past, present and future legal relations to become visible to the walker.

Second, I focus on the *Stolpersteine* ('Stumbling Stone') memorials by Gunter Demnig.[22] In German *stolpern* means to stumble or to trip, so the name refers to an interrupted gait, an impeded movement. It also has a second meaning corresponding to the second meaning of stumble in English: to stumble across something, to come across something, often by chance. *Stolpersteine* are small brass plaques, directly inlaid into the footpath. They have a simple, consistent inscription hammered by hand stating details such as: Name, Year of birth, Date of Deportation and Place if known, and details about the fate of the person, which is usually 'murdered' or 'missing'. They are made to be the same size as the cobblestones in the footpath and are inlaid in front of their entrance door or the closest place to their last known residence.

20 On the role of walking as legal method, see the chapter in this Handbook by Olivia Barr, "Wayfaring Methods." See also generally Olivia Barr, *A Jurisprudence of Movement: Common Law, Walking, Unsettling Place* (New York: Routledge, 2016).

21 The full title of the memorial (translated): "Places of Remembrance in the Bavarian Quarter: Exclusion and Deprivation of Rights, Expulsion, Deportation, and Murder of Berlin Jews from 1933 to 1945." The memorial was created by Renata Stih and Frieder Schnock in 1993.

22 See Gunter Demnig, "Stolpersteine," accessed November 29, 2019, www.stolpersteine.eu/en/.

When it came to 'write up' the results of these 'foot notes' after coming home to Melbourne, however, I was struck by the inadequacy of my descriptions. How to capture these moments in text – how to make a textual mark – when I was contending that the whole point of these memorials and their legal posturing was that these were ephemeral personal experiences. In other words, if the method of undertaking my work is based on a sense of grounded affective methodology – trying to explore the way law can also be a form of bodily movement – what happens when this has to be represented through writing, especially using a mechanised font and standardised A4 page?[23]

Be Berlin

I decided to deliberately write these concerns into the chapter, making sure there was a meta-level of commentary, in the footnotes at the bottom of the page, which attempted to draw attention to the performative shaping of the text. In addition, I structured the chapter as a walking tour, trying through this deliberate textual manoeuvre to draw attention to the artifice of the text itself.[24] Academic writing is imbued with metaphors to do with movement – first step, second step; an excursion; a detour; a logical jump – and these have implications on the structure and expected 'progression' of an argument.[25] I struggled to deploy these metaphors in my writing so that they were operating in a double-way and enabled me to speak about slipping between time, place, text and experience. I wanted to reflect the sense of Berlin and a city which is changing; the city slogan was at that time 'Be Berlin'. I like this slogan because it captures the sense of becoming, openness and 'freedom' which is now possible. But it also captures the way individuals can craft a city (and also a memorial) through their moment of visiting: you – resident, visitor, migrant – can be Berlin, and whatever 'Berlin' is, it is constantly in flux.[26] I wanted to try to make the reading experience, usually in English from left to right/up to down, also to be a form of wandering through a textual landscape.

In addition, I felt that to view a text as a monolith is to also ignore the agency of the reader and to underestimate the dynamic which evolves between a reader, a text and their time and place of reading it; it ignores the deep resonance which can develop between texts and readers. Readers bring a text alive, completing it with their own memories, experiences and predilections that evolve through taking on the responsibility of reading. In this way, Peter Fitzpatrick, bringing the insights of reception studies across to legal theory, writes: 'the work now in the

23 I don't pretend that this is a new dilemma or that the way I am presenting it here recognises the depth and complexity of such a question; this is a concern which stretches all the way back to the ontological and epistemological aspects of representation and scholarship.

24 There are a lot of similarities between going on a walking tour and reading an academic text. An academic text mirrors the role of a guide through the streets of a city – the author chooses the terrain, designs a route, speaks the narrative, and proscribes where the text pauses and the direction in which the reader is invited to look.

25 On the force of metaphor generally, see George Lakoff and Mark Johnson, *Metaphors We Live By*, 6th ed. (Chicago: University of Chicago Press, 2011). See also Alison Young writing about the walking tour: 'Whatever the format, walking tours trade upon the notion that walking-and-looking is an unmediated phenomenon.' Alison Young, *Street Art, Public City: Law, Crime and the Urban Imagination* (New York: Routledge, 2014), 160.

26 See for example: 'Their story begins on ground level, with footsteps. They are myriad, but do not compose a series. They cannot be counted because each unit has a qualitative character: a style of tactile apprehension and kinaesthetic appropriation. Their swarming mass is an innumerable collection of singularities. Their intertwined paths give their shape to spaces. They weave places together.' Michel de Certeau, *The Practice of Everyday Life*, vol. 1, trans. Steven Rendall (Berkeley: University of California Press, 1988), 97.

world cannot exist apart from the relation to its readers.'[27] I had to try to remember that my text was an address and an invitation; it was not a one-way-street.

Moving images

In order to document some of the memorials, I had taken some short video footage walking through the neighbourhood streets of Schöneberg. I hoped that the video footage would be a reminder for me of how it was to 'be there', a *souvenir* – a reliable form of 'memory' – which was to be forever captured by my pocket camera and taken to Australia.

The footage follows my pair of sandals as they walk on the footpath on a sunny day on a quiet neighbourhood street, then looks up at a sign of an adult holding the hand of a child. The camera's gaze then follows the curve of a lamppost and takes in one of the *Places of Remembrance* signs, pivoting around in the streaming sun to offer a view of both sides of the sign, zooming in clunkily to see the text. Then the camera's gaze zooms out and returns back down to the footpath, back to the sandals, as I walk a few metres down the street. Pausing again, facing downwards, the camera zooms in so that two of the *Stolpersteine* embedded at the edge of the footpath slowly fill the frame.

The video was made quickly and intuitively, the sequence was not planned. I did not intend to deliberately draw on the traditions and motifs of the language of cinema. Nevertheless, the footage does contain certain key elements which fittingly reflect (through both images and techniques) some of the processes which I am trying to get across. For example, the beginning with my own feet in the frame is a form of glorified 'shoe selfie'. However, it means the footage immediately begins with feet, shoes, the ground and walking. It means the camera follows my standpoint, my perspective, and nothing outside of this. There are no establishing shots. In a way, this fits my approach to this material – I am not a neutral observer, I am always in the frame and now I am visually there, embedded in the presentation of my work. Also, on reflection, there is a certain amount of charm to the clunky zoom. It is a technique which reminds the viewer that this is not an edited or an official representation but rather a serendipitous one. It brings one back to the personal and somewhat haphazard experience which you may have if you encounter these memorials in the street.

Address and audience

The footage was meant to be just for my private use. But then I decided to integrate the film into a PowerPoint presentation about my research at Melbourne Law School. I added some music to the footage but did not edit it in any other way. The music was from the German band *Fink*, the song: *Talking Darum Blues* (2003). I didn't translate or explain the lyrics but left them foreign, in German, so this foreignness would be part of the process of viewing. I wanted to try, as much as possible, for a viewer to feel immersed for a few minutes in the experience of being in Germany, even though they were sitting in Australia.

I also didn't translate for my audience the text of the *Places of Remembrance* sign which is shown in the video. This was a deliberate move. The German language of the memorial means it has a specific address. Compared to other memorials in Berlin which are frequented often by

27 Peter Fitzpatrick, "Reading Slowly. The Law of Literature and the Literature of Law," in *Reading Modern Law: Critical Methodologies and Sovereign Formations*, eds. Ruth Buchanan, Stewart J. Motha and Sundhya Pahuja (New York: Routledge, 2012), 197.

tourists, *Places of Remembrance* is a de-centralised memorial designed for a specific neighbourhood. It is a memorial written in German and addressed to Germans, specifically to Germans living in the present, in those streets in Schöneberg.[28]

The reaction to the video footage was fascinating. Many members of the audience were from a law school but not necessarily used to some of the methods and techniques of undertaking law and humanities scholarship. The video was the main topic of conversation afterwards. The moving images, the music and, I suppose, the novelty of showing a form of 'home-movie' in a law seminar – there was something about the process of viewing that seemed to interrupt the standard presentation format. It was also a short, simulated moment of 'being there' which (I would like to think) enabled the audience to experience a different form of understanding of my research. I don't think they would have had the same reaction if I hadn't shown the footage; I don't think I could have conveyed the same message through words alone.

Genre and medium

This reaction demonstrated to me two things about form and, in particular, designations of genre and medium. Presenting material which self-consciously names itself as being in a particular genre means to take a specific standpoint, to make an argument through form. For example, Frow emphasises the way 'all genres possess historically specific and variable *expressive capacities*: they offer frameworks for constructing meaning and value in one or another medium'.[29] As I have explained, part of the aim of my chapter in my PhD was to explore what happens when we move in those streets in Schöneberg and *how* we could view this walking as legal movement and restitutive posturing. This could be seen as a question of genre in law and humanities – or, more specifically, a question of what is at stake when we name the content of something as also forming part of a genre of 'law'.

What is your law question?

In addition, the effect of changing the format of my message away from a spoken and textual mode of presentation, to being transmitted through a film – through visuals and music – had a startling effect. But how to replicate that inside of the genre of a law PhD thesis? My question became whether I can remain tethered to and work within the constraints of a written text, acknowledging and attributing sources but not necessarily following the rigid style of traditional legal scholarship.[30]

28 Underneath every memorial sign there is another miniature sign that indicates it is part of a memorial project. This was due to concern and complaints from residents after their installation that the signs were part of Neo-Nazi propaganda. See for example, James Young: 'Thus reassured that the public had taken notice, the artists pointed out that these same laws had been posted and announced no less publicly at the time – but had provoked no such response by Germans then. At least part of the artist's point was that the laws then were no less public than the memory of them was now.' James E. Young, *At Memory's Edge: After-Images of the Holocaust in Contemporary Art and Architecture* (New Haven: Yale University Press, 2000), 115.

29 Frow, *Genre*, 79 (emphasis in original).

30 As Patricia Williams states: 'Legal writing presumes a methodology that is highly stylized, precedential, and based on deductive reasoning. Most scholarship in law is rather like the 'old math': static, stable, formal – rationalism walled in against chaos.' Patricia Williams, *The Alchemy of Race and Rights* (Cambridge: Harvard University Press, 1991), 7.

Scholarly precedents

Writing in a way which draws attention to form is to take seriously your positioning as a scholar. For example, coming out of traditions of feminist theory, where questioning methodologies has always been part of the feminist project,[31] Ann Genovese expresses her aim of accepting 'the duties of my own personae, to understand precisely what the art of writing the self – its form and content – express as an historical practice'.[32] For instance, Genovese reclaims the use of the first person, explaining the way it is formed through a persona in the text:

> when in pursuit of the question "how should I live" and how that might be written, the "I" is not directed to an authoring of self, or disclosing an authentic self, through writing. Writing in this tradition is neither romantic nor confessional. Instead the "I" attaches to the persona – be it philosopher, historian, jurisprudent or as we shall see, feminist.[33]

The vanguard of self-reflexive writing in legal scholarship was Patricia Williams. Williams creatively stages the encounter of self, institution and society in her texts, using different genres and styles to portray the everyday effects and affects of law, race and personhood. Indeed, the first line in Williams' book *The Alchemy of Race and Rights* (now almost 30 years old) encapsulates her approach:

> Since subject position is everything in my analysis of the law, you deserve to know it is a bad morning.[34]

In the next paragraph comes the line:

> So you should know that this is one of those mornings when I refuse to compose myself properly.[35]

This phrase encapsulates how she intends to write about law in a performatively un-composed, radical way. But it also reflects her refusal (and the difficulties) to keep a homogenous persona ('myself') together in a text and a world where she crosses through the identities of black female, sister, daughter, commercial lawyer and professor. Deploying a style of writing where 'little bits of law and pieces of everyday life fly out in weird combinations',[36]

31 For example, feminist scholar Wendy Harcourt is concerned to try to find 'new methods that can "perform" and capture the fluidity of changing understandings of identities, bodies, emotions, networks, power relations, and knowledge. This is particularly important for the in-between places, cyberspaces, people, places, and events that refuse to be categorized.' Wendy Harcourt, et al., "Assessing, Engaging, and Enacting Worlds: Tensions in Feminist Method/Ologies," *International Feminist Journal of Politics* 17, no. 1 (January 2015): 160, https://doi.org/10.1080/14616742.2014.988451.

32 Ann Genovese, "Inheriting and Inhabiting the Pleasures and Duties of Our Own Existence: *The Second Sex* and Feminist Jurisprudence," *Australian Feminist Law Journal* 38, no. 1 (June 2013): 49–50, https://doi.org/10.1080/13200968.2013.10854482.

33 Ann Genovese, "On Australian Feminist Tradition: Three Notes on Conduct, Inheritance and the Relations of Historiography and Jurisprudence," *Journal of Australian Studies* 38, no. 4 (October 2014): 432, https://doi.org/10.1080/14443058.2014.954137.

34 Williams, *The Alchemy of Race and Rights*, 3.

35 Ibid., 4.

36 Ibid., 14.

Williams describes her methodology as 'a way that bridges the traditional gap between theory and praxis'.[37] What is striking about Williams' work is the way her texts reflect different ways of doing legal scholarship – not only through their content, but also through their form.

Conclusion

I have offered some thoughts on form, medium and questions of standpoint in this piece. I began by emphasising how we should pay attention to the 'ritual paraphernalia' of legal scholarship and how footnotes are a textual practice concerned with authority and institutional power. But I wanted also to draw attention to the way in which including them in scholarly writing always places a text into relation with other texts. Noticing the practice of writing with footnotes means thinking about what it means to practice a scholarly ethos and join a community of scholars. I also demonstrated how doing research in law and the humanities is oftentimes outside of the boundaries of typed words on a page. It can be about trying to do scholarship in a way which is embodied and experienced and takes its authority from a momentary experience on the ground – a foot note. Taking that idea further, I explored what happens when mediums change and words become moving images.

Throughout I am trying to pay attention to the power of the 'interruption'. Footnotes are a mechanism which may disrupt an assertive monologue of legal scholarship; they are the small key to an archive, a link between the past and the present moment of reading. The film footage in my presentation was also a break in medium; luckily it was received as a welcome intrusion. And to join it all together, I note the way Lauren Berlant (another scholar highly attuned to the dynamics of form) describes the writing practice of Patricia Williams as performing and instituting an 'ethics of interruption'.[38] Perhaps, to conclude, these are all moments of what Adam Gearey describes as the aim of legal aesthetics – 'an interruption of the dialogue that the institution holds with itself'.[39]

What is your law question? I hear this refrain now as a necessary provocation; I hear it as a shorthand method to try to teach a way of thinking about legal scholarship that finds value in trying to continually understand what the questions may be. While the content is important, it was the iteration of this phrase which meant I also started to think about the way legal questions come to be shaped and passed on. What is your law question? I now hear it as an invitation, ultimately, to pay attention to the inheritances and the potential held within different practices of doing legal scholarship. There was no way to write down a simple answer.

37 Ibid., 6. Lauren Berlant describes how she 'mixes up the theoretical voice with the observational as they are already in contact.' Lauren Berlant, "She's Having an Episode: Patricia Williams and the Writing of Damaged Life," *Columbia Journal of Gender and Law* 27, no. 1 (2013): 35.

38 Berlant, "She's Having an Episode: Patricia Williams and the Writing of Damaged Life," 35. Parallel to this is the writing of Bonnie Honig, in *Antigone, Interrupted,* which is a text that stages a new approach to 'interruption'. Bonnie Honig, *Antigone, Interrupted* (Cambridge: Cambridge University Press, 2013).

39 Gearey, *Law and Aesthetics*, 99.

12

Critical humanities and the human of international human rights law

Ben Golder

How might we best understand the relationship between human rights and the humanities? In his 1993 Oxford Amnesty lecture on 'Human Rights, Rationality, and Sentimentality,' the American neo-pragmatist philosopher Richard Rorty famously takes aim at what he calls human rights foundationalism. By foundationalism Rorty means the vain attempt, on the part of philosophers from Plato to Kant (and down to the present), to adduce 'a philosophically ascertainable truth about what it is to be a human being'.[1] Arguing that such an inquiry into the nature or the essence of human being is 'outmoded and irrelevant' to the contemporary human rights project,[2] Rorty contends that the success of that project today relies much less upon developing a philosophically robust account of what makes us human (rationality, dignity, free will and so forth) than on deploying practices of sentimental education. Crucially, it is the telling and the 'hearing of sad and sentimental stories', that does most to shift the limits of moral concern and respect, 'expand[ing] the reference of the terms "our kind of people" and "people like us"' so as to extend the franchise of human rights across the globe.[3] This is doubtless why Rorty suggests, in *Contingency, Irony, and Solidarity*, that 'the novel, the movie, and the TV program have, gradually but steadily, replaced the sermon and the treatise as the principal vehicles of moral change and progress'.[4] Here the humanities (or, at least, some representatives of the humanities) are recruited to the human rights mission, figured as enriching, extending and empowering the writ of international human rights law – indeed, in some versions of this argument, as *enabling* of human rights in the first place (think for example of the historian Lynn Hunt's intriguing contention that reading epistolary novels about the plight of fictional others generates the empathetic imagination required for the *Rights of Man*).[5]

1 Richard Rorty, "Human Rights, Rationality, and Sentimentality," in *On Human Rights: The Oxford Amnesty Lectures*, eds. Stephen Shute and Susan Hurley (New York: Basic Books, 1993), 134.

2 Ibid., 116, quoting Eduardo Rabossi, "La teoría de los derechos humanos naturalizada," *Revista del Centro de Estudios Constitucionales* 5 (1990): 159.

3 Rorty, "Human Rights, Rationality, and Sentimentality," 119, 122–23.

4 Richard Rorty, *Contingency, Irony, and Solidarity* (Cambridge: Cambridge University Press, 1989), xvi.

5 Lynn Hunt, *Inventing Human Rights: A History* (New York and London: W. W. Norton & Co, 2008); cf Joseph Slaughter, *Human Rights Inc.: The World Novel, Narrative Form, and International Law* (New York: Fordham University Press, 2007).

There is doubtless far more to this complicated relation between human rights and the humanities, and much has already been written on the topic.[6] In this chapter my intention is neither to traverse this voluminous archive nor to propose a relation between international law (even, more circumspectly, international *human rights* law) and the humanities writ large, but to confine my attention more narrowly to the encounter between international human rights law and two particular humanistic modes of critique: *genealogy* and *performativity*. These genres of humanistic critique function neither (per Rorty's philosophical targets) to justify or found human rights, nor to serve, *pace* Rorty, as their cultural 'vehicles of moral change and progress', but rather to put the very human of international human rights law productively in question. In the best spirit of the critical humanities, they take something supposedly commonsensical and presuppositional and render it strange, turning it into a problem for us. Whereas genealogy (*à la* Nietzsche and Foucault, for example) evokes the groundlessness and contingencies of the human, performativity (*à la* Arendt and Butler, for example) calls for that human's reimagining and pluralisation.

In what follows, and in the tradition of handbook entries understood as manuals and guides to particular techniques, I attempt to lay out how genealogy and performativity, as particular modes of humanistic critique, work both to problematise and expose the contingencies of the human of international human rights law as well as to give us the tools to begin to remake that human differently and otherwise. In so doing I neither want to suggest that problematising the human is the special preserve of the humanities (indeed, lessons from primatology, neuroscience and artificial intelligence, to name just a few scientific disciplines, work similarly destabilising effects),[7] nor that genealogy and performativity are the humanities' only or best tools to reimagine the human. Rather, I simply select these two modes of critique as they are each representative of currently influential and productive forms of inquiry in the contemporary scholarship on international human rights law, and hence forms of inquiry with which any handbook entry should hope to reckon.

Genealogy

Embedded in most orthodox introductions to human rights or relevant chapters in international law textbooks is some version of the following, confidently asserted, phrase. '[H]uman rights', to take the exemplary instance of Jack Donnelly's *Universal Human Rights in Theory and Practice*, 'are the rights one has simply because one is a human being'.[8] As a means of distinguishing an entitlement to human rights from, say, an entitlement to citizenship rights or contractual rights, each of which clearly depend upon the rightsholder's birth or entry into a particular legal status or relation, the formulation serves a limited heuristic purpose. As a means of asserting the simplicity or straightforwardness of the legal category of the human it is, of course, a complete (yet productive) failure. For it turns out that there is nothing simple or straightforward about the human that is said to be the bearer of human rights. As I suggested earlier, there are multiple disciplinary ways of unpacking who or what is claimed to be the human of human rights, not all of them native to the humanities. Each of these disciplinary provocations to the human of human rights, however, reveals something similar: the putatively constitutive lines drawn between the human and its supposed opposite (the animal, or the sub- or less-than-human) emerge as far

6 Among many examples, see the special issue of *PMLA* dedicated to "The Humanities in Human Rights: Critique, Language, Politics" (Volume 121, Number 5, October 2006).
7 See Felipe Fernández-Armesto's beguiling *So You Think You're Human?* (Oxford: Oxford University Press, 2004).
8 Jack Donnelly, *Universal Human Rights in Theory and Practice*, 2nd ed. (Ithaca: Cornell University Press, 2003), 1.

more porous, contentious and contingent than first thought. But if it turns out that, to repurpose a famous title, we have never been human (that is to say, our operative conceptions of humanity and the rights owed to it are time-bound, contingent, variable and exclusionary) this is not necessarily to debunk or refuse the categories of the human and of human rights. If we fail to settle, simply and once and for all, the contours of the human, this is nevertheless the kind of productive failure that leads not to the end of the human (and its rights) but to the beginning of different conversations about what that human might be.

But that is to get ahead of ourselves somewhat. Let me come first to genealogy as a more particular way of articulating the historicity and contingency of human rights. What, then, is genealogy? I want to operate in this chapter with a fairly generous and non-stipulative conception of this practice of writing history.[9] This is not only because (as will shortly become evident) there is something faintly ironic in trying to police what is and what is not a genealogy (at least when one is working, as I am, with a primarily Nietzschean and Foucauldian set of references) and also because it is not entirely central to the present enterprise (which is, after all, to say what genealogy can and cannot do to our notions of international human rights law) to parse distinctions between genealogy and Cambridge School contextualism and the history of ideas, and so forth. Having said that, a starting point might be to say, with philosopher Colin Koopman, that genealogies

> are addressed to today despite ostensibly being histories about the past. . . . As such, genealogies function as critical histories of the present. Genealogies start with the present in order to trace the conditions of the emergence of the present in which we are present.[10]

(This doubtless why Foucault labelled his genealogies, bluntly yet revealingly, 'histories of the present').[11] If genealogies are forms of history writing that are written from and to a present (rather than, impossibly, from some Archimedean vantage point or with a putatively disinterested interest in the past for its own sake) then they do so precisely in order to disrupt the seeming certitude and self-evidence of present concepts and practices, denaturalising and rendering them contingent. The genealogist is not interested in establishing the lineage and pedigree of present arrangements (tracing them back to a glorious and justifying origin so as to establish temporal continuity, value and legitimacy – Nietzsche, for example, attempted the exact opposite) but rather to show how what we now think and do is in fact the product of local, haphazard and violent contests over meaning and purpose, often forgotten or repressed. The genealogist opposes herself to teleology and immanent reason in history, insisting instead on the discontinuous 'development' of history. Genealogies are irreverent counter-histories, written to trouble dominant justificatory narratives by emphasising discontinuity and breaks where the seamless historical transmission of value and identity is claimed or assumed. (It follows from the foregoing that genealogy proposes a challenge to the idea that one can narrate the origin story of a given concept or practice as a continuous development of that concept or practice through time where its meaning and self-identity remains stable. Rather, the genealogist instead proposes that

9 For a fuller treatment, see Ben Golder, "Contemporary Legal Genealogies," in *Searching for Contemporary Legal Thought*, eds. Justin Desautels-Stein and Christopher Tomlins (Cambridge: Cambridge University Press, 2017). Much of the following text in this chapter condenses analyses made at greater length therein.

10 Colin Koopman, *Genealogy as Critique: Foucault and the Problems of Modernity* (Bloomington: Indiana University Press, 2013), 24.

11 Michel Foucault, *Discipline and Punish: The Birth of the Prison*, trans. Alan Sheridan (Harmondsworth: Penguin, 1977), 31.

the meaning of, say, 'human rights', is fashioned from one historical moment and context to the next and thus has no enduring meaning 'itself', extended across time. This is why on my reading genealogy is an anti-essentialist and, broadly, deconstructive, method.)

If genealogies are counter-histories, most always rhetorically and irreverently written *against* something or someone, then it makes sense to explore what a genealogy of human rights might oppose itself to. The example of a genealogy that I am going to use in a moment is Samuel Moyn's *The Last Utopia*, and in that text Moyn explicitly opposes his own account of the rise of human rights to rival accounts that suffer from 'teleology, tunnel vision, and triumphalism'.[12] One such account is that furnished by Micheline Ishay in her 2004 book, *The History of Human Rights: From Ancient Times to the Globalization Era*. Briefly, and as its title indicates, Ishay's book narrates a longform and progressive history of human rights that connects contemporary iterations of human rights with the very dawn of civilisation, establishing the longest possible pedigree and continuity for the present human rights dispensation. Along the way, a diverse and indeed contradictory set of historical actors and movements are assimilated to the category of human rights, from Buddhism and Lenin to Martin Luther King.[13] As Moyn acerbically observes elsewhere, such accounts seek to 'ransack . . . the past as if it provided good support for the astonishingly specific international movement of the last few decades', hence furnishing appealing 'backstories to the vogue of human rights'.[14]

As has become increasingly well known, Moyn's own revisionist account of the emergence of human rights in *The Last Utopia* proceeds on very different historiographical (that is to say, genealogical) footing. I use this very well-known example in the literature not to suggest it is the last word on the history of human rights,[15] but precisely because its oft-cited account is well enough circulated and understood to release me in the present context from the duty of extensive exegesis – freeing me up instead to focus not on *what* it says so much as on *how* and *why* (and with what *effect*) it says it.

On the substance of Moyn's account, then, he insists on a radical disjuncture between contemporary understandings of human rights (which he proposes emerge in the late 1970s) and previous historical understandings of, for example, the French revolutionary Rights of Man or the rights articulated in the American revolutionary context, or indeed rights claimed in the twentieth century on behalf of decolonising peoples or, most controversially, the rights enunciated in the *Universal Declaration of Human Rights* itself in 1948. What distinguishes contemporary human rights discourse from its oft-claimed historical forebears is, according to Moyn, the fact that our present version of human rights (born in the late 1970s) is very much a creature of international law and dedicated to the transcendence of nation-state sovereignty whereas previous rights discourses founded and animated nation-state sovereignty. What explains the shift to a more minimalist and supposedly apolitical human rights at this time? Moyn contends that this vision of a minimalistic human rights protective of personal integrity rights against the state triumphs in a Cold War battle of utopias at the expense of other maximalist political projects (revolutionary communism, state socialism, decolonisation), which, at least in much of the West, had been discredited by the late 1970s as violent and flawed ideologies. *Exeunt* revolution; *enter* human rights.

12 Samuel Moyn, *The Last Utopia: Human Rights in History* (Cambridge: Belknap Press, 2010), 311.
13 Micheline Ishay, *The History of Human Rights: From Ancient Times to the Globalization Era* (Berkeley: University of California Press, 2004), 29, 175, 249.
14 Samuel Moyn, *Human Rights and the Uses of History* (London: Verso, 2014), 1–2.
15 Cf Joseph Slaughter, "Hijacking Human Rights: Neoliberalism, the New Historiography, and the End of the Third World," *Human Rights Quarterly* 40, no. 4 (2018): 735.

This adumbrated account of Moyn's argument nevertheless allows us to see how a genealogy of human rights functions and what conceptual and political work it might perform. *The Last Utopia*'s historical account introduces a radical discontinuity into the heart of the concept of human rights. Instead of a singular and self-identical concept of human rights moving through history, we are confronted with multiple discontinuous concepts of rights and of human rights, each dependent for their emergence, uptake and institutional acceptance on the confluence of particular and contingent historical factors. Rather than a time-honoured and coherent concept of human rights we are forced to reckon with the precarity and contingency of our taken-for-granted concepts in the present. Human rights could have been otherwise, indeed could still be otherwise – or (*horribile dictu*) not at all. This is the kind of vertigo the best genealogies aim to foster. Even as they withdraw the kind of temporal legitimacy often claimed on behalf of authoritative contemporary concepts and practices (like human rights), by suggesting that in fact they have a much more recent, accidental and invented history, they clearly elucidate and sharpen the political stakes of their object. They remind us that the expansion and contraction of, say, the concept of human rights, is a function not of the progressive logic of rights themselves (first white men, then white women, then racial and ethnic and religious others, etc) but of pitched and unpredictable political battles fought over who or what should fall within their remit, over who should count and be counted as a human worthy of rights. (Hans Joas reminds us that none of these battles were foregone conclusions and that political claims for full rights for women, for example, were viewed at the time 'even by the most radical universalists, partly as preposterous, and partly as a danger to the life of society'.)[16] In attending to the political constitution of the limits of human rights, genealogies of human rights also orient us away from reactivating anachronistic or nostalgic solutions to contemporary problems. A genealogist's response to the current impasse or 'crisis' of human rights (whether that be framed in terms of populism, authoritarianism, neoliberalism or a combination of the three) might well be to problematise the notion of crisis itself and to see how it configures (and perhaps invites) particular solutions rather than others, wondering what work the notion of crisis does for human rights? What it would assuredly *not* do would be to encourage us to return to a supposed heyday of human rights in the imagined past, whether that be the embedded liberalism of the post-war era or Moyn's 'original' minimalism of the 1970s ('origin' here is of course placed in the dreaded quotation marks as I want to suggest that genealogies disperse and problematise the very idea of determinate origination). If genealogies practice a ruptural historicising of the present it is not to return to the safety of the past but to sharpen our attention to the ways in which our present is presented to us, and various futures made more or less possible as a result. Finally, and as Koopman helpfully insists,[17] what genealogies are particularly good at doing is in accounting for *how* present arrangements are not only constructed in their own time but (as with the 'backstory' to human rights at which Moyn's account takes aim) retrospectively narrated.

I have briefly used the example of Moyn's critical historicisation of human rights law to lay out how genealogies trouble the self-identity of their historical object. If we have not always thought of human rights in the way we do now and the ways in which we do so are the product of particular political contestations that may not be repeated (let alone won or settled) then what vouchsafes the future of human rights? We can of course broaden the genealogical net to encompass critical historicisations not just of particular instantiations or understandings of

16 Hans Joas, *The Sacredness of the Person: A New Genealogy of Human Rights* (Washington: Georgetown University Press, 2013), 19.

17 Koopman, *Genealogy as Critique*, 130.

human rights but, perhaps more challengingly still, of the conceptions of dignity and humanity that are said to undergird human rights. The contingency, mutability and hence finitude of contemporary institutionalisations of human rights law might well be conceded but surely the metaphysics to which they refer are themselves beyond genealogy? 'If we were uncompromising mythbusters, we would tear up our human rights and start again,' suggests Felipe Fernández-Armesto, after having worked through and exposed the conceits of various attempts to distil human essences and demarcate the human from the animal. His verdict: we need to 'rethink what we mean by human life and human dignity'.[18] But if the genealogy of human rights (and indeed of concepts like humanity and dignity, and so forth) reveals their contingency and constructedness this need not lead us to paralysis and despair, or to throwing out the political and legal concepts and practices that we have to hand. Rather, genealogy issues a call to action to rethink and remake those categories without the guarantee of historical or metaphysical absolutes. Hannah Arendt called this task 'thinking without bannisters',[19] and it is to her work, and work inspired by and in dialogue with it, that I now turn in presenting a brief account of the *performativity* of human rights.

Performativity

Thinking about the performativity of human rights is to think of several, inter-related, things. On a basic level, and one which is immediately compatible with the foregoing discussion of genealogy, when we think about the performativity of human rights we commit ourselves to thinking of rights as enactments. Human rights do not exist in some immaterial *out there* (indeed have not always already existed) but are the result of practical, political claim making. Human rights are struggled for and claimed (though sometimes lost), by political groups in concrete political situations with particular political agendas who took particular political decisions and acted in particular ways (and not others). Human rights, taking this perspective, are a result of political action. As Arendt says in regard to the ideal of political equality, for example, we are equal (or, at least, some of us in political communities are equal) not because of our membership of the human species or some aspect of our human nature but rather because we decide to accord each other equal rights.[20] Rights are hence tenuous political achievements (the result, for Arendt, of speech and action in common), not timeless entailments of humanity. Thinking about international human rights law in this way orients us towards questions of doing and political practice – and away both from the transcendental claims of morality and the scriptures (and strictures!) of the sacred juridical texts of international human rights law. This is the perspective taken up (and commended) by the political theorist Karen Zivi in her book *Making Rights Claims: A Practice of Democratic Citizenship*, who argues that the democratic potential of rights inheres in the act of rights claiming itself. '[R]ights language remains of value for political movements', she argues, because it is in the very act of claiming that we 'contest and constitute the meaning of individual identity, the contours of community, and the forms that political subjectivity take'.[21] For Zivi, we need to attend to the (messy, unpredictable, and uncontainable) effects that rights claims produce in the world.

18 Fernández-Armesto, *So You Think You're Human?* 170.

19 See Hannah Arendt, "Hannah Arendt on Hannah Arendt," in *Thinking Without a Banister: Essays in Understanding, 1953–1975* (New York: Schocken Books, 2018).

20 Hannah Arendt, *The Origins of Totalitarianism* (New York: Schocken Books, 1951), 301.

21 Karen Zivi, *Making Rights Claims: A Practice of Democratic Citizenship* (New York: Oxford University Press, 2012), 7.

One of these effects, she argues, is discernible on the level of what Zivi refers to in the quotation just cited as our political subjectivity; that is to say, our conceptions of ourselves, of (legal) personhood, and of who can be the subject of human rights. This moves us closer to Judith Butler's celebrated contemporary theorisation of performativity (and of how Butler has herself applied this idea to international human rights law).[22] For Butler, at once drawing upon and radicalising the insights of a tradition of speech act theory which suggests that linguistic utterances do not simply describe the world *constatively* but intervene into it *performatively*,[23] identity is itself a performative enactment. For her, paradigmatically, the claim is that gender is performative.[24] It is precisely the reiterated and constrained performance of the social norms of gender that fabricates the sense of an inner gender identity that is said to precede its articulation and performance. There is a tension here – we 'do' gender but gender is (normatively, violently) done to us. And yet Butler nevertheless suggests that in its various doings it can go productively awry (this is the ineradicable possibility of the norms of gender unravelling and being subversively reperformed and reiterated against the grain, what she elsewhere suggestively calls the 'aberrant temporality of the norm').[25]

Butler has herself applied this way of thinking to international human rights law and in so doing holds onto both the analytic insight that the human is a regulative and regulatory category, and the promise that it can be performed differently. '[W]hen we struggle for rights, we are not simply struggling for rights that attach to my person, but we are struggling *to be conceived as persons*,' she writes in an important piece on sexual and gender diversity and human rights.[26] The human person is not simply given and it does not precede its legal articulation; rather, it is through its legal articulation that it performatively emerges:

> [I]f we are struggling not only to be conceived as persons, but to create a social transformation of the very meaning of personhood, then the assertion of rights becomes a way of intervening into the social and political process by which the human is articulated. International human rights is always in the process of subjecting the human to redefinition and renegotiation. It mobilises the human in the service of rights, but also rearticulates the human when it comes up against the cultural limits of its working conception of the human, as it does and must.[27]

And again:

> The necessity of keeping our notion of the human open to a future articulation is essential to the project of international human rights discourse and politics. We see this time and again when the very notion of the human is presupposed; the human is defined in advance,

22 For a fuller (and more complicated) account of Butler's politics of human rights, see Ben Golder, "Human Rights Trouble? Judith Butler and the Performative Refusal of Human Rights," in *Critical Perspectives on Human Rights*, ed. Birgit Schippers (Lanham: Rowman & Littlefield, 2018).

23 For the classic reference, see John Langshaw Austin, *How to Do Things with Words*, 2nd ed. (Cambridge: Harvard University Press, 1975).

24 Judith Butler, *Gender Trouble: Feminism and the Subversion of Identity* (London: Routledge, 1990).

25 Judith Butler, *Antigone's Claim: Kinship Between Life and Death* (New York: Columbia University Press, 2000), 29.

26 Judith Butler, "Beside Oneself: On the Limits of Sexual Autonomy," in *Undoing Gender* (London and New York: Routledge, 2004), 32 (emphasis in original).

27 Ibid., 33.

> in terms that are distinctively western, very often American, and, therefore, partial and parochial. When we start with the human as a foundation, then the human at issue in human rights is already known, already defined.[28]

And finally:

> I would suggest that . . . we can only rearticulate or resignify the basic categories of ontology, of being human, of being gendered, of being recognisably sexual, to the extent that we submit ourselves to a process of cultural translation. The point is not to assimilate foreign or unfamiliar notions of gender or humanness into our own as if it is simply a matter of incorporation [*sic*] alienness into an established lexicon. Cultural translation is also a process of yielding our most fundamental categories, that is, seeing how and why they break up, require resignification when they encounter the limits of an available episteme. . . . It is crucial to recognise that the notion of the human will only be built over time and by the process of cultural translation, where it is not a translation between two languages that stay enclosed, distinct, unified.[29]

The juridical framework of international human rights, on Butler's account, thus presents a promising opportunity for different cultural, sexual, religious, and so forth, groups, to argue over the meaning of the human of human rights law. On this performative view, the politics of human rights is not about uncovering an existing essence or quality of humanness and then arguing for its extension to or bestowal upon benighted others; that is to say, with Anne Phillips in *The Politics of the Human*, it is not a question of seeking recognition (of dignity, for example) but rather of demanding equality and, in the process, reperforming humanity.[30] As Butler says, the contours of this figure of the human that emerges from these human rights struggles cannot be guaranteed in advance (as the more conventional human rights language of 'foundation' might assume) but rather emerge from the fraught process of cultural translation whereby each group's different understanding of humanity is altered and affected ('yielded', as she puts it). The result is not a final or a better or a more universal rendition of the human but rather the contingent outcome of a process of universalisation that, while conscious of its own cultural embeddedness and the unavoidable exclusions it practises, nevertheless underwrites the futurity and political effect of human rights (for were there ever to be a final realisation of the human of human rights, that would itself spell the end of human rights). This is a critically self-reflective praxis of human rights that attempts to unsettle and resignify prior (and existing) inscriptions of humanness in human rights discourse in the name of new human possibilities. 'I think our current political dilemmas', Butler argues in a different context, 'are . . . challenging us to refashion what is meant by the term "human" so that it becomes more encompassing and more capacious, and finally more human, perhaps in a sense we have only begun to imagine'.[31] And this challenge 'to rethink the human', she insists in the book *Precarious Life*, is 'part of the democratic trajectory of an evolving human rights jurisprudence'.[32] To perform human rights politics, then,

28 Ibid., 36–37.
29 Ibid., 38.
30 Anne Phillips, *The Politics of the Human* (Cambridge: Cambridge University Press, 2015).
31 Jill Stauffer, "Interview with Judith Butler," May 1, 2003, accessed February 9, 2017, www.believermag.com/issues/200305/?read=interview_butler.
32 Judith Butler, *Precarious Life: The Powers of Mourning and Violence* (London: Verso, 2004), 90.

is to start from the acknowledgment that there is no human as such, no abstract set of guidelines to guide us – but to see in this prospect not the negation of human rights but their very possibility, the possibility for contestation and subversive renewal of the human.

Conclusion

To return, briefly, to the famous lecture of Rorty's with which I started, it will be recalled that whilst Rorty issued an iconoclastic challenge to philosophical human rights foundationalism (although one that is arguably less provocative than broadly unquestioned today),[33] his conception of the relationship between human rights and the (cultural) humanities was a fairly straightforward and *un*challenging one: the telling of sad and sentimental stories in various media were to assist in the extraversion of human rights globally and moral uplift and progress were set to follow, ineluctably. In the preceding pages I have simply tried to supplement this happy and simplified picture of human rights and the humanities (wherein we might well diagnose symptoms of that Moynian alliterative affliction of *teleology, tunnel vision and triumphalism*) by introducing and describing two particular humanistic modes of critique that aim not to extend the remit of an already existing human but rather to trouble its supposed foundations. Of course, to trouble something is by no means to reject it out of hand and so each of these critical humanistic methods discloses possibility even while exposing uncertainty, contingency and danger. Genealogy shows our most treasured conceptions to be recent and partial inventions (but leaves open the prospect of their renewal), while performativity exposes how our conceptions of the human become normatively solidified but at the same time can be subverted, made slippery and repurposed. It is that kind of hopeful troublemaking that is surely central to the theoretical humanities and which expresses, to finish on a Foucauldian note,[34] a certain vocation of critique in terms of exposing a hidden margin of freedom immanent in contemporary social, political and legal arrangements we previously took to be unchanging and unchangeable.[35]

33 See further Ben Golder, "Theorizing Human Rights," in *The Oxford Handbook of the Theory of International Law*, eds. Anne Orford, Florian Hoffmann and Martin Clark (Oxford: Oxford University Press, 2016).

34 See further Ben Golder, *Foucault and the Politics of Rights* (Palo Alto: Stanford University Press, 2015), especially Chapter 1.

35 I say 'a certain vocation of critique' because of course it is only one such understanding of critique, among many. For a different approach to the critique of contingency (and of human rights) that aims to think beyond the exposure of contingency, see Susan Marks, "False Contingency," *Current Legal Problems* 62, no. 1 (2009): 1 (and for an application to human rights, see Golder, "Contemporary Legal Genealogies").

World-making

13

Certain (mis)conceptions

Westphalian origins, portraiture and wampum

Jeffery G Hewitt[1]

Failure of the White man to understand and accept Indian customs and philosophy from earliest contact has led to the acceptance of certain misconceptions.

George S Snyderman[2]

Overview

There is a growing body of socio-legal scholarship focusing on the visuals of law.[3] This chapter considers international law as both story and image. In particular, I contemplate this sometimes intimate relationship of text and imagery[4] through an examination of the Westphalian origin story alongside Dutch painter Gerard ter Borch's[5] 1648 painting, *The Ratification of the Treaty of*

1 Assistant Professor at Osgoode Hall Law School. As a mixed-descent Cree man I am grateful to the many Haudenosaunne and Anishinaabe scholars and knowledge keepers, such as Bev Jacobs, Alan Corbiere, Rick Hill, John Borrows, and Brian Charles to name a few, who have taught me about various wampum belts over the years. I am particularly grateful too for the generosity of Sundhya Pahuja for including me in this larger project; and for the invitation in 2019 to speak at Melbourne Law School's Institute for International Law and the Humanities (IILAH). My visit to IILAH allowed me to explore some of my thoughts on international law and Indigenous peoples – a portion of which is the focus of this paper. Special mention to Sujith Xavier for reading an early draft, though all errors and omissions are mine. I am also grateful to Usha Natarajan, Reem Bahdi, and Ruth Buchanan, who are intellectually generous with me and in different ways encourage me to engage more with international law in my larger research interests. This paper comes out of ongoing conversations with each of them.

2 George S. Snyderman, "The Functions of Wampum," *Proceedings of the American Philosophical Society* 98, no. 6 (1954): 469.

3 Linda Mulcahy, "Eyes of the Law: A Visual Turn in Socio-Legal Studies?" *Journal of Law and Society* 44, no. S1 (2017): 111–28.

4 For insight into the relationship as between verbal processing, text and imagery see Allan Paivio and Iain Begg, *Psychology of Language* (Englewood Cliffs, NJ: Prentice-Hall, 1981).

5 Gerard ter Borch was a Dutch painter who lived during the so-called Dutch Golden Age. For more on the artist and his influence, see for example "Vermeer Was Brilliant, but He Was Not Without Influences," *The Economist*, October 12, 2017, www.economist.com/books-and-arts/2017/10/12/vermeer-was-brilliant-but-he-was-not-without-influences; and www.nationalgallery.org.uk/artists/gerard-ter-borch.

Münster[6]. Further, drawing upon wampum diplomacy, which is also both law as story and visual imagery, I then investigate a reading of certain Indigenous contributions to European international law's[7] founding narratives. How in one instance does placing ter Borch's painting in an art gallery reaffirm the Westphalian model's legitimacy, while simultaneously placing wampum in a museum, render Indigenous laws as a cultural artefact? Does expanding the legal imagination that both generates and upholds stories and visual imagery also offer a means toward more complex and comprehensive origins stories of European international law?

With limited exceptions, European international law relies heavily on written text, which is a visual medium,[8] and on other visuals, such as portraiture, as well as other cultural objects, to maintain its founding narrative. Writing (or typing) law is a physical act that produces a visual result. Curve a line without connecting the circle on the right side and one has the letter 'c', close the loop and it is an 'o'. Each letter holds its own sound(s) and meaning(s). Draw three different shapes using curves and lines, for example, and arrange them in a particular order, 'c' followed by an 'a' and 't' and the visual becomes 'cat'. Translating the visual into meaning a feline mammal, is the result of acquired literacy. Write 'cat' in another language, such as Greek, and it becomes 'Γάτα'. While visually beautiful, the Greek version of 'cat' holds no meaning for my English-trained eyes. But does that deem it meaningless? It simply illustrates that I am illiterate in Greek and thereby untrained to derive abstract meaning from the visual text, as I can in English. Text as a visual medium is learnt. Translating text into meaning requires literacy, which is also an acquired skill.

Some Indigenous sources of law, such as wampum, are also visual text and require the requisite literacy to 'read' them. Like the written treaties of Westphalia, wampum is international law.[9] Wampum is created through the use of slim, tubular beads from clam shells for white beads, with quahog clam shells supplying white and purple (sometimes referred to as black) beads which are then strung together on hemp string or sinew.[10] It was used in political and ceremonial matters,[11] as well as to record international treaties. Rather than being widely

6 To digitally view *The Ratification of the Treaty of Münster* (1648) by Gerard ter Borch online at The National Gallery, London, United Kingdom, see "The Ratification of the Treaty of Münster," *The National Gallery*, accessed March 19, 2010, www.nationalgallery.org.uk/paintings/gerard-ter-borch-the-ratification-of-the-treaty-of-munster. For a discussion on this painting as a depiction of international law as extraordinary and commemorative versus local and ongoing see Luis Eslava, *Local Space, Global Life* (Cambridge: Cambridge University Press, 2015), 31–35.

7 In keeping with this paper's proposal that 'international law' is not always accepted as universal, I use the term 'European international law' to reference the system of international law currently researched and practiced globally to reflect that while such international law may be wide in scope, it is fundamentally derived from Europe. At times, I do not include 'European' in reference to 'international law' to convey a broader framing of 'international law' that is not solely European-based (or does not have to be). I also on occasion reference 'Indigenous international law' within the context of Indigenous nations in what is now known as North America. In sum, I try throughout to be as specific as I can when referencing 'international law'.

8 For more on written text as image and the visual element of law, see for example Desmond Manderson, *Law and the Visual: Representations, Technologies, Critique* (Toronto: University of Toronto Press, 2018). For a discussion of visuals and legal theory see Neal Feigenson, "The Visual in Law: Some Problems for Legal Theory," *Law, Culture and the Humanities* 10, no. 1 (2014): 13–23.

9 For an excellent discussion of international law and the Haudenosaunee Confederacy, including wampum belts, see Beverley Jacobs, "International Law/The Great Law of Peace" (Master's diss., University of Saskatchewan, 2000), www.collectionscanada.gc.ca/obj/s4/f2/dsk3/SSU/TC-SSU-07042007083651.pdf.

10 Charles H. Gillette, "Wampum Beads and Belts," *Indian Historian* 3, no. 4 (Fall 1970): 33.

11 Kathryn V. Muller, "The Two 'Mystery' Belts of Grand River: A Biography of the Two Row Wampum and the Friendship Belt," *American Indian Quarterly* 31, no. 1 (Winter 2007): 129–64.

engaged with as international law, however, wampum are often placed in museums and viewed as material objects of Indigenous cultures.[12] In sum, wampum as an Indigenous source of law is presented in institutions, such as the British Museum, as 'cultural' artefact, which works to erase the law contained within. Conversely, a short walk from the British Museum's collection of wampum to London's National Gallery, ter Borch's painting displays European international law's origin story as a visual reinforcement of European supremacy. Ter Borch's portrait is both a commemorative statement of a key historical moment in European international law and an invitation to viewers to uphold a European-based legal narrative. Meanwhile, wampum in museums reaffirms to visitors a powerful colonial authority over a 'once-was' Indigenous culture. And yet this classification of wampum does not erase Indigenous laws. One must be able to read the language in which the law is written to fully engage with its meaning. Failure to derive legal meaning from wampum is not a failing of Indigenous legal orders; it is demonstrative of illiteracy, however widespread.

Westphalia

Though not without critique,[13] European international law's origin story is said to begin in 1648 with the Peace of Westphalia.[14] But origin stories about modern law and legal systems are often underpinned by a common characteristic – there is always more to it.[15] That Westphalia is widely considered the birth of European international law is the result of a myopic lens curved toward a particular power structure and away from a broader reading.[16] One need only give a cursory glance at ter Borch's 'Treaty of Münster'[17] to appreciate whom the genesis of European international law is for. Affluent, European, Christian, men.[18] Ter Borch's painting offers visual authority for the Westphalian story. Placing the painting in the National Gallery in London, UK, serves to sustain the ongoing narrative of European international law. It allows for a wider audience to engage with the Westphalian origin story than those who might ever view the original treaties known collectively as the Peace of Westphalia. It also reinforces a reading of European international law that is devoid of women, as well as being both racialised and devoid of Indigenous peoples.

12 The British Museum's collection of wampum is available for viewing in its digital catalogue. For an example see British Museum, "Wampum / Belt / Bead," Collection Online, accessed March 19, 2020, https://research.britishmuseum.org/research/collection_online/collection_object_details/collection_image_gallery.aspx?assetid=308190001&objectid=526662&partid=1.

13 The Westphalian origins are subject to critique by various international law scholars including: Richard Joyce, "Westphalia: Event, Memory, Myth," in *Events: The Force of International Law*, eds. Fleur Johns, Richard Joyce and Sundhya Pahuja (Abingdon: Routledge, 2011); Benno Teschke, *The Myth of 1648: Class, Geopolitics, and the Making of Modern International Relations* (London: Verso, 2003); Stéphane Beaulac, "The Westphalian Model in Defining International Law: Challenging the Myth," *Australian Journal of Legal History* 8, no. 2 (2004): 181; A. Claire Cutler, "Critical Reflections on the Westphalian Assumptions of International Law and Organization: A Crisis of Legitimacy," *Review of International Studies* 27, no. 2 (2001): 133–50.

14 Steven Patton, "The Peace of Westphalia and It Affects on International Relations, Diplomacy and Foreign Policy," *The Histories* 10, no. 1 (2019): 95.

15 Peter Fitzpatrick, *Modernism and the Grounds of Law* (Cambridge: Cambridge University Press, 2001): Ch 1.

16 Andreas Osiander, "Sovereignty, International Relations, and the Westphalian Myth," *International Organization* 55, no. 2 (2001): 251–87.

17 See ter Borch, *The Ratification of the Treaty of Münster.*

18 Herbert Arthur Smith, ed., *Great Britain and the Law of Nations: Territory (Part 1)*, vol. 2 (London: PS King & Son, 1935); Lassa Oppenheim, *International Law: A Treatise*, ed. A. D. McNair, 4th ed. (London: Longmans, 1928), 12.

Ter Borch's central, hovering placement of the golden statue of the Virgin Mary holding her infant son, surrounded by rays of golden sunlight coming from the chandelier hanging over the signing table, reinforces the blessing of Westphalia by divine authority. The main subjects, namely men, appear in their silken finery, conveying the wealth, class and socio-political stature of the participants. The men holding the paper – presumably their written oath – with two extended fingers, signifies the solemnity of their undertaking. Though, strangely all of the mouths of the men are closed as if, like the heavenly luminescence shining down on them, their silent, corporeal presence is enough to generate law. The central placement of a signatory table, sealing wax, ribbon, paper and a bound, gold-leaf book underwrite the premise that law must be written to be deemed law.

A modern positioning of European international law as a liberating force directs attention away from European international law's replication of a narrow form of masculine power that seeks to tame the savage.[19] This framing elevates laws written on paper, such as the treaties of Westphalia, and seeks to eliminate Indigenous laws (such as wampum), by also eliminating Indigenous peoples – in particular Indigenous women and girls.[20] The casting of Indigenous peoples outside of European international law as the savage is similarly echoed in visuals, such as portraiture.

This is an ongoing narrative, not an historic one. While the UK's National Gallery holds ter Borch's 1648 commemoration of the rise of the sovereign-state, in 2013 the National Portrait Gallery hosted an exhibition titled 'George Catlin: American Indian Portraits'.[21] Placing Catlin's work inside the same institutional body that hosts ter Borch's 'Treaty of Münster' furthers Euro-centric authority over the lawless North American savage, which European international law seeks to tame.

Catlin is a white, American painter whose portraiture of Indigenous peoples in nineteenth-century America plays on tropes of how Indigenous peoples are widely understood to be, with titles such as 'Scalp Dance, Mouth of the Teton River, Teton Dakota'.[22] Most of the Indigenous subjects of Catlin's work displayed in the exhibit are Indigenous men. This upholds the white, male gaze upon the noble savage-warrior narrative in sharp contrast to the affluence, civility

19 Ruth Buchanan and Rebecca Johnson, "The Unforgiven Sources of International Law: Nation-building, Violence, and Gender in the West(ern)," in *International Law: Modern Feminist Approaches*, eds. Doris Buss and Ambreena Manji (Oxford: Hart, 2005), 239–83.

20 For an excellent discussion on the many ways in which Indigenous peoples, cultures, languages, laws and people themselves are actively erased see: Eve Tuck and K. Wayne Yang, "Decolonization Is Not a Metaphor," *Decolonization: Indigeneity, Education & Society* 1, no. 1 (2012): 1–40. Such actions of colonial violence particularly impact Indigenous women and girls. See for example Josephine L. Savarese, "Challenging Colonial Norms and Attending to Presencing in Stories of Missing and Murdered Indigenous Women," *Canadian Journal of Women and the Law* 29, no. 1 (2017): 157–81; Emily Snyder, Val Napoleon and John Borrows, "Gender and Violence: Drawing on Indigenous Legal Resources," *University of British Columbia Law Review* 48, no. 2 (2015): 593; Amnesty International, *No More Stolen Sisters: The Need for a Comprehensive Response to Discrimination and Violence Against Indigenous Women in Canada* (London: Amnesty International Publications, 2009), www.amnesty.ca/sites/default/files/amr200122009en.pdf; The Final Report, National Inquiry into Missing and Murdered Indigenous Women and Girls (Canada), *Reclaiming Power and Place: The Final Report of the National Inquiry Into Missing and Murdered Indigenous Women and Girls* (Privy Council Office, 2019).

21 For the National Portrait Gallery link, see "George Catlin: American Indian Portraits," National Portrait Gallery, accessed March 19, 2020, www.npg.org.uk/whatson/george-catlin-american-indian-portraits/exhibition.php.

22 This painting by Catlin is part of the permanent collection of the Smithsonian American Art Museum and was part of the loan to the National Portrait Gallery of the United Kingdom for "George Catlin: American Indian Portraits" exhibit. For example, see "Scalp Dance, Mouth of the Teton River," Smithsonian American Art Museum, accessed March 19, 2020, https://americanart.si.edu/artwork/scalp-dance-mouth-teton-river-4347.

and respectability of European, Christian men. It is an American painter, Catlin, whose work seeks to define Indigenous peoples (notably as savage), and a Dutch painter, ter Borch, who envisions Westphalia as the capstone in civility. Both artists are engaged in supporting the same Euro-centric narrative through portraiture. These visuals situate Indigenous peoples, along with the exclusion of Indigenous women, as merely objects on display, not as living cultures capable of inventing international law. That Catlin's works were on display in 2013 underscores the modern context in which visuals and narratives combine to uphold the ongoing efforts to tame the savages who must, until civilised, remain outside Western-defined spaces,[23] including European international law. The rights of Indigenous peoples directly threaten the origins of European international law and its founding construction on the sovereign-state. As such, European international law has a 'stake in maintaining these boundaries: between male and female, inside and outside, law and violence, civilization and savagery'.[24]

There remains an ongoing marginalisation of scholarly interventions drawing on race, gender and Indigeneity, deftly deferring long overdue substantive changes to the underpinning structure of European international law. Third World Approaches to International Law (TWAIL) arose in part to respond to such a narrow reading of European international law.[25] Though TWAIL, along with feminist critiques of European international law,[26] may be on the rise, such perspectives too often continue to be categorised as outside.[27] Further, displaying Indigenous sources of laws, such as wampum, in well-lit museums as artefacts of a once-was culture contemporaneously with Catlin's portraiture of Indigenous men and ter Borch's commemoration of Westphalia, privileges European international law's narrative as a liberating force and also shapes the ways in which such visuals should be understood.[28]

Ter Borch's painting centring the affluent, Christian, European male as authoritative,[29] and Catlin's depiction of lawlessness among Indigenous peoples, contributes to the upholding of

23 For more on Vine Deloria Jr., see Vine Deloria Jr., "If You Think About It You'll See That It Is True," in *Spirit & Reason: The Vine Deloria, Jr., Reader*, eds. Barbara Deloria, Kristen Foehner and Sam Scinta (Golden, CO: Fulcrum Publishing, 2006), 40.

24 Buchanan and Johnson, "The 'Unforgiven' Sources of International Law: Nation-Building," 240.

25 For more see as examples Usha Natarajan, John Reynolds, Amar Bhatia and Sujith Xavier, "Introduction: TWAIL – On Praxis and the Intellectual," *Third World Quarterly* 37, no. 11 (2016): 1946; Luis Eslava and Sundhya Pahuja, "Between Resistance and Reform: TWAIL and the Universality of International Law," *Trade, Law and Development* 3, no. 1 (2011); Obiora Okafor, "Newness, Imperialism, and International Legal Reform in Our Time: A TWAIL Perspective," *Osgoode Hall Law Journal* 43, no. 1–2 (2005): 43; A. Anghie and B. S. Chimni, "Third World Approaches to International Law and Individual Responsibility in Internal Conflicts," *Chinese Journal of International Law* 2, no. 1 (2003): 77–103.

26 See for example Karen Knop, "Re/Statements: Feminism and State Sovereignty in International Law," *Transnational and Contemporary Problems* 3 (1993): 293.

27 For a good feminist critique of international law see for example Anne Orford, "Feminism, Imperialism and the Mission of International Law," *Nordic Journal of International Law* 71, no. 2 (2002): 275–96; Hilary Charlesworth and Christine Chinkin, *The Boundaries of International Law: A Feminist Analysis* (Manchester: Manchester University Press, 2000).

28 Svetlana Alpers, "The Museum as a Way of Seeing," in *Exhibiting Cultures: The Poetics and Politics of Museum Display*, eds. Ivan Karp and Steven D. Lavine (Washington: Smithsonian Institution Press, 1991), 25–32.

29 Derek Croxton, *Westphalia: The Last Christian Peace* (New York: Palgrave Macmillan, 2013) offers insight into some of the participants in the Westphalian negotiations as allies of the then French Cardinal Richelieu but not necessarily recognised sovereigns at the time. This is illustrative of a prioritisation of considerable Christian influence over the negotiations to the exclusion of others (in particular, non-Christians). Meanwhile, modern international law asserts universality as a strength versus its steeping in Christianity. Further, while failing to include racialised and Indigenous peoples in the founding of international law, Christianity was simultaneously seeking to convert racialised and Indigenous peoples to the faith.

European international law's origin story and the lawless savage narrative by use of visuals. Further, classifying Indigenous laws, such as wampum, as artefact while reading out race and gender and Indigeneity, shapes what is and is not international law. The constant retelling of this origin story, both as narrative in scholarship and as visual per ter Borch, privileges European international law as universal, genderless and atemporal. While European international law may be founded by elite Christian European men, TWAIL, feminist scholars and Indigenous academics work to remind us that international law is not universal, genderless or atemporal.

But the combined power of narrative and the visual is also a potent coupling that upholds the premise of universality,[30] in spite of there being little about European international law's origins that is universal. Rather, because of the varying encounters between the Crowns of Europe in their colonial expansions and Indigenous peoples globally, there is ultimately a 'factish quality of the universality of the nation state [that] is . . . settled only from within a particular juridical frame'.[31]

Positionality and international law

For me, engaging with law and legal-institutional structures takes time. I am constantly employed in the translation work of understanding what I am reading (as all learners are). As I engage with Western knowledge systems – particularly law – I work to process my readings and research into a Cree context then back again.[32] In other words, it often takes me twice as long as most to absorb legal systems that are not my own. My introduction to European international law's perceptions of its global contributions were brought to the forefront in 2014, through an 'objects of international law' workshop held at Queen Mary University, London, resulting in *International Law's Objects*.[33] Prior to this, my main engagement with European international law was through Indigenous international law practices of building relations versus hierarchically ordering them, as European international law seems to want to do. My overall sense of European international law was framed by Indigenous peoples accessing international venues and tribunals, such as the Haudenosaunne confederacy's appeal to the League of Nations,[34] or the legal advocacy of James Anaya and others at the Inter-American Court of Human Rights.[35]

At the London workshop in 2014, not for the first time, I struggled internally with trying to understand how international law, as understood in Europe, seemed so confident and self-assured.[36] It astounded me that on one hand European international law accepts only sovereign states and their successors as possessed of authority to enter into treaties, while engaging Indigenous peoples in treaty-making – while again, in the Canadian context at least, simultaneously refusing to uphold those treaties. I was further confounded by the profound erasure of Indigenous peoples' influences in the founding of international law. It was puzzling that European international law viewed Westphalia as a profound story marking a transition from medieval

30 Antony Anghie, "Finding the Peripheries: Sovereignty and Colonialism in Nineteenth-Century International Law," *Harvard International Law Journal* 40, no. 1 (Winter 1999): 1–80.

31 Sundhya Pahuja, "Laws of Encounter: A Jurisdictional Account of International Law," *London Review of International Law* 1, no. 1 (2013): 63.

32 For an exceptionally insightful explanation of this process, see Tracey Lindberg, "Critical Indigenous Legal Theory Part 1: The Dialogue Within," *Canadian Journal of Women and the Law* 27, no. 2 (2015): 224–47.

33 Ruth Buchanan and Jeffery G. Hewitt, "Treaty Canoe," in *International Law's Objects,* eds. Jessie Hohmann and Daniel Joyce (Oxford: Oxford University Press, 2018), 491.

34 Jacobs, "International Law/The Great Law of Peace," 114–21.

35 S. James Anaya and Claudio Grossman, "The Case of Awas Tingni v. Nicaragua: A Step in the International Law of Indigenous Peoples," *Arizona Journal International and Comparative Law* 19, no. 1 (Spring 2002): 1.

36 For more insight into these internal struggles, see Lindberg, "Critical Indigenous Legal Theory."

to modern Europe and as the moment sovereign states entered both our legal structures and lexicon. Meanwhile, Westphalia's creation of sovereign states ushered in a new wave of colonial expansion and violence against Indigenous peoples in North America and globally,[37] using claims of sovereign authority as justification.[38] Capitalising on the doctrine of discovery,[39] such claims of sovereignty have in turn been adopted by successor states, such as Canada,[40] as a means to continue its membership in European international law's club. Yet, Indigenous nations in Canada have also been recognised as nations,[41] which have never surrendered sovereignty.[42] Still, European international law has systematically excluded Indigenous nations and favoured the doctrine of discovery over existing treaties between European sovereigns and Indigenous peoples.[43]

There have also been less successful efforts to apply the 1961 Vienna Convention on the Law of Treaties to pre-existing treaties between Indigenous peoples and European Crowns.[44] These moves of erasure of Indigenous nationhood were criticised in the First Progress Report of the United Nations Special Rapporteur, Miguel Alfonso Martinez, appointed by the Sub-Commission on Prevention of Discrimination and the Protection of Minorities, Commission on Human Rights and the Economic and Social Council, who stated that both Indigenous and non-Indigenous peoples 'mutually bestowed upon each other (in either an explicit or implicit manner) the condition of sovereign entities',[45] and in some instances did so by way of wampum.

Consistent with the origin story of Westphalia, treaty-making in European international law requires parties to be sovereign nations and thereby authoritative for the purposes of entering into treaties. Inexplicably, as evidenced by the Crown's assertion of sovereignty in Canada, European international law simultaneously appears to uphold the premise that such treaty-making authority on the part of Indigenous leaders was temporary (like a day-pass to a circus), and expired upon placing their signatures on treaty documents.[46] This 'temporary treaty sovereignty' has no legal foundation in European international law, yet was replicated by European Crowns

37 S. James Anaya, *Indigenous Peoples in International Law*, 2nd ed. (New York: Oxford University Press, 2004), 16.

38 Ibid., 18.

39 The doctrine of discovery is intricately connected to international law, though deeper considerations of the doctrine in relation to international law are considerations for a future paper. For good critical perspectives on doctrine of discovery, see Robert J. Miller, Jacinta Ruru, Larissa Behrendt and Tracey Lindberg, *Discovering Indigenous Lands: The Doctrine of Discovery in the English Colonies* (Oxford: Oxford University Press, 2010); Robert J. Miller, "The Doctrine of Discovery in American Indian Law," *Idaho Law Review* 42, no. 1 (2005): 1.

40 See for example, *R. v. Sparrow* [1990] 1 S.C.R. 1075 wherein the Supreme Court of Canada establishes a constitutional test for Indigenous claimants to prove the existence of an 'aboriginal or treaty' right. This legal test assumes Crown sovereignty over Indigenous peoples, lands and resources and accepts the authority of Crown to extinguish and justifiably infringe the rights of Indigenous peoples.

41 Royal Proclamation No. 1 (October 7, 1763) is derived from Clarence S. Brigham, ed., *British Royal Proclamations Relating to America, Vol. 12*, Transactions and Collections of the American Antiquarian Society (Worcester, MA: American Antiquarian Society, 1911), 212.

42 For a critical analysis of Indigenous sovereignty, surrender and the Canadian state, see Arthur Manuel and Grand Chief Ronald M. Derrickson, *Unsettling Canada: A National Wake-up Call* (Toronto: Between the Lines, 2015).

43 *Island of Palmas Case (Netherlands v. United States)* (1928) 2 UNRIAA 829. See also *Johnson v. M'Intosh*, 21 U.S. (8 Wheat.) 543 (1823).

44 Jacobs, "International Law/The Great Law of Peace," 132, citing James (Sakej) Youngblood Henderson, "The Status of Indian Treaties in International Law," in *International Law in Aboriginal Rights and International Law* (Proceedings of the 1993 Conference of the Canadian Council on International Law, Ottawa, 1993), 126.

45 Jacobs, "International Law/The Great Law of Peace," 132, citing Miguel Alfonso Martinez, *Study on Treaties, Agreements and Other Constructive Arrangements Between States and Indigenous Populations: First Progress Report*, UN Doc. E/CN.4/Sub.2/1992/32, August 25, 1992, para 186.

46 John Borrows, "Frozen Rights in Canada: Constitutional Interpretation and the Trickster," *American Indian Law Review* 22, no. 1 (1997): 37–64.

as they expanded their colonial empires. But in the Canadian context there is a twist, which is explored further later in this chapter, in the form of wampum and the *Royal Proclamation, 1763*, which from the English Crown's perspective recognises Indigenous peoples as nations.

Thus I found myself in London – the heart of empire – and thinking that, when it comes to Indigenous peoples, European international law has some explaining to do.

The Westphalian origin story began with an organisation of European powers.[47] Women and racialised groups were not included. Indigenous peoples were also excluded. Moreover, if the Westphalian story is to be accepted on the face of it, Indigenous peoples were also believed to be uncivilised and without law – international or otherwise.[48] But many Indigenous nations did and do have rich legal orders that includes international law,[49] both before and after 1648. As examples, Haudenosaunne, Anishinabek and Wendat nations, along with others, engaged in wampum diplomacy – a recording of agreements between nations in wampum belts.[50] Cree, Chippewas, Metis and Assiniboine (Nakoda or Stoney) nations created an Iron Alliance among their distinct nations.[51] The Mi'kmaw Nation also actively engaged in international-law making through alliances with various nations.[52] And they did so both pre- and post-Westphalia, as European Crowns interacted with Indigenous international law-making practices. Regardless, European international law continues to ignore and fails to include Indigenous contributions to its origin story. This is particularly troublesome when, by matter of timing, the Dutch – one of the vital players in the negotiations of the Peace of Westphalia[53] – had been engaging in international law with the Haudenosaunne confederacy since at least 1613.

Wampum diplomacy and international law

As memorialised in ter Borch's painting, Westphalia was an unprecedented achievement of diplomacy.[54] Hosted by the Holy Roman Empire, various warring powers of Europe gathered to resolve longstanding battles for lands, borders, resources and power.[55] The result of such an auspicious gathering was three treaties that, among other things, established the concept of sovereign states as a new political order based on peaceful coexistence.[56] This principle

47 Konrad Repgen, "Negotiating the Peace of Westphalia: A Survey with an Examination of the Major Problems," in *1648 – War and Peace in Europe, Vol1, Politics, Religion, Law and Society*, eds. Klaus Bussmann and Heinz Schilling (Münster: Westfälisches Landesmuseum,1998), 355–72.

48 James Anaya, *Indigenous Peoples in International Law,* Ch 1.

49 John Borrows, *Justice Within: Indigenous Legal Traditions*, Discussion Paper (Ottawa: Law Commission of Canada, 2006).

50 Muller, "The Two 'Mystery' Belts of Grand River."

51 Robert Alexander Innes, *Elder Brother and the Law of the People: Contemporary Kinship and Cowessess First Nation* (Manitoba: University of Manitoba Press, 2013); John S. Milloy, *The Plains Cree: Trade, Diplomacy, and War, 1790 to 1870* (Manitoba: University of Manitoba Press, 1990); June Scudeler, "At the Same Table," *Canadian Literature* 223 (2014): 160.

52 James Youngblood Henderson, "First Nations' Legal Inheritances in Canada: The Mikmaq Model," *Manitoba Law Journal* 23, no. 1 (1996): 1–31.

53 Repgen, "Negotiating the Peace of Westphalia."

54 See Patton, "The Peace of Westphalia"; Leo Gross, "The Peace of Westphalia, 1648–1948," *American Journal of International Law* 42, no. 1 (1948): 20–41.

55 Benjamin Straumann, "The Peace of Westphalia as a Secular Constitution," *Constellations* 15, no. 2 (2008): 173–88.

56 For an excellent historical account of the negotiations at Westphalia, see Andreas Osiander, *The States System of Europe, 1640–1990: Peacemaking and the Conditions of International Stability* (Oxford: Oxford University Press, 1994).

of sovereignty, which continues to be fundamental to European international law,[57] created a model of peace through diplomacy and was premised on the non-interference in the domestic affairs of another sovereign.[58]

Perhaps in part because of the Westphalian treaties settling various European border disputes previously in contention,[59] a number of Crowns increased their outward appetite for the acquisition of new lands and resources. As a result, the seventeenth and eighteenth centuries brought another wave of colonial expansion as the sovereigns of Europe transported their continental disputes with each other to North America.[60] Subsequently, the sovereignty principle of Westphalia severely impacted Indigenous peoples worldwide and continues to do so today.[61] It seems, the 'boundaries of international law were drawn between European states as the Family of Nations on the one hand, and barbarian nations and savage entities, on the other'.[62] But there is another contribution to the founding story of European international law pre-dating Westphalia by approximately 45 years.

In 1613, the Dutch settlement in what is now the state of New York in the United States of America was a site of international law and an assertion of sovereignty. The Haudenosaunne Confederacy presented the Dutch settlers with a wampum belt, commonly known as the Two-Row wampum belt or the Guswentha/Kaswentha.[63] The Two-Row wampum established that the Confederacy and the Dutch would co-exist peacefully, without interfering with each other and respect one another as nations.[64]

Wampum belts have long been a subject of scholarly consideration.[65] In 'Wampum as Hypertext', Angela Hass states, '[d]ating back one thousand years, wampum and other material components . . . have been used by Woodlands Indians for ceremony and as records of important civil affairs.'[66] The use of wampum originates from 'the coastal [east] Indians . . . but through trade with other tribes, it traveled to the interior and western regions of the continent'.[67]

57 Knop, "Re/Statements."

58 Ibid.

59 Ibid.

60 For an historical account of the Seven Years' War between the English and French Crowns, also known as the "French and Indian War", in what is now North America, see Fred Anderson, *Crucible of War: The Seven Years' War and the Fate of Empire in British North America, 1754–1766* (New York: Vintage, 2007). For contextualisation of the importation of European-based disputes between the English and French Crowns into North America in the Seven Years' War, see Daniel Baugh, *The Global Seven Years War 1754–1763: Britain and France in a Great Power Contest* (Abingdon: Routledge, 2014).

61 Robert J. Miller, "International Law of Colonialism: A Comparative Analysis," *Lewis & Clark Law Review* 15 (2011): 847.

62 Tanja Aalberts, "Sovereign Marks," in *International Law's Objects*, eds. Jessie Hohmann and Daniel Joyce (Oxford: Oxford University Press, 2018), 456.

63 The Kawswentha (Mohawk) is also known as the Guswentha (Cayuga) and is often referred to in English as the Two-Row wampum belt. For more see Richard Hill, *Oral Memory of the Haudenosaunee: Views of the Two Row Wampum* (New York: American Indian Program at Cornell, 1990).

64 Ibid.

65 For examples, in addition to references cited elsewhere within this paper, see James Sydney Slotki and Karl Schmitt, "Studies of Wampum," *American Anthropologist* 51, no. 2 (1949): 223–36; Wilbur R. Jacobs, "Wampum: The Protocol of Indian diplomacy," *The William and Mary Quarterly: A Magazine of Early American History* 6, no. 4 (1949): 596–604; Daniel Coleman, "The Two Row Wampum-Covenant Chain Treaty and Trans-Systemic Resilience," in *Global Narratives of Resilience*, ed. Ana María Fraile-Marcos (New York: Routledge, 2019), 21–38; Curran Katsi'sorókwas Jacobs, "Two-Row Wampum Reimagined: Understanding the Hybrid Digital Lives of Contemporary Kanien'kehá: ka Youth," *Studies in Social Justice* 13, no. 1 (2019): 59.

66 Angela M. Haas, "Wampum as Hypertext: An American Indian Intellectual Tradition of Multimedia Theory and Practice," *Studies in American Indian Literatures* 19, no. 4 (2007): 78.

67 Ibid., 79–80.

The spread of wampum across an expansive geographic area larger than the size of continental Europe often meant wampum recorded agreements between more than one Indigenous nation. In this way, and as with the treaties forming the Peace of Westphalia, wampum agreements are international law expressed in a different textual form and visual medium. Whether written in ink on paper or quahog shells strung on sinew, such elements are the medium, not the legal meaning. Meaning is derived from literacy with the forms laws are expressed. The premise that international law was generated in Europe in 1648, centuries after it had been practiced among various Indigenous nations in what is now North America and with whom various European powers, such as the Dutch, Spanish, French and English, had long been engaging, is an extraordinarily narrow reading of international law and at best parochial.

The Dutch were active players in the making of the Peace of Westphalia.[68] They were also a party to the Kaswentha (Two-Row wampum) with the Haudenosauune Confederacy 35 years prior. The Dutch both understood and were engaging with the founding principles 'of kaswentha [which] emphasizes the distinct identity of the two peoples and a mutual engagement to coexist in peace without interference in the affairs of the other'.[69] Interestingly, these same principles underpin the sovereignty model of Westphalia – Europe's great contribution to international law – without any attribution to the Haudenosaunne Confederacy. Ter Borch's memorial painting also fails to include any Indigenous representative, not even so much as a wampum bead on the signing table.

Together, narrative and visual conspire to erase Indigenous peoples and their international laws while simultaneously drawing upon such Indigenous inventions and proclaiming them as European. Afterall, Indigenous peoples, such as the men of Catlin's 'Scalp Dance', could not possibly be as capable of rational thought as the elite Christian, European men in ter Borch's 'Treaty of Münster'. At least that is what the repeated narrative and visuals want us to believe.

The narrative of European international law presses onward without recognition of Indigenous contributions from the outset. To uphold the Westphalian genesis of European international law, the power of narrative and visual are carefully distributed into special networks separating law and artefact.[70] European international law benefits from continuously harnessing this power as seen in Westphalia's origin story, museums' wampum collections as well as the National Portrait Gallery's Catlin exhibit and ter Borch's portraiture, as stark examples. As such, modern international law operates in a deficit. It seeks to render Indigenous international law mute as a silenced, un-read artefact best suited to museum curation rather than acknowledge that European international law's conception of the sovereign-state was at least influenced by the Haudenosauune Confederacy with the Dutch in 1613. This practice of denial also flourishes in Canada in relation to treaties.

68 Daniel Philpott, "Westphalia, Authority, and International Society," *Political Studies* 47, no. 3 (1999): 566–89. Other European powers, such as the Spanish, French and English were also both participants in the Westphalian negotiations and had long been engaged with various Indigenous nations in what is now North America. That only once Europe decided to generate the idea of a sovereign state in 1648, does not mean international law was founded that year and was without Indigenous influence.

69 Jon Parmenter, "The Meaning of Kaswentha and the Two Row Wampum Belt in Haudenosaunee (Iroquois) History: Can Indigenous Oral Tradition be Reconciled with the Documentary Record?" *Journal of Early American History* 3, no. 1 (2013): 82–109.

70 Ruth B. Phillips, "Fielding Culture: Dialogues Between Art History and Anthropology," *Museum Anthropology* 18, no. 1 (1994): 39–46.

Treaties, praxis and international law

Treaties in international law are performative in that they are at once narrative and visual.[71] Such documents stand as *de facto* evidence that European Crowns recognised ownership of lands by Indigenous nations and that such lands were not *terra nullius*[72] nor were Indigenous nations without authority to engage in treaties:

> In countless reiterations . . . treaty literature affirms the sovereign capacity of Indian tribes to engage in bilateral government relations, to exercise power and control over their lands and resources, and to maintain their internal forms of self-government free from outside interference.[73]

The elements in the preceding mirror those of the treaties at Westphalia, according to which Crowns were free to engage with each other in diplomatic relations, were given authority and control over their own lands, and were given rights so that their own laws and governance structures would be unmolested by others.

Following the Seven Years War, the English Crown actively engaged in wampum diplomacy as international law in what is now Canada.[74] Upon dividing up Indigenous lands with the French, without any lawful right to do so, the English returned to Canada with the Royal Proclamation, 1763.[75] The Proclamation recognises Indigenous 'Nations as Tribes' and the holders of title over any lands not already sold to the Crown,[76] and forms part of Canada's Constitution Act, 1982.[77] It is specifically referenced in the Charter of Rights and Freedoms,[78] in a provision that holds that nothing in the Charter can 'abrogate or derogate from any aboriginal, treaty or other rights or freedoms that pertain to the aboriginal peoples of Canada including: (a) any rights or freedoms that have been recognized by the Royal Proclamation of October 7, 1763.' This includes nationhood found in the Proclamation.

In 1764, a year after the Royal Proclamation was issued, there was a gathering at Niagara where the Crown presented wampum to Indigenous leaders.[79] It is important to recognise that this particular wampum was commissioned and presented by the English Crown to Indigenous leaders. This praxis of Indigenous international law by the English Crown is not, as George Snyderman notes in this paper's opening quote, a '[f]ailure of the White man to understand and accept Indian customs and philosophy from earliest contact [which] has led to the acceptance of

71 Ruth Buchanan and Jeffery G. Hewitt, "Encountering Settler Colonialism Through Legal Objects: A Painted Drum and Handwritten Treaty from Manitoulin Island," *Northern Ireland Legal Quarterly* 68, no. 3 (2017): 291.

72 Robert J. Miller, "The International Law of Colonialism: A Comparative Analysis," *Lewis & Clark Law Review* 15 (2011): 847.

73 Robert A. Williams Jr., *Linking Arms Together: American Indian Treaty Visions of Law and Peace, 1600–1800* (New York: Routledge, 2013), 8–9.

74 John Borrows, "Wampum at Niagara: The Royal Proclamation, Canadian Legal History, and Self-Government," in *Aboriginal and Treaty Rights in Canada: Essays on Law, Equity, and Respect for Difference*, ed. Michael Asch (Vancouver: University of British Columbia Press, 1997), 155–72.

75 Ibid.

76 John Borrows, "Constitutional Law from a First Nation Perspective: Self-Government and the Royal Proclamation," *University of British Columbia Law Review* 28, no. 1 (1994): 1–47.

77 *Constitution Act*, 1982, being Schedule B to the *Canada Act 1982* (UK), 1982, c 11.

78 *Canadian Charter of Rights and Freedoms*, s 7, Part 1 of the *Constitution Act*, 1982, being Schedule B to the *Canada Act 1982* (UK), 1982, c 11.

79 Borrows, "Wampum at Niagara."

certain misconceptions'. It is re-inventionist to suggest as much and I wonder if Snyderman – while perhaps trying to appear empathetic to the 'Indians' – contributes to an ongoing effort to revise colonial history by recasting extraordinary violence and racism[80] as mere misunderstanding.

Like the Two-Row wampum treaty at Niagara[81] is also international law, though this time between Indigenous nations and the English Crown, versus only Indigenous nations. It serves as clear evidence that the Crown not only understood but actively engaged in international law-making utilising an Indigenous form, post-Westphalia. Similar to the conditions at Westphalia some 116 years prior, when the English Crown engaged with other nations which did not share a common legal system, those present were able to generate something new, which resulted in the Peace of Westphalia. By 1764, the Crown had been engaging with international law for over a century and understood such law may well take a form that is not solely derived from English common law; that international law called for new forms of law-making. In this instance the Crown provided wampum with an accompanying speech setting out its legal commitments woven into the treaty at Niagara. This wampum also stands as evidence that the Crown recognised, understood and acknowledged that Indigenous nations were engaged with international law in a different way from the Crown's European-based practices.[82]

Moreover, the 1764 Niagara wampum was an effort to provide symmetry to a relationship that comprised the Royal Proclamation, 1763, utilising an Indigenous form. Together the Proclamation and wampum form a text and visual narrative of a different sort than an international legal treaty written exclusively in English. But merely because it comes in a different form, does that mean wampum is not law? The actions of the English Crown to commission a wampum treaty and set out its legal obligations and relational commitments were presumably committed in good faith.[83] The Royal Proclamation, 1763 has never been overturned nor found invalid by a Canadian or international court, nor has wampum at Niagara, 1764 – though the former has constitutionally protected status and the latter does not. As such, these legal obligations at international law continue forward to present day without either being voided. None of the subsequent written treaties that followed 1764 displaced the Crown's obligations created by wampum at Niagara, though it is treaties, along with European international law's narrative, that exclude Indigenous peoples. As much as European international law has enabled imperial expansion over Indigenous nations, is there room for reconsidering European international law's history? If so, how might such (re)consideration be achieved?

Imagination, positivism and visuals of law

Human imagination is powerful. It shapes the world we live in and the one we aspire to. Imagination builds and sustains societies and social order.[84] It is both individual and collective.

80 Ania Loomba, *Colonialism/Postcolonialism* (New York: Routledge, 1998), 106.

81 Also known as Treaty at Niagara, is a large-scale wampum. For a visual of a reproduction, see: "Treaty of Fort Niagara," accessed March 19, 2020, https://d3v7qf8zyypult.cloudfront.net/maa/en/images/2014-08-01/large/5de7405a01fb96997b2934b07c20d05f.jpg.

82 As Aalberts, "Sovereign Marks," set out, treaty-making in a variety of forms found in Indigenous legal orders was also utilised by European Crowns in what is now the United States of America, as well as in a number of African countries, such as the Congo.

83 Sharon H. Venne, "Treaties Made in Good Faith," *Canadian Review of Comparative Literature/Revue Canadienne de Littérature Comparée* 34, no. 1 (2007): 4.

84 Mark Charles and Soong-Chan Rah, *Unsettling Truths: The Ongoing, Dehumanizing Legacy of the Doctrine of Discovery* (Westmont, IL: Intervarsity Press, 2019), 27.

Indeed, 'the sociological imagination enables us to grasp history and biography and the relations between the two within society. . . . It is by means of sociological imagination that men now hope to grasp what is going on in the world, and to understand what is happening to themselves.'[85] Human imagination has a number of analytical modes to engage with, including the metaphor.[86] Metaphor furthers the imaginary's construction of structure and institutions within society. Metaphor is engaged with and is central to reason.[87]

Legal positivism is based on reason and has been defined as law that is human made, versus natural, which is sourced in written rules that are negotiated, written and agreed upon by sovereign states.[88] The invention and movement from natural law to legal positivism demonstrates that human imagination is capable of moving a society from one form of understanding to another. Wampum is a human made, written set of rules negotiated and agreed upon by the relevant parties, including sovereign states, such as with wampum at Niagara. Indeed, it has been entered into by numerous Indigenous nations as well as by, for example, the Dutch and the English. Wampum is a form of legal positivism. It was relevant to the English Crown who understood wampum was law or they would not have known to engage with it in 1764. In other words, in spite of subsequently placing wampum in museums as cultural objects, in the eighteenth century the English Crown was well aware that wampum is international law. The English were also literate enough in wampum diplomacy to know how to use it.

Legal positivism also offered sovereign states a means of authority to engage in treaty-making, resulting in the production of a document recorded on paper, or in tubular beads made of clam shell. Yet, the European states viewed their own sovereignty as 'beyond history and inquiry',[89] which allowed them to solely determine what is and is not international law, who is and is not welcome.[90] The sovereignty of Indigenous nations required a feat of legal imagination of 'the international jurist to define and manage the primitive',[91] while simultaneously deploying 'a positivist methodology to examine these treaties [that] had the paradoxical effect of erasing the non-European side of the treaty even when claiming to identify and give effect to the intentions of that party'.[92] Legal positivism requires a recalibration of the necessity for Crowns to uphold their treaty obligations with Indigenous nations.

Both the Two-Row wampum and wampum at Niagara, along with a rich and extensive assemblage of other wampum, are recorded law that rely on imagery and metaphor versus text written in English (or Dutch, Latin, etc). Following the thread that metaphor is an element of reason and imagination, both the Two-Row and Niagara wampums are reasoned agreements between European Crowns and Indigenous nations. Like the Royal Proclamation, 1763,

85 C. Wright Mills, *The Sociological Imagination* (New York: Oxford University Press, 1959), 6–7.

86 Gillette, "Wampum Beads and Belts," 29.

87 George Lakoff, *Women, Fire, and Dangerous Things* (Chicago: The University of Chicago Press, 1987), xi.

88 Malcolm N. Shaw, *International Law*, 7th ed. (Cambridge: Cambridge University Press, 2014).

89 Anghie, "Finding the Peripheries," 102.

90 There was opportunity to formally recognise Indigenous nations in 1933 in Montevideo, Uruguay, with the *Montevideo Convention on Rights and Duties of States*, adopted by the Seventh International Conference of American States. Among other things, this convention held that only sovereign states already recognised in 1933 would determine present and future statehood, ensuring the existing successor states of former European colonies would continue to be recognised and upheld at international law, while ignoring the sovereignty of Indigenous nations. For more see Mikulas Fabry, *Recognizing States: International Society and the Establishment of New States Since 1776* (Oxford: Oxford University Press, 2010); Hurst Hannum, "Sovereignty and Its Relevance to Native Americans in the Twenty-first Century," *American Indian Law Review* 23, no. 2 (1998): 487–95.

91 Ibid., 65.

92 Ibid., 71.

wampum at Niagara arises of out an era of legal positivism in international law – and necessitates a realignment of current views and contributions of Indigenous laws. The classification of wampum with Indigenous nations as something other than legal positivism presents a conundrum for European international law.

Some conclusions

Returning to Peter Fitzpatrick's observation in relation to origin stories, that there is always more to it – I hope to have drawn upon a sliver of the 'more' through a consideration of portraiture and wampum. Westphalia as origin story has some explaining to do in relation to Indigenous contributions and the ongoing framing of Indigenous peoples as savages to be tamed, whose laws are outside European international laws' orderly reliance on legal positivism.

At Westphalia, the Crowns, each with a different legal order, executed an agreement in written text and ink that set out their obligations toward each other. Yet, like the text and visuals of wampum, the treaties of Westphalia were written in Latin, a language that was neither solely English, French, Dutch or Spanish, but that of their host the Holy Roman Empire. Like wampums, the treaties of Westphalia amounted to a new form of law-making seen as a benefit to the signatories.

One-hundred and fifteen years after Westphalia, the English Crown commissioned and presented a wampum belt to Indigenous leaders in Niagara, in 1764. Wampum belts were not an English form of law-making but neither was Westphalia specifically English. The Crown had over a century of experience, in practising European international law; it understood well the value of engaging in international law in a broader context, and that it accepted law taking on forms beyond the common law.

European international law continues to uphold the subjecthood of successor states by recognising treaties entered into by various heads of state, with Indigenous nations. In doing so, in some circumstances it utilises Indigenous forms of law-making, while denying the sovereignty of those same Indigenous nations. In the Canadian context, the Crown recognises Indigenous nations as sovereign nations, who hold title to lands and have capacity to enter into treaties through the Royal Proclamation, 1763, which is constitutionally enshrined. Yet simultaneously, both Canada and current international law deny the sovereignty of the Indigenous nations who entered into those treaties. Continuing on a trajectory of failing to recognise Indigenous sources of laws and Indigenous nations who also form part of the genesis of European international law's record pre-Westphalia, is not sustainable.

Similarly, the practice of placing wampum in museums and using portraiture by the likes of Catlin to uphold the savage, lawless narrative of Indigenous cultures, serves to normalise a fiction from which European international law continues to benefit. This, too, must be reimagined within a larger historical and modern context. Westphalian civility, underscored by ter Borsch's 'Treaty of Münster,' should be considered in the context of the power of visuals to uphold a male, Christian, European narrative. It should be reimagined within a context that is not as universal, genderless and atemporal as the Westphalian origin story would like us to believe. Drawing a more comprehensive narrative of European international law's origin story from our legal imagination can and should be narrated through written text and law's visuals. Otherwise, there is an ongoing risk of 'failure of the White man to understand and [uphold the] . . . acceptance of certain misconceptions'.[93] It does not have to be this way.

93 See n 2.

14

The travels of human rights

The UNESCO human rights exhibition 1950–1953

Hilary Charlesworth[1]

Introduction

International law is fixated on the written word. Think of the main activities international lawyers undertake – reading treaties, judicial decisions and resolutions as well as the writings of all those eminent publicists. International lawyers in turn produce more words – memoranda, judgments, blogposts, papers, articles and books. Central to being an international lawyer, it seems, is access to the written word. Indeed, for Jessie Hohmann, 'the production of text can come to feel like the very purpose of international law.'[2]

The dominance of the written word in international law has obscured the significance of the visual in the discipline. International law relies for much of its authority and meaning on symbols, iconography, representation, design and architecture. While there is a rich body of scholarship on the visuality of law,[3] there has been less attention devoted to the image in the field of international law.[4] Borrowing from scholars of the law and the visual we can ask: how does the visual shape and transform international law?[5] What can we see if we pay attention to the visual?

1 I am most grateful to Desmond Manderson for drawing the UNESCO exhibition discussed here to my attention and to Shane Chalmers and Sundhya Pahuja for their valuable comments on an earlier draft of this chapter. I acknowledge UNESCO's kind permission to use images from the exhibition.

2 Jessie Hohmann, "The Treaty 8 Typewriter: Tracing the Roles of Material Things in Imagining, Realising, and Resisting Colonial Worlds," *London Review of International Law* 5, no. 3 (2017): 371.

3 See, for example, R. K. Sherwin, *Visualizing Law in the Age of the Digital Baroque: Arabesques and Entanglements* (New York: Routledge, 2011); Leslie Moran, "Visual Justice," *Journal of Law in Context* 8 (2002): 431; Linda Mulcahy, "The Eyes of the Law: A Visual Turn in Socio-Legal Studies," *Journal of Law and Society* 44, no. S1 (2017): 111; Desmond Manderson, *Danse Macabre: Temporalities of Law in the Visual Arts* (Cambridge: Cambridge University Press, 2019).

4 Exceptions include Alice Palmer, "Image and Art in the Whaling in the Antarctic Case," in *Research Handbook on Art and Law*, eds. Jani McCutcheon and Fiona McGaughey (Cheltenham: Edward Elgar Publishing, 2020); Alice Palmer, "Absent Images of International Law," in this volume; Jessie Hohmann and Daniel Joyce, eds., *International Law's Objects* (Oxford: Oxford University Press, 2018).

5 See Desmond Manderson, ed., *Law and the Visual: Representations, Technologies, Critique* (Toronto: University of Toronto Press, 2018), 16.

International law has a lot to say about the visual as a matter of doctrine. Human rights law, for example, endorses a right to artistic expression.[6] International humanitarian law and international criminal law protect certain art objects from damage and destruction.[7] And the field of cultural heritage law gives some works of art protected status.[8] This chapter however does not address the international legal regulation of the visual, but rather what the visual can show us about international law. Images are enmeshed with how we see, frame, execute and legitimise law.[9]

Scholars have analysed the close relationship between visual culture and the international human rights system. They have observed the way that images have been relied on to evoke empathy with the situation of others and to found the compassion that animated humanitarianism.[10] The visual emerges as a fast track to prompting emotions that influence political action in order to protect human rights.[11]

The focus of this chapter is a travelling exhibition designed by the United Nations Educational, Scientific and Cultural Organization (UNESCO) in 1950 to introduce the Universal Declaration of Human Rights (UDHR), adopted by the United Nations (UN) General Assembly on 10 December 1948. The rights contained in the UDHR were later translated into treaty form in the 1966 International Covenant on Civil and Political Rights and the International Covenant on Economic, Social and Cultural Rights. Other specific UN human rights treaties, such as the Convention against Torture (1984), also have their genesis in the UDHR. For this reason, most jurists consider the UDHR as the foundation document of international human rights law.

The UDHR presents itself as repository of rights that are 'a common standard of achievement for all peoples and all nations'.[12] During most of its drafting, the UDHR was called the International Declaration of Human Rights, but it was changed to the Universal Declaration in late 1948 after a resolution sponsored by France. The idea was apparently to move the attention from the state delegates who drafted the Declaration to the addressees of the document – ordinary women, men and children all over the world.[13]

The assertion of universality was controversial at the time. Some states opposed the inclusion of certain rights on the basis that they were inapplicable outside the West,[14] and the American Anthropological Association argued that the UDHR would inevitably impose Western values

6 For example *International Covenant on Civil and Political Rights 1966*, 999 UNTS 171 (entered into force March 23, 1976), article 19.2.

7 For example *Rome Statute of the International Criminal Court 1998*, 2187 UNTS 3 (entered into force July 1, 2002), article 8.

8 For example *Convention Concerning the Protection of the World Cultural and Natural Heritage 1972* (entered into force December 17, 1975) 1037 UNTS 151, articles 1, 4.

9 See Roland Bleiker, "Mapping Visual Global Politics," in *Visual Global Politics*, ed. Ronald Bleiker (New York: Routledge, 2018), 4.

10 See, for example, Piers Robinson, "The CNN Effect," in *Visual Global Politics*, ed. Roland Bleiker (New York: Routledge, 2018), 62; Lilie Chouliaraki, "Humanitarianism," in *Visual Global Politics*, ed. Roland Bleiker (New York: Routledge, 2018), 161.

11 Jane Lydon, "Introduction: Visualising Human Rights," in *Visualising Human Rights*, ed. Jane Lydon (Perth: UWA Publishing, 2018), 2.

12 *Universal Declaration of Human Rights* (UDHR), UN Doc. UNGAR 217A(III), December 10, 1948, 72 (preamble).

13 Johannes Morsink, *The Universal Declaration of Human Rights: Origins, Drafting, and Intent* (Philadelphia: University of Pennsylvania Press, 1999), 33, 269–80.

14 See Mary-Ann Glendon, *A World Made New: Eleanor Roosevelt and the Universal Declaration of Human Rights* (New York: Random House, 2001).

on peoples whose cultures were misunderstood by the West.[15] The idea of universality has, however, remained a central feature of the international human rights system.[16]

I will first describe the provenance of the UNESCO exhibition and then discuss how its images relate to the rights contained in the UDHR. While designed to shore up the claims that the rights in the UDHR had a universal origin, these images tell us more than their curators intended about the specificity of the human at the centre of international human rights law.

The UNESCO exhibition

UNESCO had kept a close eye on the drafting of the UDHR. Indeed, it had rather irritated the committee established by the UN Commission on Human Rights to draft the Declaration, which suspected UNESCO of trying to take over debates about human rights.[17] In 1947, UNESCO hastily organised a survey, sent scattergun to governments, individuals and institutions such as trade unions and universities, seeking contributions on the conceptual basis of a declaration on human rights 'for the modern world'. Some 60 replies were eventually received, mainly from European intellectuals, including Aldous Huxley and Jacques Maritain.[18] UNESCO then appointed a committee, chaired by the British historian E.H. Carr, to prepare a report on the survey responses for the UDHR's drafters.[19] The report concluded that human rights rested on universal principles, even if they were expressed in terms of different philosophic traditions.[20]

From its founding in 1945, UNESCO fostered a variety of cosmopolitanism based on world citizenship. This was presented as the ineluctable route to progress from local and national communities.[21] Universal human rights were an important aspect of cosmopolitanism and UNESCO seized on the UDHR as a vehicle to achieve the 'One World' championed by UNESCO's first director-general, Julian Huxley.[22] After the adoption of the UDHR, UNESCO launched a media programme to promote the document.[23] UNESCO's goal in this respect was that '20th-century man shall not merely approve the Declaration of Rights but appeal to it constantly and

15 See "Statement on Human Rights," *American Anthropologist* 49, no. 4 (October–December 1947): 539. See Mark Goodale, "Toward a Critical Anthropology of Human Rights," *Current Anthropology* 47, no. 3 (2006): 485.

16 For example *Vienna Declaration and Programme of Action*, UN Doc. A/CONF.157/23, July 12, 1993.

17 Mark Goodale, ed., *Letters to the Contrary: A Curated History of the UNESCO Human Rights Survey* (Stanford, CA: Stanford University Press, 2018), 29–30. See also Mark Goodale, "UNESCO and the United Nations Rights of Man Declaration: History, Historiography, Ideology," *Humanity* 8, no. 1 (Spring 2017): 29.

18 A. P. Elkin, Professor of Anthropology at the University of Sydney, also contributed a reflection on 'The Rights of Man in Primitive Society'. Some of the contributions were published in UNESCO, *Human Rights: Comments and Interpretations*, UN Doc. UNESCO/PHS/3(rev.), July 25, 1948, https://unesdoc.unesco.org/ark:/48223/pf0000155042.

19 Goodale, "UNESCO and the United Nations Rights of Man Declaration," 38–40. E. H. Carr ended up disassociating himself from the process: at 40–41.

20 See Richard P. McKeon, Report of the Meeting of the UNESCO Committee on the Philosophic Principles of the Rights of Man, PHIL./9 (July 31, 1947), https://unesdoc.unesco.org/ark:/48223/pf0000124347; UNESCO, Report of the Director-General on the Activities of the Organisation in 1947, 2C/4 (September 20, 1947), 59. Goodale, *Letters to the Contrary*.

21 Glenda Sluga, "UNESCO and the (One) World of Julian Huxley," *Journal of World History* 21, no. 3 (September 2010): 393.

22 Ibid., 397–99.

23 Resolution 8 of the Third Session of the General Conference of UNESCO (1948) instructed the director-general 'to stimulate the dissemination of information' about the UDHR particularly through UNESCO's Mass Communication Department.

as a matter of course'.[24] One aspect of the media campaign was the deployment of the 'universal language' of photography to introduce the unfamiliar language of the Declaration around the world.[25] UNESCO regarded photography as an immediately accessible international language, with no need of translation, a significant tool in establishing the international public sphere underpinning One World.[26] In fact photography could constitute this world.[27]

UNESCO embraced the visual discourse of the post-war era, with its interest in forms of mass communication and gave images priority over text or voice.[28] Images were central to developing the idea of the international sphere, and photography was the primary technology for creating images. Photography was understood as an objective medium and also as an ambassador for the internationalist spirit.[29]

In 1949, UNESCO organised an exhibition on human rights at the Musée Galliera in Paris, held between October and December. The exhibition had a small organising committee: UNESCO's director-general, Jaime Torres Bodet, a former Mexican minister of education; René Cassin, a French jurist who had been one of the drafters of the UDHR; Clive Entwistle, a British modernist architect; and Roger Caillois, a French philosopher and literary critic, who was interested in surrealism and the avant-garde.[30]

UNESCO identified the aim of the exhibition as 'to show, objectively and in a spirit of international understanding, what have been the contributions of every people, every nation and every culture to the assertion and conquest of human rights'. It stated:

> By showing each visitor that the rights which are now recognised as his, and which it seems natural to him to enjoy, are in fact the reward of long struggles and many sacrifices, it will teach him . . . to be worthy of them through his better fulfillment of the corresponding duties.[31]

The exhibition was built along a winding path around over 3-metre-high pillars and installations that displayed photographs, images, documents and objects in a type of collage or montage. Some of the images, displayed at the top of the pillars, were out of viewing range, but the solid pillars emphasised the sturdiness of human rights. The idea was to present a visual history of human rights, and the exhibition was organised into 14 themes, each one devoted to a particular right or set of rights. UNESCO considered that 'the illustrations mark the stages along the road leading from the cave-man . . . to the free citizen of a modern democracy'.[32]

The Paris exhibition ended with a Treasure Room, containing originals of iconic documents of democracy, protected by armed guards. None of these documents used the language of human rights but, according to UNESCO, they were 'identical in spirit'. The documents

24 Quoted in The Human Rights Exhibition Project, "Visualizing Universalism: The Unesco Human Rights Exhibition, 1949–1953," n.d., https://static1.squarespace.com/static/521fa71ae4b01a7978566e1e/t/570fd84240261d1195924e33/1460656201979/Universalism_pamphlet.pdf.

25 UNESCO quoted in Lydon, "Introduction: Visualising Human Rights," 2–3.

26 Tom Allbeson, "Photographic Diplomacy in the Postwar World: UNESCO and the Conception of Photography as a Universal Language, 1946–1956," *Modern Intellectual History* 12, no. 2 (2015): 383.

27 Ibid., 385.

28 Ibid., 386–89.

29 Ibid., 388.

30 The Human Rights Exhibition Project, *Visualizing Universalism the Unesco Human Rights Exhibition, 1949–1953*, 13.

31 Letter from UNESCO dated April 29, 1949, reproduced in Ibid., 12.

32 See UNESCO, *A Short History of Human Rights in Human Rights: Exhibition Album* (Paris: UNESCO, 1950), 5.

included the minutes of the Dutch first free assembly in 1172, the Magna Carta (1215), Thomas Jefferson's draft of the US Declaration of Independence (1776), a draft of the French Declaration of the Rights of Man (1789), Italy's Constitution of 1840 and Abraham Lincoln's proclamation freeing slaves (1863). Omitting documents such as the 1918 Russian Declaration of the Rights of the Toiling and Exploited People, the selection reflected the tensions of the Cold War.[33]

After the inaugural show in Paris, the exhibition was converted into a portable exhibition album reproduced in 12,000 copies and sent to the UN's 50 member states. It contained 276 monochrome images on 110 sheets (each measuring 48 cm x 31.5 cm). The kit included a brochure, *A Short History of Human Rights*, whose goal was to 'enabl[e] speakers on the subject to supply their audiences with such historical background as may throw light on the meaning, circumstances and scope of the events to which the illustrations refer'.[34] There was also an instruction manual on how best to display the exhibition. The Album was designed so that it could be unpacked and exhibited in all sorts of venues, including libraries, schools and museums – in Torres Bodet's words, to 'help carry the human rights message in visual form to the peoples of many countries'.[35] The exhibition was displayed until 1953.

The exhibition was shown at a time when Europe was coming to terms with the devastation of the Second World War; the Cold War was gearing up and anti-colonial movements were becoming more powerful. In this era of tension and apparent fragmentation, UNESCO offered the history of human rights as a universal glue. This depended on an idea of historical progress – and the sense that Europe should re-articulate universal values.[36]

Torres Bodet did not share his predecessor Julian Huxley's passionate commitment to the idea of 'One World', articulating instead a more modest goal of 'international understanding' and 'friendly association between cultures' in his inaugural address to UNESCO in 1948.[37] The goal of the exhibition organisers was to establish that 'the same paths of liberty have been trodden, throughout the centuries and throughout the world, by civilizations that were very far apart'.[38] The organising committee chaired by Torres Bodet understood that the exhibition would need to contain images from outside the West. It thus invited UN member states to submit cultural and visual items that related to specific human rights 'so that the irreplaceable contributions of all countries should be represented'.[39] In the end, however, the universalism of the exhibition had a distinctly European aura. The Human Rights Exhibition Album was created by UNESCO's in-house designers. Despite the myriad contributions from UN members, UNESCO ended up sourcing much of the exhibition material from newspapers, museum and photo agencies, presumably because these images fitted the UNESCO narrative more readily.[40]

There were some strong reactions to the UNESCO endeavour. The new Islamic Republic of Pakistan complained that the exhibition failed to include images depicting Muslim contributions to human rights. In response UNESCO produced a list of such images, but they

33 Lydon, "Introduction: Visualising Human Rights," 4.
34 UNESCO, *A Short History*, 6.
35 Quoted in "Human Rights Message Will Be Spread by Travelling Exhibition," *UNESCO Courier* III, no. 1 (1950): 4, https://unesdoc.unesco.org/ark:/48223/pf0000074247.
36 The Human Rights Exhibition Project, *Visualizing Universalism the UNESCO Human Rights Exhibition, 1949–1953*, 3.
37 Quoted in Allbeson, "Photographic Diplomacy," 401.
38 Quoted in The Human Rights Exhibition Project, *Visualizing Universalism the UNESCO Human Rights Exhibition, 1949–1953*, 14.
39 Quoted in Ibid.
40 Ibid.

were simply images from India and Pakistan, and examples of Islamic calligraphy.[41] The French Catholic Church complained that the Album was overly secular and called for its withdrawal.[42]

I had read about the travelling exhibition and seen reproductions of some of its images. Australian institutions had received 20 kits in all, but the exhibition was set up in just two places – Brisbane and Adelaide.[43] I then discovered that two of the kits sent to Australia in 1950 were still held in university libraries, one at the University of Melbourne. I was thus able to leaf through the now-yellowing sheets of images in a special reading room in the Baillieu Library (Figure 14.1). This kit had clearly never been shown as the exhibition labels still had unbroken perforations.[44]

The visualisation of universality

The exhibition constructed a universal history of human rights using a European lens and flattening differences between cultures and peoples. The exhibition narrative came directly from the Enlightenment: the progress of man from a primitive state of nature to an enlightened one through language, rationality, science and law.[45] UNESCO set out to depict 'the dramatic struggle of man, from earliest times, to assert his birth right to free citizenship'.[46] On this account, the development of human rights was the culmination of all that had gone before; and its foundations were in the shared history of humanity.

Some images of the non-European world were included in the exhibition, but they tended to be presented as elements in a universal melting pot. One example is Sheet 8 which is composed of nine samples of different alphabets, including cuneiform, Devanagari, Arabic and Latin. The label for these images declared, 'All races, all civilizations, all nations have made their individual and valuable contributions to what is today the sum of Human Rights' (Figure 14.2).

The exhibition retained the organisation of the Musée Galliera show, starting with a general introduction to human rights. The first image here was of the Earth with a naked man and a woman, possibly the biblical Adam and Eve, hovering far out in space (Figure 14.3). This was a rather pale version of the original Paris exhibition which featured a planetarium with a rotating globe and the two illuminated human figures inside it, a recorded voice intoning the first two articles of the UDHR.[47] The image of the globe in the travelling exhibition, without markers of national territory, accompanied by the human figures, had no caption to explain it but was presumably designed to evoke a universally attuned outlook.[48] A statement from the UNESCO director-general was displayed to emphasise this: 'The destiny of mankind is an indivisible

41 Ibid., 15.

42 Ibid.

43 Jane Lydon, "'Visual History at its Best!': UNESCO's 1951 *Human Rights Exhibition* in Australia," in *The Social Work of Narrative: Human Rights and the Cultural Imaginary*, eds. Gareth Griffiths and Philip Mead (Stuttgart: Ibidem-Verlag, 2018), 286.

44 Unfortunately, the Album in the Baillieu Library is missing 14 of the pages of images and some of the exhibition labels.

45 This narrative is also on show in the windows in the main courtroom of the ICJ: see Daniel Litwin, "Stained Glass Windows, the Great Hall of Justice of the Peace Palace," in *International Law's Objects*, eds. Jessie Hohmann and Daniel Joyce (Oxford: Oxford University Press, 2018), 463.

46 "Human Rights in Pictures," *The News* 57, no. 8813, November 6, 1951.

47 The Human Rights Exhibition Project, *Visualizing Universalism the UNESCO Human Rights Exhibition, 1949–1953*, 17.

48 Ibid., 5.

Figure 14.1 The UNESCO Human Rights Exhibition Album, Baillieu Library Special Collections.

Figure 14.2 UNESCO Human Rights Exhibition Album, Sheet 8.

Figure 14.3 UNESCO Human Rights Exhibition Album, Sheet 2.

responsibility, shared by us all.' While the classical style of the two figures conformed with European notions of universality, it inadvertently illustrated the limitations of the idea.

The introductory images reinforced the gradual development of a universal rights consciousness. They included images of Stone Age weapons, juxtaposed with Hammurabi's Code. The associated caption referred to the 'many stages' of man:

> Man had to fashion his first tools, till his first field, conceive the first rules of morality, draw up a first rule of law, and so on, up to the most recent achievements – the guarantee of individual liberty, civic and political rights, compulsory education, social legislation.[49]

In a visual echo of the structure of the preamble of the UDHR,[50] the next section in the exhibition was titled the 'Frailty of Human Rights'. This short series of images depicted the actions of 'the totalitarian States' in the Second World War, which UNESCO presented as an interruption in the human rights journey, requiring '[a] war . . . to be fought to safeguard [the heritage of human rights]'.[51] A photograph of Hitler's Reichstag opened the section, and it finished with a photograph of the United Nations General Assembly adopting the UDHR. In between was a Plate with a photograph of three dead American soldiers on a beach juxtaposed with a photograph of a pile of decaying bodies at the Buchenwald concentration camp. The sequence thus emphasised Nazi war atrocities as an aberration from the European-led march towards universal human rights and the redemptive advent of an international institution to fill Europe's shoes. The scope of this section is strikingly narrow; for example, no images of human rights violations associated with European colonisation were included.

The largest part of the exhibition was termed 'The Conquest of Human Rights'. This depicted the development of 30 articles of the UDHR in 14 clusters, such as 'Abolition of Slavery'; 'Protection against Arbitrary Treatment, Equality before the Law'; 'Dignity of Work and Social Legislation'; 'Social Security, Family and Property'; 'Emancipation of Women'; 'Freedom of Creative Work'; and 'Participation in Government'.

The notion of struggle was integral to UNESCO's account of human rights. 'Human rights were not created out-of [sic] thin air when . . . the United Nations adopted the Universal Declaration,' the *Short History* informed readers. 'They are the outcome of a struggle that has been going on since the dawn of human history'.[52] UNESCO indeed hoped that the images would inspire 'a feeling of indebtedness towards those whose sacrifices and struggles have won us, at so much cost, the advantages we enjoy today'.[53] The final image in the exhibition, for which no caption was supplied, was a photograph of a smiling, young, European, girl holding a sheaf of blossom in a sunny rural setting. The denouement of the struggle for human rights, then, appeared to be bucolic innocence.

Each set of images tracking the 14 clusters of rights follows a rough pattern: first, representations of the absence of the right or rights in question in 'primitive communities';[54] then portraits of pioneers who campaigned for the right; followed by the recognition of the right; and finally, its spread and acceptance. The images are a mixture of photographs and reproductions of

49 UNESCO, *Exhibition Album*, Sheet 4.
50 See Shane Chalmers, "The Beginning of Human Rights: The Ritual of the Preamble to Law," *Humanity* 9, no. 1 (2018): 107.
51 UNESCO, *A Short History*, 5.
52 Ibid. See also UNESCO, *Exhibition Album*, Sheet 26.
53 UNESCO, *A Short History*, 6.
54 This was a common term in the exhibition. See, for example, Ibid., 10, 22, 33.

artworks. Images of the era of the 'absence of rights' are generally images of sculptures, engravings and paintings. The era of 'rights recognition' is depicted mainly in photographs, emphasising its modernity. Photography could at the one time capture the exoticism of difference while offering a universal language that could generate an internationalist identity, in the same way as the concept of human rights.[55] The medium and the message were thus ideal partners.

The message of universal application was reinforced by pared-back graphic art: the first sheet for each cluster of rights featured a small line drawing, apparently depicting the essence of the right in question. These images were used to publicise the UNESCO exhibition.[56] They involved white and black abstract figures, almost always male, surrounded by symbols of the relevant rights cluster. They evoke Le Corbusier's Modulor figures. Here are some examples of representations of the abolition of slavery, the abolition of inhuman treatment, the right to an adequate standard of living and social security, and freedom of thought and opinion (Figure 14.4).

UNESCO's imagery sometimes changed the emphasis of a right. We can see this in the depiction of freedom of movement, set out in article 13 of the UDHR. While the right is expressed in individual terms,[57] UNESCO translated it as essentially an adjunct to international trade through the 'opening up' of places once considered 'impenetrable'.[58] The sequence begins with a thirteenth-century picture of an Arab boat on the Euphrates and a sixteenth-century engraving of European traders in Brazil.[59] The stylised graphic on this sheet shows two men, one white and one black, clutching briefcases while crossing a dotted line, presumably an international boundary (Figure 14.5). A plane in the image suggests that this has occurred though plane travel. The next Plate celebrates the 'incalculable' value of 'pilgrimages, missions and trade' with images of Marco Polo's caravan, the arrival of Portuguese traders in Japan in the seventeenth century, and a sixteenth-century Persian painting of a pilgrimage to Mecca.[60]

Threats to freedom of movement are depicted on the next Plate by a sixteenth-century engraving of fierce 'Cannibal Indians' roasting murdered travellers over a fire.[61] This is juxtaposed with a reproduction of a 1711 decree by the French king endorsing passports as a response to such dangers faced by foreign travellers. These images are followed by a collage of depictions of different forms of travel from ancient times (a horse, a camel) to modern times (the Queen Elizabeth, a mail-carrying plane).[62] The final image, freedom of travel attained, has no human forms at all. It is the bow of a docked sleek cargo boat or ocean liner (Figure 14.6).[63] The caption makes clear that the freedom is for the benefit of interstate trade rather than for individuals. The title is 'The World Becomes a Single Unit' and the rubric states: 'The increasing speed, regularity and safety of communications and trade forged ever closer links between all the countries of the world. The prosperity of each is now largely dependent upon the well-being of the rest.'

55 Lydon, "Introduction: Visualising Human Rights," 3.

56 The Human Rights Exhibition Project, *Visualizing Universalism the UNESCO Human Rights Exhibition, 1949–1953*, 21.

57 On the drafting history of article 13, see Johannes Morsink, *The Universal Declaration of Human Rights: Origins, Drafting, and Intent* (Philadelphia: University of Pennsylvania Press, 1999), 73–75.

58 UNESCO, *A Short History*, 10–12.

59 UNESCO, *Exhibition Album*, Sheet 33.

60 Sheet 35.

61 Sheet 36.

62 Sheet 37.

63 Sheet 38.

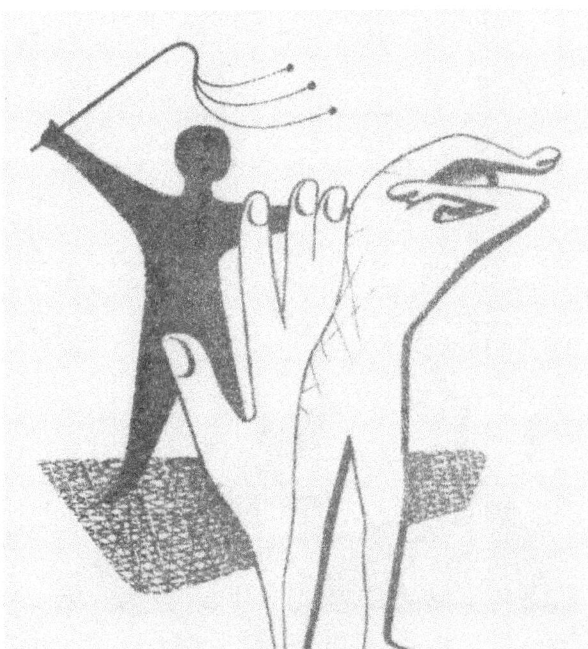

Figure 14.4 UNESCO Human Rights Exhibition Album, Sheets 27, 39, 53, 74.

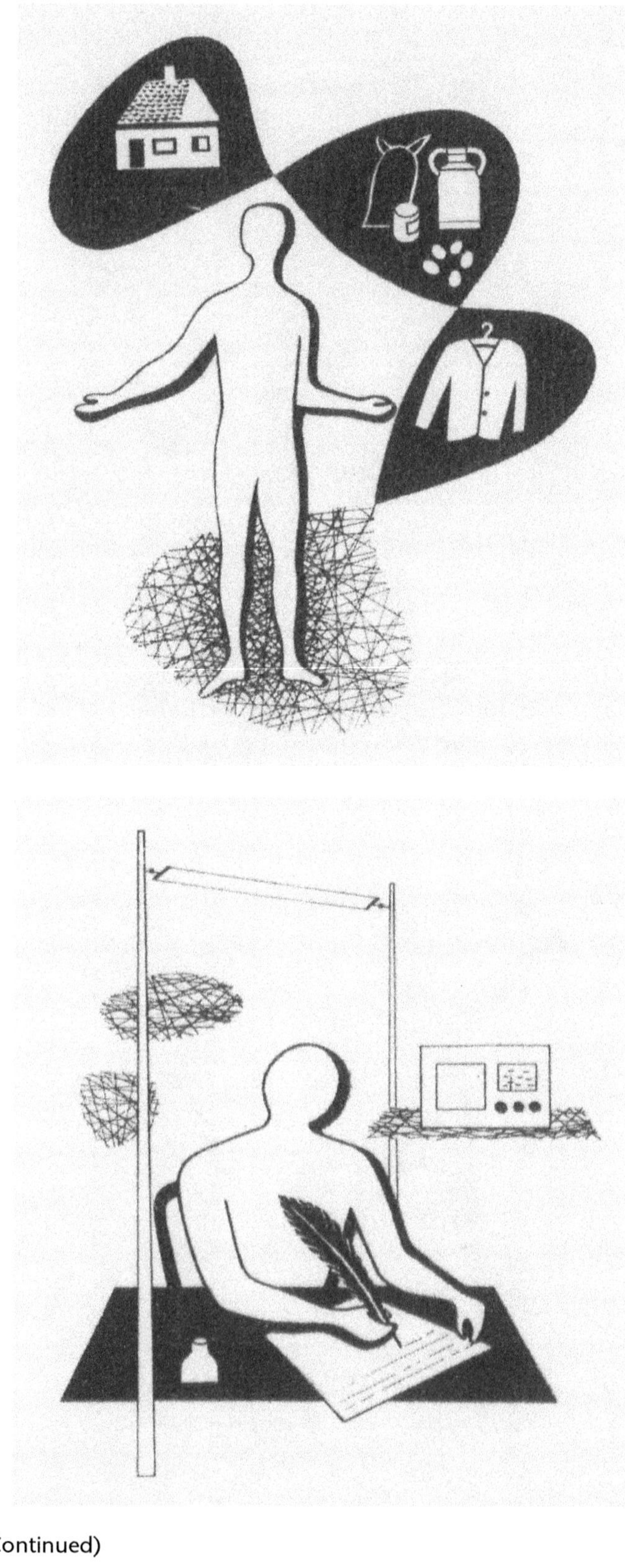

Figure 14.4 (Continued)

Figure 14.5 UNESCO Human Rights Exhibition Album, Sheet 33.

Another example of UNESCO's narrative is the cluster of rights described as 'Social Security, Family and Property' depicting articles 16, 17, 22 and 23 of the UDHR. The first Plate establishes the relevant human rights problem as 'Tyranny in the Home' with two images (Figure 14.7).[64] One is an undated, but probably contemporary, photo of, we are told, '[a] Kibuya Warrior Purchasing a Chief's Daughter for Four Goats'. The other is a seventeenth-century European engraving, 'The Wife-Beater', showing a drunken man beating a woman. UNESCO's caption states:

> In former times, the father's authority was absolute, and sometimes included the power of life and death over his children. Daughters were seldom allowed to choose their own husbands.

Displaying a twentieth-century photo of Africa with a seventeenth-century European image to illustrate tyranny in the home suggests that the problem has been transcended already in the West – it belongs to 'former times' – but that it persists in Africa. UNESCO's sketch on the edge

64 Sheet 59.

Figure 14.6 UNESCO Human Rights Exhibition Album, Sheet 38.

Figure 14.7 UNESCO Human Rights Exhibition Album, Sheet 59.

Figure 14.8 UNESCO Human Rights Exhibition Album, Sheet 59 (detail).

of this sheet reinforces European advancement by depicting the essence of the right to family security with three white silhouettes of a classic nuclear family: a man, a woman (wearing a dress) and a male child close together under a pitched tiled roof (Figure 14.8).

The second Plate in this sequence is labelled 'Domestic Happiness'.[65] It contains four photographs of families. One is of 'A Worker's Family, with Three Children, Having Dinner' showing a European man, woman and children eating around a table. One is a 'Maori Mother with Her Child'; the next is 'Mother and Children, Sierra Leone'. Despite the caption for this Plate firmly anchoring the family in a nuclear, heterosexual context, proclaiming that '[a] man and wife should find their chief happiness in the family life that they build up together', there are no fathers evident in the non-European images. The final photo of domestic happiness is a formal portrait of a youthful Franklin and Eleanor Roosevelt with five of their children, taken in 1919. Accounts of the estrangements within the Roosevelt family[66] give an ironic edge to this image, clearly unintended by UNESCO.

65 Sheet 60.

66 See, for example, Hazel Rowley, *Franklin and Eleanor: An Extraordinary Marriage* (Manchester: Manchester University Press, 2012).

Overall, the exhibition manufactured an idea of universality in its images and text by presenting human experience as similar across time and space: all men and women are part of a family; all communities have the right to protest etc. The images were however stripped of their history and context. The idea is that these are now universal claims, thanks to the UDHR. It is striking that dates are mainly given for images of Western life, while those of the non-Western world tend to be undated. This creates a sense of inescapable progression in the West, while the rest of the world is lagging and needs bringing up to speed. In this respect the UNESCO exhibition differs from Edward Steichen's famous 1955 photographic exhibition, 'The Family of Man', with which it is often compared.[67] Steichen did not use captions and restricted the information available to the viewer to the name of the photographer, the location of the image and the date it was taken.[68] The spectator is left to interpret a photo in the light of multiple neighbouring images, producing, in Ariella Azoulay's words, 'a partial repertoire of states of existence, situations, and abuses in which humans find themselves'.[69] Because '[t]he fragility of the human condition is enfolded in each and every photograph', and the images blur notions of victims and perpetrators,[70] Azoulay suggests that 'The Family of Man' is a more effective declaration of universal human rights than the UDHR itself.

The role of Western architecture in epitomising human rights culture is evident in the UNESCO exhibition. For example, freedom of religion is illustrated by nine photographs of Parisian religious buildings on a single sheet – seven churches of different Christian denominations, one synagogue and one mosque.[71] An image of the UN General Assembly meeting at the Palais de Chaillot in Paris is used as a counterpoint to the atrocities of the Holocaust.[72] Cities and scenes of urban life are also regularly deployed as the sites of the global rights-bearing community, implying that these are the crucibles of civilisation, and reinforcing a Western idea of advancement.[73]

Peter Fitzpatrick has observed that 'an obsession with origins is perhaps the most obvious substitute for the mythically transcendent'.[74] If we cannot rely on the divine, we need a clear account of our origins. We can observe this process of constructing an origin story in the UNESCO exhibition to reflect a myth of modernity: that history unfolds in a linear progression. The present is accepted as inevitable, and the past becomes simply a series of steps leading towards it.[75]

Conclusion

Visual images are perhaps more common in the field of human rights than any other area of international law: they define, promote and challenge human rights. The relationship between

67 For example Lydon, "Introduction: Visualising Human Rights," 3.

68 Edward Steichen, *Catalogue: The Family of Man* (New York: Museum of Modern Art, 1955).

69 Ariella Azoulay, "'The Family of Man': A Visual Declaration of Human Rights," in *The Human Snapshot*, eds. Thomas Keenan and Tirdad Zolghadr (Berlin: Sternberg Press, 2013), 39.

70 Ibid., 42.

71 UNESCO, *Exhibition Album*, Sheet 73.

72 Sheet 25.

73 Allbeson, "Photographic Diplomacy," 395–402.

74 Peter Fitzpatrick, *The Mythology of Modern Law* (London: Routledge, 1992), 48.

75 Richard Joyce, "Westphalia: Event, Memory, Myth," in *Events: The Force of International Law*, eds. Fleur Johns, Richard Joyce and Sundhya Pahuja (Abingdon: Routledge, 2011), 65.

art and international human rights law has been widely studied, but mainly in an instrumental way – how can each field bolster the other? For example, a major study by the EU Agency for Fundamental Rights reported in 2017:

> There are many overlaps and commonalities between the fields of the arts and human rights. Both are concerned with questions of what is (and what is not) humanity, identity, dignity, of communicating empathy, of the transformation of lives, of visions for the future and of the mission of mankind, of the full development of the person. Both are universally applicable. *There is a great deal of shared space between the disciplines, which should be captured and utilised more consistently in order to push forward with mutually beneficial agendas in both fields.*[76]

This is a recommendation for the fields of art and human rights to join forces, to gain strength from each other, presenting them as in a symbiotic relationship. The report called on artists to reinforce 'the human rights message'.[77] It argued that 'perceptions . . . are more powerful than facts. . . . And [a]rt is all about perceptions. . . . Art can [thus] transcend barriers, such as politics and language.'[78]

A more complicated relationship between art and human rights emerges when we take the visual seriously. The UDHR itself can be read as a response to the visual: Sharon Sliwinski argues that the widely published photographs from Dachau and Buchenwald taken just after these concentration camps were abandoned by the Nazis prompted the drafting process.[79] Against this visual evidence of inhumanity, the UNESCO exhibition marshalled images of human rights to tell a powerful story of the universal nature of human rights, and of the inexorable progress of the human spirit. But paying attention to these images reveals that the particular has taken on the guise of the universal; the imagined universality rests on exclusions. There is no trace for example, of the effects of colonisation on human rights.

UNESCO believed in the neutrality of photography and its capacity to generate an internationalist sensibility. And yet the exhibition shows the inevitable partiality of visualisation and the ways in which an image will always emphasise some elements while excluding others. UNESCO also regarded photography as an opportune method of comparing cultures, across space and across time, to imagine a global community.[80] This leaves little room for acknowledging differences between communities. It projects an understanding that world civilisation is simply a conglomeration of different static cultures, without any account of tensions between them or the dominance of some cultures in this mix.[81]

The international human rights system relies on an appeal to universal values. Many scholars have challenged this claim by examining, in different ways, its privileging of specific perspectives

76 European Union Agency for Fundamental Rights, *Exploring the Connections Between Arts and Human Rights: Report of the High-Level Expert Meeting in Vienna, 29–30 May 2017* (Luxembourg: Publications Office of the European Union, 2017), 6 (emphasis added).

77 See, for example, Ibid., 11.

78 Ibid., 11–12.

79 Sharon Sliwinski, "Human Rights," in *Visual Global Politics*, ed. Roland Bleiker (Abingdon: Routledge, 2018), 168.

80 Allbeson, "Photographic Diplomacy," 398.

81 Ibid., 398–99.

in the construction of universality.[82] The UNESCO exhibition offers a visual expression of that construction of a shared world culture and illustrates its inevitable biases and blind spots. Today, although the rhetoric of universality remains strong, the official imagery of human rights tends to be more nuanced. Studying the images in the 1950 exhibition offers some insight into the way that a history of human rights was manufactured at a particular point in time by obscuring the specificity of the catalogue of rights contained in the UDHR.

82 See, for example, Makau Mutua, *Human Rights: A Political and Cultural Critique* (Philadelphia: University of Pennsylvania Press, 2002); Sundhya Pahuja, *Decolonising International Law* (Cambridge: Cambridge University Press, 2011). See further the discussion by Ben Golder in this volume.

15

International law, literature and worldmaking

Christopher Gevers

Introduction

In the mid-1870s Robert Louis Stevenson completed a handwritten draft of his first novel (to be called either *The Hair Trunk* or *The Ideal Commonwealth*), but it was never published.[1] At the time, Stevenson described the novel's plot to a friend as 'the most absurd story of a lot of young Cambridge fellows who are going to found a new society' by colonising the Navigator Islands in the 'South Seas'.[2] These Cambridge fellows decide that in order to 'break with old traditions' and 'begin the *new world* unfettered and pure-minded',[3] and more importantly, in order to fund their scheme, they would require a new 'conscience', specifically an 'international' one. As their leader explains, their scheme is a 'a special case . . . [b]ecause it is *International*'.[4] As such, from the moment these Cambridge fellows signed the 'Declaration of Independence' of their 'Ideal Commonwealth', they became governed not by domestic law (or morality) but by *international law*. This law would govern not only in their relations with the soon-to-be-colonised 'inoffensive aborigines' of the Navigator Islands,[5] but also in their relations with other (European) states *and* their 'fellow citizens' in Britain, who, the group's leader assures his co-conspirators, are 'no more to us . . . and no less . . . than any tribe of painted cannibals on coral island'.[6] '[W]e shall treat the trousered proprietor in England exactly as we should treat the nude proprietor . . . on the Gold Coast', the leader declares, 'with an entire and imperturbable disregard of his rights . . . which are civic *but not international*'.[7]

1 Stevenson's complete manuscript is held by the Huntington Library, and was published (with annotations) by Roger G. Swearingen in 2014 (see Robert Louis Stevenson, *The Hair Trunk or the Ideal Commonwealth: An Extravaganza* (Kilerran: Humming Earth, 2014). An earlier handwritten draft (circa 1876) is held by the 'Beinecke Rare Book and Manuscript Library' at Yale University.
2 Sidney Colvin, ed., *The Letters of Robert Louis Stevenson to his Family and Friends, Vol I* (London: Methuen, 1899).
3 Stevenson, *The Hair Trunk*, 41.
4 Ibid., 40.
5 Ibid., 42.
6 Ibid., 43.
7 Ibid.

At around the same time, a group of international lawyers were meeting in Ghent with similar thoughts in mind. Their absurd plot involved founding an international law society – the *Institut de Droit Internationale* – that would make them the 'legal conscience of the civilized world', and by doing so inaugurate a 'modern' international law in place of the 'old fashioned' one.[8] In order to do so these 'Men of 1873' discovered a new 'international conscience' of their own, a legal one. Like Stevenson's 'Cambridge fellows', these 'Men of 1873' (as Koskenniemi labels them) imagined a world where this new international law would both (i) govern relations between the European states, and a couple of (mostly 'white') states outside of Europe, and (ii) regulate these states' interactions with the 'tribe[s] of painted cannibals' that made up the rest of humankind, and their colonisation in particular.

Seventy years later, in *The Nomos of the Earth*, Carl Schmitt would register these developments as portending the end of the spatially bound 'international order' (or 'nomos') governed by *European* international law, to be replaced by a 'spaceless' one governed by a 'universal' international law (a convenient cloak for Anglo-American imperialism, according to Schmitt). In fact, the 'international' order of Stevenson's would-be first novel was something out of Schmitt's worst nightmare. First, it allowed the extension of international law 'beyond the line' (i.e., outside territorial Europe, and into the *necessarily* lawless '"overseas" zone'),[9] in order to regulate the 'appropriation' of non-European soil by a private enterprise claiming statehood without even occupying the territory, let alone 'effectively' (it was the 'hapless confusion' of the Berlin Conference in the comic extreme).[10] Second, by turning this baseless new international law practised 'beyond the line' back onto British (i.e., European) soil, Stevenson's Cambridge fellows anticipated – and in Schmitt's version explained – the descent of Europe into an 'unbracketed' civil war of annihilation in 1914, and the establishment of the putatively 'universal' (and hopelessly normative) League of Nations – the final blow to the old order. Stevenson's fellows and the 'Men of 1873' were less concerned; their new 'consciences' placed 'the world before [them]',[11] a world that they themselves had re-imagined and re-made as 'international'.

The coincidence between Stevenson's novel and the founding of 'modern international law' is a useful place to start this essay on the relationship between literature and international law, a relationship that, after being largely neglected by the 'law and literature' movement,[12] has recently received the attention of both literary scholars and international lawyers. At its best, this emerging scholarship considers the *mutual* imbrications of international law and literature critically, without 'bracketing' either discipline, and avoiding both disciplinary retreat and escape.[13] This chapter aims to exemplify this approach to international law and literature by picking up the threads of Stevenson's unpublished novel in the 1870s, and weaving them into a discussion of John Buchan's *A Lodge in the Wilderness* (1906) and W. E. B. Du Bois' *Dark Princess: A Romance* (1928).

8 Martti Koskenniemi, *The Gentle Civilizer of Nations: The Rise and Fall of International Law 1870–1960* (Cambridge: Cambridge University Press, 2004), 23.

9 Carl Schmitt, *The Nomos of the Earth,* trans. G. L. Ulmen (New York: Telos Press, 2006), 93–94.

10 Ibid., 225–26.

11 Stevenson, *The Hair Trunk*, 40.

12 See further Christopher Warren, *Literature and the Law of Nations, 1580–1680* (Oxford: Oxford University Press, 2015), 1–30.

13 For early examples see Joseph Slaughter, *Human Rights, Inc.: The World Novel, Narrative Form, and International Law* (New York: Fordham University Press, 2007); Ed Morgan, *The Aesthetics of International Law* (Toronto: University of Toronto Press, 2007).

In doing so, the chapter aims to show how the worldmaking, and *unmaking*, practices of these novels track – both historically and theoretically – those of 'modern' international law. Buchan's *A Lodge in the Wilderness* is a useful illustration of how international lawyers could read *fictional worlds* 'historically', for how novels 'come to terms with – or "inscribe"' the contexts in which they were produced (biographical, sociocultural, ideological and discursive);[14] while Du Bois' *Dark Princess* illustrates how novels might be read for their 'subversive mappings', for their 'alternative clocks and maps'[15] that might re-orient or demystify the 'White World order' that international law took (and takes) for granted. Moreover, reading these novels alongside one another produces a rich account of worldmaking practices of both literature and international law, and what they 'do' in the world, together and apart. In doing so the chapter argues that, when it came to founding the League of Nations and establishing a 'White World order', these worldmaking practices of literature and international law were not just entangled – they were inseparable.

Worldmaking and empire: *A Lodge in the Wilderness* and the League of Nations

The new 'international' order that Stevenson and the 'Men of 1873' imagined remained, for some time, juridically inchoate. However, it was 'constitutionalized' in the Covenant of the League of Nations, the 'fundamental charter of the international society'[16] – a society composed of the 'older' states of Europe and new mostly-white states outside of it, with a standing 'international' body that was responsible for facilitating peace between these states, and monitoring their tutelage of selected 'nonwhite' peoples for possible independence, at some point (i.e., the Mandates). Under this new World order, the 'Navigator Islands' would *finally* come to be ruled over by a 'young Cambridge fellow' from the 1870s, as 'German Samoa' became a Mandate Territory in 1919, entrusted to New Zealand, and 'administered' by James Allen (who had graduated from Cambridge in 1877). However, not even Stevenson could have imagined this Cambridge fellow's subsequent role: as New Zealand's representative before the League's 'Permanent Mandates Commission', a body comprised almost exclusively of white men who were granted 'international' oversight over not just the Navigator Islands, but all Mandate territories.

Historians have recently returned to the League of Nations and the introduction of the Mandates system as a moment of 'Worldmaking'.[17] In charting the 'neglected' and 'unexplored' origins of twentieth-century internationalism and institutions in 'British imperial thought', Mazower recasts the formation of the League as a moment of 'Imperial Internationalism': a plan led by Jan Smuts to 'prolong the life of an empire of white rule through international cooperation'.[18] In these recent revisionist histories Smuts' *Practical Suggestion* figures prominently,

14 Dominick LaCapra, *History & Criticism* (Ithaca: Cornell University Press, 1985), 127.

15 Charles Mills, "Unwriting and Unwhitening the World," in *Race and Racism in International Relations: Confronting the Global Colour Line*, eds. Alexander Anievas, Nivi Manchanda and Robbie Shilliam (London: Routledge, 2015), 209.

16 Hersch Lauterpacht, "Japan and the Covenant," *Political Quarterly* 3 (1932): 175.

17 See Adom Getachew, *Worldmaking After Empire: The Rise and Fall of Self-Determination* (Princeton: Princeton University Press, 2019); Erez Manela, *The Wilsonian Moment: Self-Determination and the International Origins of Anticolonial Nationalism* (Oxford: Oxford University Press, 2007); Mark Mazower, *No Enchanted Palace: The End of Empire and the Ideological Origins of the United Nations* (Princeton: Princeton University Press, 2009); Susan Pederson, *The Guardians: The League of Nations and the Crisis of Empire* (Oxford: Oxford University Press, 2015).

18 Mazower, *No Enchanted Palace*, 13, 30.

in both the origins of the League and its Mandates system.[19] However, these 'Imperial Internationalist' worldmaking plans (and modern international law's 'constitution' that underpinned them) were anticipated more than a decade before Smuts' pamphlet, in a far less likely text: John Buchan's long-forgotten novel, *A Lodge in the Wilderness* (1906).

Before he wrote the novels for which he is remembered (*Prester John* (1910), *The Thirty-Nine Steps* (1915)), Buchan wrote some forgettable fiction, including *A Lodge in the Wilderness*, which he penned following his time in South Africa as private secretary to Alfred Milner. The novel tells the story of 'an imaginary conference' arranged by a multi-millionaire businessman, Francis Carey (modelled on Cecil John Rhodes), to discuss the future of an imperiled British Empire, facing public disenchantment at its centre and 'Colonial Nationalism' at its peripheries. The conference takes place at a lodge, Musuru, located on the East Kenyan Plateau. Its bipartisan, gender-balanced group of 18 white delegates are all drawn from Britain and the (soon-to-be) Dominions, save for one delegate who is 'the American wife of an English statesman'.[20] In their efforts to 'reconstruct the policies of the globe',[21] the group devise a worldmaking scheme that anticipates the League of Nations with remarkable precision (in an act of foreshadowing, the group meet at one point in a room styled after the Palace of Versailles).[22]

The delegates at Buchan's imaginary conference enthusiastically agree at the outset that a 'new imperialism' was emerging, one that much like the 'new internationalism' of the age, according to recent accounts, was both 'born of the "*objective* facts" of modernity' and *subjective* 'attitude[s] of mind',[23] an 'international' one.[24] One delegate defines this new imperialism – in terms very similar to how John Westlake (an original 'Man of 1873') had defined international law two years prior – as 'the closer organic connection under one Crown of a number of *autonomous nations of the same blood*', but made explicit its underlying 'racial contract' that Westlake kept silent (for reasons discussed later): 'a racial aristocracy considered in their relations to the subject peoples, a democracy in their relations to each other'.[25] The 'constitutional apparatus' that the delegates devise for this new 'United Empire' is a Federation of White States, consisting of Britain and its Settler Colonies (Australia, Canada, South Africa and New Zealand). As the 'component States' of this United Empire, these restive white 'Dominions' would gain autonomy in most matters – in recognition of their growing 'self-consciousness' (i.e., the principle of 'self-determination' for white 'peoples') – and would be given a seat on a governing 'Imperial Council'.[26]

In addition to coordinating relations between its 'component States' and other international administrative functions (managing 'currency, postage, shipping, naturalisation'[27] as well as 'native labour'),[28] the new 'United Empire' would be tasked with a far more difficult and urgent task: the administration of its 'tropical dependencies' in Asia, Africa and the Americas, those

19 J. C. Smuts, *The League of Nations: A Practical Suggestion* (London: Hodder and Stoughton, 1918), vi.

20 John Buchan, *A Lodge in the Wilderness* (Edinburgh: William Blackwood and Sons, 1906), 8.

21 Ibid., 23.

22 Ibid., 75.

23 Ibid., 14.

24 Glenda Sluga, *Internationalism in the Age of Nationalism* (Philadelphia: University of Pennsylvania Press, 2013), 12, 30.

25 Buchan, *A Lodge in the Wilderness*, 14. In 1904 Westlake defined international law as the law of '[t]he international society . . . composed of *all the states of European blood*'. John Westlake, *International Law, Part I: Peace* (Cambridge: Cambridge University Press, 1904), 40.

26 Buchan, *A Lodge in the Wilderness*, 40–43.

27 Ibid., 44.

28 Ibid., 83.

'great realms [held] . . . *in trust* for races who are *unfit to struggle singlehanded in the arena of the world*'.[29] Like the Covenant of the League, the constitutional apparatus of this 'United Empire' would grant the white Dominions a special 'mandate' (as one delegate put it) to administer these tropical dependencies *on behalf of* the United Empire.[30] While the delegates agreed that self-government for these tropical dependencies was unthinkable for the foreseeable future (or 'at any rate *for the next century or two*'), progress towards political autonomy for these 'races' was notionally possible, but would require tutelage appropriate to each tropical dependency's level of development.[31] It was necessary, the delegates decided, to distinguish between a 'long-settled' and 'fully-developed' dependent (like India), which required only 'control, amend[ment] here and there, and the benefit of our protection'; and 'lands where the fabric of civilization has to be built up *from the beginning*', most of these 'great undeveloped speculative dependencies' being located in Africa.[32]

While the initial blueprint for 'reconstruct[ing] the policies of the globe' was the *present* British Empire, Buchan's delegates agreed that their United Empire was not confined to it. In time, this worldwide racial empire might go fully 'international' – to include the British Empire's prodigal son, the United States, as well as its European cousins – as 'the greater Powers of the world' that were 'other branches of their race'.[33] As the Canadian delegate explained, the arc of 'colonial nationalism' was that British colonies begin their political lives as distinct nations which are 'extremely self-confident and bumptious', but which in time come to realise that they are 'bound by ties of *kinship and race and inherited culture to a larger world*'; eventually these 'sentimental attachments to the parent race . . . become the chief incentive to union'.[34] In the end, Buchan's delegates' imperialism, like that of Buchan's mentor Alfred Milner, knew no geographic limits, only racial ones.[35]

In the 1906 version of *Lodge in the Wilderness* this more ambitious, 'international' version of Buchan's racial fantasy was only implied. A decade later, in 1917, when it started looking like it might become a reality with the formation of the League of Nations, Buchan republished *A Lodge in the Wilderness* (and even put his name on it this time). He then wrote a follow-up novel, of sorts, in 1919, called *The Island of Sheep*.[36] This short, polemical novel told the story of a weekend gathering on a Scottish Island, with an all-white but bipartisan mix of politicians and layfolk as guests, much like the cast of *A Lodge in the Wilderness*. However, unlike in Buchan's earlier novel, the guests are not drawn from the Dominions. Rather, the British guests are joined by a French general and four Americans (a serviceman, a politician, a 'captain of industry' and a civilian living in England). Through their discussions Buchan sets out the case for, and establishes the origins of, the new 'Imperial Internationalism' that was emerging from the ongoing negotiations in Paris. The argument that the League of Nations would, as Mazower later discovered, 'prolong the life of an empire of white rule through international cooperation'[37]

29 Ibid., 45.
30 Ibid.
31 Ibid., 61.
32 Ibid., 61–62.
33 Ibid., 43.
34 Ibid., 42–43.
35 Paraphrasing Milner's 'Credo', published posthumously by *The Times* in 1925.
36 Co-authored with Susan Grosvenor, Buchan's wife, under the pseudonyms of Cadmus and Harmonia. See Cadmus and Harmonia, *The Island of Sheep* (London: Hodder and Stoughton, 1919).
37 Mazower, *No Enchanted Palace*, 30.

is most forcefully articulated by Phillip Lenchard (an 'Apostle of Empire').[38] In justifying the League of Nations to, amongst others, the doubting French general (Clemenceau, presumably), Lenchard insists that '[t]he hope for peace . . . lies in a community of law, interests, and culture over the biggest possible area' – 'a working union of all civilised people' – of which 'the British Empire was *the first instalment*'. The war had not only 'justified' Lenchard's views about British imperialism, he added, it had 'superseded them', noting: 'I used to think that the Empire was enough for the purpose, but now I see that we want nothing short of *humanity at large*.'[39] It went without saying that 'humanity at large' would be governed by white men, despite the inconvenience of 'every little faction on the globe wanting to turn itself into a State'.[40] In fact, the only reference in *Island of Sheep* to the fate of the 'dependencies' (which had so concerned Buchan's imaginary delegates in 1906) is the assurance, from Lenchard, that 'things are going very well' in Paris, as '[w]henever there was any doubt about the proper mandatory for a part of the world they generally came first to *us*' (i.e., to Britain and her Dominions, sitting as 'a group of free nations').[41]

Things did go 'very well' for Britain and her Dominions in Paris, but not quite as well for Jan Smuts as is now often suggested. Smuts had arrived in Europe in March 1917 with the clear objective of annexing 'German South West Africa' for South Africa. To this end, in his public speeches he drummed up the threat of German *Mittelafrika* (and in particular 'German-trained hordes of Africans') to the security of not only South Africa, but 'the future of the world'.[42] Unsurprisingly, then, Smuts' *Practical Suggestion* in late November 1918 was that the Mandates scheme should be purposively 'restrict[ed] . . . to the peoples and territories formerly belonging to Russia, Austria and Turkey', and that the fate of 'the German colonies' should be left to be determined by the Peace Conference.[43] It was President Wilson who proposed extending the Mandates scheme to German colonial territories, and Smuts and the rest of the British delegation only gave up on their plans for annexation late in the day, when it became clear that Wilson would not budge.[44] It was at *this* point – in order to secure annexation in all but name – that Smuts proposed his compromise: that South West Africa and the Pacific Islands become 'C Mandates', entrusted to the neighbouring Dominions. It was a last minute compromise that left the Mandates looking more like the 'United Empire' scheme of Buchan's 1906 novel than Smuts' own *Practical Suggestion* (Buchan having anticipated not only the 'staged' Mandates system, but the very language in which it was expressed in Article 22 of the Covenant).

In 1906 Buchan's imaginary delegates were hesitant to commit to a detailed plan for implementing their scheme. As one delegate put it: '[w]hen our symposium is at an end and we go back to the world . . . let us talk about methods. But do not let us confuse ourselves here by any obeisance to that intolerable fool, the "practical man"'.[45] By 1919 it was the turn of 'practical men' to implement the worldmaking project of imperial internationalism, including international lawyers, and one intolerable fool in particular, Jan Smuts. However, *A Lodge in*

38 Buchan and Grosvenor, *The Island of Sheep*, 78.

39 Ibid., 113–17.

40 Ibid., 100.

41 Ibid., 101.

42 J. C. Smuts, "East Africa," *The Geographical Journal* 51, no. 3 (1918): 141, 145. See generally, W. M. Roger Louis, "The South West African Origins of the 'Sacred Trust', 1914–1919," *African Affairs* 66, no. 262 (1967): 20–39.

43 Smuts, *Practical Suggestion*, 15.

44 See George Curry, "Woodrow Wilson, Jan Smuts, and the Versailles Settlement," *The American Historical Review* 66, no. 4 (July 1961): 980–81.

45 Buchan, *A Lodge in the Wilderness*, 86.

the Wilderness suggests that the contours of the new World order that emerged at Versailles, and the transition from empire to 'the International', took intellectual and political shape well in advance of Smuts' arrival in London in 1917.

Buchan's *A Lodge in the Wilderness* – written by an 'insider' within British imperial circles – is a useful illustration of how international lawyers might read *fictional worlds* 'historically'. The 'actual world' of an author (and a reader) is invariably inscribed into her *fictional world*, consciously and unconsciously,[46] and so novels can be read for how they 'come to terms with – or "inscribe"' the contexts in which they were produced (biographical, sociocultural, ideological and discursive), as well as the contexts of their reception and critical reading.[47] This being the case, historians of international law might read literary texts for how they 'inscribe' particular historical contexts, and their conditions of possibility (both political and intellectual).[48] Buchan's *A Lodge in the Wilderness* illustrates how intellectual historians might read literature more systemically as an 'archive of international legal thought'.[49] Similarly, literary theorists might read international law texts to explicate – to varying degrees – the 'meaning' of literary texts (and their forms), and how these change and circulate over time.[50]

But if international lawyers might read Buchan's novel 'historically' – for 'the semantic mapping of its contents upon the actual world'[51] – some literature can be read for its 'subversive mappings' thereof: for the 'alternative clocks and maps'[52] of fictional worlds that might re-orient or demystify the 'World' (and 'worlds') that international law takes for granted. One such novel is W. E. B. Du Bois' 1928 novel *Dark Princess: A Romance* whose fictional world subverts the 'worlds' that international law takes for granted on just about every level (then and now).

Unmaking 'White World Imperialism' in literature and international law: Du Bois' *Dark Princess*

In *Dark Princess*, W. E. B. Du Bois produced a *fictional world* that drew heavily on the fight against White World order that he and his fellow pan-Africanists were undertaking in the 'actual' one.[53] The novel tells the story of a secretive international organisation, the 'Great Central Committee of Yellow, Brown, and Black', representing the 'Darker Races' in the struggle against 'White World' Imperialism; and a romance between Matthew Townes (an African-American) and Princess Kautiliya, ruler of the Indian Kingdom of Bwodpur. In the novel, the World is cut in two by the 'global color line', as Du Bois understood the actual world to be. Rather than reading *Dark Princess* as simply escapism from 'White World Imperialism', Du Bois' novel (and other

46 Pavel argues that, in turn, the 'pattern[s] of interaction' between fictional worlds and the 'actual' one is itself historically contingent, but not determined. Thomas G. Pavel, *Fictional Worlds* (Cambridge: Harvard University Press, 1986), 50, 108. See further Eric Hayot, "On Literary Worlds," *Modern Language Quarterly* 72, no. 2 (2011): 137.

47 LaCapra, *History & Criticism*, 127.

48 See Christopher Gevers, "Literal 'Decolonization': Re-reading African International Legal Scholarship Through the African Novel," in *The Battle for International Law: South-North Perspectives on the Decolonization Era*, eds. Jochen von Bernstorff and Philipp Dann (Oxford: Oxford University Press, 2019), 383–403.

49 Warren, *Literature and the Law of Nations*, 3.

50 In the 'law and literature' movement this might be loosely classified as an extension of the *law in literature* approach. See Guyora Binder and Robert Weisberg, *Literary Criticisms of Law* (Princeton: Princeton University Press, 2000).

51 Pavel, *Fictional Worlds*, 84.

52 Mills, "Unwriting and Unwhitening the World," 209.

53 For a recent account see Getachew, *Worldmaking After Empire*.

Black Internationalist fiction) can be more profitably read as an attempt to subversively map the contours of White World order in and through *fictional worlds*.[54]

The war against 'White World Imperialism' in *Dark Princess* is fought on multiple fronts. It is first and foremost about the 'international' struggle of the 'Great Central Committee' of the 'Darker Races' against the *White World order*: the political and economic domination of the Earth by white empires and states (the 'international' order imagined by Stevenson and the 'Men of 1873', and 'constitutionalised' at Versailles in 1919). However, it is also about struggles of its African-American protagonist Matthew Townes against the 'global social reality'[55] of whiteness – what he identifies as the 'widespread, deep, powerful determination to make this a *white world*';[56] the 'white world' produced by what Du Bois identified in 1910 as the 'discovery of *personal* whiteness among the world's peoples', which he added was 'a very modern thing – a nineteenth and twentieth century matter, indeed'.[57]

For Du Bois, *the* White World order and 'whiteness' (or 'white worlds') were co-produced, and Buchan agreed. On an imperial 'field-trip' arranged for the delegates in *A Lodge in the Wilderness*, the millionaire Francis Carey lectures a group of settlers on the 'white man's burden', reminding them that 'the presence of the native races *makes every man of you an administrator*'.[58] He might have added that 'the administration of native races *makes every man of you white*', as this was precisely the conclusion his delegates reached about their worldmaking scheme, and the 'Mandates' in particular. Not only were the 'tropical dependencies' in Asia, Africa and the Americas 'God-given trusts . . . *for the vitality of [the white] race to exercise itself in*' through their administration, but doing so would remind '*all* imperial subjects', and the sentimentalists back home in particular, that 'our democracy is a *white man's* democracy, and we are not moved by any Rousseauism about the rights of *man*'.[59] The making of both 'white men' and 'white worlds' reached its zenith at the turn of the century, and tracing their co-production in literature and international law is the focus of this section; but first it will briefly elaborate on how Du Bois understood 'whiteness', and its tendentious relationship to the 'actual world', using the work of Charles Mills.

Making whiteness, or 'white worlds'

Du Bois' novel begins with its protagonist defending the 'Dark Princess' from the predations of a white American man, who Matthew Townes identifies as being part of the 'mighty organization of white folk' that he is at war with; the 'same, vast remorseless machine [of whiteness] in Berlin as in New York' that he labels the 'white leviathan'.[60] Philosopher Charles Mills reworks the 'social contract' of Hobbes' *Leviathan* (and others) as a '*racial* contract', in order to unmask, explain and detail this 'unnamed' sociopolitical system 'that has made the modern world what it is today': global white supremacy.[61] Like Du Bois' *Dark Princess*, Mills' Racial Contract theory

54 See, for example, Christopher Gevers, "To Seek with Beauty to Set the World Right: Cold War International Law and the Radical 'Imaginative Geography' of Pan-Africanism," in *International Law and the Cold War*, eds. Matthew Craven, Sundhya Pahuja and Gerry Simpson (Cambridge: Cambridge University Press, 2019), 492–509.

55 Charles W. Mills, *Blackness Visible: Essays on Philosophy and Race* (Ithaca: Cornell University Press, 2015), xiv.

56 W. E. B. Du Bois, *Dark Princess: A Romance* (Jackson: University Press of Mississippi, 1995), 66.

57 W. E. B. Du Bois, "The Souls of White Folk," *The Independent* (New York) 69, August 19, 1910, 339–42.

58 Buchan, *A Lodge in the Wilderness*, 73–74 (emphasis added).

59 Ibid., 45 (emphasis added).

60 Du Bois, *Dark Princess*, 7.

61 Charles W. Mills, *The Racial Contract* (Ithaca: Cornell University Press, 1997), 1. According to Mills, the racial contract is the 'set of formal or informal agreements . . . between one subset of humans, henceforth designated

brings together the making of 'whiteness' as a 'global social reality'[62] (or 'white worlds') and *the* 'White World' (i.e., the international order);[63] and sets out in their political, moral, cultural, economic and epistemological dimensions.[64]

As Mills points out, Hobbes' *Leviathan* was not *entirely* fictional, as in his mind there were 'savages' living in the state of nature in an 'actual' distant colony, which has led his disciples to dispute whether Hobbes' account was hypothetical or historical (or whether the disciplinary world of Western philosophy was founded on a fictional or real one). However, for Mills the 'racial contract' is both a *hypothetical* device 'to elicit our intuitions about justice', and more importantly, a *descriptive* account of how the modern world came to be; while not all whites are 'signatories' to the Racial Contract, all whites are beneficiaries of it (i.e., 'global white supremacy' is *structural*).[65] While acknowledging that 'no single act literally corresponds to the drawing up and signing of a [racial] contract', Mills identifies a series of global, historical events that 'can be seen, not just metaphorically but *close to literally*, as its conceptual, juridical, and normative equivalent'.[66] Notably, all of the examples he gives of literal racial contracts involve international law, including 'European discussions about colonialism, "discovery" and international law'.[67] The League of Nations was one such literal 'global racial contract', and many of its signatories were also enthusiastic signatories to the hypothetical one as well, chief amongst them Jan Smuts and Woodrow Wilson.

In Mills' account, the distinction drawn between the grand worldmaking projects of Wilson and Smuts, and the smaller 'white worlds' their makers inhabited, collapses; as, '[t]o a significant extent . . . white signatories [to the Racial Contract] will live in an invented delusional world, a racial fantasyland . . . located in real space'. This is a world of:

> white mythologies, invented Orients, invented Africas, invented Americas, with a corresponding fabricated population, countries that never were, inhabited by people who never were – Calibans and Tontos, Man Fridays and Sambos – but who attain a virtual

by (shifting) "racial" . . . criteria as "white" . . . to categorize the remaining subset of humans as "nonwhite" . . . subpersons, so that they have a subordinate civil standing in the white or white-ruled polities.' Or, put simply: 'When white people say "Justice", they mean "Just us".' Mills, *Racial Contract*, 11.

62 Charles W. Mills, *Blackness Visible*, xiv. According to Mills: 'White supremacy should . . . be seen as a multidimensional system of domination . . . extending to white domination in the economic, cultural, cognitive-evaluative, somatic, and in a sense even "metaphysical" spheres. There is a pervasive racialization of the social world that means one's race, in effect, *puts on into a certain relationship with social reality, tendentially determining one's being and consciousness*.' Charles W. Mills, "White Supremacy as Sociopolitical System: A Philosophical Perspective," in *White Out: The Continuing Significance of Racism*, eds. Ashley W. Doane and Eduardo Bonilla-Silva (New York: Taylor & Francis, 2003), 42. See further Mills, *Racial Contract*, 109–10 (noting that 'differential racial experience generates an alternative moral and political perception of social reality').

63 For Mills, the most 'illuminating framework' for understanding 'race' was 'a global one': 'the thesis that European expansionism in its various forms . . . bring race into existence as a global social reality, with the single most important conceptual division historically being that between "whites" and "nonwhites"'. Mills, *Blackness Visible*, xiv.

64 Du Bois' most comprehensive 'mapping' of this emerging transnational racial whiteness can be found in W. E. B. Du Bois, "Of the Culture of White Folk," *Journal of Race Development* 7, no. 4 (1917): 434. On the similarities between Du Bois and Mills, see Christopher Gevers, "'Unwhitening the World': Re-Thinking Race and International Law," *UCLA Law Review* (forthcoming).

65 Mills, *Racial Contract*, 11.

66 Ibid., 20 (emphasis added).

67 Ibid. The others include 'pacts, treaties and legal decisions; academic and popular debates about the humanity of nonwhites; [and] the establishment of formalized legal structures of differential treatment'. Ibid., 20–21.

> reality through their existence in travelers' tales, folk myth, popular and highbrow fiction, colonial reports, scholarly theory, Hollywood cinema, living in the white imagination and determinedly imposed on their alarmed real-life counterparts. . . . [A] cognitive and moral economy psychically required for conquest, colonization, and enslavement.[68]

It is as if, at some point, Europeans (led by European men) set off for the 'fictional' world of whiteness, burnt their ships, and never came back.[69] And yet these 'Europeans' did come back, mostly the men at first, including as writers and international lawyers.

In order to understand, historically and theoretically, the entanglements of fictional worlds (e.g., of Stevenson's fellows and Buchan's delegates), the disciplinary world of the 'Men of 1873', and the 'white worlds' identified by Du Bois and Mills, we have to begin by first setting out the co-production of late-nineteenth century 'whiteness' by both real-world imperialism and the fictional 'worlds' of literature. Then, we have to re-consider the role of 'whiteness' in the constitution and operation of the disciplinary world of international law around the same time. Doing so reveals how these processes were not only inter-linked but co-constituted, as were the 'internationals' of Stevenson's 'Cambridge fellows' and the 'Men of 1873', and those of their descendants and disciples.

'White culture' and imperialism: making 'European' men

It goes without saying that the fictional worlds of Stevenson, Buchan and their contemporaries were 'white worlds', mostly if not entirely peopled by white characters and predicated on the Racial Contract. According to Said, Kipling 'would no more have questioned . . . the right of the white European to rule, than he would have argued with the Himalayas'.[70] Even Joseph Conrad, the seemingly-unkillable critic of imperialism, was unable to imagine its alternative because he assumed 'European tutelage was a given', and so 'he could only imagine the world carved up into one or another Western sphere of dominion'.[71] As the story goes, Chinua Achebe (who, to make sure Conrad remained 'safely dead', more than once tried unsuccessfully to bury him) wrote *Things Fall Apart* as a response to Conrad's 'offensive and deplorable book'.[72] In fact, according to Achebe it was Joyce Cary, not Conrad, who inspired *Things Fall Apart*,[73] an elision that matters little for present purposes as the 'white worlds' of Conrad and Cary were indistinguishable. What does matter is Achebe's revelation that, for a while, reading 'white worlds' convinced him that *he* was white, and that it was only when he reached 'the appropriate age' that he 'realised that these writers had pulled a fast one on me!': 'I was not on Marlowe's boat steaming up the Congo in *Heart of Darkness*. I was one of those strange beings jumping up and down on the river bank, making horrid faces.'[74]

68 Ibid., 18–19.

69 See Pavel, *Fictional Worlds*, 85. One of the problems with 'white political philosophy' according to Mills is precisely its '*otherworldliness,* its ignoring of basic political realities', or reality altogether. Mills, *Racial Contract,* 11 (emphasis added).

70 Edward W. Said, *Culture and Imperialism* (New York: Vantage Books, 1994), 135.

71 Ibid., 24–25.

72 Chinua Achebe, "Image of Africa: Racism in Conrad's *Heart of Darkness*" (1977), reprinted in *Hopes and Impediments: Selected Essays* (New York: Doubleday, 1989), 14.

73 See Achebe's interview with Lewis Nkosi and Wole Soyinka, "African Writers of Today-Episode 4," *National Educational Television*, 1964.

74 Chinua Achebe, "The Song of Ourselves," *New Statesman,* February 9, 1990.

Literature, Achebe concluded, was not innocent: it can 'put you in the wrong crowd' (or the wrong *world*). Elsewhere, Achebe noted the tendency for slippage between fictional and actual 'white worlds', when he insisted that those who would defend *The Heart of Darkness* on the basis that 'racism has not become an issue in the world when [Conrad] wrote his famous African novel' 'will have to clarify *whose world* it is talking about'.[75] In response, Achebe set the 'white world' of *The Heart of Darkness*, Conrad and his defenders (past and present) against the 'world' of Du Bois, who not only mapped the 'white worlds' of Conrad, Buchan, Smuts and Wilson but understood earlier than most the co-productive or symbiotic relationship between the 'white world' metropole, and its fictional and disciplinary 'colonies'.[76]

In his 1917 essay on the 'Culture of White Folk', Du Bois was already arguing that the 'theory that "darkies" are born beasts of burden for white folk' (i.e., the Racial Contract) was being trumpeted by 'the *cultural world* with stronger and shriller accord', noting (with a swipe at Kipling):[77]

> The supporting arguments grow and twist themselves in the mouths of merchant, scientist, soldier, traveler, writer and missionary: Darker peoples are dark in mind as well as in body; . . . they are fools, unlogical idiots, "half devil and half child".

Spivak has suggested that Du Bois might be the progenitor of the literary field of 'colonial discourse studies and . . . what was to follow from it – postcolonial criticism'.[78] Postcolonial scholars have since comprehensively 'mapped' the traffic between metropolitan and colonial worlds, fictional and 'actual', and shown that imperialism was, or *is*, 'not only about soldiers and cannons but also about ideas, about forms, about images and imaginings', a struggle over geography that began 'with the charting of cultural territory'.[79] Or, as Toni Morrison succinctly put it: '[c]anon building *is* empire building.'[80]

We might use the specter of Du Bois haunting postcolonial studies to inflect the field in two ways. First, while the emphasis of much postcolonial scholarship has been on European imperialism, one – if not *the* – 'idea at the back of it' was race, and the global Racial Contract, what Du Bois called a '*White World* Imperialism'. Second, and related to this, while the focus of postcolonial scholarship has traditionally been on European literature (and *British* literature in particular),[81] American literature was also constituted by its own 'settler' (and later 'humanitarian') imperialism.[82] Inflecting postcolonial studies in this way highlights the complex dynamics that Du Bois enfolded into the concept of 'White World Imperialism': not only how the 'White World' enabled imperialism, but also how imperialism produced and circulated 'white worlds',

75 Achebe, *Hopes and Impediments*, xv.

76 See Pavel, *Fictional Worlds*, 84 (noting: 'Fictional domains can acquire a certain independence, subsist outside the limits of actuality, and sometimes strongly influence us, not unlike a colony established overseas that develops its own unusual constitution and later comes to affect in various ways the life of the metropole.').

77 Du Bois, "Of the Culture of White Folk," 439.

78 Gayatri Chakravorty Spivak, *Death of a Discipline* (New York: Columbia University Press, 2003), 97.

79 Said, *Culture & Imperialism*, 7.

80 Toni Morrison, "Unspeakable Things Unspoken: The Afro-American Presence in American Literature" (1988), reprinted in *The Source of Self-Regard: Selected Essays, Speeches, and Meditations* (New York: Vintage International, 2019), 169.

81 Toni Morrison, *Playing in the Dark: Whiteness and the Literary Imagination* (New York: Vintage Books, 1993), 7–8.

82 Aziz Rana, *The Two Faces of American Freedom* (Boston: Harvard University Press, 2010). See Said, *Culture and Imperialism*, 63–66.

and how European and American literature was entangled in both these processes, and shaped by them.

The fact that the 'prototypical modern realistic novel' written at the beginning of the eighteenth century is, as Said reminds us, 'about a European who creates a fiefdom for himself on a distant, non-European island',[83] not only shows us something about the making of novels and fiefdoms over the next 200 years. It also shows us something about the making of 'Europeans' as 'white', *globally*. In her 1990 Massey Lectures in the History of American Civilization, Toni Morrison detailed the silenced and overlooked role of early American literature in 'the architecture of a *new white man*', and in order to 'limn out and enforce the invention and implications of whiteness'.[84] More recently, Schwarz has set out a similar process in the emergence and consolidation in Britain and her 'Dominions', through popular politics and literature, of a late nineteenth-century version of 'proconsular whiteness' (for which Buchan provided the 'totem', and Smuts the 'philosophy').[85] Notably, in both these accounts it is in both the material and symbolic interactions between the (erstwhile) colony and the metropole (or New and Old Worlds) that 'whiteness' emerges and takes hold.[86] This process is represented (unwittingly, one suspects) in Buchan's *A Lodge in the Wilderness*, in the transformations in his delegates through their imperial 'fieldwork' and 'practical experiments';[87] while its global, and particularly American, dimension is evoked by the revelation by the sole American delegate – made with 'a tender melancholy' – that the tropics made her 'homesick' for 'the South'.[88]

Making the white world, or 'the International'

In this account, the new 'international' *conscience* of Stevenson's 'Cambridge fellows' was – like that of the 'Men of 1873' – also a *consciousness*: a white one.[89] What is more, their 'absurd' plans – whether to 'found a new society' or become the 'legal conscience of the civilised world' – were licensed (if not demanded) by this new, white, 'conscience-consciousness'[90] and what it entailed (i.e., the administration of the 'native' races, as part of the Racial Contract).

By tracing 'the evolution of the Western racial imagination' at the turn of century in 'the informal and formal actions of white diplomats and politicians', Furedi has shown how the 'principle of Western racial superiority [was] part of the self-knowledge of the Anglo-American political elites and . . . passed for common sense', while 'a *consciousness of white solidarity* informed diplomatic affairs'.[91] Recent revisionist accounts of international relations have shown how 'race' was central to the construction of both its American and British variants, accounts which might be

83 Said, *Culture and Imperialism*, xii.

84 Morrison, *Playing in the Dark*, 14–15, 52.

85 Schwarz, *The White Man's World.*

86 See Morrison, *Playing in the Dark*, 33–51; Schwarz, *White Man's World*, 107–64.

87 Buchan, *A Lodge in the Wilderness,* 64. In particular, the youngest delegate and least enthusiastic about Empire at the outset, Lady Flora, is transformed into a fanatic once she '[gets] the sense of space into [her] blood' (38), becoming not only her 'Better Self', but 'very like a man' (90). See further Bill Schwarz, *The White Man's World* (Oxford: Oxford University Press, 2011), 208–76.

88 Buchan, *A Lodge in the Wilderness,* 58.

89 See Koskenniemi, *Gentle Civilizer,* 41. (Noting that the 'legal conscience of the civilized world' was also a '*consciousness*' on the part of the 'Men of 1873', as 'there is an important ambivalence in the original French language'.)

90 Ibid., 49.

91 Frank Furedi, *The Silent War: Imperialism and the Changing Perception of Race* (New Brunswick: Rutgers University Press, 1998), 3, 29, 236 (emphasis added).

told through *Dark Princess* and *Lodge in the Wilderness*. Vitalis has shown how Du Bois was central to the founding of the 'Howard School', and international relations in the US more generally.[92] While Thakur et al. have traced the origins of British International Relations to 'Milner's Kindergarten' which had inspired Buchan's 1906 novel arguing that its key concepts and 'scientific' method were first developed in South Africa in the early twentieth century, where 'the creation of a racially-ordered state served as a template for the British Commonwealth and later the World State'.[93] Their account, in fact, picks up where Buchan's novel ends: with one of the delegates heading on a fact-finding tour of the Dominions, which Lionel Curtis subsequently did in 1909 and then founded not only the 'Round Table Movement' and the Royal Institute of International Affairs (i.e., Chatham House), but the discipline of international relations and its inaugural departments, chairs, journals and institutes in Canada, Australia, South Africa, New Zealand and India.[94]

International lawyers have been less willing to acknowledge the role of this 'white consciousness' in their discipline's construction and operation.[95] For example, despite being an exclusive club of only white men, Koskenniemi assures us that the shared 'legal conscience' of the 'Men of 1873' was not a *racial* one. Sure, some of them had individual racist views (and one in particular: Stevenson's fellow-countryman James Lorimer); but Koskenniemi downplays any broader theorisation of their common '*cultural* consciousness'[96] (and its relation to their new 'legal conscience'), and tells us that most of the 'Men of 1873', much like Conrad, 'simply assumed European modernity as the natural end-point of development everywhere'.[97] One could contest this, however, for present purposes, it matters little whether the common '*civilized* consciousness-conscience' of the 'Men of 1873' was arrived at via Lorimer's preferred 'science of races', Henry Sumner Maine's more sophisticated and respectable 'social and legal evolutionary ideas',[98] or simply 'assumed' as a matter of 'common sense'.[99] The point is that the 'Men of 1873' inhabited a shared (social and epistemological) 'white world' and imagined a (juridico-political) White World order, based on a 'global racial contract' amongst white states; and constructed a disciplinary world that both reflected that White World and aimed to bring it about.

One the first rules of this metaphorical 'white club', however, was not to talk about it. Whether out of what Morrison calls 'studied indifference' or as a 'graceful, even generous, liberal gesture' (or what Mills' calls an 'epistemology of ignorance'), the disciplinary worlds of literature and international law were constructed on protocols of 'silence and evasion' when it came to 'race'.[100] In the 1870s, the dangers of speaking too plainly about race were perhaps

92 See Robert Vitalis, *White World Order, Black Power Politics: The Birth of American International Relations* (Ithaca: Cornell University Press, 2015).

93 Vineet Thakur, Alexander E. Davis and Peter Vale, "Imperial Mission, 'Scientific' Method: An Alternative Account of the Origins of IR," *Millennium: Journal of International Studies* 46, no. 1 (2017): 3.

94 Ibid., 17–18. This line from *Lodge in the Wilderness* to the League of Nations was hinted at by Buchan himself in the Preface to the 1917 edition, when he noted that '[s]ome of the discussions are now out of date' – but not obsolete – and '[m]any have been advanced by my brilliant friends at the *Round Table* far beyond the stage reached at Musuru'.

95 See further Gevers, "Re-Thinking Race and International Law."

96 Koskenniemi, *Gentle Civilizer*, 70 (emphasis added).

97 Ibid., 75.

98 See Casper Sylvest, *British Liberal Internationalism, 1880–1930: Making Progress?* (Manchester: Manchester University Press, 2009), 61–100 (emphasis added).

99 See further Gevers, "Re-Thinking Race and International Law."

100 See Morrison, *Playing in the Dark*, 9–10; Mills, *Racial Contract*, 93–98. See further Charles W. Mills, "Global White Ignorance," in *Routledge International Handbook of Ignorance Studies*, eds. Matthias Gross and Linsey McGoey (New York: Taylor and Francis, 2015), 217–27.

already apparent to Robert Louis Stevenson: in the first draft of *The Ideal Commonwealth* he initially described colonialism's effects as 'the inferior race dwindles and disappears like snow burning flax before the advance of the superior'; but, on reflection, he scratched the passage out and replaced it with 'civilization advances with gigantic strides'. Much of the history of international law might be told as the re-description (ironically at times) of Darwin-inspired passages of genocidal violence as 'civilization advances with gigantic strides', and the inability even in critical accounts to name 'whiteness'. In fact, international law's most important and violent disciplinary act might be its disavowal of race, its ability to not talk about race, or at least to talk about it 'gently',[101] to construct a disciplinary world, and at its most ambitious an *actual* one, and then decadently disavow its animating racial 'dynamic'.[102]

How race became the 'unspeakable unspoken' of international law is a vast and complex matter,[103] but it had *something* to do with the making and remaking of things as 'white' and 'European' – including men, states and empires – and later as 'international'. Consider, for example, the unfolding definition of the discipline in the writings of one of the original 'Men of 1873', John Westlake. Between 1894 and 1904 Westlake's definition of international law shifted: from one in which it was 'the body of rules prevailing between states' (states being the 'nations of the *European race*'), and as the law of 'the international society of the white race',[104] to one in which: 'The international society which develops international law . . . [is] composed of all the *states of European blood*, that is of all the European and American states except Turkey, and of Japan'.[105] 'Race' became 'blood', and 'white' became 'European'.[106] It was a definition he repeated in his second edition of *International Law* in 1910. However, as Stuart Hall notes, when it comes to race and language the risk of 'a certain sliding of meaning' is ever-present, as there is 'always something left unsaid';[107] in 1910 Westlake 'slipped' when defining international law, with the prospect of extension to the 'Native States of India' in mind:[108]

> As English law is that law of England and French law that of France, so international law is that of a certain *part of the world*, which comprises if it is not exclusively composed of Europe, *all nations outside Europe but of European blood*, and Japan.

Here, 'blood' is no longer *necessarily* metaphorical (i.e., 'states' with the common metaphorical 'blood' of European political institutions or 'soil'), but links together '*all nations* outside Europe *but of European blood*' ('nations' being defined socio-historically, culturally, or perhaps biologically). Moreover, the reason that Westlake gave in *International Law* (1910) for why there could not be different 'races' within Europe, only different 'nations' (i.e., European's were all 'white'

101 See Laurence Bobo, James R. Kluegel and Ryan A. Smith, "Laissez-Faire Racism: The Crystallization of a Kinder, Gentler, Antiblack Ideology," in *Racial Attitudes in the 1990s: Continuity and Change*, eds. Jack Tuch and Steven A. Martin (Westport, CT: Praeger, 1997), 15–42.

102 See generally, Antony Anghie, *Imperialism, Sovereignty & the Making of International Law* (Cambridge: Cambridge University Press, 2005); Siba N. Grovogui, *Sovereigns, Quasi Sovereigns, and Africans* (Minneapolis: University of Minnesota Press, 1996).

103 See Gevers, "Re-Thinking Race and International Law."

104 John Westlake, *Chapters on the Principles of International Law* (Cambridge: Cambridge University Press, 1894), 1, 9, 198 (emphasis added).

105 Westlake, *International Law*, 40 (emphasis added).

106 On the 'poetics of blood', see Schwarz, *White Man's World*, 62–63.

107 Stuart Hall, *Race: The Floating Signifier* (San Francisco: Media Education Foundation Collection, 1997).

108 John Westlake, "Native States of India" (1910), reprinted in *The Collected Papers of John Westlake on Public International Law*, ed. L. F. L. Oppenheim (Cambridge: Cambridge University Press, 1914), 622 (emphasis added).

in the end),[109] meant that in this new definition 'race' (or 'whiteness') alone could be what held together his '*nations outside Europe but of European blood*'.[110]

Moreover, Westlake's modified definition of the 'international' order is not only racial but also spatial (as is 'Europe'). This international order is 'a certain part of the world' which (tellingly) both *comprises* and *is composed of* one part (objective) space called Europe (like France and England), and one part (inter-subjective) 'race' of '*European* blood'; and Japan. It seems Westlake could neither return fully to the certainty of his 1894 definition of international law (i.e., the law of states of 'the European race', or better-still 'the white race'), nor could he fall back on a spatial 'Europe' (for reasons Schmitt later pointed out).

Nevertheless, Westlake's slip – Freudian or otherwise – provides arguably his most compelling definition of international law (almost identical to Buchan's imagined delegate's definition of imperialism cited earlier), one based on neither abstractions like 'states', nor concrete geography, but on a shifting racial whiteness (expressed at times as 'race', 'blood' and 'European'). While Westlake struggled to name this thing called 'whiteness',[111] or the proper subjects of international law (people, races, nations, states), he was sure of one thing: '*These* are the peoples by whose consent [international law] exists, and for the settlement of whose differences it is applied, or at least invoked' (as his very next sentence declared). Or put another way, he was certain who this society or 'part of the world' called 'international' *could not* include: namely *non-European* European 'states' (i.e., Turkey), and wholly or doubly *non-European* 'states' (i.e., those outside of 'Europe' spatially *and* racially), such as the 'Native states of India'.

It is worth pointing out that these shifts (and slippages) in Westlake's texts, and international law more generally, mirror the way that critical race theorists (following Du Bois) have conceptualised what (and how) 'race' *means* – as 'both real and unreal', objective and 'intersubjective', personal and spatial;[112] one in which 'race' is what Mills calls a 'social ontology',[113] or as Mbembe puts it, 'at once material and phantasmic'.[114] What is more, such shifts are not limited to Westlake,[115] nor 'states': we might recast the story of 'Imperial Internationalism' told in *A*

109 Westlake explicitly rejected 'race' as the basis for distinguishing between 'nations', or 'white' nations at least. Westlake, *International Law* (emphasis added).

110 After all, aside from 'whiteness' what common 'character' might unite the 'nations' of United States and the European Settler Colonies in 'blood' and 'in feeling' (certainly not common 'language, religion, temperament, the possession of common memories, the entertainment of common political or social beliefs or aspirations'). Ibid., 4 (emphasis added).

111 On the personal and political investments in maintaining 'the sense of whiteness as mystery', see bell hooks, "Representing Whiteness in the Black Imagination," in *Displacing Whiteness: Essays in Social and Cultural Criticism*, ed. Ruth Frankenberg (Durham, NC: Duke University Press, 1997), 338–46; James Baldwin, *The Fire Next Time* (Harmondsworth: Penguin, 1964), 16–17; Mills, "Global White Ignorance."

112 Mills, *Racial Contract*, 41–53.

113 Mills, *Blackness Visible,* xiv. According to Mills: '[R]ace is best conceived of not primarily as ideational but as embedded in material structures, sociopolitical institutions, and everyday social practices that so shape the world with which we interact as to constitute an "objective" (deriving from intersubjectivity) though socially constructed "reality." Philosophy's promise to illuminate the world can be realized only by recognizing the whiteness of that world and how it affects its residents. Theorizing white supremacy as objective, systemic, multidimensional, constitutive of a certain reality that evolves over time can contribute both to understanding the world and, ultimately, to changing it.' Mills, "White Supremacy as a Sociopolitical System," 48.

114 Achille Mbembe, *Critique of Black Reason,* trans. Laurent Dubois (Johannesburg: Wits University Press, 2017), 2.

115 Simpson argues that, in international legal scholarship, 'the state . . . sometimes seems, poised between materiality and abstraction, and between unity and fragmentation'. Gerry Simpson, "Something to Do with States," in *The Oxford Handbook of the Theory of International Law*, eds. Anne Orford and Florian Hoffman (Oxford: Oxford University Press, 2016), 564.

Lodge in the Wilderness (and recently 'discovered' by historians) as a shift from 'European Empire' to 'European International' with all the same slippages of Westlake's text (including from a *spatial* to *racial* 'Europe').

Concluding remarks

Over time the term 'international' has come to stand in for all things formerly 'European', 'white' and 'imperial' in international law,[116] while in literary studies the preference remained for 'world' or 'global' – and more recently *both*.[117] With the end of formal empire through 'decolonisation', the rest of the world was 'incorporated' into the 'international' order (as states and individuals); international law became truly *international*, if not universal, and the White World became officially *the* World. As Slaughter and others have demonstrated, international law and literature continued their productive association forged during European imperialism in its afterlives, co-producing both new 'States' and 'the kinds of humans that can serve as subjects of rights' (both of which were modelled on idealised white, European archetypes).[118]

If international law today has 'something to do with States', and something to do with 'human rights-bearing subjects', then becoming and unbecoming both *by its hand* continues to have something to do with 'race'.[119] Regardless of whether or not states meet the formal material and immaterial conditions of statehood (i.e., possessing *actual* territory and *metaphorical* 'breeches'), it continues to matter how they are raced (as 'savage', 'uncivilised', 'non-European', 'undeveloped', 'African' and most recently 'shit-hole countries'). All the while, states raced as 'white' or 'European', much like Stevenson's Cambridge fellows, expect and enjoy statehood, sovereignty and, along with their 'white' citizens, the full(er) protection of international law. In an 'international' order based on the Racial Contract, 'nonwhite' statehood, sovereignty and lives remain precarious, and the 'bloodless white liberalism'[120] of 'sovereign equality' is the equivalent of 'all lives matter'.[121]

What is more, if there is a risk in 'law and literature' of losing sight of the relationship between 'legal interpretation [and] the violence it occasions',[122] then that risk is perhaps even greater when it comes to *international law* and literature. To appreciate the heightened danger of losing sight of not just the 'violence of the word' but of the imagination in this field, we might return to the analogy between the shifting grounds of 'race' (as *both* real and unreal, 'material and phantasmic'), on the one hand, and on the other hand, building-block concepts

116 On 'the international', see Samera Esmeir, "On Becoming Less of the World," *History of the Present* 8, no. 1 (2018): 88–116.

117 In arguing for a 'global world literature', Damrosch used all three in fact, noting: 'If literature has always already been international, it remains ineluctable national in today's global world.' David Damrosch, "Toward a History of World Literature," *New Literary History* 39, no. 3 (2008): 492.

118 Slaughter, *Human Rights, Inc.*, 8. Slaughter shows how the *Bildungsroman* and human rights became 'cooperative technologies of subject formation', one based on 'the Anglo-European white male' (27–28). On how 'the received categories of the territorially bounded state reach into the postcolonial imagination both to produce and discipline "independence"', see Vasuki Nesiah, "Placing International Law: White Spaces on a Map," *Leiden Journal of International Law* 16 (2003): 1–35.

119 Simpson, "Something to Do with States," 565.

120 To redeploy Lewis Nkosi's felicitous phrase. See Lewis Nkosi, "Reviewed Work(s)," *Transition* 51 (1991): 240–45.

121 See Mills, *Racial Contract*, 36–37 (noting that the 'globally color-coded distribution of wealth and poverty has been produced by the Racial Contract and in turn reinforces adherence to it in its signatories and beneficiaries').

122 Robert Cover, "Violence and the Word," *Yale Law Journal* 95 (1986): 1601.

in international law like 'states', 'sovereignty', 'the international' and 'humanity'. In critical race theory, to conceptualise 'race' as socially constructed is not to deny that it has real-world effects (often violent ones), or suggest (as liberal accounts do) that it can and should simply be wished away; rather, it is to point out how 'race' has these effects in spite of, and in some senses through, its baselessness and shifting significations.[123] The same could be said of international law's violence: that it is enabled *through* the ability of concepts like 'sovereignty' and 'humanity' to remain 'grey and inadequate' (in Mbembe's terms).

As such, the danger of losing sight of international law's violence – and how 'imaginary' cannons continue to beget actual cannons, as well as canons, and vice versa – is just as, if not more, acute. This is all the more so when one considers the ongoing relations between 'race', international law's 'grey and inadequate' words, and its violences. In this, the uneven distribution of the international legal order's immediate and structural violence, paraphrasing Claudia Rankine, continues to have something to do with the ongoing inability of 'white men [to] police their imagination'.[124]

123 See Morrison, *Playing in the Dark*, 63.
124 Claudia Rankine, *Citizen: An American Lyric* (Minneapolis: Graywolf Press, 2014).

16

Lord-healer of lost cases

Sunil Gangopadhyay† with
Debolina Dutta and Oishik Sircar[1]

There is a small village called Chingripota in the administrative district of Murshidabad. There aren't more than six or seven concrete houses in the village. There is no school, no post office, but only a Saturday market – visited by people from faraway places. Those who live in Chingripota are mostly poor Hindus and Muslims. There is nothing much to see in this village, except a pretty old statue made from white stone that stands in the middle of the market.

It is a statue of an oldish, sad-looking Bengali bhadralok,[2] dressed in choga chapkaan.[3] At the base of the statue something is inscribed in English – now hardly legible. No one in the village market knows who this man is. Our memories of old times are easily forgotten. If you ask the young boys who hang out at the tea stalls or near the river who this man was, none of them will be able to tell you. Sometimes you might hear some of them say, 'We've heard that the man was a lawyer.' Only a few very elderly people in the village will be able to tell you the history of this statue.

I once travelled across some villages in Murshidabad on foot. The day I was in Chingripota, it rained very heavily and I ran to take shelter in one of the houses in the village. The owner of the house, Abdul Rab, took very good care of me. He fed me delicious food, let me stay at his house and narrated many stories. That is how I came to know the story of Beni Laskar.

1 We are grateful to Ranabir Samaddar for reading a draft of this work and for his feedback. Translated and annotated with an afterword by Debolina Dutta and Oishik Sircar.

2 Bhadralok: literally, a decent man. However, in the colonial context the term referred to a male member of the Bengali genteel class, considered effete in comparison to imperial projections of British masculinity. See Mrinalini Sinha, *Colonial Masculinity: The 'Manly Englishman' and the 'Effeminate Bengali' in the Late Nineteenth Century* (Manchester: Manchester University Press, 1995).

3 Choga chapkaan: 'A Persian-Indian male attire', possibly indicating a syncretic sartorial practice, 'brought into vogue by the [social reformer] Rammohan Roy' as a way to mark the difference between the educated Bengali and the suited Englishman. Simonti Sen, *Travels to Europe: Self and Other in Bengal Travel Narratives, 1870–1910* (Hyderabad: Orient Longman, 2001), 94.

It's a story from very old times, when we were not yet born, our fathers were not yet born, and our grandfathers were only little kids. At that time, the British ruled our country; we were a people without freedom. When we saw white people in the streets, we moved away in fear. Even in the courts, the majority of lawyers and judges were white.

Beni Laskar was an ordinary mokhtar in one of the district courts in the city of Mahakuma in Murshidabad. A lawyer of small stature without a thriving business, in those days, was known as mokhtar – they were called Bangla-speaking lawyers. The lawyers and magistrates who worked in the courts had to speak in English. Only the mokhtars somehow managed to carry out their business by speaking a mixture of Bangla and English. Mokhtar is originally an Arabic word; its English version is mukhteer.[4]

Anyway, in that same court there were a few other lawyers and mokhtars – Barada Roy and Mohan Molla were the more well-known amongst them and attracted most of the clients. Old Benimadhab Laskar was ill-fated. Whenever he got excited, he stammered and turned into a laughing stock, so clients would seldom appoint him. Outside the court, he sat expectantly under a banyan tree looking for clients and the moment he saw people passing by, he called out to them, 'Come here, come here, g-g-good mokhtar!'

It was only poor people who came to him to get their job done for a pittance. He did not earn more than eight annas a day.[5] No one had ever seen Benimadhab smile; he always looked morose. Though that wasn't because of his meagre income – he suffered from severe headaches. He had a constant throbbing pain in his head. There weren't any modern pills then that could give him some relief. None of the kabiraji-hakimi medicines were able to ease his pain either.[6] Sometimes his headaches were so acute that he pressed his head between his two hands and squirmed in pain.

For everyone, this ordinary figure of Benimadhab Laskar soon turned into an object of major curiosity. This is how it all began . . .

One day during lunch hour, Benimadhab Laskar was sitting under that same banyan tree outside the court, in the hope of getting clients. His headache was particularly bad so he held his head with pressed hands – when a young-looking Muslim man came and stood in front of him. He said, 'Karta, I have a case of cow theft for you.'[7]

Benimadhab got excited and asked, 'What c-c-case? Sit here! T-t-tell me properly!' The man replied, 'I cannot find my milking cow, Mungli, for the last two days. Taher Ali has stolen the cow. He is hiding her in his own cowshed – several villagers have seen it.'

Benimadhab took out his notebook and pencil and was about to write something down, but suddenly he stared into the eyes of the man. He felt a spark through his head. His face turned pale. In a scared voice he said, 'No, I cannot take your case.'

4 Mokhtar, spelled in this way, appears in law reports from the early 1900s. See *The Indian Decisions* (Calcutta: The West Bengal Government Press, 1914), 2.

5 Anna: a currency unit used in colonial South Asia which was equivalent to one sixteenth of a rupee. This was 'standard currency before the introduction of the decimal system' in 1957, ten years after India gained independence from the British. See Debdas Banerjee, *Colonialism in Action: Trade, Development and Dependence in Late Colonial India* (Hyderabad: Orient Longman, 1999), xi.

6 Kabiraji-hakimi: non-western Hindu and Islamic medicinal traditions respectively that relied on herbal and Ayurvedic ingredients. See generally Madelaine Healey, *Indian Sisters: A History of Nursing and the State, 1907–2007* (New Delhi: Routledge, 2013), 45; Srirupa Prasad, *Cultural Politics of Hygiene in India, 1890–1940: Contagions of Feeling* (Berlin: Springer, 2015).

7 Karta: a colloquially used Bengali term of respect for an upper caste elderly figure of male authority based on age, knowledge or relationship. More specifically, the karta is 'a married male who had mastery (*adhikara*) over a family, was the person defined as the primary actor in a community'. Ronad B. Inden, *Marriage and Rank in Bengali Culture: A History of Caste and Clan in Middle Period Bengal* (Berkeley: University of California Press, 1976), 44.

Surprised, the man asked, 'Why not? Do you want me to pay you first? Here, I've got the money.' He took out a silver coin from his waist pocket but Benimadhad refused to touch it. 'Is your name Rajjab Ali?' he inquired.

'Yes.'

'Is the name of your village Palashdhubi?'

'Yes.'

'I cannot take your case. You go home . . .'

The man asked angrily, 'Why? Why should I go home? Isn't there any other lawyer or mokhtar? The old man has lost his mind! My cow has been stolen and I cannot file a case for that?'

Benimadhab insisted again, 'If you want your own good, go home.'

Who knows what the man understood, but he did not say another word. He turned around and hurriedly walked away.

Some lawyers and mokhtars who were nearby saw what happened. They were astounded. Benimadhab hardly gets clients, yet he refused one who offered him a shiny silver coin?

Mohan Molla came up and asked, 'What happened Benibabu,[8] you drove the man away? What's the matter?'

Benimadhab replied, 'He's not a good man.'

'Did you know him from before?'

'No.'

'Then? He brought you a case of cow theft – why bother whether the man is good or bad?'

'Nah, Molla sahib,[9] a strange thing happened. I don't know the man, but after seeing him I felt a spark inside my head. As if a voice from inside my head told me, "He is Rajjab Ali from Palashdhubi, don't take his case".'

'Really, really? This is bizarre.'

'That's not all. When I looked at the man's face, I saw something else as well, as if a picture. I saw that this Rajjab Ali attacked a seventeen or eighteen-year-old boy with a machete. He killed the boy after repeatedly chopping at his neck. This man is a murderer.'

Mohan Molla burst out laughing. 'Are you taking opium these days? Or have you started smoking pot?'

Benimadhab exclaimed helplessly, 'B-b-believe me, I really saw this!'

Mohan Molla went around narrating this story with great amusement. Everyone thought that old Benimadhab had gone mad, that he had started daydreaming! The news of the incident spread like wildfire and whenever people saw Benimadhab, they would start laughing at him.

But a few days later, Rajjab Ali from Palashdhubi was arrested by the police for committing murder. He had killed his neighbour's young son and hid the corpse in a pond under water

8 Babu: a standalone or postfix to a male person's name meant to lend respect to their status as a learned person. It has also been satirically used to refer to a community or class of educated Bengalis who want to live a life of leisure and frivolity. According to 'Yule and Burnell's Ango-Indian dictionary, *Hobson-Jobson*, published in 1886 . . . Babu . . . was not just a Bengali equivalent for the term Esquire or Mr, or a word for a "superficially anglicised Bengali . . . Babu also came to indicate a Bengali clerk who wrote English, a Bengali, who managed the pecuniary affairs of the British"'. Shompa Lahiri, *Indians in Britain: Encounters, Race and Identity, 1880–1930* (London: Frank Cass, 2000), 93; see also Kunal Chakrabarti and Shubhra Chakrabarti, *Historical Dictionary of the Bengalis* (Maryland: Scarecrow Press, 2013), 59.

9 Sahib: an Arab-Persian loanword to Bengali (and many other languages of Southasia, particularly Urdu and Hindi) that originally was used by colonised subjects as an honorific to refer to whites as lords or masters. Over time, it acquired a more generic currency where non-whites would use it to formally address or greet someone of higher status or authority. See Tej K. Bhatia and Ashok Koul, *Colloquial Urdu: A Complete Course for Beginners* (London: Routledge, 2000), 32.

hyacinths. This did surprise some people. They reasoned, Benimadhab must have witnessed the murder and only disclosed it in another away.

About nine or ten days after this incident, Benimadhad performed another strange feat. A big case was being heard in the court – a lot of people had come to see the proceedings that day. A man named Shashadhar Kundu had murdered three people. It was the day of his verdict. He would certainly get hanged.

Benimadhab was present in one corner of the courtroom. He did not have any work. His headache was severe, so he kept pressing his head with his hands. Suddenly he screamed, 'Shashadhar Kundu is innocent! Shashadhar Kundu is innocent!'

Everyone was startled. It is against the law to shout like this while the court is in session. The hakim was Charles Wilberforce,[10] a young fellow with an angry temperament. He said, 'Silence!'

Benimadhab was persistent, 'Shashadhar Kundu is innocent. Huzoor, don't h-h-hang him.'[11]

Hakim ordered, 'Silence. Throw this mukhteer out!'

Benimadhab stood up and pleaded, 'Your honour, give me one day's time. I know he is not the murderer. Shashadhar Kundu is not guilty, your honour.' Then he ran to the accused and asked him to request the judge to allow him just another day. 'I will save you. The murder has been committed by Pulin Sarkar. What, am I right, or not?'

That was a day full of chaos and commotion at the court. Benimadhab claimed that Shashadhar Kundu's friend Pulin Sarkar committed the murders and blamed it on his friend. On digging up the ground under the marigold plant in the courtyard of Pulin Sarkar's house, he said, the blood-smeared weapon and jewellery will be found. And all of which turned out to be true.

Benimadhab gathered a lot of fame because of this case and everyone started praising him. Barada Roy and Mohan Molla were very jealous as people now sought out Benimadhab Laskar to represent them in court.

But Benimadhab did not accept all cases. He looked at the accused's face very intensely for a long time, pressed his hands against his head, shook it from one side to the other. Then, after some time, he'd say, 'No, dear fellow, I cannot take your case. Go look for other options.' Or, he'd tell someone, 'I will take your case – no judge can dare punish you!' And his words would really come true. The cases that he refused to take, were lost. Every case that he accepted, he made them win.

Benimadhab came to be known as the lord-healer of lost cases.[12] He hung a signboard outside his home which said:

> Lord-healer of Lost Cases
> I take lost cases according to my own wish

10 Hakim: in formal Bengali usage, means a magistrate. From the Arabic original in *al-hakam*: 'the most qualified to judge among those who judge or the most capable of those who possess the attribute of *hikmah* [wisdom]' (emphasis in original). Hikmet Yaman, *Prophetic Niche in Virtuous City: The Concept of Hikmah in Early Islamic Thought* (Leiden: Brill, 2011), 22. It can also be used to refer to a physician, where the knowledge to diagnose illness can be akin to the capacity to judge right from wrong.

11 Huzoor: an Urdu expression used as a form of third person honorific address towards a figure of power, prestige or authority, by someone of a lesser status. See Stephan Gramley and Kurt-Michael Patzold, *A Survey of Modern English* (London: Routledge, 2002), 202.

12 We translated the word Dhanvantari – used in the original Bangla text as a metaphor – to lord-healer. Dhanvantari, in Hindu mythology is the god of medicine or healing who also served as the curer of the illnesses of gods. See generally Kum G. V. Davane, "A Critical Study of Dhanvantari," *Annals of the Bhandarkar Oriental Research Institute* 57, no. 1–4 (1976): 95–102; Louis H. Gray, "The Indian God Dhanvantari," *Journal of the American Oriental Society* 42 (1992): 232–337.

Guarantee of success 100%
Fees 4 taka per day[13]
No bargaining

Because he won so many cases one after the other in such an unearthly way, all kinds of possible and impossible rumours started circulating about Benimadhab. Even though Benimadhab's earnings had increased, it was evident that his good fortune wouldn't last very long. He suffered from constant unbearable headaches. His illness would get worse with every case. He did not have many more years to live.

Meanwhile, Madhu, son of the local zamindar,[14] Nanda Ray, got embroiled in a legal matter. A conflict broke out between the zamindar and his peasant subjects. Gun shots were fired, and four poor peasants were killed. Madhu was the one who fired the gun. But the zamindar claimed that Madhu was not even in the vicinity when trouble broke out – he was in Baharampur and there are witnesses to prove this. But the district magistrate was very strict, so he issued summons against Madhu Ray.

In matters like these you need to hire well-established lawyers and barristers, but the zamindar sent his palanquin to fetch Benimadhab Laskar. Benimadhab was very ill then – but there's no excuse when the zamindar wishes to see you. When he was about to get into the palanquin, an elderly peasant came to him crying. He said, 'Dear babu, don't take this case. The enemy has killed my son.'

'I am on the side of justice', said Benimadhab.[15] 'I don't have the power to side with injustice – I will have to die then.'

Zamindar sahib welcomed Benimadhab and requested him to take a seat. Handing over the pipe of his silver hookah he said, 'I will write 50 acres of land in Chingripota village in your name – you will have no worries in your old age.'

'Huzoor, what do I have to do?' queried Benimadhab.

'A group of hooligans attacked my guards, so they had to open fire in self-defence. I will take this matter to court later on. But these hooligans have implicated my son Madhu's name in this. Madhu was in Baharampur at the time. Fourteen witnesses – including two teachers, two lawyers, and a policeman – will swear to this fact. Madhu was not involved in this case – there is no evidence to prove his guilt.'

Benimadham exclaimed with folded hands, 'but huzoor, any good lawyer will be able to win the case then – why have you called an ordinary mokhtar like me?'

'You have a good reputation that you do not take any and every case,' the zamindar said. 'If you take this case, no one will dare to testify against him. Other lawyers are also going to fear you.'

13 Taka: the Bengla term for the rupee (which equals 16 annas).

14 Zamindar: 'A Persian word meaning a landowner', who was 'a creature of Anglo-Indian legislation' with the 'legal right to collect government land revenue from the tenants and cultivators of a tract of land [primarily including poor landless peasants], part of which is kept back as the zamindar's profit'. Chakrabarti and Chakrabarti, *Historical Dictionary of the Bengalis*, 497; Pamela G. Price, "Warrior Caste 'Raja' and Gentleman 'Zamindar': One Person's Experience in the Late Nineteenth Century," *Modern Asian Studies* 17, no. 4 (1983): 565; K. N. Chaudhuri, *The Trading World of Asia and the English East India Company, 1660–1760* (Cambridge: Cambridge University Press, 2006), 551.

15 Justice is our approximate translation for the word Nyay (from the Sanskrit Nyaya), which was used in the original Bangla text. Nyaya, as Amartya Sen writes, 'stands for a comprehensive concept of realized justice. In that line of vision, the roles of institutions, rules and organization, important as they are, have to be assessed in the broader and more inclusive perspective of *nyaya*, which is inescapably linked with the world that actually emerges, not just the institutions or rules we happen to have' (emphasis in original). Amartya Sen, *The Idea of Justice* (Cambridge: The Belknap Press, 2009), 20.

'But huzoor, I cannot do anything without seeing the accused.'

The zamindar raised his voice, 'Who are you referring to as the accused? My only son, is he a criminal? There is no need to see him – take my word for what I am telling you.'

'Huzoor, I am unable to do anything without seeing the accused. I don't have that ability.'

The zamindar's son was called in. Seeing him, Benimadhab held his head tightly with his hands, his eyes thrust out, and he fainted and fell to the ground. The zamindar's men rushed to pour water on his head. Someone held a bottle of smelling salt to his nose.

Benimadhab slowly got up. Tears were rolling down his eyes. With folded hands he pleaded, 'Huzoor, forgive me! Don't ask me to take this case.'

The zamindar asked angrily, 'Why?'

'I don't have the capacity, I won't be able to do it.'

'I will give you 500 taka. I will also give you the 50 acres of land.'

'I cannot do it.'

'1000 taka.'

'Huzoor, let m-m-me g-g-g-o.'

The zamindar was furious. 'Look, mokhtar! You have to take this case. Or else I will burn down your house and you will be finished.'

The zamindar's threats scared Benimadhab into taking the case. With a bunch of gold coins and a sunken expression, he came back home.

That night, an extremely strange thing happened. Benimadhab kept tossing and turning in his sleep. He rolled on his bed from one side to the other as if he was trying to escape from someone who was about to catch him. He started screaming, 'Leave me, leave me! I have made a mistake. I will not do it again.'

Benimadhab's children and wife gathered around his bed. He somehow managed to sit up and asked his son to fetch a pen and paper. Benimadhab immediately wrote a letter to the zamindar saying he will not be able to take the case. He is very ill. He will not go to court ever again. Benimadhab gave the letter to his son and said, 'As soon as dawn breaks, you must take the gold coins and the letter and deliver them to the zamindar. Or else, there will be no life left in me.'

Early in the morning, one of his sons left for the zamindar's house. The other one went to court and announced that Benimadhab mokhtar is leaving his profession. From today, he will go live in his native village and live a life of piety.

Soon after, events took another strange turn. That evening, one of Charles Wilberforce's peyadas[16] went and informed Benimadhab that the hakim sahib had called for him. A hakim's order was more severe than a zamindar's. Benimadhab's body was burning with high fever – but he had to hire a palanquin and travel in that condition.

Hakim sahib's bungalow was beautifully decorated. Everyone knew that he was a man of stern temperament, but he spoke with Benimadhab with an easy disposition. The hakim had learnt quite a bit of Bangla.

He asked, 'Mukhteer, why are you leaving your job?'

Benimadhab replied, 'Huzoor, I am not going to live for very long. I want to spend the rest of my life in my village house.'

16 Peyada: estate guards. '[L]arger zamindari establishments consisted of a considerable number – sometimes half or more of all estate employees – of armed men, called *jamadar, mridha, peyada, paik,* and so on, who were used against recalcitrant tenants' (emphasis in original). Partha Chatterjee, *A Princely Imposter? The Strange and Universal History of the Kumar of Bhawal* (Princeton: Princeton University Press, 2002), 29.

'How do you know that you will die soon?'

'That I have understood. I am suffering from high fever.'

Hakim sahib got up from his seat and touched Benimadhab's forehead to check his temperature. Then he opened his cupboard and took out a few medicines and said, 'Take these pills every three hours. You will recover.'

Benimadhab said, 'Even if my fever is cured, I will still die.'

Sahib smiled and asked, 'Mukhteer, is it true that by looking into people's faces you are able to tell whether they are guilty or innocent?'

Benimadhab kept quiet.

Sahib said, 'My peshkar has told me this, my munshi and some others have also reported the same.[17] People in the entire district believe this. Even the district magistrate has written to me enquiring about your abilities.'

'Huzoor, I am an ordinary man.'

'I have noticed that whichever case you take, you definitely win. What is behind this mystery? Tell me everything, don't feel scared.'

'Huzoor, I don't know whether you will believe everything that I will tell you. I have been suffering from these terrible headaches for a very long time. Nowadays, whenever I look into the eyes of a client the headache grows worse. A spark goes off inside my head – and someone whispers to me whether the man is guilty or innocent.'

'How interesting. What is the explanation behind this?'

'I don't know. But I think dead people speak to me. When someone is killed – a part of the dead person's atman enters the killer.[18] That part of the atman punishes the killer for their entire life. Through the eyes of the killer, this part of the atman tells me that he is indeed the guilty person. And when I see an innocent man, even then the dead person's atman tells me, "it's not him, it's not him! I'll tell you who is actually guilty." Do you remember Shashadhar Kundu's case? You were about to hang him. He had killed three people. There was also one little girl among them. That little girl suddenly appeared in front of my eyes and said, "not him, not him! You tell them! I will show you the actual killer." I saw everything at that moment. I had no other option but to scream out in court.'

The hakim said, 'Fantastic! How is this even possible?'

'Whether to believe it or not is your wish', said Benimadhab. 'But this happens to me.'

'Okay mukteer, tell me one thing! When you understand who is actually guilty of a crime – then you can also save the guilty person from being convicted. When you know about all the evidence that is there to incriminate someone – if you just hide it, then no one will be able to catch them!'

'Huzoor, there is a god above all of us, who is aware that knowingly I have never taken the side of injustice. If I did that – the dead people who come and speak to me – will they spare me? Yesterday only . . .'

'What happened yesterday?'

Benimadhab became a little nervous. Then he said, 'Huzoor, you are the judge. I should not give names in front of you. I had to go somewhere yesterday. I was to take someone's case.

17 Peshkar: the court reader; Munshi: the court scribe. Charles Morrison, "*Munshis* and their Masters: The Organization of an Occupational Relationship in the Indian Legal System," *The Journal of Asian Studies* 31, no. 2 (1972): 309–28.

18 Atman: 'a noun meaning "the self"' (sometimes translated as "soul") . . . the eternal, unchanging essence of the person', W. J. Johnson, "Ātman ('Self')," A Dictionary of Hinduism, Oxford Reference, 2009, www.oxfordreference.com/view/10.1093/acref/9780198610250.001.0001/acref-9780198610250-e-322?rskey=fpGxcB&result=321.

The moment I looked at him, I saw the shadowy figures of four poor peasants surrounding him – they were all pointing at him and telling me, "He is the murderer!" I did not agree to take that case. But the client threatened me, forced me to take the case. In the middle of the night those four dead people surrounded me. They said to me with a lot of hatred, "You will save our murderer? You will save him?" That is why I have decided to give up my profession as a mokhtar.'

Hakim sahib looked astonished for a while. Then he asked, 'Didn't you say that you have headaches all the time? Did you not get this treated by a doctor?'

'I have tried to get my condition treated many times, but nothing is able to cure it.'

The hakim stood up and with a worried look on this face, started pacing up and down the room. Suddenly he turned around and said, 'Mukteer, I need your head!'

Benimadhab turned pale. 'What did you say?'

'I need your head.'

Benimadhab kept staring at him in utter disbelief. The hakim asked, 'Have you heard of Roland Ross? He is a great doctor. Sitting in Calcutta, he has found out the malaria-causing virus from the stomach of mosquitoes. He is my friend. I am informing him about you.'

'What will he do after coming here?'

'Listen, we are Christians. We don't believe that spirits roam about after the death of people or that they come and speak with you. Your condition is possibly pathological – there is something in the formation of your head – that is why you imagine such things. This needs to be examined. After your death, we have to cut open your head to examine it.'

'H-h-h-uzoor, what on earth are you saying?'

'Are you scared? Once you are dead, you will not experience pain after that. Why worry?'

'Huzoor, we are Hindu! After death, if our body is not burnt on the funeral pyre, our souls . . .'

'You will only waste your body by burning it! It is better to give it up for the benefit of science. Some scientific mystery may be solved from this. You must give up your head.'

That day, Benimadhab came back home shivering. What is this dangerous proposition? The sahib is asking for him to be beheaded? This sahib is so headstrong, who knows if he will cut off my head while alive. God, what have you done?

From that day, the sahib's guards started to keep a watch on his house. Two days later, Benimadhab was completely bed-ridden. He was almost dying. At night when Benimadhab's condition deteriorated further, hakim sahib got word of this and came with his men, lest this valuable head got wasted by burning on the funeral pyre!

Meanwhile, the news had spread that the hakim sahib would not allow the burning of Benimadhab's body after his death. The mlechha doctors would cut open his body.[19] The Hindus in the neighbourhood were furious. This was an insult to their dharma.[20] They came armed with

19 Mlechha: 'In the Sanskrit literature of ancient and medieval India, foreigners were frequently described as *mleccha*. The best English translation of mleccha is barbarian, for the word clearly connotes a lack of culture and civilisation. By the end of the first millennium B.C.E., mleccha was applied not only to aliens but also to indigenous tribes – communities who were not part of the agrarian caste society of Indic civilisation. As Romila Thapar has pointed out, mleccha was hence primarily "a signal of social and cultural difference." It was a generic category into which all social groups lacking an adherence to Brahmanical norms were thrust' (emphasis in original). Cynthia Talbot, "Inscribing the Other, Inscribing the Self: Hindu-Muslim Identities in Pre-Colonial India," *Comparative Studies in Society and History* 37, no. 4 (October 1995): 698. See Romila Thapar, "The Image of the Barbarian in Early India," *Comparative Studies in Society and History* 13, no. 4 (October 1971): 408–36.

20 Dharma: in colloquial Bangla, dharma would mean religion, faith or duty. In Hindu philosophy, dharma would be understood as 'religious and moral laws', presented in the Dharmasastras, *dharma* involves two distinct sets of duties. First, there are universal duties (*sadharana-dharma*) incumbent on all, regardless of age or occupation.

sticks – they wouldn't let his dead body be taken away at any cost. The Muslims also agreed, this is grossly unjust. The whites are meddling in matters of dharma.

Sensing the possibility of trouble, the district magistrate had also arrived. He brought a doctor along with him. Everyone crowded around Benimadhab's room.

Benimadhab was lying on his bed with his eyes shut. His hands rested on his chest. He whispered something that was inaudible. Only when someone took their ears next to his mouth, could they hear him faintly say, 'Forgive me. I did not accept the zamindar's son's case. I have never supported injustice. I have never done it. God knows, I have never done it.'

The doctor was checking his pulse rate. After a while, he released his hand hopelessly and said, 'It's all over.'

Hakim sahib asked expectantly, 'Is it all over? Check carefully.'

The doctor examined him again. 'There is no life in his body.'

The hakim then said to Benimadhab's family, 'Complete whatever dharmic rituals you need to perform. I will take the dead body with me. We have to cover it with ice.'

The magistrate sahib said, 'Charles, will it be right to do that?'

'We will not let you take away his body!' exclaimed Benimadhab's son.

The hakim retorted with authority, 'I will take his body. I had spoken to the mukhteer about this. He did not have any objection.'

A commotion broke out in the room. No one could understand what anyone was saying. The women were crying, and the men were shouting.

At this moment, Benimadhab's eyes opened again. Everyone in the room was startled. The doctor exclaimed, 'By Jove, by Jove!'

Benimadhab directed a sharp look at the hakim sahib and spoke loudly in a different voice. 'Sahib, you go home!'

Many people ran out of the room in fear, one woman fainted, but hakim sahib remained unperturbed. He came closer and said, 'Mukhteer, you are still alive?'

Benimadhab said, 'Sahib, you go home right away. Don't delay any further. Your watchman is dead. Your son and wife are in trouble – go fast!'

Hakim sahib didn't stay any longer. He ran out of the room at once. His horse was kept right outside. In the middle of the night he rode the horse towards his house – the others who had gathered also followed him. Soon, some gun shots were heard one after the other. By then Benimadhab was dead again. His entire body turned cold.

That night, there was a robbery at hakim sahib's house. The robbers killed the watchman, entered the house and went to attack the memsahib.[21] The memsahib escaped with her son into another room and locked herself in. The robbers tried to break the door. At that very moment,

---

These include non-injury (ahimsa), truthfulness, patience, respect for others' property and so on. Second, and more important for determining one's particular personal responsibilities or *svadharma*, are the demands of social duty' (emphasis in original). Roy W. Perrett, *An Introduction to Indian Philosophy* (New Delhi: Cambridge University Press, 2016), 23; see also Patrick Olivelle and Donald R. Davis Jr., eds., *Hindu Law: A New History of Dharmasastra* (New Delhi: Oxford University, 2018).

21 Memsahib: the Englishwoman, stereotypically understood as 'the canonical feminine ideal of the British Raj – the good, stable wife who efficiently manages a native-run household'. Jerry Phillips, "The Mem Sahib, the Worthy, the Rajah and His Minions: Some Reflections on the Class Politics of The Secret Garden," *The Lion and the Unicorn* 17, no. 2 (December 1993): 173. Although, the hakim sahib's wife makes such a fleeting appearance in the story, the memsahib has been a controversial figure in colonial historiography. See generally, Indira Ghose, "The Memsahib Myth: Englishwomen in Colonial India," in *Women and Others: Perspectives on Race, Gender, and Empire*, eds. Celia R. Daileader, Rhoda E. Johnson and Amilcar Shabazz (New York: Palgrave Macmillan, 2007), 107–28.

the hakim sahib returned home. If he was late by a whisker, his wife and son could not have been saved. One of the robbers was killed, two of them were caught.

The hakim sahib did not wish to cut up Benimadhab's body to perform the scientific examinations anymore. Instead, he paid out of his pocket to erect a stone statue of Benimadhab and placed it in his own village. He inscribed a line from Shakespeare at the base of the statue: 'On heaven and on earth there are many such things, Horatio, that you cannot even imagine.'[22]

Cultivating a postcolonial literary legal imagination: a translators' afterword

Debolina Dutta and Oishik Sircar

As first-time translators of a literary work, we took on two roles to perform our task: first, the task of ferrying the meanings from the shores of Bangla to the shores of English;[23] second, the task of interpretation to draw out a jurisprudential account from the narrative that will make the story intelligible for a particular scholarly audience. Relatedly, our task also felt somewhat like a joyful imaginative discovery. We found ourselves journeying 'into a sea of stories, in which . . . [we] found gem after gem, with which . . . [we] began to thread together a string of pearls'.[24] What follows is an account of this stringing together, presented in the form of a rather prosaic afterword.

'In every possible sense', writes Gayatri Chakravorty Spivak, 'translation is necessary but impossible.'[25] The impossibility of our task struck us when we decided to alter the original title of this short story. In Bangla, the author Sunil Gangopadhyay had named it 'Beni Laskarer Mundu'. Literally translated into English this would be 'Beni Laskar's Head'. The word mundu, although it refers to the head, veers towards slang and is devoid of the seriousness that is attributed to the head as the physiological site of reason and scientific temperament. The Bangla word matha which is closer in meaning to the English head, appears later in the story but is not used in the title.

In 'Beni Laskarer Mundu', Gangopadhyay presents a syncretic literary-historical imagination in the form of a short story for children. It was first published in 1972 in the annual festival issue of *Anandamela*, a Bengali periodical for children and young people published from Calcutta. We had read the story in a collection celebrating 30 years of *Anandamela*'s annual festival issues.[26] The story was vividly illustrated using linocut prints by the well-known artist and book-cover designer Purnendu Patri.

22 The quote from *Hamlet* originally is: 'There are more things in Heaven and Earth, Horatio, than are dreamt of in your philosophy.' Our translation remains faithful to the version as it was worded in Bangla by the author.

23 As Teju Coles writes: 'The English word *translation* comes from the Middle English, which originates from the Anglo-French *translater*. That in turn descends from the Latin *translatus*: *trans*, across or over, and *latus*, which is the past participle of *ferre*, to carry, related to the English word "ferry." The translator, then, is the ferry operator, carrying meaning from words on that shore to words on this shore' (emphasis in original). Teju Cole, "Carrying a Single Life: On Literature and Translation," *The New York Review of Books*, July 2019, www.nybooks.com/daily/2019/07/05/carrying-a-single-life-on-literature-translation/.

24 Munshi Rezaulla, a nineteenth-century poet, quoted in Samia Khatun, *Australianama: The South Asian Odyssey in Australia* (New York: Oxford University Press, 2018), 3.

25 Gayatri Chakravorty Spivak, "Translation as Culture," *Parallax* 6, no. 1 (2000): 13.

26 Paulami Sengupta, ed., *Anandamela Pujabarshiki Galpa Sankalan* (Kolkata: Ananda Publishers, 2015), 64–74.

We also heard the story in a dramatised audio version on a radio programme called *Sunday Suspense*. While the text of the story appeared in a children's book, the audio version was not meant for the same audience. The story – its content and form – appealed to both children and adults, though our imagined readers of the translated version are not children. The multiple genres that the story is able to traverse illustrates that the genre did not predetermine its audience.[27] Interestingly, despite being written for children or a young audience, the story depicts an adult, male world and does not care to depict what can be conventionally understood as a child's world. The story has supernatural and magical elements, but the lucid form of writing does not conjure the imageries of the fable genre and remains committedly realist and historicist.

The narrative, set in a fictional post-enlightenment nineteenth-century British-India, revolves around the head of a man called Benimadhab Laskar. His head, through a series of events in the story, turns into a prospective artefact for juridical and medical inquiry. Benimadhab's head is central to the story – the original title made that apparent. Our inability to adequately translate that into English necessitated a recourse to another title – a phrase lifted verbatim – that presents the translated version as a law story: a literary text whose use of narrative, allegories, images and rhetoric can be read to gain jurisprudential insights from everyday life.[28] As we moved through the task of translation, we constantly negotiated between impossibility and necessity. It was impossible to maintain complete loyalty to the syntax and the affective intensities of the story when read in Bangla, but it was necessary that we remained loyal to our reading experience of the text when writing in English.

Our title – 'Lord-Healer of Lost Cases' – makes it possible to hold on to the discursive force of the narrative in the way in which it raises questions about law by unsettling the Manichean dualisms of reason/emotion, fact/fiction, science/supernatural, logic/superstition, modernity/tradition, religious/secular. The appeal of the story for us lies in its ability to 'unlimit' law: 'to suspend law's conventional, conceptual, doctrinal and institutional boundaries in an effort to imagine different modalities for understanding law'.[29] The line-drawing function that this dominant convention of legal theory continues to perform in order to delimit law's boundaries are organised around the dualisms which keep alive 'the myth of the absence of myth that lies at the heart of modern law'.[30]

The head as the source of reason and civilisational maturity played a key role in the founding, maintenance and reification of such mythology particularly in the context of colonialism. Arguments like J.S. Mill's relegation of the colonised races to a 'nonage' and exclusion from the enjoyment of the fruits of individual liberty because they have not yet achieved the 'maturity of their faculties',[31] founded the myths of modern law which were then used to justify colonialism as a rule of benevolence.[32] By extension, such arguments also granted sole interpretative authority

27 See generally Stanley Fish, "Working on the Chain Gang: Interpretation in the Law and in Literary Criticism," *Critical Inquiry* 9 (1982): 209–10. Fish argues contra Dworkin that Agatha Christie's novels, despite being writing that falls in the genre of the detective story, can be read as philosophy.

28 See generally Robin West, *Narrative, Authority, and Law* (Ann Arbor: The University of Michigan Press, 1993); Ann Genovese, Shaun McVeigh and Peter D. Rush, "Lives Lived with Law: An Introduction," *Law Text Culture* 20 (2016): 1–13.

29 Margaret Davies, *Law Unlimited: Materialism, Pluralism, and Legal Theory* (New York: Routledge, 2017) viii.

30 Desmond Manderson, "From Hunger to Love: Myths of the Source, Interpretation, and Constitution of Law in Children's Literature," *Law & Literature* 15, no. 1 (2003): 87; see also Peter Fitzpatrick, *The Mythology of Modern Law* (New York: Routledge, 1992).

31 John Stuart Mill, *On Liberty* (Kitchener: Batoche Books, 2001), 14.

32 See Anthony Bogues, "John Stuart Mill and 'The Negro Question': Race, Colonialism, and the Ladder of Civilization," in *Race and Racism in Modern Philosophy*, ed. Andrew Valls (Ithaca: Cornell University Press, 2005), 218;

to the coloniser who, with the aid of modern law and science – the gifts of nineteenth-century modernity – could produce knowledge about the colonised.[33] The colonised were deprived of such authority owing to their perceived intellectual impoverishment. The interpretive tools of modern law and science worked to establish that 'Eastern jurisprudential traditions were based on custom, ritual and religion, in contrast to the so-called rational and scientific legal systems of modern Western nations'.[34] Beni Laskar's head, quite literally, brings these interpretive tools into crisis.[35]

So, let's stay with the head for a bit. Beni Laskar's unique ability to accurately foretell whether a client was guilty or innocent is more than a plot point that produces a sense of mystery for the reader. The character of the hakim in Charles Wilberforce wants to treat the head – Benimadhab's mundu – as an object of scientific study. Even as a figure of colonial authority and a superior legal mind he could not dismiss Benimadhab's ability as merely supernatural, a concoction of native religious superstitions. This was because Benimadhab's predictions always turned out to be true. For Wilberforce, this meant the existence of truth, albeit without the credible rational explanations that were acceptable to the legal mind.

Benimadhab did not arrive at the truth through a distillation of facts via testimonies and evidence. His explanation was that the dead – and not God – spoke to him, led him to the truth and helped achieve justice. The pursuit of truth and justice through the registers of the afterlife and the dead was incomprehensible to the rational mind of the hakim. The colonial rationality inscribed in the Indian Evidence Act, 1872, established that '[e]vidence was above all a matter of procedure – the procedure of arriving at the truth . . . [where] truth was nothing if there was a lack of procedure'.[36] Without legal procedure, to the hakim's rational mind, there was no explanation for how Benimadhab arrived at the truth. Thus, the next available modern knowledge framework was science:[37] 'a metaphor for the triumph of universal reason over enchanting myths'.[38]

Helen Gilbert and Chris Tiffin, eds., *Burden or Benefit? Imperial Benevolence and its Legacies* (Bloomington: Indiana University Press, 2008).

33 See Aileen Moreton-Robinson, *The White Possessive: Property, Power and Indigenous Sovereignty* (Minneapolis: University of Minnesota Press, 2015), 75.

34 Eve Darian-Smith, "Postcolonial Theories of Law," in *Law and Social Theory*, eds. Reza Banakar and Max Travers (Oxford: Hart Publishing, 2013), 258. See generally Sundhya Pahuja, "The Postcoloniality of International Law," *Harvard Journal of International Law* 46, no. 2 (2005): 459–69; Dianne Otto, "Subalternity and International Law: The Problems of Global Community and the Incommensurability of Difference," *Social & Legal Studies* 5, no. 3 (1996): 337–64.

35 In trying to interpret Benimadhab's condition by studying his head, the hakim was performing an act of translation. His aim was to make the condition intelligible for the rational mind. This is not very different from the task of translation that we have undertaken – our project is also interpretive. We want to make the text intelligible as a law story. In this sense, all translations are fraught with the possibility of interpretive violence in which the text is exploited for extracting meaning. As Susan Sontag has written: 'interpretation is the revenge of the intellect upon art. . . . To interpret is to impoverish, to deplete the world – in order to set up a shadow world of "meanings".' We are mindful of this and consider our task as one that carries the ethical responsibility for treating a text with care. For this reason, we would like to acknowledge that all texts are polysemic and what our translation offers is only but one way of reading it. Susan Sontag, "Against Interpretation," in *Against Interpretation and Other Essays* (New York: Picador, 1966), 7.

36 Ranabir Samaddar, "Beyond the Frame of Practical Reason: The Indian Evidence Act and Its Performative Life," *Diogenes* 60, no. 3–4 (2015): 65.

37 'For many moderns it was the ability of science and, in a different way, law to create an objective world that creates the "great divide" of modernity both from the past and from premoderns.' Shaun McVeigh, "Law and Postmodernism," in *Law and Social Theory*, eds. Reza Banakar and Max Travers (Oxford: Hart Publishing, 2013), 233.

38 Gyan Prakash, *Another Reason: Science and the Imagination of Modern India* (Princeton: Princeton University Press, 1999), 3. Science and scientific reasoning, however, was not the preserve of Western modernity alone as

The hakim's particular recourse to science, and the subsequent story of law that we glean from this literary work, takes us in the direction of a nineteenth-century practice known as phrenology, which travelled to the colonies with the empire. The hakim considered Benimadhab's headaches and fever as a 'pathological' condition that made him delirious – much like the common symptom of malaria – so he insisted that the head be cut open and studied. The hakim also told Benimadhab that he had already referred his case to his friend, Ronald Ross. Ross was a doctor with the Indian Medical Service who won the Nobel Prize in 1902 for discovering 'the role of anopheles mosquitoes in the transmission of malaria . . . and helped to establish India as a leading site for the investigation of tropical diseases'.[39] Despite being aware that malaria was still prevalent in parts of Europe at that time, Ross and his contemporaries equated 'malaria with India, and . . . India with the tropics', to establish and pursue a body of European knowledge called 'tropical science' that considered the tropics as diseased locations.[40]

The identification of the Indian colony as the site of the disease meant the simultaneous creation of a population of diseased bodies conducive for scientific research and objects of new medical discoveries.[41] That diseased bodies were considered to house frail and weak minds is an idea which aligned with and furthered racial sciences such as phrenology that holds a significant place in the story without having been named by Gangopadhyay. For Wilberforce, sending Benimadhab's head to an expert like Ross would serve the purpose of studying the disease of the mind that he suffered from and advance European scientific knowledge production through phrenology.

As 'the most popular mental science of the Victorian age', phrenology has often been described as 'a racial science'.[42] It was prevalent in Europe and its colonies in the nineteenth century and involved the study of skulls, premised on an assumption that their shape held the key to the understanding of intellect. Phrenology, also called a 'pseudo-science' by its detractors,[43] gained popularity particularly for determining the connections between racial qualities, mental capacities and the shape of skulls. In the colonial context, the racial dimension made it both popular and controversial. However, the popularity of phrenology was not limited to the coloniser, as it seemed to have found acceptance amongst the natives. In Calcutta, a group of Bengali medical students set up a phrenological society in 1840. They fostered the same racial arguments to argue against colonialism. According to them, once the discriminatory economic measures implemented by the East India Company were removed, 'phrenology would reveal Bengalis

---

colonialism would project. See Bruce Pascoe, *Dark Emu: Aboriginal Australia and the Birth of Agriculture* (Broome: Magabala Books, 2014).

39 David Arnold, "India's Place in the Tropical World, 1770–1930," *The Journal of Imperial and Commonwealth History* 26, no. 1 (1998): 1. See also Rohan Deb Roy, *Malarial Subjects: Empire, Medicine and Nonhumans in British India, 1820–1909* (Cambridge: Cambridge University Press, 2017).

40 Ibid. In a similar vein, Sumanta Banerjee has argued that even though there is documented evidence that syphilis was prevalent in Britain in the fifteenth century, even before colonisation, the British administration in the nineteenth century blamed 'the outbreak of venereal disease among their soldiers on Indian prostitutes'. Sumanta Banerjee, *Dangerous Outcaste: The Prostitute in Nineteenth Century Bengal* (Calcutta: Seagull Books, 1998), 63.

41 See generally David Arnold, *Colonizing the Body: State Medicine and Epidemic Disease in Nineteenth-Century India* (Berkeley: University of California Press, 1993). Amitav Ghosh's novel *The Calcutta Chromosome* (1995) offers a counter-narrative to Ross's singular feat to challenge 'the traditional hierarchies that exist between the white scientist and his subaltern native assistants'. Chitra Sankaran, "Introduction: Beyond Borders and Boundaries," in *History, Narrative, and Testimony in Amitav Ghosh's Fiction*, ed. Chitra Sankaran (Albany: SUNY Press, 2012), xvii.

42 James Poskett, *Materials of the Mind: Phrenology, Race, and the Global History of Science, 1815–1920* (Chicago: The University of Chicago Press, 2019), 1, 13.

43 Ibid., 10.

to be "one of the most intelligent peoples on the face of the globe"'.[44] Nativist phrenological arguments such as this were also used to forge an Indian identity which tried to establish the idea that 'Hindu caucasians' were racially superior to 'pre-Aryan aboriginals'.[45] A contemporary version of this view can be found in circulation in the present political climate of India in its march towards a Hindu Rashtra or nation – the holy land for only Hindus.[46] By extension, the ideology of Hindutva (or militant Hindu nationalism) has long propagated a problematic 'relativist rhetoric' of ancient Hindu scriptures as the authentic and superior source of scientific knowledge.[47] Such knowledge mixes 'the mythos of the Vedas and the logos of science' leading to both 'science and spirituality' being appropriated by Hindutva.[48] An instance of such relativist bunkum was presented by Indian Prime Minister Narendra Modi in 2014, when he had said that cosmetic surgery was invented in ancient India, as evidenced by the existence of the elephant-headed Hindu god Ganesha.[49]

The historical importance of phrenology for the colonial project and its acceptance amongst Bengalis appears to have been a cue for the author of our story who is renowned for his works in the genre of historical fiction. Sunil Gangopadhyay, born in 1934 in Faridpur (now in Bangladesh), is one of the doyens of modernist Bangla literature. He moved to Calcutta (now Kolkata) at the age of 2 or 3 before the Partition of India. He studied science at the University of Calcutta and was later invited to attend the Iowa Writers' Workshop. He lived and worked in Calcutta until his death in 2012, by which time he amassed great popularity. It is said that his funeral procession saw huge numbers of people who had gathered to pay their last respects – something comparable to the 'still-talked-of frenzied scenes at [Rabindranath] Tagore's funeral' in 1941.[50]

Gangopadhyay wrote using both his own name and several *nom de plumes* across the genres of poetry, short stories, essays, travelogues, reportage and novels, but he is most popular for his detective fiction in the Kakababu series, and the novels *Shei Shomoy* (1985) and *Prothom Alo* (1996), translated into English as *Those Days* and *First Light*, respectively.[51] Both of these novels offer a daring literary reimagination of the histories of Calcutta and of the Bengal Renaissance. Many of his works have been made into films, notably by the great auteur of Bengali cinema Satyajit Ray, who had characterised Gangopadhyay as a 'visual writer. [His] Characters, incidents, relationships are all largely built up by means of sensitively observed external details'.[52]

44 Ibid., 15.

45 Rohit Chakraborty, "Resident Outsiders," *Caravan* 11, no. 12 (2019): 106. See also Subho Basu, "The Dialectics of Resistance: Colonial Geography, Bengali Literati and the Racial Mapping of Indian Identity," *Modern Asian Studies* 44, no. 1 (2010): 53–79. It is in Chakraborty's article that we found the references to Poskett's and Basu's works.

46 Tanika Sarkar, "Semiotics of Terror: Muslim Children and Women in Hindu Rashtra," *Economic and Political Weekly* 37, no. 28 (2002): 2872–76.

47 Meera Nanda, "Postmodernism, Hindu Nationalism, and 'Vedic Science'," in *Scientific Values and Civic Virtues*, ed. Noretta Koertge (New York: Oxford University Press, 2005), 220. Nanda's provocation that postmodernism and Hindu nationalism are unusual allies in advancing ideas of 'alternative science' is an important one to take on board for scholars like us who align with postmodernism.

48 Ibid.

49 Siddhartha Deb, "Those Mythological Men and Their Sacred, Supersonic Flying Temples," *The New Republic*, May 15, 2015, https://newrepublic.com/article/121792/those-mythological-men-and-their-sacred-supersonic-flying-temples.

50 Tanmay Datta, "Sunil Gangopadhyay: A Writer and a Star," *Economic and Political Weekly* 48, no. 35 (2013): 23.

51 Sunil Gangopadhyay, *Those Days: A Novel*, trans. Aruna Chakravarti (New Delhi: Penguin, 1997); Sunil Gangopadhyay, *First Light: A Novel*, trans. Aruna Chakravarti (New Delhi: Penguin, 2001).

52 Quoted in Bhaskar Jyoti Goswami, "Sunil Gangopadhyay: A Tribute," *Indian Literature* 56, no. 6 (2012): 57.

Sunil Gangopadhyay began his literary life as a poet. He founded and edited the poetry magazine *Krittibas* and had never thought that he would take to writing novels.[53] As a poet his renown led to the Beat Generation poet Allen Ginsberg mentioning Gangopadhyay's name in his poem 'On Jessore Road' written in 1971 in the wake of his visit to refugee camps in West Bengal.[54] The feminist literary scholar Gayatri Chakravorty Spivak has described Gangopadhyay's depiction of life in his poetry as a combination of 'transparency and depth [that comes] through by way of a robust careful literal reading'.[55] Later when Gangopadhyay turned to writing serialised novels in the literary magazine *Desh* (that he also edited) – because he could not earn enough to support his family by writing poetry – his works in the genre of historical fiction became so popular that the Subaltern Studies scholar Ranajit Guha had told him: 'We write so much about history but no one reads it, when you wrote it in the form of stories everyone started reading it. I think this is how history should be written these days.'[56]

'Beni Laskarer Mundu' helps us think of Southern histories as syncretic. It belies any nationalist claims to a pure past (in this case a Hindu one), ideas that are particularly significant for our current times in India, which is seeing a violent consolidation of Hindu nationalism politically, culturally and legally.[57]

Gangopadhyay's use of a colloquial Bangla, which uses words of Persian origin like mukhtar, hakim, huzoor and sahib, among others, presents a syncretic linguistic sensibility. The other references to the syncretism of the time can be found by locating the story temporally. Gangopadhyay's reference to Ronald Ross as a 'great doctor' who has already discovered the source of malaria, helps us pinpoint the period of the story to a time in the early 1900s after Ross had already won the Nobel Prize. This was also the time when the King's Viceroy, George Nathaniel Curzon, divided Bengal in 1905, inaugurating 'a divisive historical trend that separated east and west Bengal' and was the precursor to the 1947 Partition which led to the creation of the two independent dominions of India and Pakistan.[58]

53 In an interview Gangopadhyay had shared a fascinating story about how a conversation with Jack Kerouac helped him start writing a novel: 'in New York, while staying with Allen Ginsberg, I'd met Jack Kerouac. He told me one day that writing a novel was easy. I asked him, how do you find plots? He told me not to worry about plot and just to imagine one day in your life. Think about what you were doing on that day. Suppose you were standing at a bus stop waiting for a bus. Start from that: "I was standing in a bus station waiting for a bus. When I got on the bus, it started moving." Then the story would also move. So when the editor asked me to write a novel, I remembered Kerouac's advice.' Ashok Bery, "Sunil Gangopadhyay and K Sachidanandan: A Conversation," *Wasafiri* 25, no. 1 (2010): 50.

54 Allen Ginsberg, "On Jessore Road," *The New York Times*, December 17, 1971, http://movies2.nytimes.com/books/01/04/08/specials/ginsberg-jessore.html. Gangopadhyay had strong disagreements with a literary movement called the Hungryalists in Bengal that was inspired by the Beat Generation poets. See generally Maitreyi Bhattacharjee Chowdhury, *The Hungryalists: The Poets Who Sparked a Revolution* (New Delhi: Penguin, 2019).

55 Gayatri Chakravorty Spivak said this during her address at the Sunil Gangopadhyay Memorial Session at the Kolkata Literary Meet 2013. A video is available: Rudradeep Banerjee, "Sunil Gangopadhyay Memorial Session – Kolkata Literary Meet 2013," *YouTube*, February 13, 2013, 5:48, www.youtube.com/watch?v=bI96CksnjEI&t=1078s.

56 Gangopadhyay related this to the filmmaker Rituparno Ghosh during an interview on the show Ghosh & Company. Available Surma Ghosh Sarkar, "Sunil Gangopadhyay and Rituparno Ghosh – An Exclusive and a Rare Chat Show," *YouTube*, December 1, 2019, 1:09, www.youtube.com/watch?v=F3dqtreIY-I.

57 See generally Angana P. Chatterji, Thomas Blom Hansen and Christophe Jaffrelot, eds., *Majoritarian State: How Hindu Nationalism Is Changing India* (New Delhi: Oxford University Press, 2019).

58 David Ludden, "Spatial Inequity and National Territory: Remapping 1905 in Bengal and Assam," *Modern Asian Studies* 46, no. 3 (2012): 489.

Rabindranath Tagore, a critical voice in the nationalist movement for Indian independence, gives us an account of how Hindu religious ideas caught the attention of the leadership of the movement in Bengal. In a letter written in 1905 to Dinesh Chandra Sen, a researcher of Bengali folklore, Tagore provides an apposite insight into how these ideas were seen as a necessity by upper caste Hindu Bengalis of that time to induce nationalist pride.[59] This gives us a prescient sense of how the micro events circling Benimadhab Laskar's head may be connected with the macro implications of Hindu religious ideas seen in the emergence of Hindutva politics and the writing of a secular constitution, that make Gangopadhyay's syncretism pertinent for our postcolonial literary legal imagination.

Tagore writes: 'Educated Bengalis of that time out of shame imagined that our art, literature, history and religion were worthless, and they decided to imitate the West in every way as a model of progressive culture.'[60] In the letter Tagore further narrates how the Partition of Bengal led some notable native Bengali leaders to turn their own people to religious scriptures, for an unearthing of love and pride for their country that came to be missing due to the imitation of the West. In Tagore's account the turn to religious thought and shastras (Hindu scriptures) was a 'method of moving educated mind of the time towards *swadeshi*'.[61] Eventually, it is the Swadeshi movement – the boycott of British goods aimed at countering the economic extraction perpetrated by the Raj – which sowed the seeds for the consolidation of the demands for Swarajya or home rule and sovereignty and resulted in the reunification of Bengal in 1911.[62]

The 1905 Partition of Bengal, justified by the British as an administrative and economic decision,[63] resulted in the division of the population along Hindu and Muslim lines and initiated a radical territorial reorganisation of the region on communal terms. The ripple effects of this event have been immense, including in the making of the contemporary ideas of an undivided Hindu nation.[64] The wounds of the Bengal Partition are still alive in the kind of anti-minority sectarian violence and anti-Bangladeshi migration rhetoric that India lives through at present.[65] Gangopadhyay offers a reimagination of such a fraught period by placing the story in Murshidabad, a Muslim majority region in Bengal and a key urban centre for trade and culture through the eighteenth century. It was the capital of Bengal in Mughal India before the East India Company's forces, led by Lieutenant Colonel Robert Clive, defeated the last independent Nawab of Bengal, Siraj-ud-daulah, in the Battle of Plassey in 1757 and made Calcutta the capital.[66]

59 'Tagore's "dual" attitude to nationalism – supporting its emphasis on self-respect but rejecting its patriotism – was not an easy one to get across, even in India.' Krishna Dutta and Andrew Robinson, eds., *Selected Letters of Rabindranath Tagore* (New Delhi: Cambridge University Press, 2005), xx.

60 Ibid., 62.

61 Ibid (emphasis in original). Though this might appear to suggest that Tagore was a wholehearted and uncritical supporter of the ways of the Swadeshi movement, that is not the case. In his 1916 novel *Ghare Baire* (*The Home and the World*), Tagore offered a sharp critique of the Hindu nationalist turn that the movement took. Rabindranath Tagore, *The Home and the World*, trans. Surendranath Tagore (London: Macmillan and Co., 1921).

62 Sumit Sarkar, *Swadeshi Movement in Bengal, 1903–1908* (Ranikhet: Permanent Black, 2010).

63 See John R. McLane, "The Decision to Partition Bengal in 1905," *Indian Economic and Social History Review* 2, no. 3 (1965): 221–37.

64 Rimple Mehta, "Inscriptions of Race and Religion on Citizenship: 'Illegal' Bangladeshis in Akhand Bharat," *Economic and Political Weekly* 53, no. 7 (2018): 62–68.

65 See Pradip Kumar Datta, *Carving Blocs: Communal Ideology in Early Twentieth-Century Bengal* (New Delhi: Oxford University Press, 1999); Joya Chatterji, *Bengal Divided: Hindu Communalism and Partition, 1932–1947* (New Delhi: Cambridge University Press, 2002); Rizwana Shamshad, "Bengaliness, Hindu Nationalism, and Bangladeshi Migrants in West Bengal, India," *Asian Ethnicity* 18, no. 4 (2017): 433–51.

66 See Sudeep Chakravarti, *Plassey: The Battle That Changed the Course of Indian History* (New Delhi: Aleph, 2020).

The relationship between Hindus and Muslims in the Murshidabad of 'Beni Laskarer Mundu' is not marked by communal tensions. Rather the communities come together in solidarity when they protest the hakim's proposition to take away Benimadhab's body, which they see as the British meddling with matters of faith. At this time in India religion was legally governed by Queen Victoria's Proclamation of 1858, which had 'stated the policy of crown rule to be one of "non-interference" in the customs and traditions of Indians. This assurance also contained the promise that the state would protect such traditions from interference.'[67] In this sense, the protests by Hindus and Muslims against the hakim's proposition could be understood not only as an expression of cultural difference but also of the right to freedom of religion because the 'proclamation was constantly invoked as a guarantee for religious liberty in colonial India'.[68]

Our protagonist, Benimadhab Laskar, self-identifies as Hindu in the story. But Gangopadhyay's choice of surname for him is a curious one. Laskar, or its phonetic equivalent Lascar, can be historically traced back to mean an Indian, African or Arab seafarer employed to work on British ships during colonial times.[69] In the Bengal of the time being described by Gangopadhyay, Laskar was a surname that was shared by both Hindus and Muslims. With the rise of a pronounced identity-based communal divide in post-Partition Bengal, Muslim Bengalis have retained Laskar, while Hindu Bengalis have altered it to Naskar in an attempt to 'demarcate them from the Muslims'.[70] The story is thus a fictional rendition of a colonial Indian past in which syncretism is a quotidian reality even under feudal arrangements.

Writing from a postcolonial context about a historically communalised past, what might have been the source of Gangopadhyay's syncretic literary reimagination, we may ask? Though born into a Brahmin family, Gangopadhyay had maintained that he always harboured a religious scepticism.[71] His work on the nineteenth-century Bengali sufi mystic Lalon Shah Fakir presents a sustained engagement with such a syncretic past.[72] However, for us, this reimagination also appears to be shaped by Gangopadhyay's inheritance of the secular ethos of the postcolonial Indian constitution. The Indian constitution, as some have argued, understands secularism as the coexistence of multiple religions, unlike in the West where the thrust is primarily on the separation of state and church. This distinctive version of postcolonial secularism is founded on the constitutional freedom to profess and practice the religion of one's choice as opposed to the idea that to be secular one has to be non-religious.[73]

A tying of the literary and the legal whereby we can acknowledge their combined contribution to the making of Gangopadhyay's fictional universe is necessary for our interpretive task. This is because, otherwise, we would ascribe his syncretism to a literary sensibility alone. Speaking from a postcolonial position, we know that syncretism cannot be unproblematically and singularly handed over to the realm of literature, just like it cannot be done to law. For instance, 'Bande Mataram' ('salutation to the Mother'), the clarion call for solidarity and resistance during

67 Shabnum Tejani, *Indian Secularism: A Social and Intellectual History, 1890–1950* (Bloomington: Indiana University Press, 2008), 31.

68 Rohit De, *A People's Constitution: The Everyday Life of the Law in the Indian Republic* (Princeton: Princeton University Press, 2018), 66.

69 Rozina Visram, *Ayahs, Lascars, and Princes: The Story of Indians in Britain, 1700–1947* (New York: Routledge, 2015), 53.

70 Annu Jalais, *Forest of Tigers: People, Politics and Environment in the Sunderbans* (New Delhi: Routledge, 2010), 53.

71 Sarkar, "Sunil Gangopadhyay and Rituparno Ghosh – An Exclusive and a Rare Chat Show," 2:27.

72 Sunil Gangopadhyay, *Moner Manush* (Kolkata: Ananda Publishers, 2017).

73 Rajeev Bhargava, "The Distinctiveness of Indian Secularism," in *The Future of Secularism*, ed. T. N. Srinivasan (New Delhi: Oxford University Press, 2007), 20–53. For a counter to this liberal view of Indian secularism, see Ashis Nandy, "An Anti-Secularist Manifesto," *India International Centre Quarterly* 22, no. 1 (1995): 35–64.

the Swadeshi movement, was a hymn that appeared in the Bengali writer Bankimchandra Chattopadhyay's iconic 1882 novel *Anandamath*, which later turned into a 'Hindu rallying cry in moments of Hindu Muslim violence'.[74] Similarly, the constitutional imagination of a secular India is argued to have been founded on Hindu ideals. To give an example, Article I of the Constitution of India opens with the words, 'India, that is Bharat . . .', signifying 'the name to reflect the ancient pre-British and pre-Muslim era of a "glorious" Hindu past'.[75] The use of Bharat was also meant to signify 'the birth of a new India, with whose government and state the Hindus felt a sense of identification'.[76] Given this contradictory nature of the archives of both the law and literature in the making of the postcolonial condition it becomes ever more important to cultivate a literary legal imagination with responsibility – one that takes the 'double-bind' of our inheritances seriously.[77]

It was these dimensions of the narrative that made us read and translate 'Beni Laskarer Mundu' as a law story. Our motivation was primarily pedagogical. Could the story serve as a text for a jurisprudence class?[78] We feel that it can. The story inhabits a worldview that does not envisage a normative universe organised around neatly bounded realms of good and bad, rational and irrational, legal and customary, scientific and magical, the universal and particular. In short, the antagonistic world of the natives and the Europeans. Though key to the plot, the story is more complex than being one that only poses an unproblematic contestation between the coloniser and the colonised. The power implications born out of the cultural, racial and feudal hierarchies are never denied – the peasants occupy a lower class position to Benimadhab; Benimadhab, despite being a mukhtar, is subservient to the zamindar; the hakim is superior to the native zamindar in authority; and as an agent of the Raj, the stature of the hakim and the mokhtar are not comparable.[79] When the hakim demands his head, Benimadhab is in a fix. Even if he could refuse the zamindar, there is no way he could have done the same with the hakim. Yet, despite the representation of such power differentials, the story offers much more.

The narrative can be read as an invitation to think about jurisprudence from a postcolonial location that acknowledges law to be a body of knowledge formed through contradictory inheritances. The hakim, a mind trained in modern law, tries valiantly to use the Western epistemological frameworks of interpretation at his disposal to find a rational explanation for

74 Tanika Sarkar, "Imagining a Hindu Nation: Hindu and Muslim in Bankimchandra's Later Writings," *Economic and Political Weekly* 29, no. 39 (1994): 2553.

75 Pritam Singh, "Hindu Bias in India's 'Secular' Constitution: Probing Flaws in the Instruments of Governance," *Third World Quarterly* 26, no. 6 (2005): 911.

76 Ibid., 912.

77 Gayatri Chakravorty Spivak, *An Aesthetic Education in an Era of Globalization* (Cambridge: Harvard University Press, 2012), 3. On the question of inheritance being a responsible conduct, see Ann Genovese, "On Australian Feminist Tradition: Three Notes on Conduct, Inheritance and the Relationship Between Historiography and Jurisprudence," *Journal of Australian Studies* 38, no. 4 (2014): 430–44.

78 A much-used text of a short story that we had in mind as a template for a teaching text for jurisprudence when we decided to translate Gangopadhyay was Saadat Hasan Manto, "The New Constitution," in *Bitter Fruit: The Very Best of Saadat Hasan Manto*, ed. and trans. Khalid Hasan (New Delhi: Penguin Books, 2008), 206–15.

79 In 1893 Tagore had written: 'Just look at what happens with our barristers: however much they cultivate English society and the English temperament, they still cannot get on intimate terms with the sahibs living here. Even in the bar library they naturally gravitate into a dark-complexioned circle estranged from the rest like the dark spots on the face of full moon.' Dutta and Robinson, *Selected Letters*, 35. Tagore's observations seem to find echo in Homi Bhaba's formulation – ' . . . almost the same, but not quite' – about the existential racial lack in the non-white subject, who even after painstakingly mimicking the ways of the European remains the 'reformed, recognizable Other'. See Homi Bhaba, "Of Mimicry and Man: The Ambivalence of Colonial Discourse," *October* 28 (1984): 126.

Benimadhab's condition. His 'project is interpretive: he looks to decipher' Benimadhab's head.[80] When both law and science fail and Benimadhab's final words help Wilberforce to save his wife and child from being killed, he decides to suspend the pursuit for his head. Instead, he recognises both modern law's and science's failure by building a statue in memory of Benimadhab, dressed in the syncretic choga chapkan.

The line at the end from Shakespeare's *Hamlet* – even when read in literal terms – tellingly demonstrates the Western rational man's acknowledgement of his own finitude on the one hand, and on the other the judge's suspension of scientific-juridical reasoning and a resort to the speculative possibilities of literature. When we inherit Benimadhab's story in the form of the statue, we have to accommodate in our postcolonial imagination the role that both Benimadhab and Wilberforce played in the making of this memory. From being rivals, they became collaborators. In the figure of Benimadhab, a creation of the postcolonial imagination, the legal and the literary minds of the judge and the Bard, too find convergence.

80 Gayatri Chakravorty Spivak, "'Draupadi' by Mahasweta Devi," *Critical Inquiry* 8, no. 2 (1981): 381–82.

17
We are making a new world

Isobel Roele

I first saw *We Are Making a New World* (1918) at Tate Britain in London, at an exhibition of work by the English artist, Paul Nash (1889–1946).[1] It was late 2016, about six months after UK voters had opted to leave the European Union – a retreat to splenetic isolation. Initially drawn to its title by my research interests, I found myself stuck in front of the painting. Critical distance concertina'd, I was left implicated in the picture's muddy churn, both as someone who studies international organisations, and as an abashed Brit.[2] The painting implicates viewers by insisting that – like it or not – we are all engaged in world-making: the choice we have is about whether our world-making is reflective and collaborative, or not.

World-making is no longer, it seems, a valid political project. Internationalism is yesterday's news; world-making today is an investment opportunity. Political world-making has entertainment value in blockbuster movie franchises and computer games, but not a lot of credibility in a world of market forces and statistical truth. As far as democracy, dissent and deliberation are concerned, the world appears to be intractable, and Brexit is a reaction to this: if the world cannot be mastered, perhaps it can be shut out. But the association of world-making with world-mastery is just as mistaken as the notion that the world is a pre-set backdrop, which might be viewed at a safe distance.

Nash's painting suggests a way of prising these poles apart to open up a space for reflecting on world-making without descending into liberal platitudes. Like any landscapes worthy of the name,[3] his works are not views in either sense of the word: they are not reflections of the objective world, and they are not reducible to a single intention or meaning. *We Are Making a New World* shows world-making to be violent, messy and unlikely to end happily. But it also insists

1 An image of the painting is available on the IWM website, which allows visitors to zoom in or out of the image: www.iwm.org.uk/collections/item/object/20070.

2 To say that I am British feels like something between an admission of guilt and an admission of defeat. This feeling of shame, if Carlo Ginzburg is right, is the mark of belonging: Carlo Ginzburg, "The Bond of Shame," *New Left Review* 120 (November–December 2019): 35–44.

3 Christopher Neve, *Unquiet Landscape: Places and Ideas in 20th Century English Painting* (London: Faber & Faber, 1990), ix.

that world-making is inescapable, something we cannot opt-out of and are bound to do. This is the difficult landscape in which *We Are Making* implicates the viewer.

Nash was employed by Charles Masterman's Bureau of War Propaganda as an official war artist during World War One. Nevertheless, he presented the work that emerged from his stint at the Western Front in November 1917 as an indictment of those perpetuating the war. It conveys a 'bitter truth', he wrote to his wife, Margaret.[4] The quality of Nash's truth is usually taken one of two ways: heavily ironic or sunnily optimistic. In London during May 1918, when *We Are Making* was first shown at Nash's *Void of War* exhibition, irony was the order of the day: the war churned on, and Nash hoped that the optimistic message his dour painting bore would 'burn' the 'lousy souls' of the war's sponsors.[5] At around the same time, the image appeared on the front of a popular magazine *British Artists at the Front*, published by Country Life and produced by the War Propaganda Bureau.[6] The images, which neither sugar-coat nor glorify war, evidently spoke to audiences at the time.

What does the painting say today? The Imperial War Museum takes its message at face value. It featured heavily in their advertising for the centenary of the end of World War One: 'when the first war ended, a new world began' goes the tagline.[7] *We Are Making a New World* provides the back-drop for its promotional video, which celebrates the moment 'the guns fell silent'. The video tracks the flat-line of the silence left to right, across the front of the painting, which merges with John Singer Sargent's *Gassed* (1919). Singer-Sargent's line of men grope their way across Nash's landscape and off into no-mans-land. The next frames replace them with a series of photos of smiling soldiers, a couple of them black, and ends with the picture of a woman. In this video, Nash's picture is part of an inevitable progression to a new and better world. The sound-track makes this clear: as the shot tracks across a close-up of Nash's sun, bird-song replaces blasting guns. The war is over – life returns to normal – the video sighs with relief.

But in the world of Brexit – the world to which we return after watching the Imperial War Museum's video – everyone is holding their breath. Liberal certainties of peacetime progress belong to a different era. It is becoming clear that we never left the blasted landscape of *We Are Making* behind, and the painting represents the way the past is embroiled in the present. It is not just a vision of a wood in the Ypres Salient at the moment Nash sketched it in November 1917 – it is a painting which invites the viewer in, and implicates her. As Christopher Neve explained: 'landscape painting has always been about what it is like to be in the world and in a particular condition.'[8] Nash's painting was about being in the world in 1918 – but it speaks to our present condition, too, if we attend to it as active viewers engaged in world-making, rather than passive spectators of a world gone by.

Earth and emptiness

We Are Making is dominated by its churned ground; mud has swallowed two-thirds of the canvas. It is evil-looking mud. Yellowing and grey-green, bilious and infertile, and also somehow

4 Paul Nash, Letter to Margaret Nash (November 16, 1917) in *Outline: An Autobiography* (London: Faber & Faber, 1949), 211.

5 Ibid., 211.

6 The British Library has scanned a number of images from Nash's issue: www.bl.uk/collection-items/british-artists-at-the-front-series.

7 Promotional video. Imperial War Museums, "Making a New World – IWM London," www.iwm.org.uk/seasons/making-a-new-world.

8 Neve, *Unquiet Landscape*, vii.

animate – bubbling quicksand with a will of its own. The ground looks irradiated. It is unnaturally sweaty and pale, like it is sickening for something. Nash captures the quality expressed by the poet Mary Borden in her 'Song of Mud' (1917): 'pale yellow glistening mud', 'grey gleaming silvery mud'. Mud is the beneficiary of Nash's most delicate painting, a wealth of textures, colours and fine-detailing set off by the great monotone bank of rusty cloud behind it in the picture plane. Nash invites us to get embroiled in the mud, to occupy our eyes with it. It is not painted to repel us, but – a distorted echo of the soldiers sticking and sinking in it – to hold our attention.

Mud needn't signify decay. Like sunlight and water, which also feature in *We Are Making*, mud is an ingredient of growth. Nash saw this the first time he visited the front in the Spring of 1917. He told Margaret that 'flowers bloom everywhere . . . the place is just joyous, the dandelions are bright gold over the parapet and nearby a lilac bush is breaking into bloom'.[9] Nature is not regenerating in *We Are Making*. There are no sprigs or shoots of green, which might suggest future flowers. Even if it were, Nash's description foreshadows T.S Eliot's line about 'breeding/ Lilacs out of the dead land' in *The Wasteland*. Anything growing, we feel, would be compromised and fragile. Instead, the colours of flowers – dandelion yellow, wood-anemone-white, love-in-a-mist-blue – mock us from other forms: broken branches, clogs of mud, an unfathomable pool that has drowned several trees. This mud does not promise nature's regeneration. The only hope it holds out is that it sucks in the viewer, involving them in the world-making of the painting's title.

What else is there, but mud? No figures, no paraphernalia of war, no flora and fauna, no roads, parapets or dug-outs. *We Are Making* is a remarkably succinct image. But it is not empty. In it Nash contrives, oxymoronically, to manifest the void of war. This was the name of his exhibition at the Leicester Galleries in London, staged about six months after his stint as artist-at-the-front, in May 1918. *We Are Making* was one of its star attractions, and the exhibition poster picks up its smashed-tree motif.[10] Nash's endeavour to paint what is not there is typical of him. Christopher Neve explains that 'his essential subject, [was] the place where something had been'.[11] We might add that *We Are Making* is also a place where something, good or ill, *will be*.

The Imperial War Museum's promotional video treats *We Are Making* like a stage-set, correcting its lack of human figures with Singer Sargent's wounded men, as though Nash's omission was an oversight. This treatment takes the painting as a blank canvas onto which we can project our future hopes for a better world. On this reading, the absence of war signifies peace. But in projecting peace onto war, they occlude the scars, shadows and structures of war that haunt the canvas.

First of all, warfare structures the composition. The lozenge shape of the British Mark 1 tank forms a central zone in the painting, formed by the lower-most rays hitting the edges of the canvas, and a line of trees that begins, on the left, with a slanted stump that meets the ray and, on the right, with a straighter, thicker stump of around the same height. The sun provides the top of the rhombus, and the bottom is a very dark triangle embedded in the ground just beneath a central stump, of similar height to the other two. We can pick out other lozenge-shapes, too: one made by the group of five taller trees to the right of the canvas; another is made from two symmetrically sloping banks of mud at the bottom left and right corners, which answer the

9 Paul Nash, Letter to Margaret Nash (March 7, 1917) in *Outline*, 187.

10 Image available online. See Paul Nash, *Void of War* (London, 1918), https://collections.vam.ac.uk/item/O76638/void-of-war-lithograph-paul-nash/.

11 Neve, *Unquiet Landscape*, 6.

slanting sun-rays at the top of the canvas. The ghostly presence of the tanks is confirmed by the metallic greys and rusts of the sky.[12]

The churned-up ground is also marked by absences. Caterpillar-tracks are suggested in at least two places in the picture. The most obvious double-track lies immediately above the top-end of the fallen tree, black zig-zags in yellow-green ground. There is a second suggestion of tyre-track patterning in the bottom-right corner. A sparsely applied dark-brown cross-hatch, sprinkled with white, and a thin but distinct line of paint the colour of dried blood. There is also an idea that the detritus of war might have been swallowed by the quagmire of mud. In bilgy greens and yellows, Nash's mud echoes objects of war in helmet-shaped humps, and extrusions the colour of sandbags. To quote Mary Borden's 'Song of Mud' again,

> The vast liquid grave of our armies. It has drowned our men.
> Its monstrous distended belly reeks with the undigested dead.

Writing to Margaret in November 1917, Nash described the front as 'a grave'.[13] No bodies are visible in *We Are Making*, but dead soldiers haunt the scene, from the helmet shapes, to the fallen tree, to the putrefied fleshy quality of the ground.

A third way Nash makes absence visible is by suggesting a hidden trench, in a line of what might be the tops of evenly-spaced boards or planks lining its sides. The horizontal line gently diverges from the straight line above it formed by the bottoms of the five upright trunks that sit lowest on the canvas. The trench is bridged by the fallen tree, and disappears laterally into billowy, bilious mud on both sides. Mud dominates the canvas. Its puffed, messy hummocks are a foil to the straight lines of the sun's bright lateral rays, and the dark vertical uprights of the tree-trunks. The contrast foregrounds another absence – the absence of order.

The long shadows cast by the low sun also suggest absence. Scarcely distinguishable from the trees they silhouette, they remind us of the hollowness of blasted stumps, which act as substitute men. The shadows make the ground legible, punctuating it with long hyphens cast by trees, and emphatic full-stops made by shell-holes. There is also something nonsensical about the shadows. Long tree-shadows radiate outwards in a fan shape, an umbral reflection of the sun's white rays. These impossible shadows, which jut outwards in all directions, originate in a single point: the sun.

Sun and sky

The prominent sun makes Nash's painting easy to mistake for a reassertion of Enlightenment values in the wake of barbaric war. In *We Are Making*, enlightenment is grim, not complacent: 'the fully enlightened earth radiates disaster triumphant', to quote Adorno and Horkheimer.[14] Still, Nash is easily taken for a woolly English liberal. Between the wars, he was known for painting the English landscape: mystical places like Avebury, Stonehenge and the Wittenham Clumps; small towns like Swanage, Iden and Dymchurch. His decision to sign up as an official war artist might also tell against him in this regard, fixing him as an establishment figure, answerable to the War Propaganda Bureau. No less a personality than Arnold Bennett, a pillar

12 I am grateful to Ben Poore for this insight.

13 Paul Nash, Letter to Margaret Nash (November 16, 1917) in *Outline,* 211.

14 Theodor Adorno and Max Horkheimer, *The Dialectic of Enlightenment*, trans. John Cumming (London: Verso, 1997), 3.

of wartime propaganda, wrote the introductory note to *Void of War*. But *We Are Making* glorifies neither wartime heroics nor peacetime hush.

Disaster colours the sky in rust and dried blood, evoking broken tanks and dead men. The cold grey sky above the sun meets this bank of ruddy colour so abruptly as to form a mountain range – impossible, of course, in the flat landscape around Ypres. The solid wall of colour boxes the scene in, a barrier between the scene and the distant sun. If hope resides anywhere in the sky, it is in the metallic blue-grey stripe slanting down towards the left at the top of the painting. The quality of this hope is not of regenerative warmth, but of unassured openness. We can compare it in this respect to Nash's commission, *The Menin Road* (1919).[15] In that massive painting, the sky is overcast with clouds, the darkest of which cap the top right corner of the painting, emitting huge searchlight beams. The sky is forbidding and closed, suggesting a benighted world.

In the Imperial War Museum's video, the sun is a beacon of hope: life-giving after the dark days of war, the light of reason dawning on the peacetime world. Although it does not ultimately convince, there are reasons to credit this reading. After all, *We Are Making* was formed out of a drawing Nash made of the front, called *Sunrise, Inverness Copse*.[16] The painting's time of day, by contrast, is unclear. It may show the sun setting on the world, symbolising the waning of reason in war. And even if we were to take the time of day as sunrise, we should remember that dawn was the time when deserters were shot. Nash himself disparaged the difference between the two times of day: 'Sunrise and sunset are blasphemous, they are mockeries to man.'[17] The sentiment is plain to see in *The Menin Road*, which might show a night sky lit by shellfire, or daylight drowned in dust and smoke.

Richard Cork's reading of the sky is compelling. He points out that the sun appears differently from the sun in *Sunrise, Inverness Copse*, being 'restricted to a cold whiteness'.[18] But could this cold whiteness not be read as the triumph of reason, rather than the irradiation of a nuclear winter, as Cork evocatively but anachronistically suggests? Certainly the geometric precision of the sun's chilly rays could suggest a reassertion of scientific progress. Nash, however, had just witnessed technological progress slaughter millions of men in the form of mechanised war. To Jenny Uglow, the rays are 'the memory of shells scything through the fragile living world'.[19] The chalky whiteness of both sun and rays, visible if we zoom in on *We Are Making*, does not evoke the heat and light of good growing conditions. It is clinical, and chilly – a winter sun, Cork suggests.

The Earth-ward-facing rays of the sun, which do not appear in *Sunrise*, also call to mind William Blake's *The Ancient of Days*, an image of Urizen reaching down with his compasses to 'circumscribe this universe'.[20] Blake, by whom Nash was strongly influenced, struggled against such circumscription, which he took to mark the end of human ability to imagine the world

15 Paul Nash, "The Menin Road" (1919), IWM Article 2242, www.iwm.org.uk/collections/item/object/20087.

16 Paul Nash, "Sunrise, Inverness Copse" (1918), IMW Article 724, www.iwm.org.uk/collections/item/object/20067.

17 Paul Nash, Letter to Margaret Nash (November 16, 1917) in *Outline,* 211.

18 Richard Cork, *A Bitter Truth: Avant-Garde Art and the Great War* (New Haven: Yale University Press, 1994), 201.

19 Jenny Uglow, "A Painter of the Shattered World," *The New York Review of Books,* November 17, 2017, www.nybooks.com/daily/2017/02/11/paul-nash-painter-of-the-shattered-world/.

20 "The Ancient of Days" provides the frontispiece to Blake's *Europe, A Prophecy* (1794), www.britishmuseum.org/research/collection_online/collection_object_details/collection_image_gallery.aspx?assetId=38787001&objectId=1344764&partId=1. That Blake's image influenced Nash is evident in Nash's late painting, *Eclipse of the Sunflower* (1945). See http://visualarts.britishcouncil.org/exhibitions/exhibition/back-from-the-front-presents-brothers-in-art-john-and-paul-nash-2014/object/eclipse-of-the-sunflower-nash-1945-p114.

differently. Cold reason is detached and objective, not involved and personal. The idea that the landscape is an impersonal view is something that Nash pushed against. After the war, drawing on a concerted engagement with modernists in continental Europe, his English landscapes became surreal dreamscapes dotted with geometric forms,[21] or – like the *Monster Field* series – full of surreal found-objects.[22] There is an alchemy to these later landscapes of imagination, which *We Are Making*, stunted and stumped like its trees, cannot approach. The war is all too real. *We Are Making* looks like hard work, rather than magical transformation. The bright sun might be the focal point of the picture but, a small white disc, it stands distant from us, its chalky light unable to banish the shadows of war.

The trees

Nash is famous for personifying trees. It is often said that he drew trees instead of people because he was no good at drawing human figures. In his war paintings, regimented trees echo marching columns of soldiers,[23] in *Rain: Lake Zillebeke* (1918), it is difficult to distinguish the tiny marching figures from the stumps of the destroyed wood behind them.[24] In *We Are Making* the trees feel like protagonists, too. They form a troop standing to exhausted attention, amputees who have not quite lost the military habit. Nash disturbs the outline of the trunks, breaking it up with white stipples and sympathetic shades of background colour to avoid too emphatic a silhouette. Shorn of branches, they are reduced to trunks and stumps, many lean at odd angles, and one lies, uprooted, in a shell-hole. A delicate allusion to the casualties of war, the trees help to account for the picture's popularity in 1918 by pairing man with nature, and dissociating dead soldiers from the inhuman war-machine.

Paul Gough troubles this bifurcation of nature and war. He writes that 'during the course of the fighting, trees, and especially small woods, were to become death traps'.[25] Inverness Copse, the drawing of which provided the basis for *We Are Making*, was one such wood. According to the Michelin Guide of Ypres battlefields, published just after the war, 'the Germans made use for the first time of liquid fire, thanks to which innovation they succeeded temporarily in retaking the north-western corner of Inverness Wood'.[26] As Nash noted during his brief tour of duty with the Artists Rifles in Spring 1917, the destruction of trees was par for the course during war. He described to Margaret a scene closely resembling that of *We Are Making*:

> Shall I ever lose the pictures they have made in my mind. Imagine a wide landscape flat and scantily wooded and what trees remain blasted and torn, naked and scarred and riddled.

21 Like Equivalents for the Megaliths (1935), www.tate.org.uk/art/artworks/nash-equivalents-for-the-megaliths-t01251.

22 The British Government Art Collection includes a Monster Field photograph (1938), https://artcollection.culture.gov.uk/artwork/14235/.

23 As in *Men Marching at Night* (1918), www.iwm.org.uk/collections/item/object/20086.

24 Paul Nash, "Rain, Lake Zillebeke" (1918), British Museum, no. 1918,0704.4, www.britishmuseum.org/research/collection_online/collection_object_details/collection_image_gallery.aspx?assetId=269156001&objectId=699263&partId=1.

25 Paul Gough, "'Cultivating Dead Trees': The Legacy of Paul Nash as an Artist of Trauma, Wilderness and Recovery," *Journal of War and Culture Studies* 4, no. 3 (2011): 326.

26 Michelin Illustrated Guides to the Battlefields (1914–1918): Ypres and the Battles of Ypres (Michelin, 1919), www.gutenberg.org/files/36213/36213-h/36213-h.htm.

> The ground for miles around furrowed with trenches, pitted with yawning holes in which the water lies still and cold or heaped with mounds of earth.[27]

I think the trees signify people other than the soldiers 'over there'. They suggest the people 'at home', too – including, 100 years later, us. That the trees signify everyone, not only soldiers, is suggested by Richard Cork, who describes their twisted branches as 'like melancholy tresses of hair'.[28] To him they are 'chorus-like presences . . . mourning the death of the world',[29] and thus performing the traditional role of women in wartime – from Euryalus' mother in Virgil's Aeneid, to Pablo Picasso's *The Weeping Woman*. The torn branches hang like widows' weeds, with an air of exhaustion or resignation, and mourning is suggested by the dampening of Nash's primary colours into darkly subdued shades of themselves.

War rumbled on in May 1918, when the painting was first exhibited. Woodrow Wilson's Fourteen Points might have been cause to hope, but fighting was still fierce and the Germans' Spring Offensive was well underway. Visitors to the *Void of War* exhibition were living through an apparently interminable conflict, not coming to terms with something over and done with. The present tense of *We Are Making*, in that context, may simply be read as a call for an end. In his autobiography, *Outline*, Nash wrote, 'I realise that no one in England knows what the scene of war is like. . . . If I can, I will show them.'[30] The painting's presence includes its viewers – the present tense of *We Are Making* never resolves into the perfect.

Nash wanted to bring the horror of war back home to England. He traded on his dual-position as artist and soldier to do so. The exhibition advertising styled him 'Lieut. Paul Nash', emphasising that Nash was not only a witness at the front, he had seen action, too.[31] Nash himself is among those trees. Sketching *Sunrise, Inverness Copse* in mid-November 1917, he must have stood among similar trunks. He is a pivot, then, between London and the war-torn landscape of the Ypres Salient. The viewer stands where Nash stood to paint *We Are Making*. She takes part in the picture arrayed, perhaps, with other exhibition-goers in a mirror-image of the trees in the picture plane.

One way Nash achieves this implicating effect is to push the trees far up the canvas, so that the muddy bottom-half of the canvas mirrors the gallery-space between the viewer and the painting. Nash adds to the impression by making the scene totalising. If it were possible to zoom out, it feels like we would see acre upon acre of the same. That the scene is not contained by the frame is also indicated by the way that the top of the tallest tree, in the middle of the canvas, escapes the picture space. The viewer, standing in front of the canvas, is brought into its world – implicated in a painting that is not fully contained by its frame.

I want to suggest that the painting also overruns its temporal frame. This means gently prising out Nash's intention in 1918, and separating it from the work the painting does as we look at it now. We are still bogged down in Nash's highly involved mud, still rooted in it like the trees, because we have not escaped the moment of *We Are Making*. We have not emerged, as the Imperial War Museum video implies, in the sunlit uplands on the other side of that rust-red cloud

27 Paul Nash, Letter to Margaret Nash (April 6, 1917) in *Outline*, 194–95.

28 Cork, *A Bitter Truth*, 201.

29 Ibid.

30 Nash, *Outline*, 216.

31 The phrase features on the *Void of War* poster, and also the exhibition invitation. See: www.iwm.org.uk/collections/item/object/1050001821. In fact, his stint in Spring 1917 was fairly uneventful; he was invalided home after falling into a trench shortly before his regiment was decimated by a particularly bloody engagement at Hill 60.

bank. Christopher Neve said that landscape 'paintings represent one moment, continually'.[32] Nash's painting is a vehicle for this continuity in a visceral sense because he placed the viewer in the picture. Visitors to Tate Britain's exhibition, or to the Imperial War Museum's permanent collection, where the painting usually lives, do not look on from the safety of a position external to the work of world-making. Viewers, whether they yearn for a return to Great Britain's glory days of empire and wartime victory, or robe post-war peace projects in an immutable moral imperative, are implicated in the ongoing work of world-making.

Brexit rails, in various more and less sympathetic guises, against the anti-politics of the European Union. But whether the objection is to its democratic deficit, its curbing of the sovereign decision or its managerial mindset, no alternative politics of world-making is offered with the objection. Nash's painting insists that it is impossible to opt-out of world-making, but he gives us a choice about whether that world-making is reflective and collaborative, or a by-product of our individual decisions.

We Are Making is a painting of reflective attention, rather than passive waiting. The tree-figures are gathered together around the sun, an impression Nash achieves with those nonsensical shadows. It is in this congregation – not in the sunlight – that hope resides. The sun's rays encompass the trees in a common space of being together, and give its light back to the trees and earth it illuminates. In doing so it throws the trees' non-uniformity into relief: these are not ranked soldier trees. We might see in the gentle glow the trees emit a paler, politer allusion to Blake's character Orc, the passionate antithesis of reasonable Urizen, whose revolutionary ardour Blake depicted by wreathing him in flames. Demobbed soldiers, no longer under command, can choose to act rather than waiting for orders. The mood of attention in Nash's trees is not the nervous waiting of Wilfred Owen's poem 'Exposure' (1917), with its awful refrain 'But nothing happens'. *We Are Making a New World* gives us a world of agency not orders.

But in presenting a brutalised landscape, Nash reminds us that agency is not necessarily, *contra* the liberal imaginary, something to be celebrated. Blake famously came to rue the terror which followed the revolution in France. World-making is compromised and almost always disappointing. International lawyers have been disappointed in stereo: by the League of Nations, by the United Nations, by the European Union. The ugly under-bellies of these projects of international organisation – colonialism and neoliberalism above all – understandably stifle the world-making impulse. But *We Are Making* insists that world-making is necessary and unavoidable. There are alternatives to international organisation, but we won't be able to make them until we relinquish the liberal consolation of progress, and countenance the unliveable world we have made.

The sun in *We Are Making* reminds us that time passes. The ambiguity of rising or setting of the sun is perhaps part of the point, a way of emphasising that the temporality of the painting is indistinct. We can fix on either the dusky blue of the pool below the cloud, or the cold morning-light of lemon-yellows and sea-foam greys in all that mud. The mud itself bears the imprint of time. Nash has not painted a primordial ooze from which we can begin again. He has marked the mud with the scars of war, but so subtly that they do not take over. What comes next is shaped but not determined by what came before.

In his review of Tate Britain's Nash exhibition, T.J. Clark commented that 'effectiveness, in a work of art, is never to be measured in terms of honesty or accuracy or up-to-dateness – only by the power of the preserved fiction to put up-to-dateness back into the bruising flow of time'.[33] In *We Are Making* Paul Nash planted his moment in that bruising flow, a moment I encountered with rapt attention as the tumults of Brexit began in 2016.

32 Neve, *Unquiet Landscape*, 10.

33 Timothy J. Clark, "At Tate Britain," *London Review of Books* 39, no. 3 (2017): 16–17.

History-telling

18

The time of revolution

Decolonisation, heterodox international legal historiography and the problem of the contemporary

Matthew Craven

> Change is the law of life. That is the obvious truth of history. The current age is particularly an age of unprecedented speed and dynamism. The world has changed more in our time than throughout the whole of previous recorded history. The rate of change is still accelerating and its scope ever widening.
>
> Ram Prakash Anand, *New States and International Law*[1]

Introduction

'Change', 'speed', 'dynamism' and 'acceleration'. This, for Ram Prakash Anand, was the language by which one could describe the global political landscape of decolonisation. It was a landscape inflected by a particular temporality – a world shrinking through the experience of an accelerating rate of social and political change – in which the natural rhythm of time appeared to be ever shortening. For Anand, time was not simply a chronometric measure of change, but rather a form of (social or political) experience, the characteristics of which would be specific to their own historical moment ('our time'). By contrasting the experience of acceleration associated with the temporality of his own era, with the more sedate rate of change of yesteryear, Anand draws attention not only to the significance of temporality to our experience and understanding of social and political life, but also to temporality's transitional character (giving double inflection to the adage that 'time doesn't stand still').

In recent years a range of scholars have drawn attention to the apparently disjunctive temporalities of contemporary political life.[2] They point amongst other things, to the collapse of a stabilising faith in the ideas of progress, development or modernisation to which Anand,

1 Ram Prakash Anand, *New States and International Law* (New Delhi: Vikas Publishing House, 1972), 1.

2 David Scott, *Omens of Adversity: Tragedy, Time, Memory, Justice* (Durham, NC: Duke University Press, 2014), 5; François Hartog, *Regimes of Historicity: Presentism and Experiences of Time*, trans. Saskia Brown (New York: Columbia University Press, 2015).

alongside many others, was visibly drawn.[3] But my concern here is not so much to pass comment upon the political temporalities of the present day, as to work through the linkages that were at play in the work of those such as Anand – between a practice of decolonisation, a demand for the reconfiguration of international law and a latent sensitivity to the question of time or temporality. My concern is to bring to an account of international law during the period of decolonisation, an appreciation of the idea that the central problematic was not simply one of international law's spatial ambit, but of its temporal structure. My medium for bringing these ideas together will be through the articulation of a specifiable problem: the problem of 'contemporaneity'.

In its everyday sense, the 'contemporary' stands as a kind of shorthand for the 'present', for the 'hereabouts' of the now, or perhaps as that odd in-between period, as Arendt would put it, between past and future.[4] The contemporary in that sense, is that which is made intelligible by way of its contrast between a determined past, and an uncertain or unknowable future. Rather than work directly within this vein, however, I want to explore a more literal or etymological theme that is opened out by the idea of the contemporary. These themes resonate not only in terms of understanding the configurative significance of thinking in terms of the 'contemporary', but can also help us to see the place of the 'contemporary' in the legal discourses surrounding decolonisation. My interest, then, is to think through the idea that the 'contemporary', as an experiential condition, carries with it two discrete connotations: that of living 'with time' (*con tempus*), and of living 'at the same time as others' (*contemporaneus*). Although these characteristics emerged as part of a particular European historical formation in late eighteenth century, they became a theoretical problematic in the middle of the twentieth century when scholars of the 'Third World' sought to ground the terms of their engagement with international law, and to account for its relationship to a specifically colonial past.

Put simply, my argument is as follows. The 1950s and '60s was a time in which mainstream, orthodox (for which read European/Northern) international legal thought and practice was largely forward-looking: directed towards building a new global order configured around the institutions of the United Nations and its specialized agencies, forging, in Jenks' language, a new 'common law' for humankind. At the same time, an emergent generation of scholars from Asia and Africa were actively engaged in (re)describing the discipline's past – renarrating the history of international law so as to relocate the Third World within it.[5] Central to that 'heterodox' historical practice, I argue, was the problem of the contemporary – or, more specifically, the apparent 'non-contemporary contemporaneity' of the non-European

3 See Zygmunt Baumann, *Retrotopia* (Cambridge: Polity Press, 2017); Enzo Traverso, *Left Wing Melancholia: Marxism, History, and Memory* (New York: Columbia University Press, 2016), 1–21; Berber Bevernage, *History, Memory, and State-Sponsored Violence: Time and Justice* (New York: Routledge, 2012); John Torpey, *Making Whole What Has Been Smashed: On Reparations Politics* (Cambridge, MA: Harvard University Press, 2006).

4 Hannah Arendt, *Between Past and Future: Eight Exercises in Political Thought* (New York: Penguin Books, 2006).

5 A very selective array of this scholarship includes: J. J. G. Syatauw, *Some Newly Established Asian States and the Development of International* Law (The Hague: Martinus Nijhoff, 1961); Nagendra Singh, *India and International Law* (New Delhi: S. Chand, 1969); Ram Prakash Anand, *New States and International Law* (New Delhi: Vikas Publishing House, 1972); Ram Prakash Anand, ed., *Asian States in the Development of Universal International Law* (New Delhi: Vikas Publishing House, 1972); S. Prakash Sinha, *New Nations and the Law of* Nations (Leiden: A. W. Sijthoff, 1967); T. O. Elias, *Africa and the Development of International Law* (Dordrecht: Martinus Nijhoff, 1988); U. Oji Umozurike, *International Law and Colonialism in Africa* (Enugu: Nwamife Publishers, 1979).

world.[6] This 'allochronic' experience – a sense that even if we live *at* the same time we may not all live *in* the same time – was central to the analytics of savagery and civilisation that underpinned colonial legalities in the nineteenth century. It also, however, became a central pre-occupation for Third World scholars writing about international law in the era of decolonisation. The question I want to sneak up on is how we might understand that allochronic sensibility today in light of what David Scott calls 'the collapse and seeming dead-end of the projects of political sovereignty and anti-imperialist self-determination'.[7]

CH Alexandrowicz and universal international law

I want to take as my unlikely starting point on this journey the work of an equally unlikely, but nonetheless influential figure, in the heterodox tradition I seek to describe, namely, Charles Henry Alexandrowicz.[8] Alexandrowicz may be something of an odd choice here as a representative of what I otherwise speak of as an Asian and African tradition, but my reasons for looking at his work (or at least pieces of it) are twofold. In the first place his work was a key resource for later authors in the tradition, often being the primary point of reference for subsequent analyses of European-Asian legal relations in the seventeenth and eighteenth centuries.[9] In the second place, Alexandrowicz's analysis may usefully be contrasted with that of later authors so as to allow us to understand the configurative significance of the 'contemporary'.

Alexandrowicz was to become best known for a series of major works written in the 1950s and 1960s[10] on the history of international law and what he called the 'Afro-Asian world'.[11]

6 Reinhart Koselleck, *The Practice of Conceptual History: Timing History, Spacing Concepts*, trans. Todd Samuel Presner and Others (Stanford, CA: Stanford University Press, 2002), 166, where he speaks of 'the nonsimultaneity of diverse but, in a chronological sense, simultaneous histories' that resulted from the 'opening up of the world'. Koselleck's formulation appears to be borrowed from W. Pinder, *Das Problem der Generationen in der Kunstgeschichte Europas* (Munich: Bruckmann, 1961, first published 1926), 21; Ernst Bloch, *Heritage of our Times*, trans. Neville Plaice and Stephen Plaice (Cambridge: Polity Press, 1991, first published 1935) who speaks of the 'simultaneity of the nonsimultaneous' and the 'synchronicity of the nonsynchronous'.

7 David Scott, "The Temporality of Generations: Dialogue, Tradition, Criticism," *New Literary History* 45, no. 2 (Spring 2014): 158.

8 See generally, David Armitage and Jennifer Potts, '"This Modern Grotius' An Introduction to the Life and Thought of C.H. Alexandrowicz," in David Armitage and Jennifer Potts (eds), *The Law of Nations in Global History* (Oxford: Oxford University Press, 2017), 1; Carl Landauer, "The Polish Rider: CH Alexandrowicz and the Reorientation of International Law, Part I: Madras Studies," *London Review of International Law* 7 (2019): 321.

9 Armitage and Potts, "This Modern Grotius," 3.

10 For an account of his life and work see Ibid., 3–15. Alexandrowicz's earlier work at the University of Madras includes: "India and the Tibetan Tragedy," *Foreign Affairs* 31, no. 2 (1953): 495–500; "The Quasi-Judicial Function in Recognition of States and Governments," *American Journal of International Law* 46, no. 4 (1952): 631–40; *International Economic Organisations* (New York: Frederick A. Praeger, 1953); "Is India a Federation?" *International and Comparative Law Quarterly* 3, no. 3 (1954): 393–403; "The Legal Position of Tibet," *American Journal of International Law* 48, no. 2 (1954): 265–74; "Grotius and India," *Indian Year Book of International Affairs* 3 (1954): 357–67; "Mogul Sovereignty and the Law of Nations," *Indian Year Book of International Affairs* 4 (1955) 316–24; *Constitutional Development in India* (Bombay: Oxford University Press, 1957).

11 Charles Henry Alexandrowicz, *Treaty and Diplomatic Relations Between European and South Asian Powers in the Seventeenth and Eighteenth Centuries* (Leiden: A. W. Sijthoff, 1961); *An Introduction to the History of the Law of Nations in the East Indies: (16th, 17th and 18th Centuries)* (Oxford: Clarendon Press, 1967); *The Afro-Asian World and the Law of Nations* (Leiden: A. W. Sijthoff, 1968); *Studies in the History of the Law of Nations* (The Hague: Martinus Nijhoff, 1972); *The European-African Confrontation: A Study in Treaty Making* (Leiden: A. W. Sijthoff, 1973). See also, Charles Henry Alexandrowicz, "The Discriminatory Clause in South East Asian Treaties in Seventeenth

But it is in a formative article written in the British Yearbook of International Law in 1961 that he sets out the central framework for his subsequent work – namely, a thoroughgoing critique of what he saw to be traditional, 'positivist', accounts of international law that had been generated during the course of the nineteenth century. The article was titled, perchance to obscure its own radical agenda, 'Doctrinal Aspects of the Universality of the Law of Nations'.[12]

Alexandrowicz begins the article somewhat obscurely by speaking of the 'process of European consolidation' that had been gathering momentum since 1945, and how that process had its apparent origins in the work of 'positivist' writers of the eighteenth century who had identified the existence of a European law of nations based on treaties and custom. He proceeds, however, to note that this 'regional conception' was juxtaposed against, and conflicted with, an earlier 'universal and natural conception of the law of nations', giving rise to the question of 'whether the positivist European reality was reconcilable with the idea of universalism of the law of nations which drew its legal source from the declining concept of natural law but had a reality of its own'.[13]

To answer that question, Alexandrowicz turns back to the work of a little-known author – DHL Ompteda – who had written a survey of writers and treatises on the natural and positive law of nations in Regensburg in 1785.[14] Ompteda, as Alexandrowicz was to suggest, had sought to reconcile the two fields of thought – defending the universalist natural law tradition against the particularising influence of a voluntarist account of the law of nations that, in the hands of those such as Moser,[15] had apparently shrunk its spatial parameters to Europe alone. This shift from the universal to the particular, and from natural law to positive law, Alexandrowicz perceived to be both perplexing and problematic in equal measure: how was it, at a time at which the world was experiencing an expansion of world commercial relations, 'the positive law of nations was shrunk to the European area'?[16] Was this not to create a legal vacuum? How, furthermore, might one conceive of the continuity of the law of nations when faced with the postulated break between tradition and modernity?

For Alexandrowicz, following in the steps of Ompteda, the answer was not so much a thoroughgoing critique of positivism *per se* – although, at the time at which he was writing, that was a sentiment widely shared[17] – but an attempt to combine the natural and positivist law traditions by displacing a variant of the latter which he was to refer to as 'doctrinal positivism'.[18] His point, in essence, was that the nineteenth-century jurists who had taken their cue from the

and Eighteenth Centuries," *Indian Yearbook of International Affairs* 6 (1957): 126–42; "Freitas Versus Grotius," *British Yearbook of International Law* 35 (1959): 162–82; "Paulus Vladimiri and the Development of the Doctrine of Coexistence of Christian and Non-Christian Countries," *British Yearbook of International Law* 39 (1963): 441–48; "Kautilyan Principles and the Law of Nations," *British Yearbook of International Law* 41 (1965–66): 301–20; "Pufendorf-Crull and the Afro-Asian World," *British Yearbook of International Law* 43 (1968–9): 205–8; *The Law Making Functions of the Specialised Agencies of the United Nations* (Sydney: Angus and Robertson, 1973).

12 Charles Henry Alexandrowicz, "Doctrinal Aspects of the Universality of the Law of Nations," *British Yearbook of International Law* 37 (1961): 506–15.

13 Ibid., 506.

14 Dietrich Heinrich Ludwig von Ompteda, *Literatur des gesamtennatürlichen und positive Völkerrechts* (Aalen: Scientia Verlag, 1785).

15 F. C. von Moser, *Beyträge zu dem Staats und Völker-Recht und der Geschichte* (Frankfurt: J. C. Gebhard, 1764).

16 Alexandrowicz, "Doctrinal Aspects," 515.

17 See David Kennedy, "International Law and the Nineteenth Century: History of an Illusion," *Quinnipiac Law Review* 17, no. 1 (Spring 1997): 120.

18 See Charles Henry Alexandrowicz, "Empirical and Doctrinal Positivism in International Law," *British Yearbook of International Law* 47 (1974–5): 286–89.

likes of Moser and de Martens in describing international law as being, in its essence, European, had failed to take account of the empirical realities of the many, and varied, treaties and other arrangements that had been concluded between European powers and non-European sovereigns (Siam, China, Japan, India and the Ottoman Empire) over the course of earlier centuries.[19] They were, in a sense, not 'positive' enough in their method, supplanting a properly empirical account of the workings of international law, with an ideologically laden doctrine that operated on the back of an implicit distinction (which he attributes to Ranke) between those who had history and those who did not.[20] In the process, they were to compound error upon error – speaking, as a consequence, of the apparent 'admission' of Turkey to the European concert in 1856, of the subsequent 'enlargement' of the family of nations beyond Europe, and putting into practice a technology of 'recognition' as a process by which states are fictitiously endowed *de novo* with legal capacity. The family of nations could not, he suggests, 'have been reduced from universality to a regional framework' purely by means of 'a change of doctrine',[21] and to argue as much was effectively to either lapse into anachronism, or create a legal vacuum where none, in reality, existed.

As Anghie has subsequently observed, for all of his desire to recuperate the history of the non-European world within the discourse of international law, Alexandrowicz was nevertheless forced into the position of regarding the practice of colonialism itself as either essentially marginal to the formation of the discipline, or perhaps entirely extraneous to the proper articulation or understanding of the rules of international law.[22] Thus, in one direction, Alexandrowicz had to distance himself from the received tenets of nineteenth-century practice. The purported 'admission' of Turkey to the family of nations in 1856 was, in his view, 'meaningless', just as it was to suggest, as Oppenheim had done, that Persia, Siam and China were admitted at a later date than Haiti or Liberia. The 'expansion thesis' later popularised by Bull and Watson,[23] in other words, was simply wrong. In another direction, Alexandrowicz was also forced to immunise the operations of 'proper' international law from any responsibility for the establishment of colonial rule in the nineteenth century – which he did through the medium of associating imperial expansion with its violation.[24] For, if international law was universal and not merely European, its facilitation of the partition of the non-European world would have been unthinkable. Thus, on his account, African partition at the time of the Berlin Conference of 1884–1885 was not conditioned by the language of international law (*terra nullius*, occupation etc.), but rather occurred as a consequence of the violation of the various treaties of protection that had been signed with native agencies.[25]

19 See also Alexandrowicz, "Freitas Versus Grotius," 166–67; "Kautilyan Principles," 301–2.

20 Alexandrowicz, "Empirical and Doctrinal Positivism," 289: 'positivism, in its endeavor to be empirical and in its determination to do away with doctrinal international law (based on the law of nature and nations) became itself doctrinal, adopting as much of the factual historical material as it wished to, and rejecting the remainder.'

21 Alexandrowicz, "Doctrinal Aspects," 515.

22 Antony Anghie, *Imperialism, Sovereignty and the Making of International Law* (Cambridge: Cambridge University Press, 2004), 36.

23 Hedley Bull and Adam Watson, eds., *The Expansion of International Society* (New York: Oxford University Press, 1984). For earlier versions see B. V. A. Röling, *International Law in an Expanded World* (Amsterdam: Djambatan N. V., 1960); J. L. Brierly, *The Law of Nations*, 6th ed. (Oxford: Clarendon Press, 1963); Josef Laurenz Kunz, *The Changing Law of Nations* (Columbus: Ohio State University Press, 1968).

24 As Armitage and Potts point out, Alexandrowicz took the view that the exclusion of Asian states from the family of nations 'was illegitimate in legal as well as moral terms, because the Europeans did not possess the legal capacity unilaterally to expel states whose legal status they had once recognized in theory and in practice': Armitage and Potts, "This Modern Grotius," 18.

25 Alexandrowicz, "The European-African Confrontation," 117, 127, in which he describes the process of the consolidation of European titles in Africa as one in which '[i]nternational law disappears from the scene' and in which African rulers were to 'forfeit one by one the benefits and advantages stipulated . . . in treaties'.

Anand's *New States*

If Alexandrowicz's critique was to be influential in the development of the heterodox Third World historiographical tradition, it was not because the latter scholars all shared his analysis. Some certainly worked in the same analytical register, and sought, like Alexandrowicz,[26] to (re)discover and elaborate upon the lost traditions – detailing the regional Asian or African systems of international law that pre-existed colonial rule and interacted with it.[27] For others, however, Alexandrowicz's dismissal of nineteenth-century positivism as simply an erroneous ideology could not be sustained. For them, a critique of the ideology of nineteenth-century colonial international law was to be overcome not by insisting upon its 'unreality' but by admitting its historical purchase, and then positing the existence of a fundamental break between the 'colonial' and 'modern' eras brought about by the struggle for Third World sovereignty.[28] Where these latter responses parted company with Alexandrowicz was, as we shall see, on the question of how to account for the (apparent) universality of international law in the mid-twentieth century, and how to engage the received vestiges of the colonial (legal) inheritance.

A useful contrast here is found in the work of another, somewhat younger, scholar similarly working in the Indian sub-continent – Ram Prakash Anand. Anand, whilst clearly appreciative of Alexandrowicz's work, was somewhat less concerned with writing about history in the way in which Alexandrowicz had essayed, than attempting to grapple with what he saw to be the contemporary problematics of 'newness'. For him the problem was how international law might be developed or changed to take into account the interests of the newly independent states in Asia and Africa. There was a range of questions here, which included, for Anand, the conditions of international adjudication,[29] law of the sea[30] and sovereign equality.[31] But in order to engage with any of these, Anand recognised that he had, first of all, to account for history.

His approach to the question of history was outlined most clearly in *New States and International Law*, written in 1972. In that work, Anand begins with the observation that 'traditional international law' was largely a law 'developed among the Western European countries'.[32] 'Even a cursory look at the history of international law', he suggests, 'leaves no doubt about the Eurocentric nature of the law developed by and for the benefit of the rich, industrial, and

26 See especially, Alexandrowicz, "Kautilyan Principles."

27 See, for example, Syatauw, *Some Newly Established Asian States*; Elias, *Africa and the Development of International Law*. For a much earlier account of this kind see Pramathanath Bandyopadhyaya, *International Law and Custom in Ancient India* (Calcutta: Calcutta University Press, 1920). See generally Arnulf Becker-Lorca, *Mestizo International Law: A Global Intellectual History 1842–1933* (Cambridge: Cambridge University Press, 2015).

28 See, for example, Georges Abi Saab, "The Newly Independent States and the Rules of International Law: An Outline," *Howard Law Journal* 8, no. 2 (Spring 1962): 97–121; Mohammed Bedjaoui, *Towards a New International Economic Order* (Paris: United Nations Educational, Scientific and Cultural Organisation, 1979), 11.

29 See, for example, Ram Prakash Anand, *Compulsory Jurisdiction of the International Court of Justice* (London: Asia Publishing House, 1961); *Studies in International Adjudication* (New Dehli: Vikas Publications, 1969); *International Courts and Contemporary Conflicts* (New York: Asia Publishing House, 1974).

30 Ram Prakash Anand, *Legal Regime of the Sea-Bed and the Developing Countries* (New Delhi: Thomson Press, 1975); *Origin and Development of the Law of the Sea, History of International Law Revisited* (The Hague: Martinus Nijhoff, 1983); ed., *Law of the Sea: Caracas and Beyond* (New Delhi: Radiant Publishers, 1978).

31 Ram Prakash Anand, *Sovereign Equality of States and International Law* (New Delhi: Hope India Publications, 2008).

32 Anand, *New States,* 6.

powerful states of Western Europe.'[33] 'In the escort of the capital that travelled from Europe', he explained, 'went the European business practices, European civilisation, and European law.'[34] Yet, at the same time, he observes that the 'sudden expansion of the international society has upset the whole equilibrium'.[35] The alteration of what he identified as the 'sociological structure' of international society had to be accompanied by an alteration in its law. 'Law', he affirmed, 'is not a constant in society, but is a function' and hence 'ought to change with changes in views, powers and interests in the community'.[36] It was on the grounds of the functional needs of this new international society, in other words, that a universal international law could and should be built.

Whilst both Alexandrowicz and Anand thus shared a common starting point – how to reconcile their commitment to international law with an understanding of the exclusionary practices of the nineteenth-century tradition – their answers to it were radically different. For Alexandrowicz it was a question reaching back to the universal aspirations of the natural law tradition and subjecting, at the same time, nineteenth-century 'doctrinal' positivism to a form of immanent critique ('real' international law, in its empirical variety, was always universal). For Anand it was a question of affirming the Eurocentric origins of 'traditional' international law, but advocating its subversion by reference to a functionalist analytics that demanded law to be adjusted so as to bring it into line with the demands of the prevailing political or social order. 'We are', as he put it, 'entering upon a new age in the history of man, an age which has no precedent in human experience.'[37]

The stakes of history

The difference between these two standpoints was, as both were no doubt aware, of considerable significance at the time. Throughout the period of decolonisation, what were referred to as the 'new states' all had to negotiate the conditions of their formal 'entry' into international society, and the extent of their freedom in respect of inherited legal arrangements – whether that be colonial borders, concession agreements, public debts or treaties governing the presence of foreign military bases.[38] They were also concerned about the constraints imposed by the rules of state responsibility governing foreign investment and the associated practice of diplomatic protection,[39] and about the conditions under which unequal treaties might be challenged.[40] They were similarly aware of the way in which 'the same body of international law that they are now asked to abide by, sanctioned their previous subjugation and exploitation and stood as a bar to their emancipation'.[41]

33 Ibid., 45.
34 Ibid.
35 Ibid., 46.
36 Ibid.
37 Ibid., 2.
38 See generally Matthew Craven, *The Decolonisation of International Law: State Succession and the Law of Treaties* (Oxford: Oxford University Press, 2007); Okon Udokang, *Succession of New States to International Treaties* (Dobbs Ferry: Oceana Publications, 1972); Yilma Makonnen, *International Law and the New States of Africa* (New York: United Nations Educational, Scientific and Cultural Organisation, 1983).
39 See, for example, A. A. Fatouros, "International Law and the Third World," *Virginia Law Review* 50, no. 5 (June 1964): 783–823.
40 See, for example, Lung-Fong Chen, *State Succession Relating to Unequal Treaties* (Hamden: Archon Books, 1974).
41 Abi Saab, "The Newly Independent States," 100.

The routine response from the imperial Metropole on many such questions was to insist, not only that the field of established customary international law was non-negotiable,[42] but that legal continuity was a priority – insisting, for example, upon the permanence of territorial arrangements, the protection of vested or acquired rights, the localisation of debt and the internationally protected character of concession agreements.[43] By contrast, the response from scholars in the Third World was frequently to insist upon the radical character of the legal change effected by decolonisation and the need for 'new states' to re-evaluate the legal relations that appear to impinge upon the terms of their independence. Bedjaoui, for example, argued that such states were presented with a double mission: on the one hand, to establish their sovereignty and political independence; on the other, to seek to eliminate the political and economic relations of domination and exploitation that had been put in place during colonial rule. Sovereign equality demanded that the new state be free to exercise its sovereignty without being burdened by the obligations of the predecessor, and, as such, there were no

> inviolable acquired rights which can be enforced against the new sovereignty state, but only pre-existing situations which that state is prepared to take into consideration for its good reasons and not for any reason imposed upon it by some unidentified rule of international law and state succession.[44]

At this point, it is possible to discern the critical edge to the historical revisionism practiced by Alexandrowicz and Anand. Alexandrowicz's position, ironically enough, was one that would very much align with that of the imperial Metropole – legal continuity would be a basic condition underpinned by the 'discovery' that international law was already universal. The excision of colonial rule from the story of international law's history was to suggest that there was nothing to be reformed, no necessity of radical change in its local or universal content.[45] Only aberrant 'doctrine' could be impugned (and that went as much, one would suppose, to the 'doctrine' of unequal treaties as that of *terra nullius*). Anand's position, by contrast, was one in which the provincialisation of the tradition opened up a space for new states to gain for themselves a greater freedom of action in respect of the future organisation of their political or economic affairs. For Anand, thus, the narration of history went hand in hand with a desire to free the Third World from the burdens of colonialism,[46] a desire, perhaps, to overcome the infantilising condition of 'newness'.

42 See, for example, Lassa Francis Lawrence Oppenheim, *International Law: A Treatise*, 1st ed. (London: Longmans, Green, 1905), 17–18: 'No single State can say on its admittance into the Family of Nations that it desires to be subjected to such and such a rule of International Law, and not to others. The admittance includes the duty to submit to all the existing rules.' D. P. O'Connell, "Independence and Problems of State Succession," in *The New Nations in International Law and Diplomacy*, ed. William V. O'Brien (New York and Washington: Frederick A. Praeger, 1965), 12: 'it is necessary to point out that a new state is born into a world of law . . . in asserting the faculties of statehood, the new state is accepting the structure and the system of Western International law. . . . [I]t may not . . . pick and choose.'

43 See, for example, O'Connell D. P., *The Law of State Succession* (Cambridge: Cambridge University Press, 1956).

44 Mohammed Bedjaoui, *Second Report on Succession in Respect of Matters Other Than Treaties, Economic and Financial Acquired Rights and State Succession*, UN Doc. A/CN.4/216 (1969), 78, para 35.

45 Charles Henry Alexandrowicz, "New and Original States: The Issue of Reversion to Sovereignty," *International Affairs* 45 (1969): 474–75, where he notes that in case of a 'reversion to sovereignty' – such as that of Ceylon – that 'does not affect the acts of the colonial Power resulting from the legitimate exercise of its rights of sovereignty in the intervening period'.

46 Anand, *New States*, 53–60. He quotes in that context Bedjaoui's remark that the payment of compensation for property and rights acquired during colonial rule 'would almost be tantamount to repurchasing the whole country'. Bedjaoui, *Second Report*, 68.

That the same question or problem might have offered such different responses is clearly, in some respects, a function of a different understanding of how to respond to it, and what role might be assumed by international law in the process. Alexandrowicz was responding, at a very basic level, to the Eurocentrism of the received tradition by way of a straightforward denial; Anand, by a concern that denial alone was not enough, and that what was needed was struggle. Alexandrowicz was similarly concerned with conceptualising international law as being aligned with timeless principles of universal justice against which was to be counterpoised a politics of parochial interest – whereas Anand, like Bedjaoui, was inclined to think of it as a domain of social and political action. For all these differences, my suggestion is that underlying them was a more fundamental difference between Alexandrowicz and Anand. This had to do with how they conceptualised the problem itself: whereas for Alexandrowicz it appeared to be a problem associated with the putative universality of international law, for Anand it was a problem of time or, more specifically, of contemporaneity.

The problem space of history

To explain the underlying conditions of the difference, it is helpful to turn back to the subject of Alexandrowicz's article – Dietrich Heinrich Ludwig von Ompteda. As Alexandrowicz read him, Ompteda's history merely represented an attempt to reconcile an enduring dualism within the literature of the law of nations that sought to organise the relationship between principles of natural law, on the one hand, and the *jus voluntarium*, on the other.[47] In some instances, as he was to discover, the voluntary law was thought to sit alongside natural law, and in other instances, embraced within. But what was of more significance was the fact that Ompteda sought to review the literature *as history*, and in so doing marked a decisive change in orientation, not only in respect of the aesthetics by which the law of nations would come to be represented (i.e., historically), or indeed in terms of its method of law-finding (i.e., empirical/rational), but its temporal and spatial organisation.

The historical consciousness that marks out the emergent practice of international legal history from the 1780s onwards was largely configured around one principle idea – that all law would have a time and place of production, and that claims to legal authority would thereby be conditioned by the social, cultural or environmental milieu in which they were forged.[48] Not only would this direct attention to concrete historical practices as a ground of law and require the organisation of sources by reference to their temporal proximity to the present, but it would also problematise precisely that which Alexandrowicz sought to overcome: for the *place* of Moser's, de Martens or Ompteda's law of nations could not be the world on that account, but only some segment of it. And that segment for them, of course, was to be found in the emergence of Europe as a geographical domain. Thus, from the late eighteenth century, the law of nations would, in various quarters, acquire a new designation – that of the public law of Europe[49] – and would acquire at the same time a history appropriate to that formation, the origins of which would be traced from this time onwards back to Westphalia or perhaps to Rome.

47 Alexandrowicz, "Doctrinal Aspects," 507.

48 See generally, Matthew Craven, "Theorising the Turn to History in International Law," in *The Oxford Handbook of the Theory of International Law*, eds. Anne Orford and Florian Hoffman (Oxford: Oxford University Press, 2016), 21–37.

49 A. G. Heffter, *Le droit international publique de l'Europe* (Paris: Cotillon, 1857); G. de, Martens, *Précis du droit des gens modern de l'Europe*, 2nd ed. (Paris: Guillaumin et Cie, 1864); Johann Ludwig Klüber, *Europäisches Völkerrecht* (Schaffhausen: Hurter, 1851).

If the discovery of a history proper to the European law of nations, however, was to rest upon a chronology that demarcated the past from the future, it was a chronology that not only opened out the space of the present, but also gave meaning to the 'contemporary'. To live 'with time' was to live in a world in which, as Koselleck put it, the past was a space of experience that bore upon the present and the future a horizon of expectation that offered out the possibility of unrepeatable newness.[50] If the field of experience of a contemporary international law was Europe, however, then the non-European world could only exist in a condition of non-contemporary contemporaneity. It shared, in that sense, the 'natural' geological time of the modern world, but in 'human time' could only be identified as subsisting in Europe's pre-modern past. The formation of the disciplinary knowledge of what was to become known as 'international law' was thus cut through by a simultaneous process of spatial disaggregation (as seemed appropriate to the human sciences), and a temporal re-integration mediated ultimately by the language of progress, evolution and civilisation. The subsequent 'expansion' of international law was thus to take place hand in hand with the universalisation of what Mannheim called a 'mechanistic, externalised concept of time'[51] – facilitated, amongst other things, by the export of Western technologies of time-keeping ('denaturalising', as Koselleck puts it, the experience of time),[52] the establishment of the prime meridian and the 24 hour day in 1884, and the later adoption of a singular chronometric measure in the form of UTC (Universal Time, Coordinated).[53] Time, thus, was not just the meter by which experience in the world might be brought together, but a homogenising technology that itself needed to be universalised as part of that same process.

If the practice of history set the spatial and temporal conditions for the workings of international law in the nineteenth century – providing, in the process, a frame of reference for colonial expansion throughout that period – it also regulated its content. For the task of the international legal historian was not just to recount the past, but rather to recount the past of international law as a distinct disciplinary formation to be contrasted with other forms of history – whether that be diplomatic history, political history, economic history or social and cultural history. Each had their own story and their own moment of origins. However – and here was the real problem – the analytic by which one could interpret or describe the past of international law was one that could only be revealed historically. One needed to go back to locate the origins, or foundational moments, of international law in order to understand the discipline as an identifiable field of knowledge and practice. It was its origins that described its character – setting out its exact essence, or immobile form, as it moved through time. But the question left open here is whether the *res gestae* of that historiographical practice was to be the literary tradition outlined by Ompteda, or the tradition of diplomatic intercourse preferred by Moser? Was it disclosed in the writings of Grotius, or in the annals of treaty-making? Was it evidence of spirit or of experience? An ethics of diplomacy or a field of argument? The universe of reason and experience that had hitherto been held together in the natural law tradition was thus to be exploded by an historical knowledge that demanded that it locate its disciplinary identity somewhere, in some time and in some thing, but without a means to determine how that location might be found.

50 Reinhart Koselleck, *Futures Past: On the Semantics of Historical Time*, trans. Keith Tribe (New York: Columbia University Press, 2004), 241.

51 Karl Mannheim, "The Problem of Generations," in *Karl Mannheim: Essays*, ed. Paul Kecskemeti (London: Routledge, 1952), 281.

52 Koselleck, *The Practice of Conceptual History*, 104.

53 See generally Vanessa Ogle, *The Global Transformation of Time: 1870–1950* (Cambridge, MA: Harvard University Press, 2015).

The problematics of heterodox historiography: space and time

The heterodox international legal historiography of the 1950s and 1960s was by no means concerned with discarding all elements of this received historical formation.[54] Indeed, to the extent that it was still concerned with articulating accounts of the past of international law understood as a unitary phenomenon or practice (as opposed to a plurality of practices and traditions),[55] it necessarily situated itself within that tradition. Alexandrowicz's work, for example, had much in common with Lauterpacht's account of the Grotian tradition,[56] and in Anand's case, considerable reliance was placed upon the sociology of Stone[57] and Friedman[58] and upon Yale school analytics.[59] It was, as I have already suggested, the particular problem that they sought to address that delineated the heterodox tradition from mainstream, orthodox legal historiography. And this itself did not require the formation of an entirely new method for understanding the temporal or spatial organisation of the discipline. That being said, within the same general framework of inquiry, one may identify in the work of Alexandrowicz and Anand two different methodological challenges with which they sought to grapple – one being the problem of universality, the other the problem of contemporaneity.

For Alexandrowicz, as we have seen, the problem that he identified was essentially that of the universality of international law, a universality that was sustained in practice but denied in doctrine. And hence his task was the historical one of rectifying that account: bringing history back to those whose history was occluded; handing back the law, so to speak, to those from whom it had been taken. In method, however, as Onuma has observed, Alexandrowicz began with the tradition he sought to critique. Whilst he claimed to overcome Eurocentrism, 'he was fundamentally concerned with how Europeans perceived and understood the world, and not otherwise'.[60] He failed to see, in the process, 'how the treaty practice was perceived, understood and explained by Asians or Africans during those periods'.[61] Indeed one may take this further: in taking treaties and diplomatic practice as his *res gestae*, Alexandrowicz was, in method at least, to adopt much of the positivist tradition that he sought to critique. If the empirical field with which Moser engaged was unaccountably narrow when compared to the universal formations that were the subject of Ompteda's analysis, it was to Moser that Alexandrowicz looked for the method by which he would evidence what he saw to be missing. What Alexandrowicz did not appear to recognise was that the empirical, positivist methodology that he deployed was one possessed of specific content and frequently freighted with the doctrine he sought to dismiss.

54 Anand, *New States*, 52.

55 See Yasuaki Ōnuma, "When Was the Law of International Society Born? An Inquiry of the History of International Law from an Intercivilizational Perspective," *Journal of the History of International Law* 2, no. 1 (2000): 62.

56 See Hirsch Lauterpacht, "The Grotian Tradition in International Law," *British Yearbook of International Law* 23 (1946): 1–53.

57 Julius Stone, *The Province and Function of Law, Law as Logic, Justice and Social Control: A Study in Jurisprudence* (Sydney: Associated General Publications, 1946).

58 Wolfgang Friedmann, "National Sovereignty, International Cooperation, and the Reality of International Law," *University of California Los Angeles Law Review* 10 (May 1963): 739–53; "Half a Century of International Law," *Virginia Law Review* 50, no. 8 (December 1964): 1334.

59 Myres McDougal, "International Law, Power and Policy: A Contemporary Conception," *Hague Recueil des Cours* 82 (1953): 156; Myres McDougal and Associates, *Studies in World Public Order* (New Haven: Yale University Press, 1960).

60 Onuma, "When Was the Law of International Society Born?" 61.

61 Ibid. Cf, however, Anand's disagreement with Onuma on this point: Ram Prakash Anand, "Onuma Yasuaki's 'When Was the Law of International Society Born? – An Inquiry of the History of International Law from an Intercivilizational Perspective' JHIL, Vol. 2 (2000) 1–66," *Journal of the History of International Law* 6 (2004): 7–9.

If for Alexandrowicz the problem was how to shore-up the universality of international law (believing, perhaps, that it was imminently endangered), then for Anand, the problem was not a spatial one at all,[62] but a temporal one – one concerned with the challenge of living contemporaneously. In speaking of the predominant agenda of the 'new states' Anand speaks first of their 'obsession' with 'development'. The principal concern of such states, he suggests, was 'the economic continuation of the political struggle for independence, as an important means of creating a new national identity or of breaking old and restrictive ties'.[63] Despite the achievement of political independence, however, the gulf between rich and poor countries had been widening, not narrowing: 'the economic development of the Western industrialized countries . . . has been proceeding faster and more steadily than it ever did . . . [whilst] developing countries are not developing fast enough.'[64] Anand's immediate experience was one of a two-track world moving according to different temporal rhythms. It was also, and paradoxically, a world undergoing a spatial contraction as a consequence of innovations in travel and communication. The temporal conjuncture of his time was thus one marked by two simultaneous processes: on the one hand, an experience of acceleration and shrinkage as a consequence of technological innovation, travel and communications; and, on the other, a spatial differentiation in which the asymmetrical horizons of expectation and experience were weighted differently in different parts of the world. The non-European world appeared bogged down in history, whilst the European world accelerated into the future: 'the richer you are the faster you grow', as Anand was to put it.[65]

The time of decolonisation

There is, evidently enough, the remainder of a nineteenth-century historicist account of progress in Anand's argument here – no longer articulated, for obvious reasons, in the culturally laden terms of savagery and civilisation, but rather in terms of a political-economy of development, industrialisation and capital accumulation. Modernisation and development thus appeared to provide the substantive content, as Fabian observes, for the same global chronology that structured colonial thought in the nineteenth century in which the present of the West was to be the future of the rest ('evolutionary Time').[66] Even if, for Anand, his concern in highlighting the allochronic condition of the developing world was largely for critical rather than descriptive purposes, his work may still be contrasted with the more radical, 'untimely' interventions of those such as Caisaire and Senghor who resisted a straightforward conflation of decolonisation with national self-determination, and sought the articulation of alternative postcolonial futures to be brought within the political imagination.[67]

But there is a good deal more to the complex temporalities that Anand brings into play here than mere deference to the unilinear timeframe of modernity. Indeed one might say that

62 Abi Saab had already made the observation that decolonisation did not involve the 'expansion' of international law so much as the 'transformation of very large parts of the globe, mostly in Africa and Asia, from objects to subjects of international law', Abi Saab, "The Newly Independent States," 98.

63 Anand, *New States,* 86.

64 Ibid., 87.

65 Ibid.

66 Johannes Fabian, *Time and the Other: How Anthropology Makes its Object* (New York: Columbia University Press, 1983), 17.

67 See Gary Wilder, *Freedom Time: Negritude, Decolonization, and the Future of the World* (Durham, NC: Duke University Press, 2015).

his book *New States* is infused with a radically different conception of time than that which structures Fabian's critique. In the first place, the temporal calculus in operation in Anand's account was not so much an external linear temporality by which the world could be represented in terms of a sequence of instances in chronometric succession, but rather an experiential temporality – a kind of 'lived time' as Mannheim put it[68] – that placed emphasis upon the historical forces and contradictions that had shaped, and continue to shape, consciousness of social and political life. The allochronic experience of the developing world, for Anand, had thus more to do with the legacies of imperialism – the residues of practices of subjugation and exploitation – than any promise as to what the future might hold. Indeed, just as the past was hard to shake off, the future was as much a place of danger as of respite: only by reversing 'the present trends', he cautioned, would the dangerous frustrations of the developing world be fended off;[69] and only by focusing hard upon the 'problems of the present' might the world escape the imminent threat of 'endemic chaos, and the prospect of annihilation'.[70]

In the second place, the temporality of Anand's account was also far more complex, evoking a plurality of 'layers of time' or 'hybrid rhythms' that, as Buck-Morss was to observe, typically constituted the 'complex force field' of social revolution.[71] For even the objects of his title – the 'New States' – were to carry with them a dual temporality that threatened to collapse the divide between past and present. They were, at once, 'new' in the sense that they had recently acquired the 'attributes of national sovereignty' that enabled them to enjoy the full privileges of membership in the family of nations, but also 'ancient' in the sense that many 'existed long before the so-called "older" states of Europe or America were ever founded'.[72] And so far as such states were both new and old, both emerging afresh from the experience of colonial rule, yet possessing themselves a rich legal heritage,[73] so also did that condition their approach to 'traditional' international law – broadly accepting, on the one hand, the principles of sovereignty, recognition, territorial integrity, non-aggression, non-intervention, sovereign equality, reciprocity, etc, yet demanding change in relation to those elements of that tradition that were associated with the perpetuation of colonial domination (for example state responsibility, the international minimum standard and the protection of aliens).

The problem here, as Anand perceived it, was the potentially asymmetrical temporalities of law and social/political life. International law, so far as it had been developed 'in a different age, under different circumstances', threatened to operate as a stultifying influence 'lag[ging] behind life' and producing conditions of tension and violence.[74] Whilst law undoubtedly 'mirrored' the

68 Mannheim, "The Problem of Generations," 281–82. For a discussion see Scott, "The Temporality of Generations," 162–63, in explaining Mannheim and Dilthey's conception of time here he remarks: 'We do not merely live *in* history, in the commonplace sense that we inhabit a social and political environment *conditioned* by historical forces; rather, as historical subjects our consciousness is *saturated* with time. Or, to put it another way, history is not merely an *object* of consciousness, *there* to be apprehended by a timeless subject; rather, temporality itself is the object content-of-the-form of experience' (emphasis in original).

69 Anand, *New States*, 95. He emphasises this point by quoting Tagore: '[t]he weak are as great a danger for the strong as the quicksand for the elephant. They do not assist progress because they do not resist, they only drag down,' 94.

70 Ibid., 116. He does, however, speak ultimately about the 'boundless promise of the future', but that was a future available only if 'we survive the challenge of the present'.

71 Susan Buck-Morss, *Dreamworld and Catastrophe: The Passing of Mass Utopia in East and West* (Cambridge, MA: MIT Press, 2002), 67.

72 Anand, *New States,* 3.

73 Ibid., 13.

74 Ibid., 83–84.

past, it also served to 'project the future' and had to readjust itself to the needs of a changing international society.[75] And the costs of not doing so were equally clear:

> Even a static law cannot stop the historical development in a world governed by the supreme rule of change. But this dynamic development will be brought by the violation of the static law by violent methods. If peace has to be preserved the change must be brought about by an evolution within the juridical order itself. This dynamic law should strike a balance between static rules making for security, and dynamic rules providing for the necessary change by peaceful methods in conformity with the law which is to be changed.[76]

The temporal dynamism that Anand was urging upon the law necessitated the identification of new methods and new procedures for the revision and creation of international law. Customary international law and multilateral treaty-making were, for their part, far too slow and piecemeal modes of change. Recognition had to be given to the 'law-creating role of consensus of the international community' as expressed, for example, in the form of the 'quasi-legislative' character of General Assembly resolution,[77] or in the production of 'instant customary international law'.[78] In an accelerating world, international law itself had to adapt itself to the new pace of change.

If Anand was concerned both with the complex temporalities of 'newness' and the potentially disjunctive rhythms of social and legal life, it was informed also by a sensitivity to the multiplicity of social time that had been identified and developed by members of the Annales School,[79] such as Le Goff[80] and Braudel.[81] For Braudel, history in general was to be broken down into successive levels marked by distinct temporalities: an almost changeless 'geographical time' concerned with the 'history of man in relation to his surroundings'; a 'social time' concerned with the 'history of gentle rhythms, of groups and groupings' of states, economies and societies; and, finally, an 'individual time' associated with the traditional history of events (which he described as 'surface disturbances' or 'waves stirred up by powerful movement of tides').[82] History had to be told, in his view, in a way that was attentive to the multiple temporalities of the social world – to the deep structures of the *longue durée* as well as to the 'microtime' of the event – and one can sense the same concerns animating Anand's account of the moment of decolonisation.[83]

Anand saw decolonisation as having ushered in a new age or epoch[84] – one most visibly marked by the changing social and political forces in international life. 'Never before', he

75 Ibid., 84.

76 Ibid., 83.

77 Ibid., 78–83.

78 See Bin Cheng, "United Nations Resolutions on Outer Space: 'Instant' International Customary Law," *Indian Journal of International Law* 5 (1965): 35.

79 See generally, André Burguière, *The Annales School: An Intellectual History*, trans. J. M. Todd (Ithaca: Cornell University Press, 2009).

80 Jacques Le Goff, *Time, Work and Culture in the Middle Ages,* trans. A. Goldhammer (Chicago: University of Chicago Press, 1980).

81 Fernand Braudel, *On History,* trans. S. Matthews (Chicago: University of Chicago Press, 1982).

82 Ibid., 3.

83 Koselleck notes, however, that whilst '[w]e might speak, not of one historical time, but of many that overlie one another' they nevertheless depend upon 'the measures of time that derive from the mathematical physical understanding of nature', *The Practice of Conceptual History*, 110.

84 Anand, *New States*, 2: 'We are living today through the birthpangs of this wholly new world.'

remarks, 'did man have so many resources at his disposal to transform life of all mankind in a single generation.'[85] Yet, 'never before' (he continues) 'did man have power to destroy in a few minutes all that he has inherited from the past generations'.[86] Accompanying, then, the 'generational' temporalities of the creative tasks that confronted humankind, was an apocalyptic threat whose time-scale was to be measured in the microtime of the event. The work of world-making thus assumed the rhythms of social and geographical time, but was confronted simultaneously by a scientific/military/political technology whose temporal structure took the form of the near instantaneous. And here one finds a paradoxical inversion – the stultifying slowness of the developing world was yet the site of creativity and human labour, whereas the accelerated modernity of the West was the locale of its imminent destruction.

But whilst, at this moment, Anand seemed content with suggesting that the West and the Third World were moving at different speeds, he used the same analytic to destabilise those same spatial/temporal formations. For the time of the 'new states' was itself split between fields of activity. The state itself as a juridical-political entity was to be instantaneously inaugurated – the moment of independence specifying with astonishing precision the point of time in which 'emancipation' was to occur. New states were 'born' – either through the formal relinquishing of colonial (maternal) authority, or by wrestling themselves out of its embrace – yet the moment of birth was also accompanied by an overhang in the form of continued economic domination and inequality.[87] The developing state was thus shot through, in Anand's account, with two initial disjunctive temporalities – one of which imagined the state as a political entity suddenly emerging into the world in 'homogenous empty time',[88] the other which imagined it to be a project of painstaking labour and concerted action, in which the state would be worked upon, forged and fabricated, through industrialisation and production.[89] 'Development', as he put it, 'is a long-term process.'[90] On top of this was a third, challenging form of acceleration associated with the phenomenon of rapid population growth – a 'demographic revolution', as he put it, 'the pace and dimensions of which are without precedent', which threatened to 'gobble up everything that could be saved by increased production'.[91]

One can conceive Anand's work here as being concerned with the construction of the problem-space of the 'contemporary' by way of taking what Althusser referred to as an 'essential-section'[92] – the drawing of an imaginary (vertical) line through the chronology of various fields of social, cultural, political and economic activity, and observing in the process the appearance of an historical present. Whilst Althusser was to point out that such an operation was problematic (essentially 'ideological') insofar as it relied upon an abstract chronology (clock time) that lacked explication,[93] it nevertheless allowed Anand to engage in a broader critical analysis of the relationship between different fields of endeavour. For Anand it was important to recognise the inter-dependencies not only between past and present – specifically the way in which colonial

85 Ibid.

86 Ibid.

87 Ibid., 86: 'Political independence has brought in its train a desire for freedom from foreign economic domination.'

88 Benedict Anderson, *Imagined Communities*, revised ed. (London: Verso, 2006), 22–24.

89 Anand, *New States*, 90.

90 Ibid., 105.

91 Ibid., 91.

92 Louis Althusser and Etienne Balibar, *Reading Capital*, trans. Ben Brewster (London: Verso, 2009, first published 1968), 105, 115. For a scathing critique see E. P. Thompson, *The Poverty of Theory and Other Essays* (London: Merlin, 1978), 123–38.

93 Ibid., 118.

rule had come to structure the economies of the developing world[94] – but also between the demand for economic progress and the maintenance of peace,[95] between the demographics of population growth and the accumulation of capital,[96] and between the emergent structures of international society and the substantive rules of the international legal order,[97] to name but a few. For him the interdependencies were such that concerted cooperative action was both vital and urgent:

> A world still half-hungry is an appalling fact, an intolerable truth, a shocking commentary on the human condition, and a political danger of the first order. . . . Unless the international legal order is modernized by voluntary and evolutionary procedures into a welfare system it will be "thrown aside by bloody revolution".[98]

Here, finally, was the central trope that appeared to hold together the complex temporal conjunctions in Anand's *New States*.[99] His was a time of revolution(s):[100] a time in which the steady rhythms of an orderly social world, of custom and tradition, had been disrupted and pulled apart, a time in which new political agendas were being framed, new technologies were emerging, new threats and opportunities identified, and in which the entry into history of the non-European world brought into juxtaposition, rival or incommensurable fields of experience and expectation. In that context, the complex temporalities he was to evoke in his account operated in almost metaphorical guise – being both conditioned upon, but also appearing to resist, the homogenising force of a universal temporal calculus. The 'contemporary' in that sense came to operate, less as an epistemological or ontological category, than as a speculative framework of inquiry – a way of looking at the world – that brought into view, and animated, various sites of political struggle.

Conclusion

In *Imagined Communities*, Benedict Anderson notes that one of the fundamental conditions of possibility for 'imagining the nation' in Western modernity was the emergence of a new temporal calculus. What he called 'homogenous empty time' enabled a necessarily disparate, heterogenous population to think of itself as somehow bound together, moving in synchronous manner calendrically through time. Central to that formation was the idea that people's experiences of the world could be linked together through the medium of abstract time, such that they might imagine themselves occupying the same chronological space. The idea of simultaneity, however, was one that could only ultimately be imagined, not experienced, and hence depended for its socialising effects upon the productive mediation of print capitalism.[101] Chatterjee takes this argument one stage further, suggesting that homogenous empty time was not merely an

94 Anand, *New States*, 90.
95 Ibid., 94–97.
96 Ibid., 91.
97 Ibid., 110.
98 Ibid., 115.
99 It may not be entirely irrelevant to note that the word 'revolution' or 'revolutionary' appears 36 times in the text.
100 Anand, *New States*, 113: 'Man has lived through great changes and great upheavals. But now the revolutions are multiple and simultaneous.'
101 Anderson, *Imagined Communities*, 22–36.

enabling time for nationalism, but was the 'utopian time of capitalism'. This is the temporal imaginary which enables us 'to speak of the reality of such categories of political economy as prices, wages, markets, and so on', and which, when it encounters an impediment, 'thinks it has encountered another time'.[102]

At first glance, Anand might be thought to have broadly aligned himself with both the project of nation-state formation and that of the expansion of global capitalism. But as we have seen, the temporal disjunctions that appeared to structure his account of 'contemporary' international law was to foreground the limits of both. For just as each depended upon putting into operation a temporal technology – engendering a 'fictional presentness'[103] by the measuring of life against the clock – so also did that technology both reveal the asymmetrical conditions of life in the world, and the scale of the challenge placed before the world by the utopia of 'presentness'. Whether or not Anand ever believed that utopia to be realisable, he did at least recognise that the promise of 'co-existence' was dependent upon bringing the world closer together in time.

102 Partha Chatterjee, *The Politics of the Governed* (New York: Columbia University Press, 2004), 5.

103 Peter Osborne, "Global Modernity and the Contemporary: Two Categories of the Philosophy of Historical Time," in *Breaking Up Time,* eds. Chris Lorenz and Berber Bevernage (Göttingen: Vandenhoek and Ruprecht, 2013), 80.

19

A double take on debt

Reparations claims and shifting regimes of visibility[1]

Vasuki Nesiah

From debt as reconquest to debt severance as reparations

> We think that debt has to be seen from the standpoint of its origins. Debt's origins come from colonialism's origins. Those who lend us money are those who had colonized us before. They are those who used to manage our states and economies. . . . Colonizers are those who indebted Africa through their brothers and cousins who were the lenders. We had no connections with this debt. Therefore we cannot pay for it. . . . Under its current form, that is imperialism controlled, debt is a cleverly managed reconquest of Africa, aiming at subjugating its growth and development through foreign rules. Thus, each one of us becomes the financial slave, which is to say a true slave.
>
> Thomas Sankara[2]

If you were looking out to sea from the balmy beaches of Haiti in April 1825 a dozen French warships may have been visible on the horizon. Some 20 years after she was defeated by the Haitian Revolution, France remained insistent on re-litigating her loss in the domain of international law, great power diplomacy and naval power. Carried to the Caribbean Sea by the winds of the inter-imperial alliances sealed at the Congress of Vienna, those warships were the backdrop to Baron Mackau's visit to Haiti to demand protection money.[3] As an emissary of King Charles X, Baron Mackau carried the message that France and her allies would not grant recognition to the Haitian Revolution and recognise Haitian sovereignty, unless Haiti agreed to pay France the princely sum of 150 million francs as indemnity for the financial loss incurred by France and French slaveholders as a result of Haitian emancipation. If the French Revolution

1 Thanks to Ruth Buchanan and to Sundhya Pahuja for comments on this paper as it developed.

2 Thomas Sankara, "A United Front Against Debt," Speech at the Organisation of African Unity in July 1987, in *Committee for the Abolition of Illegitimate Debt*, October 27, 2011, www.cadtm.org/spip.php?page=imprimer&id_article=13533.

3 The Congress of Vienna included an agreement (a secret agreement) that the other European countries would concede to France full freedom in seeking to re-conquer Haiti.

was fought with the promise of liberty, equality and fraternity, the racial caveats to those promissory notes were clarified in Santo Domingo.[4]

To render itself visible to the world, earn recognition as a free and independent sovereign, and birth itself in the eyes of international law, Haiti was coerced into contorting itself into a debtor nation.[5] This required asserting Haitian sovereignty in the very act that corroded it – namely, accepting the terms of the extortion as 'debt' undertaken by a free and independent nation. In this way France's demands for indemnity, shifted from the hyper visibility of the warships to becoming the (ever present but also ever backgrounded) foundation of Haiti's post-revolutionary future as a sovereign nation. Assuming the debt burden that impaired and fettered Haitian sovereignty is the very process that births Haiti's 'sovereignty' as a universal category that earns recognition in the society of nations. Thus the indemnity that was imposed by the warships (and what they represented) translates into international law ledgers as a debt that sovereign Haiti owed to sovereign France through this paradoxical performative/constative structure. In fact, Haiti incurred further debt to keep up payments even after the total amount was renegotiated to 90 million francs. Haiti finally paid the principle indemnity six decades later in 1893, and settled all accounts, including related interest payments, in 1947.[6]

The impact of these payments on Haiti has been catastrophic. If the warships of 1825 manifestly threatened a violent massacre, the indemnity stealthily produced an equally brutal slow violence punishment for the temerity of Haiti's revolutionary aspirations. As Westenley Alcenat noted, 'The French indemnity crippled the Haitian state and civil society. It intensified an already predatory state and accelerated the vulnerability of the economic infrastructure, easing the floodgates for foreign exploitation.'[7] Placing the coerced indemnity into the legal framework of debt, a debt agreed to, by and for sovereign Haiti, presents in international law and development ledgers as a self-inflicted wound. Debt functions like the angling of a camera to steer our attention in one direction rather than another by operating on two intertwined registers of presence and visibility – on the one hand, the coercion that engenders and sustains sovereign debt makes its economic, military and geo-political presence felt as ever present background condition; on the

4 There were parallel indemnity bargains struck by colonial powers in other contexts too. The Dutch relinquished claims on Indonesia and recognised its sovereignty when the latter agreed to an indemnity sum of 4.5 billion guilders; Indonesia paid approximately 4 billion guilders to the Netherlands in the first decade of its independence, see Lambert Giebels, "The Indonesian Injection," *De Groene Amsterdammer*, January 5, 2000, available at: Histori Bersama, https://historibersama.com/528-2/. CLR James' observation seems apposite – 'The cruelties of property and privilege are always more ferocious than the revenges of poverty and oppression. For the one aims at perpetuating resented injustice, the other is merely a momentary passion soon appeased.' That at least was the wager that these former colonial powers made and, at least partially won.

5 Thus, at the very moment of its birth as a sovereign nation, and as a condition of that recognition, Haiti becomes less than sovereign. This may be seen in a sense as the tragic reverse of the constative/performative structure that Derrida identifies as part of the originary hypocrisy that inheres in the 'we the people' of the US Declaration of Independence – 'We the People' declare themselves sovereign when their constitution as a people is really the outcome of the declaration, rather than prior to it. If the latter case is one of an originary hypocrisy that enlarges sovereignty, the Haitian origin story is an example of an originary hypocrisy that diminishes sovereignty. See Jacques Derrida, *Otobiographies: l'enseignement de Nietzsche et la politique du nom propre* (Paris: Galilee, 1984), 21–25 as quoted, translated and glossed by Gayatri Spivak, "Constitutions and Culture Studies," *Yale Journal of law and Humanities* 2, no. 1 (Winter 1990): 142.

6 Robert Marquand, "France Dismisses Petition for It to Pay $17 Billion in Haiti Reparations," *The Christian Science Monitor*, August 17, 2010, www.csmonitor.com/World/Europe/2010/0817/France-dismisses-petition-for-it-to-pay-17-billion-in-Haiti-reparations.

7 Westenley Alcenat, "The Case for Haitian Reparations," *Jacobin*, January 14, 2017, www.jacobinmag.com/2017/01/haiti-reparations-france-slavery-colonialism-debt/.

other, debt works to focus our attention on the obligations of the indebted rather than on that coercive world order. This dynamic has provided the scaffolding for the political horizon of independent Haiti where the responsibilities attached to debt present as an indicator of Haiti's sovereign agency, even while it is the vehicle for greater and greater sovereign dependence. Alcenat recounts how dependence on loans from American financiers to pay the French debt also opened the door for US intervention in Haitian affairs that continues today.[8] Thus the Haitian sovereignty that was recognised in that 1825 deal was one that invited more warships to its shores, both ones that were visible and ones that moved with the stealth of background rules.

Refusing those warships risked even that feeble, and enfeebling, sovereignty that was birthed in the 1825 agreement. For instance, in 2003, two centuries after the Haitian Revolution, Jean Bertrand Aristide, then president of Haiti, asked for a return of the indemnity funds: 21 billion dollars in restitution when the sums were translated into their value in 2003.[9] The demand can be seen and was seen as a step towards another transition – a transition from neo-colonial oppression into a new kind of sovereign agency.[10] France was hostile to Aristide's demands for repayment; moreover, like in 1825, France was able to marshal its allies to backstop France's position. Thus, the metaphorical warships sailed into visibility again, and the guns on board those warships were immediately raised ready to fire. In 2004 there was a *coup d'état* against Aristide, and the US and France collaborated on forcibly removing him from Haiti. A post-Aristide Haiti was born and the ships once again discreetly sailed beyond the line of sight of Haiti's political horizon.[11] Haitian sovereignty was 'restored'.[12] Today Haitian national debt is in the order of 3.5 billion dollars, about a third of its GDP.[13]

The Haitian demands for restitution of the indemnity funds is an important adjunct to the demands advanced by Haiti as part of the 15-country Caribbean Community (CARICOM) plan for reparatory justice.[14] CARICOM situates the debt cycle as an inheritance of 'slavery and colonialism', arguing that: 'This debt cycle properly belongs to the imperial governments who have made no sustained attempt to deal with debilitating colonial legacies. Support for the payment of domestic debt and cancellation of international debt are necessary reparatory actions.'[15] CARICOM's ten-point plan for reparatory justice is directed at Europe, with particular attention to the historical responsibilities of Britain, France and the Netherlands for colonialism and slavery in the region. One of the most potentially consequential demands is the call for rewriting sovereign debt as central to reparations. The CARICOM vision for

8 Ibid.

9 "Haiti: Free from Slavery, Not Yet Free from Debt," *Jubilee Debt Campaign*, accessed May 22, 2020, https://jubileedebt.org.uk/countries-in-crisis/haiti-free-slavery-not-yet-free-debt.

10 Indeed it was echoed by demands from Senegal, Mali and other former French colonies in Africa for indemnity charges that France had imposed in those countries for post-independence currencies structured on the CFA Franc. "Francophone Africa's CFA Franc Is Under Fire," *The Economist*, January 27, 2018, www.economist.com/middle-east-and-africa/2018/01/27/francophone-africas-cfa-franc-is-under-fire.

11 Any effort to keep the spotlight on them was resisted; Caribbean Community (CARICOM) asked for a UN investigation of the *coup d'etat* and this request was crushed by France and the US, see Anthony Fenton, "U.S., France Block UN Probe of Aristide Ouster," *Información, Derechos*, April 13, 2004, www.derechos.org/nizkor/haiti/doc/hti34.html.

12 Mark Weisbrot, "Undermining Haiti," *The Nation*, November 23, 2005, www.thenation.com/article/archive/undermining-haiti/.

13 See https://tradingeconomics.com/haiti/gdp.

14 CARICOM includes Antigua & Barbuda, Bahamas, Barbados, Belize, Dominica, Grenada, Guyana, Haiti, Jamaica, Montserrat, St. Kitts & Nevis, St. Lucia, Saint Vincent and the Grandines, Surinam, Trinidad and Tobago.

15 Carribean Community, "CARICOM Ten Point Plan for Reparatory Justice," accessed May 22, 2020, https://caricom.org/caricom-ten-point-plan-for-reparatory-justice/.

reparatory justice takes on the politics of temporality in ways that seek to interrupt routine international relations; implicit in this vision is an analysis of how histories of colonialism and slavery are windows to the past but also constitutive of the present. They mark the political economies that figure European privilege and prosperity, and, concomitantly, the vulnerabilities of the Caribbean present, as dimensions of the contemporary lives of colonial and slave histories. If, in this analysis, colonial interests function like a silent virus crippling postcolonial futures, debt can be seen as both the virus and its symptom: shaping the postcolonial world order while also being its product. The Haiti indemnity story is a synecdoche of that larger regime of world economic order built by colonialism and slavery. This regime produced sovereign debt as the silent virus of decolonisation, birthed and nurtured by that regime in ways that have mutilated and fettered processes of political transition from colonialism and slavery through debt and dependence.

Some may point to the doctrine of odious debt as a transitional justice mechanism for such situations. The idea of 'odious debt' operates such that, upon political transition, debt obligations taken on by an odious regime are terminated. Robert Howes summarises its basic principles:

> The odious debt concept seeks to provide a moral and legal foundation for severing, in whole or in part, the continuity of legal obligations where the debt in question was contracted by a prior "odious" regime and was used in ways that were not beneficial or were harmful to the interests of the population.[16]

The core insight of the notion of odious debt is that the fact that a party submits to a contract is not proof of its validity; rather the validity of contract should depend on basic principles of fair, equitable and non-coercive conditions.[17] The doctrine originated to repudiate debt incurred by a colonial government; in particular, it was an argument invoked by the US in the aftermath of the Spanish-American War to argue that Cuba and the US should not be held responsible for debts incurred by the colonial Spanish government.[18] The Haitian restitution claims and the CARICOM demands foreground the transition from colonialism and slavery, yet that transition is itself unfinished; the world economic order built by colonialism and slavery is the co-sovereign of the postcolonial nation-state as exemplified by Haitian sovereignty emerging into the society of nations already indebted. It is this odiously twinned regime that led to debts inimical to the interests of the local population. The coercive circumstances of national debt in

16 Robert Howse, "The Concept of Odious Debt in Public International Law," *United Nations Conference on Trade and Development*, Discussion Paper 185 (July 2007): 2, https://unctad.org/en/docs/osgdp20074_en.pdf.

17 'As early as the 1898 peace negotiations after the Spanish-American War, the U.S. government contended that neither the United States nor Cuba should be held responsible for debt incurred by Cuba's colonial rulers without the consent of its people and without regard for their benefit. Although Spain never accepted the validity of this argument, the United States prevailed, and Spain took responsibility for the Cuban debt under the Paris peace treaty. The Soviet state repudiated tsarist debt in 1921 using a similar rationale. Legal scholars subsequently elaborated a doctrine of "odious debt," arguing that sovereign debt should not be transferable to a successor government if it was incurred without the consent of, and without benefiting, the people. Some scholars added the requirement that creditors must have been aware of these conditions when they issued the loans to repressive or looting governments.' Michael Kremer and Seema Jayachandran, "Odious Debt: When Dictators Borrow, Who Repays the Loan?" *Brookings Institution*, March 1, 2003, www.brookings.edu/articles/odious-debt-when-dictators-borrow-who-repays-the-loan/.

18 Michael Kremer and Seema Jayachandran, "Odious Debt," *The American Economic Review* 96, no. 1 (March 2006): 82.

the postcolony includes coercion that is visible, and coercion that is part of the background laws and institutions that cast their shadow on terms of debt negotiations; it includes the spectre of warships on the horizon, as well as the laws and institutions of economic order that sustain and reproduce systems of economic exploitation and vulnerability. Foregrounding these dimensions of postcolonial world order calls for reframing the notion of the 'odious regime' to include both visible and less-visible dimensions of global governance that structure how sovereigns both acquire debt, and negotiate its terms. How these dimensions are taken into account in defining what counts as an 'odious regime' emerges as a central dimension of how the doctrine is given force in assessing conditions for terminating debt obligations.[19]

This chapter proposes that the concept of 'odious debt' provides an especially fruitful legal framework for the Haitian and CARICOM demands for restitution and debt severance. The concept renders visible different dimensions of the background economic order that have been constitutive of postcolonial sovereignty, and the histories of trade and aid that have engendered debt. In foregrounding that visibility, the concept makes debt severance 'thinkable'. In analysing the work of different regimes of visibility I have found it useful to think with Abderrahmane Sissako's 2006 film *Bamako*, and the way Sissako illuminates the stakes of what is foregrounded and what is backgrounded in world order. Bamako unsettles the focus of the filmic gaze, shifting and reversing the camera work of viewing and being viewed so that the lens documenting the adjudication of the legal and economic framework of international debt, the act of seeing, becomes what we see. The next section engages with *Bamako* and its cinematic engagement with law and global economic governance, to cast a light on the trade and aid regime in ways that resonate with heterodox interpretations of the legal framework for debt.[20] The final section returns to the question of 'odious debt' and the way it could make resistance to the debt regime legible in international law. Visibility – both as a metaphor for what is explicit and an account of what is before our eyes – is central to the politics of reparations. In this context, the doctrine of odious debt and the cinematic considerations that frame, advance and interrupt the narrative worlds of *Bamako* provide an interpretive lens through which to make visible the background structural arrangements linking globalisation's winners and losers, and concomitantly, make evident different histories and futures for postcolonial nationhood. The reparation claims of Haiti and CARICOM can be understood as stories entailing law and economics, visibility and witnessing of the world – stories with a performative function where the telling itself seeks to interrupt how the world functions.

19 The doctrine of 'odious debt' as described by Howse, Kremer and Jayachandran, et al., and extended in this paper's interpretation of 'odious regime' as a reference to the domain of global governance (not just national territory), resonates with principles of equity in international law. Equity, present in both common law and civil law jurisdictions, has been invoked in international law through natural law principles, as well as in reference to particular doctrinal provisions built into the mandate of adjudicatory bodies such as the international court of justice and the international criminal court.

20 The extended version of this paper also engages with two other filmic registers about visibility and global governance – the feature film *Black Panther*, and the documentary film *Life as Debt*, set in Jamaica and with narration from the text of Jamaica Kincaid's book-essay, *A Small Place*. *Life as Debt* enacts invisibility with two parallel story lines – one of American tourists enjoying a vacation on the beaches of Jamaica and the other of a Jamaica devastated first by slavery and colonialism, and then, after independence, financially haemorrhaged by debt, loan conditionalities, trade and aid. The invisibility of the latter is central to oiling the wheels of the former, even as the economic devastation of Jamaica is central to the favourable currencies and tourism dependence that makes the former so enjoyable for the American visitor. The blood spilt to make the margarita on the beach has to be rendered so invisible that it is unthinkable.

Hiding in plain sight: rendering the visibility of debt visible

> If we can see the present clearly enough, we shall ask the right questions of the past.
> John Berger[21]

As the movie begins, you find yourself across the Atlantic in another former French colony. You are soon in a dusty multi-family courtyard in Bamako, Mali. A hearing is unfolding in a formal court-like setting with lawyers and witnesses making arguments and testifying before robed and bewigged judges. The hearing has been convened to hear accusations against the IMF and the World Bank for crimes against the people of Mali. Lawyers make formal arguments about a world fuelled by the continued political/economic/military devastation of the impoverished. They speak of debt, debt payments and structural adjustment conditionalities demanded by the International Financial Institutions (IFIs), pitting the people of Bamako against the world economic order. Ordinary citizens of Mali come in as witnesses; formally sworn in, they then speak of the devastation they have experienced because of the trickledown impact of the global economic order and IFI prescriptions regarding privatisation and the abandonment of public expenditure on social infrastructure. They speak of malnutrition, loss of jobs, illiteracy, lack of public transport and much more. 'Debt has brought Africa to its knees,' one lawyer argues in outlining the many vectors of dispossession. The courtyard is surrounded by shacks where people are going about their everyday chores, occasionally stopping to watch the events unfolding in the hearing. The trial unfolds against the backdrop of the day-to-day drama of people living in the courtyard; offering another kind of witness, the subplots involving these neighbours intersect with, but are also much more than, the shadows cast by the global economy. The lives of the people in the courtyard fade in and out of view as we get pulled into different characters' lives and their individual stories with work and family. Accentuating the surrealist cast of the proceedings, our view of the trial is briefly interrupted by *Death in Timbuktu*, a side movie within the movie bringing military intervention and a new take on law, outlaws and lawlessness. *Death in Timbuktu* is a spaghetti western where bands of international cowboys shoot the women and children they deem surplus. The camera returns to the courtyard to witness more lives rendered superfluous by the global economy and witnesses describing the World Bank as stone chains around their neck akin to 'the slave's sign of allegiance to his master'.

If the story of postcolonial sovereignty forged in Haiti offers one story of the future of enslavement and colonisation, *Bamako* offers a cinematic calling-to-account of the institutions that haemorrhaged the futures of the formerly enslaved and colonised. The one person who repeatedly enters the frame but then disappears is a videographer who is in the courtyard filming the trial, and by default the lives of the families whose homes border the courtyard. He darts in and out of proceedings, adjusting his lenses, shifting his camera, moving from this perspective to that one. He is witness to it all – but he is not alone. Everyone who is going about the courtyard living his or her life in a Mali shaped by the history of French colonialism and the global economy is a witness. There is no shield of invisibility over the impact of debt on people's lives and their life opportunities; as the videographer darts around, filming proceedings, their lives testify to the dystopic signature of the international economic order. If the front-stage action is the adjudication of the IFIs, the back-stage action is the witnessing. Indeed, as I watched the

21 John Berger, *Ways of Seeing* (New York: Penguin Modern Classics, 2009), 16.

film, it gradually dawned on me that the back-stage plot line steals the show by putting visibility itself on trial. Those who shape the rules engendering the debt, those who benefit from the rules enforcing debt, those who lose from the rules required to make repayment – they can all see what is going on. The videographer is not making the courtyard visible to us; he is reminding us that this is all already visible, that what is normalised as background is a scandal when foregrounded.

Indeed, for countries negotiating debt repayment conditionalities the world over, the visibility of harsh consequences for defaulting is part of the goal – as we saw even with Greece a few years ago, the EU was keen to ensure that the punishment of Greece served as an exemplary lesson for Spain and Portugal and any other potential defaulter. As Eve Sedgwick has reminded us, there are limits to a hermeneutics of exposure and suspicion in a regime where exposing atrocity is itself incorporated into a technology of atrocity.[22] In such a regime, visibility does not itself deliver solutions.[23] Spectacular violence (such as the warships in Haiti's sights) is intended not only as a punishment of particular countries, but also as a public warning to others.[24] As *Bamako* indicates, ordinary citizens are eloquent and knowledgeable about the political and economic arrangements that shape world order, and have such devastating consequences on their lives. This is not a new revelation. The trial in *Bamako* is seeking to document an aspect of how the world works, to provide a little window into historical legacies and present conditions, to expose, to lift the veil, to reveal facts and enhance knowledge. Yet, the work of the videographer is to make us attend to the act of seeing and be unsettled by that. His most unsettling intervention does not lie in making the colonial legacies and neocolonial present of Mali visible to us. Rather, it is in the reminder that this is already visible. The contours of this unsettling carry a parallel shape to the work of reparation claims today. Reparation claims have unsettled and unnerved routine politics not because they are reciting the horrors of colonialism and slavery or the grotesque inequalities of the present. They are reminding us that we already know this, that this is what we witness every day, that this is what surrounds us; it is a reminder that 'seeing' these different markers of postcolonial sovereignty are what, in John Berger's words, 'establishes our place in the surrounding world'. This is the power of noticing seeing.[25]

Viewing the Haitian and CARICOM claims through the aperture of *Bamako*, we might see the reparations demands as akin to the videographer – as making visible the visibility. What is striking is not that these reparation claims make visible the connections between atrocities from yesterday and today, from the era of slavery to the era of neoliberalism, but that they call

22 In Eve Kosofsky Sedgwick, "Paranoid Reading and Reparative Reading, or, You're So Paranoid, You Probably Think This Essay Is About You," in *Touching Feeling: Affect, Pedagogy, Performativity* (Durham, NC: Duke University Press, 2003), 123–52, Sedgewick herself builds on Paul Ricour's critique of critical habits (referring especially to Marx, Nietzche and Freud and the traditions of critical thought associated with them) as being reliant on what he first described as a 'hermeneutics of suspicion' (124–25). Sedgewick argues that such a hermeneutics can have unintended side effects that may inadvertently deter reparative reading practices that attend to 'the many ways selves and communities succeed in extracting sustenance from the object of a culture – even of a culture whose avowed desire has often been not to sustain them' (150–51). Part of the agenda of this chapter is an exploration of whether the doctrine of odious debt can be situated in such a reparative reading.

23 Or when Mali is required (as one of the witnesses in the Bamako trial testifies) to privatise as a condition of capital transfer, it is a signal to Ghana and Nigeria that privatisation is part of the package – that this is what needs to be internalised for good governance.

24 See Sybille Fischer, *Modernity Disavowed: Haiti and the Cultures of Slavery in the Age of Revolution* (Durham, NC: Duke University Press, 2004).

25 Berger, *Ways of Seeing*, 7.

attention to the scandal of that visibility. The structural arrangements linking globalisation's winners and losers are hiding in plain sight and such reparations claims are ensuring that we trip over what is in front of us when we would rather walk around it. The muscles and tissues that connect odious debt and debtor nations are functioning symbiotically in the same organism, and the reparations claims interrupt that symbiosis, they interrupt story tellers narrating theories of freedom that are also histories of enslavement. The videographer angling for a better shot in *Bamako* is producing a documentary – a realist genre with film as witness to what is really going on – and he is doing it in a surrealist world where international posses of cowboys can bring the Wild West to your doorstep.

Postcolonial sovereignty and odious debt: the aperture of legal legibility

> The role of philosophy is not to discover what is hidden, but to make visible precisely what is visible, that is to say, to show that which is so close, which is so immediate, which is so intimately linked to us, that because of that we do not perceive it. While the role of science is to communicate that which we do not see, the role of philosophy is to make us see what we see.
>
> Michel Foucault[26]

If 1804 marked the 'freedom dreams' of Haitian men and women leading to the first successful anti-slavery cum anti-colonial revolution, the 1825 recognition of Haiti as an already-indebted sovereign nation is in many ways the origin story of postcolonial sovereignty. Midwifed into the world by the twin forces of 'freedom dreams' and 'odious debt', the key foundation of postcolonial sovereignty is that shackling of freedom and duress. The call for reparation for the sovereign debt burden of postcolonial states seeks to render visible the pathologies that have been normalised into the shackling of freedom and duress. The doctrine of odious debt makes this call for reparation legible to international law; like the *Bamako* videographer, it points to the already-visible shackling of 'freedom dreams' and 'odious debt' to help render jubilee 'thinkable' within international law.[27]

The Haitian and CARICOM call for rewriting debt as reparations is not a book-keeping intervention, but a political one. There is a fundamental difference between framing it through the lens of debt forgiveness,[28] and reframing it through the lens of odious debt. The concept of "odious debt" is itself a reframing. As Howse has written:

> It regroups a particular set of equitable considerations that have often been raised to adjust or sever debt obligations in the context of political transitions, based on the purported

26 Michel Foucault, quoted in Anne Orford, "In Praise of Description," *Leiden Journal of International Law* 25, no. 3 (September 2012): 617.

27 Jubilee 2000, a global coalition spread across 40 plus countries, was formed to advocate for debt relief for the Global South. There is now a network of national jubilee committees that founded the Jubilee 2000 coalition that continue the campaign at a local level; for instance the UK organisation, Jubilee Debt Campaign, describes their work as 'part of a global movement working to break the chains of debt and build a finance system that works for everyone' (www.jubileedebt.org.uk).

28 For instance, in the World Bank's Heavily Indebted Poor Countries initiative, which predicates debt relief on Gross National Product (GNP) rather than conditions of debt acquisition.

> odiousness of the previous regime and the notion that the debt it incurred did not benefit, or was used to repress, the people.[29]

In short, it is a concept that, in the Haitian case, enables a revisiting of 1825 in the spirit of 1804.[30] 1825 cemented a compact whereby Haiti severed the radical aspirations of 1804, undertook a debt that not only impoverished Haiti and led to untold repression and hardship for its people, but it also legitimised French colonialism and slave holdings. In exchange Haiti received global recognition as a sovereign nation and integration into the society of nations. The doctrine of 'odious debt' provides a platform to revisit that compact and revive the revolutionary spirit of 1804, a spirit that was willing to take on the French empire, confident, as C. L. R. James notes, that the society of nations that it was a part of was morally odious.

> He (Toussaint) knew French, British, and Spanish imperialists for the insatiable gangsters that they were, that there is no oath too sacred for them to break, no crime, deception, treachery, cruelty, destruction of human life and property which they would not commit against those who could not defend themselves.[31]

When France formally renounced its claims to Haiti, what it recognised was the postcolonial sovereign state, not the revolution of 1804. Indeed, James argued that the ideas of liberty associated with the French (and American) revolutions had a different life in Haiti, in which even the ideals of the French Revolution 'meant far more to them than to any Frenchman'.[32] These 'freedom dreams', beyond the political horizon of the American and French revolutions, can be understood as a critique of the odious structure of the postcolonial social contract, negotiated as it is in the world constructed by slavery and colonialism.[33] It is perhaps in this sense that David Scott has argued that, for James, the Haitian Revolution was not about rights but revolution.[34] Moreover, it is perhaps in this sense that CARICOM's reparations call is a successor to the spirit of 1804 rather than the sovereignty recognised by the society of nations in 1825.

A modest case for the doctrine of odious debt relies, as Jeyachandran and Kremer argue, on two basic observations. One, debt exacerbates dispossession and misery in countries that are already impoverished. And moreover, even before we assess consequences, we may conclude that the loans were illegitimate because the parties that contracted the debt were illegitimate,

29 Robert Howse, "The Concept of Odious Debt in Public International Law," 1; UNCTAD 2007 (UNCTAD/OSG/DP/2007/4).

30 It is a proposal for a delinking from a world order of an odious regime of debt and dispossession. A refusal, a la Samir Amin, 'to submit national development strategy to the imperatives of "globalization"' – we may take here globalisation as a short hand for that odious regime of debt and dispossession. See Samir Amin, "A Note on the Concept of Delinking," *Review* (Fernand Braudel Center) 10, no. 3 (Winter 1987), 435. In his seminal *Delinking* (Zed 2007), Samir Amin argues for a refusal.

31 C. L. R. James, *The Black Jacobins: Toussaint L'ouverture and the San Domingo Revolution* (London: Allison & Busby, 1980, first published 1938), 217.

32 Ibid., 198.

33 'Freedom Dreams' is Robin Kelley's term for black radical visions. The Haitian Revolution lays bare the limits of rights talk, the rule of law and their racial caveats – or in Toussaint Louverture's famous words: 'We are black, it is true, but tell us gentleman, you who are so judicious, what is the law that says that the black man must belong to and be the property of the white man?' Robin Kelley, *Freedom Dreams: The Black Radical Imagination* (Boston: Beacon, 2002); Toussaint Louverture, *To Live Free or Die* (1791).

34 David Scott, "The Theory of Haiti: The Black Jacobins and the Poetics of Universal History," *Small Axe* 18, no. 3 (November 2014): 35–51.

or the condition in which those contracts were undertaken were illegitimate.[35] In many cases where invocation of the doctrine of odious debt has been considered (post-apartheid South Africa for instance), countries have been urged against it on the theory that reneging on debts will cast aspersions on the bona fides of the debtor nation, that it will deter foreign investors looking to make an honest deal, and inhibit integration into the international economic system.[36] Rather, the policy edicts of multilateral institutions encourage continued debt servicing. Thus, even an historically 'Third World friendly' institution such as UNCTAD works with the default assumption that the international framework for sovereign debt is free and fair. According to UNCTAD's guidelines on 'promoting responsible sovereign lending and borrowing', in some contexts of economic hardship, debt servicing may need to be restructured. However, these guidelines still encourage model debtor discipline as the default option, with language strikingly resonant with notions of financial responsibility and capitalist discipline, which are routine dimensions of quotidian tutelage regarding neoliberal citizenship. The UNCTAD guidelines teem with nuggets such as: 'Debtors should design and implement a debt sustainability and management strategy'; or, debtor sovereigns are urged to 'move in a timely fashion to communicate with its creditors'.[37] The reward of debt servicing undertaken by postcolonial sovereigns performing good financial citizenship is inclusion in this society of nations. Yet, does inclusion in the society of nations indicate the national freedom or a shackling into neo-colonial debt bondage? As *Bamako* witnesses, and as Mike Davis reminds us (in discussing genocidal famines across the globe): 'Millions died, not outside the "modern world system", but in the process of being forcibly integrated into its economic and political structures.'[38] In a certain sense *Bamako*'s stories within the story is also an argument for delinking from those structures – the IFIs are at the centre of the hearing in the courtyard, but there are other stories, other plot lines that continue without being mere subplots to the drama of the IFIs. There is the story of the singer Mele and her disintegrating marriage to Chaka. There is the spaghetti western starring Danny Glover. These 'other' stories are not romanticised – they carry all the beauty, tragedy and absurdity of life – but they continue irrespective of the outcome of the trial.

The thinkability of resistance to the debt regime

> There is another world, but it is in this one.
>
> Paul Eluard[39]

The radically utopic freedom dreams of CARICOM's reparations claims lay the ground for going beyond a plea for debt forgiveness to making the case that debt obligations should be severed on account of an illegitimate regime of economic and political governance that was used

35 Jeyachandran and Kremer, "Odious Debt," 90.

36 See Amin, *Delinking*; Mike Davis quoted in Susan Marks and Andrew Clapham, *International Human Rights Lexicon* (Oxford: Oxford University Press, 2005), 165.

37 United Nations Conference on Trade and Development, *Principles on Promoting Responsible Sovereign Lending and Borrowing*, amended and restated January 10, 2012, https://unctad.org/en/PublicationsLibrary/gdsddf2012misc1_en.pdf.

38 Quoted in Marks and Clapham, *International Human Rights Lexicon*, 165. Eric Williams offers pioneering historical analysis of these mutually reinforcing chains of profit and exploitation, see Eric Williams, *Capitalism and Slavery* (Chapel Hill: University of North Carolina, 1944).

39 See McKenzie Wark, "There Is Another World and It Is This One," *Public Seminar* (January 14, 2014), https://publicseminar.org/2014/01/there-is-another-world-and-it-is-this-one/.

to repress rather than benefit the people. Debt forgiveness implicitly legitimises the underlying contract; in contrast, the doctrine of odious debt draws attention to the fundamental illegitimacy of international economic transactions built on enslavement and colonisation directly or indirectly with sovereign debt acquired under the coercive conditions of the postcolonial economic order of Bretton Woods. If debt forgiveness invests in a certain actuarial visibility, the doctrine of odious debt invests in a political visibility. Political visibility contributes to making resistance to that default postcolonial economic order 'thinkable'.

Thinkability is a kind of *amicus curiae* in the case for the doctrine of odious debt as the framework for the CARICOM reparations claims. Michel-Rolph Trouillot has argued that the cumulative impact of the history of Western thought over the last two centuries was to make the Haitian Revolution unthinkable.[40] Trouillot says that Europeans reading news of the Haitian Revolution 'could read the news only with their readymade categories, and these categories were incompatible with the idea of slave revolution'.[41] The disappearance of the Haitian Revolution from the canon of Atlantic revolutionary struggles of that era may speak all the more to its vexed centrality as both inspiration and challenge to liberal conceptions of freedom. Liberalism entailed a complex double take of keeping your eyes on St Domingo while also looking away.

'The Eyes of the World are now on St. Domingo' – so opens an article on the Haitian Revolution in the eighteenth-century German journal *Minerva*. In *Hegel and Haiti*, Susan Buck-Morss links *Minerva*'s coverage of the Haitian Revolution to the development of Hegel's philosophy – the revolution of St Domingo was in his line of sight even if nowhere cited.[42] Slavery and colonisation were central to the conceptual grammar through which modernity has come to have meaning, and political subjectivity understood, but invisiblising that intellectual debt has been equally pivotal. The institution of slavery that emerged from the Atlantic slave trade was visible in Europe in the age of liberal modernity – from the macro scale of the ledgers of empire, to the micro scale of family paintings depicting domestic life. Buck-Morss tracks the visibility of the quotidian life of slavery in Europe. Moreover, she shows how the life of slavery as a historical institution sat alongside the increasing cultural traction with slavery as a concept that represented all that was antithetical to liberal freedom. However, these two lives of slavery were often zoned into different spheres, where one was not visible to the other. As Buck-Morss notes, slavery was a central metaphor for the theorising of freedom in European liberalism, but it was slavery as an abstraction – or as a biblical parable regarding Moses and the Egyptians – rather than the actual contemporary institutions of slavery that were the products of these same societies. Hegel was not alone. Consider John Locke who, even at a time when slavery was ostentatiously visible in Europe, in the seventeenth and eighteenth centuries, appears blind to how the actual history of slavery and slave resistance challenged his theorisation of the social contract and labour theory of value. Indeed, as a shareholder and investor in the slave-trading Royal Africa Company, which traded slaves from West Africa to the Caribbean, and then a drafter of the constitution of the Carolinas sanctifying the legality of slavery in that state, Locke can be said to be ostentatiously blind to any tension between the institution of slavery and liberal freedom. This is an analogue for how the political subjectivity of the revolutionary Haitian, the radical anti-slavery/anti-colonial position that took on a French state that heralded the 'rights of man', becomes unthinkable in the political thought of Western modernity.[43] Thus the

40 Michel-Rolph Trouillot, *Silencing the Past: Power and the Production of History* (Boston: Beacon Press, 1995). My thanks to Christopher Gevers for introducing me to Michel-Rolph Trouillot's extraordinary oeuvre.

41 Ibid., 73.

42 Susan Buck-Morss, "Hegel and Haiti," *Critical Inquiry* 26, no. 4 (Summer 2000).

43 Indeed, that is certainly how we might see the political fortunes of Aristide and his campaign for reparations – he was unthinkable for the Haiti that is visible to us as ruin.

ambitious task implicit in the call for rewriting debt as reparatory justice is not just rendering visible Haiti for Hegel (or any of the other European philosophers), but rendering visible the process of invisibilisation, to better understand how that process inflects and inhabits history.

The rewriting of debt is also about attending to the debts piling up on the other side. There is the debt to slavery and colonialism that fuelled European economic prosperity; the economies of imperial extraction that indebted Haiti were intimately intertwined with the circuits of profit in Europe. There is also the debt of the resistance to slavery and colonialism that fuelled European political thought; resistance to slavery emerges as constitutive of the very self-conception of the liberal political subject that has been so central to the identity of the West. That dialectical ground, between slave resistance and liberal freedom, is denied and rendered invisible in the work of Europe's master theoretician of the master-slave dialectic. Slavery hid in plain sight.

If the current world order is hurtling Haiti and the CARICOM world further into a long night of atrocity, the reparations claim and the story it tells about how that world functions is like a modern Scheherazade tale, both true in its wisdom and fanciful in its ambitions, magical in its idealism and realist in its account of the lives and futures at stake. In drawing attention to the fact that we are all witnesses to atrocity, it seeks to forestall the futures that have condemned the formerly enslaved and colonised, and redirect our vision to an alternative dawn. This reparatory vision interrupts our blinders to forestall the necropolitical abyss that is built into the logic of the international system through yet another story and makes such alternatives 'seeable'. In this it follows previous story-telling interventions in nights past by Toussaint Louverture, Jean Paul Aristide, the *Bamako* videographer and others yet to follow in the coming nights.

20

'The object is to frighten him with hope'

Questioning the tragic emplotments of international law and decolonisation in the Chagos Archipelago

Stewart Motha[1]

The dispossession and exile of people from the Chagos Archipelago in the Indian Ocean overlapped with the period of formal decolonisation overseen by the offices and instruments of the United Nations since the 1960s. Indeed, the Chagos litigation in UK courts over the last two decades, and in the International Court of Justice (ICJ) in 2018/2019, together comprise an invaluable legal archive revealing a process of neo-imperialism that bucked the trend of decolonisation. The Chagos Archipelago was part of the territory of Mauritius prior to the latter being granted independence from Britain. The *ICJ Advisory Opinion on the Chagos Archipelago* (February 2019) found that the decolonisation of Mauritius remains incomplete.[2] This outcome was widely seen as a triumph for the General Assembly (which had referred the matter to the ICJ) and celebrated as an achievement of international law.

These juridical interventions in relation to the dispossession of the Chagossians manifest wider stories about the hopes, defeats, successes and disappointments of decolonisation pursued through international institutions and courts. The history of international law told through these cases depends on the form of a narrative emplotment.[3] Whether successful juridical contests are an anti-colonial triumph or the perpetuation of a postcolonial tragedy in newly minted terms, for instance, depends on what stories are told of them. It is in this mode of reading cases

1 I am grateful to Laura Jeffery for her careful reading and incisive comments on an earlier draft of this essay. I would also like to thank Shane Chalmers, Balawyn Jones and Sundhya Pahuja for their helpful comments and suggestions. Any errors are mine.

2 *Advisory Opinion on the legal consequences of the separation of the Chagos Archipelago from Mauritius in 1965* (February 25, 2019) (hereafter '*Advisory Opinion*').

3 I discuss 'emplotment' at greater length later; the term is taken from Hayden White, *Metahistory: The Historical Imagination in Nineteenth-Century Europe* (Baltimore: Johns Hopkins University Press, 2014), 7. Of course, one limitation of this mode of addressing the history of decolonisation is that it is not a history that can be told through cases and international institutions alone. I recognise these limits – but for now I want to focus on the juridical and institutional.

to ascertain their literariness and what literature enables in law, that we find one of the major contributions of the humanities to the study of international law.

The Chagossian predicament and ensuing litigation is vast and complex. My book *Archiving Sovereignty: Law, History, Violence* (2018) explored how the law deploys and sustains the fictions – the 'As If' – that enabled the exile and dispossession of the Chagossian population.[4] The Chagossian case is not an aberration in this regard. Law's fictions simultaneously enable violence and its disavowal at the same time. In this chapter I focus on the more recent ICJ *Advisory Opinion* – a moment when it seemed like the relative isolation of the Brexit-mired UK, the manoeuvring of the UN General Assembly and the ICJ's confident exercise of jurisdiction might 'complete' a process of decolonisation.

The UK has been relatively isolated in UN institutions in recent times – abandoned by its European allies in the context of Brexit. States that would usually back the UK or abstain in relation to resolutions that would adversely affect the latter's interests have not done so in recent initiatives in relation to the Chagos Archipelago. The UK's pursuit of withdrawal from the European Union has also epitomised the return of sovereign isolationism as a geo-political stance. Submissions to the ICJ on behalf of Mauritius in the *Advisory Opinion* drew on these sovereigntist tropes and reflected a revived valorisation of sovereignty. However, whether sovereignty is in fact the 'thing' to be recovered in processes of decolonisation is seldom asked. There is also concern that the Mauritian recovery of sovereignty over the Archipelago (if it happens) will not necessarily end Chagossian exile and dispossession, or improve access to the islands by the descendants of the Chagossians. Arguments concerning the recovery of 'fulsome sovereignty' by Mauritius, then, run the risk of repeating both romantic and tragic emplotments of modern emancipation.[5]

Narratives of anti-colonialism and decolonisation are often viewed through the narrative forms of romance or tragedy. These literary and dramatic genres are a mainstay of critical commentary and historiographical discourse in the humanities. In romantic narratives, to put it briefly for now, emancipation is mapped in linear terms where heroic figures, movements and institutions battle valiantly towards the goal of freedom. Tragic narratives are usually more attentive to the complexity of agency and action, but more often than not, actors, institutions or movements are depicted as failing to overcome the contingencies that are the inherited terrain, and blind corners of judgment and action. These dominant emplotments for narrating the processes, journeys and aesthetic practices of decolonisation are themselves in need of interrogation.

Romance of legal triumph: the ICJ *Advisory Opinion on the Chagos Archipelago*

One reading of the *Advisory Opinion* is that it reiterates and redeems the role of international law in the task and process of decolonisation. The UN General Assembly (UNGA) by its resolution 71/292 (22 June 2017) had requested that the following questions be addressed by the ICJ:

> (a) Was the process of decolonization of Mauritius lawfully completed when Mauritius was granted independence in 1968, following the separation of the Chagos

4 Stewart Motha, *Archiving Sovereignty: Law, History, Violence* (Ann Arbor: Michigan University Press, 2018). See Introduction and Chapter 1.

5 See generally, David Scott, *Conscripts of Modernity: The Tragedy of Colonial Enlightenment* (Durham, NC: Duke University Press, 2004).

> Archipelago from Mauritius and having regard to international law, including obligations reflected in General Assembly resolutions 1514 (XV) of 14 December 1960, 2066 (XX) of 16 December 1965, 2232 (XXI) of 20 December 1966 and 2357 (XXII) of 19 December 1967?;
>
> (b) What are the consequences under international law, including obligations reflected in the above-mentioned resolutions, arising from the continued administration by the United Kingdom of Great Britain and Northern Ireland of the Chagos Archipelago, including with respect to the inability of Mauritius to implement a programme for the resettlement on the Chagos Archipelago of its nationals, in particular those of Chagossian origin?
>
> *(para. 1)*

Among other resolutions and legal instruments cited in its request for an advisory opinion from the ICJ, the UNGA recalled its:

> Declaration on the Granting of Independence to Colonial Countries and Peoples, contained in its resolution 1514 (XV) of 14 December 1960, and in particular paragraph 6 thereof, which states that any attempt aimed at the partial or total disruption of the national unity and the territorial integrity of a country is incompatible with the purposes and principles of the Charter of the United Nations.
>
> *(para. 1)*

On 8 November 1965, the Chagos Archipelago had been detached from Mauritius by British Indian Ocean Territory Order 1965, an Order in Council whereby the UK established a new colony known as the British Indian Ocean Territory (BIOT).

The UNGA resolution 71/212 of 2017 was framed to recall the frustrated past of decolonisation overseen by the United Nations. Not only was Mauritian territory dismembered when it was granted independence by the UK, the severing of the territory happened in explicit contravention of the international norms on self-determination. The reference of the matter to the ICJ is then an attempt to remedy this past and continuing wrong, and reassert the force and extension of international law.

The ICJ concluded that the decolonisation of Mauritius was not conducted in a manner consistent with the right of peoples to self-determination, and that the continued administration of the Chagos Archipelago by the UK is a 'wrongful act entailing the international responsibility of that state' (para. 177). It also determined that the UK's separation of the Chagos Archipelago from Mauritius is an 'unlawful act of a continuing character' (para. 177). It followed from this that the UK is under an 'obligation to bring an end to its administration of the Chagos Archipelago as rapidly as possible, thereby enabling Mauritius to complete the decolonization of its territory in a manner consistent with the right of peoples to self-determination' (para. 178).

The ICJ also referred to the right of resettlement on the Chagos Archipelago of 'Mauritian nationals, including those of Chagossian origin' (para. 181). It recognised that this resettlement 'relates to the protection of human rights' without specifying which rights are entailed in resettlement. The matter of resettlement was referred to the UNGA to be addressed during the decolonisation of Mauritius. As Laura Jeffery has noted:

> The particular wording – "Mauritian nationals, including those of Chagossian origin" – includes non-Chagossian Mauritians and potentially excludes people of Chagossian origin who are not also Mauritian citizens: in particular, Seychellois citizens of Chagossian origin

> and, increasingly, UK citizens of Chagossian origin who are not also citizens of either Mauritius or Seychelles.[6]

The focus on 'Mauritian nationals' is but one expression of how the problem of decolonisation is coterminous with that of national sovereignty and citizenship. Even though the focus on decolonisation enabled the UNGA to refer the matter to the ICJ for an advisory opinion in terms that would reliably enliven its jurisdiction, the notion of national sovereignty undergirds the right to resettlement in the ICJ judgment. The legal subjectivities cognisable to international law are those tied to the sovereign form, nationality and citizenship. These may well exclude the descendants of the original inhabitants who are not Mauritian nationals.

These limits of recognition and remedy are not evident from the style and swagger of international lawyers. In submissions before the ICJ, legal counsel for Mauritius, Philippe Sands QC, adopted a curious analogy when making oral submissions on 3 September 2018. Sands compared the bellicose assertions by Boris Johnson in his manoeuvrings concerning Brexit – namely, that the UK was being placed in the position of a colony of the EU with respect to the 'back stop' concerning Northern Ireland – with the UK's continuing administration of the Chagos Archipelago. Sands put it like this:

> Mr. President, no country wishes to be a colony. The mere possibility engenders strong feelings. A recent British Foreign Secretary [Boris Johnson, as he then was] made that very clear, just a few weeks ago, in a resignation letter he wrote to his Prime Minister. He complained to the Prime Minister that she was adopting a path, in relation to Britain's possible departure from the European Union, that would turn the country into one, as he called it, "headed for the status of [a] colony".
>
> The irony of his words will not be lost on those in this Great Hall. The United Kingdom does not wish to be a colony, yet it stands before this Court to defend a status as colonizer of others, of Mauritius, a significant part of whose territory it still administers. Unlike Mauritius, the coming "colony" of the former British Foreign Secretary's imagination is not in danger of having its people forcibly removed and then prevented from returning.[7]

Despite the subtle disavowal of the foreign secretary's 'imagination', Sands repeats the premise that the UK is at risk of becoming a colony of the EU to make this argument. Sands' deployment of the appellation of 'colony', and comparison of the EU's relationship with the UK under the (now defunct) Withdrawal Agreement with the status of BIOT, buys in to the most extravagant fantasies about the presence/absence of something called 'full sovereignty' that may be recovered by the UK from the EU, and by Mauritius from the UK. The tone and style of the 'story' Sands tells here is ironic. The reference is, after all, to the 'coming colony of the British Foreign Secretary's imagination'. We are not asked to believe that the UK is now, or will remain, a colony of the EU. We are invited to see Sands' disavowing 'wink', and hear the parody in his bluster. But what is the meaning of Mauritian or UK sovereignty when it is cast in these ironic terms?

6 Laura Jeffery, "The International Court of Justice: Advisory Opinion on the Chagos Archipelago," *Anthropology Today* 35, no. 3 (2019): 24–7, 26.

7 ICJ Transcript, "Public Sitting of the ICJ Held on Monday 3 September 2018 at 10 am at the Peace Palace," accessed November 6, 2019, www.icj-cij.org/files/case-related/169/169-20180903-ORA-01-00-BI.pdf, 71.

Irony, as White explained, is one of the poetic tropes in modern language theory that helps to characterise an object figuratively in discourse: 'through irony . . . entities can be characterized by way of negating on the figurative level what is positively affirmed on the literal level.'[8] While Sands' submission is delivered with an irony that figuratively dismisses the claim that the UK would become a colony of the EU, the statement is nonetheless also operating at a literal level.[9] What remains of these two levels both now and into the future? Sands arguably deploys a romantic anti-colonial narrative of the Mauritian state struggling valiantly against a hypocritical colonial power in order to recover its lost territory (the literal level vis-à-vis the UK and the EU). International law in the form of the institution of the ICJ is invited to intervene in this struggle – indeed, to complete the processes begun under the auspices and offices of the United Nations. The recovery of fulsome Mauritian sovereignty is asserted as a clear and unambiguous goal of decolonisation. There is no recognition that the Chagossian interests are not a direct concomitant of a recovered Mauritian sovereignty. The style of address – an ironic, yet heroic, bluster, urging a return of sovereignty – does not address the substance of the claim that it is, after all, the Chagossians and not the Mauritian state who were dispossessed, exiled and denied a home.

The UK has responded to the ICJ decision by stating that the Advisory Opinions are 'non-binding', and reiterated its position that the dispute is of a bilateral character between the UK and Mauritius. Sovereignty in respect of the Chagos Archipelago would be ceded by the UK to Mauritius once it is no longer required for security and defence purposes.[10] And so, despite the romantic tale of the heroic triumph of international law over the UK's ongoing colonial practices, and the symbolic power of the judgment, the status quo of displaced Chagossians and UK sovereignty over the Chagos Archipelago remains the reality.

Tragic capitulation: recalling the 'conscription' of Mauritius into modernity

Many critical approaches to decolonisation and international law have been informed by David Scott's *Conscripts of Modernity*. Scott urges a move away from anti-colonial romanticism to tragedy as the appropriate form of postcolonial emplotment. He also provides an evocative account of how anti-colonial struggles and postcolonial aspirations are conscripted into modern political formations. Let us then consider how the Chagossian predicament and the postcolonial Mauritian state may be framed in tragic terms as conscripts of modernity.

The *Advisory Opinion* returns us to the events of 1965 when the Chagos Archipelago was separated from the territory of Mauritius. By revisiting this archive of imperial power-politics, the ICJ is able to shine a light on the conditions under which Mauritius agreed to the detachment of the Chagos Archipelago from its territory. By doing this it assists the UNGA's task of 'completing decolonization'. The account offered is of a cornered Mauritian delegation having to accept terms dictated by the UK or risk the prize of their independence. If this is a tragic emplotment of a postcolonial state being 'conscripted' (Scott's term) into the modern sovereign form, then presenting Mauritian independence as a 'deal' done at the expense of the Chagossian population hardly reflects sympathetically on the Mauritians. As the *Advisory Opinion* recounts,

8 White, *Metahistory*, 31.

9 In making this observation I am drawing on White's account of figural language which I elaborate later.

10 See discussion in Jeffery, "The International Court of Justice," 26.

on 22 September 1965, a note was prepared by Sir Oliver Wright, private secretary to the prime minister, Sir Harold Wilson, in the following terms:

> Sir Seewoosagur Ramgoolam is coming to see you at 10:00 tomorrow morning. *The object is to frighten him with hope*: hope that he might get independence; Fright lest he might not unless he is sensible about the detachment of the Chagos Archipelago. I attach a brief prepared by the Colonial Office, with which the Ministry of Defence and the Foreign Office are on the whole content. The key sentence in the brief is the last sentence of it on page three.
>
> *(para. 105, emphasis added)*

That sentence read:

> The Prime Minister may therefore wish to make some oblique reference to the fact that H.M.G. have the legal right to detach Chagos by Order in Council, *without* Mauritius consent but this would be a grave step.
>
> *(para. 106, emphasis in original)*

Two events then followed on 23 September 1965. First, Prime Minister Wilson met Premier Ramgoolam. As Sir Oliver Wright's report of the meeting indicates, Prime Minister Wilson told Premier Ramgoolam that:

> in theory there were a number of possibilities. The Premier and his colleagues could return to Mauritius either with Independence or without it. On the Defence point, Diego Garcia could either be detached by order in Council or with the agreement of the Premier and his colleagues. The best solution of all might be Independence and detachment by agreement, although he could not of course commit the Colonial Secretary at this point.
>
> *(para. 107)*

Later the same day, a meeting took place at Lancaster House in which various undertakings were given to the Mauritian delegation regarding the UK using its good offices to advance the security and trading interests of Mauritius. The UK would also urge the United States to draw on labour and materials from Mauritius for construction on the islands (para. 108). On this basis, the delegation from Mauritius agreed to the detachment of the Chagos archipelago: 'On 5 November 1965, the Governor of Mauritius informed the United Kingdom Secretary of State that the Mauritius Council of Ministers "confirmed agreement to the detachment of the Chagos Archipelago"' (para. 112). Acting within the constraints of circumstances and conditions that are not entirely of their making – the contingency of action that rarely delivers all that is desired – a tragedy of dispossession and exile follows. It is, however, a tragedy visited upon the Chagossians. It is worth continuing to ask what consequences will follow from the remedy being a return of sovereignty to Mauritius.

There was apparently a degree of self-consciousness about its deviance at the time that the UK was setting itself against the pattern of decolonisation through these extortionate means:

> In a Minute sent on 5 November 1965 to the United Kingdom Prime Minister, the Secretary of State for the Colonies expressed concern that the United Kingdom would be accused of "creating a . . . colony in a period of decolonisation and of establishing new

> military bases when we should be getting out of the old ones". The Foreign Office also advised that "the islands chosen have virtually no permanent inhabitants".
>
> *(para. 111)*

The memos and notes that have emerged as part of the Chagossian litigation reveal an imperial power conscious of the emerging international institutions, laws and obligations. It is also a power capable of inscribing a 'not yet' or 'when it suits us!' in response to the aspirations of autonomy, territorial integrity and self-determination of states that are being decolonised.

The historicists will tell us that Sir Ramgoolam and his colleagues of the Mauritian delegation to London in 1965 need to be viewed in the context in which they acted. While the ICJ in 2019 has reiterated the UNGA resolutions of the 1960s – it was the fulfilment of 'hope' rather than 'right' that appeared to be the operative basis for the granting of Mauritian independence – albeit delivered with all the arrogance of an empire in decline. There is no hint that the ICJ is judging the actions of the Mauritian delegation. What would condition such judgment, in any case?

Instead, what we implicitly gather from the ICJ decision is that Sir Ramgoolam was in a tight corner; he acted within those constraints; Mauritius gained its independence, but it did so through the tragic sacrifice of the Chagossians. Moreover, the *Advisory Opinion* conveys the sense of international law completing an unfinished process of decolonisation – if only the UK would fall into line, relinquish sovereignty and cede the Archipelago to Mauritius. It is not an absence of law or relevant norms to govern international conduct that was a problem in 1965. On the face of it, the *Advisory Opinion* is trying to fill the void that was and is the ineffectiveness of international law. Then, as now, the violence flows from the UK's refusal to submit to these international legal norms, resolutions and determinations – rather than the absence of norms. Then, as now, the subsuming of Chagossian interests with the 'completion' of Mauritian sovereignty is a flawed path to justice because it assumes that all will be put right if only the UK would comply with international norms. As I set out previously, Chagossian exiles and their descendants would still then be faced with the plight of all minorities – their resettlement will be a function of their nationality and the exigencies of a 'fully' sovereign state. What insights may we draw from the humanities in seeking to understand and respond to this problem?

International law as historiography?

Part of what the humanities offer a study of international law is a means for comprehending the relationship between past, present and future. It is precisely that relationship that is being contested, ordered and re-ordered in the litany of juridical interventions in relation to the Chagos Archipelago. Confronting the successes and failures, hopes and aspirations of decolonisation in these cases can usefully be understood as a historiographical problem. To that extent, the emplotment of past, present and future in and through international law is a historiographical task.

The romantic and tragic emplotments that manifest the 'style' of international law that I have sketched through the *Advisory Opinion* are examples of narrative forms and ways of being that can be better understood through historiographical theories informed by the humanities. While it is beyond the scope of this essay to chart the full implications of understanding international law as a set of problems to be examined through a philosophy of history, we can identify the historiographical questions that arise from juridical interventions such as the *Advisory Opinion*. How might these questions be addressed with techniques and strategies drawn from the humanities?

Hayden White summed up historical theory most eloquently when he distinguished 'past reality, which is the historian's object of study; historiography, which is the written discourse about this object; and philosophy of history, which is the study of the possible relations obtaining between this object and this discourse'.[11] White argued that 'events, persons, structures, and processes of the past' can be taken as objects of study by any discipline of the human and social sciences, and indeed by the physical sciences.[12] But he insisted that it is not their pastness that makes these events and persons etc 'historical', but the fact they are written about (or spoken, sung, danced, acted and so on) 'as subject of a specifically historical kind of writing'.[13] Language as the form and conduit of discourse is not merely the carrier of 'realistic' content: 'language is both a form and a content.'[14] 'Style' is not simply the 'attractive, but by no means essential, clothing' of a historical account, but makes up the total content of the discourse as a whole.[15] It might be retorted that if a complete separation between form/content is one extreme to be avoided, then a complete dissolution of the form/content distinction is the other extreme to be resisted. In response to this we should note that we are discussing modes of representing history in and through language. It is because history can be written, performed and read as representing the object in a particular style that literary theory is so relevant for historiography and for the philosophy of history.

A mere chronology of events – such as what did and did not happen during the decolonisation of Mauritius in the 1960s – can be imbued with a plot structure through discursive techniques that White asserted were more 'tropological than logical in nature'.[16] These emplotments are tropological to the extent that, first, even temporal units of chronologies are culturally specific and not natural. To that extent the constitution of a chronicle 'as a set of events that can provide the elements of a story is an operation more poetic than scientific in nature'.[17] Second, White explained that transforming a chronicle of events into a story requires a choice from among different plot structures. There is no code that would suggest whether tragic, romantic or other plot structure is appropriate. To emplot an event as a particular kind of story it is necessary to trope those events:

> This is because stories are not lived; there is no such thing as a real story. Stories are told or written, not found. And as for a notion of a true story, this is virtually a contradiction in terms. All stories are fictions.[18]

Third, the arguments used by historians to explain the meaning of a chronicle of events will depend on the plot used to fashion the story: 'this means that the argument of a historical discourse is ultimately a second-order fiction, a fiction of a fiction, or fiction of fiction making, which bears the same relationship to the plot that the plot bears to the chronicle.'[19]

11 Hayden White, *Figural Realism: Studies in the Mimesis Effect* (Baltimore: Johns Hopkins University Press, 1999), 3.
12 Ibid., 2.
13 Ibid.
14 Ibid., 4.
15 Ibid. I return to the notion of 'style' later.
16 Ibid., 8.
17 Ibid., 9.
18 Ibid. More careful consideration needs to be given to the implications of White's account of history and stories in the context of Indigenous accounts of the relationship between stories, country and people. Suffice it to say that casting stories as fictions should not diminish their standing.
19 Ibid.

No single emplotment can be drawn on to frame the wide-ranging twists and turns in the fate of the Chagossian exiles and their descendants. There is no plot that accords with the 'real'. In the UK courts Britain's Robinsonian fantasy of sovereign solitude and self-sufficiency was contrasted to the Friday-like Chagossians.[20] This much is well known – Daniel Defoe's *Robinson Crusoe* (1719) helped to fashion the colonial imaginary through a pelagic tale about the inner life, trials and endurance of his protagonist. Crusoe and His Man Friday offered enduring racialised archetypes of coloniser and colonised, helping to create the myth of sovereign solitude interrupted only by the duties of the beneficent Master to the hapless Savage. It provided an image of a colonial state or people being alone, being as One, that persists in contemporary populist aspirations from Trumpism to Brexit.

Among the fantastic tropes mediating legal decisions is the prevailing hold of Crusoe and Friday on British judges and civil servants. In multiple judicial decisions concerning the Chagos Archipelago and its exiled people, Crusoe and Friday have featured as recurrent figures of sovereign capacity and raced being. The UK Colonial Office memos from the 1960s, Lord Hoffman's strained fictions in *Bancoult No. 2* (2009) and meetings between US/UK government officials disclosed by WikiLeaks in 2010 show the persistence of the Robinsonade for sustaining colonial and neo-imperial power.[21] For the ICJ, the grander vision of decolonisation of territories with sovereign *plenitude* remains strong. What are the other emplotments of decolonisation? What are the other postcolonial futures?

David Scott builds on White's notion of emplotment as the way 'temporarily connected events are constituted into a narrative such that readers recognize it to be a particular kind of story' – such as tragedy, romance, comedy or satire.[22] In *Conscripts of Modernity*, Scott contrasts romance and tragedy as modes of historical emplotment.[23] He suggests that 'anticolonial stories about past, present, and future have typically been emplotted in a particular narrative form, one with a distinctive story-potential: that of *Romance*'.[24] This romance usually involves heroic feats of emancipatory overcoming that moves history teleologically from past, present, to future. Scott's inquiry is inspired by Talal Asad's essay 'Conscripts of Western Civilization' in honour of the anthropologist Stanley Diamond. In it Asad eschewed Diamond's romanticism about primitive cultures being overcome by Western civilisation, but argued that, although difference is not disappearing, it is 'increasingly obliged to respond to – and be managed by – the categories brought into play by European modernity'.[25] Scott draws on these thoughts to examine the relationship between modernity and historical change.

The past and future are encountered through narrative forms that mimic literary structures of emplotment. For instance, Adil Hasan Khan usefully draws on Scott's work and extends it to examine plots of Bandung histories of catastrophe told through the narrative forms of satire, romance or tragedy.[26] As Hasan Khan points out, in the narrative of Bandung as satirical event, decolonisation is a 'futile repetition of the previously existing order rather than transformational

20 See Motha, *Archiving Sovereignty*, Chapter 1, for an elaboration of this Robinsonade.
21 Ibid.
22 Scott, *Conscripts*, 46–47.
23 Ibid., 11.
24 Ibid., 7.
25 Ibid., 9.
26 Adil Hasan Khan, "Ghostly Visitations: 'Questioning Heirs' and the Tragic Task of Narrating Bandung Futures," in *Bandung, Global History, and International Law: Critical Pasts and Pending Futures*, eds. Luis Eslava, Michael Fakhri and Vasuki Nesiah (Cambridge: University of Cambridge Press, 2017), 108–25.

change'.[27] In the 'romance of overcoming' (David Scott's term), the postcolonial transition is a triumphant one.[28] International lawyers are particularly prone to this version when international society purportedly 'moves toward true universality and leaves behind a sordid colonial past'.[29] When catastrophe invariably happens, it is 'a reversal of achievements and vision of Bandung that arrives subsequent to the moment when all was clear and the Promised Land seemed so close at hand'.[30]

Hasan Khan goes on to explain how in accounts of Bandung as tragedy, impurities and contradictions are presented as the contingent constraints in which a new order struggles to be born.[31] In this tragic narrative form of the story, catastrophe is coterminous with the event of decolonisation. Instead of the pretense of a pure moment of freedom undone later, autonomy, sovereignty and self-determination are understood to be emergent phenomena to be asserted and established through international institutions. However, the universalisation of the nation-state form becomes another way of mobilising empire.[32] The nation-state is a modern form that enables the decolonised polity to act on the world stage. It is also the international subject that is later indicted for being a 'failed state' for not managing the passions and eruptions of national identity and internal difference. Adopting the form of a sovereign and equal nation-state, then, becomes the event of a tragic 'decision'.[33]

What does this say about the expectations of tragedians? There is a sense in this account of the tragic that the Bandung generation had been expected to make decisions and act in the form of 'rupture' or 'eruption', rather than as Marx put it, in circumstances 'given and transmitted from the past'.[34] The tragedy of Bandung, when framed in that way, stems from the fact that there was no *tabula rasa*, no freedom to cast the new society. What was possible was to adopt forms and act in conditions 'transmitted' to them from the past.[35] Hasan Khan proposes an evental task for the 'heirs' of Bandung who wish to imagine a future with and through the inheritance from the past. His proposal is that Bandung be narrated as a tragic inheritance which is inherently plural, contradictory and heterogeneous. This means that there is no one, stable inheritance. It is this irresolution and incoherence that makes the Bandung inheritance transformative.[36]

For Kevin Olson, Scott's focus on tragedy 'has all of the broader limitations of any narrative genre as a mode of storytelling. Tragedy still sacrifices complexity for the sake of style'.[37] Setting a story within a genre decides in advance what kind of story is being told. Olson argues that both romance and tragedy are 'normative modes of storytelling'; romance celebrates character, and tragedy indicts the contingent circumstances in which heroes act.[38] Olson is particularly concerned with the Foucauldian episteme that this kind of history writings seems to emulate. For Foucault – and this is possibly true of Scott's orientation given the focus on the character of

27 Ibid., 109.
28 Ibid., 111.
29 Ibid.
30 Ibid., 112.
31 Ibid., 115.
32 Ibid., 116–17.
33 Ibid., 118.
34 Ibid., 120.
35 Ibid.
36 Ibid., 124.
37 Kevin Olson, *Imagined Sovereignties: The Power of the People and Other Myths of the Modern Age* (Cambridge: Cambridge University Press, 2016), 164.
38 Ibid., 164.

Toussaint Louverture in *The Black Jacobins* – the concepts deployed are individualisation, subjectification and truth-telling.[39] Instead of this, Olson suggests that modernity's greatest potential lies in developing insights about 'collective norm- and culture-formation'.[40] The focus here is on the 'political imagination' itself and the agencies, norms, institutions and sovereignties it constitutes within a 'complex play of conscription and creative improvisation'.[41] It is not clear, however, how any political imagination can avoid the aesthetic dimension. Privileging the political and normative over the aesthetic is a false choice.

Returning to Scott, we see that he is concerned with the aesthetic dimension of how a story is told. In this orientation he is inspired by C. L. R. James who disavowed the 'positivist fallacy' that facts can simply be the 'arbiter and adjudicator of historical meaning'.[42] There is also a fallacy that a truth can be produced by holding facts and literary form apart:

> For James the language in which his story is cast is no mere neutral container for the facts of the San Domingo Revolution to be poured into. For him, history is not merely the provision of useful information about "what really happened", but the endowment of events with significance and meaning. James, I am going to suggest, is a storyteller – a mythmaker.[43]

Scott returns to this motif of storytelling in the epilogue of the book. Here he compares Hannah Arendt's treatment of the American and French revolutions with C. L. R. James's treatment of the neglected Haitian Revolution.

Arendt had argued in *On Revolution* that the US had failed to establish the 'cognitive conditions of "remembrance"' of what they were originally seeking to do. Scott goes on to quote Arendt at length:

> Experience and even the stories that grow out of what men do and endure, of happenings and events, sink back into the futility inherent in the living word and the living deed unless they are talked about over and over again. What saves the affairs of mortal men from their inherent futility is nothing but this incessant talk about them, which in its turn remains futile unless certain concepts, certain guideposts for future remembrance, and even for sheer reference, arise out of it.[44]

Remembrance needed a conceptual framework through which it could exercise itself. It also needed stories to be told, over and over again. The telling of these stories, as we observed through White earlier, will necessarily involve narrative fictions.

★

In concluding these observations about emplotment it is helpful to be reminded of what Gerry Simpson has said about sentiment and style in international law. Simpson argues that it has become harder to unite literary fiction with juridical accounts of life: 'we live in a period in which it is harder to unite literature, myth, theatre, law and political life than it was, in, say, the

39 Ibid., 165.
40 Ibid., 166.
41 Ibid.
42 Scott, *Conscripts*, 39.
43 Ibid.
44 Ibid., 216, quoting Hannah Arendt, *On Revolution* (New York: Viking, 1963), 220.

classical period, and this represents a loss for us.'[45] His sentimental approach to international law seeks to overcome this. Simpson argues that much political and everyday life is not accessible to us because it is obscured by being informal, unconscious, emotional and micro-political. Accessing the sentimental lives of international law and its practitioners through legal scholarship and teaching is bound up with 'a sense if its literary style' or more strongly, that 'it *is* its literary style'.[46] Style is a matter of aesthetic judgment, but as Simpson puts it, it is also a matter of feeling and sentiment.[47] The language of international law, for instance, articulates ways of understanding, sharing, organising and inhabiting the world. Style is then not a superficial decoration but a mode of thinking and being. Observing and examining style in international law and politics is a means of accessing particular ways of thinking and being.

What Simpson relays about 'style' and international law is congruent with the influential approaches to history in the humanities – that of Hayden White, and after him David Scott, which we have been examining. However, Simpson's focus on 'style', which overlaps with but is more widely construed than the structured approach to emplotment taken by White and Scott, can enable international lawyers to comprehend ways of thinking and being without collapsing these into the established narrative genres such as romance and tragedy. It is also worth recalling the 'globa-latinisation' of the world and the homogenising literary frames.[48] The Western canon of literature and literariness, universalised in and through imperial projects, cannot be left to over-determine the narrative emplotments of anti-colonial resistance and decolonisation. Rather than the grand plots of literary archetypes (of romance, satire or tragedy) we might seek another scene – the *other* scene – of emotions, memories and unconscious commitments. These might be recovered through a 'reflective nostalgia' where time is heterogeneous and humans abandon their drive to make another history.[49] This includes questioning sovereignty – whether that be of the Chagos Archipelago, Mauritius or elsewhere – as the sole aspiration and horizon of decolonisation.

The story told in the ICJ *Advisory Opinion* of the incomplete or failed decolonisation of Mauritius is one that relies heavily on a version of international law that treats sovereignty as capable of being fulsome and complete.[50] This is a narrative that is as important to international law (perhaps even more significant for it), as the constituent ground of that law, than the rights of a displaced and exiled minority such as the Chagossians. Judged in these terms, a 'fully' decolonised Mauritius conceived solely in terms of the recovery from the UK and return to its territory of the Chagos Archipelago demonstrates a strong and somewhat archaic link between territorial integrity, the sovereignty of the nation-state and international law. Rather a lot of ink has been spilt by international lawyers trying to undo the inviolability of sovereign territory, such as in relation to the right of states to intervene in circumstances that activate the 'responsibility to protect' (R2P). That is one reason for my scepticism about the valorisation of the relationship between territory and sovereignty in the *Advisory Opinion*.

45 Gerry Simpson, "The Sentimental Life of International Law," *London Review of International Law* 3, no. 1 (2015): 3–29, 7.
46 Ibid., 8.
47 Ibid.
48 See Jacques Derrida, *Demeure: Fiction and Testimony* (Stanford, CA: Stanford University Press, 2000).
49 See Svetlana Boym, *The Future of Nostalgia* (New York: Basic Books, 2001); and the Epilogue to Motha, *Archiving Sovereignty*.
50 For an elaboration of the relation between storytelling and law as fundamental to constituting what law is, see Stewart Motha, "My Story, Whose Memory? Reflections on the Autonomy and Heteronomy of Law" (forthcoming).

Scant attention has been paid by international legal institutions or municipal courts to the actual conditions under which the exiled population of Chagossians live in Mauritius. Their right to occupy the islands of the Archipelago were also not argued in proprietary terms or as usufructuary rights. Native title or other rights that communities hold after long possession or occupation were not grounds argued in the UK cases. All this points to the narrowness and impoverished state of constitutional and administrative law in the UK. A similar charge can be levelled at international institutions. None of these observations are intended to excuse the heinous actions of the UK government in the 1960s, or its failure to take full responsibility over the last two decades of litigation and activism around the issues. Addressing these wider questions of property, belonging and exile requires international law and its institutions to step away from being the heroic defender of sovereignty tragically lost.

21

Contested histories

Revisiting the relationship between international law and slavery

Anne-Charlotte Martineau

Introduction

For the last couple of years, I have been revisiting the historical relationship between slavery and international law. In so doing, I often read and draw inspiration from the research carried out by members of the Institute for International Law and the Humanities. Many of them study the history, theory and practice of international law with a focus on inequalities and the lived realities of peoples of the Global South.[1] Because they want to grasp the role of international law in global governance, they are attentive to – and attempt to destabilise – existing narratives that portray the role of international law in an excessively positive light. In this chapter, I want to show that one such narrative pertains to slavery.

Slavery is one of the very few issues that are indisputably and unanimously condemned by modern international lawyers. The prohibition against slavery is regularly cited as a *ius cogens* norm while the long campaign to abolish the transatlantic slave trade has been presented as 'the most successful episode ever'[2] in the history of our discipline. In fact, as Frederic Mégret rightly observed, 'few causes have marked the modern development of international law as much as the abolition of slavery'.[3] The work produced by the first generation of 'gentle civilizers'[4] is a case at point: many of them celebrated the role of international law in abolishing the slave trade and slavery. They did not hesitate to condemn the conduct of Spain and other European powers after the arrival of Columbus at Hispañola in 1492.[5] They made sure, however, to contrast these

1 See for example Sundhya Pahuja, *Decolonizing International Law: Development, Economic Growth and the Politics of Universality* (Cambridge: Cambridge University Press, 2011).

2 Jennifer Martinez, *The Slave Trade and the Origins of International Human Rights Law* (New York: Oxford University Press, 2012), 13.

3 Frédéric Mégret, "Droit international et esclavage: pour une réévaluation," *African Yearbook of International Law* 121 (2013): 122.

4 Martti Koskenniemi, *The Gentle Civilizers of Nations: The Rise and Fall of International Law 1870–1960* (Cambridge: Cambridge University Press, 2001).

5 See for example Edouard Couvé, *La traite au point de vue du droit des gens* (Paris: Rousseau, 1889); Henri Lévy, *La traite des noirs et les Puissances* (Nancy: Crépin-Leblond, 1894); Henri Quéneuil, *De la traite des noirs et de l'esclavage. La conférence de Bruxelles et ses résultats* (Paris: Larose & Tenin, 1907); Michel-Louis-Ferdinand Sarrien, *La traite des*

practices with nineteenth-century colonialism and the on-going civilising mission of Africa. They insisted on the long march undertaken towards the abolition of slavery, and the need for further civilisation of 'barbaric' peoples (i.e., those who had sold their own people). Their celebratory tone called for more international law and for more intervention in the Global South.[6]

More than a century later, there is a renewed interest in the history of international law with regard to slavery. Often, the story that is told of the relationship between international law and slavery continues to be a generous one; it strengthens the thinking about slavery as a persistent phenomenon that exists in spite of international law and the good work done by international lawyers. What is characteristic of this narrative is the tendency to simplify and celebrate international law's involvement in ending the slave trade and slavery before redeploying that role in the present in order to promote some kind of humanitarian project (Part I). This is not the end of the matter, however. Over the last couple of years, a number of international lawyers have been looking at the history of international law and slavery in a more critical vein. They have shed light on the intricate relationship between the legal abolition of slavery and European imperialism. These historical studies are particularly instructive insofar as they destabilise the discipline's self-conception as an anti-slavery champion. What will need to be explained, however, is why the counterpoint ceases to be enlightening when speaking about the present and debating which institutional arrangements should address modern forms of slavery (Part II).

Standard narrative: a history of abolition

The involvement of international law on matters pertaining to slavery is generally presented through a specific historical narrative – namely, one of humanitarian progress. It is a 200-year-long story of abolition that starts with the 1815 Declaration made at the Congress of Vienna by European powers, that continues with the anti-slavery commissions set up by Great Britain in the mid-nineteenth century and that triumphs with the adoption in institutional *fora* of the 1926 Slavery Convention, the 1930 Forced Labour Convention and the 1956 Supplementary Convention.[7] Mention is then usually made of the progress achieved thanks to human rights mechanisms and the criminalisation of slavery through the Palermo Protocol and the Statute of the International Criminal Court (ICC).[8] What is certainly most disturbing about this narrative is its teleological and European-driven nature, as if abolition had been a process of expansion

---

nègres et le droit de visite au cours du XIXe siècle dans les rapports de la France et de l'Angleterre (Paris: Jouve et Cie, 1910); Karl Gareis, *Der Sklavenhandel, das Völkerrecht und das deutsche Recht* (Berlin: Deutsche Zeit- und Streit-Fragen, 1885).

6 One example among many is the doctorate thesis on the transatlantic slave trade that Henri de Montardy defended in 1906 at the Law Faculty of the University of Paris. After revisiting the carrier of African captives across the Atlantic, and after celebrating the abolition of slavery through international treaties by European states, Montardy posited that it would be a terrible mistake to grant Africans absolute freedom. Time and education were needed for the emancipation of those who had sold their own people during the barbarous slave trade. 'Only civilisation can, thanks to its slow but firm penetration, be a solution to problem of slavery': Henri de Montardy, *La traite et le droit international* (Paris: Girard & Brière, 1906), 203.

7 Ved Nanda and Mahmoud Cherif Bassiouni, "Slavery and Slave Trade: Steps Toward Eradication," *Santa Clara Law Review* 12, no. 2 (1979). The same narrative can be found in international legal textbooks. See also Seymour Drescher and Paul Finkelman, "Slavery," in *The Oxford Handbook of the History of International Law*, eds. Bardo Fassbender and Anne Peters (Oxford: Oxford University Press, 2012), 890–916; Dominique Gaurier, *Histoire du droit international. De l'Antiquité à la création de l'ONU* (Rennes: PUR, 2014), 1058–70.

8 For a survey of UN mechanisms such as the Special Rapporteur on Contemporary Forms of Slavery and the Human Rights Committee, see Vladislava Stoyanova, "United Nations Against Slavery: Unravelling Concepts, Institutions and Obligations," *Michigan Journal of International Law* 38, no. 3 (2017).

from ('enlightened') core to ('backward') periphery. But I also want to stress the heroic image it portrays of our discipline. By focussing on abolition exclusively, the standard narrative suggests that international rules and institutions stepped in only in the nineteenth century to combat, with great success, the slave trade and slavery. The ideology that is conveyed is powerful and remains pervasive still today: 'slavery', observes Anthony Anghie, 'is an abhorrence against which international law can demonstrate its commitment to protecting human dignity and furthering the cause of international law.'[9]

This narrative is not only found in general textbooks and online encyclopaedias.[10] It is also put forth in scholarly articles, especially in the fields of human rights and international criminal law. It can take the form of an introduction or shortened version of the legal history of abolition before international lawyers turn to examine contemporary case law on slavery – thereby suggesting a continuity between nineteenth-century legal developments and today's international human rights courts, the latter constituting the endpoint of a long process of humanitarian dedication and legal efforts.[11] A stronger claim can also be made whereby the legal history of abolition serves not the purpose of continuity but that of origins. One example is the special issue on slavery that was published in the *International Journal for Criminal Justice* in 2016. Although the issue was titled 'Slavery and the Limits of International Criminal Justice', the whole point was to promote the role of international criminal law in the ongoing fight against slavery. For this, the three organisers of the special issue – all of them involved in international policy-making on slavery – argued that the origins of their field lay in the slave trade abolition process. In the words of James Cockayne, Nick Grono and Kari Panaccione, 'Slavery was arguably the spur that set the international criminal justice train in motion, 200 years ago.'[12] To support this argument about their field's origins, they relied on Jenny Martinez's book, *The Slave Trade and The Origins of International Human Rights Law*.[13] They asserted that mixed commissions (renamed 'courts') established by Great Britain through bilateral treaties in the nineteenth century played a catalysing role in the emergence of international criminal law. Granted, they say, these courts could not exact penalties against crews or owners of slave ships. But they had a deterrent effect insofar as they were authorised to confiscate vessels, equipment and merchandise, and also to release captives. In addition, because courts had jurisdiction to arrest nationals of the states backing the courts, who were then obliged to try them in their own courts, mixed commissions could – and should – be seen as a 'precursor to the modern system of complementarity'.[14]

A number of critiques have already been formulated against Martinez's book after its publication in 2012. Renowned historians and international lawyers such as Samuel Moyn, Lauren

9 Antony Anghie, "Slavery and International Law: The Jurisprudence of Henry Richardson," *Temple International and Contemporary Law Journal* 31, no. 1 (2017): 13.

10 See for example Patrick Daillier and Alain Pellet, *Droit International Public*, 7th ed. (Paris: IGDJ, 2002), 707–8; Malcom Shaw, *International Law* (Cambridge: Cambridge University Press, 2008), 270; Silvia Scarpa, "Slavery," *Oxford Bibliography on International Law*, www.oxfordbibliographies.com/view/document/obo-9780199796953/obo-9780199796953-0097.xml; David Weissbrodt, "Slavery," *Max Planck Encyclopaedia of Public International Law*, http://opil.ouplaw.com/view/10.1093/law:epil/9780199231690/law-9780199231690-e874. See also Randall Lesaffer, "Vienna and the Abolition of the Slave Trade," *Oxford Public International Law*, http://opil.ouplaw.com/page/vienna-slave-trade-abolition.

11 See Andrea Nicholson, "Reflections on *Siliadin v. France*: Slavery and Legal Definition," *The International Journal of Human Rights* 14, no. 5 (2010).

12 James Cockayne, Nick Grono and Kari Panaccione, "Introduction," *Journal of International Criminal Justice* 14, no. 2 (2016): 258.

13 Martinez, *Slave Trade*, 6.

14 Cockayne, Grono and Panaccione, "Introduction," 258.

Benton and Philip Alston considered Martinez's thesis to be over-simplistic (if not utterly utopian) because she neglected to situate legal developments in the larger socio-economic and political context.[15] Her story of the abolition of the slave trade is essentially one of moral values becoming enshrined in international law that triumphed over economic and other 'great power' considerations.[16] They also criticised Martinez for having failed to bridge the past and the present in any convincing fashion.[17] According to Moyn, while it may be true that today's normative instruments and institutions look like those of yesterday, Martinez did not connect the dots between the nineteenth and twenty-first centuries in any meaningful way.[18] This proved to be particularly dangerous as Martinez did not hesitate to draw lessons from what she considered to be a successful episode.[19] Among others, she called upon the world's leading power, United States, to take inspiration from the British Empire and 'foster democracy and human rights both through the use of force and through legal institutions'.[20] Alston's response to this imperial nostalgia is unequivocal: 'to the extent that major elements of the British approach were imperialistic, albeit partly in the pursuit of an admirable goal, it becomes all the more important to exercise caution and discernment in drawing lessons for the future.'[21]

In light of this, one would think that international lawyers would have been more careful in reclaiming the (supposedly) valiant role international law played in the abolition process for the sake of today's agenda. But, as the special issue of the *International Journal for Criminal Justice* shows, this is not the case.[22] The three organisers did not attempt to provide a richer or finer contextual reading of international law's involvement in the abolition of the slave trade. In fact, their objective was not to study the past; their objective was to use history in order to advance the cause of international criminal justice today. Since international criminal courts already dealt with slavery successfully in the nineteenth century, there is no reason why they shouldn't be involved today and be successful again, right? This blunt superposition is the reason why their argument cannot be regarded as a serious historical engagement. History is merely there to support or vindicate global criminal justice – it is a noble project we should all embrace. The problem, to borrow Moyn's words, is that conjuring up the abolition process to buck up the project of international criminal justice turns into a political and intellectual trap: the special

15 Lauren Benton, "Abolition and Imperial Law, 1790–1820," *The Journal of Imperial and Commonwealth History* 39, no. 3 (2011). Martinez also failed to mention the important historical work done by international lawyers on the slave trade, such as Jean Allain, "The Nineteenth Century Law of the Sea and the British Abolition of the Slave Trade," *British Yearbook of International Law* 78, no. 1 (2008); Holger Lutz Kern, "Strategies of Legal Change: Great Britain, International Law, and the Abolition of the Transatlantic Slave Trade," *Journal of the History of International Law* 6 (2004).

16 In her response to Alston, Martinez rejected this critique, claiming that she did acknowledge that other (meaning, non-humanitarian) interests were at stake in the process: Jennifer Martinez, "Human Rights and History," *Harvard Law Review Forum* 126 (2012).

17 Lauren Benton, "The Slave Trade and the Origins of International Human Rights Law," *Victorian Studies* 56, no. 1 (2013).

18 Samuel Moyn, "Of Deserts and Promised Lands: The Dream of Global Justice," *The Nation*, February 20, 2012, www.thenation.com/article/deserts-and-promised-lands-dream-global-justice/.

19 Martinez, *Slave Trade*, 15.

20 Ibid., 15. While the United States could still do so, it should also project its 'economic and military power' into the future by supporting the International Criminal Court.

21 Philip Alston, "Does the Past Matter? On the Origins of Human Rights," *Harvard Law Review* 26 (2013): 2061.

22 For a more thoughtful approach, see Ariela Gross, "Introduction: 'A Crime Against Humanity': Slavery and The Boundaries of Legality, Past and Present," *Law and History Review* 35, no. 1 (2017).

issue obscures 'the conditions under which the cause of international criminal justice suddenly became so appealing and international courts currently operate'.[23]

International lawyers working in the field of human rights and criminal justice are not the only ones invoking international law's heroic role in the 'fight against slavery' to assert their field's authority. References to the past, and especially the slave trade, constitute a privileged discursive strategy in the context of competing knowledge communities and international legal regimes (i.e., complexes of norms and institutions) dealing with slavery. Over the last two decades, the fight against modern slavery has come to be chiefly understood in terms of 'fighting human trafficking'. This was triggered, in part, by the adoption of the UN Protocol to Prevent, Suppress and Publish Trafficking in Persons, Especially Women and Children in 2000 – otherwise known as the Palermo or Trafficking Protocol – which supplemented the UN Convention Against Transnational Organized Crimes. The fight against human trafficking has experienced a remarkable degree of success in terms of popular awareness, institutional leverage and resource allocation. In 2005, the Council of Europe adopted its own Convention on Action against Trafficking in Human Beings.[24] References to the slave trade have been commonly used. Take the speech the then US President George W Bush gave to the UN General Assembly on 23 September 2003:

> There's another humanitarian crisis spreading [beside famine], yet hidden from view. Each year, an estimated 800,000 to 900,000 human beings are bought, sold or forced across the world's borders. Among them are hundreds of thousands of teenage girls, and others as young as five, who fall victim to the sex trade. This commerce in human life generates billions of dollars each year – much of which is used to finance organized crime. . . . We must show new energy in fighting back an old evil. Nearly two centuries after the abolition of the transatlantic slave trade, and more than a century after slavery was officially ended in its last strongholds, the trade in human beings for any purpose must not be allowed to thrive in our time.[25]

In comparison to Martinez's book or the special issue of the *International Journal of Criminal Justice*, the narrative here is meant to be realistic. Bush's tone is grave, and the dangers are palpable.[26] Did Bush, by presenting himself to the UN as the leader of a large-scale campaign to end human trafficking, seek to gain support for the rather intrusive monitoring measures that the United States had put in place (and are still in place today)?[27] In any case, Bush glided over the reality that the United States' internal slavery did not end until the Civil War and the adoption

23 Moyn, *Deserts and Promised Lands*, 17.

24 See Boaventura de Sousa Santos, *The Fight Against Trafficking in Human Beings in EU: Promoting Legal Cooperation and Victims' Protection*, European Commission, www.transcrime.it/wp-content/uploads/2016/01/THB_CoopToFight.pdf.

25 George Bush, "Statement by His Excellency Mr George W. Bush, President of the United States of America. Address to the United Nations General Assembly," *UN*, September 23, 2003, www.un.org/webcast/ga/58/statements/usaeng030923.htm.

26 Imperial nostalgia also impregnates the anti-trafficking discourse. '[J]ust as the British government . . . once used the Royal Navy to stamp out the problem, today's great powers must bring their economic and military might to bear on this most crucial of undertakings': Ethan Kapstein, "The New Global Slave Trade," *Foreign Affairs* 85 (2006): 104.

27 The US has established an Office to Monitor and Combat Trafficking in Persons. The State Department also issues a "Trafficking in Persons (TIP) Report" annually, one that monitors how countries are addressing the challenges of human trafficking. See www.state.gov/j/tip/rls/tiprpt/.

of the Thirteenth Amendment to the American Constitution. He also made no mention of the slave-like conditions endured by former slaves and their descendants.[28] My point is that the so-called realism that characterises the anti-trafficking discourse depicts a highly selective 'reality' of the slave trade abolition and, in so doing, indicates the kind of law that will be privileged. The focus is no longer on the role played by courts and civil society, but on the punishment of deviant criminal behaviour and protection of 'vulnerable' people.

To say it differently, the anti-trafficking discourse presents a very narrow interpretation of the slave trade abolition, seeks to project that interpretation onto the present and extrapolates an extremely limited set of legal lessons. Critical voices have pointed out that references in the passive voice to one's own country's abolition of slavery, followed by mention of the return of slavery today, reinforces the 'denial of any complicity . . . in the slavery's re-emergence'[29] while condemning developing countries to be responsible for modern slavery. They have also warned that the contemporary fight should not be allowed to distract or deflect attention from the lasting effects of the original slavery itself. Instead of referring to the slave trade abolition as 'an emotional and historic touchstone – the blueprint against which [today's] traffic is measured',[30] the United States should address the legacies of slavery at home. Focus should be placed on the ongoing challenges confronting African-Americans, including 'the ways in which racial subordination persists in a supposedly post-racial world'.[31]

Counterpoint: a history of fragmentation

It would be reductive to relegate the entire international legal scholarship on the relationship between international law and slavery to one single narrative. Over the last decade, a number of international lawyers have studied that relationship more meticulously and thoughtfully. I am particularly appreciative of the work of Jean Allain,[32] Joel Quirk,[33] Karen Bravo[34] and Michel Erpelding,[35] who have offered a more sophisticated and nuanced understanding of the history of that relationship. Their work constitutes a counterpoint insofar as they destabilise, discredit or otherwise challenge the standard narrative. Let me give two examples.

Against Martinez et al., Quirk and Erpelding have shown that imperialism and colonialism were not side-issues in the nineteenth century but central to the law-making process on slavery. This also applies to the definitions of slavery and forced labour that were elaborated under the League of Nations.[36] These issues had become closely linked to European powers' colonial

28 Karen Bravo, "The Role of the Transatlantic Slave Trade in Contemporary Anti-Human Trafficking Discourse," *Seattle Journal for Social Justice* 9, no. 2 (2011): 562.

29 Karen Bravo, "Exploring the Analogy Between Modern Trafficking in Humans and the Trans-Atlantic Slave Trade," *Boston University International Law Journal* 25, no. 2 (2007): 221. See also Gretchen Soderlund, "Running from the Rescuers: New U.S. Crusades Against Sex Trafficking and the Rhetoric of Abolition," *National Women's Studies Association Journal* 17, no. 3 (2005).

30 Bravo, "Exploring the Analogy."

31 Anghie, *Slavery and International Law,* 21.

32 Jean Allain, *Slavery in International Law: Of Human Exploitation and Trafficking* (Leiden: Brill, 2012).

33 Joel Quirk, *The Anti-Slavery Project: From the Slave Trade to Human Trafficking* (Philadelphia: University of Pennsylvania Press, 2011).

34 Bravo, "Exploring the Analogy."

35 Michel Erpelding, *Le droit international antiesclavagiste des "nations civilisées" (1815–1945)* (Paris: Institut Universitaire Varenne, 2017).

36 To give one example, the French maintained forced labour for public works (*prestations en nature*) in their colonies until 1946: Jean Frimigacci, "L'Etat colonial français, du discours mythique aux réalités (1880–1940)," *Matériaux pour l'histoire de notre temps* 32–33 (1993).

policies: how should they condemn slavery – after all, this had been one of the justifications for colonising Africa in the first place – without jeopardising the need for a slavery-like labour force in their colonies?[37] This intricate balance was achieved by separating, in legal terms, the issue of slavery from that of forced labour, and by defining both terms narrowly. To start with, the drafters of the 1926 Slavery Convention agreed upon a formal definition of slavery as 'the status or condition of a person over whom any or all of the powers attaching to the right of ownership are exercised'.[38] From that moment onwards, the powers attached to the individual right of ownership as attributed by law became the *sine qua non* of slavery.[39] This definition made it easier for colonial authorities to close their eyes on African social mores such as domestic serfdom and servile marriage; these practices were considered either as 'soft or benevolent slavery'[40] or as falling outside the formal definition of slavery.[41] What is more, all major colonial powers opposed the inclusion of forced labour in the Slavery Convention on grounds of an infringement of their national sovereignty. This led the drafters to transfer that 'problem' to the International Labour Organization (ILO). A specific treaty was concluded in 1930 under the auspices of the ILO; it was largely the work of a committee which included four former colonial governors and the official adviser on African mine labour in the Transvaal.[42] Parties to the Forced Labour Convention agreed to progressively abolish 'all work or service which is exacted from any person under the menace of any penalty and for which the said person has not offered himself voluntarily'.[43] Otherwise, the convention required little more than the restriction of forced labour to a limited range of public works. This, again, was not incidental: forced labour was deemed necessary to colonial powers so that they could develop 'in the interests of humanity', no less, 'the riches and resources of those African countries placed under their sovereignty'.[44]

Likewise, against Bush et al., Bravo and Allain have shown that the genesis of the anti-trafficking project lies not in the transatlantic slave trade but in the white slave traffic. 'The regime of white slave traffic', argues Allain, is 'fundamental to understanding the evolution of what is today understood as human trafficking generally, and more specifically, trafficking related to sexual exploitation; and the dynamics which shaped its contemporary contours and the language used to define it'.[45] The white slave traffic arose in relation to the issue of venereal

37 Michel Erpelding, "L'esclavage en droit international: aux origines de la relecture actuelle de la définition conventionnelle de 1926," *Journal of the History of International Law* 17 (2015).

38 International Slavery Convention, 1926, Article 1(1).

39 This concerned effort to restrict the definition of slavery so that it did not apply in cases where a non-European government was the subject of inquiry (that is, Liberia): see Erpelding, *Le droit international antiesclavagiste*, 508–17.

40 Henri Queuneuil, "Conférence anti-esclavagiste de Bruxelles. Acte général du 2 juillet 1890: Application et résultats," *Revue Générale de Droit International* 15 (1908): 136.

41 See for example Fritz Weidner, *Die Haussklaverei in Ostafrica: Geschichtlich und Politisch Dargestellt* (Jena: Gustav Fischer, 1915).

42 See Suzanne Miers, *Slavery in the Twentieth Century. The Evolution of a Global Problem* (Walnut Creek: Altamira Press, 2003), 121–30.

43 *Forced Labour Convention* 1930 (no. 29), Article 2(1).

44 League of Nations, Note Submitted to the First Sub-Committee of the Six Committee by the Portuguese Delegate, General Freire d'Andrade, AVI/S.C.1/2.1925, September 11, 1925, quoted by Jean Allain, *The Legal Understanding of Slavery: From the Historical to the Contemporary* (Oxford: Oxford University Press, 2012), 202.

45 Jean Allain, "White Slave Traffic in International Law," *Journal of Trafficking and Human Exploitation* 1, no. 1 (2017): 1. See also Jean Allain, "Genealogies of Human Trafficking and Slavery," in *Routledge Handbook of Human Trafficking*, eds. Ryszard Piotrowicz and Conny Rijken (London: Routledge, 2018).

disease in the late nineteenth century and is grounded in Victorian paternalism.[46] The question was how to control women in the face of communicable diseases which were playing havoc on troops destined to engage in Europe's colonial projects. Rumours had arisen of organised networks that procured and sent women abroad for prostitution. One of the fears was that white women were being sold into slavery to non-white males. In response, a number of international instruments were adopted by European countries and the United States. The first one was the 1904 International Agreement for the Suppression of the White Slave Trade.[47] An important point of disagreement during the negotiation had been the nature of the offence for women over the age of majority versus women under the age of majority. Which offence should be given priority? Did it matter if women gave their consent? But at what age was a woman able to consent to sex?[48] These questions only found partial answers in the 1904 Agreement, and the latter proved ineffective due to the high number of reservations. In 1910, the same governments negotiated the International Convention for the Suppression of White Slave Traffic. This time, European and American (male) diplomats agreed to criminalise, on the one side, the exploitation of the prostitution of women over the age of majority and, on the other side, the prostitution of those underage. Implementation was left to state parties.

This genealogy is powerful in suggesting that today's anti-trafficking project has more to do with late nineteenth-century European sexism and racism than with 'fighting an old evil'. 'Just as the spectre of involuntary sex and despoilment of innocent white maidens seized the Western world's attention in the late 1880s and early 1890s', comments Bravo, 'overtones of that appalled, fascinated, and condemnatory prurience continued to pervade public and institutional perceptions of the traffic in human beings into the early twenty-first century.'[49] The reminiscence of Victorian paternalism is not only politically conservative; it also has important distributional implications. Today's focus on 'innocent women and children and illicit sex foisted upon them'[50] draws both attention and resources away from other forms of human exploitation and structural inequalities. It has also been noted that not unlike yesterday's scandal, today's global cause has been consolidated through the deployment of a series of dubious 'facts and figures' regarding the dimensions of human trafficking.[51]

As these two examples show, the counterpoint takes history seriously and explores the long-rooted relationship between law, economy and power. That said, I find the counterpoint less convincing when integrating studies of the past to discuss today's challenges. What are the latter? Much of the discussion revolves around the 'fragmentation'[52] of the law on human exploitation.

46 Judith Walkowitz, *Prostitution and Victorian Society: Women, Class, and the State* (Cambridge: Cambridge University Press, 1980).

47 On the racial component of the treaty, see Eileen Scully, "Pre-Cold War Traffic in Sexual Labour and Its Foes: Some Contemporary Lessons," in *Global Human Smuggling*, eds. David Kyle and Koslowski Rey, 2nd ed. (Baltimore: The Johns Hopkins University Press, 2011).

48 Allain, *White Slave Traffic in International Law*, 16.

49 Bravo, "Exploring the Analogy," 575.

50 Ibid.

51 Annie Bunting and Joel Quirk, eds., *Contemporary Slavery. Popular Rhetoric and Political Practice* (Vancouver: UBC Press, 2017). On the genesis of today's US anti-trafficking debate, see Jennifer Lobasz, *Constructing Human Trafficking. Evangelicals, Feminists, and an Unexpected Alliance* (Cham: Palgrave Macmillan, 2018). On the previous scandal, see Jean-Michel Chaumont, *Le mythe de la traite des blanches. Enquête sur la fabrication d'un fléau* (Paris: La Découverte, 2009).

52 Anne-Charlotte Martineau, *Une analyse critique du débat sur la fragmentation du droit international* (Bruxelles: Bruylant, Collection de droit international, 2015).

That slavery is now regulated by different subfields of international law (such as the law of the sea, human rights law, international criminal law, international humanitarian law, international labour law and international refugee law) raises a number of concerns. To what extent does this state of affairs give rise to conflicting interpretations of slavery?[53] In the counterpoint narrative, fragmentation is often depicted as a problem that could be resolved if we were to identify more clearly what is slavery versus lesser forms of exploitation, such as forced labour. This explains why so much ink has been spilt on the relevance of the 1926 definition: should we keep Article 1 of the 1926 Slavery Convention, which defines slavery in relation to ownership exclusively, or should we prefer an expansive definition which would focus on the degree of control and coercion? What I want to highlight is how both sides (referred to as 'restrictivists' and 'expansionists') use history to support their positions.

On the one hand, expansionists reject the 1926 definition of slavery on the ground that it was developed by the League of Nations – a European colonial club – which sought to end slavery beyond its membership while codifying forced labour in its colonies. There is no reason why we should continue to accept the colonialist argument according to which forced labour and slavery constitute substantively different practices.[54] Expansionists also argue that if we were to retain the 1926 definition, it would lead to a new form of double standard or blindness: when slavery is interpreted in such a manner as to provide for a minimalist understanding, it allows authorities to close their eyes (and support) a wide range of highly exploitative and coercive practices. 'When slavery is approached as an historical relic, rather than a dynamic problem', claims Quirk,

> blindness to contemporary problems is to be expected. To overthrow this cultural inheritance, a deeper and broader vision is required. Rather than reducing slavery to a "peculiar" historical anomaly (to be explained away), we instead need to view slavery as a widespread and deeply rooted component of contemporary life.[55]

On the other hand, restrictivists do not deny the colonial origins of the 1926 definition. But, they say, the expansion of the notion of slavery to 'practices similar to slavery' in the 1956 Supplementary Convention and then to apartheid and colonialism in the 1960s by newly independent states was equally done for political motives.[56] The result of this expansion was a confusion which is most

53 Rebecca Scott, "International Law and Contemporary Slavery: The Long View," *Michigan Journal of International Law* 38, no. 3 (2017): 352. See also Holly Cullen, "Contemporary International Legal Norms on Slavery. Problems of Judicial Interpretation and Application," in *The Legal Understanding of Slavery: From the Historical to the Contemporary*, ed. Jean Allain (Oxford: Oxford University Press, 2012). On the clash between human rights law and anti-trafficking, see James Hathaway, "The Human Rights Quagmire of 'Human Trafficking'," *Virginia Journal of International Law* 49, no. 1 (2008).

54 Nicholas McGeehan, "Misunderstood and Neglected: The Marginalisation of Slavery in International Law," *The International Journal of Human Rights* 16, no. 3 (2012).

55 Joel Quirk, *Unfinished Business: A Comparative Survey of Historical and Contemporary Forms of Slavery* (Joint Report of UNESCO and the Wilberforce Institute of Slavery, 2008), 120, https://www.jrf.org.uk/report/between-decent-work-and-forced-labour-examining-continuumexploitation. See also A. Yasmine Rassam, "International Law and Contemporary Forms of Slavery: An Economic and Social Rights-Based Approach," *Penn State International Law Review* 23, no. 4 (2005).

56 See Jean Allain, "The International Definition of Slavery and Its Contemporary Application," in *Esclavage, traite et autres formes d'asservissement et d'exploitation*, eds. Jean-François Niort and Olivier Pluen (Paris: Dalloz, 2018), 307–9.

evident in the work of the UN Working Group on Contemporary Forms of Slavery (1975–2006).[57] Under the heading of 'contemporary forms of slavery', the Working Group considered a number of social ills, including trafficking in persons, exploitation of prostitutes (1989); child pornography, children in armed conflict (1990); child soldiers (1991); removal of organs (1992); incest (1993); migrant workers, sex tourism (1994); illegal adoption (1996); early marriages and detained juveniles (1997). The problem is this: when slavery is interpreted in such a manner as to include all social injustices or human rights violations that may occur, it becomes so broad as to be meaningless.[58]

Because of their respective criticisms, both sides move on to search for a common ground. On the one hand, expansionists agree on the need to limit the issues that can be designated as species of slavery.[59] If all goes well, selected issues will acquire greater legal and political prominence, and will be addressed effectively. This is precisely what international human rights courts – with the European Court as the frontrunner – have been doing.[60] However, there remains an important downside to situating an issue within the specific historical and moral context of a human right not to be held in slavery: 'invoking slavery can be [a] polarizing move, narrowing space for ameliorative strategies that rely on the goodwill of those involved.'[61] On the other hand, restrictivists revisit the 1926 definition to suggest that it does not only cover *de jure* situations of ownership (i.e., chattel slavery), but also *de facto* situations of ownership, when one human exercises a power attaching to ownership without actually owning the other human.[62] This definition is said to be suitable because it covers contemporary practices of slavery while fitting the 'criminal law paradigm'.[63] Restrictivists believe that the ICC and the anti-trafficking regime have 'already done more . . . to advance the jurisprudence and the agenda of anti-slavery and the fight against exploitation than anything seen under the auspice of international human rights law'.[64] But who can seriously believe that the criminalisation of slavery, with its focus almost exclusively on punishment of perpetrators, will be able to address the vastly complex issue of human exploitation?[65]

What I want to convey here is that the turn to history has lost its critical bite. There is no more analysis of the ways in which, in different time and space, international law has allowed the exploitation of men by men in the name of liberal and humanistic values. There is no

57 Allain, "International Definition of Slavery," 309.

58 Jean Allain has voiced the strongest criticism against the 'conflation' of various social ills with slavery. 'In proportion to slavery's growth in breadth, has been its diminishing legal worth': Jean Allain, "The Definition of 'Slavery' in General International Law and the Crime of Enslavement within the Rome Statute," in *Guest Lecture Series of the Office of the Prosecutor* (The Hague: International Criminal Court, April 26, 2007), 2.

59 Weissbrodt, *Abolishing Slavery*, 177.

60 Michele Cavallo, "Formes contemporaines d'esclavage, servitude et travail forcé: le TPIY et la CEDH entre passé et avenir," *Droits fondamentaux* 6 (2006); Helen Duffy, "Litigating Modern Day Slavery in Regional Courts. A Nascent Contribution," *Journal of International Criminal Justice* 14, no. 2 (2016); Vladislava Stoyanova, "Article 4 of the ECHR and the Obligation of Criminalising Slavery, Servitude, Forced Labour and Human Trafficking," *Cambridge Journal of International and Comparative Law* 3, no. 2 (2014).

61 Joel Quirk, "The Anti-Slavery Project: Linking the Historical and Contemporary," *Human Rights Quarterly* 28, no. 3 (2006): 595.

62 Allain, "International Definition of Slavery," 296.

63 Jean Allain, "The International Legal Regime of Slavery and Human Exploitation and Its Obfuscation by the Term of Art: 'Slavery-like Practice'," *Cahiers de la recherche sur les droits fondamentaux* 10 (2012): 28; Emmanuel Decaux, *Les formes contemporaines de l'esclavage* (Leiden: Martinus Nijhoff Publishers, 2009), 16–17.

64 Jean Allain, "A Response to Anne Gallagher by Jean Allain," *OpinioJuris* (June 8, 2009), http://opiniojuris.org/2009/06/08/a-response-to-anne-gallagher-by-jean-allain/.

65 See Karen Bravo, "Interrogating Everyperson's Roles in Today's Slaveries," *Temple International and Comparative Law Journal* (2017): 25.

re-interpretation of the past in terms of discontinuous or unexpected genealogies. Let me be clear: the problem is not that the counterpoint uses the past for present purposes.[66] The problem is that in today's debate on the legal definition of slavery, references to history end up justifying the choice of the regime or institution allowed to rule on it. In short, history has become caught up in the fragmentation of international law.

Conclusion

In light of these shortcomings, international lawyers may wonder how to move forward and approach slavery. I do not pretend to have all the answers. But it seems to me imperative to move away from abolition. To study the relationship between international law and slavery through the lenses of its abolition privileges a history in which Europe gets to play the hero. Yet we know that abolition was imposed for multiple reasons (economic, ideological, geopolitical, cultural . . .) and by incessant struggles of slaves (suicides, poisonings, maroons, revolts, insurrections . . .). As a matter of fact, the world's most significant abolition took place as a result of a revolution by black slaves and in Haiti – not by Europeans. If there is one blind spot in the historiography of international law and slavery, here it is.[67]

Another step forward is to extend the timeframe of research. As I have shown in this chapter, the majority of international lawyers look at the field's involvement in slavery matters from the nineteenth century onwards. But international law was involved well before the nineteenth century, not in the abolition but in the actual establishment and upholding of various forms of human exploitation, including chattel slavery. This point was fundamental to the young Georges Scelle, whose post-doctoral work stands out from his later work. In his *thèse d'Etat* published in 1906, Scelle explored what he called 'the legal and political history of the slave trade to Spanish America'.[68] Instead of looking – like his peers did – at the relationship between international law and slavery through the abolition lens, he focused on what happened before the nineteenth century. He took it for granted that the enslavement of Africans was made possible, commercialised and globalised through extensive legal work. This legal work is what constituted his object of inquiry. In short, Scelle's approach contrasts with the deep-seated tendency in our discipline to celebrate the role international law has played in ending slavery. On the backdrop of such an ideological move, Scelle's work reminds us that slavery was a global legal regime and that we have to deal with it as such.[69]

66 For theoretical reflections on the relationship between past and present in international law, see Anne Orford, "The Past as Law or History? The Relevance of Imperialism for Modern International Law," in *Droit international et nouvelles approches sur le tiers-monde: entre répétition et renouveau,* eds. Emmanuelle Tourme-Jouannet, Mark Toufayan and Hélène Ruiz-Fabri (Paris: Pedone, 2013); Martti Koskenniemi, "Why History of International Law Today?" *Rechtsgeschichte* 4 (2004); Matthew Craven, "Theorizing the Turn to History in International Law," in *The Oxford Handbook of the Theory of International Law*, eds. Anne Orford and Florian Hoffmann (Oxford: Oxford University Press, 2016).

67 For an historical analysis, see Bernard Gainot, *La Révolution des esclaves. Haïti, 1763–1803* (Paris: Vendémiaire, 2017). See also Liliana Obregón, "Empire, Racial Capitalism and International Law: The Case of Manumitted Haiti and the Recognition Debt," *Leiden Journal of International Law* 31 (2018).

68 The final product is a 1610-page long comprehensive analysis of the life and death of *asientos de negros*, that is to say, contracts by which the Spanish Crown granted an individual, a company or another state the privilege – and often the monopoly – to supply African slaves to Spanish colonies: Georges Scelle, *Histoire politique de la traite négrière aux Indes de Castille. Contrats et traités d'Assiento*, vol. II (Paris: Sirey, 1906).

69 Anne-Charlotte Martineau, "Georges Scelle's Study of the Slave Trade: French Solidarism Revisited," *European Journal of International Law* 27, no. 4 (2016).

22

'Space is the only way to go'

The evolution of the extractivist imaginary of international law

Cait Storr

> Devoted to breaking the limits placed by humanity on the surface of this planet, astrofuturism forecasts an escape from terrestrial history.
>
> De Witt Douglas Kilgore, 2003[1]

In May 2019, Amazon billionaire Jeff Bezos stood on a darkened stage and delivered a televangelical monologue to a rapt crowd. His hour-long soliloquy was titled 'Going to Space to Benefit Earth'. Timed to coincide with the fiftieth anniversary of the moon landing, Bezos began by positioning himself as keeper of the faith that had animated NASA's Apollo 11 manned mission to the moon in 1969. Having invoked a hallowed US nationalist mythology, Bezos then invoked his own. He flashed an image of his 1970s high school yearbook quote to prove his lifelong ambition of becoming a 'space entrepreneur'. The teenaged Bezos, schooled in 1970s science fiction, had distilled the scripture of the commercial space industry: 'the earth is finite, and if the world economy and population is to keep growing, space is the only way to go!' Bezos – now the richest person alive – has long insisted that his motivation in accumulating his staggering private wealth via the online platform giant Amazon has been to fund this vision of space colonisation. Having established his prophetic credentials, Bezos then proceeded to step through the articles of faith upon which the burgeoning commercial space industry is being constructed. He declared a linear teleology of human progress, in which population growth and economic growth are the cardinal virtues. That growth necessarily correlates with exponential growth in energy consumption. That energy consumption is by association virtuous. As such, if the human species stays on Earth, the inevitable rationing of energy consumption would reverse this linear teleology of human development. And that, Bezos spelt out, would be a 'bad way to go'. The only alternative was therefore to 'move out into the solar system': to 'colonise space', a domain of 'unlimited resources'. Bezos arrived at his ideological *coup de grace* with the subtlety of a hammer: 'do we want stasis and rationing? Or do we want dynamism and growth?'

1 De Witt Douglas Kilgore, *Astrofuturism: Science, Race, and Visions of Utopia in Space* (Philadelphia: University of Pennsylvania Press, 2003), 1.

In his speech, Bezos replayed the spatial and temporal dimensions of what Kilgore has described as astrofuturism.[2] For Kilgore, astrofuturism is a utopian amalgam of European imperialism and liberalism that developed in the post-war United States. It is marked by a spatial fantasy of unlimited geographic expansion, 'extend(ing) the nineteenth-century notion that conquest and empire are the logical *modus operandi* of any progressive civilization'.[3] Temporally, astrofuturism is marked by a rejection of the conditions of the present: 'all astrofuturists are unreconciled to the moment of their production, the world as it exists now.'[4] Bezos' justification of his obscene personal wealth as a global good commenced the launch of the new lunar landing programme of his private aerospace company, Blue Origin. The Blue Moon lunar lander has been designed for launch under the umbrella of NASA's Commercial Lunar Payload Services programme, a lunar resources testing and exploitation programme due to commence in 2020. Aerospace companies – including Blue Origin, Elon Musk's SpaceX, the International Space Alliance and, more recently, the Google-affiliated Planetary Resources, and Moon Express – have since the early 2000s been progressively picking apart at Boeing and Lockheed Martin's half-century duopoly control over NASA contracts, established during the Cold War. As NASA funding was redirected toward the US Department of Defense following the September 2001 attacks on the World Trade Centre in New York, billionaire entrepreneurs including Bezos and Musk began to wage highly-leveraged campaigns to reconfigure the Cold War-era space sector in their favour.[5]

Outside the United States and aerospace industry circles, the prospect of mining near-Earth bodies in space is apt to invoke incredulity, for its invocation of arch science fiction themes at a time of extreme wealth inequality, climate crisis and far-right resurgence.[6] Space mining has been a standard science fiction trope since the late nineteenth century, and is all too readily dismissed as little more than that. However, the intensity of current industry activity around the technological, commercial and legal questions raised by the prospect of space resource extraction gives pause for thought. Internet platform giants including Google, Amazon and PayPal have been shifting capital into space research and development for over a decade. Resulting advancements in rocketry and applied robotics have rendered the prospect of space mining at least technically feasible.[7] According to Planetary Resources, the speculative value of mining near-Earth bodies is now in the quadrillions.[8] This figure recalls the fervour of the dot.com boom and bust of the early 2000s. It is clearly fantastical, or at least difficult to square with the immense technological and logistical challenges presented in realising it. Nevertheless, it is a clear indication of the high-profile venture capital the field has attracted over the last two decades.

As such, it is short sighted to regard space mining as a mere distraction from the daunting global challenges of the day. As multilateral climate change agreements falter and international

2 Ibid.

3 Ibid., 11.

4 Kilgore, *Astrofuturism*, 4.

5 Christian Davenport, *The Space Barons: Elon Musk, Jeff Bezos and the Quest to Colonize the Cosmos* (New York: Hachette Book Group, 2018).

6 Robert R. Heinlein, *The Rolling Stones* (New York: Baen Publishing, 2009, first published 1952). Bezos was a student of Cornell University physicist Gerard K. O'Neil, whose speculative tract on space colonisation, *The High Frontier: Human Colonies in Space* (Burlington: Collector's Guide Publishing, 2000, first published 1976), is frequently cited by space entrepreneurs.

7 Andreas M. Hein, Robert Matheson and Dan Fries, "A Techno-Economic Analysis of Asteroid Mining," *Acta Astronautica* 168 (March 2020): 104–15.

8 Asterank, accessed March 22, 2020, www.asterank.com.

collaboration itself is increasingly discredited, space resource extraction – along with seabed and polar resource extraction – is better understood as part of a systemic counter-response to those challenges. That counter-response places its faith not in international agreements but in market solutions to crisis. The new astrofuturist narratives around space mining are directly linked to the material dependency of information technology and renewable energy infrastructure – and in particular, battery storage – on rare earth metals. A clean energy future on Earth, so the rhetoric goes, will necessitate off-Earth resource extraction. Corporate proponents of seabed mining make similar claims.[9] This avant-garde of entrepreneurial activity has been shadowed by a sharp increase in exploratory activity on the moon and on near Earth asteroids by sovereign states, including China, India, Japan and the Russian Federation, and multilateral institutions like the European Space Agency. Japan's JAXA Agency landed its Hyabusa II robotic probe on the Ryugu asteroid in February 2019 and returned mineral samples to earth in December 2020, and NASA's Osiris Rex probe landed on the Bennu asteroid in October 2020, with plans to return samples in 2023. The China National Space Administration landed its Chang'e-4 rover on the far side of the moon in 2019, and is conducting mineralogical tests of the lunar surface.

As Bezos' Blue Origin performance illustrated, this new generation of space entrepreneurs actively perpetuate astrofuturist fantasies of escape – not just from the natural limits of Earth but from the contingent histories of terrestrial jurisdiction. These include, at turns, the fantasy of escape from sovereign regulatory oversight; from taxation; from operating in fiat currency; and from reliance on established forums of dispute resolution.[10] However, the purpose of this chapter is to observe the way in which such public-facing fantasies of escape misdirect attention away from the extent to which the commercial viability of any future extractive industry in space is precisely a question of law. Without legal certainty, particularly with respect to legal protections of private rights, the speculative value of space mining – and of the entire commercial space industry – cannot be realised. New scholarship in international history and international law is increasingly making the point even more strongly than that: it is law itself that will construct the value 'new' domains of resource extraction are coming to represent.[11] The constitutive role of law in producing space and value is not lost on astrofuturists like Bezos and Musk. As they have spruiked escapist tropes on stage, behind the scenes space entrepreneurs have invested heavily in standard corporate techniques of legislative lobbying, strategic anti-trust litigation and public relations campaigning. The new astrofuturists are not simply seeking to clarify the legal framework that will govern the commercial space industry. They are seeking to write it.

In practice, then, this resurgent astrofuturism has accompanied not a flight from law, but an intense engagement with lawmaking processes at all levels. The United Nations Committee on the Peaceful Uses of Outer Space (UNCOPUOS), long focused on monitoring military prohibitions, civilian satellite operations and space debris, has over recent years identified the

9 "Sustainable Supply of Minerals and Metals Key to a Low-Carbon Energy Future," *Deep Green Metals Inc.*, accessed March 22, 2020, https://deep.green/sustainable-supply-of-minerals-and-metals-key-to-a-low-carbon-energy-future/; Isabel Feichtner, "Mining for Humanity in the Deep Sea and Outer Space: The Role of Small States and International Law in the Extraterritorial Expansion of Extraction," *Leiden Journal of International Law* 32, no. 2 (2019): 255–74.

10 See for example Alexander William Salter, "Ordering the Cosmos: Private Law and Celestial Property Rights," *Journal of Air Law & Commerce* 82, no. 2 (2017): 311–32.

11 See for example Isabel Feichtner, "Sharing the Riches of the Sea: The Redistributive and Fiscal Dimension of Deep Seabed Exploitation," *European Journal of International Law* 30, no. 2 (2019): 601–33. See also Katharina Pistor, *The Code of Capital: How the Law Creates Wealth and Inequality* (Princeton: Princeton University Press, 2019).

need to revive an international diplomatic debate that ran hot in the 1960s and 1970s but was largely abandoned by the 1980s: the international legal framework that should apply to the commodification and exploitation of extraterrestrial minerals and metals as 'resources'. The post-2001 chapter in the development of the commercial space industry is part of the global reinvigoration of debate over the regulation of extractive activity in geophysical domains outside sovereign territory, including the international seabed, the polar regions and near-Earth space. Whilst this chapter focuses on current developments in the international law governing space resource extraction, the development of space law should therefore be held in counterpoint to the differential regimes that have developed to regulate resource extraction in the international seabed, the Antarctic and the Arctic.[12]

As counterintuitive as it may seem at a time of weakening international cooperation and compounding environmental and economic crises, the regulation of space mining is therefore not only a proper subject of critical analysis for international lawyers – it is an urgent one. Much extant literature on space resource extraction is industry-captured, and presumes the astrofuturist premise: that expansion of the geophysical domain of natural resource commodification is not only inevitable, but a desirable, capital-driven solution to both resource conflict and planetary limits.[13] This utopian framing of the prospect, however, should not be permitted to distract from the fact that understanding the reinvigoration of a twenty-first-century project of extra-territorial extractivism, laced with an unabashed colonial imaginary, requires clear-eyed engagement with the history of international law. This chapter argues that the advent of a commercial space resource industry signals neither an escape from terrestrial jurisdiction nor a failure of international law, but a predictable evolution of its extractivist logic. As such, the contemporary jostling over the legal regime that will govern space mining is not – or not just – a gaudy sideshow to the main event of compounding environmental and economic crisis. It is part of a systemic counter-response to that crisis which seeks to perpetuate the extractivist logic that produced it.[14]

This chapter first gives an overview of the Cold War-era space law regime and of contemporary developments in space resources law. It then considers the analytical frameworks that might productively be brought to bear on these developments, with a focus on Marxist accounts of the spatial fix and of the neo-extractivist turn in global capitalism. The chapter then argues that these concepts will need supplementation with scholarship in the history of international law, if the significance of current negotiations over the legal framework that will apply to space resource extraction is to be fully grasped. That scholarship not only offers a means of understanding the evolution of the legal framework governing space resources. It offers a means of diagnosing the real stakes of the intensive commercial, political and legal activity currently underway.

12 On the international seabed, see Surabhi Ranganathan, "The Law of the Sea and Natural Resources," in *Community Interests Across International Law*, eds. Eyal Benvenisti and Georg Nolte (Oxford: Oxford University Press, 2018), 121–35. On Antarctica, see Tim Stephens, "The Antarctic Treaty System and the Anthropocene," *The Polar Journal* 8, no. 1 (2018): 29–43.

13 See Ram S. Jakhu and Joseph N. Pelton, eds., *Global Space Governance: An International Study* (Gewerbetrasse: Springer, 2017); Ricky Lee, *Law and Regulation of Commercial Mining of Minerals in Outer Space* (Dordrecht: Springer, 2012); Priyank D. Doshi, "Regulating the Final Frontier: Asteroid Mining and The Need for a New Regulatory Regime," *Notre Dame Journal of International and Comparative Law* 6, no. 1 (2016): 189–212.

14 Isabel Feichtner and Surabhi Ranganathan, "International Law and Economic Exploitation in the Global Commons: Introduction," *European Journal of International Law* 30, no. 2 (2019): 541–46.

Space resources law: the outer space treaties and domestic legislation

As the commercial space industry booms, the skeletal treaty framework laid down between the 1950s and 1970s to regulate extractive activity in outer space is slowly returning to prominence. Although the space treaties have been enlivened more regularly around issues of militarisation, satellite operations and space debris, the regulation of extractive activity was an integral concern in international space law negotiations from the 1950s. This concern to regulate – and thereby facilitate – future resource exploitation was fundamental to the establishment of the treaty regime. From the outset, the United Nations General Assembly and the Ad Hoc Committee on the Peaceful Uses of Outer Space agreed that any future regime of resource exploitation be organised around the two principles that came to ground the space treaty framework: a prohibition on sovereign appropriation, and an assertion of common benefit.[15] As frequently noted, the conceptual basis of the space treaty framework was explicitly analogised from the Grotian principle of *mare liberum* held to ground the law of the sea.[16] The notion of 'common possession of all mankind' had been asserted in relation to the polar regions from the early twentieth century, in contestation of British claims to the Graham Land region of West Antarctica.[17]

Beyond this basic restatement of norms against sovereign appropriation and for common benefit in relation to geophysical domains beyond sovereign territorial jurisdiction, the space regime negotiated over the 1960s and 1970s is skeletal in comparison to the comprehensive UN Convention on the Law of the Sea (UNCLOS), negotiated during the 1970s and early 1980s. The UN General Assembly repeatedly cited the need to avoid limiting scientific and technological advancement, as the reason for adopting a minimalist treaty framework that would allow 'adaptive' development of space law. Yet the impossibility of fixing stable distinctions between scientific exploration, military use and commercial exploitation in space was not only presumed from the outset of negotiations in the UN General Assembly in the late 1950s – it was expressed as the principal justification for adopting a concept of common benefit as the foundational principle of international space law.[18] As Craven has recently argued, the Outer Space Treaty's silences were therefore less gaps in the space regime than deeply constitutive of it.[19] On Craven's account, a surface reading of the development of international space law tells a story of a regime grounded in 'peaceful use'. An Althusserian 'symptomatic reading' of the treaty regime's constitutive silences, however, reveals that the supposed collective suppression of the risk of space becoming a site of warfare on the one hand, and of primitive accumulation on the other, produced a regime constructed around the twin rationalities of militarisation and commodification.

The 1967 Treaty on Principles Governing the Activities of States in the Exploration and Use of Outer Space, including the Moon and Other Celestial Bodies (the Outer Space Treaty), only peripherally addressed resource extraction. The treaty declared the exploration and use of outer space as the 'province of all mankind', and freedom of exploration, use and scientific investigation for 'all States'. Article II prohibited sovereign appropriation 'by means of use or

15 See UN General Assembly Ad Hoc Committee on the Peaceful Uses of Outer Space, *Report of the Legal Committee*, UN Doc. A/AC.98/2, June 12, 1959.

16 Ranganathan, "The Law of the Sea and Natural Resources."

17 Thomas Willing Balch, "The Arctic and Antarctic Regions and the Law of Nations," *American Journal of International Law* 4, no. 2 (1910): 275.

18 UN General Assembly Ad Hoc Committee, *Report* XXX.

19 Matthew Craven, "Other Spaces: Constructing the Legal Architecture of a Cold War Commons and the Scientific Imaginary of Outer Space," *European Journal of International Law* 30, no. 2 (2019): 547–72.

occupation, or by any other means', rejecting the application of the laws of territorial acquisition to outer space, and by implication, any presumption of *res nullius*.[20] Given the extreme inequalities in spacefaring capacity during the Cold War, the assertion of common benefit was capable of sustaining irreconcilable interpretations. On the one hand, it served as a justification for commercial extractive activity structured in accordance with neoliberal ideals of global market competition.[21] On the other, it served as an argument for redistribution of profit generated by that extractive activity towards states without the capacity to participate in a competitive market. The 1967 treaty avoided altogether the question of what jurisdictional form was being invoked to ground a space extraction regime. The prospect of international territorial jurisdiction over near-Earth space presented not only a functional impossibility in the UN General Assembly of the 1960s, but also a diplomatic one, as the mandate and trusteeship models of 'international' administration that had been applied to confiscated German and Ottoman territories after World War I came into increasing disrepute.[22]

As such, the Outer Space Treaty left the door open for unilateral proprietary claims recognisable in domestic law. This permissive silence on the question of private ownership and control over minerals and metals refigured space as a 'new' frontier for resource extraction. Moreover, it did so for both decolonising and colonial states, at precisely the same time as the status of property rights in natural resources derived from colonial law came to dominate the anti-colonial agenda.[23] For former imperial states, space represented a new field of resource extraction free from the risk of post-independence nationalisation. For decolonising states, the possibility of extra-territorial resource rights in space represented an opportunity for post-independence economic development. Perhaps predictably, subsequent attempts within the UN to address the jurisdictional lacuna left by the Outer Space Treaty with respect to space resource extraction ended in diplomatic failure. The 1979 Agreement Governing the Activities of States on the Moon and Other Celestial Bodies, commonly known as the Moon Agreement, sought to remedy the jurisdictional gap that had been left by the 1967 treaty. It committed to the establishment of 'an international regime, including appropriate procedures, to govern the exploitation' of those resources, including a requirement that States Parties make public any relevant discovery.[24] Although the United States and the Soviet Union – then the only states with spacefaring capacity – took part in negotiations, neither signed the treaty. The Moon Agreement remains one of the least subscribed UN agreements. It has been ratified by 18 states, and signed by an additional four.

As the Cold War formally receded and the agendas of international institutions turned over the 1990s toward trade liberalisation, sustainable development and international humanitarian law, the concerns that had animated the establishment of the space treaty regime as it pertained to resource extraction seemed ever more remote. Within international law, the principle of

20 For a restatement of the international law of territorial acquisition during the decolonisation movements, see Robert Yewdall Jennings, *Acquisition of Territory in International Law* (Manchester: Manchester University Press, 1963).

21 Quinn Slobodian, *The Globalists: The End of Empire and the Birth of Neoliberalism* (Cambridge: Harvard University Press, 2018).

22 On mandate and trusteeship, see Cait Storr, *International Status in the Shadow of Empire: Nauru and the Histories of International Law* (Cambridge: Cambridge University Press, 2020).

23 Subhash C. Jain, "Permanent Sovereignty Over Natural Resources and Nationalization in International Law," *Journal of the Indian Law Institute* 19, no. 3 (1977): 241–56.

24 UN General Assembly, *Agreement Governing the Activities of States on the Moon and Other Celestial Bodies*, UN Doc. RES 34/68, December 5, 1979 ('Moon Agreement').

common benefit has since been refracted largely through the UNCLOS principle of the common heritage of mankind as it applies to the international seabed. In counterpoint to parallel debates in political theory, where treatments of the concept of the commons have broadened out significantly since the 1990s, treatments of the common benefit principle within international law have been whittled down to focus on the function and institutional design of the International Seabed Authority.[25] With the escalation of private investment in the space industry from the mid-2000s, international space resources law has seen a dramatic resurgence, and the questions left unanswered at the end of the Cold War era of international treaty-making are once more being raised. With notable exceptions, however, scholarly literature on the meaning of common benefit in respect of space resources has been dominated by corporate and state interests. The sub-discipline of international space law is at present largely comprised of corporate practitioners engaged by the entrepreneurial space industry and, more recently, by international lawyers revisiting the stale treaty framework at the behest of governments seeking to regain a handle on the decades-old status quo.[26]

The most significant recent developments in space resources law have been the legislative moves of the United States and Luxembourg to recognise proprietary rights in space resources at the national level. These moves have been almost entirely responsive to the private space industry, yet have pursued slightly different objectives. In 2015, the United States Congress passed the Commercial Space Launch Competitiveness Act, championed by the Obama administration.[27] Part IV of the Act, the Space Resource Exploration and Utilization Act of 2015, commits the US executive to 'facilitate the commercial exploration and utilization of space resources to meet national needs', and to 'promote the right of United States commercial entities to explore outer space and utilize space resources'.[28] The relevant section on space resource rights provides *inter alia* that a 'US citizen engaged in commercial recovery' shall be 'entitled to' any space resource obtained, 'including to possess, own, transport, use, and sell', 'in accordance with applicable law, including the international obligations of the US'.[29] The act refrains from using the direct language of property included in the bill, and includes an explicit disclaimer that the enactment constitutes a declaration of extra-territorial sovereignty. Yet in substance, the act marks yet another imperial deployment of the formal distinction between private proprietary and sovereign territorial claims, a legal technique that has characterised US empire since the nineteenth century.[30]

The Duchy of Luxembourg subsequently passed a national law recognising private property in space resources in 2017.[31] An established tax haven itself formerly dependent on mining,

25 Feichtner, "Sharing the Riches of the Sea." For treatments of the commons in political theory, see for example Camille Barbagallo, Nicholas Beuret and David Harvie eds., *Commoning with George Caffentzis and Silvia Federici* (London: Pluto Press, 2019).

26 Notable exceptions include Haris Durrani, "Interpreting 'Space Resources Obtained': Historical and Postcolonial Interventions in the Law of Commercial Space Mining," *Columbia Journal of Transnational Law* 54, no. 2 (2019): 403–60; and Feichtner, "Mining for Humanity in the Deep Sea and Outer Space."

27 *Commercial Space Launch Competitiveness Act* of 2015, Public Law No. 114–90, November 25, 2015 (USA).

28 Ibid. *Space Resource Exploration and Utilization Act* of 2015.

29 Ibid. Section 51303.

30 See for example Christina Duffy Burnett, "The Edges of Empire and the Limits of Sovereignty: American Guano Islands," *American Quarterly* 57, no. 3 (2005): 779–803; Durrani, "Interpeting 'Space Resources Obtained'," 437–42.

31 Duchy of Luxembourg, *Law of July 20th 2017 on the Exploration and Use of Space Resources*. For the English translation, see "Law of July 20th 2017 on the Exploration and Use of Space Resources," *Luxembourg Space Agency*,

Luxembourg has in recent years sought to rebrand itself as a jurisdictional launchpad for asteroid mining.[32] The Luxembourg Space Agency's marketing positions Luxembourg as

> the first European country and the second worldwide after the United States, to offer a legal framework on the exploration and use of space resources, ensuring that private operators can be confident about their rights on resources they extract in space.[33]

In contrast to the United States' old nationalist ambition to dominate space in both military and economic capacities, Luxembourg's aim is to extract resource rents from commercial space industries developing in other states. Under the new national law, in order to receive rights protection companies must be registered in Luxembourg, and any space activity must be authorised by the Luxembourg government, for a fee of between '5,000 to 500,000 euros', determined by the relevant minister. To foster industry development, Luxembourg invested directly in Planetary Resources, and established a strategic relationship with China's National Space Science Center, with plans to open a Chinese Research Laboratory of Deep Space Exploration in Luxembourg. Luxembourg is not alone is making rent-driven moves on the commercial space industry. The United Arab Emirates Space Agency has announced plans to establish a similar legislative regime, with a view to generating resource rents in a post-fossil fuel energy economy.[34]

In response to these domestic developments, the prospect first raised in the 1979 Moon Agreement of an international regime to govern space resource exploitation was discussed in the UNCOPUOS Legal Subcommittee in April 2019.[35] Preliminary proposals for the establishment of a future regime are being developed by The Hague International Space Resource Governance Working Group, commissioned by the UNCOPUOS to consult on the establishment of an international framework for 'space resource activities'. The Hague Working Group published its 'Building Blocks' in November 2019, which perpetuate rather than resolve the older contest between the appropriative and redistributive interpretations of the concept of common benefit.[36] Alongside an assertion that 'space resource activities shall be carried out for the benefit and in the interests of all countries and humankind irrespective of their degree of economic and scientific development', core principles include: 'provid[ing] legal certainty and predictability for operators'; 'tak[ing] into particular account the contributions of pioneer operators'; and 'ensur[ing] that resource rights . . . can lawfully be acquired through domestic legislation'.[37]

This move to accommodate the US and Luxembourg legislation within a common benefit regime has not, however, gone uncontested. Belgium and Greece submitted a working paper to the UNCOPUOS Legal Subcommittee in 2019, citing the need for a 'solid, unequivocal

accessed March 22, https://space-agency.public.lu/en/agency/legal-framework/law_space_resources_english_translation.html.

32 Feichtner, "Mining for Humanity in the Deep Seabed and Outer Space."

33 "Space Resources," *Luxembourg Space Agency*, accessed March 22, 2020, https://spaceresources.public.lu/en.html.

34 "UAE Eyes New Frontiers with Law to Regulate Space Tourism, Mining," *Arabian Business*, November 24, 2019, www.arabianbusiness.com/politics-economics/434048-uae-eyes-new-frontiers-with-law-to-regulate-space-tourism-mining.

35 UN Committee on the Peaceful Uses of Outer Space, *Report of the Legal Subcommittee on Its Fifty Eighth Session Held in Vienna from 1 to 12 April 2019*, UN Doc. A/AC.105/1203, June 18, 2019, 32–36.

36 Hague International Space Resources Governance Working Group, *Building Blocks for the Development of an International Framework on Space Resource Activities*, November 2019. On the contest between the redistributive and appropriative dimensions of the concept of common benefit, see Feichtner, "Sharing the Riches of the Sea."

37 Ibid., 2–4.

regime' that facilitates the 'promising future' of space resource exploitation.[38] The concern in the working paper is firmly on reserving international jurisdiction over space resource exploitation. It insists that although

> States may authorize the space activities of their nationals . . . this personal basis for the exercise of national jurisdiction does not provide any basis for legislative jurisdiction in terms of regulating the legal status of outer space itself. It follows that the legal aspects of space resource exploitation must be regulated by international law.[39]

The design of an international regime is due to be discussed at the UNCOPUOS Legal Subcommittee meeting in 2020.

Space mining as a spatial fix and the 'new' extractivism

These unfolding developments in the commercial space industry, and in the national and international law on which that industry will be built, require careful attention. As with current developments in seabed mining, the space mining industry lends itself to seemingly straightforward Marxist analysis, as yet another illustration of the inherently expansionist logic of capitalism. The advent of the space mining industry conforms, at least in part, to what Harvey described as the spatial fix to capitalism's crisis tendencies – and in particular, the crisis of capital overaccumulation.[40] For Harvey, geographic expansion is an inevitable response to capital overaccumulation and functions as a 'fix' in two senses: first, as a solution to the irreconcilable co-existence of surplus capital and labour; and second, as a mode of fixing or producing space, so that capital can move freely within and across it.[41] From this perspective, the particular appeal of space mining to internet platform entrepreneurs like Bezos, Musk and Branson – who as individuals represent some of the most extreme examples of capital overaccumulation, and who occupied determinative roles in the production of online space in the 1990s and 2000s – is clear. The advent of extractive activity in space signals a need for elaboration of understandings of the spatial fix in the seeming absence of pre-existing human labour power or productive capacity in the 'new' space being produced. Exploitation of space appears, misleadingly, to not enliven the same relations of human exploitation that produced the concentrations of capital that have made it possible.

It is precisely this apparent absence of a human subject of exploitation in space that has enabled the commercial industry to embrace the idiom of colonisation as readily as it has the idiom of common benefit. The risks in dismissing the revalorisation of colonialist rhetoric as empty or harmless are obvious. The first risk is a tacit exoneration of the global labour relations that have resulted in such extreme capital overaccumulation in the first place. The labour practices of Amazon, for instance, are notorious. A second risk is the unquestioned entrenchment of those global labour relations into the economy of any scaled industry of space resource extraction, and therefore into any post-fossil fuel energy market that depends on that extraction. A third risk is the renovation of a much older conservative discourse of environmental conservation, which

38 UN Committee on the Peaceful Uses of Outer Space, Legal Subcommittee, *Proposal for the Establishment of a Working Group for the Development of an International Regime for the Utilization and Exploitation of Space Resources: Working Paper by Belgium and Greece*, UN Doc. A/AC.105/C.2/L.311, March 4, 2019.

39 Ibid.

40 David Harvey, "The Spatial Fix – Hegel, Von Thunen and Marx," *Antipode* 13, no. 3 (1981): 1–12.

41 David Harvey, "Globalization and the 'Spatial Fix'," *Geographische Revue* 2 (2001): 24.

has long accompanied European resource imperialism.[42] As both space and seabed entrepreneurs well demonstrate with their greenwashing advertising strategies, conservational discourses work to displace extractive activity, not prevent it. The rhetorical innovation space mining entrepreneurs make is to ramp up this spatial displacement of extractive activity to planetary scale: they are, as Bezos claims, 'colonising space to benefit earth'. As useful as the concept of the spatial fix will be in mapping the development of space mining, then, the challenge for Marxist, TWAIL, South-facing and decolonial approaches to international law will be in countering mining proponents' implied argument that the seeming disjuncture of territory and population in these 'new' spaces of resource extraction obviates the terrestrial politics of extractive industry. Those politics have long been marked across the Global South by asymmetries of power between resource corporations and states, and those asymmetries are becoming increasingly pronounced in the Global North.

Staying within the Marxist framework, the role of states in the commercial space industry lends itself to analysis as an extension of the logic that has been termed neo-extractivism. The concept of neo-extractivism developed primarily within Latin America to describe the post-millennial turn of centre/left governments in Brazil, Chile, Venezuela, Bolivia, and Argentina toward 'reprimarisation' of national economies formerly dependent on resource export. That reprimarisation was undertaken in response to the failure of neoliberal restructural adjustments of the 1980s and 1990s to achieve domestic economic and political stability.[43] In this context, neo-extractivism refers to a new era of resource nationalism, in which developing states seek not to nationalise foreign investments in domestic natural resources as occurred in the 1950s and 1960s, but to actively invite foreign investment in extractive industry, in order to negotiate more favourable royalty and rent terms to direct toward social and environmental programs. Despite the progressive rhetoric of neo-extractivism, however, observers note there has been little evidence of successful redirection of resource rents toward social and environmental programs, nor of significant structural change in domestic natural resource sectors.[44] The actions of states like Luxembourg and the UAE in passing domestic legislation protecting private rights in space resources are understandable as an evolution of this neo-extractivist logic – they represent basic moves to invite foreign investment to replace dwindling or threatened flows of revenue from resource rents.

Between old and new regimes of extraction: the history of international law

The concepts of the spatial fix and neo-extractivism, then, have much to offer analyses of the astrofuturist turn in global extractive industry. Yet these framings will require supplementation if the role of law in this turn is to be understood. It is one thing to assert that this new phase of geographic expansion is a predictable evolution of the extractivist logic of capitalism. But whilst the evolution of the logic of capitalism might be predictable, the way in which that logic is evolving, and the role of law in that evolution, is not. What will require ongoing

42 Richard Grove, *Green Imperialism: Colonial Expansion, Tropical Island Edens and the Origins of Environmentalism, 1600–1860* (Cambridge: Cambridge University Press, 1996).

43 Gabriela Massuh, ed., *Renunciar al Bien Común: Extractivismo y (Pos)Desarrollo en América Latina* (Buenos Aires: Mardulce, 2012); James Petras and Henry Veltmeyer, "A New Model or Extractive Imperialism," in *The New Extractivism: A Post-Neoliberal Development Model or Imperialism of the Twenty-First Century?* eds. James Petras and Henry Veltmeyer (London: Zed Books, 2014), 36–37.

44 Veltmeyer and Petras, "A New Model," 39–40.

elaboration over the coming years is the constitutive role of law in the production of space as a field of resource extraction. It is here that scholarship in the history of international law has much to offer. Straight applications of imperial and colonial critique, including but not limited to Marxist analyses of international law, run the risk of missing what is distinctive about the legal production of these 'new' spaces of extraction in the twenty-first century. Occurring after the establishment of twentieth century norms of international administration and common heritage, this phase of expanding extra-territorial jurisdiction is defined by the prohibition on sovereign territorial acquisition. This prohibition distinguishes the current era from the oft-invoked parallel of the 'scramble for Africa' in the late nineteenth century that resulted in the Berlin Conference on the Congo, often regarded as laying the groundwork for the architecture of the international law of territorial acquisition in the twentieth century. In current debates, the prohibition on sovereign territorial appropriation has sustained contradictory interpretations with respect to the validity of claims to private property in space. The entrepreneurial vanguard has tended to assert that private proprietary claims are consistent with the Outer Space Treaties; international lawyers working for smaller States Parties have tended to assert that proprietary claims supported by domestic legislation amount to sovereign claims, and are therefore inconsistent.

These conceptual debates over the property-sovereignty relation may, however, distract from rather than illuminate the legal innovations currently being driven by the commercial space industry. Recent entrepreneurial activity indicates that the absence of international consensus on the sovereignty-property relation in space is no longer operating as a disincentive to investment. Corporations are simply devising new means of securing legal protections for their assets and investments in space resource extraction. As such, concepts of sovereignty, territory and property – concepts that have featured so heavily in understandings of the legal history of European imperialism and colonialism – may not serve particularly well to describe the political and economic powers that are being juridified to enable extractive activity in space. This is not to say, of course, that real powers amounting to what in other contexts would be identifiable as sovereign territorial rights or private proprietary rights are not being configured in other ways, or that legal histories of imperialism and colonialism will not prove crucial in mapping the historical evolution of those powers. Rather, it is to say that the concepts and practices of international administration on the one hand, and resource exploration and exploitation rights regimes on the other, are functioning together to produce these new spaces of extraction. This conjunction of internationalised administration and resource rights in the legal production of space is not unprecedented. Precursors have included forms of imperial condominium of the nineteenth century, and the mandate and trusteeship regimes of the twentieth.[45] Norms against sovereign territorial acquisition and for open door trade have in most instances been fundamental to the logic of these regimes.[46] The development of the space resource regime, therefore offers an opportunity to observe the evolution of the largely experimental regimes of international territorial administration that defined the twentieth century.

45 See generally Storr, *International Status in the Shadow of Empire*.

46 Exceptions include the Antarctic Treaty regime, and the C. Mandates.

Conclusion: space mining and this terrestrial history

> Utopia's deepest subject, and the source of all that is most vibrantly political about it, is precisely our inability to conceive it, our incapacity to produce it as a vision, our failure to project the other of what is, a failure that, as with fireworks dissolving back into the night sky, must once again leave us alone with this history.
>
> Fredric Jameson, 1977[47]

It is tempting to dismiss the prospect of space mining as a preposterous sideshow to the real event of global environmental crisis; as a gauche recycling of the tropes of twentieth-century science fiction; or simply as the vanity project of billionaire megalomaniacs, running out of terrestrial markets to dominate. All of these impressions are in some sense true. Yet without more, such a dismissal does not enable a coherent picture to emerge of the coalescing of a market-driven counter-response to climate crisis. This counter-response seeks not to dismantle the historical relations of exploitation that have produced that crisis, but to entrench them in a post-fossil fuel future. Such a dismissal also does not enable a coherent picture to emerge of the way in which law is implicated in that counter-response. The potential long-term consequences of ceding the field of space resources law to the astrofuturists are sobering. In short, Bezos' performance of astrofuturism should not be read simply as a billionaire fantasy that rejects the conditions of the present. It should be read as an attempt to reconsolidate the international order's foundational commitments to resource extraction and economic growth in the face of global inequality and environmental crisis. As Ranganathan has noted, 'capitalism's accumulative drive does not dissipate in the face of impending planetary disaster. Instead, it co-opts this disaster, extracting wealth from new commons'.[48] Chris Lewicki, CEO of Planetary Resources and former Google executive, has stated the point bluntly: space mining 'isn't a space project. It's a resource project'.[49] The history the astrofuturist utopia leaves us alone with the history of an international law that has served not to prevent staggering inequality and environmental destruction, but to perpetuate it. It is this history we must continue to revisit, if we are to resist what Harvey describes as 'the projection of the contradictions of capital onto an ever-broadening geographical terrain'.[50]

47 Fredric Jameson, "Of Islands and Trenches: Neutralization and the Production of Discourse," *Diacritics* 7, no. 2 (June 1977): 21.

48 Surabhi Ranganathan, "Seasteads, Land-Grabs and International Law," *Leiden Journal of International Law* 32, no. 2 (2019): 211.

49 Thomas Heath, "Space-Mining May Be a Decade Away as Oil-Rich Middle East Countries Look to Diversify," *Washington Post*, April 28, 2017.

50 Harvey, "Globalization and the 'Spatial Fix'," 27.

23

International law and the production of new resources

Lessons from the colonisation of Mars

Henry Jones

Introduction

In this chapter I present an analysis of how modern occidental law produces space, particularly in situations of resource extraction. Instead of a more familiar historical analysis of the deployment of occidental law in colonisation, I look at Kim Stanley Robinson's science fiction novel *Red Mars*. This literary account of the first 40 years of the human colonisation of Mars, a future history of Mars, breaks the legal analysis free of its historical and geographic specificity. Instead we see the law unleashed, and the colonial violence of occidental law repeated on a new set of facts. The writer and the characters in the novel consider the way law was used, adapted or failed to adapt to govern a new technological and geographical situation. Through a law in literature analysis we can see law's role in the production of space, material relationships and the problems of law and new technology. In this chapter I will first detail the history of the colonisation of Mars, and then consider the law relevant to this colonisation of Mars as detailed in Robinson's account. In the third part I will step back to consider the lessons for us as lawyers concerned with international law's governance of new resources. The final part will argue for the value of science fiction for helping us think about the relationship between law and changing technology.

The history of Mars

Mars is the fourth planet from the sun in our solar system. Visible from Earth with the naked eye, it features throughout human history, its distinctive red colour marking it out in the night sky. Ancient Sumerians believed Mars to be the god of war and plague; a similar position was held in the pantheons of ancient Greece and Rome. Ancient Egyptian astronomers documented Mars' apparent retrograde motion, as did Ptolemy in the *Almagest*. Mars was known to ancient Chinese astronomers as the fire star. Ancient Indian astronomers produced accurate estimates of the size of Mars.

The modern European relationship with Mars begins with the development of the telescope. Galileo is supposedly the first person to have observed Mars via telescope. That Mars had polar ice caps was observed by Cassini, who also theorised that Mars had seasons. Surface detail of Mars became visible in the late nineteenth century. Schiaparelli drew a map of Mars which included long straight grooves or channels, *canali* in Italian, mistranslated as canals in English. The canals were made famous by Percival Lowell, whose book *Mars and Its Canals* argued that the canals were built by intelligent life for the purpose of transporting water from the frozen poles to the arid desert regions at the equator for agriculture.[1] Around the same time, H.G. Wells wrote *The War of the Worlds*, in which a Martian invasion of Earth takes place.

In the second half of the twentieth century, satellite observation ended any speculation about canals on Mars. Detailed mapping of the planet started with the *Mariner* missions and the *Viking*. Eventually, the *Mars Global Surveyor* mission produced a complete and highly detailed topography of Mars. Detailed maps of Mars can be viewed at Google Mars, or NASA's Mars Trek and Experience Curiosity.[2] There have been dozens of spacecrafts sent to Mars, and as of 2019 Mars is host to eight functioning spacecraft, six in orbit and two on the surface.

In 2020 the future history of Mars began. John Boon, captain of a group of four astronauts, was the first man to set foot on Mars, with the words 'well, here we are'.[3] In 2026 the *Ares*, a joint project between the American and Russian space agencies, left Earth for Mars. In 2027 the first hundred colonists of Mars landed, and, in Robinson's words, Mars 'became a place'.[4] Those first colonists, half Russian and half American, were mostly not cosmonauts or astronauts, but were scientists, a mix of geologists, physicists, engineers, biologists and chemists. They were chosen to establish a colony, building habitats for a long-term colonisation of the planet. Separate settlements were built by Japanese colonists, the second large group to arrive on Mars in 2032. Over the next two decades the population of Mars steadily grew, as constant Earth-to-Mars shuttles brought in new colonists. Groups from the Middle East, South Africa, Ethiopia and India were notable, as was the presence of groups representing transnational corporations. The completion of the space elevator in 2057 increased emigration enormously, particularly in the context of another world war on Earth. These colonisers were both wealthy emigrants, a minority and indentured workers. During colonisation to this stage, after basic survival systems were in place, the priority for the colonists was terraforming the planet with the long-term aim of making it habitable. For the transnational corporations, the priority was resource extraction, particularly of what turned out to be an abundance of metals rare on Earth.

These different uses and understandings of Mars, habitability versus profit, were not initially in conflict. Mining projects contributed to a process of heating the atmosphere, directly and indirectly. However, a third position was held by some of the colonists: that of the need to preserve the natural Martian environment. In the view of Anne Claybourne, and those who followed her, the planet itself was the Indigenous entity, which the terraforming and mining projects were destroying. Claybourne made it her role not just to study the Aboriginal Martian environment, but also to advocate on its behalf. Although always a minority, and clearly not a successful position, this view retained a strong voice throughout the colonisation of Mars. In conflict with those who wanted to make Mars fit for human habitation, Claybourne believed 'you value consciousness too high, and rock too little'.[5]

1 Percival Lowell, *Mars and Its Canals* (New York: MacMillan, 1906).

2 Google Mars, www.google.com/mars; Mars Trek https://trek.nasa.gov/mars/; Experience Curiosity https://trek.nasa.gov/mars/.

3 Kim Stanley Robinson, *Red Mars* (New York: Bantam Books, 1993).

4 Ibid., 14.

5 Ibid., 213.

This position was known as Red, or the politics of a Red Mars. This was established in opposition to the Green, those who believed in making Mars human habitable. Both politics had within them revolutionary ideas about social and economic organisation. As Arkady Bogdanov put it, colonists on Mars at this stage 'have not been living in a money economy, that's the way scientific stations are'.[6] This dedication to a bigger project, and the physical and temporal separation from Earth, made possible new thinking and ways of conceiving social order. This included ideas such as areophany (that Mars reforms the people on it, just as they themselves try to reform Mars), and eco-economics (an economic system based around the exchange of energy). But as more people arrived on Mars with short-term interests, and as more companies imposed financial interests, the scientific station utopia broke, as it must. A utopia cannot only be for some separate few, it has to be for everyone.

The first volume of Robinson's trilogy on the future history of Mars ends in 2062. By this point there are tens of thousands living on Mars, mostly in large transparent tents covering small cities. There is a functioning space elevator making the transport of people to Mars, and valuable resources off Mars, far quicker and more efficient. Earth is in a bad state, with environmental disaster on a planetary scale, massive transnational corporations taking over all but the largest states and a global refugee crisis. Mars offers the promise of so many alternatives, from the possibility of expansion, the moving of people to Mars and the extraction of resources, to the possibilities of reshaping political organisation born on a new planet.

The law of Mars

The first human-on-Mars mission was an American operation, run through NASA with an American crew. Following that success, the project of colonisation was international, led by the USA and Russia, but under United Nations organisation. The United Nations Office for Martian Affairs (UNOMA), based in New York, was supposed to run the colonisation and exploitation of Mars. This legal organisation has a lot in common with the law of the sea. UNOMA is similar to the International Seabed Authority (ISA) and the International Maritime Organisation (IMO). Where they have responsibility for shipping and sea bed mining, UNOMA has responsibility for organising travel, settlement and mining of Mars. The first Mars Treaty did not come into effect until after the settlers set off for Mars. The planning of first settlement was simply governed under existing international law, with the Outer Space Treaty foremost.

The other major, and more conscious, international legal precedent adopted for Mars was Antarctica. This certainly occupied the minds of the first hundred settlers, perhaps because their training had all taken place in Antarctica. As the ship reached Mars and they prepared to land, the first hundred debated the organisation of property on Mars. The Russian mechanical engineer and anarchist Bogdanov argued that the Antarctic Treaty offered a model for a utopia. Land free from sovereignty and property is, in Bogdanov's words, 'land free from . . . any history at all'.[7] However, those on board were not completely ignorant of the political reality outside of the peaceful purposes and cooperation proclaimed in the treaty. The Antarctic Treaty explicitly does not renounce sovereignty claims made by contracting parties. Argentina, New Zealand, Australia, the United Kingdom, Norway, France and Chile all have territorial claims over Antarctica. The United States and Russia both reserve the right to make a territorial claim. There are a further 20 countries which have a 'significant interest' in Antarctica,

6 Ibid., 401.
7 Ibid., 110.

usually demonstrated by investing in significant scientific research stations. As Bogdanov also acknowledges, this makes the scientific stations highly political, rather than neutral, as investing in scientific research is a strong basis for a future claim, or at least involvement in any change to how Antarctica is governed.

The first Mars Treaty was modelled on the Antarctic Treaty. It had similar weaknesses. Bases on Mars belonged to the specific states on Earth which built them. The first settlers in theory were building American and Russian bases, and as such 'the nightmare of Terran law and Terran history' continued to weigh on the settlers, and even the planet.[8] As the settlement of Mars progressed, this weakness meant that a great number of different countries built bases on Mars, usually as flags of convenience for transnational corporations. Whichever transnational corporation could get the most states to allow it to build bases on their behalf would have the biggest claim to ownership of mining on Mars. The first Mars Treaty included provisions for UN licensed mining operations, with profits to be shared among every nation on Earth. How this was to be done was unspecified, but it was assumed that something similar to the mining of the international seabed would be put in place, with a tax on mining profits being collected and redistributed by the UN. It also legislated for 'measures to prevent the disruption of planetary environments'.[9] This should in principle have prohibited the mass terraforming projects which started immediately, but the provision was ignored. The treaty was upheld where it could be exploited, and failed to prevent abuse where it was not useful to those with an interest in Mars.

The Outer Space Treaty was the other significant piece of international law which formed the background for the initial settlement of Mars. This treaty, opened for signature in 1967, also forbids the claiming of sovereignty in outer space. It also restricts military uses of outer space, prohibiting the placement of weapons of mass destruction in space or on celestial bodies. Conventional weaponry is not prohibited, nor are military space forces of other kinds. One minor provision that was to prove significant when included in the Mars Treaty was Article XV, which allowed that any state party could propose amendments to the treaty. As the Mars Treaty came up for renewal in 2057, the major transnational corporations manoeuvred to have as many representatives from flag of convenience states as possible. The weaknesses of both the Antarctic Treaty and the Outer Space Treaty became very apparent when they were applied by analogy to Mars.

It should be emphasised here how speculative the mission to Mars was. Its huge mineral wealth was only known after the settlers arrived. Even then, interplanetary mining only became economically viable after the building of the space elevator, and in a period of capitalist development where the old multinationals had joined together into fewer and much more powerful transnationals. The whole mission to settle Mars was a gamble by two 'decrepit outmoded industrial dinosaurs', as Frank Chalmers, leader of the US mission puts it:

> We had all this space experience going to waste, and a couple of huge and unnecessary aerospace industries, and so we pooled them and came here on the chance that we'd find something worthwhile, and it paid off![10]

Once it became viable, there was a kind of gold rush, of countries and corporations staking claims, and emigrants seeking a new life.

8 Ibid., 111.
9 Ibid.
10 Ibid., 415.

Governance of Mars in this period was supposed to be under the oversight of UNOMA. However, it is revealed in Robinson's history that even at this stage UNOMA was not working to uphold the Mars Treaty. Helmut Bronski, senior official of UNOMA on Mars, and former EU Commissioner for Financial Affairs, awarded the first mining concession in 2047, ten years before the Mars Treaty was due to be amended, and in direct breach of the first Mars Treaty. In a conversation with Boone, he justified the decision on the basis that the treaty was superannuated, and that 'we have to try to anticipate certain aspects of the revision'.[11] The concession was granted to Armscor, originally a weapons manufacturer based in South Africa, but by this stage a transnational corporation, representing over 20 countries, and with enough capital to make it one of the world's top 20 economies, while still being one of the smaller transnationals.

Once mining concessions and terraforming were underway on Mars, the precedent of ignoring the treaty fed back into the treaties which had informed the Mars Treaty. In the same year as the first mining concession was granted on Mars, oil and gas drilling began on Antarctica. With the space elevator and the mining concessions came a huge spike in emigration to Mars, particularly of miners seeking to make their fortune and return to Earth. The emigration, far more than the mining or the terraforming, was the central issue in the renegotiation of the Mars Treaty in 2057.

By 2057, 53 states were parties to the Mars Treaty and had established bases on the planet. Working still as the United States Secretary of State for Martian Affairs, Frank Chalmers played a leading role in renegotiating the Mars Treaty, and in representing the interests of the colonists. Chalmers' first proposal was to align the interests of Mars with the interests of the Third World. Mars was a new colony, just like the former colonies, and once again the Global North was profiting by exploiting natural resources. The Global South nations present could vote together to push for profits from Mars being distributed to states rather than corporations. He persuaded these delegates that their interests should be in the money rather than mass emigration, which would be impractical and costly given the scale of the problem. To the Global North states, Chalmers sold this as sovereignty asserting itself against transnational capital, and that emigration was in the interests of these states far more than simply opening up the new planet to industrial exploitation. The interests of the Global North in emigration, and the Global South in profit sharing from resources, and of all states in asserting sovereignty against capital, brokered a sort of balanced deal, with emigration and exploitation apparently in opposition to each other.

However, it did not last long. The transnationals soon moved to different flag of convenience states to expand their mining operations. Emigration to Mars increased, in the form of workers, crammed in to rapidly built and inadequate accommodation. This increase became unmanageable after the completion of the space elevator in 2060. Workers started striking, and the transnationals sent private police and military to force them to work. In 2061 the first Martian revolution started. It was ended with extreme violence from UN-backed transnational private forces, destroying whole cities. The remaining first settlers on Mars went into hiding, and the Mars Treaty was completely abandoned, with *de facto* control of Mars handed over entirely to the transnational corporations, through UNOMA.

Old law for new wine?

There is much that we can take with us from Robinson's thinking about human settlers on Mars. The references to international law in the novel might be a little vague and imprecise for

11 Ibid., 321.

international lawyers, but the recognition of the power of legal analogy, and the interplay of law and politics, is well understood and realistic. Mars might not quite be ready for exploitation, but we are right now faced with the prospect of similar forms of commercial exploitation. The deep seabed is one worth considering, as are topics such as asteroid mining and private space exploration.

Robinsons' characters have a treaty to work with, and even a UN agency guiding them. But they are also aware of two key historical precedents in the Outer Space Treaty and the Antarctic Treaty. Today, the Outer Space Treaty is still a key pillar of any existing or potential space law. The Antarctic Treaty is more interesting, and for Robinson is regularly invoked as a kind of utopia. Overlooked in the book is the UN Convention on the Law of the Sea (UNCLOS), in which the provisions for the deep seabed could have posed a productive parallel. Instead, we can look at it the other way around, with the renegotiation of the Mars Treaty perhaps having interesting lessons for the deep seabed after the UNCLOS Implementation Agreement and with the negotiation of the Mining Code underway.

First the Outer Space Treaty. The treaty, built upon the General Assembly Declaration of Legal Principles Governing Outer Space, was adopted in 1966 and entered into force in 1967. It is very clearly a product of the Cold War space race and is a reactive piece of international legislation. By 1967 satellites had been launched, several people had been into space, and the first spacewalk had taken place. US ambitions to land on the Moon were well known, as were USSR plans for a space station. The treaty is written in very broad terms, but it does start with some useful fundamental principles – Article 1 reserving outer space and celestial bodies as 'the province of all mankind', and Article 2 prohibiting claims of sovereignty over outer space or celestial bodies.

As the relative power of states to private companies diminishes, these provisions become much weaker. Arguably, the treaty was written during a period of peak sovereignty, with the new global hegemons refusing to cooperate, and the decolonising world using its new found sovereignty in imaginative ways. The historical precedent is clear: much of colonialism was driven by private companies, such as the Dutch and British East India companies. The use of occidental law to deny Indigenous law and render settler colonies in North America, Australia and New Zealand empty are also clear comparisons. In the twenty-first century, as Robinson also sees, private companies can assert their rights in space without being limited by sovereignty. Occidental law itself makes space empty and free for exploitation. Several states have passed or are drafting legislation to permit companies operating from their states to explore space. The best known are the US Space Act 2015, which includes provisions relating to asteroid mining, and Luxembourg's Space Law 2017.[12]

The same developments are seen in the regulation of the deep seabed. In UNCLOS this area was reserved for the benefit of all humankind, but as the mining becomes possible the rights are being bought up by a few private companies operating through flags of convenience. This is seen most clearly in the case of mining company Deep Green working through Nauru.[13] Surabhi Ranganathan shows that the reserving of the deep seabed for all humankind continued a logic of exploitation.[14] Claims of territory or sovereignty are not necessary for exploiting a

12 For an excellent analysis of these developments see Isabel Feichtner, "Mining for Humanity in the Deep Sea and Outer Space," *Leiden Journal of International Law* 32 (2019): 255–74; also see Storr in this collection.

13 Nauru holds the exploration concession which DeepGreen makes use of. DeepGreen CEO Gerard Barron spoke from Nauru's seat at the ISA mining code negotiations, https://ran-s3.s3.amazonaws.com/isa.org.jm/s3fs-public/files/documents/nauru-gb.pdf. See also the analysis in Feichtner: Ibid.

14 Surabhi Ranganathan, "Ocean Floor Grab: International Law and the Making of an Extractive Imaginary," *European Journal of International Law* 30 (2019): 573–600.

resource; it is, rather, the definition of something as a resource that marks it for exploitation. Naming the seabed, or outer space, as being a resource to benefit all humankind continues to view nature through a lens of exploitation. This was clearly a struggle the colonists on Mars went through, and it is one that we are seeing right now in the drafting of the ISA mining code.

A different theory is needed. The idea of common heritage of humankind was a radical resistance to state-led imperialism. But in an age of catastrophic climate change, what is needed is an anti-extractive theory, a theory of using nature that is not exploitative. This fundamentally requires a change in science, law and economics, all of which need decolonising. To do so requires a change of theory, or of imagination, and this is the usefulness of the Martian trilogy.

Law and sci-fi: future histories, historical simulation and imagining the world differently

Science fiction offers a form of theorising that is imaginative, creative and inherently oppositional to the established order. The 'cognitive estrangement' found in *Red Mars* is one I have attempted to reproduce in this chapter, by taking the fiction seriously, even literally.[15] A similar creative liberation has been found in much of the turn to history work in international law. Perhaps it is time for a turn to the future.[16]

What then to make of the colonising of Mars? It poses as much of a legal challenge as a scientific, economic, environmental and political challenge. The later books in the Martian trilogy each include a constitutional convention – the first ideal, the second actual – echoing the treaty renegotiation in the first volume, but these are about the public law of a new and independent Mars. The first volume offers the most for an international lawyer. The characters are reasonably aware of the legal context of their mission, even if the author muddles some of the detail. But what I want to explore in this penultimate section is the usefulness of looking at international law through the novel.

It has often been said that it is easier today to imagine the end of the world than the end of capitalism.[17] That is the challenge of Robinson's science fiction: to try to think beyond what Mark Fisher called 'capitalist realism' – Fisher's term for an understanding of contemporary capitalist ideology operating as 'a pervasive atmosphere, conditioning not only the production of culture but also the regulation of work and education, and acting as a . . . barrier constraining thought and action'.[18] Robinson's novel is written as a future history, and it regularly questions what history is and how it is used. He defines science fiction as 'historical simulations' to produce a vision of the future.[19] His vision is consciously set against the 'consensus vision' of humanity in an artificial world, something like the spaceship supercomputer utopia of Iain M Banks' *Culture* novels. Robinson instead writes 'ecotopias', a science fiction world filled with

15 Darko Suvin, *Positions and Presuppositions in Science Fiction* (New York: Springer, 1998), 71–72.

16 There is of course some engagement by lawyers with science fiction and popular culture more generally, in international law see Ruth Houghton and Aoife O'Donoghue, "'Ourworld': A Feminist Approach to Global Constitutionalism," *Global Constitutionalism* 9, no. 1 (March 2020): 38–75. Houghton & O'Donoghue's article is a serious rethinking of global constitutionalism using feminist science fiction. There is also a mini-symposium in *Law, Culture and the Humanities* 14 (2018) which covers near future international law and technology issues.

17 Jameson cites this line as 'someone once said . . .' in Frederic Jameson, "Future City," *New Left Review* 21 (2003): 76.

18 Mark Fisher, *Capitalist Realism* (Winchester: Zero Books, 2009), 16.

19 Kim Stanley Robinson, *FuturePrimitive: The New Ecotopias* (New York: Tor, 1994), 9.

life and nature, combining 'the post-modern and the paleolithic' in a 'future primitive'.[20] As such, Robinson's trilogy is, in Robert Markley's words, 'a sustained, theoretically sophisticated attempt to conjure into being a future that resists the romantic dystopianism of cyberpunk, the antitechnological bias of much "green" literature, and blanket denunciations of capitalist technoscience'.[21]

This is science fiction written as a way to overcome history. The novels are 'historical simulations', that is, simulations of what historical experience might become. These novels are focused on overcoming two specific divides central to capitalist modernity – between past and present, and between science and nature. The characters of the novels are well aware that they need 'to yoke together impossible opposites'.[22] Fundamentally, as recognised by Markley and Elizabeth Leane, this is an effort of decolonisation.

Mars, like space in general, is often portrayed as a frontier. This inevitably recalls the frontier of colonialism, particularly of the westward spread of the United States. Some, like aerospace engineer and Mars exploration advocate Robert Zubrin, are explicit in their description of Mars as a new frontier, of capitalism's need for constant expansion, and of the success and plenty built upon that exploration of those earlier frontiers. Of course, this libertarian idealist viewpoint is 'founded on dubious or simplified readings of American history that repress both the human and the ecological consequences of conquest and colonisation'.[23] This view pits science against nature, with nature always and only there for human exploitation. Again, we see space repeating the ideas of the deep sea bed, as containing potentially infinite resources for continuous capitalist and human expansion and exploitation. Robinson's Mars is written in this historical moment, as well as in the legacy of all previous sci-fi depictions of Mars. He attempts a decolonised history of settling new territory.

First Robinson's Mars has no natives, unlike much work in the genre. There are no people to subjugate. This is put to the forefront by some characters in justifying an all-out terraforming of the planet, an as-fast-as-possible adaption of nature for human survival. It is only Claybourne, who becomes leader of the Red faction, who stands against this, and argues for the natural state of the planet as providing its own indigeneity. Here the tension between nature and science is rooted. It plays out as a political conflict, is a key element of the alternative economics developed and also turns into armed conflict in both revolutions through the novels. As this struggle is played out and reconciled across the three novels, the reader can see and think the frontier differently, as cooperative and ecologically driven, not as individualistic and opportunistic.

The second major reconciliation which we can learn from in Robinson's novels is between past and present.[24] In navigating the difficulties of Mars, many characters turn to history. This theme is foreshadowed on the journey to Mars, during a brief argument about history and religion.[25] While thinking about what a new Martian society might look like, John Boone describes history as 'what happened when you weren't looking – an unknowable infinity of

20 Ibid., 11.
21 Robert Markley, *Dying Planet: Mars in Science and the Imagination* (Durham, NC: Duke University Press, 2005), 355–56.
22 Kim Stanley Robinson, *Green Mars* (New York: Bantam Books, 2005), 229.
23 Markley, *Dying Planet*, 365.
24 I do not mean here to go over well trod ground on the history of international law, although what I say is relevant. Here instead I am aiming at something much bigger, the idea of human progress, from past to present, and its undoing.
25 Robinson, *Red Mars*, 69–71.

events . . . a nightmare, a compendium of examples to be avoided'.[26] The characters repeatedly struggle to apply historical analogy to the new planet. The radically different geographical setting demands a new political, economic and social organisation. Every attempt to reinstate an Earth-based system fails, whether it is Frank Chalmers' old school diplomacy or the language of the US Constitution. Instead, by the third book, the historical period on Earth that the settlers left is bracketed as feudal-capitalism, the whole period defined by private property. Mars overcomes this history by instituting a democratic economy, without private property. This is a combination of a futuristic socialism with a very traditional environmentalism. Nature combines with science, and the past with the present.

Leane centres the relationship between science and colonialism: 'like colonialism, and like patriarchy, science operates through a process of othering . . . the physical world is posited as other to the observer.'[27] She sees in Robinson's empty Mars a literal performance of what colonialist discourse does – the rendering of the colonised as natural, as objects of scientific observation in the same way the natural world is. As such, Robinson 'makes the isomorphism of the colonial and the scientific impulses explicit'.[28] The characters try to do things differently, try to 'take history by the arm and break it – *make* it. Make it new'.[29] They do this, according to Leane, by seeking what feminist scientists have called a 'successor science'.[30] This science accepts the natural world as autonomous, has 'a deep reverence for nature, a capacity for union with that which is to be known' and a 'willingness to hear what the material has to say'.[31] Law obviously also repeats this distinction between observer and object, as legislator and regulated. What would a successor international law look like, with a reverence for nature and a willingness to hear the object?

International lawyers tend to treat technological developments in two ways: either a conservative insistence on the viability of old law, or a liberal-technical desire to write new laws. The *Mars* novels suggest that both are wrong in their exclusion of the other. You cannot insist on repeating the past, but you also cannot just leave it behind. It must be overcome. International lawyers concerned for the environment can also take on the lesson that science and nature must be reconciled. An insistence on undoing science is flawed and in its worst form reveals fascist impulses. The hope of innovating out of every problem has similar totalitarian endpoints. Sax Russel, the lead terraformer of Mars, learns this over the arc of the three novels. He starts out willing to do anything to heat the planet and thicken the atmosphere, including nuclear explosions and giant space mirrors. He ends up limiting the height of the atmosphere, finding that in preserving human life he must also preserve Mars itself. Cooperation between people, and then between people and place.

Conclusion

Robinson's utopia is not a blueprint; it is a dynamic utopia. In Frederick Jameson's terms, the traditional utopia ends history; on Mars, 'it is the attempt repeatedly to begin history over again

26 Ibid., 335–36.
27 Elizabeth Leane, "Chromodynamics: Science and Colonialism in Kim Stanley Robinson's Mars Trilogy," *Ariel* 33 (2002): 85.
28 Ibid., 90.
29 Kim Stanley Robinson, *Blue Mars* (London: Harper Collins, 1996), 34.
30 Leane, "Chromodynamics," 100.
31 Evelyn Fox Keller as quoted in Ibid., 100.

which is the very subject of the work'.[32] The utopian desire is revealed through how things are done. The characters learn to do things differently. This includes law. The course of the novels takes about 300 years, and a few revolutions. The achievements of the colonists must constantly be renewed and improved. There is a lesson here, in the theorising about how to do things differently, about changing our processes to try and reconcile nature and science, past and present. This can be taken into our more practical, less idealistic, thinking about how to do international law in interesting times.

The way Sax Russel learns to do science in the second half of the second novel might be a way we could learn to do international law:

> to explore everything. No matter the difficulties! To stay open, to accept ambiguity. To attempt to fuse with the object of knowledge. To admit that there are values shot through the whole enterprise. To love it. To work toward discovering the values by which we should live. To work to enact those values in the world. To explore – and more than that – to create![33]

32 Frederic Jameson, "'If I Can Find One Good City Then I Will Spare the Man': Realism and Utopia in Kim Stanley Robinson's *Mars* Trilogy," in *Archaeologies of the Future* (London: Verso, 2005), 412.

33 Robinson, *Green Mars*, 373.

24

Revisiting *Local Hero*

Ruth Buchanan[1]

> The experience of film . . . forces the question of the relation between thinking and caring – or, as Cavell describes it, of trying "to meld the ways of thinking that have invited my conviction with the experiences of film that I have cared about".[2]

> Thinking is periodically nudged, frightened, inspired or terrorized into action by strange encounters.[3]

Sometime in the summer of 1984, I was a college student, travelling on my own through Scotland, staying in hostels and walking on beaches. One evening, possibly in the town of Ullapool, I idly wandered into a small cinema on the waterfront to see whatever was playing. The film, a romantic comedy shot in Scotland and set in a village quite like the one I was visiting, concerned the threatened purchase of the town by a Texan oil company named Knox Oil and Gas. The story of the film follows the young Houston executive named McIntyre who is sent to negotiate the purchase, as he settles into the unfamiliar routines of the tiny village and tries to navigate the ways of the locals. Walking out of the little theatre, onto the beachfront main street, I had an experience of the uncanny. Or at least, that is how I'm inclined to describe it now. This is what I said about it in 1996, when I revisited the film for a paper presented to the Law and Society Association meeting in Glasgow that year:

> The film that was playing turned out to be called *Local Hero*, and was about a small town on the northwest coast about to be bought out by a multinational oil company for the site of

1 Many thanks to Sundhya Pahuja and Shane Chalmers for the provocation, and to the editors, Rebecca Johnson, Emma Bauman and Irina Ceric, for reading this piece in draft, and to Caitlin Murphy for excellent and timely research assistance.

2 Davide Panagia, "Blankets, Screens and Projections: Or, the Claim of Film," in *The Aesthetic Turn in Political Thought*, ed. Nikolas Kompridis (London: Bloomsbury, 2014), 241.

3 William E. Connolly, *Neuropolitics: Thinking, Culture, Speed* (Minneapolis: University of Minnesota Press, 2002), 94.

> a refinery, and the Houston executive who is sent out to close the deal. In happy contrast to the hero of the movie, who falls in love with the place but in the end is inhumanely returned to his disembodied Houston office tower; when the movie ended, I found myself having the dislocating experience of walking out of the theater, right back into a utopian locality very much like (but not the same as) the one represented in the film. The romanticized and nostalgic view of the local I had picked up from the film had mapped almost directly onto my own tourist gaze to present an almost seamless transition from inside to outside the theater.[4]

Perhaps it is in the nature of uncanny experience that one is not immediately aware of its significance, that is, what it might signify or prefigure. *Local Hero* was the first film that I considered in an academic setting, but far from the last, as it turned out. Thinking, writing and teaching about film has occupied a substantial proportion of my time in the intervening decades. It's fair to say that law and film did not yet exist as a field, either in 1983 or in 1996. And yet, it turned out that I was far from alone in turning to the cinema for critical insight about the international legal order, about law and politics, and about law's violence.[5] Indeed, international legal scholarship that engages with film is by now a well-established, if not yet mainstream, subfield.[6] However, it is also a field of humanistic legal studies that is characterised by even more than the usual diversity of methodologies, approaches and orientations. It would be difficult to do justice to these approaches in a single short essay, even if one were to take a clinically taxonomic approach, which is not my intention here.

Instead, this chapter offers a decidedly subjective account of law and film scholarship, filtered through my own engagement with this particular film, which draws together some themes that have run through my work in this field, including affective encounters with strangeness and the uncanny, and the productive liminality of frontiers, telephones and beaches. As Anne Orford has observed, the discipline of international law 'operate(s) not only, or even principally, in the field of state systems, rationality and facts, but also in the field of identification, imagination, subjectivity and emotion'.[7] I have been drawn to *Local Hero* because it is a film about place, about nation, and about the international that provokes reconsideration of the complex and layered way in which we make sense of the relations among these in our lived experience as well as in legal scholarship.

Orientation: film as event

Returning to 1983, we might note that this was the year that Gilles Deleuze published the first of his two cinema books, *Cinema 1: The Movement Image*, a book that signalled a new approach to the study of film, which was neither history nor criticism, but in drawing together film and

4 Ruch Buchanan, unpublished conference paper, *Law and Society Assocation Conference*, Glasgow, Scotland, 1996.

5 Ruth Buchanan and Rebecca Johnson, "The *Unforgiven* Sources of International Law: Nation-Building, Violence and Gender in the West(ern)," in *International Law: Modern Feminist Perspectives,* eds. Doris Buss and Ambreena Manji (Oxford: Hart Publishing, 2005).

6 See for example Daniel Joyce and Gabrielle Simm, "*Zero Dark Thirty*: International Law, Film and Representation," *London Review of International Law* 3, no. 2 (2015): 295–318; see also the recent issue on film and international criminal justice in the *London Review of International Law* 6, no. 1 (2018).

7 Anne Orford, *Reading Humanitarian Intervention: Human Rights and The Use Of Force In International Law* (Cambridge: Cambridge University Press, 2003), 36.

philosophy, sought to create a particular 'atmosphere for thought'.[8] This is the spirit in which, in this short reflective piece, I am endeavouring to draw together the biographical and theoretical to offer one account of the place that film might be understood to occupy in a humanistic approach to the study of international law. I've described this elsewhere as an approach to considering film as event:

> Thinking about film as an event brings into focus the embodied and temporal dimensions of the experience of watching, hearing, and feeling a particular film as it unfolds in a particular time and place. It redirects our attention towards the components of duration, intensity, and movement – as they are apprehended by the individual. The turn, then, is from the consideration of a film on its own terms to a consideration of what is produced in the interchange between a film and a viewer.[9]

As I was developing my interest, reading scholars like Eve Sedgwick and William Connolly[10] gave me permission to write about film not as a film critic or film historian, which I was not, but simply as an embodied spectator, reflecting on the experience of watching films, and particularly the films that touched or moved me in particular ways. Had I tried to become a film 'expert' before writing about film, I might have been stopped in my tracks. And yet, the effort to try to understand how a particular film worked on me, over time, and in particular ways, whether to underscore or unsettle certain habits of thinking, seemed to me both a more modest and useful scholarly project.[11]

How I would currently explain this approach would be in terms of 'cinematic jurisprudence'[12] – but I wouldn't have used this term in 1996. With some notable exceptions, scholarship on the intersection of law and popular culture that seeks to engage with film's jurisprudential content on its own terms (and not merely for its representation of 'legal' scenes or themes that are understood as meaningfully taking place elsewhere) emerges over the following decade.[13] This approach identifies that interface between law and culture as both porous and reciprocal.

8 Gilles Deleuze, *Cinema 1. L'Image-ousement Les Editions de Minuit*, trans. Athlone Press (Minneapolis: University of Minnesota Press, 1983).

9 Ruth Buchanan, "Passing Through the Mirror: *Dead Man,* Legal Pluralism and the Deterritorialisation of the West," *Law Culture and Humanities* 7, no. 2 (2019): 294.

10 Connolly, *Neuropolitics*; Eve Kosofsky Sedgwick, *Touching Feeling: Affect, Pedagogy, Performativity* (Durham, NC: Duke University Press, 2003).

11 This approach was developed largely in collaboration with Rebecca Johnson, with whom I co-authored: Ruth Buchanan and Rebecca Johnson, "Getting the Insider's Story Out: What Popular Film Can Tell Us About Legal Method's Dirty Secrets," *Windsor Yearbook of Access to Justice* 20 (2001): 87–110; Buchanan and Johnson, "*Unforgiven*"; Ruth Buchanan and Rebecca Johnson, "Strange Encounters: Exploring Law and Film in the Affective Register," *Studies in Law, Politics and Society* 46 (2008): 36–50. Rebecca and I have continued to exchange and explore ideas about law and film throughout the past decade.

12 'To the extent that films participate in constructing as well as in reflecting upon our *nomos,* they can and should be read as jurisprudential texts.' Buchanan and Johnson, "*Unforgiven*," 134.

13 William P. McNeil, *Lex Populi: The Jurisprudence of Popular Culture* (Palo Alto: Stanford University Press, 2007); Orit Kamir, "Cinematic Judgement and Jurisprudence: A Woman's Memory, Justice and Recovery in a Post-Traumatic Society (A Study of Polanski's Death and the Maiden)," in *Law on the Screen,* eds. Austin Sarat, Lawrence Douglas and Martha Merrill Umphrey (Palo Alto: Stanford University Press, 2005), 28–82; Leslie Moran, et al., eds., *Law's Moving Image* (London: Cavendish, 2004); but see also Alison Young, "Murder in the Eyes of the Law," *Studies in Law, Politics and Society* 17 (1997): 31–58.

In Naomy Mezey's terms, it can be helpful to think of popular cultural depictions of law as translations, or 'afterlives' of law, but not in a representational sense. Indeed, she cautions that:

> to speak of "representation" and "translation" is to risk perpetuating the fiction that while popular culture continually portrays or sketches legal scenes, it always speaks in a language that is not law's language; it suggests that culture is never law. But films act as a form of juridical communication just as law acts as a form of cultural transmission.[14]

And for Kirsty Duncanson, in an article which considers two contemporary re-imaginings of key moments in Australian history and their implications for settler colonial-Indigenous relations, popular film is posited as an important site for debates over the nature of Australian sovereignty:

> Successful or critically acclaimed cinema texts are thus not only a central source of knowing what law is, how it works, and the foundations of its authority, but they also provide a space for rethinking, questioning and reimagining law: they are a venue of popular jurisprudential negotiation.[15]

For a critical legal scholar, already persuaded of the interwoven nature, and hence fundamental indivisibility of law and politics, to understand cinema as law is also then to understand it as politics. How enlivening, then, to encounter the deep and rich adjacent seam of scholarship on the interconnections of aesthetics and politics in film. There are a variety of routes that might be taken here, but for me one influential entry point was through the work of Michael Shapiro, who draws on both Deleuze and Rancière to offer up close readings of particular films as a vehicle for critical political thinking about the modern world. For Shapiro, 'thinking . . . involves resistance to the dominant modes of representing the world, whether those representational practices function as mere unreflective habit or as intentionally organized, systematic observation.'[16] And cinema, in his view, is 'a post-mimetic aesthetic . . . that inter-articulates and mobilizes images to provoke thinking outside of any narrative determination'.[17] That is, film offers itself up as a particularly rich site for thinking in this way because it doesn't just tell stories, it makes worlds, which in their aesthetic composition offer opportunities for us to consider both how they are made, and moreover, how they might have been composed otherwise.[18] This approach is informed by Rancière's politics of aesthetics which is intimately connected to what Rancière describes as the 'distribution of the sensible', or 'the see-able and the sayable'.[19] It is important to note that for Rancière, the political is also intimately connected with modes of sense perception: 'a delimitation of spaces and times, of the visible and the invisible, of

14 Naomi Mezey, "Law's Visual Afterlife: Violence, Popular Culture and Translation Theory," in *Imagining Legality: Where Law Meets Popular Culture,* ed. Austin Sarat (Tuscaloosa: University of Alabama Press, 2011), 66.

15 Kirsty Duncanson, " 'Native' Landscapes, 'Cultivated' Gardens and the Erasure of Indigenous Sovereignty in Two Recent Instances of Australian Cinematic Jurisprudence," *Law Culture and Humanities* 10, no. 2 (2014): 239.

16 Michael J. Shapiro, *Cinematic Geopolitics* (Abingdon: Routledge, 2009), 5.

17 Ibid., 11.

18 Or, as Deleuze puts it succinctly in Cinema II: 'Cinema does not just present images, it surrounds them with a world.' Gilles Deleuze, *Cinema Two: The Time-Image* (London: Continuum Books, 1989, first published 1985), 66.

19 Jacques Rancière, *The Politics of Aesthetics: The Distribution of the Sensible* (London: Continuum Books, 2005), 13: 'Politics revolves around what is seen and what can be said about it.'

speech and noise, that simultaneously determines the place and states of politics as a form of experience'.[20] Film offers us direct access to an experientially delimited landscape, and as such, well-made films can provoke us to re-examine the 'common sense' of the aesthetic-political world we collectively inhabit: 'When effectively composed, film can assist a discernment of the interrelationship between aesthetic and political registers because it can be assembled to provide critical reflection on the complex relations of the sensible, and the sayable.'[21] In this way, scholarly consideration of the aesthetic composition of a film can connect the experiential to the politico-legal in ways that can both disrupt prevailing notions of a *sensus communus*/common sense and open up space for critical analysis, or possibilities for thinking otherwise.[22]

This is the orientation that I have brought along with me as I revisit this film for the occasion of this Handbook. While *Local Hero* is a much-loved early contribution to Scottish cinema, directed by Bill Forsyth, it may not obviously offer itself as a site for the consideration of topics or themes germane to international law, in the way that films such as *Zero Dark Thirty* or *Eye in the Sky* have done more recently.[23] But, as I've explained, and will illustrate more concretely in the analysis that follows, the avenues by which I come to this work do not route through the representational, but rather through the registers of time, memory and experience. As such, the linkages to the field of international law can be expected to manifest not generally, in terms of observations on the field or discipline as a whole, but rather in terms of the particular subjects, affects or imaginative possibilities that might be revealed through the encounter. In what follows, I briefly offer my reading of two aspects of the film's aesthetic that have resonated powerfully with me over the years. The first is what I now would describe as its 'uncanniness', that is, a tendency to make the familiar strange, and the second is its preoccupation with liminality, as illustrated by, among other things, recurring wide shots of beaches and horizons, particularly as depicted at dawn and dusk.

Uncanny encounters, or making the familiar strange[24]

I begin by returning to my own temporally distant, yet vividly remembered, experience of walking out of the film *Local Hero* back into the film itself, or so it seemed. It was, as I remember it now, a striking experience of the uncanny. I had imagined that my own recollection of the main street of the town that I was most likely visiting, Ullapool had been replaced in my memories by the town of Pennan, where the film was shot. Here, a quick Google search offered up a second uncanny experience, as the images of the white buildings arrayed along the waterfront along Ullapool's main street do indeed strikingly resemble the town in the film.[25] The first time I returned to the film, in 1996, I took it up, ostensibly,

20 Ibid.

21 Ibid., 92.

22 Buchanan, "Passing Through the Mirror."

23 Joyce and Simm, "Zero Dark Thirty"; Jothie Rajah, "A Minor Jurisprudence of Spectacular War: Law as Eye in the Sky," *Law Text Culture* 21 (2017): 252–75; Matthew Robson, "Re-visioning the 'Eye in the Sky': Targeted Drone Strikes and an Ethics of the Encounter," *Critical Studies on Terrorism* 13, no. 1 (2020): 100–17.

24 I have previously written on the importance of attending to the affective aspects of cinema in an article co-authored with Rebecca Johnson, see Buchanan and Johnson, "Strange Encounters."

25 Images of Ferness are accessible here: "Local Hero: 1983," *Movie Locations*, accessed May 18, 2020, www.movie-locations.com/movies/l/Local-Hero.php, Source: Wikimedia, Tom Jervis. Some images of the Ullapool main street can be found on this site: Fiona Russell, "Exploring Ullapool," *Walk Highlands*, October 3, 2017, www.walkhighlands.co.uk/news/exploring-ullapool/0016954/.

Figure 24.1 Main street, town of Pennan, Scotland, the site of the fictional 'Ferness' in *Local Hero*.

because it was a text that represented a prevalent discourse on the global and the local as dichotomous:

> 'Local Hero' does evoke a powerful nostalgia for the concrete and everyday pull of the local, as against a dehumanizing and abstracted global, but I discovered on a recent re-viewing that it does so somewhat more ironically than I had originally perceived. The young, urban executive who is being sent out to negotiate the purchase of the seaside town by the company for the site of an (environmentally devastating) oil refinery is told he has been chosen because of his Scottish heritage; McIntyre, we discover, was a name picked at random by his Hungarian immigrant parents because they thought it sounded American. The multinational company, Knox Oil and Gas, also has a false Scottish name, as Mr. Knox, the founder, had been bought out a generation before by the father of the current American owner.

Rereading my earlier account of the film, I can see that my original viewing experience might have resonated quite differently than I had imagined. My earlier plot summary of the film uncannily mirrors my own experience of encountering *Local Hero* as a solitary traveller to the Scottish north coast, who was from the oil rich west of North America (Alberta rather than Texas), and whose Scottish name concealed an Irish heritage. The film's thematic preoccupation with naming and misnaming of people and things also evokes the uncanny, which according to Nicholas Royle is associated with 'a crisis of the proper. . . . A disturbance of the very idea of personal or private property, including the properties of proper names, of places, institutions and events.'[26]

26 Nicholas Royle, *The Uncanny* (Manchester: Manchester University Press, 2011), 1.

The concept of the uncanny is most frequently associated in film studies with fear, the supernatural and the horror genre. But it has had a wide array of usages over the past century, including the 'peculiar co-mingling of the familiar and the unfamiliar', such as encountering familiar others in strange or unfamiliar places, and varieties of doubles and doubling.[27] Freud's essay on the uncanny, published in 1919, offers a number of illustrations of these phenomena, including 'the factor of repetition' or 'this feature of the unintentional return'. The essay also offers a vivid illustration based on his own experience of walking through the narrow streets of an unfamiliar provincial town in Italy, inadvertently coming upon the same street three times in quick succession.[28]

Local Hero also plays with this sense of the uncanny. It evokes romanticised, and in the view of its critics, tired tropes of Scottishness, particularly in the ways in which the remote locality is seemingly invested with a mysterious/mystical power.[29] Paul Newland observes that the film's remote northern setting is 'a place where strange things seemingly occur' and is 'seemingly magical, otherworldly'.[30] To what extent the film reinforces, or undermines, a romanticised image that reduces Scottishness to stereotypes of the charming yet shrewd rural highlanders, known as Kailyardism, has been well debated.[31] While it may have met with some critical opprobrium at the time of its release, *Local Hero* has aged very well, becoming a much loved classic of Scottish cinema, continuing to attract tourists to the locations where it was filmed decades after the fact, and in 2019, was even restaged as musical theatre.[32] Indeed, a headline in the *Scottish Daily Mail* queried, at around the 35th anniversary of the film's release: 'Is Local Hero the most enchanting movie of all time?'[33] This enduring appeal is part of what makes it an inviting subject for a critical cultural legal studies consideration, in that it seems to offer an account of a tiny local community's face-off with a Goliath multinational corporation which many people continue to find attractive, notwithstanding – or perhaps because of – its fantastic elements.

One of these fantastic moments occurs early in the film. When the Texas-based multinational Knox Oil and Gas wants to build a refinery on the site of a (fictional) Scottish fishing village named Ferness, the film's protagonist – McIntyre, whom we know as Mac – is sent to

27 See, for example, Royle, *The Uncanny*; John Zilcosky, *Uncanny Encounters: Literature, Psychoanalysis, and the End of Alterity* (Evanston: Northwestern University Press, 2015); Cynthia Freeland, "Explaining the Uncanny in the Double Life of Veronique," in *Horror Film and Psychoanalysis: Freud's Worst Nightmare,* ed. Steven Jay Schneider (Cambridge: Cambridge University Press, 2004), 87–105.

28 Sigmund Freud, *The Uncanny*, trans. David McLintock (New York: Penguin Books, 2003), 143–44.

29 See, for example, the discussion of the film's critical reception by Jonathan Murray, *Discomfort and Joy: The Cinema of Bill Forsyth* (Bern: Peter Lang, 2011), 74. See also Paul Newland, "To the West There Is Nothing . . . Except America: The Spatial Politics of Local Hero," *Visual Culture in Britain* 12, no. 2 (2011): 171–83.

30 Newland, "To the West There Is Nothing," 175.

31 A lengthy discussion of the reception of the film, locally, nationally and internationally is found in the chapter by Ian Goode, "Mediating the Rural: *Local Hero* and the Location of Scottish Cinema," in *Cinematic Countrysides,* ed. Robert Fish (Manchester: Manchester University Press, 2007), 117. See also Stuart Aitken, "A Transactional Geography of the Image-Event: The Films of Scottish Director Bill Forsyth," *Transactions of the Institute of British Geographers* 16, no. 1 (1991): 105–18. Aitken observes 'Local Hero was roundly condemned in the British media for perpetuating the myths of Scottish culture', noting that some scholars felt that it came 'very close to falling into the Kailyard discourse. Local Hero's story-line, based upon the opposition of American entrepreneurship and Scottish couthiness, is remarkably similar to that bastion of Kailyard discourse, The Maggie (1953)', 113.

32 See Libby Brooks, "Mac's Back: Scotland's Treasured Local Hero Is Reborn as a Musical," *The Guardian,* March 11, 2019, www.theguardian.com/stage/2019/mar/11/scotland-local-hero-musical-bill-forsyth-john-crowley-david-greig-mark-knopfler.

33 John Macleod, "Is Local Hero the Most Enchanting Movie of All Time?" *Scottish Daily Mail,* May 12, 2018, www.pressreader.com/uk/scottish-daily-mail/20180512/282041917771293.

Scotland to negotiate the purchase of the town (and consequently the relocation of its residents). He arrives in Aberdeen where he is met by the Scottish representative of the company, named Olsen. After a quick visit to the company lab in Aberdeen where a scale model of the village, and the refinery which is planned to replace it, have been constructed, they take to the road in a Ford Cortina to drive north to the village. Notably, their journey is disrupted 'by the abrupt descent of an impenetrable mist. Forced to sleep overnight by the roadside, the men awake to find the mirk lifted and a breathtaking natural landscape revealed.'[34] The misty interlude recalls to mind similar scenes in other films, including the 'definitive Tartan fantasy' *Brigadoon*, from 1954, concerning a mythical Scottish village that emerges from the Highland fog only one day every century.[35] As Murray observes, the interlude in *Local Hero* might be read as rather 'ostentatious announcement of the cinematic Scotland as a world different from, and more diverting than, the modern, technologically advanced American "real"'.[36] Before continuing on their journey, Mac notices a rabbit with a broken leg on the roadside, and insists on 'rescuing' the animal by bringing it along in the car, and names it 'Trudy'. In an early signal that this film isn't content to reproduce the romanticised Scottish Eden of earlier films, Trudy turns up several days later in the form of a delicious rabbit stew cooked by the innkeeper's wife, Stella, who later becomes the subject of Mac's romantic fantasy.

Once the travellers arrive in the town, we are introduced to the character of Gordon, who is the town's unofficial mayor, its accountant, the owner of its only hotel and also in charge of the negotiations on behalf of the town. Money appears to be no object for the company, and in a bit of a twist on what one might expect, the townspeople have got wind of the pending deal, thanks to Gordon, and are eager to cash in on the riches apparently on offer, although this is scrupulously kept a secret from the newcomers. While they wait to hear back from Gordon about their offer, Mac and Olsen while away their time by taking long walks on the beach. All seems to be going according to plan, for both sides, until it is discovered that the beach is owned by Ben Knox, an eccentric beachcomber who lives in a hut with no door, who simply cannot fathom the notion that he would sell the property. From a critical legal perspective, the key problem for the dealmakers is that Ben doesn't see himself as an owner of a fungible commodity, but rather as a caretaker of the land he has inherited.[37] A tense stand-off ensues, until the billionaire owner and CEO of the company, Felix Happer (played by Burt Lancaster), arrives on the beach in a helicopter '*deus ex machina*', to climb into the hut and engage in a lengthy off-camera negotiation with Ben. Happer/Lancaster's arrival, wondrously staged as a long pan shot of the incoming helicopter's headlight in a darkening sky, across the beach foregrounded by gathering villagers who are about to confront Ben, is a pivotal moment of inchoate unease in the film. From the Scottish film critic's perspective, 'The paradox of the incoming star-hero . . .

34 Murray, *Discomfort and Joy*, 78.

35 Duncan Petrie, *Screening Scotland* (London: Bloomsbury, 2000), 33. Indeed, the trope of 'travellers from the modern world stranded in a thick fog', emerging into a community guided by older and more mysterious ways occurs in several of the films Petrie discusses in this chapter.

36 Murray, *Discomfort and Joy*, 78.

37 This is underscored in a scene where Mac, in a desperate effort to entice Ben to sell, has procured postcard images of beaches in other parts of the world (Sydney, Hawaii) and offers to buy Ben another 'comparable' beach. Mac says, 'any beach that takes your fancy, anywhere in the world'; 'I can get you 5 or 6 miles of Hawaii, no problem'. Ben replies, 'Yes, I mean they look like very nice beaches Mr Macintyre, but see I only need the one, I have this here I don't need another one. Besides, I'm not sure that there's a living in any of these beaches. I mean you've got to go into that kind of thing in detail.' Later, 'You're great at talking with the big numbers Mr Macintyre', before holding up the handful of sand and asking Mac whether he would sell it for the number of grains of sand. Bill Forsyth, et al., *Local Hero* (Burbank: Warner Bros, 2013), 1:28:00–1:29:50.

is not that he comes from an alien place to intrude upon local traditions, but that he comes from a familiar place to reveal the alienation of our traditions from our imaginative grasp.'[38] From the perspective of this North American outside viewer, the stunning cinematography of this scene also underscores the film's liminal aesthetic, to which I will shortly turn.

While acknowledging the extent to which *Local Hero* references prior cinematic depictions of Scottishness,[39] I have read *Local Hero* as only superficially nostalgic for a distanced or separate 'local'. Indeed, the film repeatedly destabilises and undermines that nostalgia – the town is periodically overflown by fighter jets from a nearby airfield; there is a young biker who periodically roars noisily through the main street, an African minister, and a charismatic visiting fisherman from the Soviet Union who holds an overseas investment portfolio managed by Gordon.

In using the film to think through the place of the local in my own research on call centres in 1996, I turned to an essay by Arif Dirlik[40] which 'attempted to think through the relationship between global capitalism and (a then) renewed interest in the local, when he describes the local as a site of both promise and predicament'. I went on to observe that:

> Dirlik also correctly noted that the turn to the local is deceptive, and consequently perilous, because one is always operating on terrain which is already globalized. In the movie *Local Hero*, the seduction of the local community is revealed through the perspective of the outsiders, which is also the perspective of the viewer (while the view of the locals, who can't wait to sell out and move, isn't really depicted).

In the context of my work then, this translated into a necessary precaution and a form of self-critique, against any tendency to privilege a turn to the 'local' in my research as a form of critique of then prevalent discourses of triumphal globalisation.[41]

Local Hero is a film that creates its effects by reorienting its view of the local village through an international perspective, a filter of past representations of remote and romanticised Scottishness on screen that both charms and distances. The international viewer, like the tourist who visits the Highlands, is 'offered pleasure through misrecognition'.[42] The disorientation I felt on initially watching the film while on holiday was perhaps effected by a doubling of that already filtered experience. To be sure, no privileged access to any truths, psychological or sociological, can be inferred from this uncanny encounter. But that is not to say that the film does not offer any insights to the contemporary viewer.

38 Murray, *Discomfort and Joy,* 82, citing Cairns Craig, 1983.

39 Ibid., 75.

40 Arif Dirlik, "The Global in the Local," in *Global/Local: Cultural Production and the Transnational Imaginary,* eds. Rob Wilson and Wimal Dissanayake (Durham, NC: Duke University Press, 1996): 'Global capitalism represents a further deterritorialization, abstraction and concentration of capital. In a fundamental sense, global capitalism represents an unprecedented penetration of local society globally by the economy and culture of capital; so the local understood in a "traditional" sense may be less relevant than ever. It is ironic then that capital itself should justify its operations increasingly in the language of the local. The irony allows us to see the local in all its contradictoriness,' 28.

41 An illustration of this style of argument is found in Boaventura de Sousa Santos, "Three Metaphors for a New Conception of Law: The Frontier, the Baroque and the South," *Law and Society Review* 29, no. 4 (1995): 569. See also the response by Rosemary Coombe, "Finding and Losing One's Self in the Topoi: Placing and Displacing the Postmodern Subject in Law," *Law & Society Review* 29, no. 4 (1995): 599–608.

42 Murray, *Discomfort and Joy*, 78.

On my return to this film in recent years, as a teacher of international law and development, I found that its carefully crafted narrative arc of seduction and betrayal by the oil company resonates more directly and more ominously;[43] and its resolution more like magical thinking than clever negotiation. We are collectively more familiar with this story now, and we know it mostly doesn't end well for the villagers, except in fiction.

David Harvey writes that 'place, in whatever guise, is like space and time, a social construct'.[44] More recently, critical geographers have moved away from the dichotomy of local/global, to examine the 'overlapping territorialities' in which we can analyse the co-production of society and space through social and political processes that also produce and connect spaces of extraction to spaces of consumption. One suggestive idea in a recent chapter by Facundo Martín is the idea that extractivism might be imagined (following Foucault) as heterotopic, in the sense that extractive zones, while they are constructed as distant, marginal 'other' spaces, are much more deeply interconnected to other places than immediately apparent.[45] Through this frame we might see that our imaginings of extractive zones, as well as places of consumption, occupy a central role in broader narratives of progress and development in our globalised economic order. Understanding the process in this way helps us to make visible how these narratives of resource extraction contribute to wider (contested) processes of social-spatial ordering. These contemporary struggles over extractive development are multifaceted, but importantly, for my purpose here, I want to suggest that they are struggles over how places are perceived and imagined, not unlike the one in the film *Local Hero*.

Returning to the end of the film, just after the scene I described earlier of the dramatic helicopter arrival on the beach, Ben and Happer spend a long and apparently convivial stretch of time discussing the fate of the beach (and possibly many other things) behind the shutters in Ben's beach hut, while the various other affected players linger, worriedly, outside. When they eventually emerge, a resolution is announced – the highest and best use for the beach is no longer, according to Happer, the planned refinery. He has now decided to build an observatory, and possibly a marine laboratory, on the site. Olsen usefully suggests that it be named the 'Happer Observatory', and is seconded to assist with the project, while Mac is unceremoniously dispatched to return to Dallas immediately, by company helicopter.

Aesthetically and narratively, this seems to have been a satisfying outcome for most viewers of the film. But for contemporary students of international economic law, all too familiar with the tragic iterations of this story, it might read, as it does now to me, both jarring and implausible, because it is an outcome that is apparently free of politics. I connect it now to the way in which international economic law scholars Schneiderman and Perrone have explained the process by which this depoliticisation (and its distributive outcomes) are naturalised.

> Depoliticized law results in the naturalization of these policy choices, unleashing the political power of multinational firms. The challenge for critical scholars of law is to identify

43 See *Chevron Corporation and Texaco Petroleum Corporation v. The Republic of Ecuador*, UNCITRAL, PCA Case No. 2009–23.

44 David Harvey, cited in Newland, "To the West There is Nothing," 173.

45 Facundo Martín, "Reimagining Extractivism: Insights from Spatial Theory," in *Contested Extractivism, Society and the State: Struggles Over Mining and Land*, eds. Bettina Engels and Kristina Dietz (London: Palgrave Macmillan, 2017), 33. As Martin explains it, in our contemporary discourse, extractive zones are imagined as 'other spaces' located far away from cities and developed countries; as deserted places where thus far 'wasted' resources abound. In this way they are only imagined as 'productive' in terms of mineral extraction, and not in any other terms.

how these choices are made and then normalized. International trade and investment lawyers prefer that we overlook this partiality, in favor of (imagining the) rules having abstract and universal forms.[46]

I cannot leave it here, however. My argument is that if we encounter it through an aesthetic rather than narrative lens, the film opens itself (and our imagination) towards a different set of possibilities. In this next and final reading, I suggest that by returning the viewer to a time that was both more naïve and more optimistic about the changes brought about by globalisation, *Local Hero* might offer up possibilities for thinking and acting differently in-between the spaces of the local and the global.

Local Hero's liminal spaces: an aesthetic of the in-between

> Thinking the global/local . . . put in its best light (is) the effort to think in lacuna, the interstice, that *gloams* at us from the transitional space between state and superstate (or no state) and the national/transnational forms of capital.[47]
>
> Gloam: n, gloam·ing | \ ˈglō-miŋ \
> 'twilight; dusk'
> 'lack', 'murk', 'shadows', 'umbra'
>
> The roots of the word trace to the Old English word for twilight, 'glōm,' which is akin to 'glōwan,' an Old English verb meaning 'to glow.' In the early 1800s, English speakers looked to Scotland again and borrowed the now-archaic verb gloam, meaning 'to become twilight' or 'to grow dark.'[48]

As I've already noted, most of the running time of this film unfolds on the edge of the ocean. Outdoor scenes were shot either in the seaside town of Pennan, situated picturesquely below a row of bluffs, with its signal red phone box on the water's edge or on the beach at Camusdarach.[49] The film's littoral aesthetic emerges from the frequent long lingering shots of the beach, particularly at liminal moments – dawn and dusk, as well as through the role of the pivotal female characters Marina the marine biologist, and Stella, the wife of the innkeeper with whom our protagonist falls in love. Sea and sky. I read the visual attention to liminality in the film's aesthetic as an invitation to explore the spaces in-between the global and the local, rather than reinforcing a dichotomy between them and/or romanticising an imaginary quarantined-off localism.

Illustrations of this in-between aesthetic abound in the film, but for reasons of space, I will only single out one in this chapter. It is striking that the visitor, Mac, almost immediately becomes enamoured with the beach, as does the camera, which lingers in long shots of Mac and Olsen walking on the beach at dusk, closely observing Mac as he stares, Narcissus-like, into tide pools, and slowly pans across the villagers in the gathering dark on the water's edge

46 Nicolás M. Perrone and David Schneiderman, "International Economic Law's Wreckage: Depoliticization, Inequality, Precarity," in *Research Handbook on Critical Legal Theory*, eds. Emilios Christodoulidis, Ruth Dukes and Marco Goldoni (Northampton: Edward Elgar Publishing, 2019), 452.

47 Paul Bove, "Afterword: Memory and Thought," in *Global/Local: Cultural Production and the Transnational Imaginary*, eds. Rob Wilson and Wimal Dissanayake (Durham, NC: Duke University Press, 1996), 372–85.

48 "Gloaming," Merriam-Webster, accessed April 27, 2020, www.merriam-webster.com/dictionary/gloaming.

49 Pascal Wyse, "A Fan's Tour of Local Hero Locations in Scotland," *The Guardian*, May 17, 2013, www.theguardian.com/travel/2013/may/17/fans-tour-local-hero-locations-scotland.

Figure 24.2 Long shot of beach at sunset.

Figure 24.3 Falling in love with the beach: Mac and a tide pool, still from *Local Hero*.

as Happer's helicopter approaches towards the end of the film. The beach, that littoral space between the land and sea, is an evocative site.[50] Manderson and van Rijswijk, considering the littoral imaginary in the Australian context, see it as a site where Australia's national insularity is fortified; 'the coast is a place of disembarkation, the sea its barrier.'[51] In this film, the Scottish

50 See Desmond Manderson and Honni van Rijswijk, "Introduction to Littoral Readings: Representations of Land and Sea in Law, Literature and Geography," *Law and Literature* 27, no. 2 (2015): 167–77.
51 Ibid., 170.

coastline plays a distinctly different imaginative role. Both narratively and visually, the viewer's attention is repeatedly drawn to the silent mysteries of sky and sea, unfolding above and behind the characters in the film. The cinematography in the film vividly captures the changing colours and moods of that dance of sea and sky. We see this dance doing its work on the characters in the film, at the same time as we are entranced by it as spectators. One commentator observed: 'the way the characters Mac, Olsen and Happer develop and change is a process of osmosis – the gradual, incremental ways they respond to the sea and the sky, captured visually by stunning cinematography.'[52]

As I suggested earlier, in the encounter with film as experience, aesthetics and politics are frequently woven together. 'The filmic experience or event is one that can be returned to, thought through, grappled with and used on the self as a technique for opening towards new political possibilities and ways of being.'[53] In my re-reading of *Local Hero*, I've encountered the aesthetic of the in-between as a productive opening out. That is, it offers up a sense of spaciousness or openness that is generative, full of political possibility. Put differently, the experience of watching the film can be understood as a kind of suspended interlude, a pause for thought.[54] For me, lingering once more with *Local Hero*'s gloamings, those slow transitions from day to night, has offered up a vivid embodied memory of the path that has brought us to this very dark moment of global capitalism: it was a journey of many steps, many opportunities for 'acting otherwise' that remain available to us, I would argue, if we can hold open the imaginative space for them.

Conclusion

I've elsewhere observed, referencing Benjamin, that one thing the study of film offers to international lawyers is a reminder that 'thinking and perception are not disconnected processes, either from each other or from history'.[55] In turning, and returning, to *Local Hero*, not only is it possible to read it affectively and critically as a cinematic text, but it also offers itself as an archive of the common sense of its own historical moment in contrast to ours. I've also argued elsewhere that revisiting film in this way can be understood as a species of critical (counter) history, and as allied with recent efforts on the part of critical international law scholars to 'broaden the archive' of international law.[56] *Local Hero* is history, and more than history. It resonates personally and also politically. It is a text to which many are nostalgically attached, and yet its story, and particularly its deeply satisfying resolution, resonates much more ominously on a contemporary reviewing than it does in memory.

The approach taken in this paper suggests that a re-examination attentive to the modes of perception (as well as discourse) that are emergent in that moment may be of interest to

52 Alistair Scott, "Local Hero at 35: Turning Hollywood's Greatest Scottish Film into a Musical," *The Conversation*, June 28, 2018, http://theconversation.com/local-hero-at-35-turning-hollywoods-greatest-scottish-film-into-a-musical-99054.

53 Buchanan and Johnson, "Strange Encounters," 56.

54 The musical metaphors are intentional here; the meditative and evocative Mark Knopfler soundtrack of the film, which I've not had space to discuss here, almost certainly amplifies these effects.

55 Ruth Buchanan, "End Times in the Antipodes: Propaganda and Critique in *On the Beach*," in *International Law and the Cold War*, eds. Matthew Craven, Sundhya Pahuja and Gerry Simpson (Cambridge: Cambridge University Press, 2019), 559.

56 Ibid., 560.

contemporary legal scholars seeking to make sense of a world in which the international ownership and operation of extractive industry has expanded to the point at which its consequences – in terms of environmental destruction, species loss and climate change – have become an existential threat to humanity, and international law's role in exacerbating that threat is very much in question.

Community

25

The politics of legibility

'The family' in international human rights law

Dianne Otto

Human rights are held out to be the 'foundation' of individual freedom, justice and peace.[1] Yet in reality, as Ratna Kapur contends, the international human rights framework operates to discipline, regulate and, at times, exclude the very subjects it purports to free.[2] In Kapur's analysis, human rights advance a 'specific way of being and of being free',[3] which she argues is oriented towards the neoliberal market. While I agree, in this chapter I enlarge on this analysis to include the governance work that international human rights law (IHRL) does in the service of the nation-state. This is often synonymous with the interests of the neoliberal market, but not always. While human rights cannot fully deliver human freedom, let alone justice and peace, they can bestow legibility and a degree of humanity on subaltern or marginalised subjects, as Kapur argues, albeit at some considerable cost to their freedom.

My specific concern is with a major contestation that has taken place at the United Nations (UN) Human Rights Council (HRC) over the past decade. As a result, feminist developments in IHRL since the early 1990s are looking frighteningly precarious, and LGBTI rights claims struggle to be granted even a glimmer of legibility. A conservative coalition of states is promoting a novel interpretation of the Universal Declaration of Human Rights 1948 (UDHR) arguing that it is based on a set of 'Traditional Values' – from which equality is conspicuously absent. At the heart of these battles is an old struggle over which 'families' are granted legibility, and therefore a measure of humanity and the associated entitlements. This dispute has simmered for many years over the question of women's equality in the family. More recently it has reached a boiling point over claims to the recognition of same-sex couple families.

Commencing with the UDHR, 'the family' has been understood as 'the natural and fundamental group unit of society' and therefore 'entitled to protection by society and the State'.[4] In an instrument concerned with the rights of individuals, the family is the only group that is

1 *Universal Declaration of Human Rights* (UDHR), UNGAR 217A(III), December 10, 1948, preamble para 1.
2 Ratna Kapur, *Gender, Alterity and Human Rights: Freedom in a Fishbowl* (Cheltenham: Edward Elgar Publishing, 2018), 228.
3 Ibid., 30.
4 UDHR, Article 16(3).

recognised as enjoying rights and protection. Contradicting the equality guarantees that apply to every other provision, the UDHR constitutes the family as a distinctly hierarchical group, headed by a male breadwinner. For instance, the right of workers to 'just and favourable remuneration' is framed as enough to ensure a life of dignity 'for himself and his family',[5] and the right to an adequate standard of living is granted to 'himself and his family'.[6] In other words, economic and social rights are largely held by the (presumed male) household head who is free to distribute these resources within the family as he sees fit, normalising gendered relations of dependence. Further, the family of the UDHR is founded on heterosexual marriage, and its primary function is reproductive.[7] Tellingly, specific reference to women occurs only twice in the substantive articles of the UDHR, in context of 'men and women' enjoying the right to marry,[8] and as 'mothers' who, along with children, are entitled to 'special care and assistance'.[9] The family is constituted as a private realm, where different rules apply than in the public realm of liberty and equality.

Constituting the family in this way serves many state interests, as well those of the socially conservative neoliberal market.[10] By prioritising a particular family form, which is rewarded by the allocation of various benefits and privileges, the state imposes a 'specific way of being' that produces a more compliant and homogeneous population that is easier to govern. Those who do not comply are marginalised, and may be vilified, pathologised and even criminalised. Further, as I will argue, the nation-state relies on reproductive, patriarchal and heteronormative family relations to reproduce the nation and its often-racialised dominant culture. This family form also reduces the burden on states for economic and social welfare by privatising responsibility for care and well-being, which dovetails with neoliberal hostility to the welfare state and its commitment to minimal state intervention in the free market distribution of wealth. The special benefits granted to families operate to keep wealthy families wealthy through inheritance rules and tax exemptions, reproducing privilege rather than serving redistributive ends. Just as neoliberals repudiate equality as a value dangerous to (market) freedom,[11] so the patriarchal configuration of the family renounces equality as detrimental to family life and the life of the nation-state itself.

It is hardly surprising then that this foundation for family legibility in IHRL has always been contentious. It denies recognition, and thus full humanity, to other family formations including Indigenous families, extended families, female-headed families, polygamous families and 'queer'[12] families, to name but a few. While many efforts have been made to 'update' and foster more inclusionary definitions of the family in IHRL,[13] the idea that we are free to form families of our own choosing remains unthinkable. Why this is so? Why are we ostensibly able to enjoy

5 Ibid. Article 23(3).
6 Ibid. Article 25(1).
7 Ibid. Article 16(1).
8 Ibid.
9 Ibid. Article 25(2).
10 Jessica Whyte, *The Morals of the Market: Human Rights and the Rise of Neoliberalism* (London: Verso, 2019), 88–89.
11 Ibid., 24.
12 I use the term 'queer' to refer to all non-heteronormative kinship relations that involve care, support and some measure of financial interdependence, including heterosexual and homosexual relationships that do not take a heteronormative hierarchical form, as well as non-sexual and non-reproductive kinship arrangements.
13 See for example Committee on Economic, Social and Cultural Rights, General Comment No. 12, *The Right to Adequate Food (Article 11)*, UN Doc. E/C.12/1999/5, May 5, 1999, para 1: 'thus the reference in Article 11.1 to "himself and his family" does not imply any limitation upon the applicability of this right to individuals or to female-headed households.'

freedom of movement, freedom of thought, conscience and religion, freedom of opinion and expression, freedom of peaceful assembly and association, and freedom to participate in government, but not the freedom to choose our family and kinship arrangements? In what follows, I explore this question. I begin my genealogy in 1995 with the Fourth World Conference on Women before examining the more recent push to (re)recognise 'traditional family values' at the HRC, as opposed to a 'diversity of family forms'. I then reflect on what is motivating states on both sides of this debate, turning the discussion to the survival of the nation-state in an increasingly interdependent world. I conclude that queer kinship relations offer a starting point for reconceiving 'families' as a site of freedom and redistributive economics, as well as a place of human belonging and care.

Struggles over 'the family' at the Human Rights Council

In order to understand the contestations at the HRC, my genealogy now leaps from the template of the UDHR to the 1995 Beijing World Conference on Women, where an uneasy compromise allowed the term 'gender' to formally enter the international legal lexicon. At this point, opposition to the term was spearheaded by the Vatican (acting at the UN through its offices as the Holy See), warning that the terminology of 'gender' threatens the 'natural' family and condones a host of 'unnatural' sexual practices, like homosexuality, bisexuality and transsexuality.[14] Along with a number of states, the Vatican placed on record an interpretive statement, appended to the Beijing Platform for Action (PFA) which outlined a set of agreed commitments to future action. The Vatican's statement made it clear that references to 'gender' should be read 'according to its ordinary usage in the United Nations context', as referring to only two sexes, male and female, 'as grounded in biological sexual identity'.[15] The PFA also condemned violence against women as a human rights violation, including in the private sphere of the family,[16] recognised women's sexual and reproductive rights[17] and that 'various forms of the family exist',[18] and called for women's rights to be mainstreamed in all the work of the UN.[19] This consolidated and extended developments in IHRL since 1948, including the adoption of the Convention on the Elimination of Discrimination Against Women (CEDAW) in 1979, which sought to redefine the family and family relations on the basis of gender equality.[20]

In the five years that followed the Beijing conference, a more organised, conservative interfaith alliance emerged at the UN. The Vatican joined with Christian-Right organisations and sympathetic states, including Russia, some eastern-European states, and members of the Group of African States and the Organization of the Islamic Conference (OIC). This new alliance cohered, despite their many differences, around defence of the 'natural' family, affirmation

14 Dianne Otto, "Holding Up Half the Sky but for Whose Benefit? A Critical Analysis of the Fourth World Conference on Women," *Australian Feminist Law Journal* 6 (1996): 11.

15 "Reservations and interpretative statements on the Beijing Declaration and Platform for Action," in *Report of the Fourth World Conference on Women (Beijing, 4–15 September 1995)*, UN Doc. A/CONF.177/20, October 17, 1995 (New York: UN Department of Public Information, 1995), para 11.

16 "Beijing Declaration and Platform for Action," in *Report of the Fourth World Conference on Women (Beijing, 4–15 September 1995)*, UN Doc. A/CONF.177/20, October 17, 1995 (New York: UN Department of Public Information, 1995), para 113(a).

17 Ibid. para 96.

18 Ibid. para 29.

19 Ibid. para 231.

20 *Convention on the Elimination of All Forms of Discrimination Against Women 1979*, 1249 UNTS 13 (entered into force September 3, 1981), Article 16.

of motherhood as women's primary role and protection of 'Pro-Family' values.[21] They stood against the 'promotion' of homosexuality and those women's rights seen as destructive to the family. This fledgling alliance tested its influence by 'storming' the Beijing +5 follow-up conference held in New York in 2000,[22] hoping to undermine the gains made in Beijing relating to women's reproductive and sexual rights and, as they achieved in Beijing, ensure that no mention of 'sexual orientation' as a prohibited ground of discrimination appeared in the official outcome documents.[23] They were determined to ensure the continuing illegibility of 'sexual subalterns'[24] in IHRL. Their interventions prevented any strengthening of the Beijing commitments and laid the groundwork for further Pro-Family cooperation.

In the early years of the new century, anxiety about the supposed 'homosexual agenda' hidden in women's rights advocacy grew, even as there was little recognition of gay and lesbian rights in practice.[25] Then, as the LGBTI human rights movement was finding its voice, the range of issues joined together under the banner of Pro-Family values expanded to include opposition to acknowledging a diversity of family forms (despite its acceptance in Beijing), refusal to recognise the multiplicity of sexual orientations and gender identities, rejection of same-sex marriage and adoption by same-sex couples, denial of access to new reproductive technologies, and opposition to sex education, gender mainstreaming and promotion of the use of condoms by safe-sex campaigns.

The Pro-Family lobby concentrated its attention on the HRC, following its establishment in 2006 when it replaced the UN Commission on Human Rights. The increasing determination of some states and human rights NGOs to have violence and discrimination based on sexual orientation and/or gender identity (SOGI) recognised as human rights violations, added grist to the Pro-Family lobby's mill of misinformation and fearmongering. Rather than rejecting the framework of human rights set out in the UDHR, the strategy that emerged from these unlikely bedfellows was to reinterpret it, locating its foundation in Traditional Values, a move that finds some support in the UDHR's representations of the family outlined previously. In 2009, a controversial HRC resolution titled *Promoting human rights and fundamental freedoms through a better understanding of Traditional Values of humankind*[26] called for a workshop to be organised on the issue. Initiated by the Russian Federation, the resolution was adopted by a majority of 26 of its 47 member states. Fifteen states voted against adoption, while six abstained.

Several years earlier, the Russian Federation, urged on by the Russian Orthodox Church, had (re)embraced Traditional Values as the hallmark of its national identity. Russia also deployed Traditional Values 'externally as a kind of exceptionalist-messianic pose to present Russia as the saviour of Europe and the leading defender of true European [traditional heteronormative] value'.[27] Subsequently, at the HRC, Russia started to use the platform of Traditional Values to

21 Doris Buss and Didi Herman, *Globalizing Family Values: The Christian Rights in International Politics* (Minneapolis: University of Minnesota Press, 2003), 117–18.

22 Ibid., 101.

23 Ibid.

24 Ratna Kapur, "*Law and the Sexual Subaltern: A Comparative Perspective*," *Cleveland State Law Review* 48, no. 1 (2000): 15–23.

25 Doris Buss, "Finding the Homosexual in Women's Rights: The Christian Right in International Politics," *International Feminist Journal of Politics* 6, no. 2 (2004): 257.

26 *Promoting Human Rights and Fundamental Freedoms Through a Better Understanding of Traditional Values of Humankind*, UN Doc A/HRC/12/L.13/Rev.1, September 30, 2009.

27 Kevin Moss, "Russia as the Saviour of European Civilization: Gender and the Geopolitics of Traditional Values," in *Anti-Gender Campaigns in Europe: Mobilizing Against Equality,* eds. Roman Kuhar and David Petternotte (London: Rowman & Littlefield International, 2017), 195.

revive its weakened position in global affairs by distinguishing itself from the 'decadent west' and asserting leadership of the 'anti-western' world.[28] Russia also cemented an alliance with the Organization of Islamic States (OIC), which is specifically concerned to promote and protect 'Islamic family values', according to Shari'ah law, by limiting women's rights to sexual and reproductive health, defending 'reciprocal' (rather than equal) roles for men and women in families, and ensuring that marriage can only occur between a man and a woman.[29] This said, it is important to also remember that practices within OIC states vary enormously and that there are many social movements working domestically for the recognition of women's and SOGI-associated rights. Women in Tunisia, for example, have for many years enjoyed a measure of reproductive rights, including access to abortion, although this remains limited by laws that perpetuate women's inequality,[30] while Pakistan adopted legislation in 2018 which allows people to choose their gender and have that identity recognised on official documents.[31]

The report of the workshop, called for by the 2009 resolution, concluded with a warning from the independent expert in the field of cultural rights, Farida Shaheed, that 'there was a danger in making something as undefined and constantly evolving as "traditional values" the standard for human rights'.[32] Nevertheless, two further Traditional Values resolutions followed. The first, in 2011, requested the HRC's Advisory Committee to prepare a study on the issue.[33] The second, in 2012, sponsored again by Russia, called for a 'better . . . appreciation' of the contribution that Traditional Values of 'dignity, freedom and responsibility' – but not equality and non-discrimination – make to promoting and protecting universal human rights.[34] The resolution referred to the family as having 'an important role . . . in upholding and transmitting these values'.[35] In a show of defiance, the second resolution was adopted before the study was finalised, after a preliminary draft revealed that the Advisory Committee was critical of the concept of Traditional Values, describing it as 'vague, subjective and unclear'.[36] Again, this resolution was adopted by a clear majority, with a vote of 25 to 15, with seven abstentions (Figure 25.1).

The Advisory Committee's completed study, released later in 2012, acknowledged that there were 'divided views' on the relationship between Traditional Values and human rights[37] and

28 Masha Gessen, "Russia is Remaking Itself as the Leader of the Anti-Western World," *Washington Post*, March 30, 2014, www.washingtonpost.com/opinions/russia-is-remaking-itself-as-the-leader-of-the-anti-western-world/2014/03/30/8461f548-b681-11e3-8cc3-d4bf596577eb_story.html.

29 Robert C. Blitt, "Equality and Nondiscrimination through the Eyes of an International Religious Organization: The Organization of Islamic Cooperation's (OIC) Response to Women's Rights," *Wisconsin International Law Journal* 34, no. 4 (2017): 755, 809–11.

30 Irene Maffi and Malika Affes, "The Right to Abortion in Tunisia After the Revolution of 2011: Legal, Medical, and Social Arrangements as Seen through Seven Abortion Stories," *Health and Human Rights Journal* 21, no. 2 (December 2019): 69–78.

31 The Parliament of Pakistan, *Transgender Persons (Protection of Rights) Act*, May 8, 2018.

32 *Workshop on Traditional Values of Humankind*, Report of the United Nations High Commissioner for Human Rights UN Doc A/HRC/16/37, December 13, 2010, para 70.

33 *Promoting Human Rights and Fundamental Freedoms Through a Better Understanding of Traditional Values of Humankind*, UN Doc A/HRC/16/L.6, March 18, 2011.

34 *Promoting Human Rights and Fundamental Freedoms Through a Better Understanding of Traditional Values of Humankind: Best Practices*, UN Doc A//HRC/RES/21/3, October 9, 2012, para 1.

35 Ibid. para 2.

36 Human Rights Council Advisory Committee, *Preliminary Study on Promoting Human Rights and Fundamental Freedoms Through a Better Understanding of Traditional Values of Humankind*, UN Doc. A/HRC/AC/9/2, June 1, 2012, para. 74.

37 Human Rights Council Advisory Committee, *Study of the Human Rights Advisory Council on Promoting Human Rights and Fundamental Freedoms Through a Better Understanding of Traditional Values of Humankind*, UN Doc A/HRC/22/71, December 6, 2012, para. 6.

2009 Res. 12/21 *Promoting human rights and fundamental freedoms through a better understanding of traditional values of humankind*, requesting the OHCHR to organize a workshop (26/15/6)
2010 Report of the UNHCHR 16/37 *Workshop on traditional values of humankind*
2011 Res. 16/3 *Promoting human rights and fundamental freedoms through a better understanding of traditional values of humankind*, requesting the HRC Advisory Committee to prepare a study (24/14/7)
2012 HRC Advisory Committee AC/9/2 *Preliminary study on promoting human rights and fundamental freedoms through a better understanding of traditional values of humankind*
2012 Res. 21/3 *Promoting human rights and fundamental freedoms through a better understanding of traditional values of humankind: best practices* (25/15/7)
2012 HRC Advisory Committee 22/71 *Study on promoting human rights and fundamental freedoms through a better understanding of traditional values of humankind*

Figure 25.1 Human Rights Council 'Traditional Values' resolutions and reports 2009–2012.

advised that while the roots of universal human rights can be found in diverse Traditional Values, some Traditional Values had helped maintain unequal social power structures, affecting women and minority groups in particular.[38] Importantly, the study also observed that families are themselves diverse and are not the only institution entrusted with transmitting human rights values, highlighting the important role of communities, societies and educational institutions.[39]

Undeterred, in the lead-up to the twentieth anniversary of the International Year of the Family in 2014, the Traditional Values lobby was in full throttle at the HRC, taking the opportunity to assert the primacy of 'traditional family values', propelled not only by the spectre of women's equality in the family and reproductive rights, but also by spreading international support for LGBTI rights. A resolution entitled *Protection of the Family*,[40] sponsored by Egypt, requesting a panel discussion, was adopted by a vote of 26 to 14, with six abstentions. Those who voted in favour included China, the Russian Federation, members of the OIC and the Group of African States. The resolution failed to recognise that 'various forms of the family exist', despite the repeated use of this formulation by human rights bodies since 1995. The resolution also made no reference to women's equality in the family. These absences make it clear that families comprising LGBTI persons, or women enjoying reproductive freedom and equality with their male partners, are not included. Nor was there any recognition of human rights abuses that occur within families. Ominously, the Concept Note for the panel discussion on protection of the family contained the same omissions.[41] Yet many participants in the discussion insisted on the recognition of family diversity and of the fact that families can be dangerous, particularly for women, children and the elderly,[42] although the silence on women's equality continued.

38 Ibid. paras 32–44.

39 Ibid. paras 57–64.

40 *Protection of the Family*, UN Doc. A/HRC/RES/26/11, July 16, 2014.

41 Frances Raday, "The Family Agenda: Promoting Traditional Values in the Human Rights Council," *Oxford Human Rights Hub*, January 8, 2015, http://ohrh.law.ox.ac.uk/the-family-agenda-promoting-traditional-values-in-the-human-rights-council/.

42 UN High Commissioner for Human Rights, *Summary of Human Rights Council Panel Discussion on the Protection of the Family*, UN Doc. A/HRC/28/40, December 22, 2014.

2014 Res. 26/11 *Protection of the Family*, requesting the UNHCHR to organise a panel discussion (26/14/6)

2014 Report of the UNHCHR 28/40 *Summary of HRC panel discussion on the protection of the family*

2015 Res. 29/22 *Protection of the Family: contribution of the family to the realization of the right to an adequate standard of living for its members, particularly through its role in poverty eradication and achieving sustainable development*, requesting UNHCHR to prepare a report (29/14/4)

2016 Report of the UNHCHR 31/37 *Protection of the Family: contribution of the family to the realization of the right to an adequate standard of living for its members, particularly through its role in poverty eradication and achieving sustainable development*

2016 Res. 32/23 *Protection of the Family: role of the family in supporting the protection and promotion of human rights of persons with disabilities* (32/12/3)

2016 Report of the UNHCHR 35/12 *Intersessional seminar on the protection of the family and disability*

2017 Res. 35/13 *Protection of the Family: role of the family in supporting the protection and promotion of human rights of older persons* (30/12/5)

2018 Report of the UNHCHR 39/32 *Intersessional seminar on the Protection of the Family: role of the family in supporting the protection and promotion of the human rights of older persons*

Figure 25.2 Human Rights Council 'Protection of the Family' resolutions and reports 2014–2018.

Undaunted, the Protection of the Family lobby sponsored a substantive HRC resolution, adopted in 2015, titled *Protection of the Family: contribution of the family to the realization of the right to an adequate standard of living for its members, particularly through its role in poverty eradication and achieving sustainable development* (Figure 25.2).[43] As indicated by its title, the resolution sought to influence discussions on the post-2015 development agenda, which were taking place later that year, notably locating responsibility for poverty eradication and sustainable development in the family, thereby embracing the neoliberal emphasis on family/private responsibility (rather than state responsibility) for individual well-being. This resolution also failed to acknowledge the diversity of families, although it did recognise 'single women-headed households, child-headed households and intergenerational households' as being 'particularly vulnerable to poverty and social exclusion'.[44] Also absent was any reference to reproductive rights, family planning or decision-making about the spacing of children. A brief mention of women's equality in the family was finally included,[45] but only after heated debate.[46] Further, the resolution treats the

43 *Protection of the Family: Contribution of the Family to the Realization of the Right to an Adequate Standard of Living for its Members, Particularly Through its Role in Poverty Eradication and Achieving Sustainable Development*, UN Doc. A/HRC/RES/29/22, July 22, 2015.

44 Ibid. para 13.

45 Ibid. para 9.

46 Frances Raday, "Recent Developments in the UN Human Rights Council: Traditional Values and Women's Right to Equality in the Family," *Oxford Human Rights Hub*, September 2, 2015, https://ohrh.law.ox.ac.uk/recent-developments-in-the-un-human-rights-council-traditional-values-and-womens-right-to-equality-in-the-family/.

family as the primary human rights-holder, which subsumes the rights of individual family members in 'family rights' effectively held by the (male) household head.[47] The 'traditional family' is lauded as an institution that needs protection, in part so that it can protect the human rights of its members,[48] without acknowledging the human rights abuses that can occur within families.

Two further Protection of the Family resolutions have been adopted. The first in 2016 concerned the family's role in helping to realise the human rights of family members with disabilities,[49] and the second in 2017 concerned the family's role in fulfilling the human rights of older family members.[50] Both resolutions urged protection of the family because it has a 'positive impact . . . on protecting and promoting the human rights of its members'.[51] Both resolutions also emphasised the 'crucial role' that families play 'in the preservation of cultural identity, traditions, morals, heritage and the values system of society',[52] speaking to the nation-state's interests in its survival. Slovenia's Statement, reflecting a different set of national values, explains its vote against the second of these resolutions:

> We believe that family policies should support all families, no matter their form, shape or size, and that all individuals within families, as well as those who may have no family at all, must enjoy equal protection of their human rights by the State. . . . In our opinion, the draft resolution before us does not adequately reflect the need to support all families, in all their diverse forms, nor does it place sufficient emphasis on the protection of the rights of individuals within families.[53]

Despite the voting patterns at the HRC, there continues to be considerable opposition to these developments from other HRC mechanisms. In 2015, at the same session that the HRC adopted its second Protection of the Family resolution, the report of the Working Group on Discrimination Against Women in Law and Practice was accepted, which stated:

> The cultural construction of gender makes women's subjection to gender-based discrimination and violence appear to be inherent and immutable. The patriarchal family is the product of this construction and the most important social mechanism for its perpetuation. Women and girls' human potential is restricted in families.[54]

Further, in 2016, the High Commissioner for Human Rights presented its report to the HRC which outlined a 'human-rights-based' approach to family policies, calling *inter alia* for legal

47 International Service for Human Rights, "States Silence Debate on Family Diversity at Human Rights Council," June 26, 2014, www.ishr.ch/news/states-silence-debate-family-diversity-human-rights-council.

48 *Protection of the Family* 2015, para 17.

49 *Protection of the Family: Role of the Family in Supporting the Protection and Promotion of Human Rights of Persons with Disabilities*, UN Doc. A/HRC/32/23, July 18, 2016.

50 *Protection of the Family: Role of the Family in Supporting the Protection and Promotion of Human Rights of Older Persons*, UN Doc. A/HRC/35/13, June 19, 2017.

51 *Protection of the Family* 2016, para 5; *Protection of the Family* 2017, para 8.

52 *Protection of the Family* 2016, para 7; *Protection of the Family* 2017, para 11.

53 Statement by the Republic of Slovenia, Human Rights Council, June 19, 2017.

54 Working Group on the Issue of Discrimination Against Women in Law and in Practice, *Thematic Analysis: Eliminating Discrimination Against Women in Cultural and Family Life, with a Focus on the Family as a Cultural Space*, UN Doc. A/HRC/29/40, April 2, 2015, para 71.

recognition of same-sex couples[55] and protection for children from discrimination based on their own or their parent/guardian's sexual orientation or gender identity.[56]

Although I am not aware of any further Traditional Values resolutions or reports at the HRC since 2018, which suggests the issue may have gone 'off the boil' for the moment, controversy over which families are made legible in IHRL continues to simmer, and many kinship arrangements remain outside the 'specific way of being' privileged by IHRL, including where same-sex relationships, in the image of the 'natural' heteronormative family, have been recognised.

Towards understanding what is at stake

What is really at stake in these struggles at the HRC over which families qualify for legibility in IHRL? It is not enough to reduce these clashes to a contest over women's equality in the family and the 'naturalness' of same-sex relationships – important as these issues are. Rather, both these human rights claims are sutured to the larger political projects of nation-state survival in a globalising world and entrenching the supremacy of neoliberal economics. We need to understand why only specific family forms are privileged and what larger governance and economic agendas this serves.

The international alliance of social and religious conservatives that emerged in the decade following the Beijing conference in 1995 has been supported and emboldened domestically by the rise of nationalist 'anti-gender' movements. These populist movements often champion the rights of the traditional family, in place of individual human rights,[57] forming part of an emerging 'anti-modernist universalism'[58] that is then reflected in and encouraged by the promotion of Traditional Values at the HRC. An important point of convergence between these disparate movements is their various commitments to national, cultural and racial homogeneity. Polish right-wing populists, for example, depict 'Brussels' (the European Union) as threatening the sustainability of the whiteness of the Polish nation, not only with the contagion of gender ideology, but also with its immigration and refugee policies.[59]

In fact, the nation-state in its current form – patriarchal, hierarchical, heteronormative and racially identified – is made possible by the putatively 'natural' kinship arrangements, which qualify as 'families' in human rights law, and are in the privileged position of enjoying state protection. That the nation-state depends fundamentally on heteronormative reproductive relations for the transfer and reproduction of national loyalty has been entirely overlooked by theorists of nationalism, including Benedict Anderson.[60] Further, as Judith Butler observes, the state's kinship configurations, in reproducing the nation and its culture, also carry 'implicit norms of racial purity and domination'.[61] This helps to explain the current anxiety of many European states

55 UN High Commissioner for Human Rights, *Protection of the Family: Contribution of the Family to the Realization of the Right to an Adequate Standard of Living for its Members, Particularly Through its Role in Poverty Eradication and Achieving Sustainable Development'*, UN Doc. A/HRC/31/37, January 15, 2016, para 27.

56 Ibid. para 42.

57 Elżbieta Korolczuk and Agnieszka Graff, "Gender as 'Ebola from Brussels': The Anticolonial Frame and the Rise of Illiberal Populism," *Signs: Journal of Women in Culture and Society* 43, no. 4 (2018): 801.

58 Ibid.

59 Ibid., 811.

60 Benedict Anderson, *Imagined Communities: Reflections on the Origin and Spread of Nationalism*, revised ed. (London: Verso, 1991).

61 Judith Butler, *Undoing Gender* (New York: Routledge, 2004), 110.

over their falling birth rates and why increasing (racially diverse) immigration is not necessarily seen as the answer. It also explains why same-sex marriage (presumed reproductive) has been so widely embraced in some parts of the world, because it promises to reproduce more citizens loyal to the nation-state, to domesticate those who were previously marked as sexual or gender outlaws and likely to develop loyalties to non-heteronormative – queer – kinship relations and communities. It is heteronormativity that makes the imagined community of the nation-state possible, giving such power to national feelings of belonging and attachment that, in Anderson's analysis, people are willing to die for it.[62] To question these arrangements, and give primacy to other forms of relational attachment, presents potentially transformative challenges to the hegemony of loyalty, based on nationality, that currently constitutes the nation-state and structures the international community and its many conflicts, hierarchies and divisions.

European powers clearly understood that the patriarchal regulation and control of sexuality was essential to their imperial state-building projects. Conjugal, monogamous, reproductive heterosexuality, closely associated with whiteness, was projected as the most civilised expression of the family. The criminalisation of 'unnatural' sexual practices was standard procedure – reflecting laws in the 'modern' European state. Colonial governance established systems of birth, sex and marriage registration that enforced gender binary, monogamy and heterosexuality, rendering perverse many local practices of kinship, inter-dependency and responsibility. Most of these imposed systems continue today in the postcolony, where there are also many counter-heteronormative movements which, as Kapur has cautioned, cannot possibly be captured by the categories of LGBTI. She uses instead the term 'sexual subalterns' to resist the assimilationism of the neoliberal project and reflect the 'extraordinary range' of these movements and familial arrangements.[63]

In the West, fears about homosexuality and gender fluidity threatening the survival of the nation-state became explicit in many of the same-sex marriage debates. For example, conservative US Senator Jessie Helms warned, in the debates that preceded adoption of the *Defense of Marriage Act* in 1996, that 'at the heart of this debate is the moral and spiritual survival of this Nation'.[64] In Russia, since the laws banning 'gay propaganda' were strengthened in 2013, the state news media has 'worked hard to portray activists as traitors doing the work of foreign powers to undermine the Russian state'.[65] A Russian judge, in sentencing the members of feminist punk rock band Pussy Riot to long terms of imprisonment for challenging homophobia and gender conformity, described their protest as 'shatter[ing] the constitutional foundations of the state'.[66]

Disconcertingly, the domestic anti-gender movements, as well as their global counterparts, do not hesitate to draw heavily on the language of human rights when it suits their purposes, as in the Traditional Values and Protection of the Family resolutions of the HRC. Frequent

62 Anderson, *Imagined Communities*, 7.

63 Ratna Kapur, "De-Radicalising the Rights Claims of Sexual Subalterns Through 'Tolerance'," in *Queer Theory: Law, Culture, Empire*, eds. Robert Leckey and Kim Brooks (New York: Routledge, 2010), 39.

64 Jesse Helms, 142 (*Congressional Record* S10068, daily edition, September 9, 1996), quoted in David L. Chambers, "Polygamy and Same-Sex Marriage," *Hofstra Law Review* 26, no. 1 (1997): 56.

65 Ivan Nechepurenko, "Russian Newspaper's Scoop? Based on Fake Letters, US Says," *The New York Times* (New York), November 21, 2015, www.nytimes.com/2015/11/21/world/europe/russian-newspapers-scoop-based-on-fake-letters-us-says.html.

66 Janet Elise Johnson and Aino Saarinen, "Twenty-First-Century Feminisms under Repression: Gender Regime Change and the Women's Crisis Center Movement in Russia," *Signs: Journal of Women in Culture and Society* 38, no. 3 (Spring, 2013): 562.

mantras include support for freedom of speech, thought and conscience, freedom of religion, cultural rights, economic and social rights, democratic rights, children's rights, family rights and even women's rights – that is, women's rights to motherhood and to be 'protected' by traditional family values. As we have seen, the transnational heteronormative alliance presents its quest for the revival of Traditional Values as offering an alternative vision of human rights that is more representative of the world's people, their cultures, religions and traditions.

Those states that support the legibility of same-sex families in IHRL are also driven by the spectre of threats to the nation-state. Their goal is to domesticate (civilise) queer expressions and communities of desire, by granting them normalising rights. Domestication stitches LGBTI loyalties to the nation-state and encourages responsible reproductive practices, minimising the potential for alternative arrangements, outside state control, which may disrupt their national projects.[67] Lisa Duggan has described this as the 'new homonormativity' which, as she says, frustrates the democratic potential – or freedoms – of sexual and gender dissidence.[68] While such legibility bestows the benefits that flow from recognition as a 'family', it does not grant people the freedom to choose their own kinship arrangements. Even full recognition of the 'diversity' of family forms in IHRL will provide only a limited form of freedom.

We must remember that human rights- and state-authorised kinship ties in the form of marriage hardly exhaust the field of life-affirming and life-sustaining relational connections. As Butler says, kinship can be 'self-consciously assembled from a multiplicity of possible bits and pieces'.[69] Around the world, queer communities exist, whether or not they are publicly visible, founded on alternative forms of kinship that allow for 'durable ties to be thought outside the conjugal frame' – opening kinship to a set of community ties that are irreducible to family, and engendering a sense of belonging and self-worth that is not dependent on state recognition. Many queer people have set about building alternative communities, based on non-reproductive kinship ties, thereby seeking to reduce the nation's hold on their loyalties and lives. They have sought to establish relations of care, intimacy, pleasure, shared values, self-esteem, economic interdependence, community obligation and public visibility, which recognise diverse sexual and intimate relations and non-binary expressions of gender as worthy of respect, affirmation, protection and celebration. Many of these communities have also challenged other exclusionary practices that anchor nation-states, like hierarchies of class, race, religion and ethnicity. Queer communities have 'cultivated unprecedented kinds of commonality, intimacy, and public life'.[70] They include long-established, still stigmatised, *hijra* communities spread across South Asia,[71] *kathoey* (third gender) communities in Thailand,[72] and the sister-girl and brother-boy networks

67 Butler, *Undoing Gender*, 104.

68 Lisa Duggan, "The New Homonormativity: The Sexual Politics of Neoliberalism," in *Materialising Democracy: Towards a Revitalised Cultural Politics*, eds. Russ Castronovo and Dana D. Nelson (Durham, NC: Duke University Press, 2002), 190.

69 Butler, *Undoing Gender*, 126, quoting Sarah Franklin and Susan McKinnon, "New Directions in Kinship Study: A Core Concept Revisited," *Current Anthropology* 41, no. 2 (2000): 275.

70 Michael Warner, "Beyond Gay Marriage," in *Left Legalism/Left Critique*, eds. Wendy Brown and Janet Halley (Durham, NC: Duke University Press, 2002), 264.

71 Dredge Byung'chu Käng-Nguyễn, "The Search for Intelligible Life in the Genderqueer Imaginary: Conceptualizing Transgenderism Independent of Homosexuality," in *The 1st Annual International Graduate Research Conference on Social Sciences and Humanities, Theme 'Harmony in Diversity'* (Proceedings of the Conference, Faculty of Social Sciences and Humanities, Mahidol University, Bangkok, Thailand, April 2–3, 2009), 258.

72 Ladda Waiyawan and Penchan Sherer, "Sexuality and Sexual Discourses of *Katheoy*: Living with HIV/AIDS in I-Saan," in *The 1st Annual International Graduate Research Conference on Social Sciences and Humanities, Theme*

of support in Australian Indigenous communities.[73] Many of these queer kinship communities are transnational, like the 'underground railway' between queer communities in Kampala and Paris that provided safe passage for Ugandan activists,[74] the members of the NGO Proud Lebanon who have welcomed queer refugees from Syria into the relative safety of their community,[75] and the bonds of solidarity and support between Palestinians and anti-occupation Jewish queer activists.[76]

The iron grip that imagined communities of nationhood have on our sense of identity and belonging presents a major obstacle to thinking in radically inclusive and plural ways about law, politics, markets, militaries, individuals and communities. Our imaginaries need to extend to the myriad assemblages of human kinship that refuse to confine loyalty and connection to the narrow and racially imbued band of 'natural' reproductive ties that provide a foundation for the nation-state.

Conclusion

In the current global conjuncture, the continued primacy of nation-state interests and neoliberal economics, underpinned by a hierarchical family form, is endangering us all. Global warming continues, a new arms race is underway, right-wing bigotry and hatred is spreading, democratic controls are faltering, states of emergency have become commonplace, and border protection has become more brutal and lawless. States are taking unprecedented measures to assert their sovereignty and ensure that it is understood that we are divided and separated along national lines. The accumulative, heteronormative, reproductive family, privileged by IHRL and state and market regulation, provides a normalising foundation for this disastrous state of affairs.

Communities based on queer kinship ties offer us hope that human solidarities and loyalties can break free of the bonds of the nation-state and the prescriptions of neoliberal economics, and extend to include others, particularly those who are most disadvantaged by the disciplinary familial ordering that is imposed on us all. We need to foster and value queer assemblages of human belonging that can withstand colonisation, patriarchy, domestication and subjection to neoliberal economic imperatives, and help to de-centre the nation-state, the market and IHRL as the arbiters of freedom. Heteronormative families are constitutive of the modern nation-state and, it follows, of the 'normal' system of state-centred international law. This system and its laws underpin the human (dis)connectedness that is endangering us all.

'Harmony in Diversity' (Proceedings of the Conference, Faculty of Social Sciences and Humanities, Mahidol University, Bangkok, Thailand, April 2–3, 2009), 59.

73 Crystal Johnson, "Napanangka: The True Power of Being Proud," in *Colouring the Rainbow: Blak Queer and Trans Perspectives – Life Stories and Essays by First Nations People of Australia*, ed. Dino Hodge (Adelaide: Wakefield Press, 2015), 21.

74 Michael J. Bosia, "Strange Fruit: Homophobia, the State, and the Politics of LGBT Rights and Capabilities," *Journal of Human Rights* 13 (2014): 256, 262.

75 James Longman, "Gay Community Hit Hard by Middle East Turmoil," *BBC News*, October 29, 2014 www.bbc.com/news/world-middle-east-29628281.

76 Sarah Schulman, *Israel/Palestine and the Queer International* (Durham, NC: Duke University Press, 2010).

26

International law at the border

Refugee deaths, the necropolitical state and sovereign accountability

Sara Dehm

Introduction

> [T]he brutality of borders is now a fundamental given of our times.[1]

On 5 September 2014, at the age of 24 years, Hamid Khazaei was pronounced dead in Brisbane's Mater Hospital. Having left Iran the previous year to seek safety and asylum in Australia, Hamid Khazaei instead had spent the last 12 months of his life in Australian-run immigration detention on Manus Island, Papua New Guinea (PNG). The subsequent coroner's report recorded the official cause of his death as hypoxic-ischaemic encephalopathy, a medical condition brought on by cardiac arrest following an acute case of septicaemia.[2] Put simply, Hamid Khazaei had died as a result of a minor leg infection 'commonly found in tropical settings' for which he had received inadequate medical treatment. While the Queensland coroner recognised that Hamid Khazaei's death occurred in the 'broader context' of Australia's immigration policy, which mandated that asylum seekers arriving unauthorised by boat in Australian waters must be detained on a 'small remote island in a developing country', they largely attributed the responsibility for Hamid Khazaei's death to the Australian government's provision of substandard healthcare under this so-called regional refugee processing arrangement. In particular, the coroner found that this substandard provision of healthcare included a lack of antibiotics

1 Achille Mbembe, *Necropolitics* (Durham, NC: Duke University Press, 2019), 3.

2 As Hamid Khazaei was detained upon arrival in Brisbane under Australia's *Migration Act 1958* (Cth), his death in Mater Hospital was officially classified as a 'death in custody'. As a result, this triggered a coronial investigation under Queensland's state jurisdiction that finally concluded in July 2018. The coroner's report makes for harrowing reading, both for clinical description of the misdiagnosis of Hamid Khazaei's condition that underplayed the urgency of his medical need in his final days and for the banality of the complex trail of bureaucratic communications surrounding the process of obtaining legal approval for his medical transfers that the report documents. Nonetheless, the coronial process and final report enable a form of scrutiny and enact practices of accountability, however limited, around Hamid Khazaei's death that have been denied to the vast majority of migrants who have died as a result of state border regimes. Coroners Court of Queensland, "Inquest into the Death of Hamid Khazaei," File No 2014/3292, July 30, 2018.

available at the detention centre's health clinic, the failure of medical staff to properly diagnose Hamid Khazaei's clinical deterioration, and a series of 'practical and operational matters' that hampered the delivery of appropriate medical care to him during his last week on PNG and that prevented his urgent medical transfer to Australia. Ultimately, the coroner concluded that Hamid Khazaei's death would have been entirely 'preventable' had he received a more accurate and timely clinical diagnosis and prompt medical evacuation to Australia.

Considered from an international law standpoint, Hamid Khazaei's death could also be attributed to the failure of states adequately to care for him. Such failures could include, for example, the failure of the Australian state to offer him proper protection and asylum under the terms of the Refugees Convention;[3] the failure of both Australia and PNG to recognise and fulfil specific human rights obligations such as the right to health towards Hamid Khazaei during his time in detention in PNG;[4] or even more fundamentally, the failure, or breakdown, in the citizen-state relationship between Hamid Khazaei and Iran as his state of nationality, forcing him to seek asylum elsewhere in the first place. While these failures may all be legally accurate and politically useful arguments to assert in order to hold states accountable for the death of Hamid Khazaei, their causal frame and analytical power to fully explain his death in the context of such state irresponsibility and brutality remain limited.[5]

This chapter instead turns to the concept of necropolitics, as theorised by Cameroonian philosopher Achille Mbembe and taken up in critical migration and border studies scholarship in the humanities, to explore the relationship between people seeking asylum and the modern state in international law. Mbembe's necropolitics, in asserting the centrality of state-produced death to the modern political order, provides a useful diagnostic for understanding the colonial history and contemporary form of state border regimes that harm migrants and refugees, and international law's role in authorising this structural violence. The concept of necropolitics allows us to apprehend refugee deaths not as aberrations, but rather as intrinsic to how contemporary international law arranges political space and legal order, with international law's principal subject, the modern territorial state, premised upon the logic of the border.

Focusing on one specific 'border encounter' between the Australian state and refugees detained on Manus Island, this chapter draws on Mbembe's theorisation of necropolitics to offer two lines of inquiry – one historical, one political – for understanding the role of international law in enabling and perpetuating state violence towards refugees. The first line of inquiry attends to international law's entanglement in the colonial histories of necropolitical spaces that inform contemporary state border regimes; while the second is concerned with interrogating international law's categories of political belonging and state responsibility that allow for the differential allocation of rights and status towards refugees in their care. Both lines of inquiry show that border logics and operations – including their fundamental function of distinguishing between people on the basis of their status as citizens or non-citizens – underpin the structures and workings of international law. Finally, drawing on articulations of migrant justice in Mbembe's work and in the humanities more generally, this chapter concludes by suggesting that understanding state violence as necropolitical offers critical potential for international lawyers to re-orient notions of community, security and belonging in international law towards less violent

3 *Convention Relating to the Status of Refugees 1951*, 189 UNTS 150 (entered into force April 22, 1954) (Refugees Convention).

4 *International Covenant on Economic, Social and Cultural Rights 1966*, 993 UNTS 3 (entered into force January 3, 1976), Art 12.

5 On the concept of state irresponsibility, see Scott Veitch, *Law and Irresponsibility: On the Legitimation of Human Suffering* (New York: Routledge, 2007).

forms of co-existence and co-habitation. Mbembe's notion of 'beings of the border' provides an opening for such a re-orientation, a re-orientation that is even more urgently needed in response to the COVID-19 global pandemic.

The necropolitical state and international law

> Nearly everywhere the political order is re-constituting itself as a form of organization for death.[6]

Necropolitics, Mbembe writes, is a modern form of power that has come to govern through death. Taking his cue and point of departure from Michel Foucault's Eurocentric theorisation of biopolitics, in his 2014 essay titled 'Necropolitics', Mbembe draws the distinction between a form of sovereignty oriented towards organising and optimising different forms of life (*biopolitics*) and a sovereignty oriented towards the imposition of death or the exposure of certain populations to death (*necropolitics*).[7] These dual forms of power, for Mbembe, can operate in the same political, social and legal spaces, in part through cultural imaginaries that classify different people 'according to different categories' with different sets of rights endowed for different, but specific, purposes.[8] Importantly, for Mbembe, necropolitical power has its origins in the colonial world, with the category of race functioning as the key organising principle for necropolitical violence. Consequently, Mbembe argues that the colonial world must be seen as the paradigmatic space of modern state violence. Mbembe shows how colonial rule kept colonised people 'alive but in a state of injury, in a phantom like world of horrors and intense cruelty and profanity'. It was through the colonial organisation of power that colonised peoples in particular contexts became exposed to conditions of death, and relegated to a 'third zone between subjecthood and objecthood'.[9]

Necropolitics thus is the enactment of a form of sovereignty that has the 'material destruction of human bodies and populations' as its target and ends.[10] As Mbembe powerfully writes, necropolitics, as a form of modern sovereignty, constitutes 'the capacity to define who matters and who does not, who is *disposable* and who is not'.[11] In this 'topography of cruelty', the ultimate expression of sovereignty is 'in the power and the capacity to dictate who may live and who must die'.[12] This has come to be epitomised in the creation of 'death-worlds', social spaces in which 'vast populations are subjected to conditions of life conferring upon them the status of living dead'.[13] In drawing attention to the systemic neglect of populations that came to take on a particular modern administrative form under colonial rule and that has continued under conditions of globalisation, Mbembe's work insists upon understanding sovereignty oriented towards human destruction as constituting the political nomos of our times.

6 Mbembe, *Necropolitics*, 7.
7 Achille Mbembe, "Necropolitics," *Public Culture* 15, no. 1 (2003). See also Marina Gržinić and Šefik Tatlić, eds., *Necropolitics, Racialization, and Global Capitalism: Historicization of Biopolitics and Forensics of Politics, Art, and Life* (Lanham: Lexington Books, 2014).
8 Ibid., 26.
9 Ibid.
10 Ibid., 14.
11 Ibid., 27.
12 Ibid., 11.
13 Ibid., 40.

In his recent book dedicated to re-reading Fanon in our present times, Mbembe expands on the interactions between biopolitics and necropolitics as two distinct political modes of organising life.[14] Here he uses the example of the pro-slavery United States before the Civil War to show how two 'orders' can historically exist within states that purport to be democracies but are premised upon racial inequality and bifurcation. In such racist democracies, there is the existence of 'a community of fellow creatures' (deemed rights-bearing citizens subject to the law of equality and considered properly belonging to the demos) and also that of 'a category of nonfellows' (deemed non-citizens through a range of categories also established and regulated by law).[15] This latter group of people instead are governed by the law of inequality 'founded on the prejudice of race'. Racism is thus the 'driver' of necropolitical power.[16] For Mbembe:

> No democracy exists without its double, without its colony – little matter the name or the structure. The colony is not external to the democracy and is not necessarily located outside its walls. Democracy bears the colony within it, just as colonialism bears democracy, often in the guise of a mask.[17]

There are several salient points one might make to indicate the power and limits of Mbembe's analysis. First, Mbembe's invocation of slavery draws attention to how particular economic systems of racial capitalism rely upon the reproduction of inequality, including through the allocation of different legal statuses, as a means of extracting surplus value from humans as labourers. This might be paralleled to the place of migrant workers, including refugee workers, from the Global South, who are often treated as a form of deposable and deportable labour within states in the Global North. Second, Mbembe does not attend to specific political, legal and social relations *within* groups of people or their relationship to particular spaces, meaning that this binary between a community of fellows and non-fellows overlooks Indigeneity in settler colonial societies.[18] This means that while Mbembe stages his analysis of necropolitical violence on stolen Indigenous lands, he does not explicitly account for Indigenous peoples or dispossession, nor for what Patrick Wolfe has termed the 'logic of elimination' at the heart of settler colonialism.[19] And third, Mbembe highlights the exclusionary and racialised logics of democracies as a matter of historical and contemporary practice, insisting on the need to decolonise modern political forms, both collective and individual, and categories of thought in order to enact a more just future, a kind of 'democracy-to-come'. He argues that under contemporary neoliberal globalisation, there has been a proliferation of racial logics of differentiation, securitisation and militarisation that result in hierarchical orders within purportedly democratic states. This shows that democracies have long embraced a politics of enmity that has had a 'propensity to violence and

14 Mbembe, *Necropolitics*.

15 Ibid., 17.

16 Ibid., 38.

17 Ibid., 27.

18 This is tied to Mbembe's theorisation of the interconnected structures and discourses of race and blackness, in which he locates the black slave of the Atlantic slave trade as the 'first racial subject' that continues to inform contemporary forms of racial exploitation and exclusion: Achille Mbembe, *Critique of Black Reason* (Durham, NC: Duke University Press, 2017), 179.

19 Patrick Wolfe, "Settler Colonialism and the Elimination of the Native," *Journal of Genocide Research* 8, no. 4 (2001): 388. See also Scott Lauria Morgensen, "The Biopolitics of Settler Colonialism: Right Here, Right Now," *Settler Colonial Studies* 1, no. 1 (2011): 52.

hostility' towards those deemed to threaten the existing order, employing necropolitical violence as 'a power that does not merely discipline but kills'.[20]

In recent years, Mbembe's work on necropolitics has been taken up within humanities scholarship on state violence towards migrants and refugees.[21] An important body of scholarship has emerged alongside or in connection with migrant activism that has traced and problematised how state border regimes have created an array of 'deathscapes' in which migrant bodies and lives are exposed to conditions of death.[22] Generally, the bulk of this scholarship has been focused on documenting and theorising migrant or refugee deaths at the edges of a state's territory. As Roxanne Lynn Doty has written of the US desert:

> Crossing the border without authorisation now [has become] an extremely dangerous proposition in which death lurk[s] in every new migrant crossing route, through formidable mountain ranges and along desolate, heat-scorched desert lands.[23]

The International Organization for Migration (IOM) estimates that at least 60,000 people have died since 2000 in the course of 'international journeys' that cross state borders.[24] It bears reiterating that there is nothing natural about such deaths. A wealth of empirical evidence has overwhelmingly shown how the actions of state decision-makers, for example, have not only forced migrants to undertake more dangerous and deadly journeys to avoid ever-proliferating state practices of unauthorised migrant detection, interception and deportation. But such state actions have also sought to leverage the physical environment as part of state regimes of border control premised on the logic of deterrence. This emergent mode of border control has been termed 'governing through death' to refer to state strategies of consciously allowing people travelling without state authorisation to be 'abandoned to the physical forces of deserts and seas'.[25] Critical border studies scholar Nick Vaughan-Williams, for example, has used the concept

20 Dorothea Gädeke, "How to Think the World? Achille Mbembe on Race, Democracy and the African Role in Global Thought," *Constellations* 25 (2018): 497.

21 It is not possible to provide a comprehensive survey of this scholarship in the humanities. For some recent interesting examples drawn from different disciplines of the humanities and touching upon different geographically located border regimes (in addition to the references cited later), see Thom Davies, Arshad Isakjee and Surindar Dhesi, "Violent Inaction: The Necropolitical Experience of Refugees in Europe," *Antipode* 49, no. 5 (2017): 1269; Jenny Stümer, "The Dead Are Coming: Border Politics and Necropower in Europe," *Cultural Politics* 14, no. 1 (2018): 20; John Round and Irina Kuznetsova-Morenko, "Necropolitics and the Migrant as a Political Subject of Disgust: The Precarious Everyday of Russia's Labour Migrants," in *Politics of Precarity: Migrant Conditions, Struggles and Experiences*, eds. Martin Bak Jørgensen and Carl-Ulrik Schierup (Leiden: Brill, 2017), 198; Ali H. Bhagat, "Queer Necropolitics of Forced Migration: Cyclical Violence in the African Context," *Sexualities* 23, no. 3 (2020): 361.

22 See in particular the collaborative, case-study based "Deathscapes Project: Mapping Race and State Violence in Settler Societies," led by Suvendrini Perera and Joseph Pugliese: "About Project," *Deathscapes*, accessed April 26, 2020, www.deathscapes.org/.

23 Roxanne Lynn Doty, "Bare Life: Border-Crossing Deaths and Spaces of Moral Alibi," *Environment and Planning D: Society and Space* 29, no. 4 (2011): 599. See also Jason De Leon, *The Land of Open Graves: Living and Dying on the Migrant Trail* (Oakland: University of California Press, 2015). For an example of the rich literature on the border in Spanish, utilising the concept of necropolitics, see Ariadna Estévez, "The Necropolitical *Dispositif* of Production and Administration of Forced Migration at the United States-Mexico Border," *Estudios Fronterizos* 19, no. e010 (2018); and Amarela Varela Huerta, "The Massacres of Migrants in San Fernando and Cadereyta: Two Examples of Necropolitan Governmentality," *Íconos. Revista de Ciencias Sociales* 58 (2017): 131.

24 International Organization for Migration, *Fatal Journeys: Volume 3* (Geneva: Missing Migrants Project, 2017).

25 Vicki Squire, "Governing Migration Through Death in Europe and the US: Identification, Burial and the Crisis of Modern Humanism," *European Journal of International Relations* 23, no. 3 (2017): 513.

of 'thanatopolitical borders' to name and analyse everyday state policies of abandonment that deliberately refuse to rescue people and instead let migrants die in the course of their unauthorised journeys.[26]

Yet, as Mbembe writes, contemporary borders are 'no longer sites to be crossed but lines that separate'; that is, rather than merely delimiting physical space and transforming it into political and juridical places, borders also function to distinguish, filter and exclude different people within a state's territory. This means that borders, or more accurately practices of 'borderisation', are not simply confined to the edges of state territory, but also take place across an array of sites within and beyond a state's territory wherever distinctions on the basis of membership and belonging are articulated, policed, enforced and contested. In this vein, scholars across the humanities have studied everyday state practices of exclusion, segregation and denial towards migrants and refugees at places within a state's territory such as at immigration detention centres, at workplaces, at hospitals, at schools or at state welfare agencies. Attending to these practices of borderisation highlights the routine and mundane kinds of 'slow violence' that can expose refugees to daily harms and enforced poverty, while also providing glimpses into everyday acts that migrants or refugees may themselves take in order to negotiate, resist or survive such border regimes.[27] Borders are, for Mbembe, then best understood as an integral part of modern necropolitical sovereignty, with borders functioning as 'the organized violence that underpins both contemporary capitalism and our world order in general'.[28]

By and large, international legal scholarship has not paid sufficient attention to the constitutive relationship between international law and state borders, nor to the form and function of borders in modern international law. This is despite the fact that modern international law is structured around the logic and operation of the border. Modern international law allocates lawful authority over space and people primarily through its principal subject, the state.[29] In legal requirements of statehood, borders are treated as an essential pre-condition for the existence of a geographically defined territory within which a permanent population can reside and over which a central government can exercise effective political control.[30] Even though a state need not have conclusively delimited its territorial borders in order to be recognised as a subject of international law, international law, in its present form, has nonetheless become structurally reliant on the concept and material enactment of state borders. Borders thus function as foundational makers and markers of juridical spaces and subjects in international law, authorising states

26 Nick Vaughan-Williams, *Europe's Border Crisis: Biopolitical Security and Beyond* (Oxford: Oxford University Press, 2015). See also Laura Lo Presti, "Terraqueous Necropolitics: Unfolding the Low-Operational, Forensic, and Evocative Mapping of Mediterranean Sea Crossings in the Age of Lethal Borders," *ACME: An International Journal for Critical Geographers* 18, no. 6 (2019): 1347.

27 See, for example, Lucy Mayblin, Mustafa Wake and Mohsen Kazemi, "Necropolitics and the Slow Violence of the Everyday: Asylum Seeker Welfare in the Postcolonial Present," *Sociology* 54, no. 1 (2020): 107; Lisa Hartley and Caroline Fleay, "'We Are Like Animals': Negotiating Dehumanising Experiences of Asylum-Seeker Policies in the Australian Community," *Refugee Survey Quarterly* 36, no. 4 (2017): 45.

28 Mbembe, *Necropolitics*.

29 As Matthew Craven and Rose Parfitt have argued, the modern territorial state is 'almost too self-evident' in international law, even if its status as the sole subject of international law has waned and is subject to challenge. Matthew Craven and Rose Parfitt, "Statehood, Self-Determination and Recognition," in *International Law*, ed. Malcolm Evans, 5th ed. (Oxford: Oxford University Press, 2018).

30 *Montevideo Convention on the Rights and Duties of States 1933*, 165 LNTS 19 (entered into force December 26, 1934), Art 1.

to enact and control their territorial bounds and to categorise and distinguish between people within their territory on the basis of state-bestowed citizenship.[31]

There are, of course, notable exceptions within international legal scholarship that take neither the specific historical locations nor form of state borders – or indeed the state itself – as a given.[32] Within the rich tradition of Third World Approaches to International Law, Makau wa Mutua, for example, has demonstrated the artificiality of contemporary state borders in Africa, imposed during the period of European colonial rule and largely affirmed in the wake of national independence. To overcome the destructive effects of historically imposed borders, Mutua argues for a 'new cartography' of map-making in order to abolish the enduring residues of the colonial state and reformulate the Eurocentric norms of sovereignty, territoriality and social organisation underpinning it.[33] More specifically within scholarship addressing international refugee and human rights law, Alison Kesby has suggested that 'international law's focus on the territorial border may render invisible other borders' and practices of bordering against migrants and refugees within states, thereby overlooking both the 'shifting location' and 'multiplication' of the border both within and beyond a state's territory as well as the changing ways that this is experienced by people rendered non-citizens.[34] And more recently, Daria Davitti has argued that there is a 'need to rethink the way in which borders are defined and used' in the context of the European Union's response from 2015 onwards to the mass arrival of refugees, primarily from Syria.[35] Drawing on Agamben's theorisation of biopolitics, Davitti showed how international law enabled and shaped 'the ordering nature of violence in EU migration policies' while also being largely ineffective in challenging EU practices of border externalisation and outsourcing.

Supplementing these existing interventions, this chapter argues that Mbembe's theorisation of necropolitics offers a productive avenue for framing the particular relationship between international law, the necropolitical state and refugees who have been exposed to 'conditions of death' through state border regimes. The remainder of this chapter is dedicated to unpacking the two specific lines of inquiry that I argue Mbembe's theorisation of necropolitics opens up for understanding international law's role in authorising state violence towards refugees. In the context of Australia's offshore detention regime, this necropolitical violence has resulted in practices of border control coming to be articulated on the incarcerated bodies of refugees themselves as a form of exclusion and deterrence, in part through the denial of adequate healthcare in immigration detention centres. Taken together, these two lines of inquiry help us to see how international law authorises the necropolitical state and thereby enables forms of necropolitical violence towards refugees.

31 This authorisation of states to control their borders is of course subject to the requirement that they do so in a manner that complies with their international legal obligations. These obligations are most typically stipulated through international human rights law (although increasingly it appears necessary to restate that the international prohibition on the use of force and international criminal law also applies to state conduct at their territorial borders). On international law's production of differentiated citizenship, see Juan M. Amaya-Castro, "'In Its Majestic Inequality': Migration Control and Differentiated Citizenship," in *The Transformation of Citizenship: Boundaries of Inclusion and Exclusion*, eds. Jürgen Mackert and Bryan S. Turner (London: Routledge, 2017), 84.

32 See, for example, Sundhya Pahuja, "Laws of Encounter: A Jurisdictional Account of International Law," *London Review of International Law* 1, no. 1 (2013): 63.

33 Makau wa Mutua, "Why Redraw the Map of Africa," *Michigan Journal of International Law* 16, no. 4 (1995): 1113.

34 Alison Kesby, "The Shifting and Multiple Border and International Law," *Oxford Journal of Legal Studies* 27, no. 1 (Spring 2007): 101.

35 Daria Davitti, "Biopolitical Borders and the State of Exception in the European Migration 'Crisis'," *European Journal of International Law* 29, no. 4 (2018): 1173.

Australia's offshore detention regime and the past and present of state necropolitical violence

Colonization was [and is] a technology for regulating migratory movements.[36]

Australia's offshore detention regime has existed as a matter of domestic law or practice since 2001, and has been marked by two distinct periods of operation: Phase I under the right-conservative Howard government (2001–2007), and Phase II under both of the two main Australian political parties (2012–current). In both periods, the policy and practice of offshore detention were justified as a necessary deterrence measure to stop unauthorised migration: both as a way of 'securing' Australia's borders and, more recently, to deter people from 'risking' or losing their lives at sea. In both periods, Australia built and maintained immigration detention centres on two Pacific Island states, Nauru and PNG, both of which have a shared history of colonisation in which Australia acted as a colonial power. Since 2001, over 4,000 people have been detained under Australia's offshore detention regime,[37] and at the time of writing this chapter, around 400 people remain in Nauru and PNG subject to this regime. Many of these people have been officially recognised as refugees and have spent the previous seven years in a mixture of closed immigration detention or substandard temporary supported accommodation.

While there is insufficient space here to explain the historical circumstances that led to the creation and maintenance of Australia's brutal offshore refugee detention regime from 2001 onwards,[38] it is critical to note that it is very much the product of international legal arrangements. International refugee law allows for 'refugee burden-sharing' arrangements, including safe third-country processing agreements. However, the 'lack of precision and clarity' around what exactly such arrangements entail has allowed states in the Global North to exploit the concept as a way of attempting to outsource and externalise their obligations under the Refugees Convention to poorer states at their peripheries.[39] In both phases of Australia's offshore detention regime, Australia concluded Memorandums of Understanding with Nauru and PNG as well as with international institutions such as UNHCR (in Phase I) and the IOM (in Phase II) and multinational for-profit corporations such as Transfield and G4S, which ran and operated the detention centres.[40] Mbembe summarises this state logic of refugee deterrence and responsibility outsourcing at the heart of Australia's offshore detention regime in the following way:

> We must close the borders. Filter those who make it across them. Process them. Choose who we want to remain. Deport the rest. Sign contracts with corrupt elites in countries

36 Mbembe, *Necropolitics*, 10.

37 The number of people detained under Australia's offshore detention regime totalled 1,637 people in Phase I and peaked at 2,450 people in April 2014 (Phase II): Janet Phillips and Harriet Spinks, *Immigration Detention in Australia* (Canberra: Parliament of Australia, 2013); Elibritt Karlsen, *Australia's Offshore Processing of Asylum Seekers in Nauru and PNG: A Quick Guide to Statistics and Resources* (Canberra: Parliament of Australia, 2016).

38 For a brief overview of this history, see Sara Dehm, "Outsourcing, Responsibility and Refugee Claim-Making in Australia's Offshore Detention Regime," in *Asylum for Sale: Profit and Protest in the Migration Industry*, eds. Siobhán McGuirk and Adrienne Pine (Oakland: PM Press, 2020).

39 See Michelle Foster, "The Implications of the Failed 'Malaysian Solution': The Australian High Court and Refugee Responsibility Sharing at International Law," *Melbourne Journal of International Law* 13, no. 1 (2012): 395.

40 During Phase I, Australian departmental officers together with UNHCR officials conducted refugee status determination on Nauru and Manus Island, whereas during Phase II, this process was outsourced to PNG and Nauruan state authorities, allowing the Australian government to project responsibility and accountability for

> of origin, third world countries, transition countries. They must be turned into the prison guards of the West, to whom the lucrative business of administering brutality can be subcontracted.[41]

For Mbembe, the enrolment of private for-profit corporations in enacting the sovereign power to exclude, and the necropolitical violence that animates the form that this exclusion takes, has led to 'the emergence of modes of domination without responsibility, as capital confiscates for itself the right of life and death over those its subjugated'.[42]

International law's entanglement in colonial histories of necropolitical spaces and practices

One line of inquiry that Mbembe's theorisation of necropolitics opens up for grasping such international legal arrangements is an insistence upon being attentive to international law's entanglement in the colonial history of contemporary necropolitical spaces as well as the enduring legacies of such colonial relations. Centring this colonial history makes visible that the choice of PNG and Nauru as locations for Australia's offshore detention centres is no historical accident. Indeed, the Australian state has a long history of exercising necropolitical violence in the physical spaces now forming part of the states of PNG and Nauru. Importantly, this historical exercise of power was authorised and enabled through international law and institutions, even if some of the particular assertions of authority or incidents of violence were contested in the past.[43]

Historians have detailed how Australian attempts to assert colonial rule over Pacific lands and peoples have formed a part of the transnational project of creating and maintaining a white Australia. Such Australian colonial ambitions can be seen, for example, in Queensland's failed attempt to annex the territories of Papua and New Guinea in 1883.[44] A German protectorate from 1884 onwards, Australia seized control of New Guinea through military occupation following the outset of the First World War in 1914. For the next seven years, the Australian Naval and Military Expeditionary Force (ANMEF) ruled the land and its people in a 'notoriously harsh manner'.[45] In the subsequent decades, Australia saw its occupation and policing of New Guinea, alongside Papua and other places such as Nauru, as key to its strategic interests in the region in general, and the realisation of its policy of Pacific sub-imperialism in particular.[46] While Australia ultimately failed in its push for outright annexation of New Guinea at Versailles, it succeeded in maintaining control over the territory under the League of Nations' Mandate system, categorised as a class C, from 1921 onwards.

processing refugee claims onto the Nauruan and PNG states as 'self-governing and responsible Pacific state[s]' while also exercising ultimate control over the arrangements as a whole. Anthea Vogl, "Sovereign Relations: Australia's 'Off-Shoring' of Asylum Seekers on Nauru in Historical Perspective," in *Against International Norms: Postcolonial Perspectives*, ed. Charlotte Epstein (New York: Routledge, 2017): 158.

41 Mbembe, *Necropolitics*, 98.

42 Ibid., 34.

43 For an imperial history of Nauru and international law, see Cait Storr, *International Status in the Shadow of Empire: Nauru and the Histories of International Law* (Cambridge: Cambridge University Press, 2020).

44 See Patricia O'Brien, "Reactions to Australian Colonial Violence in New Guinea: The 1926 Nakanai Massacre in a Global Context," *Australian Historical Studies* 43, no. 2 (2012): 194.

45 Ibid.

46 Cait Storr, "'Imperium in Imperio': Sub-Imperialism and the Formation of Australia as a Subject of International Law," *Melbourne Journal of International Law* 19, no. 1 (2018): 335.

One particularly brutal incident that occurred under Australian administration of New Guinea was the 'Nakanai expedition' in November 1926 that killed an estimated 26 Nakanai people and wounded many more as part of a reprisal mission in retaliation for the deaths of four white gold-prospectors. This official reprisal expedition, led by Colonel John Walstab, was armed with a Maxim machine gun, a lethal weapon that would become a 'grotesque metaphor for colonial violence' used for the mass killings of Indigenous people.[47] Such brutality reflects Australia's treatment of New Guinea as a 'colonial frontier' space that was distinct from but nonetheless connected to and part of a continuum of violence that was also perpetrated against Aboriginal people in Australia. It points to the transnational continuities of necropolitical violence across time within particular spaces despite changes in the international legal status of a place.

Australia's contemporary refugee detention regime builds on this history of necropolitical violence connected to projects of racial hegemony and exclusion, albeit through a different legal architecture and with different targets. Since its reintroduction in 2012, Australia's offshore detention regime has been characterised by the prolonged incarceration of people seeking asylum that has manifested in what the UNHCR has called an 'unparalleled' mental health crisis in which a collective sense of despair and incidents of self-harm among refugees are endemic. Behrouz Boochani, a Kurdish journalist and writer who himself was detained for over seven years on Manus Island, described the experience of indefinite detention as soul-destroying:

> Prison maintains its power over time; the power to keep people in line. Fenced enclosures dominate and can pacify even the most violent person – those imprisoned on Manus are themselves sacrificial subjects of violence. We are a bunch of ordinary humans locked up simply for seeking refuge.[48]

In the case of Hamid Khazaei, this necropolitical violence of Australia's offshore detention regime took the form of what Claire Loughnan has called 'active neglect'.[49] Two weeks before his death, on 23 August 2014, Hamid Khazaei sought treatment at the detention centre health clinic, run by the private for-profit entity, International Health and Medical Services (IHMS), a subsidiary of the multinational conglomerate International SOS. At the time, he had a small cut on his leg and was 'feeling generally unwell with fever, general body aches, chills/rigor, a sore throat and a runny nose'. While Hamid Khazaei was given antibiotics and monitored overnight, it would take a few more days until medical staff would request a transfer to the Port Moresby hospital and even longer for this transfer to be approved by Australian immigration officials in Canberra, who initially did not consider the request to be sufficiently urgent to warrant a transfer to Port Moresby. In fact, the process of seeking Australia's approval for the transfer was such a prolonged and convoluted web of communication involving numerous intermediaries that it resulted in Hamid Khazaei missing the only available daily commercial flight from Manus to Port Moresby as his condition rapidly deteriorated.[50]

47 O'Brien, "Reactions to Australian Colonial Violence in New Guinea", 200.

48 Behrouz Boochani, *No Friend but the Mountains: Writings from Manus Prison* (Sydney: Pan Macmillan, 2018).

49 Claire Loughnan, "Active Neglect: The New Tool for the 'Externalisation' of Refugee Protection," *Border Criminologies*, University of Oxford, July 16, 2019, www.law.ox.ac.uk/research-subject-groups/centre-criminology/centreborder-criminologies/blog/2019/07/active-neglect.

50 For example, one official involved in the approval web was Amanda Little, the Director of Health Operations within the then Australian Department of Immigration and Border Protection (DIBP). As a senior departmental official, her role was to convey requests for medical transfers to the relevant minister for approval. In the case of Hamid Khazaei, upon receiving the request for his medical transfer to Port Moresby, Ms Little opted to email

By the time Hamid Khazaei was transferred in an air ambulance in the early afternoon of 26 August 2014, he was already 'not only septic, but dehydrated and delirious'.[51] When he was eventually transferred to Australia on 27 August 2014, he was non-responsive and already showing early signs of brain death. Although the official cause of his death was in part attributed to medical errors, communication breakdowns and failures of bureaucratic medical transfers approval processes, Hamid Khazaei's death occurred in the context of an immigration detention regime that was premised on, in Mbembe's words, keeping refugees and asylum seekers 'alive but in a state of injury, in a phantomlike world of horrors'.[52] Not only were there inadequate structures in place for providing healthcare to refugees, but the overly complicated ways in which these were implemented in practice evidenced a bureaucratic callousness towards both the dignity and preservation of refugee lives. More fundamentally, the very act of expelling refugees to remote places of incarceration, and implementing a policy and bureaucratic apparatus that work to prevent medical transfers to Australia, except for in 'rare' or 'exceptional circumstances', ultimately creates a border regime that exercises the power to 'expose to death' while abandoning refugees to 'live at the edge of life'.[53]

While some scholars have already begun this work of tracing international law's entanglement in the colonial history of such spaces of necropolitical violence, it nonetheless remains a fruitful avenue for further scholarship and activism.[54] As Boochani has powerfully argued, in analysing the neo-colonial relations between Australia and PNG:

> Only a meta-historical and transhistorical approach can unpack the peculiarities associated with the issue of Manus and Nauru. Only a rigorous analysis of a colonial presence in Australia and its tactics in the region can disclose the reality of violence in these island prisons. . . . This form of affliction, inflicted on people in similarly vulnerable situations, has always existed in the history of modern Australia. Pain and suffering systematically inflicted on defenceless and vulnerable bodies.[55]

Importantly, such an analysis of international law must be extended to encompass the continuities between the technologies and practices used by *external*-facing contemporary border regimes and ongoing dispossession of Indigenous peoples *internal* to the territories claimed by settler colonial states. Joseph Pugliese, for example, documented and catalogued refugee deaths in Australian immigration detention alongside the black deaths in custody, in order to produce

back a series of questions for further information to ascertain why Hamid Khazaei could not be treated by the detention centre clinic, thus delaying the transfer process by several hours and resulting in Hamid Khazaei missing the only available commercial flight to Port Moresby that day. Amanda Little would later describe her role within the Australian bureaucratic architecture to the coroner as: 'I'm not a decision-maker; I'm an escalator in this process.' The coroner held that the Australian process for medical transfers was 'overly bureaucratic and lacked clear written procedures', and that Ms Little 'exercised significant influence as a gatekeeper in whether the transfer request for Mr Khazaei was approved by her superiors, including the timing of the approval'. Coroners Court of Queensland, "Inquest into the Death of Hamid Khazaei," 34, 99–100.

51 Ibid., 49.

52 Mbembe, "Necropolitics," 21.

53 Mbembe, *Necropolitics*, 37.

54 See, for example, Anthea Vogl, "Sovereign Relations"; Sarah Keenan, "The Blurring of Australian and Nauruan Jurisdiction," *UK Constitutional Law Association*, April 9, 2018, https://ukconstitutionallaw.org/2018/04/09/sarah-keenan-the-blurring-of-australian-and-nauruan-jurisdiction/.

55 Behrouz Boochani, "I Write from Manus Island as a Duty to History," *The Guardian*, December 6, 2017, www.theguardian.com/commentisfree/2017/dec/06/i-write-from-manus-island-as-a-duty-to-history.

'a necroethical record of deaths and self-harm produced by Australia's necropolitical immigration detention regime in the face of a systemic national forgetting' of its imperial and colonial frontier violence.[56]

International law as a law of status and differential rights of belonging

Another line of inquiry made available through Mbembe's theorisation of necropolitics is an interrogation of international law's categories of political belonging and state responsibility that allow for the differential allocation of rights on the basis of a person's status within a particular territory. International law arranges individual political belonging within the international realm through two primary means: first, according to a person's nationality (that is, their status as a citizen or member of a national community entitled to the rights and protections of their state of nationality); and second, according to a person's humanness (that is, their status as a member of 'humanity', entitled to the rights and obligations of international human rights law). Through these dual modes of belonging, international law authorises states to distinguish between different people within and beyond their territory on the basis of these statuses. As a result, states have created different legal regimes for different juridically created categories of people within the one legal space, including for people fleeing persecution entitled to the protections of the Refugees Convention under international law. For example, while the Refugees Convention stipulates that a person should not be penalised as a result of their mode of entry into a state, states in the Global North have increasingly sought to adopt an array of deterrence policies to prevent people arriving unauthorised in their territories to seek asylum. In Australia's case, this is most starkly demonstrated through the 'morbid spectacle' of "offshore processing",[57] which subjects a specific group of refugees to the torture of physical incarceration, legal limbo and political abandonment in order to deter another unspecified group of refugees from seeking asylum in Australia unauthorised by boat.

As a result, refugees themselves have come to be governed as what Shahram Khosravi, in his auto-ethnography of European border regimes, has called 'border transgressors' – people who are treated not only as 'less human and eligible for sacrifice' but also in a way that their very bodies become sites of border control:

> Borders have become invisible borders, situated everywhere and nowhere. Hence, undesirable people are not expelled by the border, they are forced to be the border.[58]

Under Australia's offshore detention regime, refugees' bodies not only become the targets of state necropolitical power to expose to death, but they have also become a site for the articulation of projects of border control and refugee deterrence. This is particularly evident through the use of the substandard provision of healthcare in immigration detention on Manus Island and Nauru as a form of both deterrence and punishment.[59]

56 Joseph Pugliese, "Geopolitics of Aboriginal Sovereignty: Colonial Law as 'a Species of Excess of Its Own Authority', Aboriginal Passport Ceremonies and Asylum Seekers," *Law Text Culture* 19 (2015): 87.

57 See Mbembe, "Necropolitics," 35.

58 Shahram Khosravi, *"Illegal" Traveller: An Auto-Ethnography of Borders* (Basingstoke: Palgrave Macmillan, 2010), 99.

59 In their historisation of incarceration as a colonial technique, Maria Giannacopoulos and Claire Loughnan write how law – and I would add international law – 'is not just exercised over geographic space, but also over particular bodies in that space', highlighting the 'persistence of punishment as a key element' of state border control

International law recognises Australia's legal responsibility to the asylum seekers and refugees transferred to Manus Island. Under the law of state responsibility, Australia is rightly deemed to have 'effective control' over the operations of the Manus Island detention centre, including through the engagement of sub-contractors. This means that international law dominantly frames the relationship as one of responsibility for state conduct and protection of refugees. This has led some scholars to argue in response that Australia's conduct indicates a profound irresponsibility towards people in its control, or even that such third country refugee detention and processing regimes are profoundly irresponsible.

Yet, the emergence of the necropolitical state that has refugees and migrants as one of its targets is more than merely the failure of responsibility of an individual state or of the particular international refugee law regime. It rather signals the conceptual limits of such international legal frameworks of responsibility. In emphasising the question of de facto control over asylum seekers and refugees, the law of state responsibility is unable to challenge the fundamental logic of the border: in this case, the act of distinguishing between citizen/non-citizen. Rather than unsettling this fundamental categorisation, the law of state responsibility works to superimpose legal relations of obligation and care, while maintaining the status of asylum seekers and refugees as non-citizens of the state that is asserting control over them. While refugees and asylum seekers are entitled to the protections of international human rights law as a matter of international law, irrespective of their status as non-citizens, in practice this has led to continued denial of many of these rights.

Mbembe's attention to how juridical status reinforces racial orders illuminates how the abandonment of asylum seekers in Australia's offshore detention regime is not simply about economic considerations. The Australian government has spent an estimated $9 billion on offshore detention since its reintroduction in 2013. Similarly, in the next budget cycle (2021–2027), the EU plans to spend an estimated $38.4 billion on funding their militarised border regime, including surveillance and boat pushbacks in the Mediterranean Sea.[60] Such operations exceed the logic of the market, even if they create a transnational border industrial complex that allows private firms to profit from these forms of enclosure.

Rather, the active neglect of refugees detained "offshore" indicates a more fundamental state rejection of the lawfulness of the claims that non-citizens (in this case asylum seekers) can make to be entitled to public goods and resources that are deemed to properly belong to a circumscribed public (in this case, the provision of sufficient healthcare) *as of right*. This rejection of asylum seekers as part of the state-conceived lawful public community takes place amid a climate of neoliberal globalisation that has been characterised by broader political assaults on public goods, the limiting of public spaces and concerted efforts to shrink the very notion of 'the public' itself.[61] These global projects of shrinking public goods, or of subjecting public goods to the logic and sacrifices of the market, are part of a larger contested project to remake the state in form and practice, one that has long been authorised through international law.[62] Mbembe's theorisation of necropolitics invites further scrutiny of international law's implication

practices. Maria Giannacopoulos and Claire Loughnan, " 'Closure' at Manus Island and Carceral Expansion in the Open Air Prison," *Globalizations* 17, no. 7 (2020): 1118.

60 Mark Akkerman, *The Business of Building Walls* (Amsterdam: Transnational Institute, 2019).

61 On the transformation of notions of the public, including public goods under neoliberalism, see, for example, Bonnie Honig, *Public Things: Democracy in Disrepair* (New York: Fordham University Press, 2017).

62 See Anne Orford, "Beyond Harmonization: Trade, Human Rights and the Economy of Sacrifice," *Leiden Journal of International Law* 18, no. 2 (2005): 179.

in the uneven global distribution of rights and resources on the basis of personal status, resulting in some lives being rendered 'disposable' and disproportionately vulnerable to death.[63]

Borders, sovereign accountability and communities of co-habitation in pandemic times

Thinking with Mbembe's theorisation of necropolitics as a way of diagnosing international law's mode of arranging political and legal order vis-à-vis people fleeing persecution does not foreclose the possibility of political contestation or resistance to contemporary border regimes. This includes contesting international law's role in arranging legal authority over people on the basis of their status vis-à-vis the territorial state in which they live or that exercises 'effective control' over them. Such challenges take various forms, including legal challenges that use international law and institutions. While it is beyond the scope of this chapter to detail these international legal challenges in full, in brief, they have primarily appealed to (i) the law of state responsibility for breaches of international refugee and human rights law; (ii) international criminal law; and (iii) the emerging global field of 'business and human rights' law.[64] Each of these legal tactics have largely worked within the established categories of international law in order to hold, for example, state and non-state corporate actors within Australia's offshore detention regime to account, with varying degrees of success in terms of advancing a politics and practice of legal, political and moral accountability.

As I write the conclusion of this chapter in April 2020, the COVID-19 pandemic has forced a rapid and drastic reorganisation of social and economic life on a global scale. Notably, many responses of states in the Global North to the pandemic have mobilised and intensified the logic of the border in order to protect particular communities of citizens from the perceived threat posed by infected 'outsiders' and to stop the global spread of the virus. In Australia, to date, this has seen the physical closure of national borders to all except for Australian citizens and permanent residents, with few exceptions; the erection of internal borders between some federated states and territories; the extension of police powers that have disproportionately targeted racialised migrant communities; and the rollout of state economic relief packages that prioritise or benefit citizens and permanent residents only. Through such bordering practices, the Australian state has expanded its necropolitical violence towards all people on non-permanent visas, treating them as unwelcome, undeserving, superfluous and even deportable, with the prime minister recently telling international students and temporary migrant workers living in Australia that 'it's time to go home now'. These practices have also exacerbated internal distinctions within communities of citizens on the basis of race, illustrated through data that suggest the disproportionate enforcement of social distancing controls against Indigenous and migrant Australians.[65] The impetus behind such measures as a form of resurgent nationalism is, in Mbembe's words, that 'enclosures must be multiplied' in order to protect 'the self' against threats and dangers from the perceived 'outside' world, even when this 'outside' is extended to encompass racialised groups of citizens within democratic states.[66]

63 On how contemporary state borders allow former colonial powers to enjoy the spoils of empire, see Nadine El-Enany, *Bordering Britain: Law, Race and Empire* (Manchester: Manchester University Press, 2020).

64 See a recent special issue on "Border Justice: Migration and Accountability for Human Rights Violations," *German Law Review* 21, no. 3 (2020), edited by Cathryn Costello and Itamar Mann.

65 See Osman Faruqi, "Compliance Fines under the Microscope," *Saturday Paper*, April 18, 2020, www.thesaturdaypaper.com.au/news/health/2020/04/18/compliance-fines-under-the-microscope/15871320009710.

66 Mbembe, *Necropolitics*, 2.

Yet, on the other hand, the COVID-19 pandemic has also starkly illuminated the particular precarious and vulnerable situation of refugees and migrants across the world who are exposed to forms of necropolitical violence, including in drastically underfunded refugee camps in the Global South with limited healthcare, in makeshift communities in refugee transit states, and in different situations of legal precarity and incarceration in states in the Global North. In Australia, this has resulted in refugee rights advocacy campaigns to urgently release people from immigration detention, including transferring people subject to Australia's offshore detention regime in PNG and Nauru back to Australia. Largely, these calls have been framed in terms of the risk that COVID-19 infections in immigration detention centres pose to both the people detained, who are unable to adhere to social distancing practices, as well as to the community at large. It remains unclear if Australian state authorities will heed these calls for release.

There is nonetheless a certain degree of irony that the historical accident and lethal force of COVD-19, which now exposes people in the Global North to the possibility of infection and death as a result of government neglect of essential healthcare systems (albeit in ways that affect people differently on the basis of race and class), may be the impetus for a loosening – or at least temporary suspension – of the carceral practices of immigration detention in the Global North. In recent weeks, several US judges have ordered the release of people from immigration detention who are at higher risk of severe illness from COVID-19 infections.[67] California has just announced a US$125 million COVID-19 disaster fund for the 2 million undocumented workers living in the state who make up 10% of the workforce there.[68] Portugal, too, has temporarily granted all migrants and refugees living within its territory full citizenship rights, including access to state healthcare, for a specified period of time.[69] Such measures, in recognising that our physical well-being is bound up in the safety of others, has the possibility of founding, in Mbembe's words, 'a relation with others based on the reciprocal recognition of our common vulnerability and finitude'.[70] There is the possibility, however unlikely or slim, of opening up a world conceived through relations of co-belonging, plurality and sharing, of holding the world 'in-common' through forms of community, solidarity and co-existence beyond the bounds of juridical status.[71]

Moreover, such state responses to the COVID-19 pandemic that break down the distinctions between citizens and non-citizens in practice offer the possibility of rethinking the self upon which such relations of community are based. Rejecting the idea of an autonomous and

67 See, for example, "Federal Judge Orders Release of Some Immigrants in Detention due to Coronavirus Outbreak, Blasts ICE," *CNN*, March 27, 2020, https://edition.cnn.com/2020/03/27/politics/ice-release-immigrants-in-detention-coronavirus/index.html; "N.J. Judge Orders Release of 5 ICE Detainees as Coronavirus Outbreak Mounts in Jails," *Daily News*, April 13, 2020, www.nydailynews.com/new-york/ny-ice-detainees-released-coronavirus-20200413-42td6yso2zcellmqmzj4r4f4oa-story.html.

68 "California Launches Nation's First Disaster Relief Fund for Undocumented Workers," *The Guardian*, April 16, 2020, www.theguardian.com/world/2020/apr/15/california-undocumented-immigrants-disaster-relief-fund-coronavirus.

69 "Portugal Gives Migrants, Asylum Seekers Residency Rights During Coronavirus Crisis," *SBS News*, April 2, 2020, www.sbs.com.au/news/portugal-gives-migrants-asylum-seekers-residency-rights-during-coronavirus-crisis.

70 Mbembe, *Necropolitics*.

71 Ibid., 40. Such measures suggest an embrace of what Étienne Balibar and Judith Butler have respectively called 'communities of fate' or 'communities of co-habitation', communities in which the borders of membership and entitlements are determined less through the accident of birth but more through a continual re-working of relations of belonging in response to historical encounters and material circulations. For a discussion, see Sara Dehm, "Accusing 'Europe': Articulations of Migrant Justice and a Popular International Law," in *Peoples' Tribunals and International Law*, eds. Andrew Byrnes and Gabrielle Simm (Cambridge: Cambridge University Press, 2018), 157.

self-determining subject, still very much a trope of international law that applies both to the state as well as to individuals, Mbembe writes that 'we have always been *beings of the border*'. Mbembe suggests that all subjects, whether individuals or political communities, are as a matter of empirical fact, and ought to be conceived of as a matter of theory, entities consisting of 'borrowings from foreign subjects'.[72] It is here that we can glimpse how it may be possible to undo the contemporary state border regimes upon which international law is structurally dependent, border regimes which have become, in Mbembe's words, 'dead spaces of non-connection which deny the very idea of a shared humanity, of a planet, the only one we have, that we share together, and to which we are linked by the ephemerality of our common condition'.[73]

72 Mbembe, *Necropolitics*, 30.
73 Ibid., 100.

27

Towards a carceral geography of international law

Kate Grady[1]

> The carceral, with its long gradation stretching from the convict-ship or imprisonment with hard labour to diffuse, slight limitations, communicates a type of power that the law validates and that justice uses as its favourite weapon.[2]

Introduction

More than 11 million people across the world are incarcerated – a population equivalent to that of Haiti. Criminologists and geographers have studied the carceral space holding these people – but rather less has been said about international law's role there. This is perhaps surprising given that incarceration concerns many themes with which international lawyers regularly wrestle. As Delaney explains:

> Prisons are the spatial, material expression of historical and cultural visions of punishment, good and evil, transgression and desert. . . . Likewise prison space is connected to other spatialities such as those constituting geographies of crime, exclusion, deviance, privilege, and injustice. They are places that exist within a wider political economy of domination. So, prison is not just a space – an inside marked off by walls, electric fences, and guns from an outside constituting the realm of freedom. Rather it is a location within more extensive carceral geographies of punishment and suffering, linking, as do other legal spaces, different scales from the micro-corporeal and architectural to the national and global.[3]

1 I'm grateful to Michelle Kelsall, Gina Heathcote, Sara Kendall and Luis Eslava for their assistance and advice, and for the feedback from participants at the Centre for Critical International Law at the University of Kent where a version of this paper was presented.
2 Michel Foucault, *Discipline and Punish: The Birth of the Prison*, trans. Alan Sheridon (New York: Vintage, 1977), 302.
3 David Delaney, "Beyond the Word: Law as a Thing of This World," in *Law and Geography,* eds. Jane Holder and Carolyn Harrison (Oxford: Oxford University Press, 2003), 72–73.

This chapter provides a preliminary sketch of the relationship(s) between international law and carceral space. In particular, I explore how practices of, and ideas about, incarceration travel between different legal spaces – examining the contingency of aspects of international law's carceral geography and connections across states, domestic and international jurisdictions, and disparate legal fields. In so doing, I draw on legal and carceral geography.

As scholars of the humanities increasingly examine the role of space in analysis of the social, for legal geographers the key question concerns law's role in this. After all, law and space do not exist separately – spaces 'are not simply the inert sites of law but are inextricably implicated in *how* law happens'.[4] Formalist accounts of law and space treat both concepts as apolitical, objective, rational and bound by their own internal logic. Yet critical lawyers and critical geographers have shown both to be explicitly political processes for ordering, and 'relational, acquiring meaning through social action'.[5] Critical lawyers and geographers thus challenge the claim to objectivity of their discipline's subject-matter, arguing instead that law and space reflect and reinforce relations of power.[6] In so doing, they intersect with each other as 'mutually constitutive' since law produces space and space enforces the law.[7] Critical legal geography thus draws on critical legal scholarship on the co-production of law and society, and critical geography scholarship on the relationship between space and social life, to consider how law, society and space constitute each other.[8]

International lawyers, of course, commonly speak a geographic language, invoking place and space in analysis of territory, borders, jurisdiction and so forth. Geography permeates the discipline, though is seldom explicitly identified. Insofar as international lawyers have turned to legal geography this has rarely concerned international criminal law or questions of incarceration. Indeed, for most international lawyers, their discipline's primary relationship to incarceration concerns conditions of detention and compliance with human rights standards. Here, I take a different tack, exploring the prison as a site through which international law operates[9] via the development of a carceral geography – a combination of geography, criminology and penology which examines places and practices of incarceration, their distributional geographies and social and spatial relations.[10] Through this, I show first how international law connects islands of incarceration in a carceral archipelago through the movement of common ideas and ideologies and shared physical spaces. As Mountz argues, '[w]hile remote detention sites may appear ad hoc, they must be viewed together to show how geographies of exclusion operate beyond local and regional scales, and actually connect national contexts with global trends.'[11] Second,

4 Irus Braverman, Nicholas Blomley, David Delaney and Alexandre Kedar, "Introduction: Expanding the Spaces of Law," in *The Expanding Spaces of Law: A Timely Legal Geography*, eds. Irus Braverman, Nicholas Blomley, David Delaney and Alexandre Kedar (Stanford, CA: Stanford University Press, 2014), 1 (emphasis in original).

5 Nicholas Blomley, "From 'What?' to 'so What?': Law and Geography in Retrospect," in *Law and Geography*, eds. Jane Holder and Carolyn Harrison (Oxford: Oxford University Press, 2003), 22, and also 20 and 29.

6 Hari M. Osofsky, "The Geography of Moo Ha Ha: A Tribute to Keith Aoki's Role in Developing Critical Legal Geography," *Oregon Law Review* 90 (2012): 1239; Keith Aoki, "Space Invaders: Critical Geography, the Third World in International Law and Critical Race Theory," *Villanova Law Review* 45 (2000): 920.

7 Blomley, "From 'What?' to 'so What?'," 24.

8 Zoe Pearson, "Spaces of International Law," *Griffith Law Review* 17, no. 2 (2008): 490, 496.

9 See Luis Eslava and Sundhya Pahuja, "Beyond the (Post)Colonial: TWAIL and the Everyday Life of International Law," *Verfassung und Recht in Übersee VRÜ* 45 (2012): 195.

10 Dominique Moran, "'Doing Time' in Carceral Space: Timespace and Carceral Geography," *Geografiska Annaler. Series B, Human Geography* 94, no. 4 (2012): 306.

11 Alison Mountz, "Mapping Remote Detention: Dis/location Through Isolation," in *Beyond Walls and Cages: Prisons, Borders, and Global Crisis*, eds. Jenna M. Loyd, Matt Mitchelson and Andrew Burridge (Athens: University of Georgia Press, 2012), 91.

I demonstrate how the movement of ideas and people within this archipelago is influenced by logics of capitalism and colonialism. I conclude by considering how critical international lawyers might resist this archipelago.

Exporting incarceration

The primary, although not the only, means through which this geography of incarceration develops in different locales is, of course, criminal justice. This enables carceral practices to move between different domestic, and domestic and international, jurisdictions. Dealing with the former, criminologists have documented a profound 'punitive turn' in the US criminal justice system since the late 1970s. The body of theoretical criminology documenting this phenomenon is vast but, to summarise, the US turned to punitive criminalisation with three important features.[12] First, criminal law was reframed as the primary remedy for social problems, with the populace 'governed through crime' as crime, criminal law and penality became expressive and politicised.[13] Second, criminal justice policy took on an increasingly punitive character with punishment seen as an end in-and-of itself. And third, this resulted in mass incarceration in harsher prison conditions, the decline of other sentencing models, and increased techniques of surveillance and control. The prison thus became a crucial instrument of this criminal justice landscape.[14]

Towards the end of the Cold War, the US expanded this domestic 'war on crime' by promoting similar practices overseas. McLeod argues that this global expansion of 'governing through crime' sought, in part, to control cross-border crime abroad in order to prevent it reaching US shores (thereby reinforcing the 'war on crime' at home). This legal transplant project operated in four ways. First, it categorised certain things as transnational or international crimes. Second, it incentivised states to address these things though US-favoured crime-control methods. Third, it sought to reform states' criminal justice systems by reference to the US model. And, fourth, it institutionalised these reforms through US-run training programmes. In consequence, since the early 1990s, the US has trained tens of thousands of foreign law enforcement officers and deployed US police and prosecutors to states across Africa, Asia, Eastern Europe, Latin America and the Middle East.[15] For McLeod, this project not only allowed the US to maintain its 'war on crime', it also engendered 'a U.S.-dominant form of global governance'[16] for the post-Cold War world order. Thus, whilst US incarceration rates are exceptional, many national penal systems have undergone their own punitive turn.

This bilateral move to incarceration has been augmented internationally in five ways. First, the UN Security Council has also proved instrumental in promoting domestic criminal justice. For example, after 9/11, it mandated the criminalisation and punishment of terrorism and related activities through the justice systems of member states.[17] Second, so-called rule of law

12 Cf Nicolas Carrier, "Anglo-Saxon Sociologies of the Punitive Turn: Critical Timidity, Reductive Perspectives, and the Problem of Totalization," *Champ pénal/Penal field* VII (2010), accessed November 15, 2019, https://journals.openedition.org/champpenal/7952.

13 Jonathan Simon, *Governing Through Crime: How the War on Crime Transformed American Democracy and Created a Culture of Fear* (New York: Oxford University Press, 2007).

14 Loïc Wacquant, *Punishing the Poor: The Neoliberal Government of Social Insecurity* (Durham, NC: Duke University Press, 2009), Ch 4 and 5; David Garland, *The Culture of Control: Crime and Social Order in Contemporary Society* (Oxford: Oxford University Press, 2002), 177 et seq.

15 Allegra M. McLeod, "Exporting U.S. Criminal Justice," *Yale Law and Policy Review* 29 (2010): 83.

16 Ibid., 103.

17 For example UNSC Res 1373 (2001), para 1(b) and 2(e).

promotion as undertaken by the UN and other international bodies, in line with US practice, largely concerns law and order, with such reform programmes often involving prison building, 'drafting criminal laws, building criminal courts and training magistrates and investigators. An entire criminal justice machinery is built and set in motion by'[18] these programmes. Third, as Engle has argued, the international human rights movement became a crucial driver of criminal prosecutions for human rights violations, following the jurisprudence of the Inter-American Court of Human Rights from the late 1980s. This embrace of criminalisation moved from domestic prosecutions to international ones via the renaissance of international criminal justice. In particular, the Security Council's establishment of the international criminal tribunals for Rwanda (ICTR) and the former Yugoslavia (ICTY) in the 1990s, coupled with work at the General Assembly on what would ultimately become the Rome Statute for the International Criminal Court (ICC), institutionalised the protection of human rights via international criminal law.[19] Since, 'at the same time that "justice" came to mean "criminal justice" in human rights advocacy, "criminal justice" largely came to mean incarceration in the United States and in its exported models',[20] imprisonment thus became international criminal law's primary sanction.

Whilst evidently this international punitive turn intersects with the domestic one via common ideology, it also does so spatially, since international criminal law co-opts domestic prison space. International courts do have prisons but these facilities usually only hold those awaiting trial, sentenced for perjury or contempt, awaiting appeal, or pending transfer.[21] In most cases, international criminals serve their sentences in domestic prisons, with the ICTY, ICTR and the Special Court for Sierra Leone (SCSL) sending those convicted to state prisons across Africa and Europe.[22] For the ICC, the Rome Statute mandates that sentences of imprisonment be served in a state chosen by the Court from a list of those willing. In so choosing, the Court should consider equitable distribution amongst states; international treaty standards on the treatment of prisoners; the defendant's views and nationality; and other relevant circumstances.[23] Thus far, the ICC has sent prisoners to the Democratic Republic of the Congo, although it has agreements with other states. The enforcement of international criminal law therefore depends on domestic incarceration and, to facilitate this, some international tribunals have paid for the development of state prisons.[24]

Fourth, for Khalili, a turn to incarceration has been an important feature of recent counter-insurgency warfare, with the 'war on terror' facilitating the circulation of carceral techniques between detention sites in Guantánamo Bay, Afghanistan and Iraq.[25] As Forman makes vividly clear in his article 'Exporting Harshness: How the War on Crime Helped Make the War on Terror Possible', the 'war on terror' internationalised US domestic criminal justice practices.

18 Stephen Humphreys, *Theatre of the Rule of Law: Transnational Legal Intervention in Theory and Practice* (Cambridge: Cambridge University Press, 2010), 170.

19 Karen Engle, "Anti-impunity and the Turn to Criminal Law in Human Rights," *Cornell Law Review* 100 (2015): 1076 and 1091 et seq.

20 Ibid., 1126.

21 Dirk van Zyl Smit, "International Imprisonment," *International and Comparative Law Quarterly* 54, no. 2 (2005): 367.

22 Barbora Holá and Joris van Wijk, "Life After Conviction at International Criminal Tribunals: An Empirical Overview," *Journal of International Criminal Justice* 12 (2014): 117.

23 Article 103, Rome Statute 1998.

24 Róisín Mulgrew, "On the Enforcement of Sentences Imposed by International Courts," *Journal of International Criminal Justice* 7, no. 2 (2009): 392–93.

25 Laleh Khalili, *Time in the Shadows: Confinement in Counterinsurgencies* (Stanford, CA: Stanford University Press, 2013), 3, 6.

The primary domestic critique of the treatment of detainees at Guantánamo Bay or Abu Ghraib has been premised upon the denial to inmates of the supposed 'benefits' of the domestic system by virtue of their off-shore detention outside the territorial jurisdiction of the US mainland. Yet, as Forman shows – via the scope of the prison complex, harsh treatment of juveniles, attacks on judicial authority and undermining defence counsel – 'war on terror' detention is an extension of existing practice within US domestic prisons.[26]

Further continuities include the deliberate adoption of detention conditions from domestic supermax prisons within extra-territorial facilities and some common instances of prisoner abuse. Indeed, one of those convicted of prisoner abuse at Abu Ghraib had previously worked at a domestic prison where there had also been a prisoner abuse scandal. The overseas treatment of detainees comes full circle as US military veterans returning home are increasingly recruited as domestic prison guards. Whilst the parallels between domestic and war-on-terror incarceration are obviously inexact, there are nonetheless important continuities which are masked by the mainstream focus on the supposed exceptionality and lawlessness of the latter.[27] In fact, far from being lawless, places such as Guantánamo Bay are, as Johns argues, 'spaces where law and liberal proceduralism speak and operate in excess'.[28] For Forman, meanwhile, focusing on exceptionality diverts attention from prisoner abuses in 'ordinary' prisons within the US (and elsewhere).[29]

Fifth, the export of incarceration practices also occurs via the increasing criminalisation of migration-related conduct. This process – dubbed 'crimmigration' by criminologists[30] – involves the intersection of immigration and criminal law via the adoption of common practices of surveillance, policing and detention. One example of this is the increasing criminalisation of immigration-related behaviour by creating new offences covering migrants' means of travel (such as using false identity documents) and provision of humanitarian assistance to migrants. Another is the increasing use of immigration detention, with states such as India, South Africa and Malaysia now detaining and deporting migrants.[31]

Again, the US has been instrumental in this practice, operating detention centres on its mainland since the 1980s, before increasingly moving off-shore, training foreign law enforcement officials to detain migrants and funding overseas detention facilities across Latin America.[32] This US off-shoring practice would become the direct inspiration for Australian migrant detention at extra-territorial sites on Christmas Island, Papua New Guinea's Manus Island, at Nauru, and in detention centres across Malaysia and Indonesia, since the adoption in 2001 of Australia's 'Pacific Solution'. Subsequently, Canada, New Zealand and Europe looked to Australia for techniques on dealing with migrants arriving by boat, with the EU and its member states

26 James Forman, Jr., "Exporting Harshness: How the War on Crime Helped Make the War on Terror Possible," *New York University Review of Law & Social Change* 33, no. 3 (2009): 331.

27 Ibid., 338–39, 348–55.

28 Fleur Johns, "Guantánamo Bay and the Annihilation of the Exception," *European Journal of International Law* 16, no. 4 (2005): 614 (emphasis omitted).

29 Forman, "Exporting Harshness," 338–39, 351–55.

30 The term was popularised by Juliet P. Stumpf, "The Crimmigration Crisis: Immigrants, Crime, and Sovereign Power," *American University Law Review* 56 (2006): 367.

31 Sujata Ramachandran, "The Contours of Crimmigration Control in India," Global Detention Project Working Paper No. 25 (August 2019), 24, accessed November 15, 2019, www.globaldetentionproject.org/wp-content/uploads/2019/08/GDP-Working-Paper-25-The-Contours-of-Crimmigration-Control-in-India.pdf.

32 Michael Flynn, "There and Back Again: On the Diffusion of Immigration Detention," *Journal on Migration and Human Security* 2, no. 3 (2014): 166 and 171 et seq.

funding migrant detention facilities in the Middle East and North Africa.[33] This move off-shore, of course, seeks to avoid migrants gaining domestic legal rights.

Much like the internationalisation of criminal justice techniques, migration detention is often militarised, involving military planes for surveillance, naval forces to intercept migrant boats, migration enforcement training at military locations and 'the recurrent use of obsolete and active duty military bases to deter, confine, and remove migrants within mainland territory and . . . offshore'.[34] Perhaps the intersection between criminal justice, militarised and migration incarceration is best illustrated by examining the repeated recycling of places of detention. Before it was a camp for detainees from the 'war on terror', the US, for example, used Guantánamo Bay as an offshore detention facility for migrants from Haiti and Cuba;[35] whilst Manus Island, before it held migrants attempting to reach Australia, was a naval base used to detain convicted Japanese war criminals after World War II.[36]

Political economy of imprisonment

This recycling of space is unsurprising considering, as prison abolitionists such as Gilmore and Davis argue, incarceration is a set of symbiotic relationships connected by gendered, racialised and capitalist power structures.[37] This latter nexus between incarceration and political economy becomes visible by analysing the transnational 'private security' companies which (in some, though by no means all, states): support domestic criminal justice imprisonment via the outsourcing of offender-management, transportation and facilities administration; undertake similar activities in the field of immigration detention; and also provide support capabilities for the deployment of military force overseas. Without underplaying the role of the state in incarceration, the public sphere often operates with support from a multi-billion-dollar international industry which unites different types of detention as part of a business model which spreads risk through this unification. This involves, for example, moving from criminal justice imprisonment to immigration detention when (criminal) prison figures plateau, recycling former prisons into immigration detention centres, and vice versa. International economic law, of course, facilitates this via conditions which allow transnational corporations to undertake outsourced public services across multiple jurisdictions.[38]

This is exemplified by G4S' recent move away from providing immigration detention facilities in the UK in favour of increasing its criminal justice prison contracts following recent proposals to expand UK prisons. This move followed allegations of abuse of immigrant detainees by G4S staff at a facility from which the company made £14 million in gross profit. G4S'

33 Ibid., 180–89; Reece Jones, Corey Johnson, Wendy Brown, Gabriel Popescu, Polly Pallister-Wilkins, Alison Mountz and Emily Gilbert, "Interventions on the State of Sovereignty at the Border," *Political Geography* 59 (2017): 7.

34 Alison Mountz and Jenna Loyd, "Transnational Productions of Remoteness: Building Onshore and Offshore Carceral Regimes Across Borders," *Geographica Helvetica* 69 (2014): 392.

35 Ibid., 394.

36 Franziska Seraphim, "Carceral Geographies of Japan's Vanishing Empire: War Criminals' Prisons in Asia," in *The Dismantling of Japan's Empire in East Asia: Deimperialization, Postwar Legitimation and Imperial Afterlife*, eds. Barak Kushner and Sherzod Muminov (Abingdon: Routledge, 2017), 130.

37 Angela Y. Davis, *Are Prisons Obsolete?* (New York: Seven Stories Press, 2003); Ruth Wilson Gilmore, *Golden Gulag: Prisons, Surplus, Crisis, and Opposition in Globalizing California* (Berkley: University of California Press, 2007).

38 See, for example Ernst Ulrich Petersmann, *Multilevel Constitutionalism for Multilevel Governance of Public Goods: Methodology Problems in International Law* (Oxford: Hart, 2017).

immigration facilities will most likely be taken over by Serco.[39] Between them, Serco and G4S manage a number of British prisons and prisoner transport services along with prison facilities in New Zealand, Australia and South Africa. Serco also has contracts with the US Department of Defence, providing logistics and support on military bases and ships, and boot camps for personnel. It undertakes similar services for the Australian military in the Middle East and UK forces in the United Arab Emirates and provides airfield communications to the Bahrain Defence Force, whilst also running immigration detention for the Australian government.[40] For Martin and Mitchelson:

> [t]he production of so much 'bed space' – for profit – imbricates a wide array of state, corporate, and non-governmental actors in the practices of detention and imprisonment. These developments beg new questions about how detention and confinement become embedded in everyday life.[41]

They also draw attention to the role of the globalised neoliberal economy in the creation of this military-prison-migration-industrial-complex.

Spectres of imperialism

Keenan argues that one key question for legal geography is how space relates to the subject, since law's uneven regulation of social and physical spaces results in the inclusion and exclusion of particular subjects – sometimes violently.[42] In consequence, in their process of co-production, law and space also produce identity. The prison is a good illustration of this since '[a] prisoner without a prison, even a virtual one, is, of course, not a prisoner'.[43] For Keenan, since 'spatial frameworks are loaded with social meaning and [are] more supportive of some identities and practices than others, legal geography poses a challenge to liberal understandings of law as universal and even-handed towards all subjects in its provision of justice'.[44] Rather than even-handed, space and law are thus racialised, gendered and class-based.

In the context of incarceration, 'geographers point to emerging relationships between space, state power, imagined geographies, and historical legacies of colonialisms. In so doing, they mark continuities between domestic prison practices and the detention of migrants, asylum seekers, and enemy combatants'.[45] As is well known, the US domestic punitive turn has led to the disproportionate imprisonment of people of colour. Koram argues that the 'war on drugs' in particular 'has fuelled a racist system of mass incarceration and state violence'[46] not only in the US but across the world, with racial disparities evident in states as diverse as Brazil, Mexico, the UK, Israel, Colombia, Canada and South Africa. In the context of international

39 Mattha Busby, "G4S to Leave Immigration Sector After Brook House Scandal," *The Guardian*, September 24, 2019, accessed November 15, 2019, www.theguardian.com/business/2019/sep/24/g4s-to-leave-immigration-sector-after-brook-house-scandal.

40 See Serco website, accessed November 15, 2019, www.serco.com.

41 Lauren L. Martin and Matthew L. Mitchelson, "Geographies of Detention and Imprisonment: Interrogating Spatial Practices of Confinement, Discipline, Law, and State Power," *Geography Compass* 3, no. 1 (2009): 472.

42 Sarah Keenan, *Subversive Property: Law and the Production of Spaces of Belonging* (Abingdon: Routledge, 2015), 29.

43 Blomley, "From 'What?' to 'so What?'," 29.

44 Keenan, *Subversive Property*, 18.

45 Martin and Mitchelson, "Geographies of Detention and Imprisonment," 460.

46 Kojo Koram, "Introduction," in *The War on Drugs and the Global Colour Line,* ed. Kojo Koram (London: Pluto Press, 2019), 2.

criminal law, scholars – especially those writing in Third World Approaches to International Law (TWAIL) – have begun to investigate the parallels between racism in domestic criminal justice systems and international criminal law's focus on, in particular, defendants from the Global South. This literature has often focused on the important question of selectivity – who gets prosecuted and who does not, and who decides.

In addition, however, there is also a question of apparatus. Less attention has been paid thus far to the manner in which criminal 'punishment was itself an instrument for projecting imperial power and culture across the globe'.[47] As Baxi shows, a penal code was established in India under British colonialism and then exported to many other colonial territories.[48] The sanction of imprisonment as a consequence of the criminal justice process was introduced to many states through colonial domination in the nineteenth century, and the general consensus appears to be that states, for example, in large parts of Africa did not use incarceration beforehand.[49] These colonial spectres of incarceration return to haunt present-day practices.[50] Khalili argues that techniques of incarceration developed via the counter-insurgency wars in Iraq and Afghanistan bear the hallmarks of earlier techniques adopted by British and French colonial powers in Algeria, Ireland, Kenya and Burma, among others.[51] Similarly, those from Japan tried as war criminals after World War II were detained in prisons across Asia, many of which had also been used to detain locals resisting colonial rule.[52] For Agozino, present-day criminology remains a colonial project on account of the exportation of Western crime control models to the Global South before their import back to the West.[53] The prison is thus an important site for understanding the operation of colonial power in the past and the present.

Colonialism moved not only ideas and techniques from, between and within colonial powers and their colonies, but also people. The emergent discipline of mobilities studies has challenged scholars' tendency to imagine prisons as fixed islands within a carceral archipelago and the resultant neglect of movement to, from and within it. As Moran explains, 'recent scholarship of the contemporary spaces of incarceration and carceral practice offers a perspective on, and empirical examples of, forced, coerced, punitive, disciplined or governmental mobility', with the result that 'authors are increasingly considering the nature of mobilities *within*, *to* and *from*, *between* and *beyond* these islands.'[54] In so doing, they challenge the traditional conception of mobility as an instrument of freedom, rather than coercion.[55] For Peters and Turner, global politics shapes 'regimes of movement which incarcerate'.[56] But thus far, the role of law – especially international law – in this process has been under-examined. One way, of course, that prisoners become internationally mobile is through extradition of those sought for criminal prosecution.

47 Kerry Carrington, Russell Hogg and Máximo Sozzo, "Southern Criminology," *British Journal of Criminology* 56, no. 1 (2016): 12.

48 Upendra Baxi, "The Colonialist Heritage," in *Comparative Legal Studies: Traditions and Transitions*, eds. Pierre Legrand and Roderick Munday (Cambridge: Cambridge University Press, 2003), 60–61.

49 Humphreys, *Theatre of the Rule of Law*, 117.

50 Eslava and Pahuja, "Beyond the (Post)Colonial," 198.

51 Khalili, *Time in the Shadows*, 8–9.

52 Seraphim, "Carceral Geographies of Japan's Vanishing Empire," 134.

53 Biko Agozino, *Counter-Colonial Criminology: A Critique of Imperialist Reason* (London: Pluto Press, 2003).

54 Dominique Moran, *Carceral Geography: Spaces and Practices of Incarceration* (Farnham: Ashgate, 2015), 71 and 75 (emphasis in original).

55 Ibid., 72–73.

56 Kimberley Peters and Jennifer Turner, "Carceral Mobilities: A Manifesto for Mobilities, an Agenda for Carceral Studies," in *Carceral Mobilities: Interrogating Movement in Incarceration*, eds. Jennifer Turner and Kimberley Peters (Abingdon: Routledge, 2017), 10.

After all, one of international criminal law's foundational principles is *aut dedere, aut judicare* (either extradite or prosecute). Similarly, as shown earlier, international criminal law effects the movement of prisoners from international tribunals to domestic prisons, whilst at the bilateral state level, treaties such as the Council of Europe Convention on the Transfer of Sentenced Persons 1983 facilitate the transfer of those in custody to serve sentences elsewhere. This movement, whilst hardly unrestrained, does not necessarily involve the absence of agency of those moved – detainees, for example, may request transfers after sentencing in order to return to their home state.

A more illicit example, however, would be the practice of extraordinary rendition by the US during the 'war on terror', moving detainees between an archipelago of black sites for the purposes of circumventing domestic and international law. Yet, this practice was not an invention of the war on terror. Like other carceral techniques, extraordinary rendition has its origins in the 1980s 'war on drugs' and was used by the US throughout the 1990s.[57] Similarly, 'managed migration' policies facilitate detainee movement. For example, under the UK 'Returns and Reintegration Fund' designed to support a policy of migrant deportation, the UK government has agreements with those of Nigeria and Jamaica for mandatory prisoner transfers and funding of prison-building programmes within Nigeria and Jamaica.[58]

These movements may invoke the colonial past. India's recent adoption of crimmigration policies, for example, relies in part on legislation originating from British colonial rule which sought to regulate the movement of colonised subjects across the empire.[59] Furthermore, whilst there are important discontinuities, it is difficult to think about present-day carceral mobility without also wondering about the history of transportation of prisoners through both slavery and penal colonies. Conviction transportation was a feature of empire – 'a coherent if locally divergent penal and labor regime underpinned by the dynamics of imperial space across a variety of global contexts'.[60] It was a form of punishment which operated multi-directionally – to, from and within numbers of states across the world, albeit with significant local differences. The routes taken by such convicts were interwoven with other movements of forced labour, including African slavery. Indeed, '[t]he existence of such 'scales' of incarceration, migration, and unfree labor were a recurrent feature of transportation across imperial geographies well into the twentieth century'.[61]

In Latin America in the 1820s, elite 'political prisoners travelled from the colonies to the metropole' to be detained in mainland Spain.[62] Almost 200 years later, there is perhaps some irony in the SCSL sending Charles Taylor, for his interventions from Liberia in Sierra Leone's civil war, to serve his sentence in the UK – Sierra Leone's former colonial power. In the penal colony, *distance* was the punishment (though economic, labour and political concerns also dictated the locations of prisoner transportation).[63] By way of comparison, one reason for Charles

57 Bruce D'Arcus, "Extraordinary Rendition, Law and the Spatial Architecture of Rights," *ACME: An International E-Journal for Critical Geographies* 13, no. 1 (2014): 80–81, 89–92.

58 Mary Bosworth, "Penal Humanitarianism? Sovereign Power in an Era of Mass Migration," *New Criminal Law Review: An International and Interdisciplinary Journal* 20, no. 1 (2017): 39.

59 Ramachandran, "The Contours of Crimmigration Control in India," 8.

60 Clare Anderson, Carrie M. Crockett, Christian G. De Vito, Takashi Miyamoto, Kellie Moss, Katherine Roscoe and Minako Sakata, "Locating Penal Transportation: Punishment, Space, and Place c.1750 to 1900," in *Historical Geographies of Prisons: Unlocking the Usable Carceral Past,* eds. Karen M. Morin and Dominique Moran (Abingdon: Routledge, 2015), 148.

61 Ibid., 147. See also 151 et seq.

62 Ibid., 154.

63 Ibid., 148–49.

Taylor's transfer to the UK was concerns about security if he were detained locally.[64] Other detainees from the SCSL were sent to Rwanda – also thousands of miles from home.[65] Under the system of prisoner transfer established by the Rome Statute, the conditions of imprisonment, whilst governed by domestic law, should be consistent with accepted international legal standards and indeed, 'in no case shall such conditions be more or less favourable than those available to prisoners convicted of similar offences in the State of enforcement'.[66] In theory, therefore, international and national prisoners today are treated equally. In reality, however, the distance from their home state (and prohibitive visa regimes) precludes family visits for international prisoners, in addition to other linguistic and cultural challenges.[67]

Conclusion: abolitionist futures?

I have argued in this chapter that it is possible to conceptualise incarceration 'as consisting of an archipelago of the specific places that constitute geographies of "correction"',[68] which is both contingent and ideological, dependant on movement of ideas, practices and people, underpinned by logics of capitalism, colonialism and international law. To conclude, I want to consider how the legal geography on which I have drawn might assist a project of critical international law. For Mahmud, geography and international law can both trace their origins to colonialism. As TWAIL scholars have shown international law's origins to be inexorably intertwined with empire, so too the early production of geographical knowledge was bound up in exploring, surveying and classifying colonised territory.[69] By the same token, however, critical legal geographies offer the potential for renewed critique of international law. For the critical international lawyer, this forces the consideration of three things.

First, this preliminary sketch of the carceral geography of international law has highlighted the connections between different spheres of international law that fragmentation serves to conceal. Peters has argued that fragmentation and the resultant diversification of international law is an opportunity for 'refinement' which 'allows accepting and reassessing diversity, conflict, and even contradiction as a positive condition which manifests and facilitates the realisation of the values of critique and contestation within international law'.[70] Yet, as Heathcote has shown, international legal scholars' embrace of this plurality is premised on its narrow construction and 'initiates a turn to functionalism that asserts that this is how the system works rather than sufficiently exploring the privileges and biases the functioning of the global order further perpetuates'.[71] In the context of incarceration, it is only by cutting through fragmented fields of international law that the full cartography of this phenomenon, and the hegemonies at work to

64 Charles Chernor Jalloh, "The Law and Politics of the Charles Taylor Case," *Denver Journal of International Law and Policy* 43, no. 3 (2015): 235.

65 Meg Penrose, "Creating an International Prison," *Houston Journal of International Law* 38, no. 2 (2016): 445 et seq.

66 Article 106, Rome Statute 1998.

67 Mulgrew, "On the Enforcement of Sentences," 385.

68 Delaney, "Beyond the Word," 72.

69 Tayyab Mahmud, "Geography and International Law: Towards a Postcolonial Mapping," *Santa Clara Journal of International Law* 5 (2007): 529.

70 Anne Peters, "The Refinement of International Law: From Fragmentation to Regime Interaction and Politicisation," *International Journal of Constitutional Law* 15 (2017): 704.

71 Gina Heathcote, *Feminist Dialogues on International Law: Success, Tensions, Futures* (Oxford: Oxford University Press, 2019), 80.

support it, become visible. In the words of Eslava and Pahuja, 'what might look like "fragmentation" from above looks a lot more like proliferation from below'.[72]

In addition to operating horizontally across sub-fields of international law, considering spaces of incarceration also collapses the vertical distinction between jurisdictions – the international, transnational and domestic. Since domestic law and practice actualise international law, law and legal practices cannot be so compartmentalised.[73] Analysing spaces of incarceration demonstrates the intersection between international and domestic criminal law since the prison is the combined site where these two fields merge. Frankland prison in the UK, for example, is prima facie a prison operating within the domestic jurisdiction. But, thanks to the presence of Charles Taylor, it is also a space in which international criminal justice manifests itself.

Second, considering spaces of incarceration also highlights paradoxes within critical international law. One such paradox might be the idea that the punishment of imprisonment can be a response to criminalised conduct which itself may be related to practices of incarceration. Indeed, critical international criminal lawyers have themselves been implicated in this in their efforts to turn the tables of international criminal law onto those who create violent spaces of incarceration. Such efforts appear seductive. Yet, one wonders whether an intellectual project committed to overturning existing hegemonies should be seeking to remedy one place of incarceration (occupied by victims) with another (to be occupied by perpetrators). This is particularly so given that the two often exist in parasitic form in the global political economy, as we have seen. The pleas to the prosecutor of the ICC to investigate EU policy in respect of migrants repatriated and then detained in Libya, or the architects of migrant detention on Manus Island, thus seem almost as ironic as the detention of Japanese war criminals after World War II in the same camps as the prisoners of war for whose mistreatment they were to stand trial.[74] I am not, of course, questioning the motives of those pursuing such cases, nor suggesting moral or legal equivalence between those occupying spaces of incarceration. Rather, I question whether there might be a logical flaw in imagining that a problem of (unlawful) incarceration may be remedied by a solution of (lawful) incarceration.

A similar paradox is revealed by examining international criminal law's recent prioritisation of prosecuting conflict-related sexual violence. If, historically, this sexual violence was the blind spot of international law, after its widespread use during the wars in Rwanda and the former Yugoslavia it became an international political and legal priority, with punitive criminalisation becoming the 'preferred vehicle for' ending impunity for sexual violence.[75] Yet, one major concern of abolitionists has been that spaces of incarceration are themselves inherently violent and this often manifests in the form of sexual violence. Davis, for example, has documented how punishment within the prison system is effected through, amongst other things, '[t]he violent sexualization of prison life'.[76] Again, this reveals a paradox: how does a feminist politics committed to ending conflict-related sexual violence come to rely on a practice of incarceration which itself suffers from the disease that it seeks to cure? Or, to (mis)quote Audre Lorde, how could the master's tools ever destroy the master's house?

72 Eslava and Pahuja, "Beyond the (Post)Colonial," 201.

73 Ibid.

74 Seraphim, "Carceral Geographies of Japan's Vanishing Empire," 132–33.

75 Janet Halley, "Rape at Rome: Feminist Interventions in the Criminalization of Sex-Related Violence in Positive International Criminal Law," *Michigan Journal of International Law* 30 (2008): 5.

76 Davis, *Are Prisons Obsolete?* 79 and Ch 4 generally.

Third, critical international criminal law is today a flourishing field, seeking to understand how international criminal justice both reflects and reinforces existing hegemonies whilst at the same time deflecting attention from how these structural power dynamics generate conditions which give rise to mass criminality. Yet, thus far, critical international criminal lawyers have largely neglected the decades of critical criminology which has already interrogated such hegemonies within the domestic context. In the US, abolitionism is a project with a long history concerned to understand spaces of incarceration as sites of discriminatory and violent legal power and is a project connected, in particular, to black feminist activism and scholarship. This activism, operating in conjunction with the prisoners' rights movement, grew in the US in the 1970s in respect of incarcerated women,

> spearheaded by radical women of colour and anti-racist white women, many of them lesbian-identified. They cultivated a distinctive left anti-violence politics that was defined by a critique of state violence; an understanding of race, gender, class, and sexuality as mutually constructed systems of power and meaning; and a practice of coalition-based organising.[77]

The aim – for abolitionists such as Gilmore and Davis – is not to deny the harms done to victims of crime by (many of) those in prison; rather abolitionism is a broader social justice project concerned with addressing the conditions which allow crime to happen.[78]

For Eslava, one effect of ignoring the operation of international law at the local level is that resistance becomes dispersed.[79] Connecting up the domestic and the international and moving across disparate legal fields by examining questions of space and place is, then, one way in which resistance can be re-connected.[80] For critical international criminal lawyers, much may therefore be learnt from scholarly consideration of more established domestic projects of resistance. In particular, black and transnational feminist abolitionism is likely to be particularly fruitful ground because, as Sudbury argues, it 'assist[s] us in unpacking the global prison by drawing our attention to the ways in which punishment regimes are shaped by global capitalism, dominant and subordinate patriarchies, and neo-colonial racialised ideologies'.[81]

77 Emily L. Thuma, *All Our Trials: Prisons, Policing, and the Feminist Fight to End Violence* (Urbana: University of Illinois Press, 2019), 2.

78 Angela Y. Davis, *Abolition Democracy: Beyond Prison, Torture and Empire* (New York: Seven Stories Press, 2005), 96.

79 Luis Eslava, "Istanbul Vignettes: Observing the Everyday Operation of International Law," *London Review of International Law* 2, no. 1 (2014): 37–43.

80 Eslava and Pahuja, "Beyond the (Post)Colonial," 221.

81 Julia Sudbury, "Introduction: Feminist Critiques, Transnational Landscapes, Abolitionist Visions," in *Global Lockdown: Race, Gender, and the Prison-Industrial Complex*, ed. Julia Sudbury (Abingdon: Routledge, 2005), xiii.

28

Law and sacrifice in Australian extra-territorial nation spaces

The residue of empire

Lee Godden

Introduction

Over a century on, the Australian nation (or at least some vociferous media commentators) still rhetorically situates its mythical origins in a distant land, and paradoxically, in a setting of violent death and sacrifice. That imagined nation space, Gallipoli, is not simply Australia's legitimation of its nationhood through the ANZAC legend,[1] which is symbolically linked to the colonial spaces of the British Empire. The legend is at once an affirmation of an earlier empire and its disavowal in a global era.[2] The 'Great War' catapulted Australian volunteer soldiers to fight and die on distant beaches at the command of empire – in what would become Turkey – a nation also forged in the First World War conflict. That territory was later to arise as a national phoenix from the ashes of the Ottoman Empire.

This chapter explores how nation, law and territory may be mediated by the intercession of bodily sacrifice, and how in the recording and aesthetic commemoration of death, the body becomes part of a national archival performance. Ultimately, the chapter focuses on efforts by the Australian government to resituate the founding myth of national sacrifice from Gallipoli to the Western Front in Europe – and more specifically to the Villers-Bretonneux region in France. In this, an extra-territorial nation space, putatively Australian, is realised within French sovereign territory. As the chapter shows, the projected extension of the Australian nation into the sovereign territory of a European nation is legitimated by reference to the constructs of sacred space and bodily sacrifice, and given material presence by the mass graves of Australian soldiers. Before discussing that extra-territorial nation space, however, the chapter first necessarily digresses into a truncated, and admittedly simplified, explanation of Australian colonial 'history' and nation founding in the context of European conflicts.

1 Australian and New Zealand Army Corps (ANZAC).

2 Andrew Mycock, Shanti Sumartojo and Ben Wellings, "The Centenary to End All Centenaries: The Great War, Nation and Commemoration," in *Memory and Great War Commemoration: Mobilizing the Past in Europe, Australia and New Zealand*, eds. Shanti Sumartojo and Ben Wellings (Bern: Peter Lang AG, 2014), 3, 7.

The Great War

The First World War was fought by many people drawn from newly-made countries and incipient nations across the world aligned with long-established empires. Germany, a relatively-recently unified nation in itself, was a main protagonist, pursuing its vision of a colonial empire and its expansion within Europe.[3] While this narrative of the origins and causes of the First World War is reductionist, it is also axiomatic that conflict in Europe over centuries was territorial in character, shaping and realigning boundaries, sovereign possessions and conceptions of law and property; either on that continent or as disputes over colonial possessions.[4] English jurisprudence regarding relationships between nations, in the period leading to the First World War, was under the sway of Austin's position on international law.[5] Yet it, too, gave expression to the bonding of nation, sovereignty and territory in a more pragmatic but no less authoritative manner. Austin's views may be more nuanced than is suggested by the conception of law as the command of the sovereign,[6] but this position may have supported well the expansion of a colonial empire. A view of international law as having only normative force[7] may have effectively aligned legal thought to the pragmatic and bureaucratic colonial administration that expanded out from the metropole, steered by the British Colonial Office.[8]

Given the intense rivalries between the European powers in the period prior to the First World War, the Eurocentric parameters of international law created a facilitative framework for European nations to subsume places and cultures within an imperial space,[9] establishing control over vast colonial empires. For the British Empire in the Great War, such constitutive networks manifested in its ability to marshal colonial populations from across the globe to the defence of empire as a concomitant of its powers to connect people and places.

Narratives of law and Australian national origins

Narratives of networks and connections have infiltrated the stories that modern law now tells of its ontology and its methodology. The space-time between points of legal connection and jurisdiction, however, can still be elided by the technical proclivities of positivist law. These proclivities can subtend the materiality of the encounter that brings peoples into a relationship with one another, and into conflict. For Australia, the counter narrative to empire, colonial law and its productive interconnections, is the subtended violence that lurks in the interstices of nation-state sovereignty, nationalism and property law. The violence of the colonial encounter between

3 See discussion in Benjamin Madley, "From Africa to Auschwitz: How German South West Africa Incubated Ideas and Methods Adopted and Developed by the Nazis in Eastern Europe," *European History Quarterly* 35, no. 3 (2005): 432–33.

4 Ibid., 429–32.

5 Michael Lobban, "English Approaches to International Law in the Nineteenth Century," in *Time, History and International Law*, eds. Matthew Craven, Malgosia Fitzmaurice and Maria Vogiatzi (Leiden: Martinus Nijhoff Publishers, 2007), 82.

6 Lobban, "English Approaches," 65.

7 Ibid., 66.

8 See generally, Catherine Hall, "Introduction: Thinking the Postcolonial, Thinking the Empire," in *Cultures of Empire: Colonizers in Britain and the Empire in the Nineteenth and Twentieth Centuries*, ed. Catherine Hall (London: Routledge, 2000), 1–33.

9 Matthew Craven, "Introduction: International Law and Its Histories," in *Time, History and International Law*, eds. Matthew Craven, Malgosia Fitzmaurice and Maria Vogiatzi (Leiden: Martinus Nijhoff Publishers, 2007), 2.

Indigenous peoples and the colonial sovereign in Australia is increasingly foregrounded, but contested in the euphemistically termed history wars.[10]

By contrast to the ANZAC legend, the origin story of the Australian nation, in law, is reimagined in the case of *Mabo No 2*[11] as arising from the High Court's displacement of terra nullius as a legal category at international law. The designation, the Court finds, was applied erroneously to the Australian colonies as the Aboriginal inhabitants were thought to have no law.[12] The leading judgment of Justice Brennan appeals to natural law and justice, in order to accord due humanity to Aboriginal peoples and Torres Strait Islanders, and then in a further appeal to contemporary Australian social values, terra nullius is revealed in *Mabo No 2* as a device of empire that must be expunged from the legal narrative in order to uncover the existence of Aboriginal and Torres Strait Islander societies, prior to the assertion of British sovereignty – and 200 years later to recognise their 'property rights'.[13] It is a narrative that keeps intact, yet reworks, the property-territory-nation synthesis. As while terra nullius is displaced, the Court retains the common law designation of a settled colony that received its property law from Britain. Those colonies later federated to form the Australian Commonwealth. The majority judgments in *Mabo No 2*, in their insistence on the primacy of the doctrine of tenure as the pivotal link of settled law between empire and colony, rethread sovereignty, property law and the nation-state. The *Mabo No 2* narrative thus only partially addresses the implicit rationale of the late-nineteenth century use of terra nullius by the Privy Council,[14] as a legitimation of colonial expropriation in Australia, New Zealand and Canada,[15] that was integral to the stability of the British imperial network of connections, its world market and ultimately its power to 'command' an imperial force in the Great War.

The two narratives at play – one of a nation formed in blood and sacrifice in the Great War, and the second that envisages the acquisition of colonial possession from a doctrinal perspective that skirts the identification of blood with law and nation – circle each other in the legal and cultural imaginary of the Australian polity. These narratives inform the contemporary constructs of sovereignty, bodily sacrifice and property that coalesce to realise an Australian extra-territorial nation space, which in turn realigns the connection between the narratives. Intersecting themes in contemporary law and humanities research, on law, violence and the archive,[16] and on the materiality and affective dimensions of place,[17] provide both method and context to examine that realisation of a nation space. The affective dimension resonates across an aesthetic appreciation of the ceremonies of memorialisation, which intersect the bureaucratic practices of registration of the places where Australian bodies from the Great War are interred in French soil. Such bodies, in effect, become a material and symbolic archive of national sacrifice.

10 See Ann Curthoys, Ann Genovese and Alexander Reilly, "Mabo and history," in *Rights and Redemption: History, Law and Indigenous People*, eds. Ann Curthoys, Ann Genovese and Alexander Reilly (Coogee: University of New South Wales Press Ltd, 2008), 37–47.

11 *Mabo v Queensland (No 2)* (1992) 175 CLR 1.

12 Ibid. Brennan J. at paras 34, 35, 36, 40, 41.

13 Ibid. Brennan J. at paras 36–42.

14 'Terra nullius' as justification for colonial appropriation was widespread in British colonies.

15 *Cooper v Stuart* (1889) 14 App Cas 286; *Wi Parata v Bishop of Wellington* (1877) 3 NZ Jur (NS) SC 72; St *Catharine's Milling and Lumber Company v The Queen* [1888] UKPC 70, 14 App Cas 46.

16 Stuart Motha and Honni van Rijswijk, "Introduction: A Counter-Archival Sense," in *Law, Memory, Violence: Uncovering the Counter-Archive*, eds. Stuart Motha and Honni van Rijswijk (Abingdon: Routledge, 2016), 11.

17 Sarah Keenan, *Subversive Property: Law and the Production of Spaces of Belonging* (Abingdon: Routledge, 2015), 39–41.

Law, body and affect

'Affect' bridges law and humanities scholarship by exploring aesthetic and experiential forms constituting 'materiality'. Aesthetics and law are no strangers. The visual turn has enlivened a preoccupation with image, expanding the attention from literature and fine arts, to now include photographs, installations[18] and the performative.[19] The concern with materialism is directing attention to movement, entanglement and affect, and how such a confluence expands the horizons of law. Germane here is a concern with how landscapes are experienced aesthetically and emotionally,[20] and how embodiment gives us the tacit knowledge of our surrounds.[21]

Such themes merge with long-standing feminist scholarship that has troubled the aesthetic of the body, seeking to disrupt conventional dualisms of subject and object, and to break open the gaze that looks on women's bodies as a spectacle. Feminist scholarship brings together the aesthetic, the body, and law's archive, through analyses of crime and evidence, for example, via the deconstruction of a forensic aesthetic.[22] Indeed, the affective dimension in its reimagination of materiality and body may have undone the reliance on the subject, rationality and human agency as the predominant explanatory mode in law.[23] If so, then affect gives a means to explore bodily sacrifice in violent conflict that moves beyond a merely representational method.

The attention to method in law typically references transdisciplinary humanities scholarship in geography, social sciences and history[24] (law, apparently, only belatedly having re-discovered that it has a 'method'). All disciplines, methodologically, may be understood as archival, as archaeologies of knowledge. Law's grasp on the archival is not confined to a cataloguing and classification exercise, nor a neutral archaeology of knowledge. Law's knowledge practices, in its intersection with imperial bureaucracies, has had devastating consequences for those colonised peoples whose history and existence have been reduced to such categories.[25] Law methodologically is instituted as archival but simultaneously inaugurated by the archival in a manner that necessarily disavows that foundation.[26]

Law and the archive

Law as archive then is a double movement, first of inauguration reliant upon institutional sources, recording and instantiation – such as the Act of the United Kingdom Parliament in 1901 that formally brought into existence the Australian nation. This teleological stance must co-exist with an ontological position of law as always in existence – not tied to any archival moment – as expressed in the natural law underpinnings of the Brennan judgment in *Mabo No 2*. The continuity of colonial possession and a contemporary national presence are made

18 Rebecca Scott Bray, "Rotten Prettiness? The Forensic Aesthetic and Crime as Art," *Australian Feminist Law Journal* 40, no. 1 (2014): 74.

19 Alison Young, *Judging the Image* (London: Routledge, 2005).

20 Alice Palmer, "Legal Dimensions to Valuing Aesthetics in World Heritage Decisions," *Social and Legal Studies* 26, no. 5 (2017): 583.

21 Ibid., 584.

22 Bray, "Rotten Prettiness," 91.

23 Greta Olson, "The Turn to Passion: Has Law and Literature Become Law and Affect?" *Law and Literature* 28, no. 3 (2016): 350.

24 See for example, discussion of critical geography and space in Keenan, *Subversive Property*, 55–59.

25 Linda Tuwahai Smith, *Decolonizing Methodologies: Research and Indigenous Peoples*, 2nd ed. (London: Zed Books, 2013), 92.

26 Motha and van Rijswick,"A Counter-Archival Sense," 11.

seamless in that moment. The power of law in its apparent completeness acts to constitute the past,[27] while presenting the instigation of law as a mere 'technology' of authority. Yet reliance upon express positivist origins in a United Kingdom Parliament and English Head of State leaves an ethical gap between law and the national polity. Without such bridging, as offered in the *Uluru Statement from the Heart*, the narratives of the coming of the Australian nation still 'circle' each other. That circling weaves through the institution of national archives, memorialisation and the political power to narrate the sacrifice that founds Australia. Indeed, '[t]here is no political power without control of the archive, if not of memory'.[28]

The function of the 'bodily' archive in constituting the public memory of a people and nation illuminates why the two narratives pivotal to Australian national consciousness are so divisive. In one instance, the commemoration of bodily sacrifice is aligned to nation status, and in another, nation status requires obscuring the memorialisation of the violent death of colonial encounter. A counter archival stance, to 'interrogate the teleological narratives of progress that law constitutes after violent events',[29] gives a point of potential resistance to the archival power of the Australian state that constitutes and continually recreates the ANZAC legend. More recently, the ANZAC mythology has been called in aid of efforts to augment the memorialisation of the First World War in the Australian national consciousness, but simultaneously to shift the actual 'place' where the inaugural sacrifice occurred.

Situating the ANZAC legend in France

2018 marked the 100th anniversary of major First World War battles in the Somme Valley in France – the region around Villiers-Bretonneux. A century earlier, 10% of the citizens of the new Australian nation had volunteered to fight in the Great War. There was a staggering loss of life for those volunteers in the war. The commemoration of that death and injury has been projected into the territory around ANZAC Cove in Gallipoli. The cove and beach mark a landing of Australian and New Zealand troops (in the wrong location due to an imperial military debacle), that left them intensely vulnerable to the Turkish soldiers positioned above on the headland. In the aftermath of the devastating loss of life, there was a growing insistence that ANZAC troops were no longer to be commanded by the imperial sovereign, but to be independently commanded by Australia and New Zealand. These small steps to independent nationhood are typically overlooked in national rhetoric of heroism, courage in diversity and glorious sacrifice that commemorates the ANZAC landing.

While the deaths and injury in Gallipoli were horrendous, the losses on the Western Front in Europe were even more extreme. The French countryside is still punctuated by Commonwealth war cemeteries. Many Australian bodies, or bits of them, remain in the wartime cemeteries that form a distinctive aesthetic of memorial places marked by row upon row of white headstones. These places, excised from the surrounding bucolic villages, are meticulously maintained by local mowing and gardening contractors, producing a sense of order and beauty that seems to neutralise the violent conflict that precipitated their existence in French territory. Despite the poppies, the roses and the garden ambience, the headstones are a tangible register that make material in the French village landscape the sacrificial deaths of a 'soldier of the Great

27 Curthoys, Genovese and Reilly, "Mabo and History," 38–40.

28 Kathleen Birrell, "An Essential Ghost: Indigeneity Within the Legal Archive," *Australian Feminist Law Journal* 33, no. 1 (2010): 95.

29 Motha and van Rijswick, "A Counter-Archival Sense," 12.

War' – the inscription that appears on the memorial plaques. Each headstone, even where the bodies were not distinguishable, is recorded in a memorial register located within each respective war cemetery.

The powers of registration collapse space and time, to ensure a continuity of the sacrificial presence of death in bureaucratic war archives. These archival techniques of the state assimilate to the powers of accounting and recording that were integral to the British colonial cultures of the nineteenth century,[30] to mobilisation of troops marshalled by the empire in the Great War, and more recently, to expanding the Australian presence in French territory. The connection of place with time as networks of 'recordings' challenges a temporal progression of change or continuity, to allow a bureaucratic manipulation of the archive whereby the pervading trauma of war consolidates but disrupts the collective memory of that violence.[31]

Recreating an extra-territorial nation place

Bureaucratic efforts to coalesce space, time and territory through the practices of commemoration and recording of national sacrifice have been utilised politically by Australian governments over many decades. Most recently, these practices have focused on efforts to resituate the collective memory of Australian sacrifice through the construction of the Sir John Monash Centre as a memorial to the Australian forces near Villers-Bretonneux.[32] The emergence of Villers-Bretonneux as a locus for Australia's extra-territorial memorialisation of the Great War can be attributed, ironically enough, to late twentieth-century diplomatic conflicts between Australia and Turkey over ANZAC Cove.[33] Gallipoli is a National Park in Turkish territory. Gallipoli is also strongly associated with Turkey's national symbolism, founded on Ataturk's leadership in the war and in building the modern Turkish nation.

Tensions flared when Australia sought to 'claim' Gallipoli as a site sacred to its nationhood. In 2003 the then Australian Prime Minister John Howard proposed to include Gallipoli as a National Heritage place under Australian law. The move was part of Howard's strategy from 1996 onward to precipitate a return to the conservative 'mainstream' by engaging in a politics of reassurance. Central to reassuring mainstream Australia was to re-establish war commemoration as pivotal to Australian nationalism. By this rhetorical reference to an imperial past, he sought to confound debate on 'identity, history and Australia's place in the world'.[34] This strategy targeted the circling narratives of Australia's national origins in contemporary Australian society. Howard sought to neutralise more robust recognition for Australia's Indigenous peoples, by aligning the reconciliation movement with 'practical' outcomes and service provision. Legislatively, the Howard government reversed several legal reforms consequent upon the *Mabo No 2* judgment,

30 Lauren Benton, *Law and Colonial Cultures: Legal Regimes in World History*, 1400–1900 (Cambridge: Cambridge University Press, 2001), 4–6.

31 Patricia Lorcin, "War and Its Spaces: Introduction," in *France and Its Spaces of War: Experience, Memory, Image*, eds. Patricia Lorcin and Daniel Brewer (Basingstoke: Palgrave Macmillan, 2009), 2.

32 The Commonwealth of Australia, *Australian Remembrance Trail Along the Western Front: A Traveller's Guide* (Canberra: Department of Veterans Affairs, April 2018), 22–25.

33 Romain Fathi, "'A Piece of Australia in France': Australian Authorities and the Commemoration of Anzac Day at Villers-Bretonneux in the Last Decade," in *Nation, Memory and Great War Commemoration: Mobilizing the Past in Europe, Australia and New Zealand*, eds. Shanti Sumartojo and Ben Wellings (Bern: Peter Lang AG, 2014), 286.

34 Ben Wellings, "Lest You Forget: Memory and Australian Nationalism in a Global Era," in *Nation, Memory and Great War Commemoration: Mobilizing the Past in Europe, Australia and New Zealand*, eds. Shanti Sumartojo and Ben Wellings (Bern: Peter Lang AG, 2014), 53.

as instituted under the *Native Title Act* 1993. Such measures included delivering 'bucket loads of extinguishment' for native title.

By contrast, the ANZAC legend was reinvigorated as central to the 'politics of reassurance'. The Howard era coincided with heightened, external deployment of Australian troops, including in United Nations' international peace-keeping efforts. The deployment resonated with growing attention to the sacrifices of the dead, who almost a century before had ventured beyond Australian shores to defend the empire. 'The mute force of their sacrifice' neutralised opposition to a nationalism grounded in a renewed fervour for ANZAC commemoration.[35]

To strengthen the popular appeal of war commemoration, the listing of Gallipoli was proposed under the Environment Protection and Biodiversity Conservation Act 1999 (Cth). This omnibus environmental legislation amalgamated several distinct earlier statutes, including the Australian Heritage Commission Act 1974. That act contained the national heritage register, an archive recording places and objects that were deemed of national heritage character, which was carried forward into the 1999 statute. The register embodied many classic features of heritage legislation of that era with references to expert committees to identify and assess the value of national places.

The potential heritage listing for Gallipoli, as exhibiting Australian national heritage value, was strongly contested by Turkey as an usurpation of its sovereignty.[36] There was a subsequent retreat by the Howard government. Currently, Gallipoli's ANZAC Cove appears, not on the register of national heritage places under the Environment Protection and Biodiversity Conservation Act, but on a 'List of Overseas Places of Historic Significance to Australia'. That secondary list, which is not a formal archive of nation, records sites outside Australian territory, in order that 'Australia can recognise and celebrate those overseas places of greatest importance to the development of our nation in a way that is respectful of the rights and sovereignty of other nations'.[37]

Having been required to duly acknowledge Turkish national sovereignty over Gallipoli, the Australian government turned its international diplomatic efforts to creating an extra-territorial commemorative space around Villers-Bretonneux.[38] This translation through ritual and ceremonial practices was theoretically anticipated by Lefebvre's analysis of abstract and sacred space.[39] The ritual practices still reference a sacrificial ANZAC narrative, but one abstracted from its material, geographic setting to form a contemporary national archival place in Europe.

The spatial redirection of the ANZAC myth, grounded by Villers-Bretonneux, intensified with the dedication of the adjacent Sir John Monash Centre and National Memorial in 2018. The curation of the installations that form the exhibition centrepiece of the Monash centre seeks to recreate aesthetically the horror and trauma of the lived experience of the war on the Western Front. The immersive aesthetic, complete with smoke, excruciatingly loud noise and graphic depictions of death, is designed to capture affective responses to a reimagined environment of Villers-Bretonneux, some 100 years before.[40] This affective experience of war contrasts with more conventional commemorative aesthetics in the architecture of the national memorial,

35 Ibid., 53.

36 Mycock, Sumartojo and Wellings, "Centenaries," 5.

37 Australian Government Environment Department, "Register of Overseas Historic Places," accessed August 12, 2019, www.environment.gov.au/heritage/places/national-heritage-list.

38 Wellings, "Lest You Forget," 57–58.

39 Chris Butler, *Henri Lefebvre: Spatial Politics, Everyday Life and the Right to the City* (New York: Routledge, 2012).

40 Australian Government, Department of Veterans' Affairs, "Sir John Monash Centre," accessed May 5, 2020, www.dva.gov.au/recognition/events-and-reminders-all-who-served/office-australian-war-graves/visitor-trails-and-4.

with its attention to the listing of the dead through representational names carved in stone. The National Memorial, through this archival aesthetic, links to registers of graves in the serene aesthetic of the war cemeteries in the picturesque French countryside. All these material expressions of Australian grieving act as spatial referents for legal, cultural, commemorative and political relationships that materially and discursively constitute an Australian sacred place in French national territory.[41] The sacrifice of Australian bodies in the Great War inaugurates a jurisdiction for the Australian state over the bodies, and the surrounding memorial archives. Pertinently, such rituals accomplish a move from absolute space, which 'unifies the living members of a community, but it also binds them to the dead'.[42]

International law, and a sense of international exchange, contribute to recreating the ANZAC 'sacrifice' in and around Villers-Bretonneux. The realisation of an extra-territorial commemorative place is enabled by a singular treaty arrangement.[43] The treaty is between France and successor nations to the British Empire that now form Commonwealth countries (the UK and former colonies, such as Australia and New Zealand). The treaty marks a reciprocal 'gift' to these nations, whose soldiers lie in carefully registered graves, row after row, in the land on which the Commonwealth war cemeteries are situated. The relevant treaty article states: 'The French government grants to the [Commonwealth War Graves] Commission, without payment and without time-limit, the free use of the land in French territory.' International law governing relations between these treaty nations appears to countenance disruption to the triad of nation, territory and sovereignty, to perpetuate the material occupation of this ritual space by bodies sacrificed to the national cause. On this foundational 'gift', the contemporary Australian government reaffirms the ANZAC legend in an extra-territorial sense, loosening its moorings from Turkish territory.

Simultaneously, the materiality of practices associated with the memorialisation of the bodies creates 'gifted' national heritage sites as a form of quasi-public, sacred property. Australian citizens are entreated to visit these sites by the Australian government as a type of national pilgrimage – complete with tourist guides to the surrounding villages and vineyards.[44] ANZAC day is now celebrated in the town of Villiers-Bretonneux, displacing an earlier commemorative holiday that marked the end of the war in this region of France. Yet these sites, at once intensely localised as holding and representing 'archived bodies', remain subject to the imperatives of sovereignty that were instrumental to conflicts that precipitated the Great War. The treaty article continues: 'this land shall remain the property of the French State.' The imprimatur of nation-state property ultimately is transcendent over sacrificial bodies and the Australian commemorative rituals re-grounding national origins in the French countryside of the Somme Valley.

The treaty, however, in its facilitation of a ritual memorialisation of Commonwealth places within French territory, now performs another function – the reiteration of a transnational alliance between France and its allies, including Australia. This is a current-day diplomatic practice that archives sacrifice and commits to memorials, which seeks to 'materialize and

41 Keenan, *Subversive Property,* 41.

42 Butler, *Henri Lefebvre*, 49.

43 Treaty series N°39 (1953) Agreement between the Governments of the United Kingdom of Great Britain and Northern Ireland, Canada, Australia, New Zealand, The Union of South Africa, India and Pakistan of the one part and the Government of the French Republic of the other part regarding British Commonwealth War Graves in French Territory.

44 Matthew Graves, "Memorial Diplomacy in Franco-Australian Relations," in *Nation, Memory and Great War Commemoration: Mobilizing the Past in Europe, Australia and New Zealand*, eds. Shanti Sumartojo and Ben Wellings (Bern: Peter Lang AG, 2014), 170.

mobilize a shared sense of the past at the intersection of collective memory and transnational history'.[45] National commemorative memory perpetuated by the Australian executive government in Villers-Bretonneux thus fulfils dual goals of supporting nationalism and consolidating European transnational alliances. It subverts a linear relationship to the ANZAC past, and to the certainties of geographic coordinates, to render the past as a present 'truth'. Time and space collapse before the project of nationalism.[46] Thus, the well-ordered cemeteries of the Villers-Bretonneux region, despite limited knowledge of them by the Australian public, will now abstractly 'mark the body and soul of the Australian nation, shaping its post-war identity'.[47]

Successive Australian executive governments, aided by national archival institutions, such as the Australian War memorial, have reshaped the ANZAC narrative to meet the exigencies of contemporary politics. The sacrifices of the Great War on the Western Front are progressively extracted from the materiality of the actual bodies that remain in French soil through an archival transformation that 'symbolizes the duty of the civilian to remember and exemplifies the desire of the state to educate'.[48] And yet, this desire of the state to 'educate' has not expunged the other origin story of the Australian nation from the body politick.

Indigenous Australians now find a place in the Sir John Monash Centre with their contribution to the war effort acknowledged and commemorated in various exhibits. But there are few official memorials to the violent deaths that attended the frontier conflicts of the colonisation of Australia by empire, while Aboriginal bodies still form part of the 'archives' of colonial museum collections.[49] Over time there have been maps and documents produced recording massacres of Aboriginal people as European settlement spread across the country,[50] but few find their way to inclusion in state archives, let alone find a place in the sacred space of the Australian War Memorial. Yet the memories of massacres and violence still run deep in the remembrance of many Aboriginal communities. This deep-seated memory surfaces in contestations over the commemorative practices of the Australian state in its proclamation and maintenance of Australia Day on 26 January each year, and its memorials to the arrival of empire in the Australian continent.[51]

Conclusion

Any moves to more honestly decolonise the national archive and its attendant institutions must contemplate not only that which is recorded and documented, but the gaps between the records that mask the violence latent in the archival moment of the Australian nation-state itself.

45 Graves, "Memorial Diplomacy," 170.

46 Romain Fathi, "A Piece of Australia," 284.

47 Lorcin, "War and Its Spaces," 5.

48 Ibid., 5.

49 Stephen Stockwell, "The Quest to Remove Aboriginal Remains from Museums," *ABC*, November 14, 2018, www.abc.net.au/triplej/programs/hack/the-quest-to-remove-aboriginal-remains-from-museums/10497952. There is an Australian government funding programme for the return of the remains of Aboriginal peoples and Torres Strait Islanders.

50 See, for example, the Colonial Frontier Massacres project at the University of Newcastle that has mapped over 300 sites of mass killings across Australia, "Colonial Frontier Massacres, Australia (Date Range: 1780 to 1930)" Map, accessed May 5, 2020, https://c21ch.newcastle.edu.au/colonialmassacres/map.php.

51 For an overview of protests on Australia day 2020 see, for example, "'Pay the Rent': Invasion Day Rallies Around Australia Protest Against 26 January Celebrations," *The Guardian*, January 26, 2020, www.theguardian.com/australia-news/2020/jan/26/pay-the-rent-invasion-day-rallies-around-australia-protest-against-26-january-celebrations.

In turn, understandings of contemporary practices of ritual, sacrifice and national archival inauguration should extend beyond the textual, to the material, affective and performative practices that attend the bodies that make material the ANZAC legend. In combination, these iterations reinforce a conservative vision of a contemporary, indivisible nation – a narrative that *Mabo No 2* both disrupts and perpetuates. Rather than historicising from the positionality of the executive state as the agent, we need different methodological insights.[52] Attention to uncovering the intersectionality of the spheres of the physical, social and ethical-legal across a space-time continuum opens the possibility of considering the affective dimensions that are inherent to the materialisation of places as sacred spaces.

The resilience of a heroic commemorative nationalism remains evident, however, in the observance of the ceremonies of Australian nationhood now performed in an extra-territorial space. While there is by no means a complete shift of collective memorial focus, from Gallipoli to Villers-Bretonneux, the Australian government has actively pursued the creation of a highly affective, sacred space as an overlay to French territory, following its rebuff by Turkey. It has fostered a naturalisation of national heritage places in the war-time cemeteries of the French countryside, to sustain the rhetorical significance of bodily sacrifice in the Great War, while attenuating the history and materiality of the actual spaces of war. 'In passing from history to nature, myth acts economically: it abolishes the complexity of human acts, it gives them the simplicity of essences.'[53]

52 Olson, "Law and Affect," 822.

53 Julien Fragnon, "Disembodied Memory: The Contemporary Legacy of the Great War Viewed Through the Lens of the Political," in *France and Its Spaces of War: Experience, Memory, Image*, eds. Patricia Lorcin and Daniel Brewer (Basingstoke: Palgrave Macmillan, 2009), 155.

29

Living together after violent conflict

Museum-making as lawful truth-making

Valeria Vázquez Guevara[1]

Introduction

The *Museo de la Memoria y los Derechos Humanos* (Museum of Memory and Human Rights), situated in Santiago, Chile, was inaugurated in January 2010.[2] The uniqueness of Chile's Museo is that, unlike museums of an otherwise similar nature,[3] its conceptualisation is informed by the account of truth established in the reports of Chile's truth commissions (TCs).[4] It was with the 1990 National Commission of Truth and Reconciliation (popularly called the Rettig Commission) and its *Informe de la Comisión Nacional de Verdad y Reconciliación* report of 1991 that international human rights law (IHRL) was formally introduced in Chilean institutional life and discourse after the dictatorship.[5] Importantly, the Rettig

1 A version of this chapter was published as "Crafting the Lawful Truth: Chile's 1990 Truth Commission, International Human Rights and the Museum of Memory," *London Review of International Law* 7, no. 2 (2019). Unless otherwise stated, all translations are my own.

2 Michelle Bachelet, "Discurso de S.E. la Presidente de la República, Michelle Bachelet, en Inauguración del Museo de la Memoria y los Derechos Humanos," accessed January 15, 2020, https://ww3.museodelamemoria.cl/wp-content/uploads/2016/01/discurso-presidenta.pdf.

3 See generally Silke Arnold-de Simine, *Mediating Memory in the Museum: Trauma, Empathy, Nostalgia* (Hampshire: Palgrave Macmillan, 2013).

4 The Chilean state implemented two TCs (1990 *Comisión Nacional de Verdad y Reconciliación* and 2004 *Comisión de Prisión Política y Tortura*) and two *ad hoc* presidential commissions (1996 *Corporación Nacional de Reparación y Reconciliación* and 2011 *Comisión Presidencial Asesora para la Calificación de Detenidos Desaparecidos, Ejecutados Políticos y Víctimas de Prisión Política*). The 1990 TC is considered the one that established the official account of the truth, and the other three commissions are considered to complement and update the account established in 1990–1991. For an historical overview of previous investigatory commissions in Chile see Elizabeth Lira, *Historia, Política y Ética de la Verdad en Chile, 1891–2001: Reflexiones sobre la Paz Social y la Impunidad* (Santiago: LOM Ediciones/Universidad Alberto Hurtado, 2001). See also, Priscilla Hayner, *Unspeakable Truths: Transitional Justice and the Challenge of Truth Commissions* (New York: Routledge, 2010), 47–49, 60–62.

5 Comisión Nacional de Verdad y Reconciliación, *Report of the Chilean National Commission on Truth and Reconciliation*, trans. Phillip Berryman (Notre Dame: University of Notre Dame Press, 1993). For an account of IHRL in the Chilean transition see Naomi Roht-Arriaza and José Zalaquett, "The Need for Moral Reconstruction in the Wake of Past Human Rights Violations: An Interview with José Zalaquett," in *Transitional Justice: Handbook for Latin America*, ed. Félix Reátegui (New York: Brazilian Amnesty Commission, Ministry of Justice/International Center

Commission and its report were especially influential in determining the creation of the Museo and its scope.[6]

In this chapter, I examine the relationship between the 1990 Rettig Commission (hereafter 'the TC') and IHRL, and how this relationship informs the work of the TC in shaping social and institutional relations in Chile after the 1973–1990 dictatorship. The argument running through this chapter is twofold. First, there is a constitutive and creative relationship between the TC and IHRL. That is, IHRL, as a 'global' legal form, *informs* the constitution of the TC as a continuing phenomenon, and IHRL *mediates* the TC's creative potential to determine the truth, while also *grounding* that truth by giving it legal authority. The second aspect of the argument is that the ways in which IHRL informs, mediates and grounds the truth involve subordination of 'local' legal forms to the 'global' legal form of IHRL. This shows how the TC's truth-making is shaped and authorised by IHRL, a 'global' legal form that carries normative socio-political, legal and economic modes of organising social and institutional relations. This 'lawful' truth-making not only silences coexisting accounts of the truth, but it also forecloses the possibility of living together after dictatorship beyond the normative forms and meanings carried by IHRL.

I develop this argument through an analysis of Chile's Museo, based on my visit there in 2018. The Museo is a type of 'memory museum',[7] and as such its 'specific forms of narration and presentation and the display tactics' use memory as the 'framework' and 'paradigm' to 'relate to the past'.[8] The Museo's description of its curatorial practices and its mission denotes its intention to represent a period of the history of Chile – Pinochet's 1973–1990 dictatorship – by articulating it as, and through, memory and human rights.[9] My argument here is that the Museo operates as a continuation of the TC. Considered to be the public place where the truth about Chile's dictatorship is memorialised, the Museo has been designed and built with the intention of preserving and transmitting the truth produced by the TC's 1991 report.[10] This is distinct from other museums built for the purpose of collective memorialisation of past violent events, which tend not to have a direct relationship with a TC or its findings. The Museo, through visual and experiential technologies, mediates and transmits to visitors the official account of

---

for Transitional Justice, 2011). On the role of IHRL in political transitions see Paige Arthur, "How 'Transitions' Reshaped Human Rights: A Conceptual History of Transitional Justice," *Human Rights Quarterly* 31, no. 2 (2009). For a critical account of 'importing' IHRL with neoliberal economics in Latin America see Yves Dezalay and Bryant Garth, *The Internationalization of Palace Wars: Lawyers, Economists, and the Contest to Transform Latin American States* (Chicago: University of Chicago Press, 2002); Naomi Klein, *The Shock Doctrine* (London: Penguin Books, 2008); Jessica Whyte, *The Morals of the Market: Human Rights and the Rise of Neoliberalism* (London and New York: Verso, 2019).

6 Museo de la Memoria y Derechos Humanos, "Visítanos," accessed January 15, 2020, https://ww3.museodelamemoria.cl/visitanos/.

7 On the difference between 'memory museum' and 'memorial museums' see Arnold-de Simine, *Mediating Memory*, 7–13. On the transformation of museums, see generally *The New Museology*, ed. Peter Vergo (London: Reaktion Books, 1989); Tony Bennett, *The Birth of the Museum: History, Theory, Politics* (New York: Routledge, 1995). See also, Jens Andermann and Silke Arnold-de Simine, "Introduction: Memory, Community and the New Museum," *Theory, Culture & Society* 29, no. 1 (2012): 4, 6.

8 Arnold-de Simine, *Mediating Memory*, 10–11.

9 For a cultural critique of practices of memorialisation in Chile see Nelly Richard, *Eruptions of Memory: The Critique of Memory in Chile, 1990–2015*, trans. Julia Sanches (Cambridge: Polity Press, 2019). I am borrowing the insight of 'representation of the past' in order to 'articulate memory' from Andreas Huyssen, *Twilight Memories: Marking Time in a Culture of Amnesia* (London: Routledge, 1995), 2–3.

10 See n 4.

the truth determined almost 30 years ago (in 1990–1991).[11] This connection between the Museo and the TC, I argue, is a metonymic relationship. I understand metonymy here as a figure of speech that is present in different means of communication or artistic expression.[12] A metonymic relationship emerges when one of two elements, which are somewhat associated or related, is used to refer to the other without losing its identity.[13] It is in this association or 'referential function' that metonymy takes place and works to 'facilitate speedy communication' about 'something that is more complex or abstract, or even sensitive', and therefore difficult to express or communicate on its own.[14] The metonymic relationship between the Museo and the TC emerges because the Museo creates an experience that facilitates the transmission of the official account of the truth of the dictatorship (as recorded in the TC Report), whilst simultaneously giving temporal continuity to the work of the TC by actualising it in a material (visual and experiential) form. Because of this metonymic relationship, visiting the Museo might also be experienced as if visiting the TC.

In the account presented in this chapter, I recreate my experience as a visitor of the Museo, paying close attention to the Museo's architectural design and conceptualisation, as well as its museological practices. In Part 1, I begin by recreating my experience encountering IHRL as a visitor of the museum. I then show in Parts 2 and 3 how the Museo gives material form and continuity to the TC, and highlight its constitutive and creative relationship with IHRL. To conclude, I discuss how the Museo manifests, materialises and reasserts not only the fundamental relationship between the TC and IHRL, but also the subordination of 'local' legal forms to the 'global' legal form of IHRL.

Encountering international human rights law at Memory Square

Inside the Museo's precinct, the grounds surrounding the building were conceived as one big space known as the esplanade or Memory Square. When the visitor enters the precinct, she does so through this esplanade. The visitor can access the museum directly from the street through the two main entrances located on Matucana Avenue and Catedral Street, as well as a third side entrance on the less busy Chacabuco Street. Upon entering the precinct the visitor encounters different objects, installations and artworks. Each piece addresses different themes, such as memory, conscience, forced exile, education and activism, or displacement, to name a few. Yet there is one theme that consistently accompanies the visitor, irrespective of her entrance of choice: 'universal human rights'. To give an example: entering through Catedral entrance takes the visitor down the inclined surface of the wide space that the esplanade offers. The esplanade, or Memory Square, is surrounded to the left and right by two small yet long walls, on which the Museo's emerald green building rests. On the right side of the rough and greyish surface of the wall the visitor can see various writings. Getting closer, the visitor sees that these are a reproduction of the Universal Declaration of Human Rights (UDHR) (see Figure 29.1).

11 On the relationship between international courts and museums (Elander) and between constitutions and museums (Douglas) see Maria Elander, *Figuring Victims in International Criminal Justice: The Case of the Khmer Rouge Tribunal* (New York: Routledge, 2018); Stacy Douglas, *Curating Community: Museums, Constitutionalism, and the Taming of the Political* (Ann Arbor: University of Michigan Press, 2017).

12 Jeannette Littlemore, *Metonymy: Hidden Shortcuts in Language, Thought and Communication* (Cambridge: Cambridge University Press, 2015), 111–13.

13 Ibid., 1–2.

14 Ibid., 1, 4.

Figure 29.1 Memory Square at the *Museo de la Memoria y los Derechos Humanos*. Photo Credit: Valeria Vázquez Guevara.

The UDHR is cast in metal letters, which have been installed all along the right wall of the Memory Square. The installed UDHR begins by reproducing the Preamble on three iron plates. At the bottom of the third plate a paragraph explains that the UDHR 'was approved and proclaimed' by the UN General Assembly on 10 December 1948, and that 'one of the leading drafters was the Chilean jurist and diplomat Hernán Santa Cruz Barceló'. By emphasising that fact, the Museo highlights that the Chilean state was an active participant in the emergence of IHRL. In a similar way, the TC's 1991 report stressed that the 'Universal Declaration of Human Rights and other relevant international documents proclaim rights which were already substantially part of Chile's legislation and its best civic traditions'.[15] The TC Report added that IHRL shows the 'shortcomings and inadequacies' of the Chilean national legislation not only during dictatorship but also before the 1973 coup d'état.[16] With this, although separated by a period of almost 30 years, both the TC Report (in 1991) and the Museo (since 2010) reassert and communicate the understanding that the violent events during the dictatorship constituted an 'exception' in the historical conduct of the Chilean state. By declaring the dictatorship a parenthesis in Chile's role as an international law-maker and law-abider, the Museo and the TC Report reaffirm the idea that IHRL is the outcome of a broad 'multicultural referendum',[17] which is therefore universal and the expression of global values.[18] This is also apparent in how,

15 Comisión Nacional de Verdad y Reconciliación, *Report of the Chilean National Commission*, 42.

16 Ibid.

17 Joseph Slaughter, "Hijacking Human Rights: Neoliberalism, the New Hisoriography, and the End of the Third World," *Human Rights Quarterly* 40, no. 4 (2018).

18 For an example of scholars supporting this view, see Steven Jensen, *The Making of International Human Rights: The 1960s, Decolonization, and the Reconstruction of Global Values* (Cambridge: Cambridge University Press, 2016); Kathryn Sikkink, *Evidence for Hope: Making Human Rights Work in the 21st Century* (Princeton: Princeton University Press, 2017). For scholarship that considers the quality of the participation of states of the Global South

to the left of the Preamble, the Museo reproduces each of the 30 articles of the UDHR. The UDHR articles cover this entire wall, ending at what the Museo's architects call the 'horizontal' part of the Memory Square, or what appears to the eye as the space's visible horizon. On this horizon, the UDHR stands out, welcoming visitors by reminding them of its promise: 'the creation of a world of the good', in this case a good Chilean state.[19]

At the gate of the Catedral entrance, the visitor can see on the left side of the esplanade a narrow space similar to a pathway running along the wall. This pathway directs the visitor to move along the wall until it ends at the entrance of the Museo's building. On the wall a plaque has been installed (in 2017) with a summary in Braille of the articles of the UDHR.[20] Also on this left wall, toward its middle point, the visitor encounters an engraving by the Uruguayan artist Luis Camnitzer. The artwork, titled *El Museo es una Escuela* (The Museum is a School), became part of the Museo's permanent collection in 2013,[21] and is part of Camnitzer's broader political work.[22] The engraving reads: '*El Museo es una Escuela: el artista aprende a comunicarse, el público aprende a hacer conexiones*' (The Museum is a School: the artist learns to communicate, the public learns to make connections). With this artwork, Camnitzer invites visitors to consider the educational relationship between the museum and society. For Camnitzer a museum should be a space where visitors are exposed to particular information, to ask critical questions about how such information or knowledge is being taught, and most importantly, for what.[23]

Thus, the visitor encounters on the walls of Memory Square two invitations for reflection (see Figure 29.2). On the one hand, the Museo presents the installation and display of the UDHR on both walls of Memory Square as a 'permanent invitation to defend and promote them [human rights] every day'.[24] On the other hand, Camnitzer invites the Museo's visitors to 'make connections' and to ask questions about what is being shown at the museum. However, Camnitzer's artwork – as part of the Museo's permanent exhibition – does not achieve its mission of challenging the museum's narrative. Rather, it complements the educational aim of the Museo in its unceasing appeal to memorialise Chile's dictatorship with IHRL. That is, the Museo, through the representations of IHRL located at Memory Square, seeks to make the visitor understand Chile's dictatorship as an IHRL story. The Museo's permanent installations – representations of IHRL (the complete UDHR and the UDHR in Braille), located in a

see Slaughter, "Hijacking Human Rights," 741–44; Sundhya Pahuja, "Laws of Encounter: A Jurisdictional Account of International Law," *London Review of International Law* 1, no. 1 (2013); *Bandung, Global History, and International Law: Critical Pasts and Pending Futures*, eds. Luis Eslava, Michael Fakhri and Vasuki Nesiah (Cambridge: Cambridge University Press, 2017).

19 Shane Chalmers, "The Beginning of Human Rights: The Ritual of the Preamble to Law," *Humanity* 9, no. 1 (2018): 111. Nesiah discusses how in political transitions the human rights and transitional justice projects mobilised 'human rights' as the normative foundation for a state's 'renewal and rebirth' in Vasuki Nesiah, "Theories of Transitional Justice: Cashing in the Blue Chips," in *The Oxford Handbook of The Theory of International Law*, eds. Anne Orford and Florian Hoffmann (New York: Oxford University Press, 2016).

20 Museo de la Memoria y Derechos Humanos, "Museo de la Memoria se transforma en un espacio de inclusión y accesibilidad universal," accessed January 15, 2020, https://ww3.museodelamemoria.cl/Informate/museo-de-la-memoria-se-transforma-en-un-espacio-de-inclusion-y-accesibilidad-universal/.

21 Museo de la Memoria y Derechos Humanos, "La Geometría de la Conciencia," accessed January 15, 2020, https://ww3.museodelamemoria.cl/exposiciones/la-geometria-de-la-conciencia/.

22 Ibid.

23 Tatiana Oliveros and Marco Fajardo, "Camnitzer en Chile: 'Un museo debe enseñarle al espectador a cuestionar lo que muestra'," *El Mostrador*, August 20, 2018.

24 Una invitación permanente a defenderlos y promoverlos cada día. Museo de la Memoria y Derechos Humanos, "Exposición Permanente – La Declaración Universal de los Derechos Humanos," accessed January 15, 2020, https://ww3.museodelamemoria.cl/exposicion-permanente/.

Figure 29.2 UDHR in Braille and Camnitzer's 'The Museum is a School' at the *Museo de la Memoria y los Derechos Humanos*. Photo Credit: Valeria Vázquez Guevara.

museological space of high-visibility such as Memory Square – show how IHRL occupies a core place in how the Museo is memorialising and presenting the truth of Chile's dictatorship. The articles of the UDHR, cast in metal on the esplanade's wall, can be seen at all times, regardless of which entrance the visitor enters the museum. In this way, by placing IHRL at the heart of the Chilean account of the truth of the dictatorship, as the TC Report has done, the Museo gives continuity and material form to the Report, and by extension the TC.

If the visitor enters the Museo through the entrance on Chacabuco Street, the UDHR is located immediately to the right of the visitor. Entering this way, the visitor passes an aircraft boarding staircase with the words '*asilo-exilio*' (asylum-exile), which symbolises the situation of asylum and exile caused by the dictatorship.[25] Beyond this, and before reaching the door to the main building, the visitor encounters an underground entrance to the Chilean artist Alfredo Jaar's installation art, titled *Geometría de la Conciencia* (Geometry of Conscience).[26] Jaar's art installation invites the visitor to sense and experience in her own way the disappearances that occurred during the dictatorship.[27] Playing with light and darkness in a closed room of 500 portrait silhouettes and mirror-walls, the visitor is prompted to consider the simultaneous presence and absence of the disappeared. The last artwork is Fernando Prats' *Acción Medular: Memorial en Homenaje al General Carlos Prats González* (Medullary Action: Memorial in Homage to General Carlos Prats González).[28] Prats' artwork reproduces excerpts of the memoirs of General

25 Museo de la Memoria y Derechos Humanos, "Asilo/Exilio," accessed January 15, 2020, https://ww3.museodelamemoria.cl/exposiciones/asiloexilio/.

26 Museo, "La Geometría de la Conciencia."

27 Ibid.

28 Museo de la Memoria y Derechos Humanos, "Acción Medular: Memorial en Homenaje al General Carlos Prats González," accessed January 15, 2020, https://ww3.museodelamemoria.cl/Informate/accion-medular-obra-permanente-en-homenaje-al-general-carlos-prats-gonzalez-y-sofia-cuthbert/.

Prats González, who was murdered along with his wife, Sofía, by agents of the Chilean state in Argentina in 1974. The letters are written with neon lights and rest on several cylindrical rock core samples that 'represent Chile's four cardinal points as a gesture that incorporates both a country's geography' and its 'historical memory'.[29] Finally, after passing by these pieces, one arrives at the doors of the Museo's building.

Although the aircraft staircase and the artworks of Jaar and Prats are museological objects that specifically refer to events of the history of Chile's dictatorship, the Museo's architectural design facilitates the visual dominance of the UDHR over them. The Museo, like the TC Report, places the UDHR, as the ultimate expression of international human rights law, at the heart of the 'truth' of the dictatorship. At the Museo, as in the TC Report, the dictatorship is presented and memorialised, and thus preserved or kept alive, as an account of human rights violations. This manifests materially in Memory Square, where the UDHR is not only visible at all times, but also physically reproduced and installed on both of the walls surrounding Memory Square. While the two artworks and the aircraft staircase work as devices that facilitate the visitor's learning of, and immersion into, important events of the dictatorship – detained-disappeared (Jaar), forced exile (aircraft stairs) and murders committed by the Chilean state's security forces (Prats) – they are subsumed within the framework of IHRL.[30] It is in Memory Square, as a space for reflection, where it becomes difficult for the Museo's visitor to hear only the 'local' stories told by the artworks and the aircraft staircase because they are overshowed by the omnipresent UDHR. The Museo, like the TC Report, places IHRL as the authority that supports and informs how Chile's dictatorial 'past' is officially articulated, by mediating and determining what the dictatorship was, and how it is and will be remembered. The grounding of this truth in IHRL gives it legal authority; it gives the TC Report and the Museo's account of truth of the dictatorship 'lawfulness'. In turn, this lawful truth displaces the plurality of truths and laws that emerge from the stories, 'feelings, [and] the knowledges of the land and territory' that Memory Square is also meant to preserve and transmit.[31]

Thus, no matter which entrance the visitor walks through to enter the grounds of the Museo, she constantly encounters IHRL as a dominant message in Memory Square. As a 'new museum',[32] the Museo aims, through 'experiential learning', to 'develop' in visitors 'more personal and immediate forms of affective engagement' with the historical past that is being represented there.[33] To achieve this, Memory Square is a museological space that has been conceptualised and designed to prepare visitors to 'connect with their state of mind' before entering into the Museo's main building.[34] The effect of Memory Square on visitors is similar to that of a 'preambular passage', which prepares visitors to enter into a sacred place to connect with her God/s.[35] Memory Square creates an 'active frame' that presents the social suffering caused by the dictatorship as a violation of IHRL.[36] As such, by preparing the visitor to enter into the Museo's

29 Ibid.

30 For 'categories' as technologies of jurisdiction see Shaunnagh Dorsett and Shaun McVeigh, *Jurisdiction* (Routledge: Abingdon, 2012), 71–76.

31 Mario Figueroa, Lucas Fehr and Carlos Dias, "Espacios Para la Cultura," *ARQ (Santiago)* 8, no. 1 (2012): 28.

32 Jens Andermann and Silke Arnold-de Simine, "Introduction: Museums and the Educational Turn: History, Memory, Inclusivity," *Journal of Educational Memory, Media, and Society* 4, no. 2 (2012): 2.

33 Ibid.

34 Museo de la Memoria y los Derechos Humanos, "Arquitectura: Propuesta Ganadora," accessed January 15, 2020, https://ww3.museodelamemoria.cl/wp-content/uploads/2016/02/Texto-arquitectos1.pdf, 4.

35 Chalmers, "The Beginning of Human Rights," 108.

36 Judith Butler, "Torture and the Ethics of Photography," *Environment and Planning D: Society and Space* 25, no. 6 (2007): 952.

building, where a detailed account of the truth of Chile's dictatorship awaits her, Memory Square 'allocates the recognizability' of the Chilean dictatorship with the articles of UDHR, as the 'broader norms' that determine what stories belong to such frame.[37] That is, it conditions what accounts of the dictatorship fit into the scope of IHRL, thus becoming true and worthy of memorialisation at the Museo. The UDHR, physically and thematically embedded in Memory Square, gives 'narrative coherence' to the plural accounts of the history of the dictatorship presented inside the Museo's building. IHRL at the Museo, like in the TC Report, works as the interpretative framework through which the violence of the dictatorship is articulated and presented as 'the' historical and truthful memory.

Curating the truth in the emerald green building

On entering the Museo's emerald green building (see Figure 29.1) the visitor is welcomed into a new museological space. This space, called Access Hall, houses a permanent exhibition titled *Derechos Humanos, Desafío Universal* (Human Rights, A Universal Challenge).[38] This display brings together four permanent collections that introduce the visitor to the Museo's articulation of memory as the truth of Chile's dictatorship between 1973 and 1990.[39]

The first to grab the visitor's attention is a giant world map, which presides over Access Hall. Although this map is visually captivating, the intended pathway through the *Human Rights, A Universal Challenge* exhibition starts to the far right of the Access Hall. The visitor is guided to start with the display *Comisiones de Verdad en el Mundo* (Truth Commissions in the World). A plaque displays a text titled 'Comisiones de Verdad' (Truth Commissions). This four-paragraph text starts by explaining that the legacy of violence across 'America, Asia and Europe has left in its wake suffering and mourning in the context of dictatorial regimes, civil wars or invasions'.[40] The following paragraph states that, 'in more than 30 countries Truth Commissions have been created. These are investigative organs, non-judicial, charged to inquire into the denunciated abuses'.[41] The third paragraph gives examples of the general object of inquiry of TCs, and establishes that 'victims . . . and their families have the right to know the truth and to a public acknowledgment of their suffering'.[42] The last paragraph then provides a brief overview of the two Chilean TCs.[43] Directly below the TCs plaque and the world map on the wall, there is a long red shelf with silver frames on it. Each frame contains a summary of one of the 30 TCs implemented all over the world.[44]

Continuing through the *Comisiones de Verdad en el Mundo*, one is guided to the world map, which displays a 'global' contemporary account of violent conflict and presents TCs as

37 Ibid., 951.

38 Museo de la Memoria y Derechos Humanos, "Exposición Permanente – Derechos Humanos, Desafío Universal," accessed January 15, 2020, https://ww3.museodelamemoria.cl/exposicion-permanente/.

39 Museo de la Memoria y Derechos Humanos, "Exposición Permanente," accessed January 15, 2020, https://ww3.museodelamemoria.cl/exposicion-permanente/.

40 Museo de la Memoria y Derechos Humanos, "Sobre el Museo – Comisiones de Verdad," accessed January 15, 2020, https://ww3.museodelamemoria.cl/sobre-el-museo/.

41 Ibid.

42 Ibid.

43 Ibid.

44 On TCs established as of March 2011 see United States Institute of Peace, "Truth Commission Digital Collection," *Margarita S. Studemeister Digital Library in International Conflict Management*, accessed January 15, 2020, www.usip.org/publications/2011/03/truth-commission-digital-collection.

mechanisms that have helped societies to live together again.[45] The images comprising the world map visualise how violent conflict has taken place in all states and societies, causing human rights violations across the globe. The world map thus presents violent conflict as a global problem, which affects all of us because it violates our human rights. According to this exhibition, TCs are able to investigate and offer a public account of the truth of the human rights violations committed during violent conflicts. The Museo represents TCs as a common mechanism that has helped states deal with the legacy of human rights violations by offering an official account of the truth. Taking together the different elements comprising the first part of *Human Rights, A Universal Challenge* (the TC plaque, silver frames and world map) the exhibition transmits a global account of violence and proposes TCs as the normative mechanism dealing with the past.[46] Furthermore, this part of the exhibition shows how, regardless of the particular context in which each of the 30 violent conflicts developed, it is a 'global' problem that concerns 'us' because it violates international human rights – 'rights' that are inherent to all.[47]

Once the 'global' context in which TCs and IHRL operate is established, the Museo introduces the visitor to how the TCs worked in the 'local' Chilean context. The collection that follows, within the exhibition, has two major parts: *Comisiones de Verdad en Chile* (Truth Commissions in Chile) and *Memoriales* (Memorials). The visitor is guided to stand in front of a table with a glass box protecting five documents on display. Inside the glass box are the reports of Chile's two TCs and two presidential commissions.[48] Above the white table, hanging from a narrow wall, a plaque states: 'The Museum of Memory and Human Rights is sustained by [*se sustenta*] the Reports of the Truth Commissions, which are the essential reference of its permanent exhibition and its heritage.' With this, the Museo proclaims that the arrangement of the museum's space and practices are integrally related to the reports produced by Chile's TCs and presidential commissions.

Opposite the table with the commissions' reports is the *Memoriales* collection. In this collection, the visitor can use an interactive screen to locate the memorial sites and monuments that have been built all around Chile to honour the disappeared.[49] This collection also shows images with a brief description of the memorial sites and monuments. Each image stands on a thin metal rod that is placed on the geographical site where each memorial or monument is located. The metal rods stand on rocky pieces that have been moulded to represent the geographical space of the Chilean state.

Apart from the Access Hall exhibition's name (*Human Rights, a Universal Challenge*) and the references that each TC silver frame might have to human rights, the exhibition does not display material objects that are explicitly about/of human rights (as in Memory Square). There is one exception: the red wall to the far end of Access Hall. This also marks the end of the exhibition.

On the way to the red wall, the visitor comes across two objects: *Cruz Patio 29* and *Pieza del Mes*. *Cruz Patio 29* is an iron cross on loan to the Museo from Santiago's General Cemetery. This cross is one of the many created to mark a mass grave in the General Cemetery, where unidentified bodies were buried during the dictatorship. The other object that the visitor encounters is the *Pieza del Mes* (Monthly Piece), a piece that belongs to the Museo's collection. By

45 Walter Mignolo, "Delinking," *Cultural Studies* 21, no. 2–3 (2007): 459.

46 Anne Orford, "Commissioning the Truth," *Columbia Journal of Gender and Law* 15, no. 3 (2006).

47 Mignolo, "Delinking," 497.

48 See n 4.

49 Museo de la Memoria y Derechos Humanos, "Memoriales (Interactive Database)," accessed January 15, 2020, http://interactivos.museodelamemoria.cl/memoriales/.

showcasing this object, the Museo highlights an historical event or moment during the dictatorship.[50] This historical object, which belongs to the Museo's archive, is rotated monthly to memorialise particular events or experiences from the dictatorship. Finally, after the visitor passes by these two objects, she stands in front of the red wall. Although the extract on the red wall does not indicate it, the text reproduces the section 'Marco Político' (Political Context) from the TC Report. This section describes the coup d'état of 11 September 1973, that removed President Allende from government, thus marking the beginning of the 1973–1990 dictatorship. In this section the TC Report affirms that it will not make a value judgment about the 11 September events. Nonetheless, it describes the Chilean state's institutional and social situation as an 'acute crisis in our national life . . . lead[ing] to the destruction or deterioration of numerous points of consensus among Chileans . . . which served to safeguard respect for *human rights*'.[51] With this description of the 1973 coup d'état as a breakdown of a way of 'living together with human rights' in Chile, the *Human Rights, a Universal Challenge* exhibition concludes.

Although the second part of the exhibition specifically refers to the work of Chile's TC (and subsequent policies of memorialisation), the arrangement of the exhibition situates the Chilean TC in a 'global' setting. That is, although the TC was Chile's ('local') way of dealing with the past, the exhibition shows how the implementation of the TC Report guaranteed that the Chilean state was addressing the 'global' concern or problem of human rights violations in an internationally acceptable way, just like other states had done since 1974.[52] With this museological arrangement, *Human Rights, a Universal Challenge* reasserts that, with the TC Report, the Chilean state was complying with IHRL, the international legal norm that the Chilean state had violated from the 1973 coup until the end of the dictatorship in 1990.[53] In this exhibition, the Museo communicates, visualises – using different means, such as a map, fact-sheets, documents, images or objects – and gives continuity to the TC Report's assertion that before the coup d'état and the dictatorship (1973–1990), living together within the Chilean state had been according to IHRL. In adhering to IHRL since the establishment of the TC, the Chilean state redressed its own dictatorial conduct.[54] By supporting an investigation into its own state-led human rights violations, the Chilean state redeemed itself from its past with the TC Report's human rights-based truth. In doing so, IHRL became (again) the foundation on which Chileans would live together after dictatorship.

Silencing 'minor' lawful truths

After visiting the *Human Rights, a Universal Challenge* exhibition, the visitor is guided up the stairs to another museological space called *Situación Pre-golpe* (Pre-Coup Situation). On the wall next to the stairs is a photographic mural, titled *Una Sociedad en Movimiento* (A Society

50 Museo de la Memoria y Derechos Humanos, "Pieza del Mes," accessed January 15, 2020, https://ww3.museodelamemoria.cl/sobre-las-colecciones/pieza-del-mes/cantata-de-los-derechos-humanos/.

51 Comisión Nacional de Verdad y Reconciliación, *Informe de la Comisión Nacional de Verdad y Reconciliación* (Santiago: Comisión Nacional de Verdad y Reconciliación, 1991), 33 (emphasis added).

52 Pahuja, "Laws of Encounter." On how Indigenous responses to violence are measured against 'human rights standards' see Phil Clark, *The Gacaca Courts, Post-Genocide Justice and Reconciliation in Rwanda: Justice Without Lawyers* (Cambridge: Cambridge University Press, 2010).

53 On human rights as a tool for global governance, see David Kennedy, "The International Human Rights Regime: Still Part of the Problem?" in *Examining Critical Perspectives on Human Rights*, eds. Rob Dickinson, et al. (Cambridge: Cambridge University Press, 2012).

54 On the 'actualization of the state' as part of the operation of international law, see Pahuja, "Laws of Encounter."

in Movement). The stairs and the mural were conceptualised to represent the social instability that Chilean society was going through before the 1973 coup. The stairs take the visitor up to a more distinct museological and architectural space: one accommodated in the emerald green building, which can be seen from the outside of the Museum. The emerald green building was conceptualised by the architects to represent 'a manifestation of [Chile's] history'.[55] As such, this part of the building houses a detailed display, arranged in chronological order, of the events of Chile's dictatorship, which follows the official account of truth presented in the TC Report.[56] The historical account in the emerald green building begins with two exhibitions, titled *11 de Septiembre de 1973* (September 11, 1973) and *Fin del Estado de Derecho* (End of the Rule of Law), which recount how the 1973 coup unfolded and outline the subsequent institutional and legal forms established by the military junta to consolidate the dictatorship. This historical account ends with two permanent exhibitions, called *Retorno a la Esperanza* (The Return to Hope) and *Fin de la Dictadura* (The End of the Dictatorship), focusing on the events, such as the 1989 plebiscite and Aylwin's 1990 presidential inauguration, which are considered to mark the end of the dictatorship and the 'return' to democracy.[57]

The transition within this architectural space, from the ground floor or 'plinth' to the emerald green building, gives physical form to the idea that Chile's 'history' rests, physically and institutionally, *on* the museological spaces of Memory Square and the Access Hall. Physically, the exhibitions concerning 'the history' of the dictatorship are located above and rest upon what the Museo's architects call the 'plinth'. In architecture, a plinth is a structure designed to support or sustain a visible part of a building, in this case the emerald green structure of the Museo. Institutionally, the Museo declares in the Access Hall's *Human Rights, a Universal Challenge* exhibition that the museological script – that is, the narrative that the Museo develops and communicates through the aesthetic arrangements of its exhibitions – is sustained by, or based on, the account of the truth established by the TCs. A truth informed, mediated and grounded by IHRL.

At the same time, in creating this lawful truth, both the TC and the Museo create 'minor' accounts of truths and lawfulness.[58] The TC presented its truth in 1991, and the Museo continues to do so, as *the* truth of Chile's dictatorship. Although this predominant account draws on the testimonies of many who experienced or were affected in different ways by the violence that occurred during the dictatorship, this truth subordinates and silences other experiences, and laws, that are not human rights-based.[59] This can be observed in how the Museo places the accounts of the Mapuche and the Arpilleristas outside the dominant account.

55 Figueroa, Fehr and Dias, "Espacios Para la Cultura," 28.

56 For an overview and analysis of those exhibitions, see Jens Andermann, "Showcasing Dictatorship: Memory and the Museum in Argentina and Chile," *Journal of Educational Media, Memory, and Society* 4, no. 2 (2012): 76–83.

57 Ibid.

58 These 'minor' lawful truths could be understood, in Goodrich's words, as 'minor jurisprudences or forms of legal knowledge that escape the phantom of a sovereign and unitary law': Peter Goodrich, *Law in the Courts of Love: Literature and Other Minor Jurisprudences* (London and New York: Routledge, 1996), 2.

59 Sundhya Pahuja, "Letters from Bandung: Encounters with Another International Law," in *Bandung, Global History, and International Law: Critical Pasts and Pending Futures*, eds. Luis Eslava, Michael Fakhri and Vasuki Nesiah (Cambridge: Cambridge University Press, 2017), 555; Mignolo, "Delinking," 460–70; Shane Chalmers, "Law's Pluralism: Getting to the Heart of the Rule of Law," *Law, Culture and the Humanities* (2017). doi.org/10.1177/1743872117707276.

The Arpilleristas were groups of women who were relatives of detained-disappeared.[60] These women collectively created patchwork tapestries, called *arpilleras*, representing images of their everyday life during dictatorship.[61] The Museo considers the *arpilleras* to be a 'testimony' that helped to 'build a wide social account' of the years of dictatorship.[62] Regardless of the importance that the Museo gives to the *arpilleras*' representation of a social 'collective memory', the tapestries are not part of the narrative of the dictatorship that the Museo displays. The tapestries are rather located as a side, or 'minor', account. The tapestries are exhibited in the last room of the Museo, on the top floor of the emerald green building. Furthermore, the exhibition of the *arpilleras* is located after a plaque titled 'Gratitude to the International Community', in which the Museo thanks foreign states and diplomats as well as international organisations for supporting the efforts to 'bring back' democracy to Chile. The location of the tapestries reveals how there is what might be called a 'major' truth, which is given a predominant, visible, authoritative position, while reducing other truths, such as that of the Arpilleristas, to a 'minor' position.[63]

Also telling of how the Museo and the TC created 'minor' accounts is the photographic exhibition, titled *Layelewün: Estar Sintiendo la Ausencia* (To Be Feeling Absence), by the Chilean artist Danilo Espinoza. The Museo houses the *Layelewün* exhibition as part of the museum's Year of Indigenous Memories, which was the 2018 annual theme.[64] Through this initiative, the Museo sought to 'give visibility to the human rights violations' suffered by the Mapuche, one of the Indigenous groups of South America.[65] Espinoza's *Layelewün* exhibition is a collection of images of the family picture albums of some of the Mapuche detained-disappeared.[66] With *Layelewün* and the Year of Indigenous Memories initiative the Museo aims to conduct an 'exercise of memory through art', because there is a '*deuda pendiente*' (a situation of owing something to someone, like a debt) to address the IHRL violations suffered by the Mapuche, since Spanish colonisation in the year 1540.[67] Importantly, the truths of the Mapuche, represented in the *Layelewün* exhibition, are part of a *temporary* initiative, thus not part of the Museo's (and the TC's) *permanent* account of the truth of the dictatorship. This reveals how, although the Museo recognises the lack of official and public acknowledgment, and redress, of the violence that the Mapuche suffered since colonisation, and that continues in the present, the Museo places Mapuche truths and laws under the dominant account of the TC's truth.[68] The Mapuche's own

60 Marjorie Agosín, *Tapestries of Hope, Threads of Love: The Arpillera Movement in Chile* (Lanham: Rowman & Littlefield Publishers, 2008), 15. See also Jacqueline Adams, *Art Against Dictatorship: Making and Exporting Arpilleras Under Pinochet* (Austin: University of Texas Press, 2013).

61 Agosín, *Tapestries of Hope*, 17, 30, 32.

62 Museo de la Memoria y Derechos Humanos, "Exposición Permanente – Arpilleras," accessed January 15, 2020, https://ww3.museodelamemoria.cl/exposicion-permanente/.

63 On how local and international organisations withdrew support for the Arpilleristas during democracy, see Adams, *Art Against Dictatorship*, 265–67; Marjorie Agosín, "Patchwork of Memory," *NACLA Report on the Americas* 27, no. 6 (1994): 13–14. See generally Agosín, *Tapestries of Hope*.

64 Museo de la Memoria y Derechos Humanos, "Exposición Temporal – Exposición sobre detenidos desaparecidos mapuche llega al Museo de la Memoria," accessed January 15, 2020, https://ww3.museodelamemoria.cl/Informate/exposicion-sobre-detenidos-desaparecidos-mapuche-llega-al-museo-de-la-memoria/.

65 Ibid.

66 Ibid.

67 Ibid. On root causes of human rights violations see Marks Susan, "Human Rights and Root Causes," *The Modern Law Review* 74, no. 1 (2011).

68 On the TC's erasure of the indigeneity of Mapuche detained-disappeared see Daniela Jara, et al., "Tracing Mapuche Exclusion from Post-Dictatorial Truth Commissions in Chile: Official and Grassroots Initiatives," *International Journal of Transitional Justice* 12, no. 3 (2018).

truth is not part of the Museo's (nor the TC Report's) aim to understand how to live together with truths which are not grounded in IHRL.[69]

The Museo's location of the accounts of the Mapuche and the Arpilleristas outside the lawful truth is thus an illustration of how the 'global' legal form of IHRL silences other accounts of truth, rendering them 'minor'. This shows how IHRL as a 'global' legal form can shape a society's relation to the past (or collective memory) after violent conflict, and thus life together in the present.

Conclusions

The importance of the relationship and arrangement between Memory Square and the Access Hall's *Human Rights, a Universal Challenge* at the plinth, and the 'manifestation of history' in the emerald green building, is that it makes manifest the relationship between IHRL and the TC. As discussed throughout this chapter, the official truth in the TC Report was the outcome of the TC's engagement with IHRL. The TC worked with IHRL to frame the object of the investigation as 'human rights violations'. Thus, through the TC, IHRL gave legal form to the violence perpetrated by the dictatorship ('the past' or 'history'). With IHRL the TC interpreted and redescribed the socio-political events of the dictatorship into legal categories susceptible to the adjudication of legal responsibility. For instance, the systematic forced disappearances of people by agents of the Chilean state were subsumed into the category of 'detained-disappeared' and conceptualised as a violation of IHRL. This is an example of how, in the TC, IHRL became the legal form that mediated what events and whose account belonged to the scope of an investigation into 'human rights violations'. In turn, the official account of truth became grounded in IHRL and in the TC Report. In a similar way, the Museo placed on its grounds in the form of the plinth, representations of IHRL and TCs. The Museo's grounds, comprising Memory Square and the Access Hall's *Human Rights, a Universal Challenge*, give physical support to the building where the history of Chile – the TC Report's truthful account – is located. But also, that museological arrangement materialises and gives continuity to the truth crafted in the 1991 TC Report. This reveals the way that IHRL informs and mediates the truth crafted by the TC, and how IHRL grounds that truth by giving it legal authority. It is this relationship with IHRL that makes the TC's, and thus the Museo's, account of the dictatorship lawful, and therefore authoritatively truthful.

69 A recent report by a Mapuche organisation shows how the violence suffered by the Mapuche during dictatorship and democracy has landownership at its core in Hernán Curiñir, *Informe Final Trabajo de Investigación, de Ejecutados y Desaparecidos, 1973–1990, Pertenecientes a la Nación Mapuche* (Temuco: Asociación de Investigación y Desarrollo Mapuche, 2016). See also Rosa Isolde Reuque Paillalef and Florencia Mallon, *When a Flower Is Reborn: The Life and Times of a Mapuche Feminist* (Durham, NC: Duke University Press, 2002).

30

The meeting of laws in Australian children's literature

Sophie Rigney

In this Chapter, I examine *The Complete Adventures of Snugglepot and Cuddlepie* (May Gibbs) and *Welcome to Country: A Traditional Aboriginal Ceremony* (Aunty Joy Murphy) to show how law, lawlessness, lawfulness and the meeting of laws is depicted in Australian children's literature. I argue that children's literature can be a helpful archive of material to help us understand the operation of law, including the ways in which different legal systems interact. The stories that we are told from the time we are very young – in children's books – are a powerful transmitter of ideas about law. In *Snugglepot and Cuddlepie*, the depiction of the 'Banksia men' suggests a lawlessness of Indigenous Australia. In contrast, in reading Aunty Joy Murphy's *Welcome to Country*, we see Indigenous laws and lawful relations between Indigenous communities and visitors. I use these children's books to examine ideas around encounters between Indigenous and settler-colonial laws; I argue that reading these books as international lawyers compels us to consider the racist ways in which international law has denied Indigenous laws, and the ways in which we can create meeting places between European/settler colonial and Indigenous international laws.

This chapter is written as an exploratory work that aims to set out some ideas, themes and possibilities, which may prove fruitful for future research. There are five parts to the chapter. First, I set out my own place as the author of this work and how I am located, in both physical and epistemic senses. Second, I set out why it is important to consider children's literature as an archive of information about international law. In the third and fourth parts, I examine the two books under consideration. Finally, I offer some conclusions, particularly in thinking through the need for European international law to engage more meaningfully with Indigenous international law.

Place

As a preliminary matter, I want to set out who I am and what my location is in this work.[1] I grew up in Hobart (nipaluna), Australia. This is the land of the muwinina people, one of the

1 Here, I am particularly inspired by Mark McMillan's use of vignettes and understanding of place in Mark McMillan, "Koowarta and the Rival Indigenous International: Our Place as Indigenous Peoples in the International,"

clans of the palawa people, the Indigenous people of the island known as lutruwita or Tasmania. The palawa people never ceded their sovereignty over this land. I am not Indigenous, and it is likely that my ancestors were actively involved in the dispossession of the palawa people from their land.

In terms of my 'epistemic location',[2] I have been trained as an international lawyer, more specifically in the form of international law which 'emerged alongside the modern European state system'.[3] This is a mode of international law that is Eurocentric,[4] and has been the handmaiden of colonisation.[5] I undertook my legal education in the territory now known as Australia, and so the international law I was taught has been maintained and progressed through a settler-colonial state.[6] This international law has also been used to justify and empower the settler state, particularly through the doctrine of *terra nullius* and the claim that Indigenous sovereignties are non-justiciable.[7] There is, therefore, a mutually reinforcing relationship between settler-colonialism and European international law.

In writing this, I am agreeing with the idea that European international law can be understood 'as simply one particular version of internationalism, rather than a universal and neutral mode according to which the relationship between nations can be mediated and managed'.[8] Once this conception is accepted, as Anne Orford writes, 'the call to live with honour according to law' requires an inquiry into how 'the European tradition of international law (might) facilitate its encounter with other legal orders in the South, as one participant among many'.[9] As a non-Indigenous woman, a settler, and a practitioner of European and colonial international law, I am increasingly aware of my responsibility to inquire into the ways in which European international law has denied Indigenous international law. These ideas guide how I read *The Complete Adventures of Snugglepot and Cuddlepie* and *Welcome to Country* as an international lawyer.

Griffith Law Review 23, no. 1 (2014): 110; and also of the 'location' work done by Katie Boudreau Morris in Katie Boudreau Morris, "Decolonizing Solidarity: Cultivating Relationships of Discomfort," *Settler Colonial Studies* 7, no. 4 (2017).

2 Boudreau Morris, "Decolonizing Solidarity: Cultivating Relationships of Discomfort," 456.

3 Anne Orford, "Ritual, Mediation and the International Laws of the South," *Griffith Law Review* 16, no. 2 (2007): 353.

4 See, for example, Martti Koskenniemi, "Histories of International Law: Dealing with Eurocentrism," *Rechtsgeschitchte* 19 (2011): 152–76; Antony Anghie, *Imperialism, Sovereignty, and the Making of International Law* (Cambridge: Cambridge University Press, 2007).

5 See particularly, Anghie, *Imperialism, Sovereignty, and the Making of International Law*; S. James Anaya, *Indigenous Peoples in International Law* (Oxford: Oxford University Press, 2000); Robert A. Williams, *Savage Anxieties: The Invention of Western Civilisation* (New York: Palgrave Macmillan, 2012); Irene Watson, *Aboriginal Peoples, Colonisation and International Law: Raw Law* (London: Routledge, 2014).

6 For more on settler colonialism, see Corey Snelgrove, Rita Kaur Dhamoon and Jeff Corntassel, "Unsettling Settler Colonialism: The Discourse and Politics of Settlers, and Solidarity with Indigenous Nations," *Decolonization: Indigeneity, Education & Society* 3, no. 2 (2014): 1–32, and the sources cited there.

7 See Dianne Otto, "A Question of Law or Politics? Indigenous Claims to Sovereignty in Australia," *Syracuse Journal of International Law and Commerce* 21 (1995): 65–66; Phillip Falk and Gary Martin, "Misconstruing Indigenous Sovereignty: Maintaining the Fabric of Australian Law," in *Sovereign Subjects: Indigenous Sovereignty Matters*, ed. Aileen Moreton-Robinson (Sydney: Allen & Unwin, 2007), 34.

8 Orford, "Ritual, Mediation and the International Laws of the South," 353.

9 Ibid. On the importance of non-Indigenous lawyers acting with 'honour' and taking account for the discipline they are a member of, see Shaun McVeigh, "Law As (More or Less) Itself: On Some Not Very Reflective Elements of Law," *UC Irvine Law Review* 4 (2014): 471; Shaun McVeigh, "Jurisprudent of London: Arts of Association," in *Lives Lived with Law* 20, no. 1 (2016) *Law Text Culture*: 188; Sundhya Pahuja, "Laws of Encounter: A Jurisdictional Account of International Law," *London Review of International Law* 1, no. 1 (2014): 63.

What's in a story? Children's literature, international law and the importance of Indigenous stories

It may seem unusual to read children's books as an archive of information about international law. After all, international law is usually understood as existing in treaties, state practice, and decisions of the United Nations and other international organisations, or in the writings of scholars – not in stories for children. However, in recent years, there has been a move to understand how international law interacts with the local lives of ordinary people. Luis Eslava and Sundhya Pahuja have described this as the 'everyday life of international law'.[10] In their words, this methodology is 'an avenue for [the political international lawyer] to start seeing international law in those places that usually escape our attention and yet regulate our lives'.[11] In this piece, I examine children's books as a source of information about law and how legal systems interact, partly as a response to this call to think of the relationship between international law and our 'everyday' lives.

While 'law and literature' is an established field,[12] the discipline of international law has largely ignored literature. It is only recently that international law has started to examine literature in any meaningful way.[13] However, these contributions have examined adult fiction. There has not yet been any sustained examination of the relationships between international law and children's books.[14] This, perhaps, is not surprising: children's literature is often dismissed, due to its 'perceived "simplicity" of language and "triviality" of subject-matter',[15] and there is, therefore, very little scholarship on understandings of law in children's literature at all.

However, children's books are a vitally important genre, as they influence how children form views on the world. These stories provide a safe space where children explore boundaries, learn shared values and engage with hypothetical dilemmas. The stories impart norms and values to children;[16] they communicate appropriate behaviours, and what to believe in. These stories are, therefore, 'an important agent of socialization . . . through which the young are taught the values and standards of their elders'.[17] In one of the few analyses of children's literature and law

10 Luis Eslava and Sundhya Pahuja, "Beyond the (Post)Colonial: TWAIL and the Everyday Life of International Law," *Verfassung und Recht in Übersee / Law and Politics in Africa, Asia and Latin America* 45, no. 2 (2012): 195–221. See also Henrietta Zeffert, " The Lake Home: International Law and the Global Land Grab," *Asian Journal of International* Law 8, no. 2 (2018): 432–60.

11 Eslaya and Pahuja, "Beyond the (Post)Colonial: TWAIL and the Everyday Life of International Law," 221.

12 See James Boyd White, *The Legal Imagination*, 2nd ed. (Chicago: University of Chicago Press, 1985).

13 For some recent examples, see Gerry Simpson, "The Sentimental Life," *London Review of International Law* 3, no. 1 (2015): 3–29; Douglas Guilfoyle, "Reading *The City and The City* as an International Lawyer," *London Review of International Law* 4, no. 1 (2016): 195–207; Ekaterina Yahaoui Krivenko, "International Law, Literature and Interdisciplinarity," *Law and Humanities* 9, no. 1 (2015): 103–22; Joseph Slaughter, "Pathetic Fallacies: Personification and the Unruly Subjects of International Law," *London Review of International Law* 7, no. 1 (2019): 3–54.

14 Some embryonic examination has commenced in the field of human rights: see Jonathan Todres and Sarah Higinbotham, *Human Rights and Children's Literature* (New York: Oxford University Press, 2016).

15 Ian Ward, *Law and Literature: Possibilities ad Perspectives* (Cambridge: Cambridge University Press, 1995). See particularly Chapter 5, Children's Literature and Legal Ideology, 90.

16 See Jack Zipes, *When Dreams Came True: Classical Fairy Tales and Their Tradition* (New York: Routledge, 2007); Jack Zipes, *Fairy Tales and the Art of Subversion* (London: Routledge, 2011).

17 Arthur Applebee, *The Child's Concept of a Story: Ages Two to Seventeen* (Chicago: University of Chicago Press, 1978), 52.

(examining Maurice Sendak's *Where the Wild Things Are*), Desmond Manderson observes that children's stories:

> are agents in the transmission of discipline to children, not merely by their immediate instructive power but through their deployment of myth and their capacity not only to narrate the stories of a civilization but to echo and to contribute to the echoes of these myths as they suffuse the child's world.[18]

Thus, the lessons that children learn from their books are enduring. It is for these reasons that it is important to examine what children are told, through these books, about systems of authority and law. In this piece, I examine in particular what children are being told about Indigenous and non-Indigenous ways of knowing and doing law, and the interactions between these legal systems.

Stories are therefore important as a method of passing on values and understandings about the world. However, for Australian Indigenous peoples, stories have a multitude of particularly important functions. First, and crucially, in Australian Indigenous societies, stories (including those told to children) remain important *sources* of law. Irene Watson has expressed the relationship between law and story for Indigenous peoples in this way:

> Many of our First Nations legal systems are embodied in stories and songs. Our ancient laws were not written down; knowledge of law came through living, singing and storytelling. Law is lived, sung, danced, painted, eaten and in the walking of ruwe.[19]

This explicit appreciation of stories as a source of law differs from a common Western approach, where many would argue children's books merely *reflect* the law, which is otherwise to be found in legislation and court judgments. Others, however, would argue that this distinction is false,[20] and that the difference is really one of acknowledgement: Western societies often deny the lawful nature of stories and myths,[21] while Indigenous societies explicitly acknowledge that stories are law.

Indigenous Dreamtime stories are now often read to all Australian children *as children's books*. As Frances Bodkin notes, 'society has come to regard the Koori Dreaming stories as something akin to the fairy tales they were told as children.'[22] However, Bodkin shows that this insistence disregards the connection of these stories to law:

> For thousands upon thousands of years, the stories in this book were used as a teaching tool to impart to the youngest members of the clans the laws which governed the cultural behaviour of clan members.[23]

18 Desmond Manderson, "Where the Wild Things *Really* Are," in *Law and Popular Culture,* ed. Michael Freeman (Oxford: Oxford University Press, 2005), 51; see also Desmond Manderson, "From Hunger to Love: Myths of the Source, Interpretation, and Constitution of Law in Children's Literature," *Law and Literature* 15, no. 1 (2003): 87–141.

19 Watson, *Aboriginal Peoples, Colonisation and International Law: Raw Law*, 12. "Ruwe" is "the territories of First Nations Peoples", see Watson, *Aboriginal Peoples, Colonisation and International Law*, 10 at note 23. See also Christine Black, *A Mosaic of Indigenous Legal Thought: Legendary Tales and Other Writings* (London: Routledge, 2016).

20 See Manderson, "Where the Wild Things *Really* Are."

21 See, for example, Peter Fitzpatrick, *The Mythology of Modern Law* (London: Routledge, 1992).

22 Frances Bodkin and Gawaian Bodkin-Andrews, *D'harawal Dreaming Stories: Wattun'goori, The Story of the Hairy Men, How the Banksias Came to Be*, Foreword by Frances Bodkin, https://dharawalstories.files. wordpress.com /2015 /05/wattungoori922kb.pdf.

23 Ibid.

Bodkin points out that the attempts to destroy Indigenous culture were unsuccessful, and 'the Dreaming Stories were able to continue in their disguise as charming legends where animals became the heroes and the heroines'.[24] But these stories contain multiple layers: the layer of secrets, the layer of law or laws that should be obeyed, and the layer of the lessons that can be learnt.[25] Stories, then, are a source of Indigenous law – no less than those expressed in legislation, or in treaties or the other sources of international law.

'Story' is also a vitally important research methodology for Indigenous peoples, and for Indigenist research – defined by Lester-Irabinna Rigney as research which is 'carried out by Indigenous Australians whose primary informants are Indigenous Australians and whose goals are to serve and inform the Indigenous liberation struggle to be free of oppression and to gain power'.[26] Linda Tuhawai Smith has outlined 'story telling' as one of 25 particular 'projects' that Indigenous people undertake to 'decolonise methodologies' in order to 'reclaim, reformulate and reconstitute' Indigenous cultures and languages.[27] Moreover, as Bagele Chilisa has written, Indigenous stories 'reflect the values of society, are socialisation instruments, are data sources and analysis tools, and provide the missing chapters on the history, philosophies, theories, concepts, categories of analysis, and interpretation in research'.[28] Indigenous stories thus have taken on particular roles in (settler) colonial states and are an important source of research for and by Indigenous peoples.

In these ways, then, stories should be seen as an integral source of information about law and how law interacts with society. I now turn to the two particular books in question, *The Complete Adventures of Snugglepot and Cuddlepie* and *Welcome to Country*.

Snugglepot and Cuddlepie: the ways settlers suggest lawlessness of Indigenous peoples

Snugglepot and Cuddlepie was published by Cecelia May Gibbs in 1918. Gibbs had lived her life between Australia and England: she was born in England in 1877 and moved to Australia at the age of 4; as an adult, she travelled between the two countries before eventually settling in Sydney in 1913.[29] *Snugglepot and Cuddlepie* was 'extremely popular', selling 17,000 copies on its first release, and to date it has never been out of print.[30] The imagery of the books is 'consciously and self-consciously Australian, her narratives are expressive and rich in demotic dialogue'.[31] For these reasons, the books continue to be popular and characters have become iconic. As Alice Mills has written,

> her images of cutely chubby, naked or semi-naked, big-eyed Gumnut babies in their nut-hats and those of the coarse-textured, villainous Banksia men have moved out of children's

24 Ibid.

25 Ibid.

26 Lester-Irabinna Rigney, "Internationalization of an Indigenous Anticolonial Cultural Critique of Research Methodologies: A Guide to Indigenous Research Methodology and Its Principles," *Wicazo Sa Review* 14, no. 2 (1999): 118.

27 Linda Tuhawai Smith, *Decolonizing Methodologies: Research and Indigenous Peoples* (London: Zed Books, 1999), particularly 142–61.

28 Bagele Chilisa, *Indigenous Research Methodologies* (Thousand Oaks, CA: Sage Publications, 2012), 139.

29 "The Story of May Gibbs," *May Gibbs Nutcote*, accessed November 17, 2019, www.maygibbs.com. au/the-story-of-may-gibbs.

30 Ibid.

31 Clare Bradford, *Reading Race: Aboriginality in Australian Children's Literature* (Melbourne: Melbourne University Press, 2001), 124.

> literature and into the realms of nostalgia. Gumnut babies and Banksia men can be found as locally made souvenirs in craft shops, both as Australiana for the international tourist and as sentimental keepsakes for the local buyer.[32]

Indeed, Gibbs's 'Gumnut Baby' illustrations grace homes and babies: the May Gibbs website now sells a variety of 'gorgeous Australian designed clothes and accessories featuring May Gibbs iconic illustrations', with a baby's onesie retailing at about $42.[33] In perhaps the ultimate show of their connection with consumerism and culture, the Gumnut Babies were featured in the Melbourne department store, Myer's Christmas window, in both 1995 and 2019.[34]

The Complete Adventures of Snugglepot and Cuddlepie contains three interlinked stories: *Snugglepot and Cuddlepie, Little Ragged Blossom* and *Little Obelia*. The three stories are each essentially adventure tales, where the characters go on quests to experience new things, and the stories detail their dangerous and exciting journeys. Such stories of 'the hero and his quest' is a dominant narrative in children's books: as Margery Hourihan points out, this story has been told 'over and over again, in innumerable versions, from the earliest times . . . it is our favourite story and it has been told so many times that we have come to believe that what it says about the world is true'.[35]

The characters of Snugglepot and Cuddlepie are two 'foster brothers' who are 'Gumnut Babies', or resemble the gumnuts of the eucalyptus tree. In *Snugglepot and Cuddlepie*, Snugglepot and Cuddlepie go on an adventure to see humans, after hearing about them from a wise old Kookaburra. The book tells of their journey and the creatures they meet along the way, including 'Mr Lizard', 'Mrs Snake', 'Ragged Blossom' and 'Lilly Pilly'.

In *Little Ragged Blossom*, Snugglepot, Cuddlepie and Ragged Blossom go on a new adventure to see different countries. Ragged Blossom and Snugglepot are captured by the Banksia Men and thrown into the sea, where they again meet new friends and enemies in the underwater world, including the baby, Little Obelia. While Snugglepot makes his way out of the ocean, Ragged Blossom stays in the sea to care for Little Obelia.[36] But the danger has not yet passed for Snugglepot: he is captured again by the Banksia men, and there is a 'terrible fight' – the crescendo of the book – between the Banksia men on the one hand and Snugglepot, Cuddlepie and their supporters on the other hand. The Banksia men are ultimately thrown into the sea, and 'never a Banksia man was left to tell the tale'.[37]

However, the third book of *Little Obelia* opens with the Banksia men resurgent at the bottom of the ocean. The story of *Little Obelia* follows the characters of Little Obelia, Ragged Blossom, Snugglepot and Cuddlepie as they battle both the Banksia men and a new enemy, the Giant Octopus. The book ends with a homecoming for the heroes: Snugglepot, Cuddlepie and Ragged Blossom all live together in a 'new big house' built by Snugglepot and end up essentially

32 Alice Mills, "Australian Children's Literature," in *A Companion to Australian Literature Since 1900*, eds. Nicholas Birns and Rebecca McNeer (Suffolk: Boydell & Brewer, 2007), 419.

33 "Clothing," *May Gibbs Shop*, accessed November 17, 2019, www.maygibbs.org/shop /category /clothing/.

34 "Myer Christmas Windows 2019," accessed November 17, 2019, www.onlymelbourne.com.au/myer-christmas-windows#.XdFcwlf7Q2w; "The Myer Christmas Windows," *State Library of Victoria Blog*, December 19, 2018, accessed November 17, 2019, https://blogs.slv.vic.gov.au/such-was-life/myer-christmas-windows/.

35 Margery Hourihan, *Deconstructing the Hero: Literary Theory and Children's Literature* (London: Routledge, 1997), 1.

36 May Gibbs, *The Complete Adventures of Snugglepot and Cuddlepie* (Sydney: Angus and Robertson, 2010), 144.

37 Ibid., 149.

adopting a large number of babies.[38] The adventures and dangers appear to have come to an end – as fits with the traditional narrative arc of children's books, where the subject is often 'disorder and order and their proper relation, beginning in order and ending there, but with disorder given its due'.[39]

As can be seen from this brief summary, the recurring villains of these stories are the 'Banksia Men'. These characters are described as 'wicked',[40] 'cowardly'[41] and 'bad'.[42] They 'snarl',[43] 'growl'[44] and make 'wicked plots'.[45] In particular, the Banksia men often kidnap Snugglepot, Cuddlepie and their friends.[46] The May Gibbs website summarises the Banksia men as 'always hatching wicked plots to capture the Nuts and Blossoms'.[47] We can see how the Banksia men and their interactions with Snugglepot and Cuddlepie are depicted in these lines:

> "Got 'im at last!" said the Banksia man, panting.
> "Is he alive?" grunted one, poking Snugglepot with his horrible bony finger.
> "Is 'e what?" sneered the Banksia man, tossing Sungglepot into a corner. "What'll we do with 'im, that's the question?"
> "The little slimy sinner!" growled one.
> "String and ring him!" said another.
> "Rack and Crack him!" snarled another.
> "Bust and rust him!" croaked a monster with three eyes.
> "Stick 'im on a bull-ant's nest; they'll kill 'im and the crows'll come and pick his bones," squeaked the smallest and ugliest of them all.
> "Oh! Ah! Throw him to the bull-dogs," shouted all the Banksia men, jumping about in wicked glee.
> "Give him a dose first," muttered one of them. So they opened poor Snugglepot's mouth and poured some horrible juice into it; and that was the last thing Snugglepot remembered.[48]

It is not unusual for adventure tales to have lawless villains; indeed, an anti-hero is a crucial element to the crisis and disorder of such a story. As we will shortly see when we examine the Indigenous story of the Banksia, the narrative of heroes, villains and victims is replicated there. Pedagogically, this triangulation can be useful when teaching, through story, about law. The villain shows – through their breaking of the law – what the law is; their 'casting out' indicates punishment for breaking law. The heroes provide a moral compass and a sense of aspiration to

38 Ibid., 222. Clare Bradford has written on the 'queering' of this scene: Clare Bradford, "The Return of the Fairy: Australian Medievalist Fantasy for the Young," *Australian Literary Studies* 26, no. 3–4 (2011): 115–32.

39 Adam Gopnik, "Freeing the Elephants," *New Yorker*, September 15, 2008, www.newyorker.com/magazine/2008/09/22/freeing-the-elephants.

40 Gibbs, *The Complete Adventures of Snugglepot and Cuddlepie*, 60, 92, 94.

41 Ibid., 65.

42 Ibid., 73, 78, 92, 147–48.

43 Ibid., 73.

44 Ibid., 206.

45 Ibid., 74.

46 Ibid. See for example 60, 147–48, 205.

47 "Stories and Characters: Big Bad Banksia Men," *May Gibbs Website*, accessed November 17, 2019, www.maygibbs.org/stories-and-characters/?ppp=274#.

48 Gibbs, *The Complete Adventures of Snugglepot and Cuddlepie*, 206–7.

lawfulness. The victims show the harm that can happen when laws are broken. In this way, then, casting some characters as villains is not without some theoretical use.[49]

However, there is a significant concern that *The Complete Adventures of Snugglepot and Cuddlepie* link lawlessness with Indigeneity. The Banksia men are highly racialised. The May Gibbs website refers to the 'Big Bad Banksia Men' as being 'based on the appearance of aged Banksia "cones" – dark, hairy, knobbly, many-eyed creatures'.[50] It is striking that the language of 'dark' is used here to describe the appearance of the Banksia men. Indeed, as Erica Hateley has pointed out, 'as hindsight has made notorious, Snugglepot and Cuddlepie's "wicked" Banksia men are illustrated as caricatures of Aboriginal people'.[51] Hateley also links this to a wider trend, and argues that when they are included in children's literature, 'Aboriginal Australians are made frightening, threatening, or strange.'[52] Evelyn Araluen has written that the Banksia men are 'aligned with savagery, animism, sexual deviancy, and Aboriginality throughout the stories'.[53]

This link between race and lawlessness is, of course, not unique to *Snugglepot and Cuddlepie*. Indeed, this is a frequently repeated trope.[54] Margery Hourihan shows us the racialised and gendered nature of adventure stories and their heroes and anti-heroes: she argues that the 'quest story' tells of 'how white European men are the natural masters of the world . . . how other "inferior" races have been subdued by them, how they spread civilization and order wherever they go'.[55] The suggestion that Indigenous people do not have legal epistemologies and ontologies of their own – and that they exist as outlaws in the Australian state – is reflected in children's books written by settlers.[56] Moreover, in her stunning piece on 'Snugglepot and Cuddlepie in the Ghost Gum', Evelyn Araluen – a descendant of the Bundjalung nation, who was 'born, raised, and writing on Dharug country'[57] – examines Australian poetics and argues that 'tropes and strategies of settler nativism are nowhere more explicit than in Australian children's literature'.[58] Elsewhere, Araluen has adopted and subverted the *Snugglepot and Cuddlepie* narratives, in her poem 'Mrs Kookaburra Addresses the Natives'.[59]

49 Nonetheless, I must include the caveat that there is often no bright light between victimhood and perpetration; casting some people (or organisations) in heroic moulds is also potentially challenging. I have written on this in Sophie Rigney, "Postcard from the ICTY," in *International Law's Objects*, eds. Jessie Hohmann and Daniel Joyce (Oxford: Oxford University Press, 2019), 366–76. On more about heroes and villains in children's stories, see particularly Hourihan, *Deconstructing the Hero*.

50 "Stories and Characters."

51 Erica Hateley, "Visions and Values: The Children's Book of Australia's Prizing of Picture Books in the Twenty-First Century," in *Canon Constitution and Canon Change in Children's Literature*, eds. Bettina Kummerling-Meibauer and Anja Muller (Abingdon: Routledge, 2016).

52 Ibid. For more on racism in Australian literature more generally, see Graham Huggan, *Australian Literature: Postcolonialism, Racism, Transnationalism* (Oxford: Oxford University Press, 2007); Bob Hodge and Vijay Mishra, *Dark Side of the Dream: Australian Literature and the Postcolonial Mind* (Sydney: Allen & Unwin, 1991).

53 Evelyn Araluen, "Snugglepot and Cuddlepie in the Ghost Gum," *Sydney Review of Books*, February 11, 2019, https://sydneyreviewofbooks.com/snugglepot-and-cuddlepie-in-the-ghost-gum-evelyn-araluen/.

54 For more on race in Australian children's books, see Bradford, *Reading Race: Aboriginality in Australian Children's Literature*.

55 Hourihan, *Deconstructing the Hero*, 1.

56 See Mills, *Australian Children's Literature*, for more examples.

57 "About Evelyn Araluen," *Sydney Review of Books*, accessed November 17, 2019, https://sydneyreviewof books.com/contributors/evelyn-araluen/.

58 Araluen, "Snugglepot and Cuddlepie in the Ghost Gum."

59 Evelyn Araluen, "Mrs Kookaburra Addresses the Natives," *Australian Poetry Journal* 9, no. 1 (2019): 14–15. I am grateful to Coel Kirkby for making this available to me.

This racist idea linking Indigeneity and lawlessness extends beyond children's books. In the context of Australian Indigenous peoples, the existence of Indigenous legal systems – of Indigenous lawfulness – has often been denied. Most profoundly, the invocation of the international legal doctrine of *terra nullius* (or 'land belonging to no-one') – which eventually became the justification for the British claim to the territory – was a denial of Indigenous systems of law and governance. This denial of systems of law is itself a form of violence.[60] The link between Indigeneity and 'lawlessness' has therefore been integral to the establishment of the Australian state.[61] Children's books link 'civilisation' and race, and international law takes this further, with 'civilisation', race, and law and lawlessness closely connected to the concept of recognition.[62]

Yet – perhaps ironically – stories of Banksia are a source of Indigenous law, as told by the D'harawal Dreaming Story of *The Story of the Hairy Man: How the Banksias Came To Be.*[63] This story starts with the existence of 'two very different kinds of people', the D'harawa'goori (the people now known as the D'harawals or the Indigenous people of the coastal area of the Sydney basin) and the Wattun'goori. The Wattun'goori were 'hairy men' and were separated into 'two different kinds': the Dooligah who were giants, and the Kuritjah who were 'little hairy men'. Although 'everybody lived together peacefully for a very long time', a 'terrible drought' came and while the D'harawals and the Kuritjah were able to survive on particular types of food, the Dooligahs became very hungry. One day, some Dooligahs were resting when some D'harawals passed by. The D'harawal children, 'instead of paying attention to their parents' instructions, were straggling along, making lots of noise . . . even breaking off branches of the trees'. The story instructs that

> everybody should know, that at all times you should be as quiet as possible whilst walking through our bushland . . . most importantly, everyone should know that you must never break off the branches of the trees . . . because it can make bushfires very much worse, especially during times of drought.

At this point, one of the Dooligahs creeps over to the children, grabs them and 'ate the fattest one and imprisoned the other' to eat later. Other Dooligahs follow his lead. On discovering their children gone, the D'harawals approach the Kuritjahs, who suspect the Dooligahs are responsible. The Kuritjahs rescue the D'harawal children from the Dooligah cave, and the D'harawal clan 'were overjoyed' and 'thanked the little Kuritjahs, giving them gifts'.

However, the children forgot the lessons they had learnt, and the Dooligahs were 'waiting for them, drooling with anticipation of a nice, juicy meal'. One day, the Kuritjahs saw the D'harawals preparing for war. The Kuritjahs were anxious to avoid this war. They managed to take the Dooligahs to the Kurrajong trees, which were hollow and contained honey and water. The Dooligahs ate and drank, and fell asleep in the hollow of the trees, and the Kuritjahs sealed up the trunks of the trees, trapping the Dooligahs. In this way, war had been averted. However, the Kuritjah were still worried that the Dooligahs might escape, and so they 'climbed a nearby tree, and there they are today, sitting along the branches, watching over the

60 See Sophie Rigney, "Indigenous Nationhood, Political Relationships, and Transitional Justice: Addressing Australia's Political Violence," *draft*, on file with author.

61 See Mark McMillan and Sophie Rigney, "Race, Reconciliation and Justice in Australia: From Denial to Acknowledgement," *Race and Ethnic Studies* 41, no. 4 (2018): 759.

62 See Martin Clark, "A Conceptual History of Recognition in British International Legal Thought," *British Yearbook of International Law* 87, no. 1 (2017): 18–97.

63 The version cited here is from Bodkin, "D'harawal Dreaming Stories: Wattun'goori, The Story of the Hairy Men, How the Banksias Came to Be."

Kurrajong trees, making sure that the Dooligah trapped inside does not escape'. The story ends: 'Today you call the little hairy men by the name of Banksia. But the D'harawals know their real name – Kuritjah.'

We therefore see that the Banksia (Kuritjah) are the protectors of the children. They can also be understood as the diplomats responsible for mediating between the D'harawals and the Dooligah. They prevent war, understand the land and the lore, and make the world safer. This emphasis on law is a far cry from the Banksia being the villains of *Snugglepot and Cuddlepie.*

In *The Complete Adventures of Snugglepot and Cuddlepie*, we see one of the most popular, enduring Australian children's books clearly linking Indigeneity and lawlessness. This link is reflected in doctrines of international law that have facilitated invasion of land and colonisation. However, this link is incorrect. As we see both in the D'harawal story of the Banksia, and in the next section when we examine *Welcome to Country*, Indigenous laws are present, clear and strong. *Welcome to Country* provides an opportunity to examine Indigenous laws, and particularly those Indigenous laws relating to visitors to Country.

Welcome to Country and the meeting of laws

Welcome to Country: A Traditional Aboriginal Ceremony is written by Aunty Joy Murphy, the 'Senior Aboriginal Elder of the Wurundjeri people of Melbourne and the surrounding area'.[64] Aunty Joy is 'a storyteller and a writer and is passionate about using story to bring people together and as a conduit for understanding Aboriginal culture'.[65] The illustrations in *Welcome to Country* are by Lisa Kennedy, 'a descendant of the Trawlwoolway people on the northeast coast of Tasmania'.[66] *Welcome to Country* was released in 2018 and won multiple awards.[67]

Welcome to Country is a picture book, but also an articulation of the ceremony provided by community elders to welcome visitors coming to Aboriginal lands. The first page of the book describes it in this way:

> The Wurundjeri Wominjeka (welcome) ceremony is a cultural greeting by the Elders (*liwik*), who give permission for *yannabil* (visitors) to enter onto their traditional lands.
>
> Aboriginal communities across Australia have boundaries that are defined by mountain ranges and waterways.
>
> To cross these boundaries or enter community country, you need permission from the neighbouring community. Each community has its own way of welcoming to Country.

In this articulation, we see concepts of jurisdiction, territory, sovereignty and governance. Indeed, there is a plethora of Indigenous jurisprudence on these legal concepts. For example, Mark McMillan has articulated Wiradjuri jurisdiction as 'Wiradjuri experiences, existences, ontologies and epistemologies' and he notes that 'in Australia all Indigenous peoples' individual (nation) jurisdictions are separated from the connection to the Anglo-Australian legal system for our

64 Aunty Joy Murphy, *Welcome to Country: A Traditional Aboriginal Ceremony* (Somerville, MA: Candlewick Press, 2018): flapjacket.

65 Ibid.

66 Ibid.

67 The book won the Environment Award for Children's Literature and Educational Publishing Award and the CBCA Notable Book; and was short-listed for the CBCA Crichton Award, the NSW Premier's Literary Award and the Speech Pathology Book of the Year Award. See "Welcome to Country," *Walker Books Australia and New Zealand*, accessed March 15, 2019, www.walkerbooks.com.au/Books/Welcome-To-Country-9781922244871.

mere existence'.[68] In *Welcome to Country*'s expression of defined boundaries that require permission to enter, we see a clear expression of Indigenous jurisdiction and authority tied to territory. Where *Welcome to Country* notes that 'We, the Wurundjeri, are the Mana Gum people – Wurun, the river white gum, and Djeri, the grub that lives in the tree', there is an explicit link between the people and the particular land. The Welcome ceremony depicted in *Welcome to Country* is a protocol of engagement between two different orders; proof of a mutual recognition of territory, sovereignty, and boundaries. Indeed, Indigenous sovereignties – never ceded – are location-specific and tied to jurisdiction:[69] Indigenous nations exercise jurisdiction and sovereignty within their mutually recognised national boundaries, as *Welcome to Country* shows.

These jurisdictions have interacted with each other over millennia, having been linked 'through trade, cultural practices and inter-community collaboration in times of crises (for example, floods and food shortages) and through ceremonial events'.[70] Ravi de Costa has outlined the 'transnational diplomacy' that occurred between Indigenous peoples in what is now known as Australia, before British invasion.[71] Yet in order to regulate these meetings between different Indigenous jurisdictions, an international law was required. As McMillan and I have written, 'the interactions between Indigenous nations has been premised on the sovereignty, jurisdictions, and governance of those nations'.[72] There has been a continued mutual recognition by Indigenous nations of the sovereignty of other Indigenous nations.[73] Indigenous international law has thus existed for thousands of years.[74]

As part of this, there is a clear sense of Indigenous sovereignty. *Welcome to Country* shows this, stating that 'we are part of the land, and the land is part of us. We feel the roots of this land beneath the soles of our bare feet.' This is reminiscent of Aileen Moreton-Robinson's articulation of sovereignty: 'Our sovereignty is embodied', writes Moreton-Robinson, 'it is ontological (our being) and epistemological (our way of knowing), and it is grounded within complex relations derived from the intersubstantiation of ancestral beings, humans and land. In this sense, our sovereignty is carried in the body.'[75] This statement of sovereignty – as something that is found in the connection between body, land, ancestors and creator spirits – is also shown in the *Uluru Statement from the Heart*, which says:

> Our Aboriginal and Torres Strait Islander tribes were the first sovereign Nations of the Australian continent and its adjacent islands, and possessed it under our own laws and

68 McMillan, "Koowarta and the Rival Indigenous International: Our Place as Indigenous Peoples in the International," 117.

69 See particularly Christine Black, *The Land Is The Source of the Law: A Dialogic Encounter with Indigenous Jurisprudence* (Abingdon: Routledge, 2010).

70 Wendy Brady, "That Sovereign Being: History Matters," in *Sovereign Subjects: Indigenous Sovereignty Matters*, ed. Aileen Moreton-Robinson (Sydney: Allen & Unwin, 2007): Part 3, Chapter 9.

71 Ravi de Costa, *A Higher Authority: Indigenous Transnationalism and Australia* (Sydney: University of New South Wales Press, 2006).

72 Mark McMillan and Sophie Rigney, "The Place of the First Peoples in the International Sphere: A Logical Starting Point for the Demand for Justice for Indigenous Peoples," *Melbourne University Law Review* 39, no. 3 (2016): 981, 993.

73 Ibid., 992.

74 For more on Indigenous international law, see also Paulo Ilich Bacca, "Indigenizing International Law: Inverse Legal Anthropology in the age of Jurisdicitonal Double Binds" (PhD Thesis, Kent Law School, Canterbury, 2018); Amar Bhatia, "The South of the North: Building on Critical Approaches to International Law with Lessons from the Fourth World," *Oregon Review of International Law* 14 (2012): 131.

75 Aileen Moreton-Robinson, "Introduction," in *Sovereign Subjects: Indigenous Sovereignty Matters,* ed. Aileen Moreton-Robinson (Sydney: Allen & Unwin, 2007), 1.

> customs. . . . This sovereignty is a spiritual notion: the ancestral tie between the land, or 'mother nature', and the Aboriginal and Torres Strait Islander peoples who were born therefrom, remain attached thereto, and must one day return thither to be united with our ancestors. This link is the basis of the ownership of the soil, or better, of sovereignty. It has never been ceded or extinguished, and co-exists with the sovereignty of the Crown.[76]

Indigenous conceptions of sovereignty are therefore in a relationship with the land as a source of life, law, culture and spirituality.[77] This relationality at the heart of Indigenous ideas of sovereignty reflects the fact that 'relational philosophy is embedded in Indigenous knowledge systems'.[78] This relationality is also reflected in several passages of *Welcome to Country*. In particular, the book discusses Bunjil, the eagle 'creator spirit' of the Wurundjeri people, who 'created man, woman and child from the land' and 'the birds, the animals, the mountains, the rivers'. The book opens with the statement: 'Our ancestors left their mark on the land for us to follow in their footsteps. We have a presence on this earth through the spirits of our ancestors.' It later reiterates, 'We thank you, for you have now joined with us to pay respect to the spirit of our ancestors, who have nurtured this land for thousands of years.' Elsewhere, the book demonstrates the mutual recognition of this sovereignty, in the statement: 'We respectfully acknowledge our elders and the community of this land and *all elders and communities of this continent and neighbouring islands*. We thank them for their courage, strength, integrity and values' (emphasis added).

Welcome to Country also outlines some of the particular protocols for engagement for visitors to Country. In particular, the book invites the reader (or visitor to Country) to 'take a leaf from the branches of the white river gum'. Accepting a leaf 'means you are welcome to everything, from the tops of the trees to the roots of the earth. But you must take from this land only what you can give back.' Here, we see the relationships and responsibilities that are inherent in visiting this sovereign jurisdiction.

Reading *Welcome to Country* as an international lawyer – and as an archive of information about international law, complemented by the writings of Indigenous jurisprudents – we read an articulation of Indigenous international legal ordering and concepts. Sovereignty, recognition, jurisdiction and responsibility are all articulated in this book. Reading the book in this way is an engagement with the lawfulness of Indigenous communities.

Creating a framework for engagement with Indigenous law

What to make, then, of these stories? We can see from the above that many children are taught stories (like *Snugglepot and Cuddlepie*) which suggest a lawlessness of Indigeneity in Australia; but we also see that there are stories (like *Welcome to Country*) which show the robust lawfulness of Indigenous peoples and nations. Further, we witness that this lawfulness includes, in the words of Orford, 'indigenous laws as another source of ceremonies, languages, privileges

76 "Uluru Statement from the Heart," *The Uluru Statement*, accessed May 26, 2017, https://ulurustatement.org/the-statement.

77 See Black, *The Land Is The Source of the Law: A Dialogic Encounter with Indigenous Jurisprudence*. See also Brady, "That Sovereign Being: History Matters," 142, who notes that 'the sovereign Indigenous nation is formed through the ancestral and communal relationship . . . each individual is part of the fabric of both authority and power that is interdependent on the other.'

78 Watson, *Aboriginal Peoples, Colonisation and International Law: Raw Law*, 13. See also Shawn Wilson, *Research Is Ceremony: Indigenous Research Methods* (Canada: Fernwood Publishing, 2008).

and obligations governing the meeting of laws'.[79] Nonetheless, as I argued at the start of this chapter, European/settler-colonial international law has long denied this. As Orford points out, there has traditionally been 'little consideration amongst non-indigenous lawyers of indigenous laws as a source of law governing relations between nations – that is, as a source of international law'.[80]

I would argue that in reading these books as international lawyers, we are invited to consider how European/settler-colonial international law – much like Snugglepot and Cuddlepie – has depicted Indigenous communities as lawless, through the application of doctrines like *terra nullius* and the concept of recognition, and has denied the very clear lawfulness of Indigenous communities. Indeed, European/settler-colonial international law has intended this denial, and has gained strength from this denial. But this is not the only way. The possibility of *Welcome to Country* is not only to acknowledge the existence of Indigenous laws to govern the relationships between Indigenous nations and others. It is possible to go further than this and create a framework for genuine engagement between European and Indigenous international laws. If jurisdiction can be understood as the act of 'speaking the law',[81] then an ethical jurisdictional encounter must involve genuine listening to the law of the other jurisdiction. The suggestion of 'genuine' engagement, and 'genuine' listening, normatively argues for a fundamentally different jurisdictional engagement than one in which one jurisdiction denies another. However, just as common law jurisprudence has 'struggled to create an appropriate form and conduct of the relations between itself and Indigenous laws and jurisprudence . . . struggled . . . to create an appropriate meeting place of laws',[82] likewise, European international law has struggled to truly consider how it may ethically and genuinely meet with other international legal orders.

In reading these books as non-Indigenous international lawyers, then, perhaps we can be encouraged to 'live with honour according to law',[83] and to take 'responsibility for the practices our own conduct as jurists authorises'.[84] Part of this must be a consideration of the ways in which we can envisage an ethical and genuine meeting of Indigenous and European international laws.

79 Orford, "Ritual, Mediation and the International Laws of the South," 353.

80 Ibid.

81 See Shaunnagh Dorsett and Shaun McVeigh, *Jurisdiction* (New York: Routledge, 2012); see also Pahuja, "Laws of Encounter: A Jurisdictional Account of International Law," 63–98; McMillan, "Koowarta and the Rival Indigenous International: Our Place as Indigenous Peoples in the International," 110.

82 Shaunnagh Dorsett and Shaun McVeigh, "Conduct of Laws: Native Title, Responsibility, and Some Limits of Jurisdictional Thinking," *Melbourne University Law Review* 36, no. 2 (2012): 470.

83 Orford, "Ritual, Mediation and the International Laws of the South," 353.

84 Pahuja, "Laws of Encounter: A Jurisdictional Account of International Law," 92.

Concepts for our time

31

International law and the humanities in the Anthropocene

Kathleen Birrell and Julia Dehm

In this chapter, we will address the various ways in which key concepts that frame and animate thought and scholarship in international law and the humanities are being rethought and reanimated in response to the 'Anthropocene'.[1] The Anthropocene thesis, originating in geological and Earth systems science, controversially proposes the inauguration of a new geological epoch, in accordance with which the impact of the *anthropos* – the human – has assumed geological proportions. While this appellation remains relatively undertheorised in legal scholarship,[2] we draw upon an expansive literature in the humanities and social sciences to consider its implications for international law. The ascription of this term to the present moment is highly contested, invoking a variety of normative claims and imperatives. Given that understandings and implications of the Anthropocene thesis are subject to political contestation and normative choice, we emphasise that it does not impel a singular mode of engagement but, rather, poses critical questions about the futures we wish to collectively build. Described as a 'portmanteau term',[3] the Anthropocene concept might be also considered a galvanising idea that marshals different interdisciplinary engagements between law and the humanities, and indeed draws attention to the inhuman in the humanities.[4] We foreground the inherent political choices in different ways of engaging the Anthropocene thesis that could variously reinforce dominant frames or unsettle and pluralise international law. While acknowledging its critical reception, we suggest that as a conceptual frame and provocation as well as a proposed epochal demarcation, the Anthropocene might be adopted in more counter-hegemonic ways to illuminate rather than perpetuate the hierarchies and abstractions implicit within its nomenclature. Further, it might prompt legal scholars to relinquish modernist claims to mastery in the pursuit of a determinate trajectory or universalising law. Ultimately, we suggest that an embrace of the plurality of

1 We use single quotation marks to acknowledge contestation surrounding this term. While continuing to acknowledge this, quotation marks are dropped hereafter.

2 See however, Louis Kotzé, *Global Environmental Constitutionalism in the Anthropocene* (London: Bloomsbury, 2016); Louis Kotzé, ed., *Environmental Law and Governance for the Anthropocene* (London: Hart Publishing, 2017).

3 Jedediah Purdy, *After Nature: A Politics for the Anthropocene* (Cambridge: Harvard University Press, 2015), 4.

4 Elizabeth Grosz, Kathryn Yusoff and Nigel Clark, "An Interview with Elizabeth Grosz: Geopower, Inhumanism and the Biopolitical" (2017) 34(2-3) Theory, Culture and Society 129-146, 131.

the broader Anthropocene concept enlivens new collective possibilities and encounters within and between communities as well as scholarly disciplines, and might facilitate a more responsive, radical and open international law.

To begin, we discuss the contested reception and interpretation of the Anthropocene thesis and suggest ways in which these critical engagements could compel alternative conceptualisations of a more radical counter-Anthropocene. Turning to emergent critical thought on approaches to history and temporality enlivened by the Anthropocene, conceived as both scientific thesis and conceptual provocation, we then examine the proposed collapse of distinctions between geological and human world history and different temporal modalities illuminated. We particularly consider the implications of these temporal recalibrations for international law, including the reappraisal of linear temporal accounts and distinctions between human and geological timescales. We reflect upon the spatial abstractions that the Anthropocene concept reveals within the global imaginary of international law, and the different ways in which the 'globe' of 'globalisation' and the 'global' of the planetary are imagined. We emphasise the need for new imaginaries and representational strategies to render visible incremental violence and injustice and to bear witness to grounded and more extensive articulations of justice. We consider broader conceptualisations of agency inaugurated by the Anthropocene, including the need to account for the agency of the more-than-human and the implications of this for international legal scholarship. Finally, we suggest that the Anthropocene prompts a rethinking of modes of connection and inter-species entanglements, as well as of the nature of obligations, responsibilities and relationships arising from lawful encounters, with particular reference to Indigenous jurisprudences. We conclude with reflections on the opportunities provided by a critical and political engagement with the Anthropocene to imagine the pluralisation of international law.

The very idea of the Anthropocene, as a new global narrative, conceptual apparatus and provocation, as well as a proposed new geological epoch, has been met with both approval and censure. Initially presented in the International Geosphere Biosphere Program *Global Change Newsletter* in 2000 and subsequently published in the journal *Nature* in 2002, Dutch geochemist Paul Crutzen and American biologist Eugene Stoermer identified 'the central role of mankind in geology and ecology'.[5] Whether conceived as epoch,[6] ideology,[7] condition,[8] thesis,[9] trope[10] or turn,[11] this concept has provoked enormous contestation surrounding its interpretation in

5 Paul Crutzen and Eugene Stoermer, "The Anthropocene," *Global Change Newsletter* 41, no. 1 (May 2000): 17.

6 Ibid.; Paul Crutzen, "Geology of Mankind," *Nature* 415, no. 1 (January 2002): 23.

7 Jeremy Baskin, "Paradigm Dressed as Epoch: The Ideology of the Anthropocene," *Environmental Values* 24, no. 1 (2015): 10–11.

8 Purdy, *After Nature*, 4.

9 Jean Luc Nancy, "The Existence of the World Is Always Unexpected," trans. Jeffery Malecki, in *Art in the Anthropocene: Encounters Among Aesthetics, Politics, Environments and Epistemologies*, eds. Heather Davis and Etienne Turpin (London: Open Humanities Press, 2015), 87; Daniel Matthews, "Law and Aesthetics in the Anthropocene: From the Rights of Nature to the Aesthesis of Obligations," *Law, Culture and the Humanities* (2019), https://doi.org/10.1177/1743872119871830.

10 Anna Grear, "Deconstructing Anthropos: A Critical Legal Reflection on 'Anthropocentric' Law and Anthropocene 'Humanity'," *Law and Critique* 26, no. 3 (2015): 226–27. See also Louise Kotzé, "Reflections on the Future of Environmental Law Scholarship and Methodology in the Anthropocene," in *Perspectives on Environmental Law Scholarship: Essays on Purpose, Shape and Direction*, ed. Ole Pedersen (Cambridge: Cambridge University Press, 2018), 140.

11 Manuel Arias-Maldonado, "The 'Anthropocene' in Philosophy: The Neo-Material Turn and the Question of Nature," in *Anthropocene Encounters: New Directions in Green Political Thinking*, eds. Frank Biermann and Eva Lövbrand (Cambridge: Cambridge University Press, 2019), 50.

the sciences, social sciences, humanities and arts. Beginning as a tentative proposition in the physical and earth sciences[12] – a proposition that remains under review by a special working group of the Subcommission of Quaternary Stratigraphy – the Anthropocene thesis contemplates the naming of a new geological epoch to reflect the relatively recent and catastrophic impact of humanity upon the Earth. Attribution of meaning to the term has now extended beyond geoscientific authority as the concept has rapidly entered broader scholarly, political and cultural discourse.[13] Irrespective of its confirmation as a geological epoch, the Anthropocene is understood to be both 'a collective assemblage of scientific enunciation', as well as 'an inherently political concept',[14] which operates as an 'invitation to rethink conventional philosophical and political categories'.[15]

The premise of the Anthropocene thesis – namely, that humans have become a 'geological force'[16] and so fundamentally changed our environment that distinctions between nature and society have collapsed[17] – could operate to both authorise and destabilise assumptions of human mastery over the natural world. Some commentators lament 'the poverty of our nomenclature',[18] and suggest that this term facilitates the troubling pursuit of 'active planetary management'[19] on the understanding that, for Crutzen and German journalist Christian Schwägerl, 'we . . . decide what nature is and what it will be'.[20] The thesis has been further and pejoratively described as 'an homogenizing abstraction',[21] 'a discursive development . . . with shadowy repercussions',[22] a 'narrative tool' for domination, 'which gathers discursive steam',[23] an 'intervention by geoscientists into politics' and an ideological 'paradigm dressed as epoch'.[24] Jeremy Baskin has argued that while the Anthropocene thesis is presented as a scientific account, it is simultaneously invested in a particular 'ideational underpinning', which universalises and elevates the (male) Anthropos,

12 Crutzen and Stoermer, "The Anthropocene"; Crutzen, "Geology of Mankind"; Paul Crutzen and Christian Schwägerl, "Living in the Anthropocene: Toward a New Global Ethos," *Yale Environment* 360, accessed September 10, 2019, https://e360.yale.edu/features/living_in_the_anthropocene_toward_a_new_global_ethos.

13 Jamie Lorimer, "The Anthropo-scene: A Guide for the Perplexed," *Social Studies of Science* 47, no. 1 (2017): 117–42, 132.

14 Heather Davis and Etienne Turpin, "Art and Death: Lives Between the Fifth Assessment & the Sixth Extinction," in *Art in the Anthropocene: Encounters Among Aesthetics, Politics, Environments and Epistemologies*, eds. Heather Davis and Etienne Turpin (London: Open Humanities Press, 2015), 7.

15 Frank Biermann and Eva Lövbrand, "Encountering the 'Anthropocene': Setting the Scene," in *Anthropocene Encounters: New Directions in Green Political Thinking*, eds. Frank Biermann and Eva Lövbrand (Cambridge: Cambridge University Press, 2019), 3.

16 Dipesh Chakrabarty, "The Climate of History: Four Theses," *Critical Inquiry* 35, no. 2 (Winter 2009): 201.

17 Bruno Latour, "Fourth Lecture: The Anthropocene and the Destruction of (the image of) the Globe," in *Facing Gaia: Eight Lectures on the New Climatic Regime*, ed. Bruno Latour (Cambridge: Polity Press, 2017). See also Purdy, *After Nature*, 3.

18 Eileen Crist, "On the Poverty of Our Nomenclature," in *Anthropocene or Capitalocene? Nature, History, and the Crisis of Capitalism*, ed. Jason Moore (Oakland: PM Press, 2016), 27.

19 Baskin, "Paradigm Dressed as Epoch," 10. See earlier reference to 'planetary management' in Andrew Ross, *Strange Weather: Culture, Science and Technology in the Age of Limits* (New York: Verso, 1991), 207–12.

20 Crutzen and Schwägerl, "Living in the Anthropocene."

21 Manuel Arias-Maldonado, *Environment and Society: Socionatural Relations in the Anthropocene* (Switzerland: Springer, 2015), 6.

22 Crist, "On the Poverty of Our Nomenclature," 14.

23 Zoe Todd, "Indigenizing the Anthropocene," in *Art in the Anthropocene: Encounters Among Aesthetics, Politics, Environments and Epistemologies*, eds. Heather Davis and Etienne Turpin (London: Open Humanities Press, 2015), 244.

24 Baskin, "Paradigm Dressed as Epoch," 23; especially 10–11.

'promotes instrumental reason' and legitimates 'non-democratic and technophilic approaches', such as geoengineering.[25] Further, he identifies a troubling connection between the Anthropocene concept and normative accounts of 'global justice' and development.[26] This connection is exemplified in the increasing application of the concept of resilience to human populations in the context of climate change, as informed by the imperatives of sustainable development. For Brad Evans and Julian Reid, political subjects are interpellated in accordance with an 'an ideal of *resilience*'.[27] This ideal depoliticises localised climate change narratives and reinforces the ontological and epistemological violence and subsequent structural inequalities of colonisation[28] that preceded climate change,[29] addressed now only in the language of disproportionate and increased exposure and vulnerability to its effects.[30] Indeed, some argue that the central claim of Anthropocene discourse to unprecedented ecological crisis constitutes a denial of the 'catastrophic ruptures' of empire: 'the apocalypse has already happened'.[31]

Alternative epochal nomenclature has been proffered – the 'Manthropocene',[32] the 'Econocene',[33] the 'Capitalocene',[34] the 'Technocene'[35] and the 'Plantationocene',[36] among others. For Donna Haraway, these terms should all be abandoned in favour of the 'Chthulucene', a term derived from but exceeding Greek linguistic roots. Drawing upon Jacques Derrida's notion of 'response-ability', as an active responsibility, which 'assigns [us] even in [our] liberty', Haraway defines the chthulucene as 'a timeplace for learning to stay with the trouble of living and dying in response-ability on a damaged earth'.[37] Eschewing orientations toward either 'apocalyptic or salvific futures', including 'a comic faith in technofixes', she urges the acknowledgment of our overlapping temporal, corporeal and ontological entanglements.[38] Countering Haraway and others in rejecting the term, Latour presses us to consider the radical potential of the Anthropocene, as a concept inaugurating wide-ranging reorientations. Emphasising its broader implications, he argues that the Anthropocene provides a linguistic and conceptual apparatus with which to describe immense geological and atmospheric change (without

25 Ibid., 9, 11.

26 Jeremy Baskin, "Global Justice and the Anthropocene: Reproducing a Development Story," in *Anthropocene Encounters: New Directions in Green Political Thinking*, eds. Frank Biermann and Eva Lövbrand (Cambridge: Cambridge University Press, 2019).

27 Brad Evans and Julian Reid, *Resilient Life: The Art of Living Dangerously* (Cambridge: Polity Press, 2014), 2.

28 Silja Klepp and Libertad Chavez-Rodriguez, "Governing Climate Change: The Power of Adaptation Discourses, Policies and Practices," in *A Critical Approach to Climate Change Adaptation Discourses, Policies and Practices*, eds. Silja Klepp and Libertad Chavez-Rodriguez (London: Routledge, 2018), 8–12.

29 See Slavoj Žižek, "Against the Populist Temptation," *Critical Inquiry* 32, no. 1 (Spring 2006): 555, discussed in Erik Swyngedouw, "Apocalypse Forever? Post-Political Populism and the Spectre of Climate Change," *Theory, Culture & Society* 27, no. 2–3 (2010): 222.

30 United Nations, *World Economic and Social Survey 2016* (New York: United Nations, 2016), Ch 2, www.un.org/development/desa/dpad/wp-content/uploads/sites/45/2_Chapter_WESS2016.pdf.

31 Elizabeth DeLoughrey, *Allegories of the Anthropocene* (Durham, NC: Duke University Press, 2019), 7.

32 Kate Raworth, "Must the Anthropocene Be a Manthropocene?" *The Guardian*, October 20, 2014, www.theguardian.com/commentisfree/2014/oct/20/anthropocene-working-group-science-gender-bias. See also Giovanna Di Chiro, "Welcome to the White (M)Anthropocene? A Feminist-environmentalist Critique," in *Routledge Handbook of Gender and Environment*, ed. Sherilyn MacGregor (Abingdon: Routledge, 2017), 487–505.

33 Dipesh Chakrabarty, "The Seventh *History and Theory* Lecture," *History and Theory* 57, no. 1 (March 2018): 6.

34 Moore, *Anthropocene or Capitalocene?*

35 Nancy, "The Existence of the World Is Always Unexpected," 88.

36 Donna Haraway, *Staying with the Trouble: Making Kin in the Chthulucene* (Durham, NC: Duke University Press, 2016).

37 Ibid., 2.

38 Ibid., 1, 3.

necessarily providing prescriptive 'solutions'),[39] and to reveal our entanglements with rather than 'mastery' over the Earth, where the latter is no longer 'triumphal'.[40] Further, it facilitates the abandonment of the modernist ideal of the globe, and the recognition of an epoch that is not universal and universalising but 'post-natural, post-human, and post-epistemological'.[41] Accordingly, we might imagine (and perhaps embrace) the Anthropocene as a descriptor for this '*postnatural* period' – that is, a period in which dominant narratives must relinquish the foregrounding of human life and endeavour and attachments to 'nature' as existing in 'equilibrium' or as 'systematic, deanimated, global'.[42] Given that scholarly engagement with the Anthropocene concept is now a veritable 'cottage industry',[43] we follow and extend Latour in urging that 'to stay with the trouble it's better to stay with the word'.[44] Yet, we stress that the meanings signified by the 'Anthropocene' remain open and subject to destabilisation and pluralisation.

We suggest that for international law, an embrace of the Anthropocene as a radicalising conceptual apparatus could facilitate an unprecedented interdisciplinarity, with important implications for the theory and praxis of decoloniality.[45] For Andreas Philippopoulos-Mihalopoulos, the Anthropocene inaugurates a new 'grammar, perspective and methodology'[46] and provides the productive impetus for epistemological ruptures.[47] Indeed, the Anthropocene introduces new possibilities for productive intersections between international law and the sciences, humanities, and arts, which might be also understood in terms of 'ecotones'.[48] As described and adapted by literary scholar Rob Nixon, this term refers to border zones between adjacent communities of vegetation, which generate new possibilities in the creation of 'edge effects'.[49] Interdisciplinary encounters in 'scholarly ecotones' might facilitate 'new dynamic combinations' and 'connective corridors' in the context of growing scholarly 'habitat fracture'.[50] Some scholars have further proposed a 'counter-Anthropocene', which requires a 'rethinking' of modernity and political conversations about viable 'future Anthropocenes'.[51] Such alternative renderings might resist the implicit hierarchies of the *anthropos* (to which we will return); indeed, Zoe Todd has proposed the 'gleeful disruption' of hegemonic understandings of the Anthropocene through academic and artistic engagement with the local '*in situ* challenges' of climate change.[52]

Debates surrounding the Anthropocene thesis, as a descriptor for a geological unit of time, process and strata, frequently coalesce around its date of commencement and how to understand the figure of the *anthropos*, humanity or the human-species that is positioned as a 'geological agent'. The majority of the Anthropocene Working Group has now voted to date this new

39 Baskin, "Paradigm Dressed as Epoch," 13.
40 Latour, "Fourth Lecture," 115.
41 Ibid., 144.
42 Ibid., 142.
43 DeLoughrey, *Allegories*, 2.
44 Latour, "Fourth Lecture," 121, footnote 30.
45 Todd, "Indigenizing the Anthropocene"; Catherine Walsh and Walter Mignolo, *On Decoloniality: Concepts, Analytics, Praxis* (Durham, NC: Duke University Press, 2018).
46 Andreas Philippopoulos-Mihalopoulos, "Critical Environmental Law as Method in the Anthropocene," in *Research Methods in Environmental Law*, eds. Andreas Philippopoulos-Mihalopoulos and Victoria Brooks (Northampton: Edward Elgar Publishing, 2017), 132.
47 Ibid., 131, 139–40.
48 Rob Nixon, *Slow Violence and the Environmentalism of the Poor* (Cambridge: Harvard University Press, 2011), 30.
49 Ibid.
50 Ibid., 30–31.
51 Arias-Maldonado, *Environment and Society*, 88–90.
52 Todd, "Indigenizing the Anthropocene," 252.

geological epoch to the mid-twentieth century, pending formal confirmation.[53] Others have proposed 'a time-transgressive Anthropocene', lacking a single impetus or chronology,[54] a pluralisation of origins that could perhaps better acknowledge the accretive impacts of colonisation, capitalism and industrialisation.[55] The Anthropocene compels a reconfiguration of the temporal relationships between the past, present and future, and the ways in which these are experienced, envisioned and enacted.[56] The different temporal narratives deployed to structure accounts of climate change all have considerable shortcomings and risk frustrating present action, decision and responsibility. Climate change is commonly narrated as an inexorable catastrophe, yet such accounts may generate impotence and foreclose action in the present. Alternative accounts narrate climate change as a clarion call to action, resistance and collective agency, yet these may overemphasise the regenerative capacity of collective agency and resistance in the face of past action and inaction.[57] One response has been to disrupt assumptions of a singular chronology, with some activist/scholars suggesting that ecological crisis generates 'shadow time', the sense of experiencing two timescales simultaneously.[58] Indeed, Astra Taylor suggests that conventional chronology might itself present a barrier to sustainability, where climate change merges the past, present and future.[59]

Similarly, an attentiveness to imperial histories and colonial violence provides a basis for interrogating the figure of the *anthropos* as undifferentiated humanity or the human-species that debates surrounding the Anthropocene invoke as both culpable and responsible agent. Dipesh Chakrabarty somewhat reluctantly accedes to the necessity of 'species thinking' and a 'universal history of life' in the face of the existential threat of climate change, in a context where there are 'no lifeboats here for the rich and privileged'.[60] Countering these claims and the ways in which the dominance of natural science displaces engagements with social and cultural theory, Andreas Malm and Alf Hornborg highlight the 'differentiated vulnerabilities at all scales of human societies' and show that the catastrophe of climate change is 'not universal, but uneven and combined'.[61] Similarly, Jason Moore has warned that the positioning of humanity as a 'largely homogenous, acting unit' in dominant Anthropocene discourses operates to obscure inequality, commodification, imperialism, patriarchy, racism and more.[62] Indeed, Anna Grear

53 Meera Subramanian, "Anthropocene Now: Influential Panel Votes to Recognize Earth's New Epoch," *Nature News*, May 21, 2019, www.nature.com/articles/d41586-019-01641-5?utm_source=fbk_nnc&utm_medium=social&utm_campaign=naturenews&sf213192063 = 1.

54 Ibid.

55 Simon Lewis and Mark Andrew Maslin, "Defining the Anthropocene," *Nature* 519, no. 1 (2015): 171.

56 See Anna Grear, "'Anthropocene Time?' – A Reflection on Temporalities in the 'New Age of the Human'," in *Routledge Handbook of Law and Theory*, ed. Andreas Philippopoulos-Mihalopoulos (Abingdon: Routledge, 2019), 297–315.

57 This is discussed further in Julia Dehm, "International Law, Temporalities and Narratives of Climate Crisis," *London Review of International Law* 4, no. 1 (2016): 167.

58 "Shadow Time," *The Bureau of Linguistical Reality*, accessed October 30, 2019, https://bureauoflinguisticalreality.com/portfolio/shadowtime/.

59 Astra Taylor, "Bad Ancestors: Does the Climate Crisis Violate the Rights of Those Not Yet Born?" *The Guardian*, October 1, 2019, www.theguardian.com/environment/2019/oct/01/bad-ancestors-climate-crisis-democracy; Astra Taylor, "Out of Time: Listening to the Climate's Clock," *Lapham's Quarterly*, accessed January 20, 2020, www.laphamsquarterly.org/climate/out-time.

60 Chakrabarty, "The Climate of History," 221.

61 Andreas Malm and Alf Hornborg, "The Geology of Mankind? A Critique of the Anthropocene Narrative," *The Anthropocene Review* 1, no. 1 (2014): 67.

62 Jason Moore, "The Capitalocene, Part I: On the Nature and Origins of Our Ecological Crisis," *Journal of Peasant Studies* 44, no. 3 (2017): 596–97.

argues that reference to 'human *species* responsibility' both disguises and replicates the very 'discursive and material hierarchisation' that created and perpetuates the conditions for the climate crisis and its injustices.[63] Tracing the ontological and epistemological foundations of the *anthropos* in the 'disembodied Cartesian *cogito* and Kantian transcendent person' as foundational to the legal subject of modernity,[64] Grear reveals the inherent 'intra- and inter-species hierarchies' and associated historical and structural inequalities subsumed within the Anthropocene thesis.[65] The Anthropocene refers to universal human responsibility, she argues, without interrogation of the *anthropos* itself, which is a mere 'cypher' for a human subject that is 'emphatically *not* its "others"', human and non-human.[66] Given that these hierarchies are foundational to the 'exclusions enacted by "anthropocentric" law and constructions of juridical "human" subjectivity', Grear advocates a more 'critical-creative' theorising and deployment of legal personhood and the consequent embrace of the plural subjectivities of 'an open juridical ecology'.[67] As a call to reframe our 'industrialized present' as simultaneously 'evolutionary and geologic',[68] it prompts a reassessment of dominant accounts of sovereignty, governance, rights, obligations and legal subjectivity in international law.

The Anthropocene, therefore, necessitates novel international legal engagements with the past. With methodological implications for the broader 'historical turn' in international law, such engagements compel a reconsideration of the purpose and effects of historical accounts and their modes of enunciation and disclosure.[69] Moreover, the Anthropocene illuminates the limitations of international legal accounts of temporality, and especially the way in which 'international law continues to construct/be constructed by the idea of progress'.[70] Dipesh Chakrabarty has proposed transformative implications for thought on human history in the context of climate change,[71] identifying a 'conceptual traffic between Earth history and world history'.[72] The recognition that humans now wield geological force, he argues, collapses the putatively 'age old' distinction between human and geological timescales, unsettling the humanist distinction between 'natural history' and 'human history'.[73] This account, however, fails to properly historicise the distinction between human and geological history, the context in which it came to be made, its effects and consequent displacements.[74] Reinhart Koselleck has traced the conceptual distinction between natural and human history to the emergence of modernity in the late eighteenth century.[75] During this period, modes of historical writing were transformed: historical narratives were imbued with the poetry and linearity of epics, and the concept of a philosophy of history emerged alongside the temporalisation of history and was fused with the

63 Grear, "Deconstructing Anthropos," 245.
64 Ibid., 231–42.
65 Ibid., 233.
66 Ibid., 237, 241.
67 Ibid., 230, 231, 246.
68 Davis and Turpin, "Art and Death," 6.
69 See Matthew Craven, "Theorizing the Turn to History in International Law," in *Oxford Handbook of the Theory of International Law*, eds. Anne Orford and Florian Hoffmann (New York: Oxford University Press, 2016), 21–22.
70 Thomas Skouteris, "The Idea of Progress," in *The Oxford Handbook of the Theory of International Law*, eds. Anne Orford and Florian Hoffmann (New York: Oxford University Press, 2016), 940.
71 Chakrabarty, "The Climate of History," 198.
72 Dipesh Chakrabarty, "Anthropocene Time," *History and Theory* 57, no. 1 (2018): 6.
73 Chakrabarty, "The Climate of History," 201–7.
74 We are indebted to Adil Hasan Khan for this insight.
75 Reinhart Koselleck, *Futures Past: On the Semantics of Historical Time* (New York: Colombia University Press, 2004), 36.

notion of 'progress'.[76] These transformations were integral to modernist conceptions of the purpose and method of historical narrative and, as Matthew Craven suggests, bore consequences for the formulation of international legal knowledge.[77] Orthodox sources of international law were limited by the notion of history as linear and recognised only in accordance with the customs and practices of European states, thereby obscuring other laws.[78] Progress narratives affirm faith in the notion of 'universal justice' that enlivens international law,[79] even as the Anthropocene might be better perceived as a catalyst for interrogating these assumptions and rethinking relations between law, progress and temporality.[80]

These conceptual shifts, including the occidental distinction between human and natural histories, involved the displacement of alternatives and valuable modes of engagement with the past. Exemplar history, practiced by the Greeks and Romans and predominant until the nineteenth century, was a didactic and inductive method of intergenerational instruction and transmission of virtues. Principles of conduct and morality were taught through the past experience of others, rather than the precepts of moral philosophy.[81] Rather than temporalising narratives of the climate crisis that risk foreclosing action, decision and responsibility in the present, this rival practice of exemplar history may offer ways of engaging the past in order to learn modes of conduct for living ethically in the Anthropocene. The work of Sioux scholar Nick Estes on resistance to the Dakota Access Pipelines, which is informed both by '*traditions* of Indigenous resistance' and contemporary resurgent resistance, resonates with practices of exemplar history.[82] Describing the traditions of Indigenous resistance that preceded the #NoDAPL movement alongside the experience of the camp at Standing Rock, Estes illustrates, by example, the virtues of courage and determination necessary to resist settler-colonialism and extractive capitalism and forge decolonial futures. This work is underpinned by a temporal continuity in Sioux ontology, which does not separate past, present and future but considers them to be structured by the ancestral past.[83] Resistance practices are perpetually engaged in processes of reconnecting to 'Indigenous places and histories' and revitalising these 'suppressed practices' to allow them to 'make a crack in history' and thereby challenge the 'colonial present'.[84]

The spatial imaginary of international law, in accordance with which the world is confined to a 'territorial matrix' that conditions and reproduces understandings of international order,[85] is also challenged by the Anthropocene concept. This imaginary has narrowed 'the active boundaries of geopolitics and geo-economics',[86] privileged specific practices of spa-

76 Ibid., 34, 36–37.
77 Craven, "Theorizing the Turn to History in International Law," 27.
78 Rose Parfitt, "The Spectre of Sources," *European Journal of International Law* 25, no. 1 (2014): 297–306.
79 Cait Storr, "Islands and the South: Framing the Relationship Between International Law and Environmental Crisis," *The European Journal of International Law* 27, no. 2 (2016): 521.
80 Julia Dehm, "Reflections on Paris: Thoughts Towards a Critical Approach to Climate Law," *Revue québécoise de droit international* 1, no. 1 (2018): 71.
81 George Nadel, "Philosophy of History before Historicism," *History and Theory* 3, no. 3 (1964): 298; Kosseleck, *Futures Past*, 36.
82 Nick Estes, *Our History Is the Future: Standing Rock Versus the Dakota Access Pipeline, and the Long Tradition of Indigenous Resistance* (London: Verso, 2019).
83 Ibid., 14.
84 Ibid., 18.
85 See Nikolas Rajkovic, "The Visual Conquest of International Law: Brute Boundaries, the Map and the Legacy of Cartogenesis," *Leiden Journal of International Law* 31, no. 2 (2018): 272.
86 Ibid., 269.

tial authority and disciplined postcolonial imaginaries of 'independence',[87] and delimited the possible relations between law and place. What sort of spatial literacy does the Anthropocene require? International relations scholars have proposed that their discipline's conceptual and analytical division of the globe into distinct nation-states is 'undone' by the infinite assemblages of the planetary.[88] Nonetheless, the alternative spatial imaginary of the planetary that informs Earth system science and governance is premised on a 'transcendental subjectivity that sees the world from the point of view of the cosmos itself'[89] and reflects an epistemic standpoint that is both totalising and withdrawn.[90] Reflecting the universalising 'figure of the Globe', imprinted in our collective consciousness by the 'blue planet image' of the Earth as viewed from space,[91] this vantage point reflects a highly modernist paradigm that flattens heterogeneity and elides 'the particularities of places'.[92] For Latour, the globe epitomises the singularity of Western philosophy, science, theology and politics, and fails to pay attention to 'the way in which the Globe might be built, tended, maintained and inhabited'.[93] Indeed, he suggests, the 'immense danger' that global thinking presents is of 'unifying too quickly what first needs to be composed'.[94]

This warning, however, also suggests an alternative orientation toward the global that is not premised on a 'leap beyond the world' and conceptual abstractions and totalisations but, rather, a situated view of the global as the product of interactions and interconnections. For Chakrabarty, the 'globe' of 'globalisation' differs markedly from the 'globe' of 'global warming', with each conjuring different ways of picturing the planet and the place of humans.[95] The former suggests a 'whole' that is 'discovered on the ground', constituted by human connections and thus also 'crisscrossed by issues of identity and difference', while the latter is perspectival, envisaging this planet in the context of others.[96] Although Chakrabarty suggests that climate change unsettles the former, activist strategies to mitigate climate change are increasingly attending to global connections that enable fossil fuel extraction, circulation and combustion or deforestation[97] through global supply chains, logistics and infrastructures,[98] as well as banking, finance,

87 Vasuki Nesiah, "Placing International Law: White Spaces on a Map," *Leiden Journal of International Law* 16, no. 1 (2003): 2.

88 Anthony Burke, et al., "Planet Politics: A Manifesto from the End of IR," *Millennium: Journal of International Studies* 44, no. 3 (2016): 501.

89 Vassos Argyrou, *The Logic of Environmentalism: Anthropology, Ecology and Postcoloniality* (New York: Berghahn Books, 2005), 96.

90 Dipesh Chakrabarty, "Planetary Crisis and the Difficulty of Being Modern," *Millennium: Journal of International Studies* 46, no. 3 (2018): 265.

91 Latour, "Fourth Lecture," 130.

92 Brian Cook, Lauren Rickards and Ian Rutherfurd, "Geographies of the Anthropocene," *Geographical Research* 53, no. 3 (2015): 235. See also Kathryn Yusoff, "The Anthropocene and Geographies of Geopower," in *Handbook on the Geographies of Power*, eds. Mat Coleman and Jon Agnew (London: Edward Elgar, 2018).

93 Latour, "Fourth Lecture," 123.

94 Ibid., 138.

95 Chakrabarty, "Planetary Crisis and the Difficulty of Being Modern," 260.

96 Ibid., 261, 263, 265.

97 For example, in response to Amazon fires, Indigenous communities have called for a boycott of Brazilian agribusiness engaged in invading and deforesting protected areas, but also of foreign companies implicated through transnational supply chains: Marianne Brooker, "Brazilian Indigenous People Propose Boycott," *The Ecologist*, May 16, 2019, https://theecologist.org/2019/may/16/brazilian-indigenous-peoples-propose-boycott; on transnational supply chains and fossil fuels see Julia Dehm, "Post-Paris Reflections: Fossil Fuels, Human Rights and the Need to Excavate New Ideas for Climate Justice," *Journal of Human Rights and the Environment* 8, no. 2 (2017): 280.

98 See Deborah Cowen, "Infrastructures of Empire and Resistance," *Verso Blog*, January 25, 2017, www.versobooks.com/blogs/3067-infrastructures-of-empire-and-resistance.

asset-management and the provision of insurance.[99] Moreover, an understanding of the global as constituted through interconnections rather than as an abstract representation of 'common concern' could foster the building of commonalities through grounded material practices of solidarity.[100] This sense of the international as a 'meeting place' represents a different 'jurisdictional form' of international ordering than that of cosmopolitanism, in which the 'international domain' is independent.[101] The Anthropocene could thus also pose an imperative to pluralise the representation of the international, and perhaps also the global and plenary, by recalling and experimenting with different 'jurisdictional forms'. Accordingly, international legal ordering could enable a political ecology that acknowledges the different 'worldings' of an expansive 'pluriverse': a 'practice of a world of many worlds'.[102]

Rather than pursuing modernist divisions between the particular and the universal,[103] Latour suggests that the Anthropocene might provide the impetus for a provincialisation or 'relocalization of the global',[104] realised in a world that is '*slowly* composed'[105] of autonomous yet entangled ontological and epistemological commitments. Borrowing from and adapting Dipesh Chakrabarty's influential work on the provincialisation of Europe,[106] literary scholar Elizabeth DeLoughrey further proposes that we might 'provincialize the Anthropocene'.[107] This 'provincialisation', and its decolonising implications, is exemplified in the work of Kathy Jetñil-Kijiner, a poet from the Marshall Islands who received a standing ovation at the United Nations Climate Summit in 2014. The mobilisation of Pacific climate activism has been described as an 'Oceanic cosmopolitanism', which attempts to elevate Indigenous voices in the pursuit of climate justice and a decolonised world politics.[108] For DeLoughrey, while Marshallese diplomats have been active and influential at climate change summits and in garnering the support of other postcolonial island states, Jetñil-Kijiner's articulation of local experiences in a global forum presents a particular 'cultural geologic', which exceeds the 'universalized climate science of the Anthropocene'.[109] Indeed, the political, affective and activist force of her poem, titled 'Tell Them', renders visible forms of 'slow violence'[110] and injustice accompanying ecological degradation, including the discourses of resilience and adaptation now embedded within international law.

99 See Bill McKibbon, "Money Is the Oxygen on which the Fire of Global Warming Burns," *New Yorker*, September 17, 2019, www.newyorker.com/news/daily-comment/money-is-the-oxygen-on-which-the-fire-of-global-warming-burns.

100 Julia Dehm, "Carbon Colonialism or Climate Justice? Interrogating the International Climate Regime from a TWAIL Perspective," *Windsor Yearbook of Access to Justice* 33, no. 3 (2016): 159.

101 Shaun McVeigh and Shaunnagh Dorsett, *Jurisdiction* (New York: Routledge, 2012), 117–18.

102 Marisol de la Cadena and Mario Blaser, *A World of Many Worlds* (Durham, NC: Duke University Press, 2018), 4.

103 Peter Fitzpatrick, *Modernism and the Grounds of Law* (Cambridge: Cambridge University Press, 2001), 193.

104 Latour, "Fourth Lecture," 135–36.

105 Bruno Latour, "Whose Cosmos, Which Cosmopolitics?" *Common Knowledge* 10, no. 3 (2004): 457. See also Rosi Braidotti, "Becoming-world," in *After Cosmopolitanism*, eds. Rosi Braidotti, Patrick Hanafin and Bolette Blaagaard (New York: Routledge, 2013), 42.

106 Dipesh Chakrabarty, *Provincializing Europe: Postcolonial Thought and Historical Difference* (Oxford: Princeton University Press, 2008).

107 DeLoughrey, *Allegories*, 2. This notion was proposed earlier by Kathleen D. Morrison, "Provincializing the Anthropocene," *Seminar* 673 (September 2015): 75–80.

108 Samid Suliman, et al., "Indigenous (Im)mobilities in the Anthropocene," *Mobilities* 14, no. 3 (2019): 298–318, 300, 303.

109 Ibid., 4.

110 Nixon, *Slow Violence*, 13.

International law has been concerned with distinctions between violence that is legal and illegal, legitimate and illegitimate.[111] Critical scholarship, however, has exposed an intimate relationship between violence and the origins and exceptions of law and its promises of non-violence.[112] The Anthropocene also draws attention to the necessity of revealing – and theorising – forms of violence that are 'neither spectacular nor instantaneous'.[113] As opposed to violence as spectacle, Rob Nixon describes the 'slow' and 'environmentally embedded violence' and '[a]ttritional catastrophes' of ecological degradation, displacements and subsequent amnesia.[114] These displacements, he writes, are 'temporal, geographical, rhetorical, and technological displacements that simplify violence and underestimate, in advance and in retrospect, the human and environmental costs', and reflect the occlusion of a 'vernacular landscape'.[115] Nixon dwells upon the temporal erasures and spatial abstractions revealed by the Anthropocene, which intersect with its newly configured temporal constraints and the geographical specificity of its impacts. The urgency of immediate action to curb human planetary impact is rendered abstract by the relative slowness of ecological degradation and attendant political inertia, and the dispersals and displacements of 'slow violence' across time and space are concealed.[116] For Nixon, the violence inflicted by 'petro-imperialism' renders people displaced in place, 'stranded in a place stripped of the very characteristics that made it inhabitable'.[117] This attritional violence disentangles human and non-human communities, and their relationships and obligations to and in place.

Alongside the need to reveal 'incremental and accretive' harms,[118] the Anthropocene also impels a reimagining of forms of agency exhibited by human and non-human 'actants',[119] in a context where 'entanglement of natural and political processes of violence has reached a point where it is difficult to differentiate between their causalities'.[120] The 'new materialist' or 'ontological' turn in the social sciences has shown how 'agency is distributed across a vast range of entities and processes', such that a vast range of beings and entities have the ability to produce effects, affects and change in the world.[121] Directly challenging Cartesian dualism, scholars have conceptualised matter as vital and active parts of 'agentic assemblages' that produce culture, subjectivity and the social world.[122] Such accounts echo the key tenets of many Indigenous cosmologies, in accordance with which ancestral land may be considered sentient and a source

111 David Kennedy, "Lawfare and Warfare," in *The Cambridge Companion to International Law*, eds. James Crawford and Martti Koskenniemi (Cambridge: Cambridge University Press, 2012): 174–75.

112 Robert Cover, "Violence and the Word," *The Yale Law Journal* 95, no. 8 (1986): 1601.

113 Nixon, *Slow Violence*, 2.

114 Ibid., 7.

115 Ibid., 7, 17, citing John Brinckerhoff Jackson, *Discovering the Vernacular Landscape* (New Haven: Yale University Press, 1984).

116 Nixon, *Slow Violence*, 2, 7, 10.

117 Ibid., 5, 19–20.

118 Ibid., 2.

119 This term comes from Latour's actor-network theory: see Bruno Latour, *Reassembling the Social: An Introduction to Actor-Network Theory* (Oxford: Oxford University Press, 2005).

120 Nabil Ahmed, "The Toxic House," in *Forensis: The Architecture of Public Truth*, ed. Caroline Sturdy Colls (Berlin: Sternberg Press, 2014), 632.

121 Arias-Maldonado, "The Anthropocene," 53.

122 See for example Jane Bennett, *Vital Matter: A Political Economy of Things* (Durham, NC: Duke University Press, 2009).

of human and non-human agency.[123] Whereas international law reduces the 'environment'[124] to an 'object' of international regulation, the materialist turn impels a reconsideration of juridical distinctions between subject and object and, further, of 'the locations of agency, will and intention in international law'.[125] Philippopoulos-Mihalopoulos further advocates a recognition and embrace of the inherent materiality of law as applied to the non-human, which would allow for a 'planetary jurisprudence'.[126] That is, a 'planetary' (rather than global) and 'agenerational' (rather than intergenerational) equity, and an interdisciplinarity that would allow for a newly 'material' and 'situated' law.[127] Critical readings of the Anthropocene concept do indeed prompt a reconsideration of juridical distinctions and associated instrumentalism and might illuminate the possibilities of more material and situated laws. With what strategies and methodologies might we approach this reframing? Upon which sources of inspiration, legitimacy and authority might we draw?

Critical analysis of the limitations of international legal doctrines and orthodox theories of recognition and legal personality and their contribution to global inequality[128] have been amplified by the Anthropocene concept. Influenced by theories of 'Wild Law', 'Earth Jurisprudence' and 'Ecological jurisprudence',[129] broader recognition of the legal personhood of parts of the non-human world has emerged.[130] The attribution of legal personhood to four rivers in Aotearoa New Zealand, India and Colombia in 2017[131] raises complex doctrinal and theoretical questions regarding the expansion of juridical personhood beyond established categories. Nonetheless, models of juridical personhood and its abstracted notion of the 'human' – the white, European, male property-owner, which reaches its 'apotheosis' in the corporation as juridical person[132] – have operated in exclusionary and marginalising ways. Given the limitations of rights discourse as applied to humans, constrained by institutional limitations and contained

123 Vanessa Watts, "Indigenous Place-Thought & Agency Amongst Human and Non-Humans (First Woman and Sky Woman go on a European World Tour!)," *Decolonization: Indigeneity, Education and Society* 2, no. 1 (2013): 21. See also C. F. Black, *The Land Is the Source of the Law* (Milton Park: Taylor & Francis, 2010); Deborah Bird Rose, *Nourishing Terrains: Australian Aboriginal Views of Landscape and Wilderness* (Canberra: Australian Heritage Commission, 1996), 26.

124 Paul Warde, Libby Robin and Sverker Sörlin, *The Environment: History of the Idea* (Baltimore: John Hopkins University Press, 2018); Perrin Selcer, *The Postwar Origins of the Global Environment: How the United Nations Built Spaceship Earth* (New York: Colombia University Press, 2018).

125 Jessie Hohmann and Daniel Joyce, "Introduction," in *International Law's Objects*, eds. Jessie Hohmann and Daniel Joyce (Corby: Oxford University Press, 2018), 7.

126 Philippopoulos-Mihalopoulos, "Critical Environmental Law as Method in the Anthropocene," 142, 144.

127 Ibid., 149–52.

128 See Rose Parfitt, "Theorizing Recognition and International Personality," in *The Oxford Handbook of the Theory of International Law*, eds. Anne Orford and Florian Hoffmann (New York: Oxford University Press, 2016), 584.

129 Cormac Cullinan, *Wild Law: Governing People for Earth*, 2nd ed. (Claremont: Siber Inc., 2011); Peter Burdon, *Earth Jurisprudence: Private Property and the Environment* (Abingdon: Routledge, 2015); Cristy Clark, Nia Emmanouil, John Page and Alessandro Pelizzon, "Can You Hear the Rivers Sing? Legal Personhood, Ontology, and the Nitty Gritty of Governance," *Ecology Law Quarterly* 45, no. 4 (2018).

130 The classic in this area is Christopher Stone, *Should Trees Have Standing? Towards Legal Rights for Natural Objects* (Los Altos, CA: W. Kaufmann, 1973). For an overview of this movement, see Ariel Rawson and Becky Mansfield, "Producing Juridical Knowledge: 'Rights of Nature' or the Naturalization of Rights?" *Environment and Planning E: Nature and Space* 1, no. 1–2 (2018).

131 See Erin O'Donnell, *Legal Rights for Rivers: Competition, Collaboration and Water Governance* (Milton: Routledge, 2018).

132 Grear, "Deconstructing Anthropos," 237.

within 'liberal imaginations',[133] there are real risks in transposing these legal forms to the non-human world.[134] Instead of expanding anthropogenic models of personhood, the demands of the Anthropocene provide the impetus for a critical reconceptualisation of the model of the 'bounded self'[135] and the subject/object distinction upon which it is premised.

Beyond the juridical reconstruction and reanimation of the non-human within a modernist rights frame, international law might usefully draw upon the environmental humanities, particularly multispecies studies, which focuses on relationality and obligation in the material semiotics of place.[136] This scholarship is informed by a vast literature in multispecies ethnography, anthropology, extinction studies and more-than-human geographies,[137] and explores an ethics of interspecies entanglement. Cultivating 'arts of attentiveness' and 'cosmopolitical care', for Thom Van Dooren and Deborah Bird Rose, entails a collapse of modernist dualisms – nature/culture, non-human/human, ontology/epistemology – and the acknowledgement of our co-habitation and co-constitution as 'a single assemblage'.[138] Following Isabelle Stengers and Latour, this ethic extends the notion of a 'subalternist cosmopolitics', with its focus on 'cohabitation, coexistence, and hospitality', to embrace the non-human.[139] Moreover, it requires deliberate and sustained attention to stories as 'world-making, life-shaping technologies', and to the generative possibilities of acts of 'storying'.[140] For Haraway, '"World" is a verb' rather than a descriptor or repository, involving 'risky co-makings, speculative fabulations'.[141] Storytelling might therefore reinscribe the very constraints we wish to resist or, alternatively, facilitate new encounters and impose different obligations.[142]

As opposed to 'an ever-expanding and diversifying "rights-talk"',[143] critical legal scholars have sought to resuscitate the legal, ethical, sociological and political questions surrounding obligations and their centrality to community. Scott Veitch and Daniel Matthews explore a particular historical positioning of humans as 'bound beings' – bound to law and its institutions,

133 Ben Golder, *Foucault and the Politics of Rights* (Stanford, CA: Stanford University Press, 2015), 86. See also Radha D'Souza, *What's Wrong with Rights? Social Movements, Law and Liberal Imaginations* (London: Pluto Press, 2018), 55.

134 Anna Grear, "It's Wrongheaded to Protect Nature with Human-Style Rights," *Aeon*, March 19, 2019, https://aeon.co/ideas/its-wrongheaded-to-protect-nature-with-human-style-rights.

135 Jennifer Nedelsky, "Law, Boundaries and the Bounded-Self," *Representations* 30, no. 1 (Spring 1990): 173–35.

136 Haraway, *Staying with the Trouble*. For an overview of multispecies studies, see Thom van Dooren, Eben Kirksey and Ursula Münster, "Cultivating Arts of Attentiveness," *Environmental Humanities* 8, no. 1 (2016).

137 Van Dooren, Kirksey and Münster, "Cultivating Arts of Attentiveness," 5. For early work on the more-than-human in human geography, see Sarah Whatmore, *Hybrid Geographies: Natures, Cultures, Spaces* (London: Sage, 2002).

138 Ibid., 1, 16. The authors cite Gilles Deleuze and Félix Guattari, *A Thousand Plateaus: Capitalism and Schizophrenia* (New York: Continuum, 1987), 34.

139 Matthew Watson, "Derrida, Stengers, Latour, and Subalternist Cosmopolitics," *Theory, Culture & Society* 31, no. 1 (2014): 87–88.

140 Thom Van Dooren and Deborah Bird Rose, "Lively Ethography: Storying Animist Worlds," *Environmental Humanities* 8, no. 1 (2016): 89.

141 Donna Haraway, "Jeux de ficelles avec les espèces compagnes: Rester avec le trouble," in *Les animaux: Deux ou trois choses que nous savons d'eux*, eds. Vinciane Despret and Raphael Larrère (Paris: Hermann, 2014), quote taken from earlier English language draft, cited in van Dooren and Rose, "Lively Ethnography," 89.

142 Van Dooren and Rose, "Lively Ethnography," 89.

143 Daniel Matthews and Scott Veitch, "Law, Obligation, Community: Introduction," in *Law, Obligation, Community*, eds. Daniel Matthews and Scott Veitch (London: Routledge, 2018), 1. For a useful discussion and critique, see Peter Burdon, "Environmental Human Rights: A Constructive Critique," in *Research Handbook on Human Rights and the Environment*, eds. Anna Grear and Louis Kotzé (Cheltenham: Edward Elgar Publishing, 2015).

place, community, memory and the social institutions of collective life – and the centrality of obligations to 'lawful relations'.[144] Drawing upon the work of Simone Weil, Matthews suggests that obligation, 'with its etymological root in *ligare*, to bind', foregrounds the 'normative force that inheres in the vital processes that sustain human habitation of the earth', and indeed predates and assumes priority over rights.[145] We are bound to one another in community and in the 'rootedness' of place,[146] which inform lawful relation. While suggesting that the nature of 'connection to place' advocated by popular activists such as Naomi Klein 'remains elusive',[147] he proposes a juridical and political return to obligation, as that which binds us in community and in place. While Matthews draws upon an occidental etymology and the 'primordial bonds that constitute community'[148] in English and European epistemology and jurisprudence and grounds the pursuit of 'connection to place' in obligation, Kombumerri/Munaljahlai scholar Christine Black describes an Indigenous Australian 'talngai-gawarima' jurisprudential structure that is sourced in the land.[149] This jurisprudence, Black asserts, arises from the movement of knowledge through storytelling, which leads an individual into lawful behaviour. Lamenting the economic abstraction of land,[150] Black emphasises the importance of *feeling* (as opposed to emotion) to Indigenous epistemologies and lawful conduct.[151] In his book, *Story About Feeling*, with which Black engages, Senior Law Man Bill Neidjie describes a visceral connection between oneself and one's land, and 'the body as a site of law', through a poetic jurisprudential account:[152] 'This story e coming through your body.'[153] This jurisprudential rendering of lawful relationships and a situated ethics of responsibility provide a vital counter to the 'rights-talk' to which Matthews and Veitch refer. While attending to the ethic of responsibility that inheres in the meeting of jurisdictions and that must animate the meeting places of laws[154] – Indigenous and non-Indigenous, human and more-than-human – the acknowledgement of a plurality of laws is of critical importance to new imaginings of lawful relations, and of international laws.

The Anthropocene, initially articulated as a scientific proposition but subsequently engaged discursively, provides a novel impetus for interdisciplinary conversation and contestation. Construed as an opening rather than a closure, it does not necessarily compel a determinate response but, rather, facilitates critical dialogue about our collective futures. The interrogation of its premises and implications illuminates the inadequacy of juridical renderings of the human subject – the *anthropos* – as a legal person and reveals the 'intra- and inter-species hierarchies' and inequalities of international law and the 'slow' and unacknowledged violence of

144 Matthews and Veitch, "Law, Obligation, Community," Introduction, x.

145 Matthews, "Law and Aesthetics in the Anthropocene," 18, citing Simone Weil, *The Need for Roots* (Abingdon: Routledge, 2001); Simone Weil, "Draft Statement for a Statement of Human Obligations," in *Simone Weil: An Anthology*, ed. Sian Miles (London: Penguin, 2005).

146 Daniel Matthews, "Obligations in the New Climatic Regime," *Critical Legal Thinking Blog*, accessed October 24, 2019, http://criticallegalthinking.com/2018/07/16/obligations-in-the-new-climatic-regime/.

147 Matthews, "Law and Aesthetics in the Anthropocene," 18, citing Naomi Klein, *This Changes Everything: Capitalism vs The Climate* (London: Penguin, 2014).

148 Matthews, "Obligations in the New Climatic Regime."

149 C. F. Black, *The Land Is the Source of the Law* (Milton Park: Taylor & Francis, 2010), 178.

150 Ibid., 168.

151 Ibid., 176, 184.

152 Bill Neidjie, *Story About Feeling* (Broome: Magabala Books, 1989), 1, cited and discussed in Black, *The Land Is the Source of the Law*, 27.

153 Black, *The Land Is the Source of the Law*, 27.

154 Shaunnagh Dorsett and Shaun McVeigh, "Conduct of Laws: Native Title, Responsibility, and Some Limits of Jurisdictional Thinking," *Melbourne University Law Review* 36, no. 2 (2012): 471.

ecological degradation. Interrogation of the Anthropocene, as both thesis and conceptual provocation, does not necessarily render it inadequate to the challenges of the present moment but rather galvanises a 'rethinking' of modernity and the dualisms, temporal modalities and spatial abstractions that define international law and its subjects. Embracing the notion of a 'counter-Anthropocene' as articulated in critical humanities scholarship, which is attentive to the ethics of encounter and entanglement beyond the human, invites us to imagine the radical pluralisation of international laws.

32

Who, or what, is the human of international humanitarian law?

Matilda Arvidsson[1]

> Human is not a value-neutral term. It is a term that indexes access to power. So, can we have a human that looks like this? Can a woman represent humanity? Can the woman be the measure of all things? . . . Can 'the universal' be carried by turns other than white masculinity, can we have alternatives to this?
>
> Rosi Braidotti, '*Posthuman, All Too Human*'

Introduction

Contemporary critical international humanitarian law (IHL) scholarship concerned with intelligent technologies in warfare rarely employs feminist or posthumanist theories in its analyses. Moreover, technology as a whole is often positioned as an overwhelmingly destructive force rather than an already present and necessary condition for human existence. This chapter, in contrast, engages in a posthumanist feminist analysis that embraces life, death and technology. It takes targeting in intelligent warfare as its example in order to reframe the relevant question for IHL scholarship. This requires a shift from critiquing technological and digital practices in contemporary intelligent warfare, to asking (also or instead) who or what the 'human' of international *human*itarian law is and can be in the posthuman condition.

Recalling queer and postcolonial critique, the question of the 'human' is foregrounded by Rosi Braidotti's work.[2] Her posthumanist feminist scholarship is helpful when describing and analysing contemporary intelligent warfare as it attends to the intersection of issues well known to war, in particular human-tech agency and relations.[3] Moreover, in taking a feminist stance,

1 Adapted from Matilda Arvidsson, "Targeting, Gender, and International *Posthuman*itarian Law and Practice: Framing the Question of the Human in International Humanitarian Law," *Australian Feminist Law Journal* 44, no. 1 (2018), copyright © Taylor & Francis Ltd (2018), reprinted by permission of the publisher.

2 Rosi Braidotti, *The Posthuman* (Cambridge: Polity Press, 2013); see also Rosi Braidotti, "Posthuman, All Too Human," filmed January 25, 2017 at Durham University, video, 11:00–12:00, www.youtube.com/watch?v=JZ7GnwelrM0&t=721s.

3 See also Matilda Arvidsson, "The Swarm That We Already Are: Artificially Intelligent (AI) Swarming 'Insect Drones', Targeting and International Humanitarian Law in a Posthuman Ecology," *Journal of Human Rights and the Environment* 11, no. 1 (2020): 114.

it asks about the ways in which the privileged 'human' figure emerges through power-relations of intra- and inter-species gendered domination and subjugation. Braidotti considers nature and culture as self-organising and co-produced through entanglement between different 'natural' and 'non-natural' elements or aspects. Rather than understanding technology in warfare as affording 'humanity greater control over the world' – as if humanity existed apart from or above the world – or 'for machines to do the "seeing" for us' in targeting practices – as if the 'human' and the 'machine' could ever be fully told apart – posthumanist feminist theory de-thrones the 'human' as a given or 'natural' entity distinctly separate from other species and technologies.[4] A posthumanist feminist analysis recognises that '[t]here can no longer be a pre-given boundary between a body and its environment', regardless of that 'environment' consisting of other species, digital platforms, or technology at large.[5] The 'posthuman predicament' in which we live enforces, as Braidotti argues:

> the necessity to think again and to think harder about the status of the human, the importance of recasting subjectivity accordingly, and the need to invent forms of ethical relations, norms and values worthy of the complexity of our times. This calls for a re-definition of the aims and structures of critical thought.[6]

In this chapter I respond to her call for new 'forms of ethical relations, norms and values worthy of the complexity of our times'. What, I ask, is the 'human' of IHL and what if it cannot be fully distinguished from its 'other(s)'? 'Keeping the human in the loop' is a major theme in contemporary debates on intelligent warfare, especially those concerning lethal targeting in drone warfare and in the development and deployment of autonomous weapon systems (AWS), which, 'once activated, can select and engage targets without further intervention by a human operator'.[7] But who or what can this 'human' be? What if 'humans' are already *not* in control – or indeed, are already 'more-than-human', at least as warfighters (following the inauguration of posthuman warfare in the wake of WWI)?[8] What if the incapacities ascribed to 'non-human' intelligent entities in contemporary warfare – such as insect-simulating swarming autonomous drones – are also 'human' (and 'humans' are already swarming insects)?[9] What if humans are unable to fully know the cause of 'human agency', be the sole authors of 'human-made' decisions and, as a consequence, be held accountable for belligerent acts in warfare? The argument in this chapter is twofold: first, that this is where we are already at in the posthuman condition and, second, that this calls for an ethical and normative order worthy of our time – an international *posthumanitarian* legal ordering able to recognise subjectivity and accountability of 'non-human'

4 Peter Asaro, "On Banning Autonomous Weapon Systems: Human Rights, Automation, and the Dehumanization of Lethal Decision-Making," *International Review of the Red Cross* 687 (2012): 709; Christopher Coker, "On Humanising War," *Politics, Religion & Ideology* 1, no. 2 (2000): 77, 84.

5 Andreas Philippopoulos-Mihalopoulos, "Lively Agency: Life and Law in the Anthropocene," in *Animals, Biopolitics, Law: Lively Legalities*, ed. Irus Braverman (Abingdon: Routledge, 2016), 193, 199.

6 Braidotti, *The Posthuman*, 186.

7 Noel Sharkey, "Staying in the Loop: Human Supervisory Control of Weapons," in *Autonomous Weapons Systems: Law, Ethics, Policy*, eds. Nehal Bhuta, Susanne Beck, Robin Geiβ, Hin-Yan Liu and Claus Kreβ (Cambridge: Cambridge University Press, 2016), 23.

8 Joanna Bourke, "Killing in a Posthuman World: The Philosophy and Practice of Critical Military History," in *The Subject of Rosi Braidotti: Politics and Concepts*, eds. Bolette Blagaard and Iris van der Tuin (London: Bloomsbury, 2014), 29.

9 Arvidsson, "The Swarm That We Already Are."

entities in warfare alongside and in conjunction with 'human' and 'more-than-human' entities, not as separate and superior/subordinate, but as relationally responsible posthuman becomings.[10]

In order to think the questions of 'the human' through, I start this chapter by explaining how IHL frames the 'human' as material and binary-gendered, while warfare practice first and foremost understands the 'targetable human' in terms of convergingly material and digital aspects. Against this background, and taking seriously the concern expressed in much of contemporary IHL scholarship that the 'machine' will overtake the 'human' in targeting decisions, I go on to ask who and what the 'human in the loop' performing the targeting is or can be. Drawing on Judith Butler's notion of the subject, this 'human' is re-read, via Braidotti's posthumanist feminism, as the always-already digital and material, more-than-human: neither fully 'machine' nor fully 'human'; neither autonomous nor free. In the final part I set out a tentative framework for thinking about the 'human' in an international *posthumanitarian* legal ordering of posthuman relations.

Targeting, the 'human', and its genders in international humanitarian law and practice

IHL is said to strike a balance between 'the need for military necessity and concerns for humanity' in warfare.[11] Its telos is the survival of the 'human species' through regulating the modes of lawful killings in armed conflicts, privileging the 'human' over other species and entities in an anthropolegal logic of gendered separation, hierarchisation and domination.[12] 'Humanity' is, in this logic, the master of its own destiny, which IHL operationalises through a series of distinctions: the binary-gender distinction defining the targetable 'human', as well as the 'human'/'other' distinction defining the first (the 'human') as the only subject capable of accountability in military decision-making.

In conducting war lawfully, a warfighter – 'human' or 'other' – must distinguish between civilian and non-civilian targets. This is the principle of distinction in IHL. The laws of targeting, in short, involve checking the lawfulness of killing a specific target against IHL before and after an armed attack. Military operational, strategic and tactical objectives are weighed against the potential damage a military attack may cause. Damage must be proportional in relation to its estimated concrete military advantage (the principle of proportionality in IHL). The principle of precaution, moreover, imposes a set of obligations on belligerents ranging from seniority in decision-making to risk assessment, advance warnings, use of weaponry and means of warfare. It is against this detailed and well-established process of recognition, assessment, judgment and evaluation that the debates on 'human' and 'non-human' agency and action in contemporary intelligent warfare must be understood.

Within the IHL targeting context, an individual becomes a lawful target based on her perceived performance: who and what she appears to be and do. Identification within the targeting

10 Building on Hans Lindahl's concept of legal order*ing* ("Inside and Outside Global Law," *Sydney Law Review* 41, no. 1 (2019): 1, 14), the notion '*posthumani*tarian legal ordering' is further developed in Arvidsson, "The Swarm That We Already Are."

11 Brian Rappert, Richard Moyes, Anna Crowe and Thomas Nash, "The Roles of Civil Society in the Development of Standards Around New Weapons and Other Technologies of Warfare," *International Review of the Red Cross* 94, no. 886 (2012): 765, 766.

12 Arvidsson, "The Swarm That We Already Are"; Anna Grear, "Deconstructing *Anthropos*: A Critical Legal Reflection on 'Anthropocentric' Law and Anthropocene 'Humanity'," *Law and Critique* 26 (2015): 225.

context is described in IHL and its doctrines as hinging on whether or not the potential target is in military uniform and bearing weapons openly. This identification/self-identification is a way of entering into the production of subjectivity through, as Butler puts it:

> a stylized repetition of acts . . . which are internally discontinuous . . . [so that] the appearance of substance is precisely that, a constructed identity, a performative accomplishment which the mundane social audience, including the actors themselves, come to believe and to perform in the mode of belief.[13]

Relying on such visual performance, the identification as to whether the potential target is either combatant/targetable or civilian/non-targetable is made. Quite literally, an ocular inspection of garments and a cultural analysis of performance becomes the basis of who, or what, an individual 'passes' as. The combatant performs the 'one' male form (the *uni*form co-constituting the combatant) which in turn creates the 'other' civilian/female (wearing non-uniform clothes, performing non-maleness). Combatant(male)/civilian(female) identity/identification emerges through IHL as a 'style-guide' on how to 'pass' as a particular gender/identity as well as how to identify the 'human' as a particular gendered form of life for the purpose of targeting.

In contemporary intelligent warfare, however, targeting is not done exclusively on the basis of these conventional identifications of cultural gendered performance. Rather, a large portion of the identification is digitally done through automated and self-learning systems programmed to identify potential targets. This renders the digital performance of individuals – digital bodies – central. Digital bodies comprise the diverse set of data generated through digital technologies and platforms, often availed through the everyday use of cell phones, e-mail programs, smartphone apps and 'smart' household items such as 'connected' refrigerators, TV's and 'smart' home security systems. The digital-embodied visibility – the digital body – often remains undisclosed to the individuals ('humans' and others) whose digital performance becomes the backbone of targeting identification in contemporary intelligent warfare.

Discussing US military targeting practices, Amin Parsa has shown how what I term 'digital performance' and 'digital bodies' and life are identified as 'seeds', 'identifiers of interest', and 'targets'.[14]

A 'seed' (Figure 32.1), Parsa explains, is '"an identifier of a communications endpoint" and is deemed a potential threat'. The 'seed' is not equivalent to any 'human' individual as separated from technologies, but rather refers to:

> a communication channel such as a phone number, an Internet Protocol (IP) address or an email address that a target (or many others at many different times) may use. . . . Analysts use a particular seed identifier, e.g. a cellphone number, to dig into a vast database and gather information about other persons or networks that are in communication with the particular seed.[15]

13 Judith Butler, *Gender Trouble: Feminism and the Subversion of Identity*, 10th ed. (New York: Routledge, 1999), 179 (emphasis in original).

14 Amin Parsa, "Knowing and Seeing the Combatant: War, Counterinsurgency and Targeting in International Law" (PhD diss., Lund University, Lund, 2017), 182.

15 Parsa, "Knowing and Seeing the Combatant," 183.

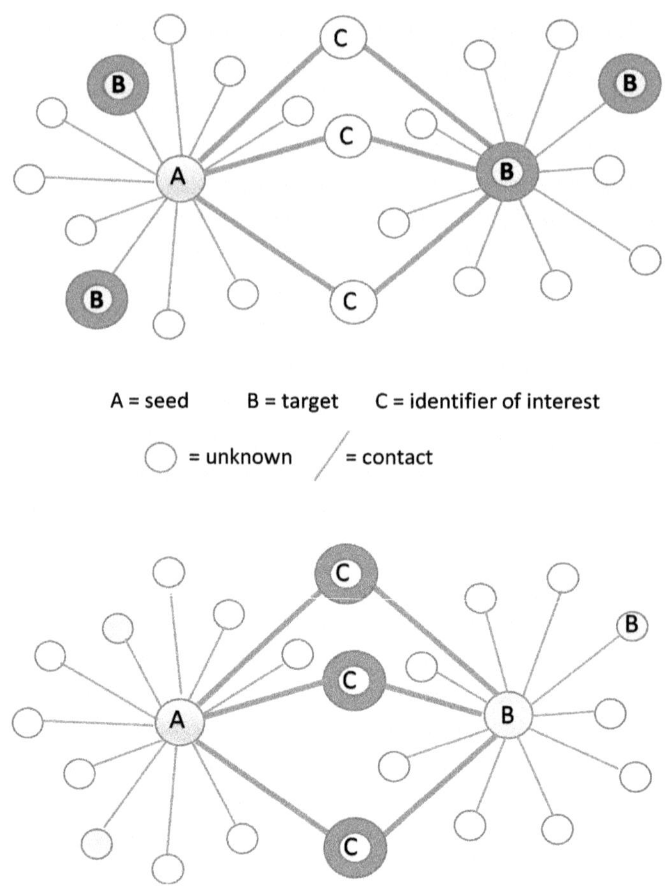

Figure 32.1 Contact-chaining graph: a network of contacts amongst identifiers.[16]

Recalling the principle of distinction in IHL, the digital body does not necessarily perform 'one' (male/uniform/combatant) or 'other' (female/non-uniform/civilian) form of life or gender: it 'entangles with', but should not be conflated with, material bodies. Moreover, digital bodies comprise several different digital aspects, which makes them ephemeral and ever-changing yet, at the same time, unaffected by time. While material, biological bodies fall sick, die and decompose (material states of becoming), digital bodies remain in a digital state of becoming – they converge with 'human' (and other) material bodies, yet relations are fluid, ephemeral and infinite.

'Human targets' identified in contemporary intelligent targeting warfare are thus quite different from the ones recognisable through IHL's binary-gendering distinctions. Converging digital and material bodies *as military targets* queer IHL's categories, and distinctions between

16 See also: *Bulk Collection of Signals Intelligence: Technical Options*, 2015, Committee on Responding to Section 5(d) of Presidential Policy Directive 28: The Feasibility of Software to Provide Alternatives to Bulk Signals Intelligence Collection; Computer Science and Telecommunications Board; Division on Engineering and Physical Sciences; National Research Council, www.nsa.gov/about/civil-liberties/resources/assets/files/BulkCollectionofSignalsIntelligenceTechOptions.pdf; Parsa, "Knowing and Seeing the Combatant," 182.

'human'/technology and nature/culture become conflated. On a practical note, this conflation of the binary-gender distinction renders the IHL principle of distinction quite impossible to pursue. After all, how could anyone (or anything) tell a combatant/male apart from a civilian/female based on a potential target's digital performance alone (what is the gender of an IP address, a 'seed' or a 'target'? And indeed, can it ever become 'human')? The ways in which digital bodies emerge and converge with material ones conflates the binary-gender distinction and reveals IHL as resting on the assumption of 'humanity' as necessarily being of one (male) or the other (female) gender. Moreover, in contemporary targeting practice belligerents are left with a legal framework which seems unfit to grasp – let alone 'regulate' – intelligent warfare and the relational work of life and death, digital and material convergence, through which contemporary targeting is done. The result is not only unsatisfying on an abstract or theoretical level. It introduces a paradoxical situation: in order to perform targeting in accordance with IHL requirements, belligerents in contemporary intelligent warfare must identify – in a first step – converging digital and material bodies as targets, after which – in a second step – they must, as a/the gesture to satisfy the IHL requirements of distinction, gender targets for the purpose of lawfulness-dressing. If IHL can offer little more than the protection of digital-material bodies being identified as performing civilian/women cultural identificatory factors, such as wearing 'bright garments' and 'jewelry', then surely more can be asked of a legal framework aiming at ordering the posthuman condition in life and death.[17]

Technology, warfare and the 'human in the loop'

In the analysis earlier, the 'human' of IHL has emerged as a binary-gendered combatant/man or civilian/woman target/non-target. Through contemporary intelligent warfare and targeting practices, the 'targetable human' has, moreover, emerged as equally and convergingly material and digital, co-produced through the targeting process as such. In the following I will attend to how 'the human in the loop' emerges.

In contemporary legal debates on intelligent warfare – drone warfare as well as debates focusing on the development and deployment of new AWS – 'human' decisions are analytically kept distinct from the drone/AWS, the latter of which is considered a technological extension of 'human' agency and decision-making. Artificial intelligence (AI) – in particular data-driven agency – may, in these accounts, aid 'humans', yet decisive decisions in the targeting process call for a 'human' who can, as a subject of IHL and international criminal law (ICL), be held ethically and legally accountable. In setting the 'human' apart from the 'non-human' in the targeting process Mireille Hildebrandt gives us the following explanation of what data-driven agency is and does:

> Data-driven agency refers to a specific type of artificial intelligence, capable of perceiving an environment and acting upon it, based on the processing of massive amounts of digital data. Data-driven agents can be more or less embodied, ranging from robots (drones, self-driving cars or even companion robots) to software bots (search engines, advertising auctions, smart energy grids).[18]

17 Lauren Wilcox, "Embodying Algorithmic War: Gender, Race and the Posthuman in Drone Warfare," *Security Dialogue* 48, no. 1 (2017): 11, 12; see also "Transcripts of U.S. Drone Attack," *Los Angeles Times*, April 8, 2011, http://documents.latimes.com/transcript-of-drone-attack/.

18 Mireille Hildebrandt, "Law *as* Information in the Era of Data Driven Agency," *The Modern Law Review* 79 (2016): 1, 4.

In the intelligent warfare targeting context, data-driven agency denotes a capacity to see, know and act based on digital data (in Figure 32.1, this is identified as the seed, identifier of interest and target). The kind of AI involved in processing the large quantities of data through which digital bodies emerge, as well as in selecting, suggesting and executing actions within the targeting process, becomes part of what the 'targeting human' is and does. The data, as well as the reasons for deciding and selecting (that is, the reasons on which the 'human decisions' are based), are partially opaque and unavailable to the 'human decision-maker'. The 'human in the loop' cannot fully know the reasons for 'her' decisions because these reasons are in part locked into a black-box of advanced AI that cannot fully be known (even to specialists) and made explainable to the 'human' decision-maker.

The problem of keeping the 'human' in the loop, and thus distinct from a 'non-human' (artificial) intelligence that the 'human' is supposedly only augmented by, may seem new, but military history tells us otherwise.[19] The question of human-other interaction and agency in warfare – of how to tell a 'human' warfighter apart from (its) warfare technologies – is embedded in the quest for regulating warfare within a legal ordering. Is the 'human' warfighter on horseback a 'human' augmented by horsepower and 'non-human' animal agency? Or, rather, is the horse a 'non-human' (who appears to have an agency on its own) aligned and entangled with a 'human' in what Gilles Deleuze and Felix Guattari would call 'a war machine' that has its own aim (and cannot be restricted to safeguarding 'humanity' for the sake of the survival and prosperity of 'humankind' alone)?[20] Is fire a natural element or a lethal weapon in warfare of which 'humans' are in control? These are only examples of questions that have had to be decided for the purpose of regulating warfare in the quest for 'humanising' warfare through IHL.

'Technology', in contrast to (or, perhaps, the same as) horses and fire, is human-made, and as such, it is already designed to serve 'human' purposes and telos. Data-driven agency and similar intelligent warfare technologies emerge through the military-industrial complex precisely because they serve necropolitical (and capitalist) purposes.[21] If a new weapons system – artificially intelligent or not – does not enhance the warfare capacity of a belligerent, the system is of little use. Moreover, and from a perspective endorsing adherence to IHL, technologies which cannot be made to (or used to) perform the basic *human*itarian principles of distinction, proportionality and precaution, alone or in conjunction with other ('human' or 'non-human') intelligent warfighting entities, cannot be lawfully deployed in warfare. It has sometimes been argued that data-driven agency is superior to 'human' agency, in particular in AWS, due to its capacity to process large amounts of data and act autonomously at a high level. However, 'autonomous systems may', as Christoph Heynes puts it, 'sometimes respond in unpredictable ways, and are, to the extent that this happens, outside human control'.[22] But what makes 'human' intelligence different from 'artificial' or other intelligence within the context of contemporary intelligent warfare and IHL?

'Human' agency generally implies a capacity to see, know and act based on human cognition and consciousness, and in particular the human capacity to control one's actions and act

19 Bourke, "Killing in a Posthuman World."

20 Gilles Deleuze and Félix Guattari, *A Thousand Plateaus* (London: Bloomsbury, 2013); Arvidsson, "The Swarm That We Already Are."

21 Achille Mbebe, "Necropolitics," *Public Culture* 15, no. 1 (2003): 11 (trans. Libby Meintjes).

22 Christof Heynes, "Autonomous Weapons in Armed Conflict and the Right to a Dignified Life: An African Perspective," *South African Journal of Human Rights* 33, no. 1 (2017): 48.

intentionally in the world. Agency, David Kyuman Kim explains, 'reflects the conditions of freedom, autonomy, and liberation'.[23] To 'freely' and 'autonomously' see and know the enemy (as gendered) in a war scene is what IHL affords to the 'human' warfighter. Yet, such 'freedom' and 'autonomy' are restricted insofar as they are performed within a particular body of knowledge (of gendering distinction) and insofar as they rely on non-human material and digital entities and agencies. Moreover, Butler's scholarship on subjectification has convincingly shown that we all emerge as individuals entangled with our 'human' others. To be an individual 'human' with agency and intentionality means, in Butler's view, to constantly emerge in relationality. We can, she points out, neither recall our own psychic emergence, nor can we, as a consequence, fully know who we are: we cannot fully give an account of ourselves, our actions and the causes of those actions.[24] There is, Butler argues, an opacity to the subject instilled through the process of subjectification in which the other becomes part of the self, including the other's unconscious. This makes parts of our basic psychic structure irretrievable to us and we become irreversibly bound to our others through subjectification. To consider the 'human' capable of assuming accountability for her acts based on notions of 'autonomy' and 'freedom' appears, against this background, purely fictitious.[25] Human intentionality – that which many describe as the reason why 'man' and not 'machine' can be trusted to safeguard 'humanity' and must be kept 'in the loop' – appears as a 'human' desire rather than an attribute that sets 'humans' apart from their 'non-human' digital and material others.

Drawing on Butler again, we may say that the 'human' in the targeting loop can neither fully account for her acts, nor secure the cause of those acts as fully and only hers. IHL and ICL, at this point, demand a transcendental subject. The only thing asked of such a subject is the ability to tell a persuasive story: a sequential-linear narrative of events where cause (intentionality) and effect (targeting decision and execution) follow.[26] It does not matter if the 'targeting human' has the psychic capacity to know her intentions and how those are linked to the effect of her actions, as long as her narrative capacity remains intact. The narrative becomes, as Butler puts it, 'a performative accomplishment which the mundane social audience, including the actors themselves, come to believe and to perform in the mode of belief'.[27] The application of IHL, and the international and domestic legal provisions ensuring accountability within the targeting context, thus works on the basis of narrative capacity and performative belief. The 'human in the loop' is presumed to have, as Alex Sharpe puts it, a 'capacity for reason' and 'a conclusion of corporeal integrity'.[28] The latter is a body that passes as 'human' – performing 'humanness' – yet which may be technological and digital in various degrees. 'Humans', in IHL, are attributed psychic and bodily-material core features which are neither, following Butler, indicative of the psychic structure of the human species, nor consistent with how 'human' existence is interdependent with technology in contemporary intelligent warfare and in the posthuman condition. That which may set 'the human in the loop' apart from its artificially intelligent 'other' is the narrative capacity – the cultural skill of convincing and capturing storytelling. Or, is it?

23 David Kyuman Kim, *Melancholic Freedom: Agency and Spirit of Politics* (Oxford: Oxford University Press, 2007), 84.

24 Judith Butler, *Giving an Account of Oneself* (New York: Fordham University Press, 2005).

25 Ibid., 37.

26 Ibid., 12.

27 Butler, *Gender Trouble*, 179 (emphasis in original).

28 Andrew Sharpe, *Foucault's Monsters and the Challenge of Law* (Abingdon: Routledge, 2010), 114.

Posthumanist feminist re-descriptions of law/life/technology

If such bold and fictitious assumptions as those set out previously can be made about the 'targeting human' in IHL could something similar – in a posthumanist feminist turn – be imagined about other entities and agents otherwise partaking in the targeting process? Could we imagine a range of entities, 'human' as well as 'others', who are able persuasively to author, narrate and give accounts of the reasons for their actions, whereby they will be held accountable for their acts undertaken within the targeting process? Would constructing (additional) legal subjectivity and accountability for a range of 'entities' in 'the loop' (including warfighting 'entities' with data-driven agency and converging digital and material entities), be a step in the direction of Braidotti's call to 'recast subjectivity' and 'invent forms of ethical relations . . . worthy of the complexity of our times'?[29]

A *posthuman*itarian international legal ordering – one that aims to regulate and continuously order (hence the verb form) – worthy of the complexity of our posthuman condition would need to recognise ephemeral and entangled legal subjectivities of 'human, 'non-human' and multiple intelligence and entities in warfare. Such a recognition would risk reintroducing IHL's problem of 'seeing' and 'knowing' along categories such as gender, race and species. Yet, in understanding entangled legal subjectivities as relational between 'human' and 'more-than-human' entities the legal ordering would have to move into closer contact with contemporary technological developments and digital, material and biological ways of life. 'Humans' would, in such an understanding, neither necessarily be separate from or superior to other forms of life – be it material or digital. The only 'humanism' of such a posthuman ethical-legal ordering would be the insistence on legal configurations of responsibility which privilege 'humans' (as responsible for others). As Andreas Philippopoulos-Mihalopoulos puts it, we are required to take on such a responsibility while living 'in sync with [our] nonhuman extensions and mediations'.[30] This is the difficult task of *becoming with* and *among* 'others', as Deleuze and Guattari describe it, while at the same time assuming ethical and legal responsibility in ordering.[31]

To remake IHL as we know it could imply an opportunity to build on existing legal figures for accountability of artificial persons, such as corporations, organisations and professional offices, as opposed to 'natural' persons (individual 'humans'). Yet, to further set apart digital and material bodies and lives, persons and things – to further fragment international law by creating specialised legal provisions (ex post facto) for each new entity appearing in the context of intelligent warfare – rather than to embrace the convergence, would be as unhelpful as leaving IHL as it is. A posthumanist feminist ethics serving as a foundation for an ethical-legal ordering worthy of the complexity of our times would, as a start, facilitate the survival of life (material and multi-species as well as digital), *tout court*, in the posthuman condition. At the same time, it would celebrate the fact that both digital and material death (and decomposition) is a necessary and inevitable part of the posthuman ecology. 'Humankind' would be among the species and entities for which the telos of the new legal ordering could be made to work, but humanity's survival as set above and apart from its others could not be its purpose. Rather than furthering subordination, exclusion and othering/gendering, a posthumanist feminist normative-ethical ordering would facilitate recognition, protection (insofar that law can at all protect in war or

29 Braidotti, *The Posthuman*, 186.

30 Andreas Philippopoulos-Mihalopoulos, "Critical Environmental Law as Method in the Anthropocene," in *Research Methods in Environmental Law*, eds. Andreas Philippopoulos-Mihalopoulos and Victoria Brooks (London: Edward Elgar Publishing, 2017), 133.

31 Deleuze and Guattari, *A Thousand Plateaus*.

otherwise), and allocate responsibility and accountability among relations. Recognition of the other is, as Butler has argued, the only viable ground on which ethical responsibility can be built.[32] To this I add that a legal ordering operative in the posthuman condition needs to be able to recognise and offer recognition to the relational, entangled and converging digital and material ways in which life and death appear.

Conclusion

In this chapter I have brought Braidotti's posthumanist feminist questioning to bear on the question of who, or what, the 'human' of IHL is or can be. I have shown that the binary-gendered 'humanity' that IHL aims to safeguard is already a digital-material converging 'more-than-human', which, insofar as it is 'human', is opaque to itself, cannot know the reason for its actions, and emerges as a subject capable of ethical and legal responsibility only to the extent that it can perform a narrative capacity – the cultural skill of convincing and capturing storytelling. This, I have argued, calls for an ethical and normative order 'worthy of the complexity of our time'.[33] I have suggested that it must be an international *posthuman*itarian legal ordering able to recognise subjectivity and accountability of 'non-human' entities in warfare alongside and in conjunction with 'human' and 'more-than-human' entities: not as separate and superior/subordinate, but as relationally responsible posthuman becomings.

Ending on a cautiously optimistic note on the possibilities of thinking about law/life/technology in terms of legal ordering in the postmodern condition, I find that the analytical tools posthumanist feminist scholarship avails to critical scholarship are particularly apt for thinking about ethics and law in our times – IHL included. In embracing the vitality of auto-poietic life in the posthuman condition we (more-than-)'humans' might find it in ourselves to worry less about what technological advancement may do to us as a species in a more or less developed dystopia of cybernetic-robotic cataclysmic war-takeover of the world, and think more about what we, as the converging digital-material entangled assemblages that we always already are, do to and for our others.

32 Butler, *Giving an Account of Oneself.*
33 Braidotti, *The Posthuman*, 186.

33

Automating authority

The human and automation in legal discourse on the Meaningful Human Control of Lethal Autonomous Weapons Systems

Connal Parsley[1]

Introduction

Lethal Autonomous Weapons Systems (LAWS) are commonly defined as weapons that are capable of operating without human guidance. In the US Department of Defence Directive 3000.09, they are systems that 'once activated, can select and engage targets without further intervention by a human operator'. Depending on how autonomy is defined, this is either a feature of existing weapons technology or a near future possibility – but the challenge LAWS present to legal and diplomatic regulatory discourse is already apparent. Legal debate on LAWS reveals three main sites of anxiety: whether and how these technologies can adhere to the existing law of armed conflict, the ethical deficit of LAWS (or at best their specific ethical texture), and more generally, the question of early twenty-first century 'smart' technology's challenge to existing underlying paradigms of law and normativity.

This chapter addresses a possible site of consensus for the regulation of LAWS: the emerging regulatory concept of Meaningful Human Control (MHC), and particularly its central reliance on the figure of the human. Focusing on the legal figuration and institution of the human, I suggest, is important to the growing debate on 'law and technology'.[2] Not because it is necessary

1 I would like to thank Gregor Noll, Shane Chalmers, Sundhya Pahuja, Claerwen O'Hara and all of the IILAH colleagues past and present who have influenced this work in so many ways, particularly Matilda Arvidsson.

2 For recent work interrogating the figure of the human in relation to LAWS and human-machine hybridity in contemporary war, see the forthcoming Matilda Arvidsson, "The Swarm That We Already Are: Artificially Intelligent (AI) Swarming 'Insect Drones', Targeting and International Humanitarian Law in a Posthuman Ecology," *Journal of Human Rights and the Environment* 11, no. 1 (2020): 114–37; as well as Matilda Arvidsson, "Targeting, Gender, and International Posthumanitarian Law and Practice: Framing the Question of the Human in International Humanitarian Law," *Australian Feminist Law Journal* 44, no. 1 (2018): 9–28; Emily Jones, "A Posthuman-Xenofeminist

to reassert the normative relevance of human agency, but because contemporary technologies are putting latent notions of humanity and its agency under a strain that is not well absorbed by modern law's ingrained conceptual vocabulary. In this context, an expanded understanding of the problem of the human and humanisation is important for facing the specific challenges levelled by 'smart technologies', like those used in LAWS, against the conceptual and normative frameworks of legal discourse – and their claim to authoritatively govern an emerging techno-social world.

Whilst these challenges are often acknowledged, 'regulation' is typically championed without considering the extent to which its ontological premises are threatened.[3] This chapter, conversely, takes up Gregor Noll's recent suggestion that the machine learning used in LAWS is fundamentally incompatible with current legal paradigms of normativity. I connect this problem to the question of how and why MHC poses the 'human' as the non-technological, non-automated limit to automation technology. I argue that when sophisticated knowledge about human-machine interrelation is deployed in legal regulatory discourse, it passes through a 'conceptual bottleneck': a latent conception of the human as non-automated; the conscious, reflective decision-maker that is for that reason able to ground legal authority. The nature and function of this bottleneck is presented as part of a broader process of 'anthropogenesis', or the always ongoing production of human ontology. Automation, I suggest, plays a key role as the constitutive 'other' of this concept of humanity within a broader anthropogenic arrangement of life, and it is intrinsic to the arrangement of matter within the production of authoritative legal jurisdiction.

Using this framing, I suggest that MHC discourse's explicit proposition of the non-automated human as the negatively-defined criterion of lawfulness is historically significant. MHC would positivise the anthropogenic principle, reinforcing legal regulation just as the imminent failure of its brand of normativity to meaningfully govern the subjects of LAWS comes into view. As such, I suggest, the anthropogenic function central to law's presupposed life-world and authority has itself been *automated*, representing a shift in the relation between law, authority and life. Whilst the effects of the legal regulation of LAWS remain to be seen – potentially including their legitimation, constraint, and the production of new norms and practices – the chapter concludes that it is important to register this shift in legal ontology. As new approaches to technology and social life call for the exploration of humans' technological nature, it is important to recall that our imagination is limited by an instituted image of regulatory and decision-making authority that is deeply premised on the separation of the human from the technological. It falls to a 'new (law and) humanities' – in which law, science and the human are indistinguishable – to discover a new criterion of value and evaluation that does not insist on anthropogenically separating human life from technology.

Laws, regulation and Meaningful Human Control

An increasingly sophisticated commentary – informed by robotics, Science and Technology Studies, and critical legal and humanities studies – sees Lethal Autonomous Weapons Systems

Analysis of the Discourse on Autonomous Weapons Systems and Other Killing Machines," *Australian Feminist Law Journal* 44, no. 1 (2018): 93–118. See also Matilda Arvidsson's chapter in this volume.

3 Julia Black and Andrew Murray, "Regulating AI and Machine Learning: Setting the Regulatory Agenda," *European Journal of Law and Technology* 10, no. 3 (2019): 1–21.

(LAWS) not only as a novel object of regulation, but also as an intensification of pre-existing political-ontological conditions.[4] LAWS are the screen through which some of the twentieth century's most defining techno-political dramas are re-coded. These range from 'purely technological' anxieties (the lethal malfunction of complex armed systems) to 'techno-economic' ones (the emergence of ever-more asymmetrical warfare). Yet LAWS also accent new qualities of human-machine interface, which are increasingly the 'hard case' re-posing definitional and theoretical questions about the juridical nature of humanity. Such questions have revolved around notions of autonomy and agency; their necessary humanness or otherwise; and their concentration in single actors or dispersal through decision networks or ecologies.[5] Amongst theoretical and practical debates on what weapons autonomy means, there emerge fundamental questions about the nature of human decision-making and judgment. Through an accounting of the kinds of information that go into making lethal strike decisions, the accuracy of that information, structures of command, and the involvement of algorithms and machine learning within them, there re-emerge political questions about accountability and transparency, and juridico-moral questions about responsibility (including criminal responsibility) for the decision to kill. As human judgment is (partially) handed over to machines that – it is often presumed – cannot be enmeshed in social, normative or political systems in the same way as humans (but may be faster, and more cognitively stable and 'accurate'), there has been renewed reflection on the fallibility and undesirability of *human*-wrought death. Conversely, the evolutionary direction of such technologies has been critically analysed as intensifying the political power relations embedded in legal norms and human judgment.[6]

What is so striking about this regulatory discourse is that when these sophisticated knowledges about human-machine interaction in contemporary warfare are shaped for legal definition, they pass through a conceptual bottleneck: the notion of the human, via the term 'Meaningful Human Control' (MHC). Introduced by the NGO Article 36 in 2014,[7] MHC has emerged as the site of an initial regulatory consensus, expressing the 'widespread understanding that both the legal and ethical acceptability of a weapon system would require some kind of human control'.[8] It has been regarded as 'the most promising starting point for a more holistic approach' to the regulation of LAWS,[9] and is the centre point of a possible additional protocol to the Convention on Certain Conventional Weapons. Numerous calls have been made for its inclusion as a basic principle of international humanitarian law (IHL).

Though novel in important ways, MHC should be seen as an extension of an underlying political and legal status quo. Scholars have noted that by definition MHC amounts to at least a

4 See, for example, Sara Kendall, "Law's Ends: On Algorithmic Warfare and Humanitarian Violence," in *War and Algorithm*, eds. Max Liljefors, Gregor Noll and Daniel Steuer (London: Rowman & Littlefield International Ltd, 2019), 105–25.

5 Mireille Hildebrandt and Antoinette Rouvroy, eds., *Law, Human Agency and Autonomic Computing: The Philosophy of Law Meets the Philosophy of Technology* (Abingdon: Routledge Glass House, 2011).

6 See generally Nehal Bhuta, et al., *Autonomous Weapons Systems: Law, Ethics, Policy, Autonomous Weapons Systems: Law, Ethics, Policy* (Cambridge: Cambridge University Press, 2016).

7 Article 36, "Key Areas for Debate on Autonomous Weapons Systems," Briefing Paper, May 2014, www.article36.org/wp-content/uploads/2014/05/A36-CCW-May-2014.pdf.

8 Michael Biontino, *Report of the 2015 Informal Meeting of Experts on Lethal Autonomous Weapons Systems (LAWS)*, UN Doc. CCW/MSP/2015/3, June 2, 2015, 11.

9 Nehal Bhuta, Susanne Beck and Robin Geiss, "Present Futures: Concluding Reflections and Open Questions on Autonomous Weapons Systems," in *Autonomous Weapons Systems: Law, Ethics, Policy*, eds. Nehal Bhuta, et al. (Cambridge: Cambridge University Press, 2016), 381.

partial 'ban on full autonomy over certain (critical) functions of a weapons system'.[10] As Gregor Noll points out, anything 'truly autonomous' is not only not yet regarded as existing, but is by definition not regulable by human control. In this way, the only relevant LAWS are already-existing weapons that are 'not really LAWS' (not 'really', or completely, autonomous),[11] and this definitional sleight of hand underwrites the manageability of the problem by the existing legal regime, thus ensuring, for now, the ongoing relevance of law and its normative frameworks in addressing this significant problem. Further, support for this notion – particularly on the part of states – has underlined the *practical* utility of the concept in augmenting adherence to existing norms of the law of armed conflict; namely, that to be lawful attacks must distinguish between lawful and unlawful targets (the distinction requirement), not cause excess collateral damage relative to military benefit (the proportionality requirement) and minimise incidental injury (the feasible precautions or humanity requirement). States, the thinking goes, are more likely to endorse very general ideas first, and achieve consensus on more difficult details later.

The presupposed human of Meaningful Human Control (MHC)

A deeper legal conservatism is at play here, in the centrality of the figure of the human. The 'human' is the limit-principle of MHC; marking the acceptable boundary of weapons systems and determining when their concrete features and use-practices will be lawful. Consider the three sets of definitions posed by different organisations between 2014 and 2016, as set out by Rebecca Crootof:

> In early 2014, the International Committee for Robot Arms Control (ICRAC) proffered three 'minimum necessary conditions for meaningful [human] control':
>
> 1 "[A] human commander (or operator) must have full contextual and situational awareness of the target area and be able to perceive and react to any change or unanticipated situations that may have arisen since planning the attack";
> 2 "[T]here must be active cognitive participation in the attack and sufficient time for deliberation on the nature of the target, its significance in terms of the necessity and appropriateness of attack, and likely incidental and possible accidental effects of the attack"; and
> 3 "[T]here must be a means for the rapid suspension or abortion of the attack".
>
> Soon after, the Center for a New American Security (CNAS) reviewed the existing literature and concluded that there are three 'essential components' to Meaningful Human Control:
>
> 1 Human operators are making informed, conscious decisions about the use of weapons.
> 2 Human operators have sufficient information to ensure the lawfulness of the action they are taking, given what they know about the target, the weapon and the context for action.
> 3 The weapon is designed and tested, and human operators are properly trained, to ensure effective control over the use of the weapon.

10 Ibid.

11 Gregor Noll, "War by Algorithm: The End of Law?" in *War and Algorithm*, eds. Max Liljefors, Gregor Noll and Daniel Steuer (London: Rowman & Littlefield International, Ltd., 2019), 77.

More recently, Article 36 has argued that 'Meaningful Human Control' requires:

1 '[p]redictable, reliable and transparent technology';
2 '[a]ccurate information for the user on the outcome sought, the technology, and the context of use';
3 '[t]imely human judgement and action, and a potential for timely intervention'; and
4 '[a]ccountability to a certain standard'.[12]

Despite the 'human' element being the very basis for the cogency of the concept and its consensus, these examples show that efforts to confront the problem of MHC in a way that would satisfy the regulatory/IHL context devote all their definitional energy to the 'meaningful control' aspect and none of it to the 'human'. (Crootof, earlier, even had to correct the omission of the word 'human' from the ICRAC conditions).

The human, in MHC, is entirely presupposed. Though remarkable, this omission is commonplace. The presupposition that our interlocutors (or even ourselves) are human is fundamental – and perhaps humanness even consists in simply not ruining this illusion.[13] Not even Asimov's laws of robotics concern themselves with what a 'human' is, despite premising the safe development of robotics on *human command* and a prohibition against *harming humans* (and later, 'humanity').[14] Further, unlike personhood – which is an indispensable function of the grammar of legal process and vision (in the sense of allowing entities to appear to juridical relations and processes) – the 'human' is not, on its own, a *legal concept*. Since the 'human' can be a legal *object* like any other, it can be defined, for any number of specific and thus potentially variant or incompatible legislative contexts (even where that object has the complexion of a subject, as in the case of personhood or human rights).

The fact that the 'human' is not a positive concept in legal discourse, however, does not prevent it from serving as a conceptual bottleneck. On the contrary, it has an organising, facilitating and legitimating role that requires greater attention as new technologies put the presupposition of humanness under strain. Liberal legal modernity's imaginary casts the human as a 'natural', 'individual', 'biological' entity, 'self-contained' and temporally prior to any exercise of its 'free will' in the act of decision. To say nothing of decades of cultural theory to the contrary, in an age of increasing human-machine hybridity (or 'hybrid cognitive architectures'[15]) this presupposition is increasingly untenable – yet it remains the default for regulatory paradigms. Gregor Noll's recent work on LAWS explains that the premise that a human agent rests 'at the top of the decision hierarchy' ('exercising something akin to free will' via 'conscious human cognition') is central to military procedure and the law of war. Noll explains four developing aspects of algorithmic war that on the contrary involve 'situation-specific

12 Rebecca Crootof, "A Meaningful Floor for 'Meaningful Human Control'," *Temple International & Comparative Law Journal* 30, no. 1 (December 2016): 56–57 (references omitted).

13 Brian Christian, *The Most Human Human: What Artificial Intelligence Teaches Us About Being Alive* (New York: Penguin Random House, 2012).

14 Even those helpfully updating these laws adopt this presupposition of humanness. See Frank Pasquale, "Toward a Fourth Law of Robotics: Preserving Attribution, Responsibility and Explainability in an Algorithmic Society," *Ohio State Law Journal* 78, no. 5 (2017): 1243–55; Jack M. Balkin, "The Three Laws of Robotics in the Age of Big Data," *Ohio State Law Journal* 78, no. 5 (2017): 1217–41.

15 Paul Scharre, "Centaur Warfighting: The False Choice of Humans vs Automation," *Temple International & Comparative Law Journal* 30, no. 1 (2016): 152.

constellation[s] of human and machine' in which neither can be separated.[16] In robotics and in AI, 'the human's embodied mental states' are moved into external bodies and 'artificial mental states created by computers' that are used pervasively, for example in target selection.[17] In neurotechnology, such as the brain-machine interfaces being investigated by Elon Musk, 'human neuronal signals' are assembled with 'artificial mental states' to maximise the advantages of each. Finally, potential applications of genomics 'transfer the artifice of coding into human flesh' by selecting military personnel based on genetic characteristics or, in the future, genomic enhancement.[18]

This problem goes beyond an outdated legal approach that could be easily updated. Scholars addressing MHC are well aware of the intrinsic dependence of human command on automation and machine learning, but the MHC concept is inherently tautological (or rather it 'begs the question'), because it is precisely the boundary of this human that latently determines the cogence of the proposed MHC norm, as well as what 'meaningful control' might practically mean. To presuppose a cognitively, temporally and biologically discrete entity, understood as the self-evident negation of 'automated processes', presumes the very conditions it ostensibly seeks to articulate and enumerate.

It is more helpful – but no less problematic – to consider the 'human' who is presupposed in MHC legal discourse as the figure of a human *judgment*. This human is positioned as *by definition* capable of intervening into and arresting automated decision-making. Recourse to the 'human', then, stands in for a *quality* of decision-making that is paradigmatically not automated, and not technological. (Indeed, some LAWS experts have expressed a preference for the term 'appropriate human judgment' over MHC). Even if such a quality of judgment, disjoined from a 'human' operator, could be exercised by machines – a possibility not discounted in the literature – the current regulatory discourse poses an antinomy between a *non*-human 'other' (technology, and its blind, cold, lawless, calculating destruction) and a humanness presupposed as always *conscious*; the human of moral, evaluative judgment who is *trained* and, for all these reasons, both capable of fulfilling IHL's principles of distinction or proportionality and *accountable* for any failure to do so.

Floating human signifiers and legal legitimacy

If human-machine hybridity is commonly accepted even by legal scholars, why must it pass through this conceptual bottleneck of autonomous humanity? The earlier suggestion that it is required for compliance with legal norms is central. Yet this does little to explain the historical stakes of insisting upon humanity's autonomy from technology in legal discourse today. A more familiar example will allow us to reorient the problem. In the IHL context, Costas Douzinas has shown with particular clarity how 'humanity' is a floating signifier: 'empty of all meaning' and able to be 'attached to an infinite number of signifieds'. It cannot be limited to a 'particular conception because it transcends and overdetermines them all'.[19] Precisely because the human

16 Noll, "War by Algorithm: The End of Law?" 78.

17 More generally on embodiment and autonomic computing, see Hyo Yoon Kang, "Autonomic Computing, Genomic Data and Human Agency: The Case for Embodiment," in *Law, Human Agency and Autonomic Computing: The Philosophy of Law Meets the Philosophy of Technology*, eds. Mireille Hildebrandt and Antoinette Rouvroy (Abingdon: Routledge Glass House, 2011), 104–18.

18 Noll, "War by Algorithm: The End of Law?" 79–80.

19 Costas Douzinas, "The Many Faces of Humanitarianism," *Parrhesia*, no. 2 (2007): 4.

'carries an enormous symbolic capital, a surplus of value and dignity', he argues, 'combatants in political, social and legal struggles want to co-opt [it] to their cause'.[20] Never politically inert, this 'human' enables the securing of power relations by augmenting legitimacy. According to Douzinas, humanitarianism has turned the invocation of humanity from a tool of resistance against the power and reason of state into the very principle of their exercise. Humanitarian concern comes to underpin the lawfulness of lethal force – the so-called humane war – with the result that 'human rights are today a main weapon for generating governmental legitimacy'.[21]

From this point of view, what is 'human' is *not* a synchronic question – whatever is presupposed from time to time as the content of the signifier 'human' – but should be identified with the broader processes that construct it. Such processes are as eminently historical as the legal acts and authorisations that enable them and that they in turn enable. In Douzinas' example, an international, post-political Western subjectivity for humanity is made by the tragic dramatisation of an idealised form of human by pitting it against its 'others'. Douzinas suggests a tripartite production of, first, a monstrous threat (a barbaric *in*-humanity) that threatens, second, a helpless victim (a suffering and disempowered *sub*-humanity), who is aided by, third, a *fully* human saviour. The saviour's war and law are just and humanising only insofar as positioned by this dramatisation of roles. In this way, the very 'humanisation' of law comes to coincide with the legitimation of the exercise of force.[22]

MHC: from the presupposed human to the humanity of presupposition

What is the equivalent function of the anti-automation human of MHC? It has something in common with the humanitarian: the discourse against LAWS, once made a norm, will legitimate a determined use-case, benefiting those states that have them and validating their asymmetrical power. But this 'humanisation' of law is not only ironic: it is flatly self-contradictory, because it coincides with the legitimation of the technologisation of the exercise of force. To understand this contradiction, it should be situated in relation to a more fundamental operation of presupposition that is important for legal authority generally. For Italian philosopher Giorgio Agamben, the presuppositional structure of language posits 'positive' identities, but this covers over their lack of inherent content. Drawing on Heidegger, Agamben suggests that this is fundamental to Western ontology, which addresses the question of *being* negatively such that the foundation of the human (what is proper to the human, or the human's inherent task or place), is always something 'negative' or absent.[23] From his earliest writings, Agamben identified legal discourse as a special site for producing this (undetermined) nature of the human, casting it as 'the foundation of legal behaviour'.[24] Agamben's aim is to move from a presuppositional linguistic ontology towards one of *exposition*, whose aim is to reflexively *reveal* this specific kind of 'truth' about human life to itself.

Law may thus be central to the generation of a recognisably human life, but it is important to understand that producing the 'humanity' of Western ontology is not a specific 'task' undertaken by law, but a far broader linguistic-ontological condition that shapes law's nature

20 Ibid.

21 Ibid., 10.

22 Ibid., 15–24.

23 See generally Giorgio Agamben, *Language and Death: The Place of Negativity*, trans. Karen E. Pinkus and Michael Hardt (Minneapolis: University of Minnesota Press, 1991).

24 Ibid., 105.

and praxis. In his later work, Agamben identifies that condition with 'anthropogenesis' (the process of becoming human), and the 'anthropological machine' of the human sciences. This makes clear that law is not something apart from or above life, but is a key participant in the immanent generation of the self-recognition of life. The human names a style of 'thinking life' that is based on self-recognition, not a determinate content: more than in any 'clearly defined species' or specific 'substance', for Agamben humanity must be sought within the 'machine or device' that produces 'the [self]-recognition of the human'. This is always achieved negatively, presuppositionally, by '[self-]recogniz[ing] that [which] it *is not*'.[25] Further, in Agamben's work, this device is something inherently *technological*: for Agamben, following Foucault, the device is not some*thing*, but 'a set of practices and mechanisms (both linguistic and non-linguistic, juridical, technical and military) that aim to face an urgent need and to obtain an effect'.[26] It can include anything that has the capacity to 'capture, orient, determine, intercept, model, control or secure' living beings, including 'not only prisons . . . schools . . . factories . . . juridical measures' but also 'the pen, writing . . . agriculture, cigarettes, navigation . . . cellular telephones and . . . language itself', with the result of producing 'subjects'.[27]

The anthropogenesis of (legal) automation

This view of law's role within a broader linguistic ontology allows us to probe the central contradiction within MHC. In literalising and positivising the presuppositional quality of the negative invocation of humanity, it literalises also the 'machine' or technology of anthropogenesis. We have seen that what becomes visible in this literalisation, first of all, is the investment of legal discourse in a self-image of the human as non-automated. It is important to understand the depth of this investment and the peculiar role of automation within it. Humanity has habitually been attributed a 'higher' element (soul, or reason, for example) that masters and governs its material or animal 'lower' part. This 'something higher' has been invoked at decisive moments to resist increasingly sophisticated accounts of all life as 'mechanical' or 'automated' – and not only by theological, idealist and vitalist thought. To take one central example, Thomas Huxley ('Darwin's bulldog'), in his 1874 extension of the experimental reasoning underlying Descartes' 'animal automatism' to humans 'in fulness and entirety',[28] ultimately pulls back from the 'logical consequence' of his reasoning for humanity ('Fatalism, Materialism and Atheism'). Yet even Huxley's 'compromise' image of humans as 'conscious automata', reserving a strong but limited place for subjective consciousness, remained deeply controversial. It not only precipitated staunch objection amidst Victorian legal and psychological thinking (with their emphasis on

25 Giorgio Agamben, *The Open: Man and Animal*, trans. Kevin Attell (Stanford, CA: Stanford University Press, 2003), 26.

26 Giorgio Agamben, *"What Is an Apparatus?" And Other Essays*, trans. David Kishik and Stefan Pedatella (Stanford, CA: Stanford University Press, 2009), 8.

27 Ibid., 14–15.

28 Thomas Huxley, "On the Hypothesis That Animals Are Automata, and Its History," *Nature* 10 (1874): 362–66, 366. See also Joseph Needham's pithy 1925 evaluation of 'mechanistic biology', affirming that 'such a thesis cannot without grave logical difficulty be extended to cover the sphere of mind'. Joseph Needham, "Mechanistic Biology and the Religious Consciousness," in *Science Religion and Reality*, ed. Joseph Needham (London: Sheldon Press, 1925), 250.

volition, agency and responsibility), but provoked widespread fascination (and parody), entering common parlance through literary-cultural exploration.[29]

Just as the Western traditions of thought that underpin the legal 'conceptual bottleneck' have often defined the 'human' in opposition to automatism, automation is explicitly understood as 'not-human'. It is difficult to find a definition of automation that does not rely fundamentally on the *figure of the human* who is excluded: 'Automation . . . implies operating or acting, or self-regulating, independently, without human intervention.'[30] But this is no *simple* exclusion, since it 'has always been developed by people', for their benefit.[31] Socially, too, automation seems to exist insofar as it charts the usurped space of a past 'human life' (and often human *labour*), marking out the negative terrain where humans once busied themselves. Correspondingly, automation takes up ever-more space *within* human life, dwelling within it as the inherent inhuman dimension that humans seamlessly negotiate, liberate themselves from and define themselves against. (Considering the well-known quip that a cooking recipe is a kind of algorithm, it should be clear that this is not something inherently dramatic or negative.) Seen in this light, automation is an intrinsically *human* problematic. Automation is not the opposite of the human, but necessary to the specific sense of human life that is produced by the negatively-defined process of humanisation.

We have said that MHC discourse is a literalisation of this 'anthropogenesis'. But why is this significant? Why must sophisticated knowledge about humanity's technological imbrication pass through this conceptual bottleneck, and what is at stake in its *appearance* in legal discourse? One answer is that automation serves as a *productive* counterpoint to the notions of free will and deliberation that are fundamental to a legal humanist view of life, justice and judgment. Automata are problematic *objects* of legal thought,[32] at least since the late nineteenth century.[33] But the question of automated or calculative decision-making, with its own long history[34] and embraced by several schools of jurisprudence,[35] concerns more directly the nexus between the nature of decision, juridical subjectivity and the authority of legal jurisdiction. This problematic catalysed the late twentieth-century faultline between justice and mere legality. For Jacques Derrida, particularly, it is clear that a decision 'worthy of the name', and the possibility of justice, requires the dissociation of law from the mere calculation that modern legality-fairness seems organised to deliver.[36] Yet even Derrida's post- and ultra-human decision on the undecidable (as between differing subjects) is possible only if considered against the material organisation of the elements that enable it. In the neurological context, automation processes 'hard-wire' the synaptic 'life-process' of a living organism by growing more synaptic connections. Richard Patton

29 See Suzy Anger, "Thomas Huxley, 'On the Hypothesis that Animals are Automata' (1874)," *Victorian Review* 35 (2009): 50–52.

30 Shimon Y. Nof, "Automation: What It Means to Us Around the World," in *Springer Handbook of Automation*, ed. Shimon Y. Nof (Berlin: Springer, 2009), 14.

31 Ibid., 22.

32 See, for example, the several papers by Giovanni Santor on 'Cognitive Automata and the Law'.

33 See Ugo Pagallo, "From Automation to Autonomous Systems: A Legal Phenomenology with Problems of Accountability," *Proceedings of the Twenty-Sixth International Joint Conference on Artificial Intelligence (IJCAL-17)* (2017): 17–18.

34 See remarks on Savigny and the mechanisation of jurisprudence in Carl Schmitt, "The Plight of European Jurisprudence," *Telos*, no. 83 (1990): 35–70.

35 Most famously the law and economics movement, but in the LAWS context see Duncan MacIntosh, "Autonomous Weapons and the Nature of Law and Morality: How Rule-of-Law-Values Require Automation of the Rule of Law," *Temple International & Comparative Law Journal* 30 (2016): 99–117.

36 See Jacques Derrida, "Force of Law," *Cardozo Law Review* 11 (1990): 919–1045.

and Peter Patton have written that 'this, in effect, automates a *volitional* process by making it more mechanical and . . . more highly automated'.[37] This is an everyday part of the growth and learning of trainable neurological systems.

In the context of legal judgment, we could say that the same dynamic applies, as seen in the example of the evolution of dedicated courtroom spaces and later their internal organisation. Even before the recent turn to legal materiality, spatial, aesthetic and 'decision ecology' approaches[38] have equipped us to read legal processes in terms of automation. To take one detail of Norm Spaulding's argument that 'due process . . . is itself intimately bound up with the location, design, and use of law's administrative space',[39] the eighteenth century in the USA saw the division of court spaces into dedicated zones for participants. Instead of officers of the court having to negotiate the space each time it was entered, they were able to enter a pre-organised space from 'off-stage' and take an elevated position. Whilst 'the authority of the law might be contested', that contest came to occur in a space 'formally organized and decorated to induce deference to the administration of justice'.[40] Spaulding focuses on how spatial arrangements orchestrate the 'inclusive exclusion' of 'outsiders' (other humans and their 'non-legal' perspectives), but it would be possible to see this process as the 'automation' of spatial elements to foreclose them from the unstable operation of contested human volition that is in issue. Put differently, the volition to jurisdictional authority becomes 'hard-wired', or automated. This, of course, does not make it uncontestable, but it renders the object of contestation less transparent, and requires it to take a different form (in harmony with the automated process) or become an act of destruction or refusal rather than a negotiation. From this point of view, automation is a latent precondition within Dorsett and McVeigh's notion of jurisdiction as 'how to do things with law',[41] a not-doing that organises and 'naturalises' the doing, by inheriting, repeating and developing older forms.

Matter that is automated with respect to judicial process is any matter that supports authoritative decision-making by *constituting* but *being excluded from* the space of deliberation and the human act of decision. Juridical anthropogenesis describes this ongoing organisation of matter. Whether or not contemporary scientific debates on matter, consciousness and 'emergence' seriously contest or newly confirm the presupposition just described, the human of juridical anthropogenesis exists – and governs – by not accounting for the conditions of its organisation of matter, thus ensuring its separation from it.

The waning authority of law's humanity

This anthropogenesis is relatively stable, in that its automation of matter is *functionally* similar at different times, presuming and reproducing a humanity defined as that which is not automated but decides upon, and with, what is automated. That is not to say there are no 'historical' differences between any two individual moments. We could in fact call 'historical' the difference

37 Richard D. Patton and Peter C. Patton, "What Can Be Automated? What Cannot Be Automated?" in *Springer Handbook of Automation*, ed. Shimon Y. Nof (Berlin: Springer, 2009), 305.

38 See, for example, David Pan, "Carl Schmitt and Barack Obama on Political Identity in a Multi-Polar World," *Telos*, August 10, 2010, www.telospress.com/carl-schmitt-and-barack-obama-on-political-identity-in-a-multi-polar-world/.

39 Norman W. Spaulding, "The Enclosure of Justice: Courthouse Architecture, Due Process, and the Dead Metaphor of Trial," *Yale Journal of Law & The Humanities* 24, no. 1 (2013): 315.

40 Ibid., 324.

41 Shaunnagh Dorsett and Shaun McVeigh, *Jurisdiction* (Abingdon: Routledge-Cavendish, 2012).

between two states of automation within this basic image of human life. But paradoxically, where an 'automated' system becomes an 'autonomous' one, 'automation' ceases by definition (because it takes on its own, unintended agency). In this case, it ceases also to be human since it ceases to be defined in relation to human volition and the measure of human progress. It then becomes unrecognisable as the same (human) 'life'. As Patton and Patton write, 'if an automated process began to self-organise into something else, then it would not be a very good piece of automation. . . . It would perhaps be a brilliant act of creating a new form of *life* (i.e., a self-organizing system)'.[42]

This presents the central question raised by legal discourse as its anthropogenesis encounters LAWS and results in its basic contradiction. Unlike in other legal contexts where 'automation' is shifting to 'autonomy',[43] MHC's literalisation of anthropogenesis forces legal discourse to name, rather than only perform, its *self-understanding* as human against the foil of automation technology. The question then arises whether LAWS regulation arrives not merely as historical, but as an *epochal* struggle for a determinate paradigm of law and governance that can continue to be premised on anthropogenesis; and the definitional rejection of automation. To repaint this epochal struggle in Agamben's terms, the technology of anthropogenic governance arrives at a special historical moment. Management, or *oikonomia*, is identified with the 'device' itself; 'a set of practices, bodies of knowledge, measures, and institutions that aim to manage, govern, control, and orient – in a way that purports to be useful – the behaviours, gestures, and thoughts of human beings'.[44] For Agamben, the coming to visibility of this 'governmental machine', in a parody of theological *oikonomia*, leads to a 'catastrophe'.[45] The question then becomes, as the anthropogenic device reveals its hand in MHC: can the *legal* human as an image of a technologically governed life survive this, or must it give up its image and give way to a new form of life? Can the law *of* this legal human prevail, or will it be reduced to the technological element it must pretend to eschew?

We return to Gregor Noll's account, to see how this catastrophe can be seen as the loss of law's 'human' to automation technology and its corresponding paradigm of normativity. Recall that for Noll, the subjects of LAWS regulation are always 'situation-specific constellation[s] of human and machine'. Whereas for optimistic commentators this allows systems to 'leverage the advantages of each',[46] for Noll it harbours incompatible paradigms of normativity: 'legal' and 'cybernetic'. In the 'legal' (monotheistic) paradigm, Noll explains, humans are imagined as incarnate, and the 'Written' law (modelled on the word of God) is 'excarnate'.[47] The goal is to incarnate law through study and internalisation, requiring conscious individual effort. Conversely, in AI, the natural world relieves 'God' of the place of the Author, and it is 'nature' that is supposed to (re-)emerge through cybernetic processes. Its code is not 'law' but the programme, and it is not law that is studied but training data (originally classified by humans).[48] Human study and the internalisation of norms then serve as neither process nor goal; they are replaced by a

42 Patton and Patton, "What Can Be Automated? What Cannot Be Automated?" 305 (emphasis in original).

43 See, for example, Madeleine de Cock Buning, "Autonomous Intelligent Systems as Creative Agents Under the EU Framework for Intellectual Property," *European Journal of Risk Regulation* 7 (2016): 310–22.

44 Agamben, *"What Is an Apparatus?"* 12.

45 Ibid., 24.

46 Scharre, "Centaur Warfighting: The False Choice of Humans vs Automation," 152.

47 Noll, "War by Algorithm: The End of Law?" 95.

48 Ibid., 97.

'collective, anonymous and decontextualized classification' that displaces (but is based upon) a world 'unconsciously pre-figured by the classifying human'.[49]

Notwithstanding the humanity driving and training the system, even if it could then be effectively studied by humans, what is studied is a 'non-human intelligence', a judgment beyond human appeal that cannot be effectively evaluated. This judgment *replaces* rather than being able to be *subjected to* law 'under the monotheistic form'.[50] Where an algorithmic weapons system participates in any act, that act is qualitatively distinct because the system 'consumes space otherwise available for the responsibility of human authors'.[51] Military AI *co-authors* such acts, bringing to bear on the world 'norms that can no longer be traced back to a human intention'; revealing *human* processes and cognition that *require* AI to become known; offering 'truths' that are produced within algorithmic processes that cannot be understood or validated '*outside* or *beyond*' AI; and that cannot be subjected to realistic testing.[52] As such, for Noll there is no way for IHL to ever effectively address the question of human-machine assemblages in its rules, which (even in IHL) imagine self-contained individual legal subjects to whom a determinate mental state must be attributable. New legislation is ineffective in governing algorithmic war because of this 'epochal rift' between emergent technology and the 'only understanding of law we currently have', meaning that here, all 'worldly law has come to an end'.[53]

In this light, the presupposed human of MHC regulatory discourse is more than another critical discourse that is absorbed by the existing political texture and technological trajectory of state violence. What is at stake is nothing less than the efficacy and authority of human law *qua* human, and its capacity to maintain the world that it recognises, and that is capable of recognising it as (its) law.

Conclusion: automating (what was) authority, and the task of a 'New Humanities'

What makes this problem of presupposed humanity in MHC compelling is that it shows us both the increasing *impossibility* of that human and its *necessity* within current paradigms of legal regulation, which I have called the 'conceptual bottleneck'. Noll's account does not equip us to mediate or choose between two forms of normativity, as other leading scholars have attempted to do in more amenable regulatory contexts.[54] When read through the lens of anthropogenic governance, it is rather a warning that it is precisely the habitual reapplication of that system of legal regulation and decision, in extension to incompatible subjectivities and normative paradigms, that will take us into a different political ontology, a different law.[55] If automation technologies embed contextual judgment, thus becoming 'open systems' and ceasing technically to be automated systems, this would indeed amount to a 'brilliant . . . creat[ion of] a new form of *life* (i.e., a self-organizing system)', with a new principle of normativity that genuinely threatens the ones we know.

49 Ibid.
50 Ibid., 98.
51 Ibid., 90.
52 Ibid., 89.
53 Ibid., 78, 98.
54 Mireille Hildebrandt, "Algorithmic Regulation and the Rule of Law," *Philosophical Transactions of the Royal Society A* 376, no. 2128 (2018): 1–11.
55 See also Brian Sheppard, "Warming Up to Inscrutability: How Technology Could Challenge Our Concept of Law," *University of Toronto Law Journal* 68, no. 1 (2018).

Even if what we are witnessing today is just another legal epistemological battle (like that, say, with medical science) or internal revolution (like the rise of modern social science),[56] it is qualitatively distinct. For Mireille Hildebrandt, unreflexively allowing law to encompass the so-called onli*fe*[57] world's data-driven agency 'will drain the life from the law, turning it into a handmaiden of governance'.[58] Joining this to the analysis of anthropogenesis I have made here, we could see the resulting *literalisation* of law's humanness (and at the same time its maximal conditioning by technology) as a concrete example of Giorgio Agamben's lament: that our era is the zenith of law as both 'in force' and 'without significance'. It corresponds ever-less to new objects and subjectivities, but its anthropogenic governance persists. In this sense, we could say that the basis for law's authority – its grounding in life – has itself become mechanised, or automated. Only in the effort of scholars on the edge of this process, straining to make a techno-social world conform, 'somehow', to something like the rule of law as we know it, is this rule of law not mechanised.[59]

This problematic can also serve as a response to Luciana Parisi's observation of a 'strong mistrust of technoscience . . . [and] the instrumental reason embedded in cybernetic and computational communication' and their continued identification 'with control as governance'.[60] Parisi rightly laments that it would be 'self-delimiting' not to explore the mode of thinking that is engendered by these new technologies, accenting Deleuzian 'creative unfolding of potentialities' over the Heideggerian 'un-concealing' of human finitude that, in my analysis, is visible in the regulatory problem of LAWS. By understanding this in terms of anthropogenesis, the legal discourse examined here can be seen as exactly that principle self-delimiting self-recognition that structures an otherwise immanent field of life; the continuation of the reflexive 'institution of a relation to life' that, in Pierre Legendre's terms, is the work of law.

From this point of view, the problem signalled by MHC's anti-technological human is not a failure to understand the extent of human-machine hybridity in the LAWS context, nor poor regulatory formulation. Neither is it some mistrust of technology, or a simple refusal to take up what Parisi calls 'techno-philosophy', a 'parallel articulation of philosophies of machines contributing to the reinvention of worlds, truths and facts' that can overturn 'the new brutality of technopolitics'.[61] Rather, it tells the story of the deep embeddedness of a particular form of self-delimitation based on a non-technological concept of humanity. Notwithstanding possible creative re-uses of existing legal apparatuses,[62] moving past the 'new brutality of technopolitics' requires that some other institution of a relation to life at the level of self-recognition could

56 See W. T. Murphy, *The Oldest Social Science? Configurations of Law in Modernity* (New York: Oxford University Press, 1997).

57 Today's 'transformative life world, situated beyond the increasingly artificial distinction between online and offline', according to Mireille Hildebrandt, *Smart Technology and the End(s) of the Law* (Cheltenham: Edward Elgar, 2015), 8.

58 Mireille Hildebrandt, "Law as Information in the Era of Data-Driven Agency," *Modern Law Review* 79, no. 1 (2016): 2.

59 Amongst innumerable examples, see Pasquale, "Toward a Fourth Law of Robotics"; Jake Goldenfein, "Algorithmic Transparency and Decision-Making Accountability: Thoughts for Buying Machine-Learning Algorithms," in *Closer to the Machine: Technical, Social and Legal Aspects of AI*, ed. Office of the Victorian Information Commissioner (Melbourne: Office of the Victorian Information Commissioner, 2019), 41–60; Hildebrandt, "Algorithmic Regulation and the Rule of Law"; Mireille Hildebrandt, "Law as Computation in the Era of Artificial Legal Intelligence: Speaking Law to the Power of Statistics," *University of Toronto Law Journal* 68 (2018): 12–35.

60 Luciana Parisi, "Reprogramming Decisionism," *E-Flux Journal* 85 (2017): 11.

61 Ibid.

62 See, for example, Susan Schuppli, "Deadly Algorithms," *Radical Philosophy* 187 (2014): 2–8.

emerge, fashioned by the future subjects of a life where 'all life is artificial life',[63] rather than from the legal-anthropogenic opposition between artifice and humanity. If a self-recognition for that life does emerge, this may provide the basis for a new criterion of value and evaluation to rival the extraordinary success of law as we know it.[64] The task of seeking a notion of value and evaluation for an inherently technological humanity is underway in the post-humanities, and is very explicit in the work of, for example, Bernard Stiegler. Such research responds directly to Derrida's call for a 'new humanities' – dissolving boundaries between science, the human and law.[65] This, more than simply reasserting the juridical human, its value and its anti-technological account of its agency, should be a central task for law and legal thinking. As the discourse on regulating LAWS shows us, few inherently *legal* problems are more urgent.

63 Claire Colebrook, "All Life Is Artificial Life," *Textual Practice* 33, no. 1 (2019): 1–13.

64 For an account of both the human-nonhuman division as foundational to Western law, and displacements of that division from 'within' the contemporary legal academy, see Margaret Davies, *Law Unlimited: Materialism, Pluralism, and Legal Theory* (Abingdon: Routledge, 2017).

65 See Jacques Derrida, "The University Without Condition," in *Without Alibi*, ed. Peggy Kamuf (Stanford, CA: Stanford University Press, 2002).

34

Rainbow family

Machine listening, improvisation and Access to Justice in international family law[1]

Sara Ramshaw[2]

As I write, I ask my iPhone's Siri: 'Hey Siri, I am getting a divorce. What should I do?' The response: 'I'm sorry to hear that.'[3] No further information is offered. Siri, for once, is speechless. Need this be the end of the story, though? What if, instead, we could develop a machine listening device that would provide creative and deeply attuned resolutions to those experiencing family conflict? Would this satisfy Access to Justice concerns felt throughout the world concerning the provision of accessible, timely and cost effective solutions? Yet, also provide the ability to listen creatively and deeply to the specifics of a family matter and offer not a generalised solution, but a bespoke one – also a prerequisite for Family Justice?

1 Strictly speaking, there is no such thing as 'international family law'. Instead, the label is often used to signify the application of domestic family law to international aspects of a case, if there are any: Jeremy D. Morley, "What Is International Family Law?" *International Family Law Firm*, April 21, 2015, www.internationalfamilylawfirm.com/2015/04/what-is-international-family-law.html. I am using the term here as an entrance to the current and potential use of technology and Artificial Intelligence (AI) in the area of Family Justice in a few international jurisdictions, namely Canada, The Netherlands, the United Kingdom (UK) and Australia.

2 I would like to thank Michael Griffin and Mitchell Ferreira for their research assistance on law, justice and technology, particularly the use of Online Dispute Resolution (ODR) in Canada and elsewhere throughout the Commonwealth. This chapter owes much to the feedback from participants at the public event, *Machine Listening*, held at Melbourne Law School on 24 July 2019 and hosted by Liquid Architecture. In particular, I would like to thank fellow panelists Seth Kim-Cohen and James Parker (also co-organiser), and Chair and Co-organiser Joel Stern. For more information, see https://liquidarchitecture.org.au/events/machnelistening. A version of this chapter was also presented at the 2020 Association of the Study of Law, Culture and the Humanities (ASLCH) conference in Connecticut, USA in March 2020. I am also extremely grateful to Johanne Blenkin, Director of University of Victoria's Access to Justice Centre for Excellence (ACE), for her invaluable advice, suggested readings and enthusiasm for this research, all of which has helped solidify many of my views. Finally, I am very appreciative of the support and patience of the editors of this Handbook, Shane Chalmers and Sundhya Pahuja. As always, all errors are my own.

3 When I engaged Siri with this question before the ASLCH conference in New Haven, Connecticut on 7 March 2020, I received a slightly different, although equally hollow, response: 'That's too bad. But I'll always be here for you.'

With the preceding in mind, this chapter interrogates how and why Digital Family Justice, as currently conceived, falls short of meeting Access to Justice requirements in the international context. As will be detailed later, justice is not just about increased accessibility to legal advice and/or judicial decision-making. It also requires that individual cases are listened to with the depth, attentiveness and creativity that the singularity of the situation demands. On the assumption that online family dispute resolution is presently wanting due to its restricted listening capacity, the real issue, and the one that propels my research here, is whether machine listening technology can bridge the divide between the desire for digitalisation as a facilitator of Access to Justice and the necessity for more deeply attuned listening and creative decision-making in the family law realm.

This research follows on from previous work I have undertaken, which found that Family Justice requires an improvisational approach to dispute resolution.[4] Such an approach invites responsiveness, adaptability, and creativity by judges and legal professionals when they apply general rules to a specific legal matter.[5] Moreover, I have found that litigants are more likely to accept a legal decision, even one that goes against them, if they feel they have actually been listened to by the judge and had their case properly considered.[6]

This chapter combines my research on improvisation, attentive listening and creativity in family law with an interest in the interdisciplinary work being undertaken on machine listening, especially by the interdisciplinary research network, Humanising Algorithmic Listening (HAL).[7] HAL explores the active role that technologies play in mediating our relationship with the world. This chapter will examine the potential of this technologically mediated listening in the area of family law by critically assessing the role of technology and Artificial Intelligence (AI) in relation to international Family Justice. While always attentive to the serious legal and

4 In January 2014, I (PI) and Paul Stapleton (Co-I) were awarded a UK Arts and Humanities Research Council (AHRC) Early Career Research Grant for a project titled *Into the Key of Law: Transposing Musical Improvisation. The Case of Child Protection in Northern Ireland*. This project united the fields of Family Law and Critical Studies in Improvisation (CSI), viewing improvisation not just as a musical, but also as a social practice, one that teaches us how to actively listen to the singularity of a situation and its relationship to context and the surrounding circumstances. For more information, see http://translatingimprovisation.com.

5 See, for example, Sara Ramshaw, *Justice as Improvisation: The Law of the Extempore* (London and New York: Routledge, 2013); Sara Ramshaw and Paul Stapleton, "From Prepeace to Postconflict: The Ethics of (Non) Listening and Cocreation in a Divided Society," in *Playing for Keeps: Improvisation in the Aftermath,* eds. Daniel Fischlin and Eric Porter (Durham, NC: Duke University Press, 2020), 300–23; Sara Ramshaw and Paul Stapleton, "Just Improvisation," *Critical Studies in Improvisation/Études critiques en improvisation* 12, no. 1 (2018): 7, www.criticalimprov.com/index.php/csieci/article/view/3977/4192; Sara Ramshaw and Paul Stapleton, "Unremembering: Countering Law's Archive. Improvisation as Social Practice," in *Law, Violence, Memory: Uncovering the Counter-Archive*, eds. Stewart Motha and Honni van Rijswijk (New York: Routledge, 2015), 50–69; Sara Ramshaw and Seamus Mulholland, "The Improvising Judge: An Interview with Her Honour Judge Patricia Smyth, Northern Ireland County Court," *Critical Studies in Improvisation/Études critiques en improvisation* 12, no. 1 (2018): 13, www.criticalimprov.com/index.php/csieci/article/view/3915/4189; Sara Ramshaw, "The Creative Life of Law: Improvisation, Between Tradition and Suspicion," *Critical Studies in Improvisation/Études critiques en improvisation* 6, no. 1 (2010): 13, www.criticalimprov.com/index.php/csieci/article/view/1084/1700; Sara Ramshaw, et al., "*Hydra*: A Creative Tool for Critical Legal Advocacy and Ethics," *Critical Studies in Improvisation/Études critiques en improvisation* 12, no. 1 (2018): 14, www.criticalimprov.com/index.php/csieci/article/view/3751/4190.

6 Ramshaw and Stapleton, "From Prepeace," 312; Ramshaw and Mulholland, "The Improvising Judge," 10–11.

7 See the UK Arts and Humanities Research Council (AHRC)-funded project, "Humanising Algorithmic Listening," accessed March 21, 2020, www.algorithmiclistening.org/about/.

ethical issues associated with machine listening,[8] this chapter questions whether Online Dispute Resolution systems should be pursued by legal systems throughout the Commonwealth and beyond, or whether sonic or acoustic-based technology may be better suited to providing justice in the family law realm. Can machines, in other words, ever listen deeply and attentively to the singularity of a family law case such that they are able to offer the creative and bespoke solutions that Family Justice demands?

The preceding questions are important. Whether we agree with it or not, family law is becoming increasingly digitised in contemporary society. It is timely and necessary to undertake a careful investigation of the current and potential use of digital family law and to develop a critical framework for examining the role that listening algorithms may play in resolving family disputes to ensure that what is dispensed by machine 'judges' approximates something like justice. This chapter provides a brief overview of the key issues in this area and the reasons why (machine) listening as improvisation might offer some hope for the future of international Family Justice.

With this said, Part I will look specifically at Online Dispute Resolution systems currently in place in various jurisdictions before moving on to the question of whether machine listening as improvisation is something worth pursuing in the international family law context.

Digital Family Justice

> Governments around the world know that digital technology is probably their only saviour in coping with the massive demands of . . . family justice.
>
> – David Hodson[9]

Online Dispute Resolution[10]

The current 'global leader'[11] in Online Dispute Resolution (ODR) is British Columbia (BC)'s Civil Resolution Tribunal in Canada.[12] It is the first court-designed and publicly financed ODR system in the world and is a mandatory path for certain defined categories of disputes, namely motor vehicle injury (up to $50,000 CAN), small claims (up to $5,000 CAN), strata property

8 Unfortunately, there is not enough space in this chapter to discuss the 'dark side' of machine listening in any detail. For more information, see, for example, Ethan Zuckerman, "Beware the Listening Machine," *The Atlantic*, June 17, 2015, www.theatlantic.com/technology/archive/2015/06/listening-machines/396179/; Marcia Ford and William Palmer, "Alexa, Are You Listening to Me? An Analysis of Alexa Voice Service Network Traffic," *Personal Ubiquitous Computing* 23 (2019): 67–79.

9 David Hodson, "The Role, Benefits, and Concerns of Digital Technology in the Family Justice System," *Family Court Review* 57, no. 3 (July 2019): 432.

10 For a report on ODR in England and Wales, US (Michigan and Utah), Australia (New South Wales and Victoria) and Canada (BC), see Cambridge Pro Bono Project, *A Comparative Analysis of Online Dispute Resolution* (Cambridge: University of Cambridge, February 2019).

11 Roger Smith, "Classical Lessons from the Rechtwijzer: A Conversation with Professor Barendrecht," *Law, Technology and Access to Justice*, June 22, 2017, https://law-tech-a2j.org/odr/classical-lessons-from-the-rechtwijzer-a-conversation-with-professor-barendrecht/.

12 Earl Johnson Jr, "BC's Civil Resolution Tribunal – Rechtwijzer 2.0 on Steroids: Some Early Observations" (Chapter Presented at the International Legal Aid Group (ILAG) Conference, Ottawa, Canada, June 17–19, 2019), 1, http://internationallegalaidgroup.org/index.php/conferenecs/ottawa-2019/conference-chapters#.

(condominium) (any amount), and societies and cooperatives associations (any amount).[13] The Civil Resolution Tribunal, and technology generally, is said to align with Access to Justice objectives in that it removes 'barriers like cost, time, and information asymmetry',[14] by providing free legal information and tools via the Internet, enabling litigants to resolve their disputes online, 24/7, thereby saving 'time, money and stress', with the end result being 'accessible, timely and fair resolutions'.[15]

Civil court matters in Canada are financed by the private citizen. With the average cost of a two-day civil trial costing over $30,000 (plus possible travel and childcare expenses, along with any wage loss from absences from employment), it is not surprising that a large percentage of small claims and family law disputes involve at least one self-represented litigant.[16] Coupled with a lack of support and long delays in legal processes, this can lead to severe stress and have serious effects on 'the health and emotional well-being of participants and on the public's confidence in the administration of justice'.[17]

To address these issues, the Civil Resolution Tribunal is designed to prevent and manage civil disputes using a four-stage process. (1) *Preliminary Phase*: before a claim is commenced, participants can access a free online tool called Solution Explorer, which uses guided pathways to help potential litigants learn more about their options in order to make informed decisions about the resolution of their disputes. They are asked a series of questions about the dispute and provided with specifically tailored information and resources. (2) *Commencement of Action Phase*: if unable to resolve a dispute using the Solution Explorer, they may launch a tribunal claim via the online intake process in which information from Step 1 is carried forward. After the other party to the dispute is served with notice of the claim, there is a brief opportunity to negotiate directly with one another, with little intervention from the tribunal. (3) *Facilitation Phase*: if negotiation is unsuccessful, the parties move on to the facilitation phase in which they are assisted by an expert facilitator, with the goal of reaching a consensual agreement. This will involve not only digital communication channels, such as the tribunal platform and e-mail, but also text, phone, video conferencing, fax and post. Salter explains: 'Despite being online, the CRT is a very human-driven organization. Leveraging technology, the CRT democratizes access to dispute resolution services by connecting the public, wherever they may live, with expert facilitators and tribunal members.'[18] Any agreement reached at the facilitation stage may be converted into a binding agreement of the tribunal, which is then enforceable in court. (4) *Adjudication Phase*: if the parties were unable to reach an agreement using a facilitator, the dispute is transferred to a tribunal member who is a lawyer specialising in the relevant matter. Typically, written evidence is submitted, which the member considers and then issues a binding decision of the tribunal.

13 See "Civil Resolution Tribunal," *Civil Resolution Tribunal Website*, accessed March 21, 2020, https://civilresolutionbc.ca. See also Johnson Jr, "BC's Civil Resolution Tribunal," 1.

14 Shannon Salter, "Online Dispute Resolution and Justice System Integration: British Columbia's Civil Resolution Tribunal," *Windsor Year Book of Access to Justice* 34 (2017): 113.

15 See "Civil Resolution Tribunal." For those unable or unwilling to use the online technology, paper- and telephone-based services are available: Salter, "Online," 114.

16 For example, in 2017–2018, 41% of family law and 69% of small claims litigants were self-represented at the British Columbia Provincial Court, see: "We Report to You," 2017/18 Annual Report, Provincial Court of British Columbia, April 9, 2019, www.provincialcourt.bc.ca/enews/enews-09-04-2019.

17 Salter, "Online," 119.

18 Ibid., 120–21. Facilitators may or may not be lawyers; they usually have a strong mediation background. It is anticipated that this phase will resolve up to 70% of disputes in this area: Ibid., 121.

The entire process is intended to take no more than 30 days and cost approximately the same as a Small Claims Court dispute: $200 CAN.[19]

Digital Family Justice: in BC and beyond

At present, BC's Civil Resolution Tribunal does not take family law cases. Yet, separation and divorce may be the 'biggest personal [and legal] challenge most people will ever face'.[20] Is it then not a worthwhile endeavour to try and innovate the legal process of divorce/separation, reducing its adversarial nature and making it more understandable and easy to follow?[21] With this in mind, in August 2019, BC's Legal Services Society (LSS),[22] also known as BC Legal Aid, launched a free online mediation platform called MyLawBC Family Resolution Centre[23] to help couples negotiate parenting time, vacations and other important details regarding their child(ren)'s care upon divorce or separation. It is the first service of its kind in Canada (and perhaps the world) and aims to enable low income parents who would not be eligible for referral to a legal aid lawyer[24] to create a 'parenting plan'[25] together online,[26] which can then be finalised into a consent order or a binding legal agreement. If the couple is unable to agree on certain topics, they can access up to five hours of free online assistance with a professional mediator qualified under the BC *Family Law Act* to assist with this task.[27]

19 This cost will obviously be less if the dispute is resolved in Phases 1–3 and there are fee exemptions for litigants experiencing financial hardship. The fees are meant to be high enough to discourage frivolous claims, but not so high as to prevent access to the legal system: Ibid. For more information on the Civil Resolution Tribunal, see Johnson Jr., "BC's Civil Resolution Tribunal."

20 Roger Smith, "Rechtwijzer: Why Online Supported Dispute Resolution Is Hard to Implement," *Law, Technology and Access to Justice*, June 20, 2017, https://law-tech-a2j.org/odr/rechtwijzer-why-online-supported-dispute-resolution-is-hard-to-implement/. While many divorce cases are quite simple with regard to the legal issues, they are often 'psychologically complicated with far-reaching consequences for (former) partners and their children': Bregje Dijksterhuis, "The Online Divorce Resolution Tool '*Rechtwijzer uit Elkaar*' Examined," in *Digital Family Justice: From Alternative Dispute Resolution to Online Dispute Resolution?* eds. Mavis Maclean and Bregje Dijksterhuis (Oxford: Hart Publishing, 2019), 193.

21 Smith, "Rechtwijzer."

22 BC's LSS is a non-profit organisation, providing legal information, advice and representation services. It is funded by the British Columbia provincial government, with additional support from the Law Foundation of BC and the Notary Foundation of BC. It is accountable to the public and remains independent of the government. For more information, see "We're Here to Help," *Legal Services Society*, accessed March 21, 2020, https://lss.bc.ca.

23 See "Get Help with the Issues Families Face When They Separate," Separation, Divorce and the Law, My Law BC, accessed March 21, 2020, www.mylawbc.com/paths/family/.

24 In BC, referrals are extremely limited and primarily occur where family violence is a factor: "What Is Legal Aid?" *Family Law, Legal Services Society*, accessed March 21, 2020, https://familylaw.lss.bc.ca/bc-legal-system/legal-help/legal-advice-and-legal-aid/what-legal-aid.

25 According to the Canadian Department of Justice: 'A parenting plan is a written document that outlines how parents will raise their children after separation or divorce': "Create a Parenting Plan," *Department of Justice, Government of Canada*, accessed March 21, 2020, www.justice.gc.ca/eng/fl-df/parent/plan.html.

26 This does not address Access to Justice for parties who are unable to afford or do not have access to Internet or digital services: David Hodson, "The Role, Benefits, and Concerns of Digital Technology in the Family Justice System," *Family Court Review* 57, no. 3 (July 2019): 425. While Internet access is nearly universal (92%) in urban areas of BC, the Canadian Radio-Television and Telecommunications Commission (CRTC) notes that only 33% of rural communities and 35% of rural Indigenous communities have access to the recommended broadband internet speeds (50 Mbps): "Connectivity in BC," *Government of British Columbia*, accessed March 21, 2020, https://www2.gov.bc.ca/gov/content/governments/connectivity-in-bc.

27 See "Family Mediation," *My Law BC*, accessed March 21, 2020, https://mylawbc.com/mediation/. As the platform is relatively new, no public data currently exist to assess its usage or rate of resolution. As with other

Internationally,[28] Digital Family Justice is similarly growing in recognition and support.[29] The invention and design of MyLawBC originated from the Hague Institute for the Internationalisation of Law (HiiL),[30] an organisation at the forefront of digital family law.[31] In partnership with the Dutch Legal Aid Board and the US firm Modria (now part of Tyler Technologies),[32] HiiL developed a digital platform called *Rechtwijzer* in 2007,[33] which is described as an online diagnostic and triage tool that assists users in obtaining the information they need to resolve their legal problem.[34]

The original version, *Rechtwijzer 1.0*, provided a questionnaire to be filled out by those in a legal conflict and aimed to provide them with relevant information such as referrals to (legal) experts, and relevant websites, and/or offering checklists, films and interactive online self-help tools to assist with parenting plans, divorce and calculating child support.[35] It has been lauded as 'a game-changer in showing how information/advice websites could become interactive and tailor information to an individual user'.[36] A re-vamped version, titled *Rechtwijzer 2.0*, was

---

international jurisdictions, it is also possible to obtain a desk-order divorce in BC without actually going to court or hiring a lawyer. Using the provincial government's Online Divorce Assistant, "Online Divorce Assistant," *Department of Justice British Columbia*, accessed March 21, 2020, https://justice.gov.bc.ca/divorce/ – and other online advice provided by the LSS, parties going through an uncontested divorce in which all property and support matters and/or issues relating to children have been agreed in advance, either through a separation agreement or an agreement about the terms of a consent order, can fill out the requisite forms and pay the fees online. Their divorce can be processed in as little as three or four months and cost less than $500, see: "Do Your Own Uncontested Divorce," *Separation & Divorce, Family Law, Legal Services Society*, accessed March 21, 2020, https://familylaw.lss.bc.ca/separation-divorce/getting-a-divorce/do-your-own-uncontested-divorce. For more on Digital Family Justice in BC and the withdrawal of the neo-liberal state in ensuring that access to Family Justice is possible, see Rachel Treloar, "My Problem, My Solution? Private Ordering and Self-Help in British Columbia, Canada," in *Digital Family Justice: From Alternative Dispute Resolution to Online Dispute Resolution?* eds. Mavis Maclean and Bregje Dijksterhuis (Oxford: Hart Publishing, 2019), 17–41. In England and Wales, parties can apply online for divorce through the government website: "Apply for a Divorce," *Government of the United Kingdom*, accessed March 21, 2020, www.gov.uk/apply-for-divorce. When there is agreement to and valid grounds for the divorce, parties do not need to instruct a divorce solicitor and can instead apply for a desk-order or 'DIY' divorce online: "How to Apply for a Divorce Online (UK)," *Divorce Online*, accessed March 21, 2020, www.divorce-online.co.uk/blog/how-to-apply-for-a-divorce-online-uk/. See Mavis Maclean, "The Digital Contribution to Reforming the Traditional Family Justice System in England and Wales: Reaching for the Best of Both Worlds?" in *Digital Family Justice: From Alternative Dispute Resolution to Online Dispute Resolution?* eds. Mavis Maclean and Bregje Dijksterhuis (Oxford: Hart Publishing, 2019), 225–28. Online filing is also available in Australia, see: "How Do I Apply for a Divorce?" *Federal Circuit Court of Australia*, accessed March 21, 2020, www.federalcircuitcourt.gov.au//wps/wcm/connect/fccweb/how-do-i/divorce/apply-for-a-divorce/apply-for-divorce.

28 For a list of some other Online Dispute Resolution courts, see: "Courts Using ODR," *The National Center for Technology & Dispute Resolution*, accessed March 21, 2020, http://odr.info/courts-using-odr/.

29 Hodson, "The Role," 425.

30 See "What We Do," *Hague Institute for the Internationalisation of Law*, accessed March 21, 2020, www.hiil.org.

31 Legal Aid, "LSS and HiiL Announce MyLawBC Partnership," October 24, 2014, http://elan.lss.bc.ca/2014/10/24/lss-and-hiil-announce-mylawbc-partnership/.

32 Roger Smith, "The Fate of Rechtwijzer's English Daughter: Relate Suspends Online Family Dispute Resolution Project," *Law, Technology and Access to Justice*, September 28, 2017, https://law-tech-a2j.org/odr/rechtwijzers-english-daughter-relate-suspends-online-family-dispute-resolution-project/.

33 *Rechtwijzer* means "Signpost [or Roadmap] to Justice" in Dutch: Sharon MacLennan, "HiiL Leads the MyLawBC Scrum," *The Factum MyLawBC*, October 9, 2014, https://factum.mylawbc.com/blog?offset=1426701383509.

34 MacLennan, "HiiL."

35 Dijksterhuis, "The Online," 196.

36 Roger Smith, "Classical Lessons from the Rechtwijzer: A Conversation with Professor Barendrecht," *Law, Technology and Access to Justice*, June 22, 2017, https://law-tech-a2j.org/odr/classical-lessons-from-the-rechtwijzer-a-conversation-with-professor-barendrecht/.

launched in 2012, incorporating a more ambitious ODR element in 2015.[37] It was designed to go beyond signposting (*Rechtwijzer 1.0*) to provide a method of resolving disputes online.[38] (Former) partners would be required to use the platform together, which combined self-help advice along with assistance from lawyers, mediators and other experts,[39] thereby lessoning the overall expense, delay and stress of going to court.[40]

Rechtwijzer 2.0, however, was scaled back in July 2017 because, as a *private* ODR system, it failed to attract enough users to remain financially sustainable.[41] It was replaced by *Uit-Elkaar.nl*, a less internationally focused service and one more aimed at a domestic Dutch audience.[42] This platform, managed by the start-up Justice42,[43] launched the 'Online *Scheidingsloket*' (Online Divorce Desk) in July 2019, which provides parties going through or considering divorce with suitable tips, advice and information on local support agencies. According to the website, '[t]he tool is free, anonymous, reliable, easy to use, and has the potential to become a guide for other (legal) problems in the future.'[44]

One lesson learnt from the demise of *Rechtwijzer 2.0* in 2017 is that a fully online divorce process may remain 'too much for people'. While it will work for some (whose numbers are growing), there are still those who want and need individual assistance in the 'traditional way'.[45] More modest in its ambitions, *Scheidingsloket* provides a hybrid system of on- and off-line legal assistance and advice, with mediation as a 'kind of top up optional module in addition to the services of the case manager and the final involvement of the lawyer who approves the settlement'.[46]

Access to Justice remains a key driver in the provision of this service. According to the co-founder and chief operating officer of Justice42, Laura Kistemaker, although the Dutch Legal Aid Board is no longer involved as a partner, it has a 'special arrangement' with Justice42, such that applicants eligible for legal aid are recommended and encouraged to use *Scheidingsloket* as

37 Smith, "Classical Lessons."

38 Dijksterhuis, "The Online," 201. MyLawBC is very much based on the *Rechtwijzer 1.0* model, while MyLawBC Family Resolution Centre is similar to the *Rechtwijzer 2.0* platform.

39 Dijksterhuis, "The Online," 202.

40 MacLennan, "HiiL." According to Hodson, an English-language version of *Rechtwijzer* was used for a time by the UK NGO, Relate, but it had to suspend the project due to the financial burden: Hodson, "The Role," 431. See also Smith, "The Fate." For more information on Relate, see "Relationship Support for Everyone," *Relate*, accessed March 21, 2020, www.relate.org.uk. For more on *Rechtwijzer*, see Hague Institute for the Internationalisation of Law, "Rechtwijzer – Signpost to Justice," *YouTube*, April 14, 2020, www.youtube.com/watch?v=400eNEsZ6S4.

41 Roger Smith, "Goodbye, Rechtwijzer: Hello, Justice42," *Law, Technology and Access to Justice*, March 31, 2017, https://law-tech-a2j.org/advice/goodbye-rechtwijzer-hello-justice42/. For more on why *Rechtwijzer uit Elkaar* did not work out, see Dijksterhuis, "The Online," 205–10.

42 Roger Smith, "Classical Lessons from the Rechtwijzer: A Conversation with Professor Barendrecht," *Law, Technology and Access to Justice*, June 22, 2017, https://law-tech-a2j.org/odr/classical-lessons-from-the-rechtwijzer-a-conversation-with-professor-barendrecht/.

43 Roger Smith, "The Rechtwijzer Rides Again," *Law, Technology and Access to Justice*, December 7, 2017, https://law-tech-a2j.org/odr/the-rechtwijzer-rides-again/. For more on Justice42, see "About Justice42," *Justice42*, accessed March 21, 2020, https://justice42.com/?lang=en.

44 See "Uitelkaar.nl Presents the 'Online Scheidingsloket' (Online Divorce Desk)," *Justice42*, accessed March 21, 2020, https://justice42.com/2019/07/18/uitelkaar-nl-presents-the-online-scheidingsloket-online-divorce-desk/?lang=en.

45 Roger Smith, "The *Rechtwijzer* Rises from the Ashes: An Interview with Laura Kistemaker of Justice 42," *Law, Technology and Access to Justice*, February 9, 2020, https://law-tech-a2j.org/odr/the-rechtwijzer-rises-from-the-ashes-an-interview-with-laura-kistemaker-of-justice42/.

46 Ibid.

it remains the cheapest option, costing only 36 euros as opposed to the unsubsidised cost of 450 euros.[47]

Private ODR platforms such as *Rechtwijzer* (and now *Scheidingsloket*) have been praised for providing significant benefits to users in terms of allowing them to avoid traditional public justice processes. However, as Shannon Salter notes,

> they do little to transform existing public judicial processes. Rather, by creating a buffer around the justice system, these private ODR systems may insulate the justice system from well-founded pressure from the public to transform their processes to better meet public need. Justice system transformation requires more than simply limiting direct interactions with existing processes.[48]

David Hodson, writing in relation to UK family law, argues that the necessarily flexible and highly discretionary nature of family law in common law jurisdictions, with its focus on fairness considerations, is 'not easily adaptable to online dispute resolution' and, where children are involved, 'there are often nuanced issues to consider alongside the need to take account of their best interests'.[49] Thus, digital systemisation becomes far more difficult and problematic than perhaps in other areas of law, such as strata and small claims disputes.[50] That said, Hodson is very keen to digitise family law, encouraging 'more settlements and more use of formulaic-based approaches'.[51] 'The law', he argues, 'must be adapted to digital processes':

> The law must not be so sophisticated and keen to produce a tailor-made outcome for every individual case as to make it so expensive, so complex, and so hard to predict as to put off both lay parties and digital programmers. Of course, IT is the servant of the law, but the law must adapt to work best with IT. This is not a challenge to fairness. It is a challenge to produce an accessible justice system.[52]

It is my position in this chapter, though, that, regardless of whether the ODR platform is private, public or non-profit, justice in the family law realm is not just about accessibility, or saving time, money and stress. Family Justice requires deep and attentive listening to the singularity and unique circumstances of a family conflict and finding creative solutions to these disputes. As one family law judge, who I interviewed for a previous research project, noted: 'every child is an individual, every family problem is individual, and needs a bespoke solution.'[53] Creativity and attentive listening are thus essential features of Family Justice.

47 Ibid. See also Dijksterhuis, "The Online," 211.

48 Salter, "Online," 116.

49 David Hodson, "The Role, Benefits, and Concerns of Digital Technology in the Family Justice System," *Family Court Review* 57, no. 3 (July 2019): 426. The Best Interests of the Child (BIoC) principle has international legal origins in the *United Nations Convention on the Rights of the Child*, see: Margrite Kalverboer, et al., "The Best Interests of the Child in Cases of Migration: Assessing and Determining the Best Interests of the Child in Migration Procedures," *International Journal of Children's Rights* 25 (2017): 114. Many jurisdictions, including Canada, The Netherlands and Australia, use BIoC as the paramount consideration in family law decision-making concerning children. The UK applies a variant, the 'welfare of the child'.

50 Hodson, "The Role," 429.

51 Ibid.

52 Ibid.

53 Ramshaw and Mulholland, "The Improvising Judge," 4.

In support of this argument, Part II outlines the use of algorithmic or machine listening in the fields of improvised music and the sonic arts and queries whether advancements in these areas might be transposed into the legal realm to assist with the attainment of Digital Family Justice.

Can machines offer Family Justice?

As mentioned earlier, I have written extensively about the improvisational nature of justice as a negotiation between the singularity of a particular case and the pre-existing rules or laws to which it must adhere or follow. As a 'social practice' that is 'learned and culturally embedded',[54] improvisation, as will be detailed later, is crucial to any discussion of Digital Family Justice. Focussing on a key feature of improvised activity, namely deep and attentive listening, Part II of this chapter will ask: (1) can computers improvise? and (2) why do we want them to? As a pioneer in and staunch supporter of creative machine listening, I will look to the work of improvising trombonist, composer and computer/installation artist George E. Lewis to guide this discussion.

Can machines improvise?

The idea of machines improvising may sound strange, non-sensical even. Is not machine behaviour the exact opposite of improvisation? Predictable, programmable, systemised, routinised and generalised?[55] And, yet, it is important to note that musical improvisation by human actors, although often defined or categorised as providing 'substantial *fresh* input' to a work in the time of the performance,[56] for the most part must be based on pre-existent materials, structures and rules.[57] Thus, while conventional wisdom holds that musical improvisers simply 'make it up' as they go along, or just let 'sounds be themselves', as Lewis reminds us, creating within the conditions of the moment requires immense discipline and skill and must be based on 'one's history, culture, and practices'.[58] That said, the simple application of rules will not guarantee a successful improvisation – be it in a human or in an automated player.[59] Thus, improvisation in both humans and machines requires simultaneous structure and a certain degree of autonomy such that one is able to not only implement the 'rules' for improvisation, but also facilitate non-deterministic, surprising, perhaps even creative and aesthetic, decision-making.[60]

Judicial decision-making and dispute resolution in family law requires considerable creativity. Thus, equally vital is that listening machines not only improvise, but do so creatively,

54 Lewis, "Mobilitas," 114.

55 Gunter Lösel, "Can Robots Improvise?" *Liminalities: A Journal of Performance Studies* 14, no. 1 (2018): 185.

56 Roger Dean, *Hyperimprovisation: Computer-Interactive Sound Improvisation* (Wisconsin: A-R Editions Inc., 2003), xiii.

57 Ibid.

58 George E. Lewis, "Notes (2004/04/28)," *American Composers Orchestra*, April 28, 2004, www.americancomposers.org/improvise-new/notes20040428-htm/. For an introduction to this critical approach to improvisation, see George E. Lewis and Benjamin Piekut, "Introduction: On Critical Improvisation Studies," in *The Oxford Handbook of Critical Improvisation Studies, Vol. 1*, eds. George E. Lewis and Benjamin Piekut (Oxford: Oxford University Press, 2016), 1–35.

59 Lösel, "Can Robots Improvise?," 187.

60 Ibid.

that is, with the ability to offer bespoke solutions to individual family law problems. Looking to the fields of aesthetics and computational creativity, there is evidence that machines can produce artistic outputs.[61] However, still unsettled is whether the process of machine creation is itself creative, or whether algorithms as artistic agents have anything to offer us regarding the nature of human art and creativity,[62] or the relation between technology and art.[63] These are significant concerns. However, due to limited space, they must be left unexplored in this text.

Looking to the writings of Gordon Pask, Lewis outlines four features of an aesthetically potent, and therefore creative, algorithmic system:

1 Creative machines must provide a variety of offerings, but not so many as to make the environment unintelligible.
2 Creative machines must offer material that a human interactant can learn to interpret at various levels of abstraction.
3 Creative machines must provide cues or tacitly stated instructions to guide the learning process.
4 Creative machines may, in addition, respond to the human interactant, engage them in conversation, and adapt its characteristics to the prevailing mode of discourse.[64]

All of these elements would be necessary if machine listening technology were to be employed in the family law realm.

Digital Family Justice would require one more thing: algorithmic software that mirrors the *emotional* state of the human participant(s). This process, which Lewis calls 'emotional transduction,' is centred on machine-human interactivity:

> This notion ['emotional transduction'] constructs physicality and performance as an intentional act, that is, an act embodying meaning, and announcing emotional and mental intention. On this view, interaction and behavior are carriers for a complex symbolic signal, and that notes, timbres, melodies, duration, and other music-theoretical constructs are not ends in themselves. Embedded in these objects is a more complex, indirect, powerful signal that we must train ourselves to detect.[65]

Machines can, as Lewis and others have demonstrated, be creative improvisers. The next question that must be addressed, though, is why do we want them to be?

61 See, for example, a neural network that creates art in the style of Van Gogh: Michael Culpan, "This Algorithm Can Create an Imitation Van Gogh in 60 Minutes," *Wired*, September 1, 2015, www.wired.co.uk/article/art-algorithm-recreates-paintings.

62 Mark Coeckelbergh, "Can Machines Create Art?" *Philosophy & Technology* 30 (2017): 285–86.

63 Ibid., 209. See also Heidegger's linking of *techne* to *poesis* in, for example, Martin Heidegger, *The Question Concerning Technology and Other Essays*, trans. W. Lovitt (New York: Harper & Row, 1977).

64 George E. Lewis, "From Network Band to Ubiquitous Computing: Rich Gold and the Social Aesthetics of Interactivity," in *Improvisation and Social Aesthetics*, eds. Georgina Born, Eric Lewis and Will Straw (London: Duke University Press, 2017), 101, referring to the work of Gordon Pask.

65 George E. Lewis, "Interacting with Latter-Day Musical Automata," *Contemporary Music Review* 18, no. 3 (1999): 106.

Why do we want machines to improvise?[66]

> [P]erhaps our improvising computers can teach us how to live in a world marked by agency, indeterminacy, analysis of conditions, and the apparent ineffability of choice. Through improvisation, with or without machines, and within or outside the purview of the arts, we learn to celebrate our vulnerability, as part of a continuous transformation of both Other and Self.[67]

The question of the possibility of improvisation in machines is very much tied to the 'why' question: why do we want machines to improvise? Put another way, what do humans gain by creating improvising machines, or what does technology offer improvising musicians, for example, which would tempt them to interact with computers? To answer this, it is worth mentioning that even the most skilled improvisers experience certain constraints on their ability to process information with the speed required for virtuoso improvisation. As Jeff Pressing notes:

> The improviser must effect real-time sensory and perceptual coding, optimal attention allocation, event interpretation, decision-making, prediction (of the actions of others), memory storage and recall, error correction, and movement control, and further, must integrate these processes into an optimally seamless set of musical statements that reflect both a personal perspective on musical organization and a capacity to affect listeners. Both speed and capacity constraints apply.[68]

Accordingly, one response as to why we want our machines to improvise is that, by teaching machines to improvise and/or exploring creative machine improvisation, we not only learn something about AI and technology, but we also learn something about the processes of improvisation in humans[69] and 'about ourselves, and our environment'.[70] For George Lewis, questions about the possibility of improvisation in machines 'encompass not only technological or music-theoretical interests but philosophical, political, cultural and social concerns as well.'[71]

While there is anxiety felt by improvising musicians, just as there is by lawyers and judges,[72] that humans will be replaced by machines or robots,[73] Lewis believes whole-heartedly in the benefit that humans acquire by studying and honing cyborg sociality,[74] particularly as it relates to the skills of interactivity and attentive listening. The techno-human creative process is very much

66 Lewis has explored this question in more depth in his chapter, George E. Lewis, "Why Do We Want Our Computers to Improvise?" in *The Oxford Handbook of Algorithmic Music*, eds. Roger T. Dean and Alex McLean (Oxford: Oxford University Press, 2018), 123–30.

67 Lewis, "Why," 128.

68 Jeff Pressing, "Improvisation: Methods and Models," in *Generative Processes in Music: The Psychology of Performance, Improvisation, and Composition*, ed. John A. Sloboda (Oxford: Clarendon Press, 1988), as cited in Dean, *Hyperimprovisation*, xx.

69 Gunter Lösel, "Can Robots Improvise?" *Liminalities: A Journal of Performance Studies* 14, no. 1 (2018): 185. See also George E. Lewis, "Too Many Notes: Complexity and Culture in *Voyager*," *Leonardo Music Journal* 10 (2003): 33.

70 Lewis, "Why," 128.

71 Lewis, "Too Many Notes," 33.

72 Dana Remus and Frank Levy, "Can Robots Be Lawyers? Computers, Lawyers, and the Practice of Law," *The Georgetown Journal of Legal Ethics* 30 (2017): 501–58.

73 Lösel, "Can Robots," 185. See also Lewis, "Why," 124, referring to anthropologist of technology, Lucy Suchman.

74 Lewis, "Why," 127.

dependent on listening, or what Lewis calls, 'the exchange of sonic features lead[ing] to a form of sociality'.[75] Listening is by its very nature an improvisational act, one that is 'engaged in by everyone'. It is an 'expression of agency, judgment, and choice, conducted in a condition of indeterminacy', which places us 'in a condition of momentary subalterity [sic], whatever our designated social, racial, gender, or class position'.[76] According to Lewis, working with creative machines offers a means of 'creating a politically inflected, critically imbued aesthetic space'[77] and (machine) listening *as* improvisation 'announces a practice of active engagement with the world, where we sift, interpret, store and forget, in parallel with action and fundamentally articulated with it'.[78]

Rainbow Family (1984) was the first of Lewis' 'interactive virtual orchestra pieces'.[79] It featured up to four human musical improvisers performing with a network of four computers. Three of the machines represented autonomous 'performers' connected to synthesisers producing sounds. A central computer functioned as an 'ear', analysing the individual offerings of the computers and the collective performance of the human-computer musical interaction.[80] Celebrated as a 'groundbreaking work', *Rainbow Family* 'employs proto-machine-listening software to analyze an improviser's performance in real time, while simultaneously generating both complex responses to the musician's playing and independent behavior arising from the program's internal processes'.[81]

Drawing upon AI and practices of free improvisation, *Rainbow Family* includes 'machine subjectivities as central actors'.[82] The creative machine, in other words, is not only able to analyse a fellow (human) improvisor's performance in real-time and respond to it, but also provide its own musical contribution in accordance with the programme's internal processes.[83] Lewis designed these creative machines to perform in a manner that utilises key elements of improvisation, both within and outside music, such as staking out territory, assessing and responding to conditions, and asserting identities and positions.[84]

In his article, '(Machine) Listening as Improvisation',[85] Lewis offers *Rainbow Family* as a 'provocation concerning the act of listening'. He explains:

> The ontologies of "creative machines," and the hybrid ontologies of encounters between them and human musical improvisors (or even with other machines like themselves), depend upon a fundamental construction of something that we are pleased to call "listening," in

75 George E. Lewis, "(Machine) Listening as Improvisation," *Technosphere Magazine*, December 23, 2018, www.technosphere-magazine.hkw.de/p/5-Rainbow-Family-5Aj9nAxzG6zFRAAd9icEvH.

76 Ibid.

77 George E. Lewis, "Mobilitas Animi: Improvising Technologies, Intending Chance," *Parallax* 13, no. 4 (2007): 111.

78 Ibid., 113.

79 For a short video of the 1984 performance of *Rainbow Family* with Douglas Ewart (alto-saxophone, flute and clarinet), Joëlle Leandre (double bass), Derek Bailey (electric guitar) and Steve Lacy (soprano saxophone), see *Technosphere Magazine*, "Machine Listening, George Lewis, Rainbow Family Premiere," *YouTube*, December 22, 2018, www.youtube.com/watch?v=i4bS-0tsVEg. Rainbow Family was recently released on Carrier Records on 30 October 2020. See https://carrierrecords.bandcamp.com/album/rainbow-family.

80 George E. Lewis, "Listening for Freedom with Arnold Davidson," *Critical Inquiry* 45, no. 2 (Winter 2019): 434. See also the description of *Rainbow Family* in Lewis, "(Machine) Listening."

81 Lewis, "(Machine) Listening."

82 Ibid.

83 George E. Lewis, "Interacting with Latter-Day Musical Automata," *Contemporary Music Review* 18, no. 3 (1999): 103.

84 Lewis, "(Machine) Listening."

85 Ibid.

> which the exchange of sonic features leads to a form of sociality. At some level, framing machines as listeners becomes phenomenological and social as well as technological; in fact, all three aspects of the listening experience need to be considered together as we construct technologies of both human and machine listening, the modalities of which are similar to each other, yet different as well.[86]

With the questions regarding whether machines can improvise and why we might want them to, if not answered satisfactorily for readers, at least given synoptic attention, I now move on to some preliminary thoughts about the potential benefits and pitfalls of introducing machine listening into the family law realm.

Rainbow family law: improvisation as (machine) listening with litigants

> What we say about human/computer interaction is all too frequently dictated by an already determinate picture of the boundaries of the possible and the impossible. If we detach ourselves from this picture so that we can begin to listen, perhaps we will come to experience these creative machines as posing and provoking the challenges of self-transformation and social meaning from yet another perspective. And then we will be in a position to realize that multiplication of perspectives means multiplication of possibilities.[87]

When I first began to investigate the increased digitisation of family law throughout the Commonwealth and beyond, impulse told me that my research on justice as improvisation[88] would be of limited value. Is not improvisation naturally the preserve of *human* (legal) actors?[89] Something we humans all do, every day?[90] Yet, after delving more deeply into the subject of improvising automata, particularly the interactive, computer-driven systems created by George Lewis, such as *Rainbow Family*, I found myself perhaps not yet a convert, but definitely more open to the possibility and potential of Digital Family Justice.

In particular, I am intrigued with the concept of machine listening as a 'listening *with*', that is, as a listening alongside machines in a manner such that our skills as human listeners might be enhanced.[91] Creative machines listen not so much for what is happening now, but for what is likely to happen next.[92] This is perhaps why listening has been described by some as 'fundamental to human evolution'.[93]

The question with which I would like to leave readers, is how might technology and machine listening enhance human skill and understanding in relation to Family Justice?[94] Laura

86 Ibid.

87 Lewis, "Listening," 445, quoting Arnold Davidson, "Free at Last" (programme note for concert of Lewis and Geri Allen, Institute for the Humanities, Wellesley College, February 10, 2012).

88 Ramshaw, *Justice*.

89 Lösel, "Can Robots," 203.

90 Lewis, "Notes."

91 Simon Emmerson, "Listening *With* Machines: A Shared Approach," *Organised Sound* 20, no. 1 (2015): 68.

92 Ibid., 69.

93 Ibid., 70.

94 Ibid.

Kistemaker of the Dutch start-up Justice42 highlights that '[t]rust is key for people going through divorce'.[95] People must feel like they are being listened to by those dispensing legal advice or making decisions in relation to their disputes.[96] Thus, any ODR system focused on family law issues must make attentive listening and social interactivity or relationality with the participants a priority. As evidenced by Lewis' interactive computer-driven systems, it is possible to programme machines such that they produce outputs that not only embody meaning, but also announce 'emotional and mental intention' and, perhaps most importantly for Digital Family Justice, mirror the emotional states of those (e.g., musician, machine or litigant) to whom they are listening (or with whom they are improvising).[97]

One final aspect of machine listening that holds both considerable promise and potentially serious risks is that, due to its inherent sociality and interactivity, algorithmic creations are never objective or universal; instead, they represent 'the particular views of their creators'.[98] This is noteworthy when focused on one of Lewis' later computer music compositions (and the most widely performed), *Voyager* (1987–present),[99] which he programmed to specifically embody 'African-American aesthetics and musical practices'.[100] The so-called aesthetics of multidominance[101] that inspired *Voyager* looks to multiple colours, textures, patterns, shapes and rhythms routinely found in African visual art and music.[102] Embedding the aesthetics of dominance into the software itself, Lewis created a machine listening that is 'culturally contingent, historically emergent and linked to situated structures of power and dialogue'.[103] Applied to the international family law context, it is critical that any machine listening in this area vigilantly guards against algorithmic logics that simply reassert stereotypical visions of the 'proper' family in society. This is especially true where family violence may be an issue. As noted earlier, every family is unique and justice demands bespoke, not generalised, solutions to legal disputes. Moreover, although (machine) listening as improvisation can be 'reproduced transnationally, transculturally and even transhistorically',[104] would there be wide variation internationally, and would we want there to be?

95 Smith, "The Rechtwijzer."
96 Ramshaw and Stapleton, "From Pre-Peace," 312; Ramshaw and Mulholland, "The Improvising Judge," 10–11.
97 Lewis, "Too Many Notes," 36.
98 Ibid., 33.
99 I was fortunate to be in the audience for a performance by George Lewis, bassist Barry Guy and the *Voyager* computer pianist on 24 April 2007 at the Sonic Arts Research Centre (SARC), Queen's University Belfast, as part of the programme for the 2007 Sonorities Festival. For more information, see "Archive," *Sonorities*, 2016, accessed March 21, 2020, www.sonorities.org.uk/archive.html#1. For a review of this concert, see Erdem Helvacioglu, "Sonorities 2007 – Belfast, Northern Ireland, April 20–25, 2007," www.erdemhelvacioglu.com/content/sonorities-2007-belfast-northern-ireland-april-20-25-2007. To watch the International Contemporary Ensemble play George Lewis: Voyager (1987/2018) at the Mostly Mozart Festival 2018 at the Lincoln Center, New York City, see https://vimeo.com/288885065.
100 Lewis, "Too Many Notes," 33.
101 Ibid.
102 Ibid., 33–34. Lewis notes, though, that 'multidominance is not present in all trans-African music and art and certainly must not be applied as a sonic litmus test': Ibid., 34. That said, in a society dominated by Eurocentric conceptions of what constitutes 'music', the sounds produced via an 'aesthetics of multidominance' are often heard as simply '"noise", "frenzy" or perhaps "chaos",' which is, according to Lewis, the same for 'virtually every extant form of black music': Ibid.
103 Ibid.
104 Lewis, "Mobilitas," 114.

A great deal more can be written on this topic. And the question of whether it is desirable – or even possible – to create an interactive computer-driven system aimed at assisting family law litigants with ODR processes remains open for debate.[105] Ultimately, though, paraphrasing Lewis, the subject in question here is not technology or computers, but justice itself.[106] How we respond both domestically and internationally to the call for increased digitisation in the name of Family Justice says as much about us as a global legal community as it does the machines themselves.

105 Hodson predicts that 'complete replacement of the judiciary by the digital is unlikely' and, although an advocate for Digital Family Justice, he argues that '[u]nder no circumstances is it suggested that all justice must become digital. Justice is human. An algorithm is an equation. Justice is not being privatized to the digital community': Hodson, "The Role," 430.

106 Lewis, "Interacting," 110.

35

In the name of the victim

Representing victims in international criminal justice[1]

Maria Elander

'In the name of the victims'

International criminal courts and tribunals (ICTs) are today a standard approach in dealing with the aftermath of conflicts and atrocities. At the heart of this approach lies a number of promises, from personal accountability, deterring future atrocities, restraining wars, to simply knowing the 'truth'. Yet, as an enterprise, international criminal justice (ICJ) is held together not only at a level of facts, institutions or moral principles but also by the language used. Certain forms of suffering and losses during conflicts and atrocities are perceived as 'crimes', those who are responsible for these crimes as 'perpetrators' and those who have suffered as 'victims'. Through the allocation of subject-positions and by labelling conduct, experiences and events are expressed and heard. In this way, at the foundation of ICJ's promises is a promise of representation.

The figure of the victim appears in relation to these promises of ICJ in general and to the promise of representation in particular. Its practices and relations are manifold. For example, victims are invoked in arguments for setting up a court and in the rationales for its practices.[2] Notwithstanding comments that victim survivors have no place in the proceedings, prosecutors of the international criminal courts take on a position as spokespersons and representatives of victims,[3] while it is in the name of the victim that justice is served.[4]

1 This chapter builds on my book, *Figuring Victims in International Criminal Justice* (Routledge, 2018).

2 *Rome Statute of the International Criminal Court*, opened for signature July 17, 1998, 2187 UNTS 90 (entered into force July 1, 2002), Preamble ('*Rome Statute*'): States parties are '[m]indful that during this century millions of children, women and men have been victims of unimaginable atrocities that deeply shock the conscience of humanity'.

3 See for example statements by ICC Prosecutor Fatou Bensouda and former ICC Prosecutor Louis Moreno Ocampo. These are discussed at length by Sara Kendall and Sarah Nouwen, "Representational Practices at the International Criminal Court: The Gap Between Juridified and Abstract Victimhood," *Law and Contemporary Problems* 76 (2014): 235.

4 'When the judges have delivered their verdicts, we hope that Cambodians and all who support us will feel a load lifted from our backs as we finally bring justice in the name of the victims': Prime Minister Hun Sen, "Preface," in *An Introduction to the Khmer Rouge Trials*, 4th ed. (China: Public Affairs Section, Extraordinary Chambers in the Courts of Cambodia, 2004).

Victims feature in news articles, NGO reports, academic writings and legal texts; they appear as figures of the past and present, in descriptions that are positive and negative. The plight of victims is often invoked as a call for action,[5] and a description of their situation becomes a description of the need for criminal courts to act. Within judicial institutions, victims figure in and through the proceedings: victims' experiences take the form of evidence, their statements appear as testimonies, and their comments about the court are often taken in media and NGO reports as indications of whether the court and its proceedings are successful. In relation to international criminal law and justice, victims figure in significant ways.

Recent years have seen an explosion of scholarship that in different ways engages with the relation between victims and ICJ.[6] Because of perceived connotations with passivity and helplessness, the terms 'survivor' and 'agent' are often invoked. This 'Agent-Not-Victim' trope[7] has become a preferred, even dominant, form to describe those who have suffered injustices and violence.[8] Nevertheless, the term 'victim' retains a strong position in ICJ, in part because of its longevity in law and legal writing, but also because of the fact that not all who figure as victims of international crimes have survived. Indeed, victim survivor is but one iteration of the victim figures.

How do we understand the way victims figure in international criminal justice? Much of the scholarship on victims in ICJ is dedicated to analysing particular practices or mechanisms with the purpose of demonstrating how these either benefit or harm victims. Much of this scholarship also takes the subject position of 'victim' for granted. By taking victim subjectivity as ontologically prior, it assumes there is a subject (named) 'victim' who engages or seeks to engage with a court, a court which in turn responds more or less appropriately. While this approach may provide important insights into the successes and failures of courts, it leaves unattended the question of how the practices of international criminal courts and tribunals play a part in constituting the subject position of the victim.

In this chapter, which draws on my book on figuring victims in international criminal justice, I ask the question of how practices of international criminal justice represent victims of atrocity – if and when representation is understood as a practice of subject formation. How does it contribute to our understanding of the constitution of victim, for and in international criminal justice? In asking these questions, I draw on a body of critical scholarship that seeks to unpack the imaginations and presentations of subjects such as victims in ICJ, and the way that international courts and tribunals contribute to discourses on victimhood.[9] Doing so

5 See, for example, Anne Orford's work on the discursive production of the call for action in the context of humanitarian intervention: Anne Orford, *Reading Humanitarian Intervention: Human Rights and the Use of Force in International Law* (Cambridge: Cambridge University Press, 2003).

6 Scholarship on victims in ICJ is too extensive to provide in full here. For collections see, for example, "Special Issue: Reconsidering Appropriate Responses to Victims of Conflict," *International Journal of Transitional Justice* 10 (2016); Thorsten Bonacker and Christoph Safferling, eds., *Victims of International Crimes: An Interdisciplinary Discourse* (The Hague: TMC Asser Press, 2013).

7 Gudrun Dahl, "Sociology and Beyond: Agency, Victimisation and the Ethics of Writing," *Asian Journal of Social Science* 37 (2009): 391.

8 See Rebecca Stringer, *Knowing Victims: Feminism, Agency and Victim Politics in Neoliberal Times* (New York: Routledge, 2014).

9 See, for example, Kendall and Nouwen, "Representational Practices at the International Criminal Court"; Christine Schwöbel, ed., *Critical Approaches to International Criminal Law: An Introduction* (Abingdon: Routledge, 2014), 181; Christian De Vos, Sara Kendall and Carsten Stahn, eds., *Contested Justice: The Politics and Practice of the International Criminal Court Interventions* (Cambridge: Cambridge University Press, 2015), 272; Nesam McMillan, "Imagining the International: The Constitution of the International as a Site of Crime, Justice and Community," *Social & Legal Studies* 25, no. 2 (2016): 163.

enables a richer account of not only victims but also of the practices of international criminal justice.

In the following sections, I provide two examples, or illustrations, of instances in which the figure of the victim is constructed and negotiated. While much of my work centres on the Khmer Rouge Tribunal in Cambodia, the two examples here are from trials dealing with the crimes of Nazis. I take these as examples here in order to destabilise a certain canon that has been established on 'victims' in international criminal law. The first example from the International Military Tribunal at Nuremberg demonstrates how the identity of the victim may shift over time, while the second example from the Eichmann trial at Jerusalem demonstrates how subject formation is not simply a power imposed on a person but how subjectivity is negotiated and can be resisted.

Iconic trials

> That four great nations, flushed with victory and stung with injury stay the hand of vengeance and voluntarily submit their captive enemies to the judgment of the law is one of the most significant tributes that Power has ever paid to Reason.
>
> Justice Robert H. Jackson, US Prosecutor at the Nuremberg IMT[10]

> When I stand before you here, Judges of Israel, I am not standing alone. With me are six million accusers. . . . Their blood cries out, but their voice is not heard. Therefore I will be their spokesman and in their name I will unfold the awesome indictment.
>
> Attorney General Gideon Hausner at the Israeli trial against Eichmann[11]

Two iconic trials with two iconic opening speeches. The opening address at the International Military Tribunal (IMT) at Nuremberg by US Prosecutor (and Supreme Court Associate Justice) Robert H. Jackson stands as a milestone in international criminal justice for its eloquent invocation of the power of law as a form of reason. In 'stay[ing] the hand of vengeance', the victors of World War II called upon reason, understood as being codified in law, to pass judgment on the leaders of the Nazi regime for its committed atrocities. This turn to law and the affirmation that 'crimes against international law are committed by men, not by abstract entities',[12] are represented as landmarks in fostering post-conflict justice. Here, the suffering experienced by victims was told by the prosecutors and by witnesses, of whom only a few were victims themselves.

In contrast, the opening address by Attorney General Gideon Hausner at the Israeli trial against Adolf Eichmann[13] explicitly invoked victims as the figure in whose name the trial

10 Robert H. Jackson, "Opening Statement Before the International Military Tribunal (21 November 1945)," *The Robert H Jackson Center*, accessed January 23, 2020, www.roberthjackson.org/speech-and-writing/opening-statement-before-the-international-military-tribunal ('*Jackson Opening Address*').

11 Transcripts of Proceedings, "*Attorney General v Adolf Eichmann* (District Court of Jerusalem, Criminal Case 40/61, 17 April 1961)," accessed January 23, 2020, www.nizkor.org/hweb/people/e/eichmann-adolf/transcripts/Sessions/Session-006-007-008-01.html ('*Eichmann Transcripts*').

12 Judgment in International Military Tribunal, *Trial of the Major War Criminals Before the International Military Tribunal, Nuremberg 14 November 1945–1 October 1946*, vol. 1 (Nuremberg: The Tribunal, 1947), 171, 223.

13 See, for example, Hannah Arendt, *Eichmann in Jerusalem: A Report on the Banality of Evil* (New York: Penguin Books, 1963); Lawrence Douglas, *The Memory of Judgment* (New Haven: Yale University Press, 2001); Shoshana

proceeded. This was a trial conducted in the name of victims and then driven by victim testimonies. The trial became iconic for the way it focused on the Jewish victims of the Nazi regime and for inaugurating what Annette Wieviorka termed *L'Ère du témoin* – the Era of the Witness.[14] This has been considered a paradigm shift in the giving and hearing of testimonies by survivors of the Shoah.

The two trials are taken in scholarship on victims and ICJ to signify opposing poles of a spectrum in two fundamental ways. First, the trials differ fundamentally in the way the victims relate to the *telos* of the trial. Second, the relationship between victims and evidence that come together in the role of victim-witness differs drastically in the two trials. This has led to a claim that the distinction between the two trials is one between an absence and a presence of the victim figure. I disagree. Instead, based on a close reading of the two trials, I suggest that the trials and commentary around them provide useful insights into the construction of victim subjectivity, across time and place.

The Nuremberg IMT and the absent victim

In contemporary scholarship about international criminal justice, the victim at the Nuremberg IMT is represented as an absent figure.[15] Susanne Karstedt, for example, positions the IMT as a point of departure on 'the road from absence to presence'.[16] According to her, victims held a 'near-complete absence' in the post-World War II tribunals.[17] As she describes it, at Nuremberg IMT, the proceedings were 'conducted without their presence'[18] and the voices heard at the trial were not those of victims but of perpetrators.[19] For Sam Garkawe, this 'victim-free trial'[20] made the trial parsimonious, as the presence of victims would 'have enhanced the proceedings . . . provided a greater sense of justice . . . [and made] the trial much more dramatic and memorable'.[21] For him, the lack of active involvement by victim survivors was simply 'unjust'.[22] In contrast to the assertion by Karstedt and Garkawe that victims at Nuremberg were characterised by an absence, I suggest that the question of the role of victims depends upon whom the victim is considered to be, and that victim identity constantly changes – slips – with regards to victims at Nuremberg.

Felman, "Theaters of Justice: Arendt in Jerusalem, the Eichmann Trial, and the Redefinition of Legal Meaning in the Wake of the Holocaust," *Critical Inquiry* 27, no. 2 (2001): 201; Martti Koskenniemi, "Between Impunity and Show Trials," *Max Planck Yearbook of United Nations Law* 6, no. 1 (2002).

14 Annette Wieviorka, *The Era of the Witness*, trans. Jared Stark (Ithaca: Cornell University Press, 2006).

15 This was less the case in the successor trials to Nuremberg under Control Council Law 10, where the plight of victims was more frequently invoked by the prosecutor. See Paul Weindling, "Victims, Witnesses, and the Ethical Legacy of the Nuremberg Medical Trial," in *Reassessing the Nuremberg Military Tribunals: Transitional Justice, Trial Narratives, and Historiography*, eds. Kim Priemel and Alexa Stiller (New York: Berghahn Books, 2012), 74.

16 Susanne Karstedt, "From Absence to Presence, From Silence to Voice: Victims in International and Transitional Justice Since the Nuremberg Trials," *International Review of Victimology* 17, no. 1 (2010): 9.

17 Ibid., 10.

18 Ibid.

19 Ibid., 10, 14.

20 Sam Garkawe, "The Role and Rights of Victims at the Nuremberg International Military Tribunal," in *The Nuremberg Trials: International Criminal Law Since 1945–60th Anniversary International Conference*, eds. Herbert Reginbogin and Christoph Safferling (München: KG Saur, 2006), 86, 93.

21 Ibid., 88.

22 Ibid., 89.

First, there is an absence. During the trial's almost year-long proceedings, very few victim-witnesses[23] addressed the court. A Jewish writer and partisan fighter called by the Soviet prosecution told of the persecution of the Jews of Vilna,[24] and a French resistance veteran, who had spent three years at Auschwitz, told the court of the terrible regimen of the camp, the medical experiments and the gassing of Jewish people,[25] but the victim-witnesses were few. According to Karstedt, the lack (or at least small number) of victim-witnesses is directly linked with the lack of (Jewish) survivors in Germany at the time of the trial. Of those who had survived, many had left Germany. This meant that not only were there few witnesses, there were also few Jewish victims who sat in the audience of the trial and who participated in the public debate.[26] This (almost) absence of Jewish survivors as witnesses and as audience members is taken to mean an absence or silence of 'victims' at the Nuremberg IMT. Is, however, the lack of victim-witnesses and of Jewish survivors in the audience necessarily an absence of victims? Here is a slippage between the presence of victims and the presence of survivors, where the absence of (or more accurately the few) survivors and survivor testimonies are taken as a lack of victims *tout court*.

In certain ways, victims were particularly manifest during the trial. In the indictment, references to murder and to ill-treatment are elaborated at length. The text of the counts on war crimes and on crimes against humanity described the means of killing, including gassing, beating and starvation.[27] During the trial, the prosecution presented their case, not based upon witness-testimonies, but through written material and records that were the defendants' 'own making' and whose authenticity could not be challenged.[28] In these Nazi documents were detailed accounts of the taking and mistreatment of hostages[29] and the poor conditions at camps, and there were numerous references throughout the proceedings to the killings of 'civilians'. Defendants such as Rudolf Höss appeared as witnesses and told of the killings, including the 'destruction' of '2 million Jews' at Auschwitz.[30] It was in this way that victims appeared during the trial – through references and spokespersons. When Karstedt claims that 'there was no visible presence of victims at the IMT, not even of representatives who could speak on their behalf',[31] she ignores the victims who figured *through the evidence*, in the arguments made by the prosecution and the testimonies by the defendants. While there were few victims who addressed the court directly, victims were placed at the centre of the proceedings through descriptions of the crimes and their evidence, spoken on their behalf. Although Karstedt correctly observes

23 Of these few, most were French former interns at concentration camps and three were Holocaust survivors. See testimonies in International Military Tribunal, *Trial of the Major War Criminals Before the International Military Tribunal*, vol. 5, 167 (from January 11, 1946) and vol. 6, 183 (from 25 January), 231 (28 January), 242, 263, 278 (29 January), 289, 302.

24 Testimony by Abram Suzkever in Michael Marrus, *The Nuremberg War Crimes Trial 1945–46: A Documentary History* (Boston: Bedford Books, 1997), 197–201.

25 Testimony by Marie Claude Vaillant-Couturier: Ibid., 154–57.

26 Karstedt, "From Absence to Presence," 12.

27 International Military Tribunal, Indictment, October 6, 1945, Counts 3 and 4 in Marrus, *The Nuremberg War Crimes Trial 1945–46*, 57–70.

28 Justice Jackson in Stephen Breyer, "Crimes Against Humanity, Nuremberg 1946," *New York University Law Review* 71, no. 5 (1996): 1161–62; Sonali Chakravarti, "More Than 'Cheap Sentimentality': Victim Testimony at Nuremberg, the Eichmann Trial, and Truth Commissions," *Constellations* 15, no. 2 (2008): 223, 225.

29 Secret report addressed to Göring on February 15, 1940, quoted by French Prosecutor Charles Dubost in Marrus, *The Nuremberg War Crimes Trial 1945–46*, 152.

30 Testimony by Rudolf Höss: Ibid., 202–7.

31 Karstedt, "From Absence to Presence," 13.

that there were very few victim-witnesses and no lawyers who represented victim participants of the kind we see today at the International Criminal Court and Extraordinary Chambers in the Courts of Cambodia, it is difficult not to hear the suffering of victims while reading the evidence.[32]

Victims also figured as part of the *telos* of the trial. However, this victim is not whom we today might consider the primary victim of the Nazi regime. To get a sense of the telos of the tribunal and its proceedings, consider again the opening address of Justice Jackson. While all four prosecutors gave opening addresses,[33] it is that by US Prosecutor Justice Jackson that has become iconic. For him, the trial was held because 'the wrongs which we seek to condemn and punish have been so calculated, so malignant, and so devastating, that civilization cannot tolerate their being ignored, because it cannot survive their being repeated'.[34] Moreover, the purpose of holding a trial was to 'stay the hand of vengeance'.[35] Karstedt takes Justice Jackson's reference to vengeance to be a fear that victims would, as had occurred in France and Belgium, turn against former collaborators for revenge, something that had 'instilled widespread fears of disorder, violence and massive conflicts'.[36] Alongside the victim figure described earlier by Karstedt as silenced because of absence, here is another figure that is silenced because of a potentially vindictive nature. The oscillation between absence and vindication in the victim figure becomes clearer when taking into consideration the focus and scope of the trial. Karstedt's absent victim is that of the survivor of the Shoah, whose absence enabled a state of denial in Germany and elsewhere about the crimes against the Jewish people.[37] Indeed, there were few victim-witnesses and even fewer who had been victimised because of their Jewish identity. However, the main focus at Nuremberg, the 'crime of crimes' articulated in the IMT Charter, considered by the tribunal to contain the 'accumulated evil of the whole',[38] was not crimes against humanity (which at the time encompassed genocide) but the crime against peace, now called the crime of aggression. This is the crime that, for US Prosecutor Jackson, 'comprehends all other lesser crimes'.[39] Here is a victim figure, but not 'humanity' and not one targeted because of a Jewish identity.

It is not that the crimes against the Jewish people were completely ignored at the trial. In his opening address, Justice Jackson dedicated a section to 'crimes against the Jews', stating that the 'most savage and numerous crimes planned and committed by the Nazis were those against the Jews . . . [whom] Nazis were fanatically committed . . . to annihilate'.[40] Referring to the 'conspiracy or common plan to exterminate the Jew', Justice Jackson states that 'history does not record a crime ever perpetrated against so many victims or one ever carried out with

32 See for example descriptions of the torture and killing of 30,000 hostages in a secret report addressed to Göring on 15 February 1940, quoted by French Prosecutor Charles Dubost in Marrus, *The Nuremberg War Crimes Trial 1945–46*, 152.

33 For French prosecutor Francois de Menthon, the trial proceeded on the basis of 'the craving for justice of the tortured peoples'. Francois de Menthon, Opening address January 17, 1946 in Marrus, *The Nuremberg War Crimes Trial 1945–46*, 89.

34 *Jackson Opening Address.*

35 Karstedt, "From Absence to Presence," 12.

36 Ibid., 12–13.

37 Ibid., 21.

38 Arendt, *Eichmann in Jerusalem*, 255.

39 Gerry Simpson, *War, Law and Crime: War Crimes Trials and the Reinvention of International Law* (Malden: Polity Press, 2007), 145.

40 *Jackson Opening Address.*

such calculated cruelty'.[41] But as Gerry Simpson has pointed out, 'this was [considered] largely a product of one over-arching scheme to wage a war of aggression'.[42] As Jackson himself had argued during the set-up of the tribunal,

> this isn't merely a case of showing that these Nazi Hitlerite people failed to be gentlemen in war; it is a matter of their having designed an illegal attack on the international peace . . . and the other atrocities were all preparatory to it or done in execution of it.[43]

The 'matter' was thus one of 'international peace', and Nazi Germany's 'illegal attack' on it was the foremost of crimes committed. When this focus on the crime of aggression is taken into consideration, it is less surprising that the victims of persecution, murder and destruction appear only through second-hand reference. The primary victim of the Nazis as represented through the Nuremberg IMT was not those of the Shoah or any other form of persecution, but the victim of aggression. So who is this figure victimised by aggression? For Justice Jackson, the victim was 'civilisation'; for French Prosecutor de Menthon, it was 'the spirit . . . all spiritual, rational, or moral values' that distinguishes humanity from barbarism.[44] Civilisation perhaps, spirit perhaps, or in a less ideational vein, the target – the victim – of the aggressive war was the group of Allied states.

From this perspective, the Nuremberg IMT tells us several things about representations of victims. First of these is that representations are unstable and changeable. In contemporary readings of the trial, the absence of victim-witnesses of the Shoah that Karstedt and Garkawe lament is striking. But the lack of witness-survivors who, through individual testimonies and appearances, represent all the victims of the Shoah is not the same as a general absence of victim figures. The victim Jackson produces through his speech, which is then reinforced during the trial, is not the individual or collective victim of persecution but the Allied states that had been targeted by an aggressive war. It is in their name that the trial was conducted. So while the Nuremberg trial has gone down in history as the event recognising that crimes are committed by men and not abstract entities, it was precisely as an abstract entity that the victim figured.

The Eichmann trial and the victim as survivor testifier

In contrast to the Nuremberg IMT, at the Eichmann trial 15 years later, the crimes committed against the Jewish people were the focal point of the proceedings – and beyond. This second iconic trial, with an iconic opening address, is that against Adolf Eichmann, held in Israel in 1961. While both the Nuremberg IMT and the trial against Eichmann dealt with the atrocities of the Nazi regime, they appear with respect to victims as fundamentally different in several aspects. At the Eichmann trial, the victim figured in an explicit way as the foundation of the trial. In his dramatic opening address, Israeli Attorney General Gideon Hausner positioned himself and the prosecution as spokespersons – representatives – for the 6 million deceased victims.[45] For him, it was a trial that went beyond the mere finding of guilt or innocence. As he explained after the trial, he 'knew we needed more than a conviction; we needed a living record

41 Ibid.
42 Simpson, *War, Law and Crime*, 145.
43 Quoted in Marrus, *The Nuremberg War Crimes Trial 1945–46*, 122.
44 de Menthon, Opening address January 17, 1946 in Marrus, *The Nuremberg War Crimes Trial 1945–46*, 91.
45 *Eichmann Transcripts*, April 17, 1961.

of a gigantic human and national disaster'.[46] The trial was the forum where this record would be created and hence, the victims of the Shoah were represented as the figure behind the trial. Appearing then at the Eichmann trial is a victim, presented as the rationale for the trial, but one whose conditions for appearance were in constant negotiation.

Victims were not only placed as the *telos* of the trial, but also acted as its drivers through testimonies. During the 14 weeks of the trial, half of the trial sessions – 62 of 121 sessions – were devoted to the 100 witness testimonies. Ninety of these acted as victim-witnesses, having survived Nazi concentration camps.[47] The victim here appeared as a *survivor*, narrating their story. As described by Lawrence Douglas, Attorney General 'Hausner encouraged testimony to take a narrative form, permitting the witnesses to speak for minutes on end between brief questions'.[48] Prompted by the (few) questions by Hausner, the testimonies were framed to produce a certain figure, not vulnerable and weak, but a hero, constructing what Lawrence Langer calls a 'heroic memory', 'a version of Holocaust reality more necessary than true'.[49] Here, the representations of the victim of the Shoah as absent or silenced were challenged, calling into effect a speaking victim subject.

Victims at the Eichmann trial spoke through their testimonies and through the speech of Attorney General Hausner. In addition, the audience at the Eichmann trial mostly consisted of victims.[50] Most photographs from the trial are not of Eichmann or even of witnesses, but of courtroom spectators,[51] showing members of the audience gasping in horror, tightly holding handkerchiefs or sobbing. The event of the Eichmann trial was in many ways *made* through the presence of the audience. Thus, the example of the Eichmann trial provides a sharp contrast to the Nuremberg IMT: here the victim was an individual and a collective of individuals with a manifest presence either through the frequent references to the dead, or as a survivor who testified or sat in the audience.

Commentators were split over how to read this manifest presence of victims at the Eichmann trial. Hannah Arendt, perhaps the most famed critic of the trial, dismissed the victim testimonies as 'time consuming' and legally irrelevant.[52] According to Arendt, the testimonies went beyond and against 'the purpose of a trial [which] is to render justice, and nothing else'.[53] The victims appeared as a distraction, and a potentially dangerous one, and should have had no active role to play in the proceedings. Instead, she found their role at the Eichmann trial to be dangerously close to complicity in a state-orchestrated show trial, similar to those in the Soviet Union.[54] For Douglas, the Eichmann trial does something else than simply put on a show on behalf of the state. When he turns to the Eichmann trial, it is not because he ignores the ways in which the trial was used for the state's purposes. On the contrary, he makes a point of Hausner's orchestration of the testimonies that figured the victim as a hero of resistance and which ran a specific ideology of Israeli nationhood and Jewish identity.[55] Nonetheless, Douglas argues that this

46 Hausner in Douglas, *The Memory of Judgment*, 106.

47 Arendt, *Eichmann in Jerusalem*, 223. Note that not all witnesses were victims. For instance, an American judge who had questioned the defendants at Nuremberg IMT testified here on remarks made by Herman Göring on Eichmann.

48 Douglas, *The Memory of Judgment*, 134.

49 Lawrence Langer quoted by Douglas, *The Memory of Judgment*, 128.

50 Ibid., 109.

51 Ibid., 107–9.

52 Arendt, *Eichmann in Jerusalem*, 122.

53 Ibid., 253.

54 Ibid., 15.

55 Douglas, *The Memory of Judgment*, 3, 156.

orchestration was not completely successful, but resisted by the survivors themselves. Through their testimonies, survivors such as Michael Podchlewnik, who seemed to have 'survived not as a result of his personal will, but in spite of it',[56] infused tensions in the heroic images of the victim survivor.[57] These tensions demonstrate the possibility of resistance. Hausner's attempts to move the victim from a sign of weakness to a symbol of heroism were not completely successful. The victims' addresses – their position as heroes and their testimonies – were under negotiation.

It is despite (or because of) this that Douglas attends to the Eichmann trial. For him, 'it transformed understandings of what the law can and should do in the wake of traumatic history'.[58] What he demands or seeks from a trial is not only that it does 'formal justice to the perpetrators' but also '*representational* justice to the Holocaust qua event'.[59] Against Arendt's legalistic dismissal of the victim testimonies as (irrelevant) evidence of Eichmann's guilt, Douglas argues that an equally crucial question to ask is 'did the trial do justice to the testimony of the survivors?'[60] For him, the Eichmann trial illustrates 'competing conceptions of the law itself'.[61] On the one hand, trials serve as the reinstatement of 'rule-bound authority . . . by bringing perpetrators of atrocity to justice'.[62] But on the other hand, a trial 'produces and suppresses narrative and clarifies and obscures history',[63] 'serv[ing] the interests of history and memory'.[64] The court, in this aspect, becomes 'less . . . a forum for judging a specific defendant than . . . an occasion for narrative, a public event and solemn forum staged to satisfy the need of those who have survived to bear witness'.[65] For Douglas, then, the victim serves as a figure whose address symbolises the different conceptions of law. Depending on these conceptions, the speech of the victim is given different meanings. The victim's position within the trial, both physically and symbolically, provides a link to the very purpose of the trial.

The competing conceptions of law and the trial – between the parties of the case, between Douglas' narrative justice and Arendt's legalism, and between Hausner's nationhood of heroes and the survivors' testimonies – are seized within the figure of the victim as a survivor testifier. In slightly different ways, Hausner and Douglas both see in the victim a figure in whose name a trial proceeds and justice should be and can be served. Against this stands what is described as a legalistic conception of the law and trial, wherein the surviving victim plays at most a limited role, and only in relation to the determination of the guilt of the accused. In this way, within the figure of the victim are manifold and at times contradictory representations, between which the victim constantly slips.

Together, the trials against Eichmann and the Nuremberg IMT illustrate how the practices that represent victims are determined to some extent by the address of the institutions. It is not only the judicial institutions that regulate the appearance of victims, but also those writing about it. The different trials, the various actors of the trial, the commentators of the trials – they all present varying accounts of victim, producing alternating and at times conflicting representations of victims. At the same time as norms are developed, there remains the possibility for

56 Ibid., 169.
57 Ibid., 156–73.
58 Ibid., 174.
59 Ibid., 113 (emphasis added).
60 Ibid.
61 Ibid., 260.
62 Ibid.
63 Ibid., 113.
64 Ibid., 260.
65 Ibid., 126.

challenge and difference. Accordingly, the places and forms of speech accorded to victims at these trials appear as potential tensions that continue to be played out in international criminal justice.

Figuring victims

To return to the main question: how to understand the subject position of victims within international criminal justice. As becomes evident from the two earlier examples, 'victim' operates as a category that holds together manifold and at times contradictory representations that are nevertheless composed in and condensed by one figure. While the category of the victim is singular, its figurations are many, and sometimes incoherent.

Given this multiplicity and incoherence, how can certain hegemonies about 'victims' and their (stable) interests be destabilised? One approach would be to turn to people who have suffered from the crimes that are (or should be) adjudicated at international criminal courts and tribunals and try to ascertain, on the basis of their responses, how well they consider the institutions provide justice. Empirical scholars such as Eric Stover have in this vein argued for a move away from 'wishful and uncritical thinking' about the benefits of criminal justice and through interviews with people in 'affected communities' sought to 'ground it in the everyday lives of those most affected by violence'.[66] One such example is the work by Luke Moffett who describes his study on the ICC's activities in Uganda as based on the 'importan[ce] to meet with individuals and communities who had suffered from international crimes . . . so as to understand their views on and concerns about the Court . . . and to provide a general sentiment on the Court'.[67] And as Laurel E. Fletcher and Harvey M. Weinstein put it, their work seeks to provide 'empirical evidence to substantiate claims about how well criminal trials achieve the goals ascribed to them'.[68] Similarly, large-scale population-level surveys on the attitudes of people who have experienced conflicts[69] are used to ascertain both the views of victim survivors and to evaluate the impact and responses to international criminal tribunals in so-called affected communities. In this vein, the Human Rights Center at Berkeley uses 'empirical research methods to give voice to survivors of mass atrocity'[70] on which it then bases recommendations to concerned institutions and donors. In these studies, the voices of victims hold a status of empirical data – they appear as bearing the standards of justice.

However, at the same time, empirical work that seeks to shed light on the court practices on the basis of interviews with victim subjects remains wedded to the discursive realm where courts and institutions 'respond' to subjects already formed. The voices of the victims are presented as unmediated, as simply allowing the victims 'themselves' to describe their experiences of the international criminal courts and tribunals. These empirical studies conceive of the subjects'

66 Eric Stover, *The Witnesses: War Crimes and the Promise of Justice in The Hague* (Philadelphia: University of Pennsylvania Press, 2005). See also Diane Orentlicher, *That Someone Guilty Be Punished: The Impact of the ICTY in Bosnia* (New York: Open Society Institute, 2010).

67 Luke Moffett, *Justice for Victims Before the International Criminal Court* (New York: Routledge, 2014), 4–5.

68 Laurel Fletcher and Harvey Weinstein, "Violence and Social Repair: Rethinking the Contribution of Justice to Reconciliation," *Human Rights Quarterly* 24 (2002): 573, 585.

69 Human Rights Center, University of California, Berkeley. Their reports are available at Human Rights Center, "Reports," accessed January 27, 2020, www.law.berkeley.edu/centers/human-rights-center/publications/reports.

70 Phuong Pham, et al., *So We Will Never Forget: A Population-Based Survey of Attitudes About Social Reconstruction and the Extraordinary Chambers in the Courts of Cambodia* (Berkeley: Human Rights Center, University of California, 2009).

identity as victims as exogenous and ontologically prior to court practices. That is, their subjectivity is determined by something other than court prescribed criteria. Notably, this positions victim survivors as outside (and prior) yet in relation to the institutions of international criminal justice.

This raises a question about the practices of representation. Notwithstanding their differences, international criminal prosecutors who claim to act on behalf of victims and empirical scholars all write about subjects in order to either give them voice or to claim them a presence. This activity of writing to give a subject voice prompted Gayatri Chakravorty Spivak to ask whether the subaltern can speak.[71] Spivak was concerned about research on subjects perceived as others – such as victims – that seek to reveal an 'authentic' or 'true' voice. According to her, this activity requires the scholar to erase his/her own positionality, and assumes a 'transparency' that ignores the ways the scholar and writing contribute to the constitution of the represented figure.[72] Whilst scholars writing on 'complex victims' question the way courts deal with certain subjects and the complexity of human life, they still seek to make sense of 'who' the subjects are. The subjectivity of 'complex subjects' is still taken as determined and existing exogenously, outside of the legal processes. Furthermore, while this scholarship is often critical of the international criminal justice institutions, it nevertheless partakes in the furthering of the enterprise. As it is not possible to overcome the violence that is inherent in representation, it is instead important to attend to what Spivak called the *mechanics* of victim figures, the very practices through which they figure.

To conclude, victims figure in a range of practices at the criminal justice institutions. By attending to these practices as the workings of representation and performativity,[73] it is possible to discern a range of victim figurations. The figurations shift and change, depending on the practice, but remain in relation to the institution. Together, the practices constitute a victim as moving through the legal institution, a movement that involves both repetition and difference. And together, the practices of the institution provide for manifold and indeterminate victim figurations. This claim of indeterminacy is not a suggestion that the victim representations are ambivalent or unclear, but indeterminate in the sense that there is nothing self-evident about 'who' the victim appearing through the practice is. This indeterminacy enables the figure to constitute a performance of the international criminal legal order as a politics of transition.

71 Gayatri Chakravorty Spivak, "Can the Subaltern Speak?" in *Marxism and the Interpretation of Culture* (London: Macmillan Education, 1988).

72 Ibid., 280–18, 285, 294.

73 See Judith Butler, *Gender Trouble: Feminism and the Subversion of Identity*, 2nd ed. (New York: Routledge, 2007); Judith Butler, "Gender as Performance," *Radical Philosophy: A Journal of Socialist and Feminist Philosophy* 67, no. 1 (1994): 32; Judith Butler, *Excitable Speech: A Politics of the Performance* (New York: Routledge, 1997); Judith Butler, *The Psychic Life of Power* (Stanford, CA: Stanford University Press, 1997); Hanna Fenichel Pitkin, *The Concept of Representation* (Los Angeles: University of California Press, 1967).

36

A sovereignty that is 'useless to fascism'

Richard Joyce

The rise of globalisation as a field of study in the mid-1990s brought with it a concern about the fate of national sovereignty.[1] The general sweep of the scholarship of the time was to account for (and understand the implications of) a shift away from national control over law, politics, the environment and the economy, towards control by international organisations, capital and markets. Since the global financial crisis of 2008 and the subsequent rise of populist – and explicitly right-wing nativist – politics, and with it aggressive reassertions of national sovereignty in various parts of the world, the opposite concern has come to light. The immediate challenge for many commentators is to work out what went wrong to drive the lurch towards nativist populist politics and how the international system has been weakened by this development. The concomitant challenge is to work out what can be done to defend and restore that system and with it the liberal democratic values it is imagined to carry. If the trend towards right-wing nativist populism continues unabated in these states, so one influential strain of the argument goes, these states may fall into authoritarianism and possibly fascism.[2] These commentators understand there to be a symbiotic relationship between a liberal-democratic form of sovereignty prevailing against nativist populism at the national level, and a liberal international order prevailing against it at the supranational level.

The apparent opposition between a liberal form of sovereignty which is consistent with the international order, and an authoritarian or proto-fascist form of sovereignty which threatens it, overlooks the commonalities between these two forms of sovereignty. In particular, it overlooks the way in which the concept of sovereignty at work in liberal national and international law contains within it the seeds of sovereignty's authoritarian and fascist forms. At the heart of this commonality is a claim to represent the authority of the people contained within an enduringly bounded community and to exercise that authority through law and by way of the organs of the state. In the passage from liberal democracy to authoritarian politics and beyond, the claim

1 See, for example, Saskia Sassen, *Losing Control? Sovereignty in an Age of Globalisation* (New York: Columbia University Press, 1996).

2 Madeleine Albright, *Fascism: A Warning* (London: William Collins, 2018); Steven Levitsky and Daniel Ziblatt, *How Democracies Die: What History Reveals About Our Future* (New York: Viking, 2018).

to represent the sovereignty of the people simply becomes more direct and centralised. In this light, recent developments expose not only the excesses of demagogues to represent popular sovereignty, but of what remains latent within the same claim when mediated by parliaments and moderated by an independent judiciary and media.

That such commonalities exist, and that these enable a movement between these two forms of sovereignty, is implicit in the argument presented in this chapter. In short, the problem common to both fascist and liberal politics, and the source, perhaps, of the potential (under certain political, social and economic conditions) to slide from liberalism towards fascism, can be framed in terms of an attachment to the idea of a singular people as a structuring principle of national sovereignty. The same idea grounds the conceptual structure of liberal theories of international law in which nation-states are taken to be foundational actors which pre-exist, and whose consent determines, the rules of international law. I will touch on the character of this idea briefly, but my focus will be on attempting to sketch out a conception of sovereignty which is not susceptible to co-option by authoritarian or fascist politics. Or, more precisely, a conception in which its inherent resistance to such co-option lies at the surface, ready to be activated – rather than buried deep beneath an apparently solid conceptual and legal infrastructure. The inspiration for the attempt comes from Walter Benjamin's attempt to 'introduce into the theory of art' concepts which are 'completely useless for the purposes of fascism' and which are, by contrast, 'useful for the formulation of revolutionary demands in the politics of art'.[3]

In this chapter, I want to explore a conception of sovereignty inspired by that same imperative – that is, a sovereignty useless for the purposes of fascism and useful for the formulation of revolutionary demands in law. In short, this is a conception of sovereignty which acknowledges that, at most, a sovereign's claim is no more than a claim to determine law and determine the boundaries of community *for the time being* – where *the time being* is nothing more than an *instantaneous moment*. This insight enables a recognition of the role that sovereignty plays in the conceptual structure of modern law, but which, contrary to received wisdom, emphasises not its power, but its weakness.[4] It also requires us to recognise the possibility of sovereignty taking shape without being founded on the idea of a singular people.

This chapter is intended not as setting out a formula for opposing fascist and authoritarian sovereignty, but as a building block for a particular type of resistance. In particular, I argue that the canon of modern sovereignty contains resources which enable us to disrupt it from within. To look within the canon begs the question of why we should not simply jettison the concept outright, nor look explicitly to forms of sovereignty (or – if the word itself carries too much baggage – forms of identity, authority and responsibility) which have been developed outside that canon. And so, before sketching out the basic elements of a sovereignty which is useless to fascism, I will first address the question of why we should look within the canon of modern sovereignty for elements which are resistant to fascism. Importantly, this chapter should not be

3 Walter Benjamin, "The Work of Art in the Age of Its Technological Reproducibility," in *Selected Writings, Volume 3: 1935–1938*, trans. Edmund Jephcott, Howard Eiland and others, eds. Howard Eiland and Michael W. Jennings (Cambridge: Belknap Press, 1996–2006), 102.

4 Specifically, sovereignty's vulnerability to a 'weak force' of what Derrida calls 'unconditionality', or of a 'messianic faith . . . without messianism' drawing on Walter Benjamin's reference to a 'weak messianic power'. See Jacques Derrida, *Rogues: Two Essays on Reason*, trans. Pascale-Anne Brault and Michael Naas (Stanford, CA: Stanford University Press, 2005), xiv; Jacques Derrida, *Spectres of Marx: The State of the Debt, the Work of Mourning, & the New International*, trans. Peggy Kamuf (New York: Routledge, 1994), 181; Walter Benjamin, "On the Concept of History," in *Selected Writings, Volume 4: 1938–1940: 1935–1938*, trans. Edmund Jephcott and others, eds. Howard Eiland and Michael W. Jennings (Cambridge: Belknap Press, 2006), 390 (thesis II).

read as a celebration of the concept or an ode to its capacity for redemption (either of itself or of us). Rather, it is an attempt at a particular juncture in history to try to set out a way in which we can live with the concept without unwittingly conspiring with fascism.

Why sovereignty?

In her chapter 'What Is Freedom' in *Between Past and Future*, Hannah Arendt argues that 'if men wish to be free, it is precisely sovereignty they must renounce'.[5] The particular form of sovereignty Arendt rails against is one which understands freedom as free will – rather than of freedom as action in the public sphere – and of sovereignty as supreme and indivisible. Here, Arendt differentiates between the publicly oriented, action-based 'I can' of freedom (which she derives from Greek thought) and the power-thirsty, solipsistic, in-ward looking 'I will' of sovereignty (which she attributes to a combination of Christian thinking and modern political theory).[6]

For Arendt, the link between free will and sovereignty reaches its apogee in Rousseau. Of his theory and its implications, Arendt writes:

> Politically, this identification linking freedom with sovereignty is perhaps the most pernicious and dangerous consequence of the philosophical equation of freedom and free will. For it leads either to a denial of human freedom – namely, if it is realised that whatever men may be, they are never sovereign – or to the insight that the freedom of one man, or a group, or a body politic can be purchased only at the price of the freedom, i.e., the sovereignty, of all others.[7]

In this telling, modern sovereignty is susceptible to co-option by fascism, or tyranny, for Arendt, because it replaces the freedom of public political action with the imposition of a general will which is always imposed rather than self-generated. Moreover, it denies the world-making possibilities and potentiality of freedom as action. Indeed, she hypothesises that 'action and beginning are essentially the same'.[8] So, by replacing freedom of action, sovereignty would thus deny spontaneity and the possibility of things being other than they are. It would prevent humans from recognising their 'capacity for performing miracles' by which she means their capacity for bringing into the world and making real 'infinite improbabilities'.[9]

In so arguing, Arendt aligns sovereignty with tyranny, and freedom with non-sovereignty. As James Martel argues in *Divine Violence: Walter Benjamin and the Eschatology of Sovereignty*, Arendt does so with some ambivalence.[10] As Martel points out, the Arendt of *The Human Condition* makes a distinction between a sovereignty 'which is always spurious if claimed by an isolated single entity, be it the individual entity of the person or the collective entity of a

5 Hannah Arendt, *Between Past and Future: Eight Exercises in Political Thought* (New York: Penguin Books, 1977), 165.

6 Ibid., 156–65.

7 Ibid., 164.

8 Ibid., 169.

9 Ibid., 169–71.

10 James Martel, *Divine Violence: Walter Benjamin and the Eschatology of Sovereignty* (Abingdon: Routledge, 2012), 32–36.

nation',[11] and a sovereignty which refers to the useful political effect of mutual promising.[12] For this Arendt:

> sovereignty as a body of people bound and kept together, not by an identical will which magically inspires them all, but by an agreed purpose for which alone the promises are valid and binding, shows itself quite clearly in its unquestioned superiority over those who are completely free, unbound by any promises and unkept by any purpose.[13]

For Martel, Arendt's attempt to articulate a form of sovereignty which preserves the constitutive and contingent, plural qualities of mutual promising, but which does not ultimately give itself over to the imposed sovereignty of entities claiming the authority to represent the people, ends, inevitably, in failure. He writes that sovereignty, as an 'illegitimate, violence based-form of arbitrary force' (which Arendt rails against), destroys all systems based on promises (which Arendt seems to celebrate) 'each and every time'.[14] Arendt's ambivalence, argues Martel, shows 'how insidious sovereignty can be and how it must be resisted utterly rather than partially'.[15]

Certainly critics of Western sovereignty in the anti-colonial tradition have developed fundamental critiques of that form of sovereignty and, specifically, of its tendency towards fascism. Aimé Césaire famously made the link between colonial violence and Nazism in his *Discourse on Colonialism*, writing of the European bourgeoisie that 'before they were [Nazism's] victims, they were its accomplices; . . . they tolerated that Nazism before it was inflicted on them . . . they absolved it, shut their eyes to it, legitimized it, because, until then, it had been applied only to non-European peoples.'[16] But while Germany's genocidal colonial history can be understood as pre-cursor to Nazism,[17] it is also the case that 'the states with the longest and ultimately most violent colonial record – France, Britain, the United States, and the Netherlands – remained democracies throughout the twentieth century'.[18] Here the exercise of authoritarian rule in the colonies established ideas and techniques of differential rule by liberal states which remain operative today. Ideas of centre and periphery, fear and difference, and racial hierarchy can be seen at work in, for example, the current treatment of refugees within Western liberal democracies and international legal rules prioritising the protection of foreign investment. These ideas make it possible to distinguish between people within liberal states to whom freedoms are extended (and who exercise and enjoy the powers and protection of sovereignty), and those from whom such freedoms, powers and protections are denied. These distinctions also facilitate the development of techniques, both physical and conceptual, by which exertions of sovereign

11 Hannah Arendt, *The Human Condition*, 2nd ed. (Chicago: University of Chicago Press, 1958), 245.

12 Martel, *Divine Violence*, 34–35.

13 Arendt, *The Human* Condition, 245; Martel, *Divine Violence*, 34.

14 Martel, *Divine Violence*, 35.

15 Ibid., 36.

16 Aimé Césaire, *Discourse on Colonialism*, trans. Joan Pinkham (New York: Monthly Review Press, 1972), 35–36.

17 Jürgen Zimmerer, "Colonial Genocide and the Holocaust: Towards an Archeology of Genocide," in *Genocide and Settler Society: Frontier Violence and Stolen Indigenous Children in Australian History*, ed. A. Dirk Moses (New York: Berghahn Books, 2004), 49–76; Benjamin Madley, "From Africa to Auschwitz: How German South West Africa Included Ideas and Methods Adopted and Developed by the Nazis in Eastern Europe," *European History Quarterly* 33 (2005): 429–64. See also Frantz Fanon, *The Wretched of the Earth*, trans. Constance Farrington (Harmondsworth: Penguin, 1967), 80.

18 Robert Gerwarth and Stephan Malinowski, "Hannah Arendt's Ghosts: Reflections on the Disputable Path from Windhoek to Auschwitz," *Central European History* 43 (2009): 279.

authority can take on fascist dimensions. These include experiments in authoritarian policing, confinement, demonisation of racial 'others' and the priority given to the protection of capital over social and environmental values. Critiques drawing on these themes speak to an unholy alliance between sovereignty, racism, capital and violence that puts in question the possibility of extracting sovereignty away from the others such as to avoid its potential for supporting fascist forms of governing.

Yet, despite these critiques, and my sympathy for them, I want to hesitate before adopting broad claims about utter resistance to sovereignty. Sovereignty continues to be the term used by groups seeking to assert identity and legal authority separate from, and directly challenging to, dominant political and social forms. Claims of Indigenous peoples, for example, commonly use the word as a source of power, independence and resistance. In that sense, it seems to have work to do. Perhaps this is because it is the only language the dominant system understands. Perhaps it is because it reflects something already deeply felt and able to be captured in a word capable of (imperfect) translation across different languages and cultures. This will no doubt be a source of continuing debate, and I am certainly open to being convinced that when considered against the broader background of the relations between colonial and former colonial powers and their current and former territories, the concept of sovereignty offers nothing good. For now, however, I will take its continued use by Indigenous and independence movements as a sign that the word has work to do and that it is important that its potential for resistance to power be recognised.

Certainly for critics of sovereign formations within the Western tradition, the word has some work to do. As Jacques Derrida writes, '[o]ne cannot combat, *head on, all* sovereignty, sovereignty *in general*, without threatening at the same time, beyond the nation-state figure of sovereignty, the classical principles of freedom and self-determination.'[19] He argues that sovereignty's deconstruction must occur while 'recognising that all the fundamental axiomatics of responsibility or decision are grounded on the sovereignty of the subject, that is, the intentional auto-determination of the conscious self'.[20] This suggests a strong argument that some form of sovereignty is required for the formation of individual and collective identity capable of being actualised in the world. In the absence of a transcendent overarching authority governing the world, how else can we assert a position which could hold a community in place, or determine its law (however transitorily)? This is a point which is not engaged by Arendt's distinction between the 'I will' of sovereignty and the 'I can' of political action.[21] If 'sovereignty' has this force, and this purpose, it may be in some sense inescapable. If so, then for all my sympathies with sovereignty's more radical critics, it strikes me that at least one urgent task is to see whether it is possible to arrive at a conception of sovereignty which enables the formation and pursuit of individual and collective identities without being susceptible to fascist co-option. Further, regarding sovereignty as something that must be utterly opposed suggests that it is, itself, incapable of being understood otherwise than in its pernicious forms and incapable of being subverted. Given both the power of the concept and uncertainty about its meaning, my view is that one should avoid ceding its meaning to only its worst (or even its most common) forms, even

19 Derrida, *Rogues*, 158 (emphasis in original).

20 Jacques Derrida, *Without Alibi*, trans. and ed. Peggy Kamuf (Stanford, CA: Stanford University Press, 2002), xix.

21 By contrast, it is a crucial aspect of Derrida's critical conception of sovereignty as articulated in *Rogues*, where the 'I can' refers not just to one's action in and on the world but also one's 'self-representation, the sovereign and reappropriating gathering of the self': Derrida, *Rogues*, 10–11.

in order to oppose them. It is for these reasons, rather than an inherent desire to redeem the concept, that I focus here on how best to separate sovereignty from fascism.

To work out the point at which Western sovereignty can be subverted such that it becomes useless to fascism, one must look to its roots. Here we can return briefly to Arendt, and her argument that in modernity, we have a loss of authority and tradition which leaves us bereft of stable grounds for our political and legal formations. In her telling, the loss of authority:

> is tantamount to the loss of the groundwork of the world, which indeed since then has begun to shift, to change and transform itself with ever-increasing rapidity from one shape to another, as though we were living and struggling with a Protean universe where everything at any moment can become almost anything else.[22]

To speak of the 'loss of the groundwork of the world' is to evoke Nietzsche's madman and his warning of the Death of God.

But this loss is also an opportunity. For Derrida, '[t]he "deaths of God," before Christianity, in it and beyond it, are only figures and episodes' of a fundamental absence.[23] 'Everything', he writes, 'begins with the presence of that absence.'[24] Derrida's 'deconstruction' operates in view of this lack. It 'tries to show that convention, institutions and consensus are stabilisations (sometimes stabilisations of great duration, sometimes micro-stabilisations) of something essentially chaotic'.[25] This 'chaos and instability' is 'fundamental, founding and irreducible'.[26] Now, Arendt's concern is that in modernity a deterministic form of sovereignty – one saturated with violence and overblown representative claims to activate law in the name of the general will – fills the empty place left vacant by the loss of authority. But rather than focus on the problems with the forms of sovereignty which purport to fill the empty place of authority, I think we should focus on the fact that this place is never filled. That is, we should recognise that even after the attempt to impose sovereignty, there is always a void.

Identifying this void and recognising its persistence does not depend on an external critique of the canon of texts making up the conception of modern sovereignty in the Western tradition (of which I will touch on some central figures, without claiming comprehensiveness). Rather, it can be glimpsed by exposing the paradoxes and contradictions inherent in the theories of sovereignty within that tradition.[27] This is a different form of critique than emerges from Wendy Brown's examination of the canon of Western sovereignty in *Walled States, Waning Sovereignty*.[28] There, Brown seeks to trace the contemporary remnants of the early moderns' political theology of sovereignty in which temporal authority was understood as having a close parallel to

22 Arendt, *Between Past and Future*, 95.

23 Jacques Derrida, "Faith and Knowledge: The Two Sources of 'Religion' at the Limits of Reason Alone," trans. Samuel Weber, in *Acts of Religion*, ed. Gil Anidjar (New York: Routledge, 2002), 65. See also Richard Joyce, *Competing Sovereignties* (Abingdon: Routledge, 2012), 4.

24 Derrida, "Faith and Knowledge," 65.

25 Jacques Derrida, "Remarks on Deconstruction and Pragmatism," trans. Simon Critchley, in *Deconstruction and Pragmatism*, eds. Simon Critchley, Jacques Derrida, Ernesto Laclau and Richard Rorty (London: Routledge, 1996), 83.

26 Ibid., 83.

27 This Martel does brilliantly in respect of Hobbes in James Martel, *Subverting the Leviathan: Reading Thomas Hobbes as a Radical Democrat* (New York: Columbia University Press, 2007). For the others, see Joyce, *Competing Sovereignties*, chapters 1 and 3.

28 Wendy Brown, *Walled States, Waning Sovereignty* (New York: Zone Books, 2010).

the absolute nature of divine authority. Brown's concern is to show how, under contemporary conditions of fragmentation, in which such a theory cannot explain or justify the exercise of legal authority, sovereignty remains potent as the source of practically impotent but symbolically powerful violent phenomena – the exemplary one being wall-building.

Here, my concern is to hint at how a critical reading offers a way of showing how, in the canon, the impossibility of fully grounded human authority gives way to a contradictory reliance on divine authority. In this way, the political theology of modern sovereignty is not a source of strength, but an exposure of weakness. This, I argue, indicates a chink in the armour by which assertions of sovereignty, both symbolic and practical, are justified. And so, one can observe how Jean Bodin's sovereign – the absolute, perpetual, indivisible power over the law of a commonwealth – turns out on closer inspection to be less than absolute, limited in time and divisible.[29] And rather than being utterly ascendant over law and the commonwealth, Bodin's sovereign finds itself in fact dependent on both to ground its authority.[30] Similarly, even Hobbes's Leviathan – often taken to be a figure of absolute, unchallengeable sovereign power – betrays a strange dependence on the people in its formation, and remains bound by laws both natural and customary (i.e., not of its own making) after its formation.[31]

As the Enlightenment dawned, the contradictions persisted – most tellingly in the central theme of replacing claims to divine authority with an authority grounded in society itself. Rousseau, for example, in a project ostensibly aimed at establishing how human authority can be made legitimate,[32] finds that the sole source of legitimate authority, the general will, is not something that can actually be put into effect by human institutions. For this reason, writes Rousseau, 'the founders of nations have been forced in every period to resort to divine authority and attribute their own wisdom to the gods.'[33] Kant likewise suspends his enlightenment mantra of *sapere aude* to argue that, as a principle of practical reason, 'presently existing legislative authority ought to be obeyed, whatever its origin', and must be 'thought as if it must have arisen not from human beings but from some highest, flawless lawgiver', namely God.[34] In his attempt to ground sovereignty not in the realm of the gods, but (as a good modern) in the territory of the nation, Sieyès swaps contradiction for tautology. Of the nation's place at the heart of legal authority, Sieyès writes that 'nation exists prior to everything; it is the origin of everything. . . . A nation is all that it can be simply by being what it is'.[35] All of that is reassuring until we need to locate the nation itself, prior to any law establishing it. To the question 'where is the Nation?' Sieyès answers: 'Where it is.'[36]

To the extent that the work of these theorists has been used to explain and justify the power of the form of the nation-state, one can say that it has done so without establishing a solid

29 Joyce, *Competing Sovereignties*, Chapter 1.

30 Ibid.

31 See Ibid., 69–70; Richard Joyce, "Sovereignty, Faith and the Fall," *Polemos: Journal of Law, Literature and Culture* 7, no. 2 (2013): 285, 297–302; Peter Fitzpatrick, "Legal Theology: Law, Modernity and the Sacred," *Seattle University Law Review* 32 (2009): 321, 330–32.

32 Jean-Jacques Rousseau, *The Social Contract* (Oxford: Oxford University Press, 1994), 45.

33 Ibid., 78; Peter Fitzpatrick, "'Gods Would Be Needed . . .': American Empire and the Rule of (International) Law," *Leiden Journal International Law* 16, no. 3 (2003): 429.

34 Immanuel Kant, *The Metaphysics of Morals*, trans. Mary Gregor (Cambridge: Cambridge University Press, 1996), 95.

35 Emmanuel Sieyès, *Political Writings*, trans. Michael Sonenscher (Indianapolis: Hackett Publishing Company, 2003), 136–37.

36 Sieyès, *Political Writings*, 140. See also Joyce, *Competing Sovereignties*, 73–74, 81–88.

ground for such arrogations of power. Rather, the gaps, contradictions and paradoxes have been variously ignored, smoothed over or forgotten. A critical reading of the canon, one which brings back into focus the groundlessness of sovereign claims, may therefore offer a useful corrective. It would reveal, perhaps, and contrary to Arendt's concerns in 'What Is Freedom', that the consequence of there being a lack of solid grounds for authority is not that space is opened for a pernicious form of sovereignty in its place. Rather, the lack of grounds is the opening space for thinking about sovereignty differently. What makes authoritarian and fascist politics (and some forms of liberal politics) so dangerous is not sovereignty itself, but that their forms of sovereignty claim to fully overcome that lack by deploying violence and insisting on a dogmatic and deterministic conception of law and singular conception of community.

By characterising sovereignty as a pernicious replacement for authority, Arendt's formulation does not make space for an account of sovereignty in which its *failure* to replace authority is an important, productive attribute. Indeed, sovereignty's revolutionary potential lies precisely in that fact. The key is to keep in view sovereignty's lack of grounds and its manifest failures to live up to the promises made in its name; not so that we renounce it, but that we can activate its potentiality to be otherwise. It is precisely in, and not despite, the pretentions inherent in claims to sovereignty that they can be seen to contain the seeds of their own undoing. Here lies the possibility of sovereignty's articulation in a form which is useless to fascism and useful for the formulation of revolutionary demands in law.

What form of sovereignty is useless to fascism?

In my view, modern sovereignty is not an essence or a quality but rather a type of claim. Specifically, it is a self-grounded claim to determine the boundaries of a community and the content of its law. What makes it 'sovereign' is not that it emanates from a state apparatus, but that it depends on no higher authority than that of the entity making the claim. This is a feature of claims by nation-states to sovereignty (which are largely accepted within the international legal order) and rival claims by regional sub-national groups (which are infrequently accepted) and by Indigenous peoples (which have a complex relationship to international law).[37] Such claims are made possible, indeed required, as a result of modernity's groundlessness.

When made in the name of nation-states, such claims have the capacity, perhaps even the tendency, to become pernicious and overblown in precisely the ways Martel and Arendt warn. The recent rise of populist and authoritarian claims by national leaders to claim a capacity to truly and directly represent 'the people' is a clear example. As Jan-Werner Müller argues, populist leaders including Victor Orbán of Hungary and Donald Trump of the United States have used such claims even where electoral results indicate only minority support. This is possible because the claims are 'moral and symbolic' rather than empirical.[38] For example, Orbán met his 2002 electoral defeat with the response that 'the nation cannot be in opposition'.[39] Trump's failure to secure a popular majority has remained an open sore for the duration of his presidency. This has not stopped him from claiming that his supporters alone constitute 'real Americans'

37 To say that sovereign claims are self-grounded is not to say that they are necessarily without territorial, historical or cultural basis. Rather, it is to recognise that there is no common higher authority that can determine the validity of rival claims, especially those which arise from different territorial, historical or cultural bases.

38 Jan-Werner Müller, *What Is Populism?* (Philadelphia: University of Pennsylvania Press, 2016), 31–32.

39 Ibid., 32, 39.

and accusing his political opponents of treason.[40] For Trump, 'the only important thing is the unification of the people – because the other people don't mean anything.'[41]

For Müller, the problem with such claims is that they fail to acknowledge the legitimacy of plural political voices within the polity. Hence for Müller, there is a bright line between liberal acceptance of the mediating institutions of representative democracy and the populist claim to directly represent a unified people, which Müller, quoting Kelsen, regards as a 'metapolitical illusion'.[42] Müller writes that:

> run-of-the-mill democratic politicians [do not] necessarily subscribe to a high-minded ethics according to which, beyond all our partisan differences, we are engaged in a common project of perfecting the political community's foundational political values. But most would concede that representation is temporary and fallible, that contrary opinions are legitimate, that society cannot be represented without remainder, and that it is impossible for one party or politicians permanently to represent an authentic people apart from democratic procedures and forms. Which means that they implicitly accept a basic claim that was clearly articulated by Habermas: "the people" appear only in the plural.[43]

This suggests that there is also a bright line between liberal and populist conceptions of sovereignty – one tempered by mediating institutions and one invoked directly. But a close examination of this quote suggests that this may not be the case. Müller's pluralism is one which occurs within the bounds of the polity. Despite legitimate internal differences within the political community (and the ever-present possibility of change to the composition of the community by birth, death and migration), the community itself remains a singular entity bound by a single set of foundational principles (even if their proper interpretation is contestable). In short, liberal representative democracy and its mediating institutions do not avoid the problem of the so-called metapolitical illusion or, perhaps more precisely, myth,[44] of a singular people. While populist, authoritarian or fascist politics might place that quality within the grasp of a single party or individual leader in the context of domestic politics (while liberalism does not), liberalism nonetheless holds to it as a structuring concept of political theory. Moreover, the idea of a singular people is frequently operationalised by politicians otherwise committed to domestic political pluralism when justifying decisions to deploy military force beyond their borders and in both legislative and police response to certain security threats within.[45] The same idea also lies at the foundation of international law. The question therefore remains as to whether sovereignty can exist as a structuring concept of modern political life without an attachment to the illusion or myth of a singular people. In my view it can, provided that our conception of community

40 Katie Rogers, "As Impeachment Moves Forward, Trump's Language Turns Darker," *The New York Times*, October 1, 2019, www.nytimes.com/2019/10/01/us/politics/trump-treason-impeachment.html.

41 Müller, *Populism*, 22 (citing a speech by Trump in May 2016 reported on CBS Weekend News, May 7, 2016).

42 Müller, *Populism*, 28. The reference to Kelsen is: Hans Kelsen, *Vom Wesenund Wertder Demokratie* (Aalen: Scientia, 1981), 22.

43 Müller, *Populism*, 40. The reference to Habermas is: Jürgen Habermas, *Faktizität und Geltung: Beiträge zur Diskustheorie des Rechts und des demokratischen Rechtsstaats* (Frankfurt am Main: Suhrkamp, 1994), 607.

44 On myth and its significance to Enlightenment conceptions of modern law, see Fitzpatrick, *The Mythology of Modern Law*.

45 See, for example, President Barack Obama, "Remarks by the President at the National Defense University," May 23, 2013, accessed May 27, 2020, www.whitehouse.gov/the-press-office/2013/05/23/remarks-president-national-defense-university.

departs from the image of a self-contained and fully determined polity. Here we can look to the work of Franz Fanon and Jean-Luc Nancy, before returning to Arendt.

Fanon's position here is complicated. On the one hand, Fanon calls for the development of a national consciousness (which he distinguishes, not altogether consistently, from 'nationalism')[46] as both a philosophical and political project in which the dignity, ideas and needs of the masses as a whole could be actualised. This is set against chauvinistic tribalism, bourgeois nationalism and pan-continental (Arab or African, specifically) cultural consciousness. To this end, national military and civil service are promoted as necessary to 'raise the level of national consciousness, and to detribalise and unite the nation'.[47] Fanon also draws repeatedly on the language of sovereignty. In *The Wretched of the Earth*, the term pertains both to a people and a nation, is the goal of decolonisation, must be defended against (local and foreign) neo-colonial governing practices and exists as the 'exact equivalent' of dignity, such that 'a free people living in dignity is a sovereign people'.[48] As such, Fanon appears at times to combine sovereignty and nationalism in a way which might, in the terms outlined in this chapter, make his notion of sovereignty susceptible to fascist co-option.

Fanon's target, of course, is colonial and neo-colonial forms of government. His political and philosophical commitments (inseparable from one another) make him less concerned with the problems inherent in the idea of national unity and sovereignty, than with specific malign forms. Specifically, Fanon's concern is with the way in which an inclusive nationalism espoused by middle-class leaders of independence movements soon gives way, upon independence, to the 'sole motto of the bourgeoisie': '"Replace the foreigner."'[49] With replacement rather than economic and political transformation as its goal, the new bourgeois leadership transforms the institution of the party into an expression of its own, narrow desires, and the police and military into an instrument of controlling the masses and protecting foreign investment.[50] The bourgeois leadership also fans ethnic rivalries while claiming 'to speak in the name of the totality of the people'.[51] By contrast, what is needed, for Fanon, is the active participation of the masses – not as a 'blind force that must be continually held in check'[52] but rather as 'men and women . . . included on a vast scale in enlightened and fruitful work' through which 'form and body are given to [national] consciousness'.[53] For Fanon, the 'popular will', for which 'no leader can substitute himself' should be the basis for a 'national government' which gives the citizens 'back their dignity' precisely 'because conscious and sovereign men dwell therein'.[54]

It is possible to read Fanon's conception of sovereignty as being founded on something other than the myth of a singular people. First, we have to reconcile his call for national consciousness and national unity with his opposition to the notion of strong leader as speaking for the people and his rejection of 'the flag and the palace where the government sits' as the 'symbols of the nation'.[55] Then, we have to recognise the inherent plurality of collective consciousness in Fanon's work. For Fanon, collective consciousness is the product of education, discussion and

46 Frantz Fanon, *The Wretched of the Earth*, trans. Constance Farrington (Harmondsworth: Penguin, 1967), 199.
47 Ibid., 162.
48 Ibid., 160.
49 Ibid., 127.
50 Ibid., 82, 146.
51 Ibid., 147 (for the quote); 136, 146–47 for the broader propositions.
52 Ibid., 146.
53 Ibid., 165.
54 Ibid.
55 Ibid.

mass participation in the production and implementation of new ideas. It is 'decentralisation in the extreme' and involves the creation of a new form of human subject.[56] Fanon's programme is not one, therefore, geared towards the sovereignty of the people as expressed through a singular person, party, constitution or concept (even the concept of 'nation'). Rather, it is a dynamic process through which the sovereignty of each person is expressed and 'responsibility on the historical scale' assumed and experienced from the bottom up.[57] Further, the concept of self which emerges (both at the individual and collective level) is not one which is complete in and of itself. For Fanon, the 'consciousness of self is not the closing of a door to communication. Philosophic thought teaches us, on the contrary, that it is its guarantee.'[58]

The tradition of philosophy on which Fanon appears to draw here, which emphasises the mutual dependence of the individuated self and the context of communication and relation in which it is embedded, is one carried forward by Jean-Luc Nancy.[59] Importantly for present purposes, Nancy's conception of the impossibility of detached singular existence (either as a person, or as a collective form such as 'nation') is particularly instructive for thinking about a sovereignty which is useless to fascism especially in confronting the illusion of a singular people in whose name fascist politics may be exercised. It is to his work I now turn.

In Nancy, we see two different conceptions of collective life articulated. The first would be one based on the myth of its own completeness, which emphasises its own immanence and (impossibly) its separation from that with which it relates. It is singular and absolute. The second is what Nancy calls community. Community, for Nancy, is not to be found in some internal characteristic or quality, but in exposure and relation to that which is outside it (or, more precisely, that with which it might otherwise be). The first conception Nancy explicitly aligns with is a logic that leads towards fascism. Nancy writes, in the context of a discussion of Nazism, 'Political or collective enterprises dominated by a will to absolute immanence have as their truth the truth of death. Immanence, communal fusion, contains no other logic than that of the suicide of the community that is governed by it.'[60] This is not only because of its extermination of the other based on categories of blood and soil, but also because of the inward-turning logic of an ever narrower criteria of racial or ideological purity. By contrast, community, for Nancy, 'assumes the impossibility of its own immanence'.[61] This means that community can have no enduringly fixed or determinate content but must be ever open to challenge and change.

By the same token, the openness to challenge and change cannot be such as to prevent the possibility of holding a position for the time being. Indeed, an entity cannot relate to others without itself holding a position in relation to that which is other. Since we must avoid claims to communal fusion in order to keep our conceptual distance from fascism, this determinate position cannot be based on some enduring and essential feature exclusive and common to the members of a polity. Nor can it be a question of transcendent abstractions. It must engage with the concrete circumstances of relational life. The challenge then becomes to think through the possibility of holding an instantiated position which is an essential aspect of relation, while not being susceptible to an immanentist logic.

56 Ibid., 157–59.

57 Ibid., 159, 161, 165.

58 Ibid., 199.

59 See especially Jean-Luc Nancy, *The Inoperative Community*, trans. and ed. Peter Connor (Minneapolis: University of Minnesota Press, 1991); Jean-Luc Nancy, *Being Singular Plural*, trans. Robert Richardson and Anne O'Byrne (Stanford, CA: Stanford University Press, 2000).

60 Nancy, *Inoperative Community*, 12.

61 Ibid., 15.

It is here that a certain conception of sovereignty itself becomes both useful to a critical conception of community and useless to fascism. Sovereignty provides a community with a form of claim to determine its character and content which can cut through what Nancy would rightly identify as its inoperability and its essential and eternal changefulness. The crucial point is that it does so groundlessly, contingently and only for the time being. Since community is ultimately uncontainable, sovereignty over any such instantiated community would be, in Nancy's terms, nothing other than the 'sovereign exposure to an excess (to a transcendence) that does not present itself and does not let itself be appropriated (or simulated)'.[62]

This same conception of sovereignty is not only contrary to a settled singular polity on which fascist politics could be built, but also upsets claims to fully and finally determine the content of law. Like community, law requires sovereignty precisely because its content cannot be fixed and stable. As no more and no less than the conditions of our being with each other in the world, law must be open to being refashioned – in Peter Fitzpatrick's terms: to being other than it is.[63] This openness can be activated by the call to justice, which is inherent to law but cannot be conditioned or determined in advance.[64] In this tension between a law determined through the exercise of power, and a claim to justice which exceeds all such determination, lies the potential for new, revolutionary demands in the name of law.

Emphasising, as Nancy does, the primacy of relation brings us back to Arendt's project in productive ways which can help explain her antipathy to the concept and how her apparent resort to sovereignty via mutual promising might not be quite the compromise Martel suggests. Her antipathy towards sovereignty expressed in 'What Is Freedom' can be explained by the way in which she aligns sovereignty with a solipsistic emphasis on the position of the individual actor (a person or a collective) rather than on relationality itself. By the time Arendt returns to sovereignty in *The Human Condition*, the question of mutual promising is not set in the context of attempting to justify the authority of, or within, a political community. Rather, it is set in a context in which plurality is established as a foundational aspect of human life. Promising is, in this context, one form of political action which arises out of, but does not overcome, the irreducible plurality of human life.

As Andrew Benjamin argues, for Arendt, to *be* is to be *in relation*.[65] He draws on her characterisation of the Romans, in the early pages of *The Human Condition*, as 'perhaps the most political people we have known', for whom 'the words "to live" and "to be among men" (*inter homines esse*)' were synonyms.[66] Benjamin stresses here that what is 'central in the formulation "inter homines esse" is the "inter" rather than those between whom relationality obtains'. Taking this one step further, Benjamin argues that Arendt 'opens up . . . the need to move from the sovereignty of the subject to the sovereignty of the relation'.[67] In the terms advanced in this chapter, it would be the sovereignty of the subject and, by extension, of the polity which is useful to fascism in so far as it is understood as a fixed, originary position which pre-exists its relation to others.

However, once we recognise its primacy, it is not clear to me that 'relation' itself needs to bear the name 'sovereign'. More useful, I think, is to focus on the role of sovereigns, and of

62 Ibid., 19.

63 Peter Fitzpatrick, *Modernism and the Grounds of Law* (Cambridge: Cambridge University Press, 2001), Chapter 3.

64 Jacques Derrida, "Force of Law: The 'Mystical Foundation of Authority'," trans. Mary Quaintance, in *Acts of Religion*, ed. Gil Anidjar (New York: Routledge, 2002), 251–58.

65 Andrew Benjamin, "The Problem of Authority in Arendt and Aristotle," *Philosophy Today* 253 (2016): 60.

66 Arendt, *The Human Condition*, 7–8.

67 Benjamin, "The Problem of Authority," 261.

sovereignty, *in* the relation. It is this form of sovereignty, in which relationality is prime, but sovereignty is needed to be able to articulate and hold instantiated positions of actors within that relation for the time being, which can provide a conceptual framework for claims to individual and collective identity, and the authority to speak the law of a community, without being useful to fascism. Most importantly, keeping in view the primacy of relation ensures that sovereign claims must be made in full view of their ultimate groundlessness and of their need to be open and responsive to all that challenges them, and all that they may become. Unlike liberal forms of sovereignty, this plural relation must inhere not just within a bounded polity, but *between* different polities – other forms of community and people. This is a form of sovereignty open to the illimitable potentiality of human relation, or in Arendt's terms, as-yet-unrealised infinite improbabilities.

Index

For Product Safety Concerns and Information please contact our EU
representative GPSR@taylorandfrancis.com
Taylor & Francis Verlag GmbH, Kaufingerstraße 24, 80331 München, Germany

www.ingramcontent.com/pod-product-compliance
Ingram Content Group UK Ltd.
Pitfield, Milton Keynes, MK11 3LW, UK
UKHW050053200926
475702UK00019B/2809
* 9 7 8 0 3 6 7 7 7 3 4 5 8 *